On Social Facts

On Social Facts

Margaret Gilbert

PRINCETON UNIVERSITY PRESS
PRINCETON, NEW JERSEY

Published by Princeton University Press,
41 William Street,
Princeton, New Jersey 08540
In the United Kingdom,
Princeton University Press, Oxford
Copyright © 1989 by Margaret Gilbert
Reprinted by arrangement with Routledge,
publishers of the 1989 edition;
first Princeton Paperback printing, 1992
All Rights Reserved

Library of Congress Cataloging-in-Publication Data
Gilbert, Margaret.
On social facts / Margaret Gilbert.
p.   cm.
Originally published: London; New York, 1989.
ISBN 0-691-07401-1 (cloth)—ISBN 0-691-02080-9 (pbk.)
1. Sociology—Methodology. 2. Social groups. 3. Social action.
4. Collective behavior. I. Title.
[HM24.G479   1992]
301'.072—dc20   91-38727

Princeton University Press books are printed on acid-free paper,
and meet the guidelines for permanence and durability of the
Committee on Production Guidelines for Book Longevity of the
Council on Library Resources

10 9 8 7 6 5 4 3 2 1 (pbk.)

Printed in the United States of America

For Miriam Gilbert

CONTENTS

Contents

PREFACE AND ACKNOWLEDGEMENTS

I have been thinking about the topic of this book for many years. During this time my views on the character of social phenomena among humans have changed rather radically, becoming more holistic. Around 1982 I came to sense that what I refer to here as the conceptual scheme of singular agency was incapable of properly characterizing the experience of social connection. This initially inarticulate perception has found its expression in the present work, which was completed in 1986.

I have tried to make the book accessible to those previously unfamiliar with the issues and texts I discuss, presenting fairly detailed expositions of the texts in question. Meanwhile, I make no attempt to mention every related work. I have of course attempted to make it clear if anyone has influenced the specifics of what I say here. But I have kept undiscussed references to a minimum.

David Lewis introduced me (and the learned world) to the important notion of what is now generally referred to as 'common knowledge'. He also provided an elegant account of social convention that demanded attention, and set a new standard of depth, clarity, and precision for such accounts. At one point I favoured an account of social phenomena which took common knowledge phenomena to be paradigmatically social. Later I began to feel that this was not so. Thus I came to appreciate the scepticism about common knowledge that Charles Taylor had been expressing. Though I continue to hold that common knowledge is an intriguing phenomenon of major importance in the context of human interactions, Taylor's expressions of doubt helped to encourage my sense of the need for more holistic conceptions in the characterization of social phenomena.

My work on the topic of this book has been facilitated over the years by stipendiary research fellowships at St Anne's College,

Oxford University, St Hilda's College, Oxford University, and the Institute for Advanced Study, Princeton. I have also enjoyed the privileges of a Visiting Fellow in the philosophy department at Princeton University on a number of occasions. I thank these institutions and the faculty members involved for this invaluable support. I should mention in particular Gwynneth Matthews and Gabriele Taylor, Jean Austin, and Morton White. I am also grateful to Albert Hirschmann and to Pat Sher.

I thank the following friends and colleagues for reading and commenting on part of the book manuscript or on related material: Polly Allen, Martha Bolton, Myles Burnyeat, Richard Collins, Raymond Geuss, Martin Gilbert, Tim Elder, Gilbert Harman, Rom Harré, Anne Hiskes, Ted Honderich, Anne Jacobson, Leonard Krimerman, Charlotte Katzoff, Saul Kripke, Joel Kupperman, David Lewis, Steven Lukes, the late John Mackie, A.S. McGrade, Judith May, Ruth Millikan, Mark Sainsbury, Thomas Scanlon, Amartya Sen, Jerome Shaffer, Frank Stewart, John Tienson, John Troyer, David Vance, Steven Wagner, Samuel Wheeler. I hope that I will be forgiven for any inadvertent omission. Being read in the course of writing has meant a very great deal to me. In addition, I thank John Albanese, Marie Becker, Richard Collins, Zlatan Damnjanovic, and Shelly Korba, for help of various important kinds.

I dedicate this book to my mother, Miriam Gilbert, who has so often provided a supportive and peaceful setting in which to write. I hope that the book reflects to some degree her clear-sightedness, honesty, and good sense.

Errata and additional bibliographic material may be found on p. 521.

I

INTRODUCTION: EVERYDAY CONCEPTS AND SOCIAL REALITY

1 PREAMBLE

The relationship between human individuals and the social groups to which they belong has long been disputed. Much passion and puzzlement has been associated with this issue.

What precisely is a social group? Does group membership involve a deep transformation of the human individual? If so, what is the nature of the transformation? It is natural to look to the social studies for answers to these questions, and more generally to find out what a social phenomenon is, as opposed to phenomena of other types. But social scientists have disagreed widely over the proper characterization of their subject matter, beginning with the acknowledged founders of sociology, Max Weber and Emile Durkheim. Durkheim sees social groups as dynamic 'new' entities, phenomena *sui generis* that arise when individual humans associate with one another. Weber shuns such description, urging that it is solely the actions of individual humans that constitute human social life.

Such disagreement suggests that the core phenomenon at issue in the human social domain has not yet been isolated. Yet only when this has been done can we properly understand our situation and our tasks as human social animals. In this book I provide a solution to this problem.

2 THE FOCUS AND THESIS OF THIS BOOK

We think of certain phenomena as 'social' phenomena. Here are some examples: two people talking on a street corner; a football game; a meeting of the Town Council; the mob storming the Bastille. But what do we mean by 'social'? What restrictions are

1

there on what we would consider a social phenomenon? How is the everyday, intuitive concept of a social phenomenon to be explicated? This question prompted the investigations in this book. The title is meant to recall Durkheim's view that the phenomena particularly apt for the label 'social' are significantly special. (Durkheim calls these phenomena 'social facts'.) I agree that our paradigmatic social phenomena have a very special nature. In this book I explain why. My reasons have something in common with Durkheim's, though I do not claim to be a Durkheimian.

I shall be parsimonious in my initial assumptions about our everyday concept of a social phenomenon. So as not to exclude in advance certain approaches to the issue, I shall not assume at the outset that 'social' means something like 'having to do with a society or smaller social group'. I shall take it for granted, however, that human social groups and their properties are social phenomena *par excellence*. So a key question can be put in terms which echo Georg Simmel: 'What makes a collectivity out of a sum of living human beings?' I construe this as a conceptual question: under what conditions do we count a set of human beings as a collectivity or social group? I maintain my focus on the question of *human* collectivities until the very end of the book, where the question of nonhuman animals is considered briefly.

In the main body of the book I focus on three everyday concepts relating to group life among human beings: the concept of a collectivity or social group; the concept of the belief of a group; and the concept of a social convention. I also discuss the concept of a group's language. Investigation of these concepts leads to important results. These results enable us to say something interesting and precise about the concept of a social phenomenon in general. They also bring into focus a consequential range of phenomena.

The main thesis of the book will be that our collectivity concepts incorporate the concept of a *plural subject*. The nature of plural subject phenomena will be carefully explained. They are so special, and so apt for the label 'social' that one can argue it should be reserved for them. My main aim is not to produce an argument about a label, however. Rather, it is to draw attention to the concept of a plural subject and to the precise nature of plural subject phenomena. Thought about our use of the label 'social' can lead to such awareness.

There is little question that plural subject phenomena are of the utmost importance in human life. Awareness of these phenomena and clarity about them is essential for the understanding of many issues in philosophy and elsewhere. These

2

issues include large theoretical questions such as the nature of language, the nature of politics and political obligation, and more practical and detailed questions such as the morality of lying and the conquest of loneliness.

I shall not be able to examine all the implications of the existence of plural subjects in this book. Among other things, however, I argue that the results presented here allow us to adjudicate the longstanding controversy between 'individualism' and 'holism' about social groups. Many great thinkers, both philosophers and social scientists, have spoken on the different sides of this controversy. On the individualist side, along with Max Weber, we find among others John Stuart Mill, who forcefully asserts, in *A System of Logic*, that people 'do not form a new kind of substance' when they come together in society.[1] But in *Utilitarianism* Mill describes the members of a social group as the 'members of a body', sounding closer then to Durkheim and his view of society as a 'synthesis' *sui generis*, and to those who like Plato in the *Republic* see group members as united (ideally at least) in a single organism.[2] The fact that Mill can be cited on both sides is significant. Others also fall into this category. I shall suggest that this is because both types of statement contain an important truth. Each of these truths can be clearly and unequivocally stated, as I hope to show.

The results presented here suggest that one risks the impoverishment of social theory if one ignores plural subject concepts. An understanding of them should do more than improve our understanding of human possibilities. If we are blind to our own possibilities, how can we make good decisions about the conduct of our lives? How can we have a reasonable scale of values, if we do not know what is there to be valued? Since much of what follows will be quite abstract and general, it is worth making this point at the beginning. The investigations undertaken are not simply exercises in pure theory or semantics, or matters of mere logic-chopping. Sometimes logic must be chopped, in order that both the way we think, and the way we are, may be seen clearly.

3 SOCIAL SCIENCE AND EVERYDAY CONCEPTS

My primary aim is to make explicit the structure of certain everyday concepts. The articulated concepts appear well suited for the conceptual quiver of social theory.[3] In pressing the claims of these concepts on social scientists I run counter to influential ideas expressed by Emile Durkheim and Max Weber. Let me explain.

In his classic work *Suicide*, discussing how he will define 'suicide' for sociological purposes, Durkheim observes that his own technical notion diverges from what is apparently meant by 'suicide' in everyday speech. He defines suicide as action undertaken in the knowledge that one's own death is a highly probable result. Thus a soldier's maintaining his position in the front line under orders would count as suicide. Meanwhile, the vernacular notion is, rather, the idea of an act in which one aims at one's own death. Consistently with this, in his methodological treatise, *The Rules of Sociological Method*, Durkheim strongly attacks the idea of conducting sociological enquiry in terms of vernacular notions, or 'preconceptions'. After alluding to Descartes's method of doubt he writes:[4]

> the sociologist, either when he decides upon the object of his research or in the course of his investigations, must resolutely deny himself the use of those concepts formed outside science and for needs entirely unscientific. He must free himself from those fallacious notions which hold sway over the mind of the ordinary person, shaking off, once and for all, the yoke of those empirical categories that long habit often makes tyrannical. (p. 73)

One of the things Durkheim says here is quite plausible: our everyday concepts were not formed for scientific purposes. His methodological recommendation in the light of this, however, is unexpectedly strong: the sociologist must not use these concepts. A more plausible conclusion is that social science could use a careful examination of everyday notions. These will in any case tend to inform all our endeavours, as Durkheim suggests. If we find them wanting or insufficient to our needs we can act accordingly. The possibility remains that on close examination they may surprise us with their complexity, beauty, and theoretical utility. The 'analytic' branch of philosophy may be expected to be a useful adjunct to social science in the articulation of everyday concepts.[5]

Possibly under the influence of the founders of sociology, social scientists have tended stipulatively to define a set of technical terms, on the one hand, and, on the other, to use vernacular concepts relatively uncritically and without examination. There are often good reasons to do these things. Meanwhile I want to urge the importance of carefully examining the structure of the vernacular concepts relating to the social world.

My putting Weber in the sceptical camp may seem surprising. His attitude to vernacular concepts is in fact complex. One of Weber's central tenets certainly dictates that sociologists should steep themselves in these concepts. As is well known, Weber believes that sociologists must attempt to grasp the *meaning* that pieces of human behaviour have for the persons concerned. More will be said about this view later. But it evidently requires that sociologists both grasp and employ the concepts that are in play in people's minds when they act. To give a simple example, a man moving his arm in a certain way might be doing this with the intention of saluting his country's flag. In order to describe the man's intention correctly, it seems that an observer must himself employ the concept of a salute.[6]

If he would allow that in order to describe people's intentions sociologists must employ those people's vernacular concepts, Weber would also insist that in describing other aspects of the world sociologists must adopt a critical stance to vernacular concepts. Such concepts should only be used if they conform to certain scientific requirements.

According to this view, the social scientist may be expected sometimes to be in the position I would be in were I to tell you that 5-year-old William is looking for goblins in the garden. I know what goblins are – or are supposed to be – so I know what I am talking about when I say that he is looking for goblins. I know that William believes that there are goblins, small human-like creatures with wings, and whatever. I myself do not think that there are any goblins, and I do not mean to commit myself to the existence of goblins when I say he is looking for goblins. Unlike William, I could not myself seriously set out to look for goblins in the garden. But I can take an interest in how he goes about it, listen with understanding to his progress reports, and report them back to others.

The view that social scientists should not apply vernacular concepts to the world uncritically seems utterly reasonable. It may be your duty as a developmental psychologist to discover the contours of the concept of a goblin, if many children believe in goblins. But it surely cannot be your duty to share their belief. The same goes for all manner of concepts that the social scientist may need to grasp in order to proceed – witchcraft, phlogiston, and so on. One need not believe what others believe, in general, in order to know that they believe it, to investigate why, and so on. Which concepts one applies to the world *in propria persona* should be a function of the way one takes the world to be.

As described so far, Weber's position on the role of vernacular concepts in theoretical sociology seems eminently reasonable. He does not deny the theoretical utility of all vernacular concepts, but presumes that such concepts should not be adopted uncritically. There is a more problematic aspect to his views, however.

4 WEBER ON EVERYDAY COLLECTIVITY CONCEPTS

In his classic discussion of the 'fundamental concepts of sociology' in *Economy and Society*, Weber expresses scepticism about one of the very concepts one would expect to demarcate the subject matter of sociology: the everyday concept of a collectivity. His discussion is both complex and compact and it is not entirely obvious what he means to claim. With that caveat, let us look at the details of Weber's discussion.[7]

On the one hand, Weber accepts that in everyday life people operate with a number of 'collective concepts', such as the concept of a 'state', a 'family', an 'army corps', and so on. In so far as people do operate in terms of these concepts, the sociologist 'cannot afford to ignore' them. On the other hand, Weber evidently has some trouble accepting that states, families, and so on, *exist*. This may seem bizarre. How could one deny that families, for instance, exist?

Weber's reasons are not entirely clear. One thing that troubles him is that people in possession of the vernacular concept of a family, say, allow themselves to speak as if families themselves can act. They also ascribe rights and duties to them. Possibly Weber thinks it obvious that nothing but an individual human being can act, have rights and duties, and so on. He says at one point: '. . . for sociological purposes, there is no such thing as a collective personality which acts'. It seems reasonable to assume that we can read 'for the purposes of scientific description' in place of or in addition to 'for sociological purposes'. It is possible, then, to discern in what Weber writes something like the following line of argument. According to the vernacular concept, a collectivity can act. But then there can be no collectivities in the sense in question.

As I have noted, Weber allows that the sociologist cannot afford to ignore the 'concepts of collective entities which are found both in common sense and in juristic and other technical forms of thought'. But this is because 'actors . . . in part orient their actions' in terms of these concepts. In other words, the sociologist will use these concepts in the description of people's thoughts. Weber also implies that sociologists will undoubtedly find themselves talking about 'families', 'nations', and so on, because the terminology is at hand, and (I suppose) may seem the natural terminology to use to describe some actual phenomena. However, 'If purposes of sociological terminology alone were involved' it would be possible, though 'extremely pedantic and cumbersome', to eliminate such terms entirely, and substitute 'newly coined words'. It seems that we are to understand that in so far as sociologists may say that 'there are collectivities' and so on (using terms referring to specific kinds of collectivity), such utterances must be interpreted or handled differently from the vernacular statements of everyday life (and of the law).

Weber writes elsewhere that it is the task of sociology to reduce such concepts as those of a state, an association, and so on, to '"understandable" action, that is, without exception, to the actions of participating individual men.'[8] What does Weber mean by 'reduce' here? Taken out of context his words might be thought to express the view that our common-sense, everyday concepts of 'collective entities' can be *explicated* in a certain way. Given the rest of what he says, the more likely alternative is that the sociologist must *replace* our common collectivity terms with new ones which are explicable in terms of the actions of individual human beings, the so-called 'members' of the 'collectivity'.

I take it that Weber has one main guiding criterion for an acceptable sociological definition of 'collectivity' or of any theoretical term in social science. Reasonably enough, Weber evidently supposes that sociological concepts must be realistic in some sense.[9] I shall not try to elaborate an appropriate criterion of realism here. Presumably such a criterion will exclude any concept which we know cannot apply to the world, because it is internally inconsistent, for instance.

Weber indicates that he accepts a second criterion, which he seems to see as derivable from a criterion of realism. Witness his remarking that everyday collectivity concepts are to be 'reduced' to '"understandable" action', to 'the actions of participating individual men'. He makes many similar claims: such as 'these collectivities must be treated as solely the resultants and modes of organization of the particular acts of individual persons, since these alone can be treated as agents in a course of subjectively understandable action'. We might sum up this criterion as follows: the existence of a human collectivity must be a function of the acts of individual human beings.

In one sense this criterion is unexceptionable. However, it is subtly ambiguous and suggests a criterion against which this book will, in effect, provide an argument. The distinction in question will best be made in the light of ideas I will develop. This issue is discussed fully in the concluding chapter. At this point we may simply note three questions that Weber's remarks on collectivity concepts in general raise. First, how are our everyday collectivity concepts to be explicated? Second, do these concepts definitely not meet Weber's criteria for acceptable sociological concepts, as he suggests? Third, are Weber's criteria reasonable?

This book focuses on the first question. In the light of my answer I shall argue that in so far as the two Weberian criteria noted are reasonable, everyday collectivity concepts do meet them. These concepts are thus freed to be candidates for the role of foundational concepts of social science. I shall argue that from an intuitive point of view this is indeed their proper role. That is, the vernacular concept of a collectivity and its relatives initially locate the concerns of the disciplines most aptly referred to as social sciences. In that sense they will be foundational concepts of social science. This is by no means an unimportant sense. For the concepts which are accepted as foundational in this sense give direction to subsequent enquiry in a given discipline.

5 THE EVERYDAY CONCEPT OF A COLLECTIVITY

It will be useful to preface more detailed analysis with some general remarks about our everyday collectivity concepts.

How do we begin to determine the boundary of our everyday concept of a collectivity? Sociologists and others sometimes make lists of types of social group, of collectivities, or, more grandly, 'social systems'. For example, Weber lists: a state, a nation, a family, an army corps. Durkheim lists, among the 'smaller social groups' which are part of larger societies, religious organizations and literary societies. Some put into their lists some very transient and small-scale affairs, such as a pair of conversationalists on a street corner.[10] I too could make some such list. The conjunction of the above examples, ending with 'and so on', will do.

In dealing with such lists the reader is evidently supposed not to balk at an 'and so on' at the end. If one is in this position, this suggests that one has grasped a concept or an intuitive principle of some kind, linking all the examples mentioned. What is this intuitive principle? To ask this is another way of asking for an explication of the everyday concept of a collectivity.

Consider the questions: What have typical families in common with schools? What has an army corps in common with two people chatting on a street corner? These questions could be addressed as empirical questions. First we might consider a sample of what we took to be typical families, then a sample of schools, and ask ourselves what in the world they had in common. Evidently, differences might be as salient as commonalities, and it might be quite hard to see where to start such an

8

investigation. But the question about an intuitive principle is of a different order. If it could be given an answer, one would have a special way of answering these other questions: a family and a school have the following in common, in so far as both are collectivities . . . (there would follow an explanation of the nature of collectivities in general).

The question about an intuitive principle is, in effect, a question about what lies behind our listings. On what basis are we willing to put families in, but loth to put in King James the First, or the population consisting of Rudyard Kipling, Julius Caesar, and David Hume? It is clear that most people would not put King James, or the latter trio, in one of these lists. Thus, though there could be disputes about cases, there are also areas of clarity. It should not be said that 'it's all a matter of arbitrary choice'.

Let me make a few clear points at once, to fix ideas. It is generally acknowledged, and my example of Rudyard Kipling and the other two randomly chosen people shows, that not just any set of people, in the logician's sense of set, forms a social group intuitively. Again, it is not enough for certain persons to have some feature or other in common. Thus the population of left-handed people, or the population of women, is not automatically a social group by virtue of having members with a common property. Again, merely inhabiting the same geographical area of the world, perhaps one cut off from others by a surrounding sea or mountain range, is not sufficient to make a population a social group, intuitively. So much, I take it, is common ground. Having said only this much, however, a caveat is in order.

Groups or populations of some of these kinds may be of great interest to demographers and others. For instance, one might be curious to discover whether those with a given feature in common (left-handedness, say) had any other common properties (higher or lower intelligence than right-handed or ambidextrous persons, say). One might be curious to know whether sameness of interests, whatever the particular interests were, tended to make people like one another more, or whatever. So to say that some type of population is not by its nature a social group, intuitively speaking, is in no way to judge the interest of some or all populations of that type from a scientific or other point of view.

A study of some such populations may make good sense within the framework of an interest in the nature and workings of a particular society or type of society. For instance one could usefully study the question of the relative contentment of those at the low end of the economic scale in different types of society.

Such a study could be undertaken by someone we are pleased to call a social scientist, without it being the case that the poor in a given society necessarily constitute a collectivity in any intuitive sense. Thus it must be clearly understood at the outset that to argue that populations of certain types are not social groups intuitively implies nothing about when, why, or by whom populations of that type may be studied, nor about their importance in whatever way in the scheme of things. The question here is: when does a population count as a collectivity, and what is especially interesting about this class of populations? I have focused on this question because I think the intuitive concept of a collectivity picks out a phenomenon of the greatest interest.[11]

6 METHODOLOGY

My approach to the business of conceptual analysis is quite standard. Two points are worth noting at the outset for those unfamiliar with this type of project.

First, I do not simply present my own accounts of the concepts at issue, but will first examine certain plausible alternatives and argue that they are unacceptable. I regard it as an important part of the defence of my own accounts that the inadequacy of these alternatives be clearly seen. In addition, the delineation of alternatives will help to locate the answer I myself propose in what might be called the space of concepts. For every proposed analysis is in effect a definition, the construction of a new concept if not the analysis of an old one. Part of what I want to say about the collectivity concepts that I in effect *construct* here is: look how different they are from the concepts delimited by other possible analyses.

Second, in assessing a proposed account I will often bring a counterexample against it. This can be a real or an imaginary case in which, say, purported sufficient conditions hold but the concept at issue does not apply. Now, the cases may sometimes seem bizarre or unrealistic, and quite possibly *silly*, to those unfamiliar with this enterprise and this method of approach. But the main test of the adequacy of a counterexample is not that it describes something which could quite likely happen, but that it describes something logically possible. Mere bizarreness is not a flaw in such examples. They must be taken seriously if our judgments about them contradict a proposed analysis.

We can tell much that we need to know about concepts by telling science fiction tales and such. Some may find it irritating to try to understand anything without constant recourse to the world of flesh, bones, and stones. But nonexperimental, unempirical research can reveal conceptual structures. Once revealed their applicability to the world can be ascertained. Thus the imaginary, the bizarre, and even the silly can help us come to grips with what is real.

There is clearly a question whether, for a given concept, any useful analysis or account in terms of logical entailments or entailers can be given. In advance of work on a given concept, I know of no general argument strong enough to rule out the possibility of such an account a priori.

A note on the terms 'intuition' and 'intuitive' may be useful. When I speak of our 'intuitive' concept of an X, I refer to the concept that is implicit in the judgments we are most immediately inclined to make about what counts as an X and what does not. When I say that something is 'counterintuitive' or 'contrary to our intuitions', I mean that it does not accord with such judgments. Clearly, 'intuition' here is not supposed to be the exercise of some faultless faculty of seeing into the essence of things.

A standard and important route to the analysis or explication of concepts is a consideration of how we use certain key words or phrases, such as 'social group', or 'social convention'. Of course words can be ambiguous. I shall sometimes argue that I have captured *a* sense of a certain term in English. I may suggest it is the *central* sense, on the grounds that it is the narrowest and richest sense and other senses can be seen as looser uses. (Consider in this connection the word 'game'. We may talk about the games people play in their daily interactions, yet at the same time be happy to deny that these are really *games*.) Or I may speak of *a* central sense, meaning that I think that there is this sense and it is a distinctive and common one.

I believe that the ultimate interest of what I have to say lies in the articulation of a scheme of vernacular concepts that attaches to important real phenomena. We could possess a given concept without possessing some neat phrase or a single term with which to express it. We could simply tend to agree that certain lists of items looked right; we could have convoluted ways of expressing our views on what the items in question have in common. Meanwhile, the importance of the concepts and the phenomena at issue here would be supported by the fact that they have compact reflections in language. Hence at times I have found it worth arguing that they are indeed so embodied in everyday talk.

11

7 THE MAIN THEMES

Each of the following chapters represents part of an assault on our everyday concept of a social phenomenon. A major theme running through the whole discussion is: how are we to explicate our everyday collectivity concepts? Until this is decided, we cannot hope to solve the more general problem. Two important issues in this connection are what I shall call *singularism* and *intentionalism*. Let me explain roughly and briefly what these are. (Later discussion will help to make things clearer and more precise.)

The issue of singularism concerns a certain restricted conceptual scheme. This may be called the conceptual scheme of *singular agency*. At its core is the idea of a (human) agent with goals of his own.[12] One acts as a *singular agent* in so far as one acts in the light of one's own goals. It may be thought at first blush that the conceptual scheme of singular agency is the only scheme of *agency* that there can be. That issue will be addressed later. Meanwhile it may be noted that the conceptual scheme of singular agency informs some influential recent attempts to model social processes in terms of the mathematical theory of games. A similar type of modelling is suggested by the scheme of fundamental concepts of sociology that Weber presented in *Economy and Society*. In the context of an investigation of our vernacular collectivity concepts, *singularism* is the thesis that these concepts are explicable solely in terms of the conceptual scheme of singular agency. If singularism in relation to our vernacular collectivity concepts is false, then the question of the adequacy of a singularist scheme of technical concepts to describe social processes becomes pressing. The falsity of singularism will be suggested by the results of the next chapter, and later chapters will reinforce this suggestion. My eventual stance, then, will be against singularism. In concluding I shall connect singularism with individualism, arguing against certain precisely specified forms of individualism, as opposed to the contrasting forms of holism.

Intentionalism is the view that according to our everyday collectivity concepts, individual human beings must see themselves in a particular way in order to constitute a collectivity. In other words intentions (broadly construed) are logically prior to collectivities. Intentionalism is surely plausible. Human beings appear to be in an important sense powered by their ideas and views of their situation. Thus many things human may be expected to depend on the existence of certain perceptions and thoughts in people's minds. Now there are philosophical arguments derived from Wittgenstein to the effect that, as a matter of logic, thoughts or intentions are logically dependent for their existence on the existence of social groups. If the arguments are valid, and intentionalism about everyday collectivity concepts is true, these concepts will be incoherent and there will be nothing to which they apply. I shall argue that intentionalism about everyday collectivity concepts is true, but that this does not mean these concepts are incoherent.

As the falsity of singularism would throw doubt on the adequacy of game theoretic and related approaches to social phenomena, so the truth of intentionalism would suggest the inadequacy of approaches in terms of externally observable structures or systems. Some theorists would propose that the essential mark of a human collectivity is an externally perceivable organization or structure, or systematic relations between the parts, that is, the human members. While there is doubtless something to be said for the view that human collectivities may be viewed externally as systems or structures, I shall argue that according to our intuitive conception they are not systems from an external point of view only. The participants must see themselves as bound together in a highly specific way. This suggests that an *explanation* for the existence of objective systemic features in collectivities may be found in an internal sense of unity. This would not be surprising, in so far as we accept that human beings are powered by their own perceptions of the situation. There is therefore reason to suppose that the perceptions indicated in our everyday collectivity concepts are the real 'glue' of the human social world.

Clearly, it is not enough to argue for the coherence of intentionalism. In order to argue convincingly for an intentionalist account of everyday collectivity concepts, one must attempt to specify precisely what thoughts, conceptions, and perceptions, are the binding glue of collectivities according to that conception. Here my anti-singularist, pro-intentionalist stance finds its positive basis. I argue that people must perceive themselves as members of a *plural subject*. As will become clear in the course of the book, this thought takes them (and the observer) beyond the conceptual scheme of singular agency.

So much, then, for the main themes. In the next section I sketch the contents of each chapter. The chapters are organized into a pointful sequence and together constitute a lengthy argument. At the same time, each one but the last is to a large extent self-contained. Different readers may wish to concentrate on different chapters. Although each chapter revolves to some degree around the ideas of a particular sociologist or philosopher, this is not primarily a work of exposition or comparison of texts. I have attempted, rather, to come to grips with the issues I am interested in by taking provocative, central statements in the work of others, and discussing and developing them in my own terms.

8 OVERVIEW OF CHAPTERS

Chapter II focuses on Max Weber's influential technical concept of 'social action'. Roughly, a person performs a social action when he acts with someone else in mind. For instance, if I tell you something, if I wave goodbye to you, I perform a social action in Weber's sense. In *Economy and Society* Weber claims, in effect, that his concept of social action is the fundamental concept of sociology: it is the existence of social actions in his sense that provides social science with a subject matter. Of course there are social actions of many different kinds, and many different types of complex of social action are possible. The sociologist is to develop categories which pick out types or complexes of social action that are deemed to have some special importance. Weber himself articulates a number of such categories. However, the fundamental social fact, if you like, is the fact of social action itself. Weber's view has been influential. Numerous writers in the social sciences and the philosophy of social science write as if 'social actions' in something like Weber's sense are the central subject matter of social science.

Weber's placement of his concept of 'social action' at the heart of his scheme of sociological concepts is importantly suggestive in two ways. It implies that sociological concepts will appeal to human intentions. It also suggests that the conceptual scheme of singular agency is adequate for sociology.

In Chapter II I consider whether an effective unitary characterization of sciences which could be called social sciences with intuitive aptness can be given in terms of Weber's concept of social action. I argue that this is not so. I argue that one thing that should trouble us is that Weber's concept does not enable us to explicate the vernacular concept of a collectivity. I argue for its insufficiency in this respect by considering and rejecting a number of possible simple accounts of a social group using Weber's notion. Clearly, the relation of Weber's concept to our collectivity concepts will best be ascertained when a satisfactory analysis of those concepts has been given. Meanwhile, the ground is cleared here to the extent that certain attractively simple analyses in terms of Weber's concept do not work.

In concluding I argue that it is doubtful whether an action social in Weber's sense is naturally thought of as a 'social' phenomenon in itself. Paradoxically, Weber's vision of human life gives every indication of leaving out its intuitively social dimension. In my view, it is not Weber's allusion to intentions that creates the problem, but rather the implied suggestion that sociology stick to the conceptual scheme of singular agency.

As I have indicated, faith in the adequacy of the conceptual scheme of singular agency is still alive in modern social science and is exemplified in attempts to model social processes in terms of the mathematical theory of games. I take a further look at the consequences of this approach when I examine – and reject – the influential game-theoretical account of social conventions proposed by the philosopher David Lewis, in Chapter VI. Chapters IV and V will also consider accounts of social phenomena which embody the limited perspective of singular agency.

There are traces in Weber's writing of the view of social phenomena that I shall put forward here. Why did this view not surface more? I am inclined to conjecture a disinclination to acknowledge certain facts, a disinclination which is expressed in Weber's animadversions against the existence of collectivities which act. There is doubtless a sense of 'action of a collective' such that Weber's negative existential claims in this regard are warranted. However, it will be the main thrust of this book that there is an important and theoretically respectable sense in which collectivities can act, and, indeed, think, have attitudes, and hold to principles of their own. I am in little doubt that Weber was aware of that sense at some level and that it informed his own daily life. So it would not be surprising if this awareness manifested itself at times in his writing. I say this not because I know anything significant about Weber's daily life, but because I think we all know this at some level. Normal human beings regularly, if not always and inevitably, see themselves as members of a collective agent or, more generally, of a collectivity with specific psychological properties. Moreover, they constantly act in terms of this perception. This book as a whole will be an explanation of why I say this. In the concluding chapter, I explain how the structure of our intuitive collectivity concepts makes it understandable that someone might wish to deny the existence of collective psychological properties.

Recall that intentionalism concerning our collectivity concepts is the view that an explication of these concepts will appeal to human intentions. In Chapter III I defend the coherence of intentionalism in general against some well-known arguments derived from Wittgenstein's work. Many whose primary interest has been the philosophy of social science have first encountered

Wittgenstein's thought through the interpretation in Peter Winch's monograph *The Idea of a Social Science and its Relation to Philosophy*. Winch claims that Wittgenstein has shown it is logically impossible for a being outside society to have intentions. That is, our concept of a being with intentions involves our concept of a society or social group. This would clearly be a problem for intentionalism. Winch's understanding of Wittgenstein has points of contact with that of many others. As I shall explain, however, the argumentation he presents is inconclusive. At a crucial point he assumes rather than argues for the unavailability of an acceptable 'nonsocial' model of language and, ultimately, of intention.

Not only is this assumption crucial to Winch's argument for the society-dependence of both language and thought. It is also deeply disturbing. For, as I argue, our everyday notions of language and thought imply that an acceptable nonsocial model is indeed available. If Winch's assumption is true, there can be no such thing as language or thought as intuitively conceived. Though Winch does not see the import of his assumption this way, it does seem to have this powerful consequence. In other words, if Winch is right about this assumption, then language and thought do not have a social nature; they are simply impossible: they cannot exist.

Is there a philosophically acceptable nonsocial model of language and thought, then, or is there not? This was a main focus of Wittgenstein's concerns, according to the interpretation proposed in Saul Kripke's *Wittgenstein on Rules and Private Language*. Kripke derives from Wittgenstein powerful arguments against a nonsocial or 'private' model. I argue that in spite of the power of these arguments one type of private model has not been shown to be incoherent and can be argued, then, to be philosophically acceptable.

Kripke suggests that rather than concerning himself with the formulation of necessary and sufficient conditions for thought and meaning, or with the analysis of the concepts of thought and meaning, Wittgenstein prefers to drop such an enterprise and consider what 'language game' we play with words such as 'thought' and 'meaning'. I argue that were we to accept this approach, it would be possible to accept a form of intentionalism. My conclusion in relation to intentionalism, then, is that it can be allowed to stand, as far as the arguments in Winch and Kripke go. Thus the ground has been cleared for an intentionalist approach to the logical construction of collectivities.

Though I do not accept a society-dependence thesis of thought and language in general I believe that a full understanding of the

16

nature of human linguistic phenomena demands special consideration of what it is for a group, as opposed to an individual, to have a language. Indeed, awareness that a radical distinction can be made between a group's language and that of an individual may help to defuse a fairly prevalent sense that language as such is society dependent, and a possibly consequent judgment on the nature of thought. I therefore conclude Chapter III with a brief account of the concept of what I call a *group language*. This is a subtle and important collectivity concept. To my knowledge, it has not been explicitly noticed, let alone examined with any care, in previous literature on Wittgenstein or on language in general. I shall explain how Wittgenstein's remarks on *criteria*, which have puzzled many commentators, are strikingly appropriate to an account of a group language, as opposed to the language of an individual. (I do not claim that Wittgenstein was prepared to make the distinction I am stressing here.) A fuller understanding of group languages requires an understanding of the concept of a social group, the topic of Chapter IV.

Chapter IV is perhaps the core of the book. I develop a new account of our concept of a human collectivity, inspired by a remark of the sociologist Georg Simmel's in 'How is society possible?'. Simmel says that humans must see themselves as *unified* in some way in order that they constitute a collectivity. This is clearly an intentionalist view. It is distinguished by the precise content of the thought supposed to be crucial. The account I develop from this beginning has points of contact with other authors also, in particular with Rousseau.

I argue that our concept of a collectivity is the concept of a plural subject of action, belief, attitude, or other such attribute. Such subjects exist when people do things together, for instance. A very simple example of people doing things together is that of two people going for a walk together. (I am happy to be committed to the existence of small, ephemeral collectivities. I believe that these are the bedrock of human social life.) I argue that in order to do things together people must view themselves in a certain special way.

I discuss in some detail what it is for people to do things together, or to *share in an action*. After considering various possible conditions on sharing in an action I conclude that it is necessary that the participants express to each other willingness to be part of a plural subject of a certain goal, for instance the goal that A walks in the woods and B walks in the woods and that they do so in one another's company. Their being part of a plural subject of this goal is, importantly, not equivalent to each one's accepting the goal as his own.

17

There are various ways of attempting to say what it is to express willingness to be the plural subject of a goal but none of these appears to involve what would normally be thought of as an analysis. For instance, one might say that each participant must manifest willingness jointly to accept responsibility for achieving the goal in question. But such willingness is in its turn best explicable as willingness to constitute a plural subject of the goal.

What I have said so far, then, does not give us a definition of what it is to be the plural subject of something. Rather, it gives us a logically necessary condition for the existence of such a subject. The statement of this condition itself *uses* the notion of a plural subject. It is a notion the members of a plural subject must have in order to become members of a plural subject. For they must experience and manifest willingness to be members of such a subject.

To illuminate the plural subject notion further we must turn to a description of a kind used by Rousseau. One is willing to be the member of a plural subject if one is willing, at least in relation to certain conditions, to put one's own will into a 'pool of wills' dedicated, as one, to a single goal (or whatever it is that the pool is dedicated to). It is logically sufficient for the existence of such a pool that it be 'common knowledge' among the people in question that, roughly, everyone has expressed his personal willingness that his own will be part of it. (Common knowledge is a technical term that will be defined later.)

I argue that the English pronoun 'we' has a central sense in which it refers to a plural subject. Its referents are not only the plural subjects of *goals*. 'We' is also properly used at least of those who are ready to share in certain actions when the time comes, or *jointly ready*. Joint readiness involves a plural subject. This makes it more plausible to define a *social group* in terms of 'we'. Intuitively speaking, not all social groups involve the current pursuit of a goal or end, in spite of the impression given by some writers.

I conjecture that plural subjecthood is the crucial constituent of a social group. In brief, social groups are plural subjects. In the following two chapters plural subject phenomena other than joint readiness for action or actual joint action are discussed in detail. Further consequences and aspects of plural subjecthood are discussed in the concluding chapter.

In the remainder of Chapter IV I address various aspects of my account of collectivities. These include the processes of group formation, the relation of group formation to language, the crucial minute phenomenon of mutual recognition, the possibility of large groups and inactive groups, the occasionally striking

18

phenomenology of plural subjecthood. I reply to a set of possible objections, and note the relation of my account to the remark of Simmel's which provoked it.

Chapter V addresses the topic of a group's beliefs. I do not assume at the outset that the account of a social group proposed in the previous chapter is correct. This enables the discussion here to serve as a test of the idea that social groups are plural subjects. I start with the fact that we often say things of the form 'Group G believes that p'. Under what conditions are such locutions most appropriate intuitively? Which actual phenomena most clearly warrant this kind of description?

It is widely assumed that any account of collective belief must be 'summative'. As I use the term, a *summative* account of collective belief holds it to be a necessary condition of a group's believing that p that all or most members of the group believe that p. A weaker requirement on an account is that it merely be 'correlativist'. A *correlativist* account holds it to be a necessary condition of a group's believing that p that *at least one* member of the group believe that p. As far as they have been characterized here, correlativism and summativism are consistent with a singularist view of collectivity concepts. In an exegetical passage of some length I argue that Durkheim, in *The Rules of Sociological Method*, held an account that was not even correlativist, let alone summative. I shall myself argue for a nonsummative, noncorrelativist stance.

I give summative theory a good run for its money. I start with an account that many would accept, what I call the *simple summative view*. This holds that in order for a group to believe that such-and-such it is both necessary and sufficient that most members of the group believe that such-and-such. I consider two other summative accounts, each one more complex than the preceding account, whose problems it attempts to avoid. One account brings in a common knowledge condition, and one is a 'causal' account. ('Causal' is in quotation marks since the causal nature of the account could be disputed.) Before describing and assessing these accounts I formulate some intuitive tests by which the aptness of the label 'belief of a group' can be assessed.

Summativism does not do well on the intuitive tests. A detailed example of a situation in which a group may be held to have formed a belief is then presented (the case of the poetry discussion group). Given the details of this case I argue that correlativism is false as a general theory of the conditions under which a group believes something. *A fortiori*, so is summativism.

I argue that the poetry group example and other data considered support a radically different type of account of collective belief: roughly, a group belief is a *jointly accepted view*. That is, it is a view that each of a set of persons has shown willingness to accept jointly with the others. A jointly accepted view is not to be confused with a view that all or most of the people concerned personally accept. One may accept a view jointly with certain others but not believe it personally.

That a certain view is jointly accepted by certain persons is an extremely important type of fact. It can influence what people themselves think, and in any case it constrains their behaviour in important ways. I conjecture that the phenomenon I characterize under the label of 'jointly accepted view' is both widespread and influential. It would be too bad if misinterpretation of everyday language, or anything else, resulted in obliviousness to this phenomenon.

As it turns out, the account of a group's belief arrived at here supports the account of a social group proposed in the previous chapter. That which jointly accepts a view is a plural subject.

Chapter VI proceeds in much the same way as Chapter V. It consists of a relatively independent and self-contained investigation of the everyday concept of a social convention. I first present a detailed critique of David Lewis's influential game-theoretic account of social convention. (There is a brief introduction to game theory for readers who are unfamiliar with it.) This is an account of a social convention as, in effect, a 'certain kind of sequence' of 'actual and possible social actions' of certain specific types. (The quoted phrases are from Weber.) I then consider an alternative which resembles a number of the available accounts of 'social norms' or 'social rules' in making no appeal to the concept of a plural subject. (In H. L. A. Hart's influential account in *The Concept of Law*, for instance, there is no explicit appeal to plural subjects. What is only implicit is hard to gauge.) Both accounts are argued to be inadequate as accounts of the intuitive concept of a social convention.

Having arrived on the basis of discussion of these accounts at a precisely articulated set of criteria for evaluating an account of social convention, I propose a new account which satisfies the criteria better than the others do. According to my account a social convention is a principle of action jointly accepted by the members of some population, a principle of the 'fiat' form. Intuitively, a population which jointly accepts such a principle thereby constitutes a collectivity. This is an intuitively appealing result from the point of view of social convention, and at the same time helps to confirm the plural subject view of social groups. For by virtue of joint acceptance of a principle members of a population constitute a plural subject. In the course of this chapter the connections of social conventions to a number of other phenomena are investigated. In particular, I distinguish between social conventions and what I call 'linguistic conventions', and between a group's morality, its conventions, its agreements, and its laws.

In the concluding chapter I summarize the positive results of the previous chapters and then turn to some applications of these results. I discuss three main issues. The first is Weber's proposed constraint on admissible collectivity concepts in sociology, to the effect that these are to be analysable in terms of the 'actions of participating individual men'. The second is the general issue of individualism versus holism about social phenomena. The third is the question with which this book began: the nature of social phenomena in general as intuitively conceived. The thesis that we have and live in terms of the conceptual scheme of plural subjects has implications for all these issues, and more. I explain by brief reference to examples why I take our possession of this scheme of concepts to be relevant to political philosophy, and to psychology.

Should the reader wish to concentrate on my own positive accounts of the various collectivity concepts considered, this material is largely to be found in the following parts of the book: Chapter III, section 6; Chapter IV; Chapter V, section 7; Chapter VI, section 8; and Chapter VII. I should stress that the reasons for preferring them will be clearer if the surrounding material is read also.

II
'SOCIAL ACTION' AND THE SUBJECT MATTER OF SOCIAL SCIENCE

1 INTRODUCTION

Max Weber's technical concept of *social action* (*Soziales Handeln*) is, roughly, the notion of an action by one person which takes account of someone else. (I shall give a more precise account of it shortly.) Weber regarded this notion as a fundamental sociological concept. He explicitly delimited sociology in terms of it. Thus in *Economy and Society* he writes:[1]

> Sociology (in the sense in which this highly ambiguous word is used here) is a science which attempts the interpretive understanding of social action. (p. 88)

And he says that social action is sociology's

> central subject matter, that which may be said to be decisive for its status as a science. (pp. 114-15)

In this chapter I consider a question that is naturally provoked by Weber's claims. It is not concerned specifically with the kind of sociology Weber wished to develop, but with the idea of a social science (or social study) in general. I take it that the idea of a social science is equivalent to the idea of a science with (or connected to) a specific ('social') type of *subject matter*. Can an effective, unitary characterization of those sciences aptly referred to as social sciences be given in terms of Weber's technical concept of social action?

If the answer to this question is positive, this will have a direct bearing on the issue at the centre of this book, the issue of how the intuitive concept of a social phenomenon is to be explicated. For suppose Weber's concept can give an effective unitary characterization of any science aptly referred to as a social science. It is reasonable to expect that it will at the same time

22

effectively characterize our intuitive concept of a social phenomenon. (Perhaps it could fail to do this, if the range of our intuitive concept included things that for some reason must be excluded from the scientist's domain.) It is possible, then, that Weber's concept of social action can solve for us, without further ado, the problem of characterizing the nature of social phenomena in general, as intuitively conceived.

Since Weber, many writers in the social sciences and in philosophy have evidently supposed that social science concerns something called 'social action'. Talcott Parsons's classic general work on sociology is entitled *The Structure of Social Action*. One could go on citing similar references for a long time.[2] It is fairly clear that there is no universally accepted sense of the phrase 'social action'.[3] An explicit definition, however, is rarely given by particular authors. As far as there is an everyday sense of the phrase 'social action' (there seems to be at least one, connoting something like 'action aimed at improving the structure of society'), this is not the sense of the phrase as used by most writers in the fields concerned. Authors may well be following Weber in their use of the phrase, but this does not entail that they use it in his sense.[4] Some clearly do use the phrase in Weber's sense, in so far as they cite his definition.[5] Meanwhile, in some cases the context suggests a sense different from Weber's.[6] To compound confusion, 'action' and 'social action' are often used as if they are interchangeable.[7] Sometimes, I suspect, the phrase 'social action' is used without any special understanding, that is, we have mere mouthing of a prevalent phrase.

A variety of technical definitions of 'social action' seem appropriate enough, given the meaning of the qualifier 'social'. A definition which would be inappropriate is, say, 'action performed by a person with brown hair'. Meanwhile the following, for example, appear to be relatively natural definitions of the phrase, whatever their own obscurities: 'action aimed at some feature of a society', 'action influenced by social factors', 'action by a person who is a member of a society', 'action performed in the context of a society'. This compounds the difficulty of interpretation. Of course we could just 'interpret' the phrase thus: 'action which is social (in some way or other)'. Given the plethora of possible ways, this leaves the term supremely vague, not a virtue in a technical term.

The writers cited so far in the text and notes, including Max Weber himself, all assign to the phrase 'social action' a meaning such that individual people perform social actions. In other words, the phrase is not interpreted as 'action of a group'. 'Action of a group', meanwhile, would be quite an appropriate meaning to assign to the phrase in question. This suggests something like the following shared motivation for the relatively casual but at the same time insistent use of the phrase 'social action'. On the one hand, there is the belief that social phenomena are, at base, constituted by the actions of individual persons, and/or that what social scientists study is the actions of such individuals. On the other hand, there is a desire to retain the idea that social scientists are concerned with things intuitively social. And, on the face of it, there is nothing obviously social about an action as such. (Consider the case of someone scratching an itch say, or stretching his leg.)[8] The apparent problem of disappearing socialness is then addressed by adopting the assumption that social science is concerned with a particular species of action by individuals, a species appropriately labelled 'social action'.

Whether or not one shares these views, the facts about usage noted raise the following general question: is there a sense of 'social action' such that (a) individual people perform such actions and (b) one can give an effective unitary characterization of social sciences as those concerned with such actions? Let us see whether social action in Weber's sense can do the trick.

2 WEBER'S ACCOUNT OF 'SOCIAL ACTION'

2.1 Introduction

What exactly is Weber's notion of a 'social action'? At the beginning of *Economy and Society* Weber gives an explicit definition for 'social action' and discusses cases in an attempt to clarify its range of application. In spite of the care Weber takes, there remain some obscurities in the notion, as in his more basic notion of 'action'. I hope that the following account will be reasonably clear, reasonably faithful to Weber's gist, and adequate to my purposes here. We should start, as Weber does, with his definition of 'action' *simpliciter*.

2.2 'Action'

Weber says:

> In 'action' is included all human behavior when and insofar as the acting individual attaches a subjective meaning to it. (p. 88)

24

He adds that, in effect, action in his sense need not involve any obvious physical movement; it is enough that one deliberately refrain from 'positive intervention' in a situation, for instance.

The full subjective meaning of a piece of behaviour may, as Weber understands it, be quite complex. First, there is the 'subjective meaning of a given act as such' (see Weber, p. 94). It appears that this would be captured by the answer to the question, asked of a particular 'behaver', 'What does he mean to be doing?' To cite one of Weber's examples, a man wielding a chopper in a certain way may be *chopping wood* – the stressed words may capture the subjective meaning of his act 'as such' (p. 95). (Note that they may not. Even if he is in fact moving in such a way that wood is being chopped by his chopper, he could, for example, be in a state of automatism such that he 'attaches no meaning' to his behaviour. Or he could be hallucinating and think that he is hacking his way out of a snowdrift, say.)

Presumably the core of Weber's notion of 'subjective meaning' lies here. That is, we can give a rough account of it thus: when a person A behaves in a certain way, he attaches a subjective meaning to his behaviour if and only if something of the form 'A means to be doing so-and-so' is true of A. Alternatively, we might refer to A's *intention* in acting. A must *intend* to do so-and-so.

In order to arrive at the full subjective meaning of a given act, further questions are relevant. (Only, I suppose, on the assumption that the first question is relevant.) In particular, 'What is his *motive* in, say, chopping wood?', and perhaps also 'Why does he have this motive?' Weber gives examples of motives: the wood chopper may be working for a wage, or chopping a supply of firewood – chopping in order to gain his wages, or to obtain a supply of firewood. One who is aiming a gun at a target may have been 'commanded to shoot as a member of a firing squad', thus aiming in order to shoot, in obedience to commands made to him as a member of a firing squad. We might also describe this last case, more naturally perhaps, as the man aiming in order to shoot, and purposing to shoot, or shooting, because the leader of his squad has so commanded the members. One's motives in doing something may of course be manifold. A motive which may frequently coexist with others is a desire to do what one does for other reasons in a socially acceptable way. For example, one's saying 'I'm awfully sorry old chap, but . . .' to X could be motivated by the desire to rebuke X *and* one's standing desire to do whatever one does in a socially acceptable manner.[9] It is clear that such an aim, even though in some sense subsidiary to the main one, should be included in an action's subjective meaning.

We will not go far wrong, then, if we take it that the full subjective meaning of a piece of behaviour will be given by the answer to the question: 'What does the person concerned mean to be doing, what does he hope to achieve by doing it, and what is his reason for seeking such an achievement?' One modification to this characterization should, however, be made.

Weber mentions the case of one who is 'working off a fit of rage' by his woodcutting. He calls this 'an irrational case' (pp. 8-9), and distinguishes between such cases and others. Let us consider the locution 'He's working off a fit of rage' as an answer to the question 'Why is he chopping wood?' This could be interpreted in terms of what have been called 'in order to' motives. That is, it could be interpreted as telling us what the agent hopes to achieve by chopping wood, as in 'he's doing that *in order to* get rid of his rage'. Here there is the connotation of some deliberate attempt on the agent's part to rid himself of his anger, but the original locution will also cover a case where the above interpretation is not appropriate. It is rather that he is angry, and *in his anger*, he is chopping up the wood. He is *expressing his anger*, rather than deliberately doing something to get rid of it. In so far as we place the act in its 'context of meaning' by stating that it is an expression of anger, this case has not so far been covered by our account of Weber's conception of subjective meaning.

We may take it, then, that the subjective meaning of a piece of behaviour is given, roughly, by the answers to the questions: 'What does he mean to be doing, what does he hope to achieve by doing it, and what is his reason for seeking such an achievement? (and so on)' where these are appropriate; and in answer to the questions: 'What does he mean to be doing, what emotion is being expressed, and what or whom is this emotion directed at? (and so on)' where these are appropriate.

This takes account of the main aspects of 'subjective meaning' that Weber mentions, and hence of the core of his notion of 'action'.[10] (Weber's notion of *'Verstehen'* – usually translated 'understanding' – is closely tied to his notion of 'meaning'. Understanding an action is, basically, grasping the action's meaning (see pp. 94–6). I shall not discuss this notion further here.)

Weber's idea that behaviour with a subjective meaning is crucial for sociology is often regarded as a distinctive approach. Yet it is surely a very natural one, corresponding to our common-sense understandings of the way human beings function. It is part of everyday discourse to ask: 'What are you doing?' and 'Why did you do that?', to ask, that is, for the agent's intentions in acting and his reasons for acting the way he did. 'Did you want the money to spend or to save?' is the kind of question the pointfulness of which is taken for granted in everyday life. It is assumed that human behaviour may be powered by ideas; that, speaking broadly, the way a person conceives of his situation, and his reasoning about that situation, may in some sense *lead him* to act.[11]

The everyday concept of an intentional action, expressed in such statements as 'She raised her arm', 'She waved goodbye', and so on, embodies the assumption of the powerfulness of intentional states. Weber's concept of action is not, as defined, identical with the everyday concept for he does not posit the powerfulness of subjective meaning. There is every reason to think, however, that Weber's implicit understanding of the nature of human behaviour does correspond to the understanding embodied in the everyday concept of intentional action. As we shall see, his sense of the powerfulness of intentional states is brought out more clearly in his definition of social action than in his definition of action.

Assuming the powerfulness of human intentional states, one might infer that such intentional states are the basic ingredients of many phenomena involving human behaviour, and, in particular, of social phenomena among humans. It would not be surprising to find that everyday concepts of social phenomena involve the assumption that intentional states have this status, given that the powerfulness of intentional states is assumed in the everyday concept of intentional action as well as in everyday discourse regarding such action.

Weber's conception of subjective meaning at the core of social phenomena among human is, then, a conception which coheres perfectly with the everyday conceptual scheme relating to intentional states. The question remains whether Weber's notion of social action is the key to the everyday conception of social reality.

2.3 'Social action'

According to Weber, action is social when:

> by virtue of the subjective meaning attached to it by the acting individual(s) it takes account of the behavior of others and is thereby oriented in its course. (p. 88)

A few comments on this account are in order.

The *behaviour* (*Verhalten*) of others does not have to involve overt physical behaviour, or itself be action in Weber's sense.

Thus according to Weber, one's production of something would be a social action if it were 'oriented to the future *wants* of others' (my stress). In an earlier essay in the journal *Logos*, Weber counts action intended to give pleasure to another person as social action.[12]

Weber writes: 'Overt action is nonsocial if it is oriented solely to the behavior of inanimate objects' (p. 112). I shall take this to mean (at least) that one who performs a social action must take the other or others in question to be animate. Paradigm 'others' will be human persons but it appears that 'others' is intended to apply in principle to non-human animals. (At one point Weber refers to the 'theoretical possibility' of 'a sociology of the relations of men to animals' (p. 104).)

For there to be a social action, it is not enough that the agent merely has someone else 'in mind' while acting. Thus a woman gathering firewood might happen to be thinking about her mother. Unless this thought contributed in some way to the subjective meaning of her act, it would not help to make it a social action. If the woman were gathering wood so that her mother might keep warm in winter, this would bring her mother into the subjective meaning of her action.

Whether reference to someone else is part of the subjective meaning of one's act may not always be simple to determine. Suppose we ask someone what she is doing, and she says 'I'm going to look at the clock my father gave me.' Is the action she describes social? In order to ascertain this, we need a more precise account of the subjective meaning of her action. Perhaps her intentions are most aptly described as follows: she intends to look at a certain clock (which, she is aware, was given to her by her father) in order to tell what time it is. Then we might want to say that what she really means to do is to look at the clock in question, in order to tell the time. That is, we might want to drop out of our description the reference to her father and his action. But perhaps she wants to look at the clock in question in so far as it is the clock given to her by her father (perhaps because she is intent on reflecting on his generosity). Then it seems that the reference to her father's behaviour has an essential role to play in capturing the subjective meaning of her act.

I shall take it that a social action in Weber's sense must take account of a condition of another which is seen as an expression or aspect of the other's animate nature. It is not enough that some aspect of the condition of another be addressed, while that other is seen as animate. The following two cases illustrate the distinction I have in mind. First case: Green turns to the right because otherwise he will bump into Brown and cause him pain.

Second case: Black turns because otherwise he will bump into White. White has been strapped to a chair which is in Black's path. Black has no interest in White's past, present, or future states of mind. He is only interested in avoiding immediate physical harm to himself. White's animacy, then, in no way enters into Black's calculations, though he is well aware that White is animate. Were this so, it would seem that White's animacy, or rather, Black's perception of it, has no essential role to play in the generation of Black's action. Putting things in terms of subjective meaning, reference to White's animacy is not necessary to characterize the intention or motive, and so on, of Black's act. Black wanted to avoid bumping into a certain physical object, the body of White, in order to avoid getting hurt himself. This seems to capture what is essential to the subjective meaning of his act, and it makes no reference to anyone's animacy except that of Black himself. Indeed we could say it does not refer to another person, in so far as White's body is really all Black is concerned with, White himself having no present control over it.[13]

My way of construing Weber here will presumably allow for the following case, where it is indeed the other's animacy which is at issue: Gold turns because he wants to avoid bumping into Silver, in so far as Silver is (believed by him to be) an animate being. (Perhaps Gold has a phobia of contact with animate beings as such.)

In my characterization of Weber's concept of social action, I shall not attempt to refine further the condition that an expression or aspect of the animacy of another being must be involved in the subjective meaning of a social action. There are hints, particularly in Weber's *Logos* essay, that orientation must be to the subjective meaning of another's act, even to subjective meaning of a certain sort. Meanwhile the sufficiency of a reference to other's wants and pleasures implies a wider concept, in terms of a more general notion of animacy. The *Logos* essay, particularly the first paragraph p. 1376, suggests that Weber was struggling there with a decision between different definitions of social action. (I say a little more about this shortly.) Still, he did opt for a wide official definition in *Economy and Society* and this is what has predominantly been echoed in the literature. There are good reasons, therefore, for considering the utility of this particular notion.[14]

Weber says that a social action must be 'oriented in its course' by virtue of the reference to another in its subjective meaning. I take this to be intended to require a causal or quasi-causal role for the subjective meaning, a requirement made in the light of the assumption that typically a person's having a given motive and intention helps to bring about or maintain behaviour appropriate to the meaning in question. (The suggestion of causal role, as I have noted, is not brought out so explicitly in Weber's definition of 'action'.)

2.4 What Weber's social action is not

Weber contrasts social actions in his sense with certain other kinds of action. In drawing the particular contrasts he does, Weber is in part engaged in distinguishing his conception of the subject matter of sociology from the conceptions of certain others. Action which is merely *influenced* by the presence of other people is not by virtue of that fact social in Weber's sense. For example, an action is not social just because the agent is somehow influenced by being a member of a crowd.[15] Again, the *imitation* of others' actions is not necessarily a social action, though it may be; it depends on the precise nature of the imitative action. Thus compare seeing the Queen in a certain hat and later making a similar hat because 'that was a nice hat I saw the other day', and making a hat of a certain kind 'because the Queen has one like it'. In the former case 'one's action is causally determined by the action of others, but not meaningfully'.[16]

Action *similar* to that of many other persons is not thereby social action (p. 113). An example (from Weber): We all put our umbrellas up at the same time. Rain has started to fall and each of us is responding to it. Another example: All over the country, *every morning*, people wake up, stretch, and yawn. Given that they mean to stretch, they may well have no further 'motive' than that they feel like stretching. They need have no thought of what others are doing, have done, or will do. As this example shows, not all society-wide uniformities in action are uniformities in social action.

Weber in fact stresses the importance for sociology of 'uniformities in the orientation of social action' (pp. 120ff). An example of such a uniformity would be everyone driving on the right by reason of 'a mutual declaration to the effect that a certain kind of action will be undertaken or is to be expected'.[17] Weber stresses the case where 'the corresponding type of social action is in the nature of the case best adapted to the normal interests of the actors as they themselves are aware of them' (p. 122). In other words, uniformities generated by the exercise of what might be called 'means–end' rationality. (To foreshadow a criticism I shall later make of Weber's concept of social action:

his *uniformities in social action* evidently form a motley crew. Means–end rationality can be exercised without any orientation to others; and it is the exercise of such rationality in a similar context on the part of many people which is responsible for the uniformities it generates, not the fact that the action regularly performed is oriented to others.)

In general, just any plethora of social actions does not produce any (further) homogeneity in action. Weber would presumably agree with this, but there is a passage which could give a different impression. In the *Logos* essay, written before the part of *Economy and Society* on which I am focusing, Weber remarks:[18]

> it is by no means only social action (*Gemeinschaftschandeln*) which makes it appear 'as if' action was determined by a consensual order. (p. 1377)

Weber uses his example of the umbrella-raisers here too, as an example of homogeneous mass behaviour (*Massenhandeln*) which, he says, can produce the appearance of determination by a consensual order 'equally and even more drastically' than social action can.

Weber's remark could be seen as advice to a sociological observer. Mere homogeneous mass behaviour may involve salient 'patterns' on the ground that are not different in outward form from patterns resulting from, say, actions making reference to past agreement or social convention. So the observer should not assume that all such regularities involve social action, let alone such specific references.

Weber is here explicitly concerned to refute a form of 'organicism' which implies that human social life can be characterized in terms of regularities in human behaviour. Given that social actions in his sense are constitutive of social life proper, he points out that not all regularities involve social actions. This will only worry the organicist, of course, if he already accepts that social actions in Weber's sense are constitutive of social life. Meanwhile, it is worth pointing out that many behavioural regularities, even those uniquely characterizing particular human groups, will not be the result of any intentional connections between the people concerned. This might well make one pause if one were at first inclined to think of at least nonbiologically determined regularities in behaviour within human populations as social from an intuitive point of view.[19]

In the passage quoted Weber does not make it clear that there can be a great deal of social action going on *without* there being the appearance of 'determination by a consensual order'. Though he does say elsewhere that this is so, in reading these early

31

passages one hardly feels clear that it is social action according to Weber's official definition that is felt to be central for sociology, as opposed to behaviour involving 'determination by a consensual order', whatever precisely that is. However, the 'official doctrine' is certainly that the broader category of social action is fundamental; it is this official doctrine, and that broad category, that are under scrutiny here.

According to Weber's official notion, a social action can be performed when an agent is alone. The idea of social action is not the idea of action 'directed at' someone in the agent's present environment. Moreover, Weber would agree that the other or others to whom social action is oriented need not be known personally to the agent in question. What Weber says is:

> The 'others' may be individual persons, and may be known to the actor as such, or may constitute an indefinite plurality and be entirely unknown as individuals. Thus money is a means of exchange which the actor accepts in payment because he orients his action to *the expectation that a large but unknown number of individuals he is unacquainted with* will be ready to accept it in exchange on some future occasion. (p. 112; my stress)

In spite of the great care Weber takes to clarify his concepts, queries remain. For instance, must one's orientations be to others one knows to exist, even if one does not know them personally? Or must one simply *believe* that some particular other or others have existed, do exist, or will exist? What then of one who lights a fire just in case there are any other survivors of a certain war on this island, while not truly believing that there are? Does such a person perform a social action in Weber's sense? Note that if either belief or hope and the like are sufficient, then from a logical point of view a social action could be performed in a universe containing only a single person.[20]

Without a clear understanding of the motivation behind Weber's definition as it stands, one can have little basis for deciding where he would draw lines he has not explicitly drawn. I shall therefore only assume one restriction here, relating to the beliefs of the agent about the other person in question. It would seem to be in accord with Weber's concerns that the agent must believe that the 'other' in question *may* exist. This would rule out someone's acting with a known-to-be fictional character in mind, deciding quickly, say, so as not to become like (Shakespeare's) Hamlet. At a later point in the discussion I introduce some further restrictions, in order to see whether Weber's concept can do a certain kind of work better with such restrictions introduced.

In advance of a discussion of the work the concept is to do, we can leave things here.

As it stands in my exposition, Weber's technical concept of social action has two general features worth stressing at this point. First, it involves a strongly intentional conception of what makes a piece of behaviour social: whether one performs a social action or not depends not on factors such as the influence of others or consequences for others, but rather on the ideas and conceptions of the agent. In particular, the agent must have the conception of an animate being other than himself, and the social meaning of his act must involve that conception. Second, at least on the face of it, the definition of social action involves *no collectivity concepts*. One who performs a social action in Weber's sense need not, from a conceptual point of view, either be or see himself as a member of a *social group* or see that other to whom his act is oriented as the member or co-member with himself of any group. In this respect, Weber's concept is well suited to provide an account of the concept of a collectivity entirely in terms of 'the actions of participating individual men'. One who says that collectivities are complexes of social action in Weber's sense does not use the concept of a collectivity in his explanation, either in relation to the intentions implicitly imputed, or in any other way. Perhaps this is one reason Weber found his concept of social action attractive.

So much, then, for Weber's technical concept of social action. My concern will now be with the role, if any, which this particular notion can play in the elucidation of the nature of the social sciences.

2.5 My approach to Weber's concept

I shall put forward a number of arguments which suggest that Weber's 'social action' notion is not apt for a useful characterization of social science. I first argue that there is reason to believe that we cannot give a satisfactory *unitary* characterization of social science in terms of Weber's notion. I then argue that Weber's notion leaves much to be desired even if we wish only to give a partial account of social science. Though I concentrate on the efficacy of *Weber's* notion of 'social action', my arguments can be brought to bear on a variety of claims about social science, for instance the quite common claim that 'meaningful action' in general is what social science is about.[21] My first argument returns us to the topic of everyday collectivity concepts.

33

3 THE QUESTION OF COLLECTIVITIES

3.1 Introduction

One might wonder how we, in an attempt to grasp the nature of social scientific subject matters, could accept the claim that 'social action' in Weber's sense was the 'central subject matter'. At least one line of thought throws doubt on this: are not many social scientists concerned with such phenomena as social conventions, with, quite generally, the properties of collectivities, or social groups? And would not a study which aimed at perspicuous descriptions or explanations of these phenomena be for that reason worthy of the title 'social study', whatever its connection or lack of connection with social action?

This line of thought was, I think, one that occurred to Weber. As noted in the last chapter, Weber's attitude to everyday collectivity concepts was complex. He suggests that the sociologist must redefine the relevant words in terms of the 'actions of participating individual men'. He appears to believe that such redefinition will allow the sociologist to capture what there really is in the social world.

In the following brief statement, Weber suggests the form such a redefinition will take.[22]

> When reference is made in a sociological context to a 'state', a 'nation', a 'corporation', a 'family' . . . or to similar collectivities, what is meant is . . . only a certain kind of sequence of actual or possible social actions of individual persons. (p. 102)

Of course this is merely a sketch. None the less, Weber may have felt able to hold a unitary theory of social scientific subject matters in terms of social action in his sense, because he believed that the concepts closest to our everyday collectivity concepts which are empirically viable are definable in terms of a certain kind of sequence of social actions.[23]

I shall consider the question: how close a relation does social action in Weber's sense bear to the intuitive concept of a collectivity? In advance of a careful examination of everyday collectivity concepts, we cannot be sure that these are unrealistic, as Weber supposes. Possibly they can be explicated in terms of Weber's notion. If they cannot, then unless we are sure that they are unrealistic, we should be sceptical of the idea that Weber's concept of social action provides us with a satisfactory *unitary* account of the range of possible social scientific subject matters. In the rest of this section, then, I consider whether Weber's concept of social action bears a close relation to the everyday concept of a social group. In particular, I consider whether the intuitive notion of a social group is explicable in a relatively simple and direct way, in terms of Weber's notion.

I first consider a number of relatively precise accounts of purported *logically sufficient* conditions for social group existence. In each of these Weber's notion of 'social action' or a close cousin of that notion plays a central role. Since none of these accounts works, I argue that the burden of proof is on one who claims that 'social group' is explicable in terms of Weber's notion. The question of whether social actions in Weber's sense are a necessary component of any social group is then briefly touched upon.

3.2 A solitary social actor

Consider first hypothesis W1: the very simple idea that a plethora of social actions entails group existence. This is refuted easily enough. We have seen that a person can perform social actions when alone. So consider the situation of Rose, who has been shipwrecked. She once lived in a community; she is now alone on an island. She knows where and what the island is, and knows that ships pass fairly close by three or four times a week. So she lights a huge fire and keeps it burning, hoping that those unknown others who, she knows, will pass by (and who do indeed pass by) will see the fire and find her there. If a *social actor* is one who frequently performs Weberian social actions (and let us define 'social actor' thus for the present), then Rose is a social actor, but she herself does not thereby constitute a one-member group, or so I would judge.

Perhaps a one-person social group is possible. Even if so, it seems clear that 'There is a society' or 'There is a social group' is not best analysed as 'Numerous social actions are performed in a certain area over a period of time.'

3.3 Assuming a many-person framework

In considering the concept of a social group, the obvious question is: 'what makes a social group out of a *plurality* of persons?' For the notion of a social group is standardly applied to a plurality of beings, the members, so-called, of the group. So let us now assume a many-person framework.

A really simple and straightforward use of Weber's notion here is still unacceptable. Hence consider hypothesis W2:

Given a population (call it 'P') of more than one agent, P is a social group if most members of P most of their waking lives perform social actions.

Fairly clearly, a plurality of persons could perform social actions much of the time and there none the less be no social group of which they are all members. The following intergalactic fantasy shows this quite clearly. Consider three people, Smith in our galaxy, G; Jones, in galaxy G'; and Robinson in galaxy G''. Suppose the galaxies have never been in contact with each other, and these people have no conception that there are other galaxies. Each often acts, meanwhile, with members of *his own* galaxy in mind. He performs Weberian social actions with respect to his own friends and so on. The three people mentioned, however, never act with *one another* in mind. This seems to be a clear case of Smith, Jones, and Robinson *not* being members of one social group and certainly not *forming* one.

Hypothesis W2 can be refuted by intragalactic examples also, such as the following case. One person, Annabel, spends a lot of time doing things to please another, Beatrice; Beatrice spends a lot of time doing things to please Clarissa (who is unknown to Annabel); we continue on, down a chain of twenty-six people ending with Zena. Surely the people involved in the chain are not *by reason of this chain* members of a collectivity intuitively speaking. This case, of course, is not simply intragalactic; all the members of the chain could live in the same town.[24]

3.4 The mushroom pickers

It is not obvious where one should proceed after hypothesis W2. I shall move to W3, which is considerably stronger:

Given a population P of two or more agents who much of their time perform (and may be expected to perform) demonstrative social actions with respect to one another, P is a social group.

By a 'demonstrative social action' I mean a social action in which the other referred to is, and is referred to as being, in the agent's presence. For example, one who sees another standing in his path moves forward with the intention of pushing *that person* out of his path. W3 is intended to refer to a population such that, if the members of the population are, say, Sam, Naomi, and Phyllis, then, over a period of time, Sam performs a number of demonstrative social actions aimed at Naomi, and a number of such actions aimed at Phyllis, and similarly, *mutatis mutandis*, for the other two. W3 thus rules out both the intergalactic and

36

intragalactic cases cited so far, and in this agrees with intuitions on those cases.

In my discussion of W3, I shall introduce a set of people whose situation passes through various stages. At first they will perform no social actions, then social action will be introduced. We shall see whether, in moving to the situation in which according to W3 they should form a social group, they do so intuitively.

Stage 1: Our population consists of a plurality of people living within walking distance of each other. We shall not ask how each came to be where he is; we shall assume each has a language, not inquiring how. If you like, we can imagine that each arrived at his own place from a society in which he grew up, having grown restless and come to settle here. The emotions and attitudes of these people may remain somewhat obscure to us, but we can assume they are not savage, nor as needy as Hobbesian men. Each grows food, and sufficient food for his needs, off the plot of land in which he has pitched his dwelling. We can picture each person living alone on the perimeter of a forest, out of sight of the others, but within walking distance of them. As the *first stage*, let us take it that these people, though physically close, never come in perceptual contact; each assumes he is many miles from another person. Here there are no demonstrative social actions performed, and our population does not form a social group.[25]

Stage 2: We can let our people come into physical and perceptual contact without introducing social actions. Here is one possibility: every now and then members of our population go on solitary mushroom picking expeditions in 'their' wood. When one is picking mushrooms with his head bent down, he sometimes inadvertently collides with another, who is doing the same. We might suppose that each is stunned for a while by the head-on collision, and when each awakes his first thought is not for the one he collided with, but to get back home and lie down. So they take no account of each other; each struggles to his feet when he recovers, and staggers painfully home. As yet, though in a physical sense these people have come in contact (interacted?) they have performed no Weberian social actions; and at this point it would surely seem that they form no society either. Compare Weber's example of two cyclists:

> A mere collision of two cyclists may be compared to a natural event. On the other hand their attempt to avoid hitting each other, or whatever insults, blows, or friendly discussion might follow the collision, would constitute social action. (p. 113)

Stage 3: Now let us introduce Weberian social action. After their unpleasant experiences of bumping into things in the woods, the members of our population might begin to tread warily, looking up every now and then to see what was in their path. So now every so often one looks up and sees another coming toward him picking mushrooms, and moves away in order not to collide with this mushroom picker. It appears that we now have a set of social actions, in particular demonstrative social actions. If so, we have social actions, but no collectivity.

It could be objected that the avoiders here are not yet social actors, since for all that they do and believe, the *others* they have in mind might be inanimate objects, like trees (which they will also avoid) or (a more appropriate example) like mushroom-picking machines. There seems to be some point to this objection. Perhaps it is sufficient rebuttal to say, by fiat, that our agents move away *in order not to bump into that other human mushroom-picker*, seen precisely as someone with intentions, feelings, beliefs and so on. That is, in this case, though not in the case where they avoid the trees, the subjective meaning of their action involves reference to another animate being as such. We might add, further, that in the human case, but not in the case of the trees, each avoider has two reasons for his avoiding action; one is to avoid pain himself, the other is to avoid pain for the other, whom he assumes will be hurt if they collide. If we add in this complex motive for avoidance, the actions involved appear to be truly Weberian social. However, if this is all that went on, I do not think that our population would thereby become a society. Hypothesis W3 appears to have been refuted.

Perhaps it will be objected that at stage 3, we have precisely the kind of situation in which people will form a social group. They will, surely, get together around this point. Perhaps they will establish an apportionment of territory to each individual and agree that each is only to work his own land. Perhaps they will set up a committee to watch for boundary violations.

In answer to such an objection, I would claim that it does not really matter whether or not it is true that after finding themselves in this situation people would naturally get together and form a social group. As long as they would not yet constitute one at stage 3 as described, this case refutes hypothesis W3, which purports to give logically sufficient conditions for the existence of a social group.

Moreover, if there ever were a population like that of the mushroom pickers, it could be that its members would fail to form a group in the way suggested. For it could be that were they actually to make eye contact, were they to subject themselves to one another's look, they would panic and rush away from each other. Perhaps each fled from his respective society before because he had eye contact phobia. Perhaps now he will refuse to leave his dwelling in case he risks encountering the looks of others. I spell out this fantasy in order to show that even if one feels strongly that the situation described contains the germ of a society, the germ needs a special atmosphere in which to flourish. Even competent performers of demonstrative social actions need not as a matter of fact be able to provide the right atmosphere.

Another possible objection is this. Will not the following inevitably be true of the mushroom pickers as described? Each will know, after a certain amount of time has elapsed, that there is a collection of people, including himself, each of whom picks mushrooms in this wood. Each will know that all the other mushroom pickers know the same thing. In other words, it will be clear to all members of the population that they have a special shared way of life (picking mushrooms in this wood) based on an interest they have in common (an interest in finding mushrooms) and that all know this. Is this not enough to make them a social group? This objection can be countered in various ways. One might question whether general knowledge that there is this kind or degree of 'shared way of life' and 'interests in common' is sufficient to constitute group-hood. At this point, however, it is enough to note that given the mushroom pickers' situation at stage 3, the development described is not logically inevitable. It is logically possible that the mushroom pickers are all afflicted with a special form of amnesia. Each is incapable of remembering any encounter with another human being in the wood. Consequently none of them will make any inferences about the population of mushroom pickers as a whole. None the less – and this is the important point here – the conditions posited in W3 will have been satisfied, without a social group being formed.

It is worth noting that my conclusion on the mushroom pickers implies that in so far as they can be said necessarily to have – if not to know about – a *shared way of life* and *common interests*, then these properties alone cannot be logically sufficient to make a population into a collectivity intuitively. Quite possibly we can make out different senses of the phrases in question here. Indeed, the conceptual framework of plural subjects that I shall develop in later chapters will, in effect, provide a basis for richer concepts of *shared* ways and *common* interests than are exemplified by my mushroom pickers. Such shared ways and common interests will indeed be sufficient for collectivity production.

A more vivid kind of counterexample to W3 than that of the peaceable mushroom pickers would be a form of 'war of all against all'. Not a war formally declared, of course, but something very primitive. Imagine a population of misanthropic humans who live scattered around in a large forest. If one sights another, he stalks him in the attempt to kill, or at least to inflict pain. Thus they bite, scratch, and wound one another. They only pause to slip away to tend their own wounds, feed upon berries, and sleep. Their need for food and sleep satisfied, they are once again inflamed with anger at the thought that other humans inhabit the forest, and return to stalking their human prey.

Such people perform a variety of Weberian social actions over a period of time in relation to each other, but their activities by no means give them the right to the title 'collectivity'. Once again, we can propose that such a situation will not be stable, that eventually these people will start caring for one another or banding together against other people from other areas, and so on. But, as the case has been described so far, nothing of this sort has happened. There is, however, a proliferation of Weberian social actions. Once again hypothesis W3 has been presented with a counterexample.[26]

Given that we have cleared away the distractions of certain logically inessential possible developments from them, then, I believe that hypothesis W3 is refuted both by stage 3 of the mushroom pickers story and by the story of the misanthropes. It would not be a real blow to my argument if someone were inclined to call the mushroom pickers or the misanthropes 'social groups'. It is, after all, possible to come to use any term in a relatively broad way, when others use it more narrowly. Someone who uses 'social group' rather broadly may still agree that my imaginary populations are significantly different from typical families, clubs, discussion groups, and so on. If so, then we agree that there is the following problem: how can we alter the mushroom pickers' situation so as to have something which is less obviously different from these other populations, the paradigmatic collectivities? Is there perhaps some crucial general feature which is both necessary and sufficient for this?

Possibly there is someone who finds it natural to include the mushroom pickers' type of population after 'families, discussion groups, clubs, tribes, . . .' This would not be totally surprising, since populations of these various sorts can be subsumed under many different rubrics (including 'population' itself). None the less, as I shall argue in Chapter IV, populations including typical families, tribes, clubs and discussion groups do in fact fall into an important and distinctive class that does not include the mushroom pickers. Members of this class are standardly classed as collectivities. Neither Weber's concept of social action nor the narrower notion of demonstrative social action considered here can serve effectively to characterize this class. In particular, hypothesis W3 does not suffice for the purpose. For now, let me press on with some further general remarks on the everyday concept of a collectivity as I understand it.

3.5 Further observations

In my description of the mushroom pickers, though each mushroom picker performed social actions with respect to every other, with some frequency, nothing we would very naturally think of as a 'social interaction' occurred between any two individuals. If we made the mushroom pickers' one-to-one encounters richer, we might well judge that the two people involved in each separate encounter formed a fleeting mini-collectivity at the time of the encounter. Suppose, for instance, that as one looks up, another does also. Their eyes meet, and, in this case, a firm 'Hi!' from one is met by a similar 'Hi!' from the other. Each surmises he has happened upon a fellow English speaker. They stand up, shake hands, and start conversing about the weather, the abundance of mushrooms, and so on. After a few minutes one says 'Well, I must go!' and they go their separate ways with a friendly goodbye. Suppose that such a scene was taking place, at the same time, all over the wood. Then, we may want to say that at 3 p.m. on Thursday, say, fifty little collectivities, in particular, fifty little conversational groups, sprang into being in the wood. However, failing further facts not so far noticed, *the population of mushroom pickers as a whole* would not yet form a social group, intuitively.

Two conclusions suggest themselves. First, if we want to find some relatively general, logically sufficient conditions on collectivity-hood, we could do well to consider everyday conversations. These are indeed among the phenomena that I shall refer to later in elaborating and defending my own positive accounts of collectivity-hood and specific features of collectivities. There is no obvious reason to think that the best way to analyse the conversations constitutive of groups is to start by thinking of them as sequences of actions social in Weber's sense, attempting to discover precisely what subspecies of Weberian social action is at issue.[27] Second, a proliferation of conversations, or more generally, communications, in a population does not make that population a collectivity. In other words, were hypothesis W3 replaced by W4, in which something like 'successful acts of communication' were substituted for 'demonstrative social actions', we would still not get an acceptable hypothesis.

41

Let us consider W4:

Given a population P of two or more agents, if successful acts of communication between the various members regularly occur over time, then P is a social group.

I have claimed that W4 is false. Let me briefly consider one aspect of this issue. Someone might argue as follows: in a population whose members regularly communicated, people would come regularly to use one particular language. The population would then have a language of its own, and, hence, it would be a collectivity. There are various ways of countering this line of thought, however.

One is to ask: in what sense if any of 'Population P has a language of its own' does this entail that P is a social group? My own view on that question should be clear by the end of this book.[28] Meanwhile, let me just say that in my view P must have a language of its own in a sense which implies more than that members regularly communicate with one another in a given language.

Another way of countering this line of thought, which attacks it further up, so to speak, concerns the logical relation between regular communication and regular use of a given language. Briefly put, it can be argued that a proliferation of communication successes in a given population does not logically entail the prior, past, or eventual future *regular use of a given language* by members of that population. From a logical point of view it seems that there could be beings so equipped that in individual encounters they always understood each other (and had reason to think they did) even though in each different encounter a different language was used by the speaker. This is not to say that under specifiable conditions in populations with a given type of member a population-wide regular use of a given language will not inevitably or with a high degree of probability occur. The concept of regular successful communicative behaviour alone, however, will not get us wherever we might think the concept of regular use of a given language will get us.[29]

3.6 Necessary conditions and 'states of nature'

I shall not make any further attempt in this chapter to give a set of logically sufficient conditions for collectivity-hood in terms of Weber's concept of social action. It is clearly unlikely that we shall get something in which Weber's concept plays a central role. Note that I have already gone beyond Weber's concept in using the more specific concept of demonstrative social action (in W3) and of action with communicative intent (in W4). (In later chapters some complex patterns of social action will be looked at. I argue there that these patterns are not sufficient to give us a collectivity.)[30]

I now turn to the idea that a proliferation of social actions in Weber's sense provides us with a necessary condition for a collectivity.[31] Let us consider W5:

> If a population P of two or more agents is to form a collectivity, then the members of P must regularly perform Weberian social actions in relation to one another.

Given such a formulation, a problem arises. *Assume* that W5 is true, that social actions must be performed in any collectivity. Now, of course there are some states of nature – situations where no collectivity is present – in which no social actions are performed. Such was stage 1 of the mushroom pickers' story. At the same time, however, there are states of nature which involve much social action. Indeed, the 'war' of all against all described above, a striking example of a noncollectivity, has as *its* necessary condition a proliferation of Weberian social actions. The problem, then, can be put thus: It seems that even a correct statement of necessary conditions for a social group will not genuinely illuminate the concept of a social group if the conditions are also necessary for a paradigmatic noncollectivity such as the 'war' of all against all.[32] Whether or not W5 is true, then, it does not provide an *illuminating* necessary condition for a social group.

The question remains, of course, as to whether W5 is true. In so far as this is not solvable quite readily, it is of some interest. However, I shall waive this question here. The point I want to make here is this. Whether or not W5 is true, we need to go beyond it if we are to gain any real insight into collectivities. One reason for thinking this is that it does not meet the condition on an illuminating necessary condition noted above.[33]

3.7 Conclusions

I conclude that Weber's generic notion of 'social action' as defined in *Economy and Society* can make little contribution to the analysis of intuitive collectivity concepts. We may feel happier about this when we have settled on the concepts that can make a contribution. But even in advance of this the conclusion seems quite firm.

It would be a real achievement to provide a sufficient condition for the existence of a social group of the form 'a proliferation of actions of kind K performed by all or most members of a population P makes P a social group or society'. It would also be an achievement to provide an illuminating necessary condition for the existence of a social group of the form 'a proliferation of actions of kind K performed by all or most members of a population P is necessary to make P a social group'. It is not clear that we can find any action concept which enables us to provide a condition of either type mentioned, let alone one which enables us to provide conditions of both types at once. It should now be clear, however, that Weber's notion of social action is not of the right kind, and at least to this extent it can make little contribution to the analysis of collectivity concepts.

Regarding the subject matter of sciences appropriately referred to as social sciences we have one conclusion forthwith. If such sciences may be about what are intuitively social groups and their properties, the claim that they are in general about social actions in Weber's sense is highly misleading at best. (It will be highly misleading rather than outright false, if Weberian social actions are logically necessary components of collectivities.) And on the face of it, it is at least as plausible to claim that the study of social groups and their properties would be a social study, as to claim that the study of social actions in Weber's sense would be. I now move on to give arguments to show that Weber's notion of social action leaves much to be desired even if we release it from the task of providing a unitary theory of social scientific subject matters, and ask only that it gives us a helpful partial account.

4 FURTHER CONSIDERATIONS ON WEBER'S CONCEPT

4.1 Introduction

I now turn away from the problem of analysing collectivity concepts in an illuminating way, and indeed stop focusing on these concepts altogether. Let us consider whether reference to Weberian social actions can play some other useful role in the description of natural expectations about what a social science would deal with.

Given that Weber's concept of social action is, after all, the concept of a kind of action that individual persons perform, the following question is a natural one: Is social action in Weber's sense going to be *the* type of action of interest to social scientists, when and in so far as they are concerned with kinds of action that individual persons perform? In this section I argue for a negative answer to this question. My argument involves appeal to existing studies of suicide.

4.2 Concerning suicide

As far as the actual subject matter of sociology goes, I suspect many would agree with Jack Douglas when he writes:[34]

> The theoretical treatment of suicide is one of the few classical subjects in sociology... it was of great importance in the establishment of sociology as an independent discipline... as a result of Durkheim's work on suicide.

Durkheim's work on suicide was particularly striking, in that it attempted to show, using statistical studies of suicide rates in various countries, that suicide, apparently an individual and 'private' act *par excellence*,[35] was actually closely associated with quite specific large-scale features of the surrounding society. For instance, Durkheim claimed to have shown a positive correlation between relatively high suicide rates in a society and 'anomie', the lack of well-defined norms in that society. As far as I know, it is generally not disputed that Durkheim's claims, if they were clearly established, would show that suicide is a proper subject for sociology or, more generally, for social science.

While the existence of important sociological 'suicide studies' may lend plausibility to the idea that sociology is at least to some extent concerned with the study of human action, or types of human action, it at the same time appears to disprove the claim that it is social action in Weber's sense which is sociology's concern. It is worth discussing the nature of suicide and of Durkheim's interest in suicide in enough detail to show what is true and what is false in both of these impressions.

(i) The definition of 'suicide'

How precisely to define 'suicide' has been an important issue for the sociologist, and definitions have differed.[36] As I noted earlier, Durkheim's definition of suicide is somewhat at odds with intuitive 'pretheoretical' conceptions, a fact of which he is aware and which he makes a point of saying does not worry him. He insists that suicide, as the sociologist conceives of it, should not definitionally involve one's aiming at his own death. We should count as a suicide, for instance, one who does not act expressly in order to bring about his own death, but rather sees his death as an evil which will inevitably come about as he pursues some other

45

aim. Thus Durkheim urges that we should not define 'suicide' narrowly as 'deliberately killing oneself' but more broadly as 'dying as the result of an act one knows will produce one's own death'. (It appears, then, that no particular meaningful content, in Weber's sense, is ascribed to suicidal acts in general by Durkheim. The only condition for an act's being an act of suicide is the agent's *knowledge that*, in doing a certain thing, he will bring about his own death.)

Whatever the merits and demerits of this account from a sociological or an intuitive point of view, it seems to square with intuitive notions at least in this: committing suicide involves doing something intentionally, where the meaning of one's action is such that it is not necessarily Weberian social action.[37]

On no natural definition of 'suicide' will suicide be a Weberian social action as a matter of logic. It seems, then, that the existence of sociological studies of suicide, in particular Durkheim's, disprove the claim that in so far as social sciences are concerned with types of human action, they are concerned with social action in Weber's sense.

(ii) 'De facto' social action

It may be objected that I am wrong to suppose that Weber, or anyone else, would say that the act *types* with which social sciences deal are social in Weber's sense *by definition*. They could say, rather, that the particular, dated actions with which the sociologist deals are *in fact* social. That is, they are indeed often tokens of act-types such that an act may be of that type without being oriented to others, but they are, none the less, oriented to others *de facto* as it were, rather than *de iure*. A case of suicide, for instance, may be oriented to others in various ways, even though *qua* suicide it does not have to be so oriented. One may kill oneself out of revenge, out of spite, out of despair that one will never be loved by a certain person, and so on.

What then of the claim that social scientists are concerned with particular acts which are in fact social in Weber's sense? Do sociological studies provide a counterexample to *this* claim? I take it that the questions to ask are these: Do sociologists study actions which are in fact always social in the relevant sense? Are they interested in such actions *qua* social actions?

On the face of it, it is by no means obvious that all actual cases of suicide are in fact social actions in Weber's sense. Of course this is ultimately an empirical matter. However, one could cite the possibility of someone's killing himself in a fit of 'objectless depression'. Moreover there are many cases where the depressed state, though having a clear conscious object, does not make an action involving it qualify as social in Weber's sense. A scientist might be severely depressed over his inability to explain some phenomenon; someone might fall into despair on hearing he has contracted a fatal disease. No other person is the object of the person's depression in these cases.

Recall that for Weber it is not enough that the agent is *influenced by* the people who surround him, unless this leads the 'subjective meaning' of the act to refer to them. Nor is it enough for thoughts about others to be running through the suicide's head, unless he decides to act *in order* to spite them, say, or *because* they have spurned him. Our empirical knowledge surely does not make it clear, moreover, that there is always at least an unconscious orientation to others. Weber might accept such an orientation as entailing that an action is social, but we surely do not know that motivations of the relevant kind occur in every case. The aetiology of the various forms of depression is a highly complex matter about which there is surely no such knowledge, at least at present.

Suppose that we were to agree for the sake of argument that *all* suicide cases were in fact cases of social action (obviously very many are, at least). This would not show that sociologists studying these cases were concerned with suicide *qua* social action. This feature of all cases might never be mentioned by the sociologist, either as part of his characterization of his initial concern, or as part of an explanatory theory. In trying to characterize the subject matter of social science we are presumably interested in saying what the precise concern of the social scientist is.

(iii) The Durkheimian approach to suicide

How then is it with sociology as we find the subject? Are those who study suicide interested in it *qua* oriented to others or not? If we look at Durkheim's *Suicide*, and at a 'Durkheimian' approach in general, it appears that the initial interest is not in *individual cases* of suicide as such, but rather in differences in *suicide rates*, in particular in differences in the suicide rate between different social groups. Durkheim thought he could explain such differential rates in terms of 'social facts': 'social structure', 'currents of opinion', and the like. Given a certain type of society, as opposed to some other type, and other things being equal, there is more (or less) suicide per head of population.[38]

According to this style of sociology, sociologists might be said to be interested in suicide or any other phenomenon of human action only in so far as they can explain its incidence in a social group by reference to properties of the group in question. Thus these sociologists will be interested in suicide, say, *qua* action of a type whose incidence is somehow dependent on or influenced by certain particular kinds of collectivity states.

It is evident that for sociologists of this type, a particular species of human action cannot in general be known a priori to be of sociological interest. Thus it might have been that the incidence of suicide in a group was a function not of its social structure, but of the weather in the region in which it occurred.[39] Perhaps it is in fact so dependent, and sociologists who have argued on behalf of 'social causes' are mistaken. If so, then suicide studies would only be 'sociological' by mistake, as it were; they would play no part (as far as explanatory theories for suicide were concerned) in a perfected sociological theory.

This approach gives us, in effect, another possible definition for the phrase 'social action'. On this definition, a social action would be an action of a kind whose incidence in a society is influenced by particular states of collectivities. This seems unlikely to be extensionally equivalent to Weber's notion and it clearly gives a different meaning to the phrase. As we have seen, by 'social action' Weber does not mean *action influenced by certain states of other people*, let alone *action whose incidence is affected causally by states of the relevant collectivity*. (This latter sense of 'social action' obviously does not fit Weber's 'individualist' orientations with respect to a fundamental concept of sociology.)

Durkheim's approach to suicide, then, did not focus on suicide *qua* Weberian social action. Yet I assume that as this approach has been roughly characterized here, it would intuitively be thought of as a sociological or social scientific theory. The theory aims to explain the variation in the suicide rate between different groups, and the general form of the theory is that, roughly, these rates are a function of the kind of group in which they occur. None the less the theory is quite naturally thought of as concerned with a type of human action. Studies of suicide of a more 'understanding' nature may be found.[40] None the less, the very possibility of a theory of this general form makes it clear that to say that a social science will concern itself with types of action only if they are social in Weber's sense, and indeed only *qua* social in Weber's sense, is at best highly misleading. One might prefer to be less generous and argue that it is simply false.

It may be objected that it is unfair to use the Durkheimian approach as a counterexample to Weber's claims about the centrality of social actions, because Durkheim's approach is

48

precisely antithetical to Weber's. My reply is that we are here considering what types of theory about human actions, by whomsoever, would intuitively count as social scientific theories, and Durkheim's surely counts as such a theory.

Someone might possibly argue on behalf of Weber, at this point, that Durkheim's approach to suicide is considered sociological because it appeals to states of collectivities, as intuitively conceived, as explanatory variables. That is, it is considered sociological because of its appeal to something constituted by social actions in Weber's sense. While I would agree with the first of the above statements, it is not really germane to the point at issue in this section. As to the second point, I have already argued that the claim that social scientists are concerned with social actions in Weber's sense is misleading, if it is intended to capture the idea that collectivities and their states, as intuitively conceived, are appropriate subjects for social science. Thus in so far as the point about Durkheim is right, it constitutes, if anything, a mark against Weber's social action concept with respect to the characterization of social scientific subject matters, and in favour of the pre-eminent importance of everyday collectivity concepts.

(iv) 'Verstehen' approaches to suicide

Approaches to suicide with a greater concern for '*Verstehen*' than Durkheim's are possible. Given that this is so, it is unlikely that these will focus on Weberian social action as such. On the one hand they may be expected to be concerned with a broader concept, on the other hand they may well concern narrower notions. Let me explain.

One might attempt simply to catalogue or categorize *motivations* agents typically have for suicide. Now it is possible that one might find out that suicides generally divide into a few basic categories, say, for the sake of argument, into revenge suicides, and suicides constituting calls for attention. If these were the categories in question, then it would have turned out that suicides were generally social actions in Weber's sense. But whether or not this was so, the initial concern would have been suicide in general. Moreover, it is not obvious that without some prodding from a knowledge of Weber's concept one would find it salient or particularly interesting that the result could be described in terms of that concept. It is true that someone could in principle set out specifically to discover what are the ways (if any) in which suicides take others into account. Indeed if someone took the view that he was engaged in a discipline whose central subject

49

matter was Weberian social actions he probably would limit his enquiries into suicide, if he made any, in some such manner. In advance of a defence of the importance of Weber's category, however, any such limit is likely to appear arbitrary. If one's interest is in human suicide, its modes and reasons, there seems little point in dividing the subject up *in advance* into the bit which considers orientations to others and its kinds and the bit which considers other orientations.

It is plausible to suppose that where the scientist's interest in explaining or categorizing suicide *is* restricted to suicides of a certain type, the type will tend to be more specific than action social in Weber's sense. Consider, for instance, the following possibility. Someone impressed by political self-immolations by Buddhist monks and others could start an inquiry into the conditions under which a person might seriously consider and actually undertake such suicide. Then the intended topic would not be suicide *qua* social action in Weber's sense, in spite of the fact that all political action *is* at the same time social in this sense. The focus would, rather, be suicide *qua* action aiming at improving one's society, or *qua* political action.

(v) Suicide studies and social science

It is possible that many who find the Durkheimian approach to suicide unattractive hunger for a kind of account which is hardly that of a scientific study at all. Such an account might perhaps be provided by a subject we could call 'phenomenological psychology' or it may best be left to novelists and poets. Thus Sylvia Plath's poem 'Daddy' may seem to give one more insight into the mind of someone with an urge to suicide than anything Durkheim ever wrote. (Of course Durkheim did not set out to provide any such insight.) The idea of investigating 'typical motivations' and the like may give a better approximation to this sort of insight than Durkheim gives us. It is not clear that either the phenomenological approach or the typical motivations approach would very naturally be thought of as constituting, in themselves, branches of *social* science. For these approaches to suicide do not, in setting out their appointed tasks, mention anything which is obviously to be labelled a 'social phenomenon'.

Sociological studies like Durkheim's can be closely related to motivational questions. For example, assume that there is a highly negative correlation of suicide rates with the existence of clear-cut, well-known, well-established norms in a society. In itself, this tells us nothing about individual motivation, but it can point to or suggest hypotheses about individual motivation which can be investigated at the individual level. Not only can studies at the level of the group point to explanations at the individual level, but the data about individuals' motivations may sometimes explain how the correlations between large scale variables come about. In so far as the psychological data would then play an important role in explaining the facts about groups, such data could be considered 'part' of social science.

(vi) Conclusions, and a further question

In conclusion, it appears that, first, suicide need not be social action in Weber's sense, though it may be. Second, the Durkheimian approach to suicide, which may be complemented by psychological studies, is not concerned with suicide *qua* social action in Weber's sense. This approach would be intelligible and would not be any less sociological even if suicides never in fact took account of the behaviour of others. This is enough to refute the claim that social action in Weber's sense is going to be the type of action of interest to social scientists.

I have noted, in addition, that there is a variety of possible '*Verstehen*' approaches to suicide. Not all will be concerned with suicide *qua* action of a certain kind, where that kind is indeed a species of Weberian social action. Suppose, though, that we restrict ourselves to studies that are so concerned. It is not obvious that these will naturally be referred to as social studies. That will depend, it seems, on whether Weberian social action is intuitively a social phenomenon, a question I take up later. But even if we waive this issue, it is clear that the claim that Weberian social action is the type of action we can expect to interest investigators with a special interest in '*Verstehen*' is misleading. For the focus of interest may be expected not to be suicide *qua* Weberian social action, but rather *qua* some specific type of Weberian social action. We need not restrict the point to suicide studies alone. For instance, Erving Goffman wrote on *Behavior in Public Places*. Such behaviour may tend to be other-oriented, but the specific concern of the study is not with its other orientation as such but rather with behaviour in a certain rather special kind of context.

Now the facts just mentioned suggest that Weber's category of social action is not an especially salient or interesting category. Which brings us (as we become less and less ambitious for Weber's concept) to the last question: Is social action in Weber's sense going to be *a* type of action of interest to social scientists? One way to address this question is by considering whether the category of Weberian social action is a scientifically promising one.

4.3 Weber's 'social action' as a scientific concept

I shall now argue that, on the face of it, the category of Weberian social action is not itself a promising candidate for a scientific concept.

In the literature on such concepts, the following two features have been seen as particularly desirable: clear criteria of application, and aptness for use in the statement of scientific laws or, more modestly, of scientific theories.[41] Suppose we accept that Weber's concept has the first feature to a high degree. What, then, of the second? It might seem that we cannot possibly say a priori – in advance of the development of successful theory – that any given notion will or will not prove to be scientifically fruitful. Given a certain background of knowledge of the world one can, however, make plausible judgments along these lines.

Considering the range of meaningful actions, we might draw up two columns; one for nonsocial action and the other for social action (in Weber's senses). Under 'nonsocial action' we would find: performing a private superstitious ritual intended to promote one's own good fortune; kicking a stone in anger; committing suicide in a fit of 'objectless' depression. Under 'social action' we would find: performing a private superstitious ritual intended to promote one's child's good fortune; committing suicide in order to earn someone's pity; kicking a man in anger in order to hurt him and thus relieve one's own feeling of misery. Thus kicking a man in anger in order to hurt him is social, kicking a stone in anger is not. Kicking a man in order to hurt him is a social action, and so is performing a private superstitious ritual to help one's child, but performing the same ritual to help oneself is not social action.

This is the way Weber's social action category would have us divide things up, but intuitively the divisions seem to fall elsewhere. For example, performances of superstitious rituals, on behalf of oneself or another, appear to call for investigation as a single category. Again, the study of aggressive angry behaviour might be expected not to distinguish between stone-kicking and man-kicking in so far as its purview went. In short it is not clear that any theory is likely to need the broad Weberian distinction between social action and nonsocial action in demarcating its subject matter. The onus is on the Weberian to show that his concept divides things up into importantly distinct kinds, the Weberian social and the Weberian nonsocial.

Weber himself was not unaware of or unconcerned with this issue. In what I take to be an important observation in the *Logos* essay, he observed:

In principle, it appears at first sight irrelevant whether a person's action is guided by the expectation that certain natural events will occur, with or without his purposive intervention, or that human beings will act in a certain way. (p. 1376)

Note that Weber is already implicitly concerning himself with a notion narrower than his official notion of social action (which does not only concern one's taking account of the *expected future actions* of others). Moreover, in the interesting but obscure passage which follows, he seems to envisage far more restrictive accounts of social action and hence rather different phenomena. Since my brief is to hold still his official notion of social action for investigation, I shall not attempt to follow Weber here, or consider possible changes in his concept which might meet the criterion at issue in this section.

At this point, with respect to Weber's concept of social action, well known as it is and often quoted (though also misquoted), it seems reasonable to agree with Rolf Dahrendorf when he says:[42]

There floats over Weber's 'Basic Sociological Terms' a slight air of irrelevance: one may use these concepts if one wishes to, but one is not forced to, and it is difficult to demonstrate that one should.

Indeed, it seems reasonable to say something stronger: one should not wish to use, or use, this concept unless someone has demonstrated that one should. Dahrendorf is surely too complaisant: sociologists and philosophers of social science should not complicate their thought and ours with a concept whose introduction has no obvious justification, and of which it is tempting to say that it obviously has no justification.

4.4 Are Weberian social actions intuitively social phenomena?

Are actions social in Weber's sense *social phenomena* intuitively? If they are, then something like the following, at least, could be said in defence of Weber's concept: in so far as actions falling under it are the topic of an investigation, or are otherwise focused upon, then that investigation would naturally be thought of as a part of social science.

It might be thought that the fact that they have been labelled 'social' actions shows that social actions in Weber's sense have been felt to be social phenomena. I was probably once inclined to think so.[43] But the import of this usage can be questioned. It would be possible to find the label 'social' appropriate because one thinks of acts of the type in question as the building blocks of collectivities and their states. In other words, the label may be used solely because of a presumed relation to what one conceives of as a social phenomenon proper. Then 'social' actions would be considered social only in a derived sense, in the sense of 'constitutive of (some) social phenomenon proper'. It is not clear how Weber saw the reason for his labelling, but this is quite possibly it.[44]

The status of Weberian social actions as social phenomena in a nonderived sense is doubtful. I do not wish to address this issue at length here. I return to it in the book's conclusion. However, a few related points may be noted.

One way to elicit the reaction that an action social in Weber's sense is not as such a social phenomenon intuitively is to stress such facts as these: social actions in Weber's sense can in principle be performed even if only one agent exists or has existed in the world; a social action can be performed with another person in mind even when that other never learns of it or guesses at it; I can perform a social action in relation to you and you perform one later, in relation to me, without us 'interacting' in any intuitive sense; my punching another from behind in order to get him to see stars is a social action in Weber's sense.

It may also be useful to look at things from another point of view. What features of Weberian social action might incline one to think that the performance of such an action brings the social into the world? First, one might cite the fact that Weberian social action by its nature 'has to do' with a plurality of persons (to put it vaguely). Now, it appears a single Weberian social action does not entail the actual existence of such a plurality. This surely militates against our having a social phenomenon proper here. None the less Weberian social actions do at least 'have to do with' a plurality of persons. (Compare, say, acts aimed at solving a problem in mathematics; or acts aimed at shortening one's hair.) Second, Weberian social action involves a type of intentional connection between one person and another (or hypothesized other). That is, one person has the other in mind in some way. Again, it might be thought that for there to be a social phenomenon proper among humans there must be a plurality of persons each of whom has some sort of intentional tie to the others. This may be why Weber's example of a set of people all holding up umbrellas because it is raining has intuitive appeal as a case to rule out of the domain of social phenomena. Of course, people holding up umbrellas in the rain could have a variety of orientations to their fellows or to members of the wider society. But in so far as each one's motive is purely to protect himself from rain, the simple fact that they all do the same thing does not seem to make the phenomenon of simultaneous umbrella raising a social phenomenon in itself.[45]

Given that these two things – plurality of persons, and mental connection between them in terms of each conceiving of the other or others in some way – are features of anything we would think of as a social phenomenon proper, one can see why it might not seem *bizarre* to call action social in Weber's sense 'social' action. None the less, given these two facts it also seems clear that social actions in Weber's sense, as such, are not themselves social phenomena intuitively. In addition, I think it doubtful that we have an intuitively social phenomenon even when we have a demonstrative social action, in which two actual people are, by definition, involved, or a 'pair' of such actions, in which one person performs such an action towards another, and later the other performs such an action towards the original person (as happens in the case of each pair of mushroom pickers at stage 3) – so that each does conceive of the other in some way.

It might be urged that I now try to construct an example of an intuitively social phenomenon out of a particular type of complex of actions social in Weber's sense or in some refinement of that sense. But I see no reason to constrain inquiry further by focusing on Weber's notion of social action. (Later discussion of social conventions, however, will demonstrate, in effect, that certain interesting sequences of social action in Weber's sense are not collectivity-creating, as could be supposed.)

5 CONCLUSIONS

I have mentioned four reasons one might have for labelling one particular kind of action as 'social' action in the philosophy of social science. Negative conclusions on Weber's concept emerge on all counts.

First, a certain concept of action might play an illuminating role in the analysis of vernacular collectivity concepts. These concepts are, Weber contends, inevitably going to figure in sociological thinking. I see no reason to dispute this claim. If it is true, then students of sociology or the philosophy of sociology may well need some form of analysis of these concepts in order to understand fully what they are talking about. If they need this, then, I have argued, Weber's concept of social action is not what they need.

Second, if we could illuminatingly mark off all those types of action which might, intuitively, provide a focus for a social science, by reference to some precisely specified type of action, the concept of that special type of action might justly reign supreme in the social sciences and the philosophy of social science. We could then justify a casual use of the phrase 'social action' in these disciplines. If there is such a kind of action, Weberian social action appears not to be it.

Third, a particular concept of action might pick out some obviously important natural class of events which were intuitively 'social' and for which one might hope some science could provide explanations and/or understanding. It does not appear likely that Weber's notion of social action picks out a class of events of such a kind. One reason is that it does not appear to 'carve nature at the joints', in so far as one can tell such a thing a priori.

Fourth, actions of a particular type might be social phenomena in a nonderived sense. It is not clear that Weber's notion *is* a notion of an intuitively social phenomenon.

A main conclusion of this chapter is that Weber's notion of 'social action' cannot provide a satisfactory *unitary* theory of social scientific subject matters, or of social phenomena in general. Let me summarize my argument. Given that there are social groups or collectivities, societies, business associations, clubs, and so on, these are clearly social things or phenomena of some kind. Weber himself, we recall, says that sociologists cannot 'afford to ignore' collectivity *concepts*. Now if these concepts *do* apply to things in the world, what they apply to will, presumably, be subjects or potential subjects for social sciences. The social sciences are quite commonly characterized, indeed, as 'sciences of society'. It seems then that a unitary social action theory of the social sciences could only work if it could somehow be argued that statements about social groups said 'nothing' over and above certain appropriate statements about the occurrence of social actions, as such. The only clear way of showing this would be to show that the concept of a social group was analysable rather simply in terms of social actions. I have argued that as far as Weber's social action notion goes, social groups cannot usefully be argued to be 'nothing but sequences of social actions'.

One further point may be noted. I have not wanted to insist that action social in Weber's sense is not already a social phenomenon, whatever its connections to other things. But if someone judges that it is, and we go with this judgment, then it begins to look doubtful whether we can have any illuminating unitary theory of social science subject matter, given that collectivities are conceivable foci for science, and a science of collectivities would intuitively be a social science. For we have seen in the case of Weber's notion that if a theory of potential social scientific subject matters must embrace social groups, a

56

theory that social sciences are about Weberian social actions may well be false and will certainly not be very helpful. However, there is the reverse problem also. It seems absurd to suggest that Weberian social actions are constituted by collectivities. Nor is it plausible to suppose that whatever the basic elements of collectivities actually are, Weberian social actions are also constituted by such elements. In short it is hard to see how there can be an illuminating unitary theory of social phenomena that embraces these two radically distinct phenomena, collectivities on the one hand, and Weberian social actions on the other. It is on the cards that there can be no such theory. Meanwhile, one thing is clear: collectivities are intuitively social phenomena. This is a good reason to continue the search for an account of social groups.

III
ACTION, MEANING, AND THE SOCIAL

1 INTRODUCTION

1.1 The intentionalist programme

None of my criticisms of Weber's technical concept of social action in the last chapter goes against the idea that, if we are to give an adequate account of our everyday concept of a social group, we will have to appeal to the intentional or meaningful acts of human beings. If this *intentionalist* programme is correct, then thought is part of the foundation of human social groups as intuitively conceived: thought is logically prior to society.

In this chapter I address a philosophical position whose correctness would raise problems for the intentionalist programme, and argue against it. This will clear the ground for my own accounts of our concept of a social group and related concepts. For these are intentionalist accounts. In so far as the main argument of this chapter does not develop or defend the specifics of my particular intentionalist accounts, it would be feasible for a reader to cover the rest of the material in the book without prior consideration of this chapter. However, in rounding out my argument I shall have reason to sketch an account of one important collectivity concept, the concept of a group's language.

1.2 The society-dependence thesis

A number of philosophers and social scientists, influenced in particular by Wittgenstein, have attributed a social character to language and related phenomena. Thus the philosopher Michael Dummett espouses 'the social character of language' and 'the social character of meaning' (1974, p. 424), and anthropologist

Clifford Geertz writes that 'meaning is public' (1973, p. 12). Perhaps the strongest of these claims occurs in a well-known work in the philosophy of social science, Peter Winch's monograph *The Idea of a Social Science*. Winch claims that 'all meaningful behaviour must be social' (p. 116). He refers, apparently, to all intentional action as such.[1] Meanwhile, the exact import of the claims made is not always clear.

According to Winch, for one, we cannot say what meaningful behaviour is without bringing society in. That is, meaningful behaviour is logically impossible for anyone who has had no experience of a human society (see op. cit., p. 33). If this *society-dependence thesis* were true, for whatever reason, an intentionalist account of our collectivity concepts would be circular. In this chapter I argue against the society-dependence thesis. My argument will at the same time count against the possibly more general idea that meaningful action as such has an intrinsically social nature, and the parallel claim about language as such. The argument will go quite deeply into questions about the nature of both thought and language.

The simplest argument against the thesis that meaningful behaviour is society-dependent is as follows. The thesis is counterintuitive on the face of it: the idea of one whose actions are meaningful though he has never participated in the life of any society appears at first sight to be perfectly coherent. Surely it is logically possible for someone to kick a stone or reach for food intentionally without any prior experience of a human society? Some may feel that this argument is all that is needed to refute the thesis that meaningful behaviour is society-dependent. But it will not satisfy those who think there are good arguments for society-dependence. They will naturally demand that these arguments be considered before society-dependence is rejected.

The thesis that language is social might seem more plausible at first. And some may, indeed, link the two theses via the assumption that thought is itself logically dependent on language. However, if the claim is that it is logically impossible to have a language if one has not participated in group life, it is similarly counterintuitive on the face of it. It appears that we can at least conceive of a congenital Crusoe – a being socially isolated throughout his life – who was initially endowed with, or invented, a language all his own. In other words, it appears that such a being is at least a logical possibility. Of course some philosophers have argued to the contrary, and I shall examine some such arguments in what follows. But at least before acquaintance with these arguments, untutored intuition seems to take the other side.

Someone might react to this along the following lines. 'Surely it is not fortuitous that a language such as English is an efficient means of interpersonal communication? Surely, therefore, such a language cannot be viewed as a mere sum of idiolects, a phenomenon resulting from a chance coincidence of "privately owned" languages? This suggests that by its very nature language is a social phenomenon. In other words, what has just been alleged to be conceivable is not really so.'

In my view, it can indeed be argued that a *group's* language, of the sort group members standardly use when they communicate with one another, is not a mere sum of idiolects. And a group's language is a paradigmatically social phenomenon. But it does not follow from this that language as such is social from a logical point of view. Nor do I believe that it is. Hence, were thought impossible without language, this would not itself justify the claim that thought as such was social. These positions will be supported in the course of my attack on the idea that meaningful behaviour is society-dependent. This attack goes beyond the simple appeals to direct intuition that have just been noted.

1.3 My strategy

I begin with a close examination of the arguments for society-dependence presented by Peter Winch in *The Idea of a Social Science*, arguments he finds in Wittgenstein's *Philosophical Investigations*. This is an obvious and, as it turns out, a useful place to start. Of course Winch's is not the only available interpretation of Wittgenstein's notoriously obscure text. But Winch has not been alone either in ascribing the arguments he does to Wittgenstein or in finding them convincing in their own right. (Some of those in agreement have fairly clearly worked independently, others appear to have been influenced by Winch.) Others, of course, have not been convinced by these arguments. At the same time, as I shall explain, some of the explicit criticisms that have been made miss the point, faulting too easy a target. A thorough and decisive attack must go deep, and, indeed, beyond the issues Winch himself explicitly addresses. A close examination of the arguments he presents, then, proves to be a good way into the fundamental problem area at issue in this chapter. Since Winch clearly accepts the arguments in question, and their relationship to Wittgenstein is less clear, in what follows I shall refer to them as 'Winch's' arguments, for short.

I shall contend that these arguments involve a number of unjustified moves. These moves are worthy of notice, however, for they are obviously tempting and easy to overlook. Engagement with the arguments, meanwhile, forces us to consider some crucial and difficult questions about language and thought. Is it possible to give a coherent account of the nature of language and thought as such that does not bring society in? In particular, can such an account allow that, roughly, there can be a right (and a wrong) way to go on in the application of concepts?

I first briefly argue that our everyday concepts of thought and language assume the coherence of a particular type of 'nonsocial' account. But Saul Kripke has noted a crucial set of problems for any such account in his book *Wittgenstein on Rules and Private Language*. This leads me to defend the coherence of a platonist or fregean account. I take this to be the only account of the required type that is salvageable given the considerations Kripke puts forward. Thus there is a high premium attached to this defence. If the defence fails, we have to conclude that there is no such thing as language and thought according to our everyday concepts. Meanwhile, if our concepts of thought and language are indeed coherent, then we must allow that it is possible in principle for there to be a creature without experience of a society which thinks and uses language. Hence the logical society-dependence thesis must be rejected.

In sum, my attack on the logical society-dependence thesis has two main elements. On the one hand I reject as flawed or inconclusive some common ideas that appear to support the thesis, focusing for the purposes of argument on Winch's text. On the other hand I provide a defence of a nonsocial account of intention against some considerable and profound objections. I conclude that intentional acts are logically independent of participation in a collectivity.

Two important further issues will be dealt with. On the one hand, I consider what might be said if, despairing of the acceptability of any nonsocial account of the nature of language and thought, one were to adopt the positive approach that Kripke ascribes to Wittgenstein. Suppose that rather than considering *the nature of language and thought*, we concern ourselves with the 'assertability conditions' for the sentences in which we talk about language and thought, with questions about when it is proper to say such things as 'George knows what "counterdependent" means' and so on. I argue that if we adopt this approach, an analogue of the intentionalist programme is by no means obviously ruled out.

On the other hand, suppose we accept a platonist account of thought and meaning. Such an account entails that when one uses language one's meaning, if not quite in the head, is not necessarily discoverable by observation of one's behaviour. Now this poses a problem. If meanings are not open to public view, how can we communicate, how can there be a language that people share and know they share? Or can such things not take place on this view, something which would be at best a disturbing consequence? I provide an answer to these questions. I argue for a radical distinction between a language 'owned' by a single individual and a group's language (or 'group language'). This involves giving a sketch of an analysis of the important notion of a group language. I argue that, on the one hand, this uses the basic semantic concepts needed to characterize the language of a single individual, or an idiolect. On the other hand, the notion is not that of a simple aggregation of idiolects. From a structural point of view, it can be argued that a group language is the most efficient means of communication among humans. But, as I show, there is no need to reject a platonist understanding of thought and language in general in order to accommodate group languages.

1.4 The claim that meaningful behaviour, as such, is intrinsically social

My discussion starts with the provocation of Winch's claim that all meaningful behaviour must be social. I take this to be the claim, more precisely, that meaningful behaviour as such is intrinsically social. (I explain what I have in mind shortly.) This I take to be a radical claim, and, indeed, to be false. At the same time, a number of similar but distinct theses are fairly obviously true. Let me briefly mention a number of these more plausible views, in order to make it as clear as possible what I am *not* arguing against.

There is of course a variety of uses of the term 'meaning'. Raising one's hat to someone counts in some circles as a sign of deference. We may say that hat raising has a certain established meaning in these circles. Thus we may talk about 'meaning' when we have something like meaning-by-social-convention in mind. (The phrase 'social meaning' seems quite apposite in such contexts.)[2] Someone might say that all meaningful behaviour was social if they had in mind meaning by social convention, and intended to stress that such meaningfulness was the product of a social group. But the arguments at issue in this chapter are not about meaning by social convention. They concern, rather, meaning in roughly Weber's sense, a sense to be further articulated in the next section. The social nature of behaviour which is meaningful in this sense is hardly obvious. Argument is clearly needed when we are concerned not with meaning-by-social-convention, but with different forms of meaning.[3]

The claim that meaningful behaviour, or action, *as such* is social concerns the content of our concept of an action. It is therefore distinct from a number of reasonable and important empirical claims with which it could be confused. For instance, it may be that human infants require the nurturance of other members of their species in order to develop their capacities for more than rudimentary actions.[4] Again, given that adult humans in general live in a social milieu, many if not all of their actions may be expected to bear the stamp of this. For instance, we may expect many human actions to be performed in the light of knowledge that they are considered obligatory or at least permissible in a certain group. Such claims are of obvious interest, and indicate the wide range of phenomena that may turn out to be in some sense or to some degree intuitively social. None the less they do not have to do with the very concept of meaningful behaviour.

The assertion that actions as such are *intrinsically* social, ascribes a social nature to actions by virtue of what they are in themselves, rather than by virtue of their potential for bearing some relation to other things. One might perhaps think of actions as social because one believed that it is out of actions and their ilk that social phenomena are constituted. (A belief Weber, of course, would have accepted, though he evidently wished to stress that a particular type of action was needed to make a society.) The claim at issue is not of this sort.

Even the carefully qualified claim that actions as such are intrinsically social could be used to express a thesis distinct from the one at issue here. It could be used to sum up a methodological thesis about how action may best be understood, or accurately characterized. Given that an action is a piece of behaviour which has a certain meaning from the point of view of the agent, it seems reasonable to argue that one who wants to understand another's action must if possible enter into social relations with the agent. This seems to follow from the quite humdrum point that one would do well to *ask* the agent what he or she is doing.[5] Asking this will presumably involve both parties in a social relationship, albeit of a transitory kind. (The nature of the situations where questions are asked, and so on, will be discussed further in the next chapter.) Such a point does make plain one rather clear distinction between the methodologies of the natural sciences and the study of human action. Nor is it without serious practical consequences. Once asking questions of the subject of study is part of one's investigation, new skills become helpful research tools. One needs skills of the kind which dispose those studied to frankness, for instance. Students of elementary particles or numbers are not in this position.[6] The dictum that actions as such are intrinsically social, if used to express such a view, will in effect be ascribing socialness to each action for the reason that, if a certain operation upon it (understanding) is to come about, then something intuitively social in itself (social relations) will first have to be brought into being. The socialness of actions in this sense is not at issue in this chapter. The question is rather whether all actions, like all social relations, are social irrespective of any consideration of the conditions under which they are best investigated.

A final note: people sometimes write as if the subject matter of the social sciences was, simply, the acts of individual humans, with no special restriction on the context or content of the acts and thoughts.[7] I doubt that this is because people see action as such as intrinsically social. The identification could derive from the idea that social phenomena are partly constituted by the actions and thoughts of individual human beings. Or it could stem from a conscious or unconscious denial that such putative phenomena as the collectivities of everyday thought are in fact real, which leads to an insistence that if there is to be any scientific study of the 'social' it must relate not to collectivities at all but to the actions and thoughts of the human beings who invent them. Again, it could result from a simple lack of interest in the collective aspects of human life, from a sense that the active individual person is what is important, of value, and hence of primary interest to the social sciences. Certainly, to character-ize social science as a whole in this way has the effect of devaluing collectivities and collective phenomena. The fact, then, that people have sometimes characterized the subject matter of the social sciences as the actions of human beings, does not show that it is natural to think of actions as such as intrinsically social phenomena.

2 THE DEEP LEVEL OF THE DISCUSSION

2.1 Introduction

Winch's claim that 'all meaningful behaviour must be social' occurs in the context of a criticism of Weber's distinction between 'behaviour which is merely meaningful and that which is both

meaningful and social' (*The Idea of a Social Science*, p. 116).[8]
Winch continues:

> It is evident that any such distinction is incompatible with the
> argument of Chapter II of this book: all meaningful behaviour
> must be social, since it can be meaningful only if governed by
> rules, and rules presuppose a social setting.

In decrying Weber's distinction, Winch could have been
arguing that all action must be social action in Weber's technical
sense, and that Weber's technical distinction between social and
nonsocial action marks no real distinction among phenomena for
this reason. However, it looks rather as if Winch's claim is this:
given the meaning of the qualifier 'social', all actions are and
must be social in a certain way, and therefore no absolute
distinction in principle between actions which are 'social' and
those which are not can be made. This claim could then generate
the following criticism of Weber: his use and stipulative definition
of the phrase 'social action' obscures the important fact that all
action is social in some way to be specified.

One way of describing the social character of action, according
to Winch, is apparently this: in order to be meaningful,
behaviour must be 'governed by rules, and rules presuppose a
social setting' (p. 116). An earlier claim appears to provide a
gloss on the point about rules and social settings: in order to
follow a rule one must 'have had experience of human society'
(p. 33). In other words, what is ultimately alleged is a form of
logical society-dependence for actions as such.

As I shall shortly argue, there is a way of construing the claim
that all actions are 'governed by rules' which makes this hard to
doubt. If we interpret Winch in the relevant terms, the pressing
question is whether the society-dependence of rules of the
relevant type can be made out.

I should note at the outset that Winch's own discussion is often
obscure, and though my discussion of it is quite thorough, I do
not claim that no other reading is possible. The reading that
follows is in important ways a sympathetic one. On this reading
the discussion concerns a fundamental issue and proceeds at a
deep enough level to stand a chance of proving the society-
dependence of meaningful behaviour. I shall, of course, contend
that Winch ultimately fails to prove this. But the reasons for this
failure are instructive, and it brings us face-to-face with what is
perhaps the most profound issue in the philosophy of language
and thought.

2.2 The deep level of the discussion

In my view Winch's argument is best seen as proceeding at a particular, deep level. This has not always been appreciated. Let me explain.

The argument starts from the assumption that all meaningful behaviour involves the agent in *following a rule* of some kind. What sort of rule is at issue? Winch wants to argue that all rules of the type in question presuppose a social setting. Knowing this, someone might assume that it is social rules or conventions, such as the convention that men open doors for women, that are at issue in the initial assumption. For it is easy to accept that rules or conventions of this kind presuppose a social setting. But then an obvious problem arises: surely it is possible to act without following such a social rule or convention?

More generally, many have objected as follows to the linking of meaningful behaviour with rules. Surely one is not in fact following rules all the time, surely one can act without following any rules? What about someone who deliberately disobeys a rule, someone, say, who deliberately smokes beside a sign saying 'Smoking not allowed in this area'? And surely there are many particular things one does which do not involve the following of rules of any kind? For instance, walking alone in the country, I might turn round in order to discover the source of a sudden noise. Winch himself imagines such objections and reacts at one point by saying that even an anarchist's way of life is a *way of life*, and hence involves the adoption of a type of principle (p. 58). But he does not need to rely on this sort of point, which seems hard to sustain for all cases that might be cited.

The objections noted are all avoided once one sees that Winch's argument can be construed as invoking a very special kind of rule, a concept. If, and probably only if, it is so construed can the assumption that all meaningful behaviour is 'governed by rules' be sustained. For one can argue plausibly for a necessary link between meaningful behaviour and the use of concepts.

2.3 Meaningful behaviour and concept possession

I say more about concepts as rules shortly. Let me first make clear how concept possession is involved, intuitively, in meaningful behaviour.

I take it that Winch's 'meaningful behaviour' (or, more briefly, action) may be equated with Weber's, and hence with intentional action in so far as that involves 'meaning to be doing something'. In particular, behaviour may be 'meaningful' whether or not the people in question have or have not any particular motive for what they do, or whether or not they are trying to communicate anything to anyone else. Further, its content may be as complex or simple as you like. For instance one may (as in one of Winch's favourite examples) be meaning to *vote in an election*, or one may be meaning to *scratch one's ear* or to *eat a fig*. The essential thing about meaningful behaviour is precisely that it has some subjective content: the agent endows it with some specific subjective meaning.

Though some of Winch's remarks may give a different impression, in my view this gloss best fits his remarks taken as a whole. One example that Winch would regard as an example of behaviour which is *not* meaningful is 'the pointless behaviour of a berserk lunatic'.[9] It is not entirely clear how much Winch wants us to ascribe to his berserk lunatic. Does he mean to be doing things but for no good or particular reason? Or is he just 'flailing about' without any awareness of what he is doing? In the discussion surrounding this case it may look as if acting meaningfully is for Winch meaning to do something for a particular reason.[10] Yet in earlier passages Winch stresses that this is not so. Thus he says:

> The category of meaningful behaviour extends also to actions
> for which the agent has no 'reasons' or 'motive' at all in any of
> the senses so far discussed. . . . Suppose N votes Labour
> without deliberating and without subsequently being able to
> offer any reasons, however hard he is pressed...although N
> does not act here for any reason, his act still has a definite
> sense. What he does is not *simply* to make a mark on a piece of
> paper; he is *casting a vote*. (pp. 48-9)

(I say something about Winch's further comment on this case shortly.) It should also be noted that Winch takes himself to be giving us Weber's notion of meaningful behaviour, and I take it that my gloss best squares his account with Weber's in *Economy and Society*.

Evidently we can usefully distinguish, as Weber does, different 'levels' of subjective meaning of behaviour. Winch's argumentation can be taken to apply to behaviour's subjective meaning at its deepest level, on which the existence of all other types of subjective meaning depends. That is, it can be taken to apply to all behaviour such that the agent means to be doing some particular thing.

Now it is natural to construe 'X means to be doing A' as

entailing something like 'X sees himself as doing A' or 'X thinks he is doing A'. The last two phrases indicate that a certain *thought about* or *conceptualization of* what is going on, is involved. It seems reasonable, then, to sharpen things with the following assumption: meaning to be doing A involves the use of and hence the possession of the concept of doing A. (Precisely how that use is best characterized is a question that I need not go into here.) For example, a man cannot be said to mean to be going for a walk if he does not have the idea of 'going for a walk'; he cannot mean to be running if he does not have the concept of running; he cannot mean to be working for a wage if he does not have the concept of a wage, or working. In short, we can take it that meaningful behaviour involves concept possession.

Now, the intuitive ideas of an (interpreted) language and of a concept are closely linked.[11] Roughly and briefly, to use a term, say 'grass' or 'green', in a certain sense, is to associate the term with a concept, in this case the concept (or a concept) of grass, or of greenness. One uses the term to express the concept.[12] One could, evidently, approach the conditions on concept possession somewhat obliquely through a consideration of what it is to have a language.

The following can now be seen as a recipe for producing an argument for the social nature of meaningful behaviour: *show, either directly or as a by-product of an argument about language, that concept possession is a social matter.* Since meaningful behaviour involves concept possession, it will follow that meaningful behaviour is a social matter.

The claim that concept possession as such is a social matter purports to be completely general and a priori. It is important to appreciate the status of the argument since it is too easy to slip into acceptance of this conclusion by confusing much less contentious, albeit important theses with it. Thus consider the following statement from a textbook in social psychology: 'Concepts are products of interaction of many people carrying on the important business of living together in groups.'[13] As Winch notes, someone saying this may only mean to claim that 'particular concepts may be a product of the peculiar life of the society in which they are current'. Clearly, the claim that concept possession as such is a social matter is much stronger than this.

The question here could be put thus: suppose we are interested in the question of whether an asocial creature we have observed or created (on a distant planet or in the laboratory or wherever) possesses concepts and hence is in a position to perform meaningful actions. Can one argue a priori for the impossibility of such a creature's having concepts?

2.4 Concepts as rules

Let me now explain how concepts can be seen as rules. I turn first to a remark of Winch's that can be developed in a deeper way than is obvious from the way he puts it. He says that one requirement on N's casting a vote is that he 'must be aware of the symbolic relation between what he is doing now and the government which comes into power after the election' (p. 51). Winch claims, moreover, that *any* action with a sense 'is symbolic': it 'goes together with certain other actions in the sense that it commits the agent to behaving in one way rather than another in the future' (p. 52).

One might wonder about this. Is it really a general requirement on meaningful behaviour that any instance of such behaviour involves a commitment regarding the future? If so, what is the content of the commitment? Winch's comment on the particular case of voting does not imply that voting commits the agent to the future performance of any particular action. This seems right for the voting case and also for another case Winch cites, that of using a bookmark to mark one's place. Evidently, however, the claim is at least that some understanding regarding the future is necessary. And in the bookmark case, it is hard to see how one can intelligibly be said to be using a piece of paper as a bookmark if one has no conception that it may serve later to show how much of the book one has read. But what of my eating a fig, or my viewing a painting? What, if anything, must one understand about the future in cases like this? What we are looking for, evidently, is some sort of commitment common to the voting and the fig-eating cases. Is there any such thing?

The following roughly sketches an answer, though Winch does not develop his remarks in this way. It seems possible to regard any action, in so far as it involves the agent in classification or conceptualization of what he is doing, as 'symbolic' in Winch's sense, that is, as 'committing the agent to behaving in one way rather than another in the future'. The commitment, however, is not a simple commitment to perform some specified action at some future time, but is of a more subtle sort. Intuitively, concepts collect things, or, more generally, bits of the world, together. To see something as an instance of a given concept is to see it as a member of a certain class of things or situations. These things, in so far as they fall under the same concept, may be thought of as similar to one another in the relevant respect. From these points it seems we can derive the following point about commitment: in taking *this* to be an instance of concept C, I at one and the same time commit myself to taking anything relevantly similar that I am presented with in the future as an instance of C also. My application of C in a given instance is full of implications for other situations. This point clearly applies to all general concepts from the concept of voting to that of eating a fig.[14] The correlative point about action, then, would apply as much to my eating a fig as to my voting Labour. I shall return to this point about concepts shortly.

So far the term 'rule' has not been used, and it is not clear that it has to be used in this discussion. None the less it is intuitively plausible to connect up the notions of language, concept, and rule, in roughly the following way. That concepts as such can be seen as rules has already been indicated, in effect, in other terms. I have noted that, for example, if I take some particular thing to be a fig, I take it to be an instance of a characteristic that many things can have; I ought to take anything relevantly similar to be a fig also. Note that one quite naturally writes 'ought' here. If concepts are rules, then using a word in a certain sense involves associating it with a rule. For using a word in a certain sense involves associating it with a concept which then constitutes a rule for the use of the word.

One can argue, thus, that using a word in a certain sense involves the user in a certain rather complex kind of commitment. Roughly, things look like this. Suppose I use the word 'fig' in a certain sense today. This means that, today, I use the word 'fig' to express a certain concept, call it F. Then a certain complex counterfactual will be true of me. If, tomorrow, I want to use 'fig' in the sense that I use it in today, then it will be incumbent upon me, tomorrow, to accept 'that is a fig' of whatever concept F applies to, at least if I desire to speak truly. There is, one might say, *a right and a wrong way to go on.* In this way, it may be said that *senses, like concepts, are normative for future behaviour.* I shall call this the *rule* thesis (for concepts and senses).[15]

Nothing in the rule thesis entails that in principle I cannot use a word (that is, a certain phonetic array or symbol) in a different sense every time I use it. The thesis just claims that *if* I am to go on using a term in a given sense, *then* I *must* do or say certain things in certain circumstances.[16] Similarly, it seems one could apply a certain concept once, and then forget or otherwise lose it. But if one is faced with applying or not applying a given concept, one's original grasp of it already had implications for whatever one would be faced with in the future.

A note on phraseology may be pertinent. I have freely used such locutions as 'using a phrase in a given sense', and say that, for instance, 'concepts are rules'. Possibly influenced by their

70

reading of Wittgenstein, some may think such language 'reifies' senses and concepts in an unwarranted way. However, these ways of talking as such would probably not be disallowed by Wittgenstein himself. Moreover, a rephrasing that is less likely to provoke a charge of unwarranted reification can generally be managed, though such rephrasing may sometimes seem rather awkward. For instance, instead of saying 'Concepts are rules' one might more long-windedly say 'To grasp a concept is to grasp a rule' (as indeed I sometimes do). Talk of 'grasping a concept' could itself appear to involve the reification of concepts. But taken by itself this phrase need not necessarily be construed as implying anything about what is involved in the acts of so-called 'concept grasp' or 'meaning'.[17] In any case, however much they suggest that concepts are real objects, the locutions in question are quite natural. I have therefore made no special attempt in this and the following sections to avoid phrases that could appear to involve the reification of concepts. I have simply written whatever seemed sufficiently perspicuous and germane to the purpose in hand.

To sum up the discussion in this section, I have argued that meaningful behaviour involves concept possession and that to grasp a concept is to grasp a special type of rule. It is now time to see whether Winch provides a convincing argument for the claim that rules of this sort presuppose a 'social setting' or, more specifically, a society with socially established rules.

3 WINCH ON RULE-FOLLOWING

3.1 Some acceptable negative claims

I have noted that if the basic issue is the nature of concept possession, then one way to approach it is by considering what it is to have a language. In effect, this is the route Winch takes. His general conclusions about 'the concept of following a rule' (p. 25) come at the end of a discussion which begins with a question about thought ('What is meant by saying that I am "thinking about Mount Everest" ?'), but moves quickly – 'sharpening' the issue – to one about language: 'What is it about my utterance of the words "Mount Everest" which makes it possible to say that I *mean* by these words a certain peak in the Himalayas?' (p. 25). Winch notes that his example's being one of reference to a particular is not essential to it (p. 25). Thus he introduces the general issue of how to set up and follow a 'rule governing the use' of a word (p. 27) and, more generally, what is it to *follow a rule* (p. 29).

Winch's discussion is couched in slightly different terms at different points. I take his main aim to be the *analysis of a concept*, that of following a rule, with special reference to the rules (concepts) which we take to govern the use of words. There is a good basis in his text for taking him this way. First, the crucial section in his book is entitled 'Rules: Wittgenstein's analysis' (p. 24), and he refers in the first paragraph to 'Wittgenstein's discussion of the concept of following a rule' (p. 25). Second, Winch's strongest statements of his position are in terms of logical possibility, logically necessary prerequisites, logical dependence and so on; in short, they are couched in the sort of language appropriate to conceptual analysis. There is no doubt that he uses a variety of other types of locution appropriate to different forms of claim. At the same time, these shifts are never explained.[18] There is reason, then, to construe Winch's main topic as I do, and to undertake a judgment of his discussion from this standpoint.

Something should be said here about the stress on rule-*following*. Given the framework of concepts as semantic rules, various questions about rules for the use of words can be asked. In particular: (1) What is it to grasp a concept, to have or possess a concept? (2) What is it to set up (establish) a certain concept as the rule for the use of a given word? (3) What is it to follow – and to go on following – a rule for the use of a word? Evidently, both rule-following and rule-establishing in this context involve concept grasp or possession. From the point of view of elucidating the basic intuitive concept of concept grasp, the issues of rule-following and rule-establishing may not seem very important. However, one line on the ultimately deeper question evidently is: What is it to follow a rule for the use of a word? With that caveat, I proceed.[19]

Now, one might expect that someone out to say what it is, quite generally, to follow a rule for the use of a word, would explain that one must accord with the commitments generated by one's association of the word with a particular concept. What Winch stresses, however, is rather the following:

> first, that it must be in principle possible for other people to grasp [any rule a person is following] and judge whether it is ‧ being correctly followed; secondly, that it makes no sense to suppose anyone capable of establishing a purely personal standard of behaviour if he never had any experience of human society with its socially established rules. (p. 33)

Given that this is supposed to apply to rules for the use of words, to the logical requirements on using a word in a certain sense, it seems counterintuitive. For it seems logically possible for a congenital Crusoe to use a language. So how does Winch think he can argue for it?

Winch starts along lines one might expect, in effect asking what it is to associate a given concept with a term. (We can divine hidden in this question the deep one: what is it to grasp a concept?) Clearing the ground for his positive remarks, he first notes and rejects several relatively natural suggestions about what it is to set up and henceforth follow a rule for the use of a word. Though the following points will be familiar to many, it is appropriate briefly to run through them here. (In what follows I alter the order of Winch's discussion, and put the points I find there in my own terms.)

One suggestion that turns out to be useless is that to set up and follow a rule for the use of a word is to make a certain type of conscious decision about one's future use of the word, and then act in accordance with one's decision (thereby following the rule one previously laid down). An example of such a decision is: 'I will use this word ['Everest'] only to refer to *this* mountain' (p. 28). Evidently one who makes (and understands) a verbal stipulation about the use of a word uses certain words in certain senses, thus implicitly following rules for the use of those words. Any purported explication of the notion of following a rule for the use of a word in terms of such activity is circular.

Suppose someone were now to suggest the following way to set up and follow a rule for the use of a word. Give an ostensive definition, pointing to Everest, for example, and uttering only 'Everest', the word you are defining. Then act in accordance with this ostensive definition. Winch in effect rejects this too, and rightly. What is it to 'act in accordance with' an ostensive definition? Is this to 'follow the rule laid down or encapsulated in the definition?' If so, the suggestion simply assumes that we know what it is to define a term ostensively, to associate a term, by ostension, with a certain rule for its use. It by no means explains what it is to do this. It too, then, is circular.

In considering the question of following *another person's* ostensive definition (pp. 26–7) Winch writes: 'as far as immediate external appearances go, the ostensive definition [of 'Everest'] simply consisted in a gesture and a sound uttered as we were flying over the Himalayas'. Winch points out, there, that 'with that gesture' the teacher might have been defining the word 'mountain' rather than 'Everest'. Presumably, indeed, such a gesture and utterance need not have anything to do with language at all. Both could be the result of involuntary muscle movements; or the 'teacher' could be stretching his arm and clearing his throat in a rather peculiar way. Thus we can certainly take from Winch the basic point that *mere gesturing in the direction* of, say, Mount Everest, and utterance of the sound 'Everest' does not decide what, if anything, 'Everest' means in the mouth of the utterer.

Moreover, even if we allow ourselves to assume that a certain 'utterer' does mean something by the sound uttered, and that the object he is pointing at does fall under the relevant concept, what he means is not thereby determined by his behaviour. As Winch points out, someone pointing to Mount Everest could mean *mountain*, or *Everest*, for example.

Now it is perhaps natural to assume that things would change if we considered a longish sequence of ostensive uses, but it turns out that this is simply not so. Suppose we assume that a certain utterer, Felix, uses a certain sound 'S' in a constant sense on every occasion that he utters it, and that all his ostensive uses are correct (the objects pointed out instantiate the relevant concept). Suppose further that there is a long sequence of instances of Felix's using 'S' ostensively: he points to several hundred objects. Someone might suggest the following as a useful (if trivial) negative condition on Felix's rule-following in this connection: Felix can only be following a constant rule for the use of 'S' if there *is* a concept such that the objects he pointed to all fall under it. This condition, however, cuts no ice. For any set of objects, there always is a rule of the relevant type, a concept instantiated by all these objects. As Winch indicates, any sequence of utterances of the type in question can be brought within the scope of some rule, if we are prepared to make it sufficiently complicated.[20] We might call this the *rule availability point*. If an example is needed consider a case where someone points first to a green tree, then to a red table, then to a red umbrella, and says, on each occasion, 'trable'. Presumably he could always mean 'physical object' or 'existing thing' by this word. If we are allowed negative instances, like his indicating that, say, a blue chair is not a trable, then we must get into a more complicated rule for trable, where it means something like 'tree or red object'. Clearly, if we increase the number of utterances and negative and positive instances, we may be forced to suggest more and more complicated rules, but it seems that, as a matter of logic, something can always be found.

A striking and related Wittgensteinian point that Winch does not explicitly make here is this: as far as 'immediate external appearance' goes, any given finite sequence of utterances of a term is subject to *infinitely many* possible interpretations, or rules with which such behaviour accords. (In the case of the 'trable' example, 'trable' could mean 'tree or umbrella or red object', 'tree or red object or mathematical symbol' and even 'tree if sighted before June 1981 and red object if sighted subsequently'.)[21] We might call this the *multiple rules point*.

All this shows that the condition that one's linguistic behaviour be coverable by a rule is useless, even when applied to large finite sequences of utterances and pointings, and under the stated assumptions about stability of meaning and correctness of judgment. Presumably these assumptions are not always warranted in real cases – people certainly can be wrong about what is facing them, and can use the same term in different senses. Clearly, the number of interpretations possible for a given ostensive use is compounded enormously if we allow for the possibility of mistakes and variability of sense across time.

The negative points noted here indicate, first, that in attempting to say what it is to follow a rule for the use of a word we have to be careful to avoid circularity, in particular we cannot appeal to any use of verbal rule formulations which the speaker understands. Second, an individual's overt behaviour is insufficient in itself to determine what rule he is following and indeed his behaviour cannot in itself determine whether or not he is following a rule at all.

Clearly, these points do not prove anything positive about what it is to follow a rule for the use of a word. Let us now look at Winch's positive remarks, and at how he gets to his strongest conclusion.

3.2 A positive claim

Winch centres his positive remarks around an example, which I quote in full.

> Imagine a man – let us call him A – writing down the following figures on a blackboard: 1 3 5 7. A now asks his friend, B, how the series is to be continued. Almost everybody in this situation, short of having special reasons to be suspicious, would answer: 9 11 13 15. Let us suppose that A refuses to accept this as a continuation of his series, saying it runs as follows: 1 3 5 7 1 3 5 7 9 11 13 15 9 11 13 15. He then asks B to continue from there. At this point B has a variety of alternatives to choose from. Let us suppose that he makes a choice and that A again refuses to accept it, but substitutes another continuation of his own. And let us suppose that this continues for some time. There would undoubtedly come a point at which B, with perfect justification, would say that A

was not really following a *mathematical* rule at all, even though all the continuations he had made to date *could* be brought within the scope of some formula. Certainly A was following a rule; but his rule was: Always substitute a continuation different from the one suggested by B at every stage. And though this is a perfectly good rule of its kind, it does not belong to arithmetic.

Now, B's eventual reaction, and the fact that it would be quite justified, particularly if several other individuals were brought into the game and if A always refused to allow their suggested continuations as correct – all this suggests a very important feature of the concept of following a rule. (pp. 29–30)

Note that Winch's discussion here is couched in terms of justification. We are asked to consider when someone would be justified in saying something.[22] Meanwhile, the existence of a logical link between 'X is justified in saying that p' and 'p' is not obvious.

As far as justification goes, when would B be justified in saying that A was not really following a mathematical rule? It is not clear that he would have to be in the circumstances Winch describes. Has he considered the following possibility? A may have deliberately thought up, in advance, a formula which will generate a series such that, when faced with the first four numbers, B will naturally go on a certain way, but will be wrong from the point of view of the formula; such that facing a certain longer stretch he will be wrong again, and so on. It is true that in such a case A would have been guided in his devising of his formula by a rule like: 'for a long while produce, at intervals, a continuation different from the most natural one'. But even if this were true of him, the formula he developed, on the basis of this rule, would be a mathematical one. *It* would make no reference to 'B', 'natural continuations', and the like. Faced with such a possibility, before B tries to continue the series he could presumably ask A to write out the formula for the series, if he has one in mind, in a place where B cannot see it. Then, if B feels he has to give up at some point, he can see what, if anything, A has written down. He may then have to agree that A had indeed been following a mathematical rule, mechanically following a certain mathematical formula with which he started out in the first place. So, as the example is presented by Winch, it is not obvious that B would be perfectly justified in reaching his conclusion, given that he has omitted to do something which could have led him to say the opposite.

We can reformulate the example somewhat so as to avoid this particular problem. 'Grasping a principle for a series of numbers' does not seem to have to involve conscious realization of the principle in question. When B goes on '11, 13' and so on, we do not assume that he can only grasp such a rule if he has explicitly formulated one. So we can stipulate that A's claim is that: (a) he has not explicitly considered the rule involved; (b) he has none the less grasped a rule for the series beginning: 1 3 5 7. B can be construed as aiming at grasping A's putative rule, though not necessarily at formulating it explicitly. It will not then be a relevant move for B to ask A to write out the formula for the series he has in mind. This brings us closer to the case of grasping a rule for the use of a word at its most basic, where no definition or rule formulated in words already understood is or can be involved.

Now, perhaps even without formulating it explicitly, A could just happen to have a peculiarly complex function in mind. Suppose that A is the mathematician Kurt Gödel at the height of his powers, and B is an undergraduate with no special mathematical ability. In such a case, assuming he knows who A is, B would surely not be justified in concluding that A was not following a mathematical rule, however long B tried to work out what it was by looking at the numbers, and the way A went ahead with them. So it looks as if we should also stipulate that it is true and known to all parties that A, B, and any others involved in trying to grasp A's rule have (otherwise) the same level of mathematical ability and knowledge. (Even this may not be enough, as is suggested by the historical example of the great mathematician Zermelo, who was never able to accept Godel's proof of the incompleteness of arithmetic.)

Let us now consider how a linguistic analogue of Winch's example would go. The analogue of 'grasping a rule for a series' will presumably be 'grasping a rule for the use of a word'. An analogue of 'continuing the series in a certain way' will be 'continuing to use the word ostensively on a range of occasions'. In Winch's mathematical case one takes it that the participants are assumed to communicate in a common language; let us, then, for the linguistic analogue, feel free to assume a framework of a shared language in which the participants talk. The linguistic analogue of Winch's mathematical case, then, might run like this: A* claims to be using word 'W' in a certain constant sense. He then uses 'W' ostensively on a number of different occasions, pointing at a variety of objects. He asks his friend B* how to 'continue to use' 'W'. For instance, A* points to a cat, then to another cat; B*, asked to continue, points to a third cat. A*

shakes his head, indicating that this is not what he would do. A*
then points to a table, uttering 'W'. B*, seeing that the first two
cats were black, the third white, and that the table is black, next
points to a black cushion. A* shakes his head, and so on.

Given his remarks on his own example, presumably Winch
would say here too that there would 'eventually come a point'
when B* would be 'perfectly justified' in saying that A* was using
'W' in no sense at all, or, more specifically, that 'W' had no
constant sense in A*'s mouth.

It does seem that, in a real case, someone in B*'s position
would eventually feel he had good reason to deny that 'W' had
any constant sense in A*'s mouth, and that he could then be said
to be 'perfectly justified' or 'quite justified' in making such a
denial. So far, then, one can agree with Winch regarding this
type of case. To say this is not to say, of course, why he would
feel or be justified. In any case, being perfectly justified in the
relevant sense, whatever exactly this is, does not seem to entail
the *truth* of the denial. Particularly if one bears in mind the rule-
availability point made earlier, and in any case intuitively, B*
would not be right if he said 'It is logically impossible – given my
evidence – that A* is following a rule here'.

Winch would presumably claim in the linguistic case presented
here, as in his own mathematical case, that B*'s eventual reaction
would be especially justified if 'several other individuals were
brought into the game', and did no better than he. Something
like this seems to be right. At least someone in B*'s situation
could only feel more confident of his judgment, not less, if
several others were also unable to get A* to agree that their
ostensive use of 'W' was correct. Why exactly this is needs
explanation. Perhaps it is because the others' failure would
indicate that B* had not simply failed to notice some relevant
feature of the situation through inadvertence, or through an
idiosyncratic blind spot which was crucial in this case. But once
again, the fact that none of a whole crowd of well-endowed
observers got to the point of going on with word 'W' as A*
claimed they should (according to his rule) does not seem to
entail that A* is not using 'W' in a constant sense, in accordance
with a rule he has grasped.

Similar points about justification seem to be available with
respect to concepts lacking a verbal vehicle. Suppose A* simply
points to various objects, wordlessly. Were he to point consistently to trees, say, it is possible that we would feel some tendency
to say he had – or seemed to have – the concept of a tree. But
what if he points in what seems to us like a random way? It seems
that we will feel happiest and best justified about denying that his

behaviour indicates concept grasp if we cannot in any way 'get the hang' of what he does, if our best hypothesis about what is going on is that he is just pointing to whatever he happens to feel like pointing to at the moment. In spite of these points about justification, there is an intuitive distinction between A*'s actually failing to be continuously reapplying a given concept, and our having the best possible behavioural evidence that this is so. Could he not, in principle, be reapplying a (to us) bizarre or hugely complex concept? Our concept of a concept appears to allow us to suppose so without contradicting ourselves.

Having presented his example of A and B and made the remarks about justification I have commented on, Winch goes on to say that the example suggests a 'very important feature' of the concept of following a rule. He then makes a number of related suggestions:

[1] . . . one has to take account not only of the actions of the person whose behaviour is in question as a candidate for the category of rule-following, but also the reactions of other people to what he does. (p. 30)

The phrase 'one has to take account' here raises a familiar question of interpretation. Is it argued that others' reactions are somehow partly *constitutive* of someone's following a rule? Is something to do with others' reactions a logically necessary condition of one's rule-following? Or is Winch still talking about the conditions under which one is justified in saying someone follows a rule?

A second claim, characterized as *more specific*, is couched in terms of when it would be 'intelligible to say' that someone is following a rule:

[2] . . . it is only in a situation in which it makes sense to suppose that somebody else could in principle discover the rule which I am following that I can intelligibly be said to follow a rule at all. (p. 30)

In further discussion, Winch notes that in his example, B continued the series with 9, 11, and so on, as a matter of course. He then claims that:

[3] . . . going on in one way rather than another as a matter of course must not be just a peculiarity of the person whose behaviour claims to be a case of rule-following. His behaviour belongs to that category only if it is possible for someone else to grasp what he is doing, by being brought to the pitch of himself going on in that way as a matter of course. (p. 31)

Here it is clear that Winch is making a claim about a logically necessary condition on rule-following: 'His behaviour belongs to that category only if . . .'. As I have noted, it seems that one cannot infer any such condition from the related claim about when one is justified in saying that someone is following a rule.

Winch is certainly not alone in making a positive claim to the effect that it must be possible for 'someone else to grasp' what a rule-follower is doing. His statements to that effect find clear correspondences in the writings of Wittgenstein himself and many commentators. Wittgenstein writes negatively of a language which is 'private', that is, which is such that 'only I myself can understand' it (*Philosophical Investigations*, pt. 1, sec. 256).[23] And on his behalf doubt has been cast on the possibility of a language which 'not merely is not but cannot be understood by anyone other than the speaker' (Malcolm, 1954, in Fann (ed.), 1967, p. 182). Or the problematic type of language is characterized as one that 'it is logically impossible that anyone but the speaker should understand' (Thompson, 1971, p. 183). And it has been asserted that 'What is ruled out in the . . . private language argument is . . . one whose concepts, rules, and opinions are essentially unshareable rather than contingently unshared' (Hacker, 1972, p. 222). In short, statements much like Winch's have with some justification been considered by many to express a central Wittgensteinian thesis about language. This thesis may then be regarded as itself implying that language as such is 'social'.

Now, in spite of the sense that such writers evidently have that their formulations are precise expressions of a position, all of the locutions quoted subsume two importantly distinct theses. As I shall argue in the following sections, one of these is relatively trivial and easy to accept, while the other is false on the face of it and therefore clearly in need of support. Meanwhile, the existence of the kind of ambiguity involved could easily have the effect of lending unwarranted support to an otherwise counter-intuitive claim. It is clearly important to be aware of the existence and nature of this ambiguity.

3.3 The meaning-shareability condition

There is a plausible non-epistemic claim about language that could be expressed in terms similar to those of Winch and the others just cited. I shall call it *the condition of meaning shareability*. It can be formulated thus:

(1) If one person, P1, uses a word in a certain sense (with

80

certain semantic properties), then as a matter of logic there could be another person, P2, who uses that word in that sense (with those properties).

To put this succinctly: senses or meanings are in principle shareable.

I shall call the analogous point for concepts *the condition of concept shareability*:

(2) If one person, P1, has grasped concept C, then as a matter of logic there could be another person, P2, who grasps that concept.

In other words, concepts are shareable.

Note that nothing is said here regarding any other person's coming to know anything *about P1*. In particular, nothing is said regarding anyone's coming to know that P1 grasps the concept in question. I believe that these conditions are genuine conditions given our intuitive understanding of what concept grasp and language use are.

Let me deal briefly with one possible objection. This concerns concepts that pick out the felt or phenomenological qualities of an individual's experiences. Must it always be possible in principle for some other person to have those particular concepts? It seems that, from an intuitive point of view, this may be answered affirmatively. Surely a second person, P2, could in principle have experiences with exactly the same felt qualities as those of person P1? (Clearly this is not to say that P2 could experience P1's experiences.) But if so, then surely P2 could in principle have the concept of any phenomenological quality that P1 experiences? This could be so, whether or not these people know, or have any way of telling, that they share the concept in question.[24]

It seems a little strong to think of claims (1) and (2) above as claims about the social nature of language or thought. For one thing, though more than one person or individual is mentioned in these formulations, surely not just any state of affairs in which two people are involved (even when both are actual) is properly described as a social state? Nor does it seem that the (potential) relationship between P1 and some possible being P2 here – namely, their both having a given concept – is enough to give us one. The fact that Jones in Galaxy J had concept C, and that Xenon in Galaxy X also had concept C, does not seem to be an example of an intuitively social fact, though it may be a necessary condition of various intuitively social facts, such as Jones's buying a car from Xenon, or whatever. I shall not try to argue further here for the correctness of the meaning-shareability condition.

Correct or not, I believe that it is the most plausible version of Winch's claim.[25]

Now, even if we assume that the meaning-shareability condition is a logically necessary condition on a given person's using a word in a certain sense, it is circular. (It appeals to another person's *using a word in a certain sense*.) The wish to avoid circularity may be what leads Winch himself to write in terms not of grasping a putative rule-follower's rule, but rather of grasping 'what he is doing' (p. 31).

Can we in fact explicate the meaning-shareability condition in a noncircular fashion? Let us consider Winch's claim that it must be possible for another person to be 'brought to the pitch of himself going on in that way'. Call this the 'condition of the possibility of congruent behaviour'. Winch also says that it must be possible for some other person to be 'brought to the pitch' of himself going on congruently *as a matter of course*. It is not absolutely clear what the quoted phrase means, but it is probably something like 'without hesitation', 'without thinking', 'spontaneously', 'as if this is obviously right'. (Compare Wittgenstein's remark: 'When I obey a rule, I do not choose. I obey the rule *blindly*' (sec. 219).) Putting the two conditions together, we have what may be called the 'condition of the possibility of congruent behaviour with spontaneity'. It might be suggested that this condition is fundamental, and that Winch is not, or need not be, relying on any circular condition of meaning-shareability. The latter condition is, it may be claimed, eliminable in favour of the noncircular condition of the possibility of congruent behaviour with spontaneity. Unfortunately for the programme of analysing the notion of meaning in a noncircular way, this appears not to be so.

Consider first the idea of a condition of congruent behaviour. As I noted earlier, Winch was right to see a problem in the claim that if I point to Everest when I say 'Everest', then it follows that I use the term 'Everest' as a name of Everest. I may, rather, be using 'Everest' as a term for mountain, for instance. What does seem to be true, intuitively, is that my pointing to Everest when I say 'Everest' may be explicable in part by the fact that I (now or in general) use 'Everest' as a name of Everest. In other words, on a natural understanding of language use, it is because one uses a word in a certain sense that one goes on behaviourally as one does in one's use of that word. Similarly, it does not follow from the fact that one goes on putting shells together that one has the concept of a shell. Intuitively speaking, concept grasp is not a function of behaviour, however 'classificatory' it looks. Rather, to take behaviour to be of a classificatory sort, is to take it as behaviour explicable in terms of the application of a certain concept.

It now appears that the condition of congruent behaviour, in so far as it is a logically necessary condition, is circular, and, moreover, redundant given the condition of meaning-shareability. For apparently what must be possible for another person, P2, with respect to someone, P1, who is following a rule for the use of a word 'W' is this: to be brought to the pitch of going on as P1 does (in his overt use of 'W') *just to the extent that, and in so far as, this capacity for congruent behaviour will be generated by P2's following the same rule for the use of 'W' that P1 follows.* The qualification 'in so far as' is not of purely theoretical significance. For one thing, if a given concept applies to the phenomenological qualities of experience, P2 may rarely if ever be justified in applying the concept in relation to P1's experiences, and so can hardly be expected to get to the pitch of applying a term expressive of the concept to all and only the very things P1 applies it to. (How often does one realize that another person has a mild toothache, for instance?) For another, people often make mistakes of identification, sometimes for reasons of a highly idiosyncratic sort. Presumably we do not require that others must be able to get to the point of reproducing someone's mistakes.

Similar points may be made with respect to spontaneity of behaviour. Of course it does not follow from the fact that I spontaneously utter the sound 'chien' in pointing out a dog to you, that I mean *dog* by 'chien'. Mere spontaneous use of a term in a certain context, or sense of certainty that it is to be uttered in that context, does not logically imply that one is using the term in any sense at all. (Of course I do use the word 'chien' in the sense of *dog*, if my spontaneously uttering the sound 'chien' on this occasion is in part explicable by the fact that I mean *dog* by 'chien'!)

It seems then that the possibility of congruent behaviour with spontaneity cannot be accepted as a condition genuinely independent of the circular condition of meaning-shareability. Intuitively, it is acceptable as a necessary condition on linguistic rule-following only if understood to involve the idea that the spontaneous behaviour in question (in the case of both rule-follower and the other person) results from, or is an expression of, grasp of the relevant concept or sense. The condition in question then becomes *circular*, on the one hand, and *redundant*, given the condition of meaning-shareability, on the other.

So far, then, we have not yet come beyond the plausible, circular condition of meaning-shareability. I suspect that this condition is as far as one can legitimately go in linking one person's grasp of concepts with other people. As far as one can go, that is, with respect to logically necessary conditions for concept grasp.

3.4 Meaning-identifiability

The plausible condition of meaning-shareability must be distinguished from what I shall call a *condition of meaning-identifiability*, such as the following:

> (3) If one person, P1, uses a word in a certain sense, then some other person, P2, should in principle be able to discover that P1 is doing so.

In other words, someone else must be able to discover something *about P1*, in particular, to discover what he means by the word in question.

Now, given all the logically possible ways of knowing, this condition as it stands may not seem to be either strong or counterintuitive.[26]

Winch and others, however, seem to hold to rather a strong and counterintuitive form of meaning-identifiability condition. Winch's various formulations of what must be in principle possible, in their context, suggest something like this, which I shall call *the condition of strong meaning-identifiability*.

> (4) If one person, P1, uses a word in a certain sense, it must be possible for some other person, P2, *by monitoring P1's behaviour* (a) to be able to grasp the sense involved; and (b) to be able to tell that P1 has grasped it.

Like the meaning-shareability condition discussed above, this condition is circular as stated. What it seems to come down to, meanwhile, is not so much something about what others must be able to discover about someone, as the claim that, roughly, *there must be behavioural correlates of meaning*. More specifically and strongly, Winch suggests that these behavioural correlates must be sufficient to enable those observing the speaker to grasp the meaning in question *and* tell whether the person in question is following the relevant rule correctly.

An obvious objection to (4) points out the apparent logical possibility of a case in which someone has what I shall call a 'pure sensation term', that is, a term for a sensation quality whose presence has no distinctive behavioural correlates accessible to ordinary observers. ('Behavioural' will be broadly construed so as to include such correlates as being stuck with a pin.) I shall return to the apparent logical possibility of a pure sensation case several times in what follows. Here is a hypothetical example of such a case. Stella has had two phenomenologically distinct types of ache in her shoulder. She decides to call one of these types of ache an 'r-type' ache, and the other type an 's-type' ache. There are no distinctive behavioural correlates associated with either type of ache. (Perhaps Stella is paralysed.) She frequently correctly exclaims: 'Oh, I have an r-type ache', 'Now I have an s-type ache.' In other words, she has grasped and continues to follow one rule for the use of the word 'r-type' and another rule for the use of the word 's-type'. Intuitively this seems easy to imagine and the description has nothing obviously self-contradictory about it. Yet it is clear that on the basis of the behavioural evidence no one could grasp either one of Stella's rules and so know that she has grasped that particular rule.[27] We can contrast with this a case where someone who is judged to be 'of sound mind' uses a term like 'tree' while pointing to various items in the public world. From such a series of ostensive uses one may (as we would say) get to grasp a concept, and have reason to suppose it is the concept the speaker grasps (though not conclusive reason).

3.5 A crucial ambiguity

Now, why might someone be inclined to deny that, after all, a pure sensation case is possible? Winch ultimately allows that

> It is . . . possible, within a human society as we know it, with its established rules of language and institutions, for an individual to adhere to a private rule of conduct. (p. 33)

He insists, however, that it must always be possible for others to 'grasp that rule and judge when it is being correctly followed'. This rules out the pure sensation case, in so far as the 'grasping' and the judgments in question are to be based on a putative rule-follower's behaviour.

Now of course someone may believe that there is a good argument for the existence of the strong meaning-identifiability condition on meaning. I discuss one such argument later. Meanwhile there are some routes to a strong meaning-identifiability condition which one might slip into unawares, but which must be avoided. Let me explain.

Recall the plausible condition of meaning-shareability. There are, it turns out, a number of ways in which, having easily accepted this condition, one might slip to a stronger, less plausible one.

Someone could have arrived at the view that meaning-shareability entailed strong meaning-identifiability by reasoning as follows: 'How might P2 *come to share* P1's concept? By P2 learning P1's concept from P1. How might that be? By P2's observation of how P1 proceeds.' Or the underlying thought might be: how would P2 *know* he shared a concept with P1? The answer may seem to be that behavioural evidence is necessary. But, surely, that one shares a concept or meaning with another does not entail one's having come to share it by learning it from that other, nor that one knows that one shares.[28] Thus consider a case in which each of two people have sensations of both the r-type and the s-type, neither of which has any easily observable behavioural or environmental correlate. By sheer coincidence, they might each independently decide to call these 'r-type' and 's-type' respectively. Thus they use these terms in the same senses. None the less, neither has any serious evidence that they do so. Meaning-shareability, then, does not appear to entail strong meaning-identifiability.

In moving from a meaning-shareability condition to something strong and contentious one may not be relying on argument, but may rather be influenced by an unnoticed ambiguity. For the meaning-shareability thesis can be given a quite ambiguous formulation, whose ambiguity may easily be overlooked. Given the nature of the ambiguity, it is easy to slip from the uncontentious meaning-shareability condition to a strong meaning-identifiability condition. It is important to be clear about this.

Consider the following formulation:

(5) If one person, P1, follows a rule, it must be possible for someone else, P2, to grasp P1's rule.

This could be interpreted as stating the requirement *either* that P2 come to grasp a certain rule, *or* that P2 come to learn something *about P1* (as well as grasping a certain rule).

Now, if someone has slipped even to a weak meaning-identifiability condition via the ambiguity I have pointed out, he may feel that some behavioural or environmental correlate of language has to be essential to it, since how else could other people be expected to have any confidence regarding what rule one is following? Thus we have a fairly simple route, via an ambiguity, to the assumption of a strong meaning-identifiability condition on meaning.

Many of Winch's formulations, and those of others, are ambiguous in the way noted. One also finds what may be unconscious shifts in the literature. Once one has become attuned to the ambiguity, and to the difference between the meaning-shareability condition and the strong meaning-identifiability condition, passages in various authors become unclear, and seem to call for more perspicuous formulation. It seems quite possible that many people have failed to notice the ambiguity in question, and have had their conviction of the necessity of strong meaning-identifiability illegitimately strengthened by virtue of the intuitive correctness, if not obviousness, of a meaning-shareability condition.

3.6 Shareability, identifiability, and communication

Earlier I quoted from Hacker a formulation of the point of Wittgenstein's 'private language argument', in terms of the essential 'shareability' of concepts. It hardly seems ambiguous, apparently expressing a point which is immediately plausible intuitively. This point hardly seems like a possible philosophical breakthrough, however, certainly not an anti-platonist one. Does Hacker not mean something stronger? Just previously to the passage I quoted, he writes:

> the necessary conditions involved in the existence of language (and hence of thought) imply . . . only possible sociality, . . . the possibility of interpersonal discourse. (1972, p. 222)

Now Hacker does not spell out what he takes the conditions on 'sociality' to be, nor on 'interpersonal discourse'. Consider, then, what I shall call *thin communication*. Thin communication, as I define it, takes place just in case on some occasion, some person, P1, uses (means) term 'T' in sense S; another person observes P1's utterance of 'T' and understands 'T' in sense S. This does not require that either person has any reason to believe that they interpret 'T' in the same way. Such communication could occur by sheer coincidence and without the knowledge of the parties.

Now meaning-shareability is certainly a *necessary* condition on thin communication, whereas strong meaning-identifiability is not. Does meaning-shareability, meanwhile, 'imply its possibility'? Certainly it does not seem to be very close to sufficient to secure the occurrence of communication in the thin sense. Just because some concept I possess is shareable obviously does not mean it is actually shared or even that anyone who wanted to could come to share it by observing me. (Consider the case of Stella's use of 'r-type' and 's-type' earlier.) Meanwhile, strong meaning-identifiability in something like Winch's sense does imply at least the latter.

So much for the case of thin communication. Now, when we think of interpersonal discourse and communication among humans we tend to have in mind not merely communication in the thin sense, but a more complex phenomenon in which communication in the thin sense is embedded. A standard feature of such discourse is that people do have some grounds for assuming their words will be taken in the right way, in part at least because of some observed correlation between utterances and the world. Within this context, people can form and act on the intention to communicate. Thus a second possibility regarding what is meant by 'interpersonal discourse' is that it is or essentially involves *intentional* achievement of thin communication. Probably one cannot *intend* to communicate in the thin sense (as opposed to hoping to do so, say) unless one believes one has grounds for thinking one's words will be interpreted aright. Meanwhile, as noted above, it is clear that meanings can be *actually shared* without anyone having grounds for thinking they are, and hence without one who properly assesses the evidence being able seriously to intend to communicate. Meaning-shareability, then, is far from ensuring the possibility of *seriously intended* communication, should it be desired. There is reason to think that it is not meaning-shareability, but meaning-identifiability, if either of these, which makes it possible.

Now it is fairly clear that Hacker means to appeal to a fairly strong meaning-identifiability condition, whose fulfilment would enable another person to engage in seriously intended communication, given a bit of time and effort. Meanwhile, his summary of his point in terms of shareability can only tend to confuse the issue, and facilitate acceptance of a counterintuitive thesis. For we can all agree on the necessity of meaning-shareability if there is to be meaning at all. But it is by no means clear that there must be something which 'implies the possibility' of interpersonal discourse.

Writing of Frege's views on language, Michael Dummett (1974, p. 424) says that

> Frege insisted on the objective character of sense: sense is something which can be communicated from one individual to another (in a way in which he thought mental images and the like cannot).

Dummett's reference to sense being something which can be 'communicated' from one individual to another may now give us some pause. Apart from questions about the proper exegesis of Frege, in emphasizing the objectivity of senses or meanings one might be expected to have in mind the shareability of meanings or concepts. For from an intuitive point of view two people can use a word in one and the same sense, while (to allude to Dummett's statement) they cannot associate numerically the same mental image with it. This is what at least suggests the objectivity of senses. Meanwhile, in spite of the availability of a technical concept of thin communication, Dummett's statement would most naturally be interpreted in terms of standard intentional communication. But then a quick move from objectivity to communicability is not what one would expect. It leads one to wonder if a general strong meaning-identifiability condition for all language use is being assumed. I am not saying that it is, only that given the prevailing ambiguities some clarification of Dummett's terms would be helpful.

3.7 Further considerations on strong meaning-identifiability

(1) If someone were to claim that it is a logically necessary *precondition* of my using a word in a certain sense that someone else can discover this on the basis of my behaviour, their claim would be incoherent. For I must already use the word in the sense in question in order for anyone to be able to *discover* that I do. It appears that in order to avoid incoherence and retain strong meaning-identifiability as a logically necessary precondition, my meaning something must, first, be construed as in part at least *constituted by* behavioural facts about me, as a matter of logic. The view requiring strong meaning-identifiability could then be construed as requiring that these facts must be such that on the basis of awareness of them (in part) others can conclude that I mean what I do. Positing a behavioural precondition of some sort does not appear to be incoherent. Coherence may, then, be retained. The price is counterintuitiveness given the apparent logical possibility of a pure sensation term, among other things.

(2) Suppose someone is tempted to assume that it is a logical precondition of one's meaning something by a word that one's use of it involves behaviour on the basis of which others could discover one's rule. He should consider the following line of argument. Assuming such a condition, and reasoning only from a priori principles about meaning, it appears to reach what may be called an anti-Crusoe conclusion. That is, a conclusion entailing

89

that in order to mean something by a word I cannot have lived in total isolation from other language users all my life.

The argument starts with the assumption that when one means something by a word one knows that one means something, and what one means, with fair certainty. (In section 3.9 below I briefly defend the idea that this assumption is part of our intuitive notion of meaning.) But suppose it is a precondition of one's meaning something by a word, that one's behaviour in using it is such that others can by observing it come to learn one's meaning in a relatively short time. One might think it would be hard to be really sure that others could do this, if they had not in fact already done it. After all, our assumption is that we know what we mean, when we mean, with fair certainty. So we must be as sure as possible that others really could grasp our meaning. If this seems to be getting us to too strong a conclusion, it might be argued that once I know that I really have meant various things in the past, because others have come to learn my meaning on the basis of my behaviour, I can then be confident enough in the appropriate circumstances that they could learn my meaning, even when they are not around to confirm this. Then we would still reach an anti-Crusoe conclusion. For the argument would conclude that I must once have been among other people who got my meaning, as a result of observing my use, and that I must have observed this happening, in so far as it could be observed. (Winch refers to the necessity of an early experience of a 'society' with 'socially established rules', but he nowhere attempts any careful elucidation of what he or anyone means by 'society' and 'socially established rule', and we do not need to bring in such terms to have an anti-Crusoe conclusion.)

As noted earlier, such a conclusion is counterintuitive on the face of it. So if it can indeed be derived from a strong meaning-identifiability precondition, that counts against such a condition.

(3) A meaning-identifiability thesis in terms of the 'availability to others' of one's language through correlated nonlinguistic behaviour and circumstances might, I suppose, be termed a thesis about the 'social nature' of language. This is rather a strong way to describe it, however. The thesis states that one individual cannot use or 'exercise' a language unless others could, by observing him, get to share his language and know that they share his language. To have a language, then, would involve being at least potentially part of a set of people with that language, some of whom had learnt the language from oneself. If the argument to the anti-Crusoe conclusion sketched above works, then the thesis also implies that the language user must

have lived among people who did learn his language by observing him, and must know this.

In spite of these considerations, it is more natural or perspicuous to describe meaning-identifiability in terms of the 'public' rather than the 'social' nature of language. The notion of 'publicity' itself, meanwhile, is a somewhat slippery one. One thing that strong meaning-identifiability clearly implies is that one's meaning must be 'public' in the sense of not wholly residing, as it were, 'in the sphere of the mind'.[29] This explication of 'publicity' still leaves things open, evidently. We might think of something as not residing wholly in the sphere of the mind, for the reason that it is or involves some relation to an abstract, objective particular. With respect to strong meaning-identifiability, however, the publicity of meaning is not a matter of its necessary relation to an abstract objective particular, but rather its openness to everyone's view in the way in which tables and chairs are open to view: its residing in the physical world of objects open to sensory perception.

Strong meaning-identifiability seems to imply that to mean something is to have a body or at least to be able to affect the rest of the world in some way. It would then be logically impossible for a bodiless mind to talk or think. This, it seems to me, would be quite a powerful conclusion to reach. Though some may find it congenial, I find it hard to accept the idea that such a mind is a conceptual impossibility.

I have not been claiming that it is impossible to support a strong meaning-identifiability condition of some kind by argument. But it is important to see that any such condition is badly in need of support, and, in particular, that it is not to be confused with the far less contentious condition of meaning-shareability.

3.8 An argument from the necessity for a standard of correctness

In a passage towards the end of his exposition of Wittgenstein on rules, Winch presents an argument that he sees as both supporting a strong meaning-identifiability condition and as showing that without prior experience of an actual society no one could follow a rule. He seems to regard this as a self-contained argument from obvious premises. It is important to see that the argument does not have this complete and obvious character. Other expositors have derived similar conclusions from similar premises. Like Winch they take the argument to be relatively self-contained and based on obvious assumptions about the nature of rules as 'standards of correctness'.[30] Probably in some cases later expositors have been influenced by Winch's own exegesis.[31] Meanwhile, in viewing the argument as complete in this way expositors seem ultimately to be relying largely on a famous passage of Wittgenstein's.[32] Whether or not Wittgenstein himself regarded this passage as a self-contained argument from obvious premises is, however, open to question.[33] In any case, let me now look at the details of Winch's presentation.

I first quote or paraphrase three points which might be taken as truistic.

(1) 'the notion of following a rule is logically inseparable from the notion of *making a mistake*. If it is possible to say of someone that he is following a rule that means that one can ask whether he is doing what he does correctly or not'. (p. 32)

(2) 'A mistake is a contravention of what is *established* as correct.' (p. 32)

(3) Whether or not I make a mistake in following a rule for the use of a word cannot just be a matter of my decision or say-so.

So far, one might say, so good. These points appear to be immediately acceptable from the point of view of naïve intuition. The crucial question here is: what, if anything, follows from these premises? I shall argue that conclusions of Winch's type are derived from them only by overlooking a crucial gap in the argument. Winch alleges:

(4) 'if I make a mistake in, say, my use of a word, other people must be able to point it out to me. If this is not so, I can do what I like and there is no external check on what I do; that is, nothing is established.' (p. 32)

One might think that Winch is claiming something like this here: all rules or standards must be *socially* established. If you like, establishing a rule is a collective activity requiring a multiplicity of participants. Winch denies that this is exactly his point. He says that at least within 'a human society as we know it, with its established language and institutions' it is possible for someone to adhere to a 'private rule of conduct' (pp. 32–3). However,

(5) One who follows any rules must initially have had some experience of 'human society with its socially established rules' (p. 33).

and

(6) There must always be the possibility of an 'external check on what I do'.

92

In other words, Winch infers a strong meaning-identifiability thesis for *all* meanings. (See p. 33.)

The main question I want to press here is this. Why should anyone think that such conclusions follow from the truisms about rules and mistakes in (1) to (3) above?

Suppose we start by accepting that a rule governing the use of a word ('zod', say) will determine what things I may correctly call 'zods'. It will place constraints on such behaviour. We then imagine someone 'going on' in a certain way, calling each of a certain set of things 'zods'. We ask: what is it that decides the correctness of such calling? What constitutes the standard? As I see it, this is the crucial point at issue in Winch's and similar arguments.

Winch apparently holds that only one type of answer is even available for consideration. Roughly, what determines whether one goes on right or not must have to do with facts about people other than oneself. The detail of Winch's answer is complex; key terms are not articulated (he does not elaborate on 'socially established rule'); and it is not made clear how the qualified nature of (5) is to be justified. In any case, Winch evidently sees actual 'socially established rules' as somehow basic or primary. One must have experience of such standards if one is to accord with any. Thus Winch reaches an anti-Crusoe conclusion from a set of truisms about rules and mistakes. Something seems to have gone wrong. Has it? And if so, what is it?

It has been argued rather generally against Winch's type of conclusion that it is not self-contradictory to suppose that 'someone, uninstructed in the use of any existing language, makes up a language for himself'.[34] We can do more than this, however. We can approach the 'standards of correctness' argument on its own terms. For we can read the argument as in effect proposing a task: the location of an appropriate standard of correctness for a person's word use as such. According to Winch and others, the only possible locus for such a standard is in facts about people other than oneself. As I shall now explain, however, a quite different locus is possible, and this is the possibility implicit in our intuitive conception of concept grasp and language use. This has serious consequences for the standards of correctness argument.

3.9 The 'natural view' of concept possession and language use

The six theses to be set out below all appear to be components of our intuitive conception of concept possession and language use. For the sake of a label, I shall call this conception as a whole *the natural view.* It might also have been characterized as the intuitive, or common-sense, or pretheoretical, or, indeed, naïve view.

Perhaps because they have believed the natural view to be philosophically untenable, Wittgenstein's followers have tended to deny its status as the natural or pretheoretical view. They characterize it, rather, as a mistaken 'philosophical' theory, one arrived at by a misunderstanding of the games we play when we talk about language and meaning. I shall later argue, in effect, that there has been no conclusive philosophical demonstration of the unacceptability of the natural view. This should make it easier to accept that it is indeed our intuitive conception.

Let me now list some of the theses that appear to constitute the intuitive conception of concept possession and language use. I shall not attempt a lengthy justification of my inclusion of any given thesis. None the less, I believe that at least prior to exposure to Wittgenstein's or other opposing philosophical positions most people would accept each of the theses listed below as partially constitutive of their notion of meaning.

It is not in fact crucial to the argument I shall give in defence of the intentionalist programme that each thesis be part of our intuitive conception. The basic line of argument can, I think, be sustained given only the first two. Meanwhile, the fuller set of theses presented below allow us to take some short cuts. And my first intention is to show how the fuller set implies a particular locus for a standard of correctness in the matter of concept grasp. So let us proceed.

The pivotal *rule thesis* was, of course, noted earlier. Grasp of a concept is grasp of a rule: a given concept is either correctly or incorrectly applied to a given object. To grasp a concept is to grasp a standard for sorting: one sorts things correctly or incorrectly in accordance with the standard. In so far as I now associate a general concept with a certain word 'W' as determining its sense, then, *if* I wish to use 'W' in the same sense in the future, it is now already determined of what I may correctly say 'This is W.'

An additional component of the natural view involves a further spelling out of the rule thesis. I shall call it the *infinity thesis*. It runs thus. If I now use 'red' in the sense of *red*, for instance, then it is already determined *for all of the infinitely many possible candidates* whether or not I can truly say 'X is red' of them. I associate 'red' with the concept of redness, and by its nature this concept determines for all possible cases – an infinite number – whether or not it applies to them. When I say 'That is red' of a certain book, say, I imply that it has a certain quality which in principle is instantiable infinitely many times. I implicitly co-classify that book with all actual and possible red things. In some sense I know how such things are to be distinguished from other things: I know what redness is.

I have already indicated that another part or consequence of the natural view is this: a person has a language or grasps a concept as long as he possesses a certain property, and whether or not he possesses that property can be ascertained by considering how it is with him considered in isolation from all other people. If on a certain occasion I use the term 'red' in the sense of *red*, then this is solely a matter of how it is with me now. It does not concern how it is or has been or will be with any other person. It seems to follow that in principle a being could use a word in a certain sense even if he has always been entirely alone in the world. For his doing so is, after all, only a matter of how it is with him. Whether or not a being possesses a concept is, one might say, a 'private' matter, though one others may be able to find out about in at least some instances. So let us call this the *privacy thesis*.

How plausible is it to say that the privacy thesis is part of the natural view of concept possession? One datum in favour of this is one's immediate suspicion of an argument that purports to rule out as a matter of logic the possibility of a congenital Crusoe who has a language. I shall return to this case again later. It also seems reasonable to cite monotheism's conception of a unique creator who deliberately created the universe. The entrenchment of this conception suggests that this idea has been found accessible and not baffling to generations. It therefore seems reasonable to take it as evidence for the claim that the privacy thesis is the natural one. Careful theologians have had difficulty in the past with the concept of omnipotence: was an omnipotent being possible? Did omnipotence imply the power to falsify mathematical claims? They have not similarly questioned the concept of a solitary being with intentions. Such a doubt would strike at the heart of a monotheistic cosmology of the universe. Though philosophers are sometimes tempted to write off certain standard imaginings or hypotheses as bizarre, it should surely give us some pause that certain stories have been accepted not only by children but also by mature and sophisticated adults through the ages. An argument to show that any such stories are inherently *unintelligible*, that they fail *to make sense*, is going to have to be unusually powerful and convincing.

We might also consider how it seems to be with ourselves. You, the reader, now interpret my words in a certain way. That this is so may seem rather obviously to be a fact about you and you alone, as opposed to any other people. (Whether our interpretations tally is, of course, not a fact about you alone.)

The privacy thesis, then, is apparently a part or consequence of our everyday conception of concept possession and language use. Other elements of that conception in fact provide a certain backing for the privacy thesis. They at least strongly suggest that thesis. Before explaining this, let me run through the rest of the components that I wish to list here.

One of these is what I shall call *the subjectivity thesis*, according to which the use of a word in some sense or other requires the occurrence of subjective phenomena of a special kind. One can hold the subjectivity thesis without taking a stand on the relation of mental to physical phenomena. The thesis concerns facts like the following. There is, it seems, a subjective experience of 'using a word in a certain sense'. A related experience, noted by Wittgenstein, is the experience of 'losing the meaning' of a word. If one repeats a single word, 'bucket', say, many times, one often experiences a sudden '*gestalt*-shift' in which 'bucket' suddenly appears to be a meaningless sound. One has lost the 'experience of meaning'. Is this a trivial or a crucial fact? I personally find it very tempting to say that should a being's utterances never be accompanied by the 'experience of meaning' then that being does not *mean* anything by its words, lacks any *understanding* of the words, and so on. In other words, I am tempted to see the experience of meaning as conceptually crucial to the acts of meaning and understanding.

The following conjecture seems intelligible: Sally, who appears to be talking to us, is not really assigning any sense to her words. We can make this conjecture even if her words are interpretable by us as words in a language we understand. It can be argued that this is the conjecture people most naturally make about what is happening with machines whose output is readable as words and sentences of the English language. It is plausible, meanwhile, to interpret this conjecture in terms of the absence of certain subjective phenomena. Hence there is reason to suppose that subjective phenomena are conceived of as playing a crucial role in acts of meaning.

The next thesis I want to mention is an epistemological one. People have observed that in carrying out his famous method of doubt in the *Meditations*, Descartes never doubts that he knows the meanings of his words. In particular, he never doubts that he means something by '*cogito*' and that he *knows* what he means by it. He appears to assume that fact is accessible to him (and indubitable) even when the existence of the whole physical world is in doubt. So now, continuing to consider our notion of concept grasp, it seems we should add *the content certainty thesis*. Briefly, this is the thesis that when I use a word in a certain sense I *know* what sense it is. When I apply a concept to a thing I know what concept it is.

This is not to say that people cannot use words without knowing their meaning *in the language of their group*. It is not to say, either, that if I use a word in a certain sense, I know whether I am now using the word in the sense in which I used it before. (I could have forgotten what sense I used it in before.) Nor is it to say that one cannot 'mouth' words without any understanding of them, or that it will not require much care and probing to become explicit about one's meaning. In this book I take many pages to arrive at carefully articulated hypotheses about the precise senses in which I (at least) use certain words, phrases, and sentences. But I appear to be articulating and making explicit a form or structure which is already known in some sense. I ask myself lots of questions about *what I mean*. I presume myself to be authoritative about the answers. Our concepts of language use and concept possession apparently make this presumption reasonable. Again, meanings and concepts can, it seems, be intuitively vague or fuzzy edged, so that one may realize that all one can say of a given case is that, say, 'it seems to be a sort of book' or whatever.

It may now seem that the content certainty thesis as that is understood here is practically tautological. In any case, I suggest that on at least one natural construal its denial would be counterintuitive. Let me make a brief attempt to convince on this point. Consider how bizarre the following dialogue would be. Mr Jones: 'Well, I'm off to the bank!' Ms Jones: 'Tom, do you mean "river-bank" or "money-bank"?' Mr Jones: 'Hmm. I'm really not sure'. The symbol 'bank' is ambiguous, in English. But, if someone is using it in one of its senses, we expect that person to *know which sense it is*. More can and should be said on this topic.[35] Now, however, I must leave it there. I shall assume, then, that part of our concept of language use runs roughly as follows: to use a word in a certain sense is to know, of some sense or concept, that one uses that word in that sense.

Descartes evidently assumed that he could be certain of his meaning and the content of his concepts by virtue of the nature of his subjective state. Given the subjectivity thesis, such an assumption is not surprising. And it suggests that we may add to the natural view the thesis of a *subjective grounding* for certainty about meaning.

We should think hard before giving any of these theses up, for to give any of them up may well amount to giving up our intuitive conception of concept possession and language use, rather than properly elucidating it. I shall in what follows assume that each thesis does indeed partly characterize our intuitive conception: each is a component of the natural view.

If we put the above theses together something like the following complex account of the nature of concept grasp emerges. With respect to a person, P, and a concept, C, it is by virtue of facts about P alone that P grasps C. More specifically, it is by virtue of being in a certain subjective or mental state that P grasps C. The fact that it is C which is grasped has an infinity of normative implications, implications known to P by virtue of his grasp of C. That is, P knows how he ought to go on in his use of any term 'T' which is intended to express C, or how to go on collecting things together as instances of C, for all the infinite number of possible contexts.

The natural view, so characterized, may be regarded as a theory or partial theory of concept grasp. It is, more specifically, a theory of our concept of concept grasp, and is therefore not an empirical theory. However, it is quite complex, and in the light of it we can do more than merely state that from an intuitive point of view a congenital Crusoe is possible. In other words, we can do more than simply affirm the privacy thesis. We can present a relatively complete, wholly individual-based account of what is going on in hypothetical Crusoe cases. The natural view thus serves to some extent at least to *explain* how a congenital Crusoe could mean something.

Consider Maude, who, by hypothesis, comes into being on a desert island, and starts and goes on using the word 'noum' in the sense of *mountain*. In order for this to be so, she must have grasped a rule for the use of 'noum'. But can this be so? It can, given the details of the natural view. Recall those of Winch's points about rules which could be read as truisms: if someone follows a rule one can (intelligibly) ask whether they are doing what they do correctly or not; a mistake contravenes what is *established* as correct; whether a person makes a mistake cannot just be a matter of their own say-so. If we accept the natural view, we can accept that all these truisms apply to Maude. She has grasped a concept, the concept of a mountain. This means that she has grasped a rule which can effectively determine when 'noum' is used correctly and when not. That is, *if Maude wishes to go on using 'noum' to express this concept*, it is already determined what is correctly called a 'noum' and what is not. So we can intelligibly 'ask whether she is doing what she does correctly or not'. The concept in question establishes what is correct, and whether or not she makes a mistake is not up to her, it is a function of the nature of this concept. It seems, then, that Maude can have a language and this is a function of facts about her considered in isolation from any society. In particular, *it is a function of her grasping 'in her head', as it were*, certain determinate concepts or rules, which provide the standard for her rule-following linguistic behaviour.

In response to claims about possible language-using isolates in Strawson, 1954, and Ayer, 1954, Winch writes, roughly, that they have begged the question in saying that Crusoe 'has a language'. By what right do they speak of his having a language here, Winch asks (pp. 34ff)? If we start from the standpoint of what is acceptable intuitively, however, there is need of an argument to show that those who write of language-using isolates have no right to do so. In other words, this question may indeed be begged, until it is shown that such statements are incoherent or otherwise inadmissible. More precisely, some flaw must be clearly shown in the picture of how it is with Maude that I have sketched.[36]

If the natural view as characterized above is coherent, the story of Maude and similar stories are coherent also. At the same time, it follows that society is not the only possible source for a standard according to which an individual's linguistic behaviour can be judged right or wrong. We do not find any serious discussion in Winch of the possibility envisaged in the natural view. But now the problem for Winch's argument appears more drastic than the presence of a simple lacuna. On the one hand, it seems that he would have to show that there is something unacceptable about those aspects of the natural view that allow for privacy, if his implicit claim that the only possible locus of rules is society were to be sustained. On the other hand, it appears that to show this would be to show that our intuitive conception of concept possession is incoherent, rather than to pave the way for an improved *analysis* of that notion. Instead, it would lead to the drastic conclusion that there can be no such thing as meaning as intuitively conceived.

At this point it is time to leave Winch's argument. Our discussion has now brought us face-to-face with the following fundamental question: is the natural view as so far characterized coherent? Is it philosophically tenable? If we can show that it is, then both intention itself and its society-independence will have been saved together. Winch's discussion cannot help us here. Meanwhile, Kripke's exposition of Wittgenstein is much to the point. To this I now turn.

4 KRIPKE'S WITTGENSTEIN

4.1 Introduction: Kripke's Wittgenstein and the issue of intentionalism

In Kripke's discussion of Wittgenstein, one finds material for a systematic attack on what I have called the natural view of concept grasp. Kripke does not set out an explicit characterization of our intuitive conception of concepts and linguistic meaning of the sort I have just given. Nor would he necessarily be willing to endorse the characterization I have given here. Meanwhile, he suggests that Wittgenstein has developed 'the most radical and original sceptical problem philosophy has seen to date' *(Wittgenstein on Rules and Private Language*, (1982), p. 60.)[37] And he argues that if Wittgenstein's sceptical argument works, 'There can be no such thing as meaning anything by any word' (p. 55).

It turns out that if the sceptical argument Kripke envisages does work, then it will have been shown that there cannot be such a thing as concept grasp or language use according to the natural view as characterized here. I shall argue in what follows that powerful though the sceptical argument is, it does not show this view to be philosophically untenable. This should help to sustain confidence in the idea that the natural view as that is characterized here is indeed the natural view. The main strand of my defence of intentionalism will thereby be completed. For it will have been argued that the conception of language and intention characterized in the last section is our everyday intuitive conception, that it is indeed coherent, and that it does not involve the concept of a collectivity. Given that all this is so, the claim that the possession of intentions is logically dependent on membership in a social group will have been refuted.

As a complement to the sceptical argument, Kripke sees Wittgenstein as suggesting an altogether new positive approach to linguistic and related phenomena. It will help to complete my defence of intentionalism in the context of Wittgensteinian attacks, if I can show that given this approach a form of intentionalism can be sustained. So I shall not only consider the argument that seems to present a challenge to the natural view, but pay attention to Wittgenstein's positive approach to language as Kripke construes it.

I should stress that in this section I shall not attempt to give a step-by-step account of Kripke's own careful exposition. Rather, I present an independent exposition of 'Wittgenstein's views according to Kripke as I understand him', slanting my exposition in the direction of the concerns of this chapter. I occasionally cite places in Wittgenstein's text that Kripke does not explicitly cite, but that support his general line of interpretation. Occasionally, also, I include a supporting argument of my own for a conclusion Kripke reaches. If ever it is not made entirely clear whether or not Kripke himself has endorsed a particular point, the reader should refer to his book rather than assuming that he has endorsed it.[38]

One reason I do not refer to 'Kripke's argument', and so on, in these sections, is that, unlike Winch, Kripke does not commit himself to the overall acceptability of what he takes as Wittgenstein's position, powerful and important though he rightly takes this position to be. Precisely what Wittgenstein himself intended in his difficult, aphoristic text may be expected to remain a disputed question, and it is not my aim to enter that debate. Meanwhile, Kripke's interpretation clearly has much to recommend it. With this caveat, I shall feel free sometimes to refer simply to 'Wittgenstein's argument', and so on, in what follows.

4.2 The sceptical argument

As noted earlier, in the application of his 'method of doubt', Descartes did not even raise the issue of whether he could doubt the meanings of his words. The whole issue of the knowledge of meaning and the nature of concept possession was left untouched. Hume, the famously radical sceptic, seems likewise never to have raised a doubt about meanings or concepts. At the same time, he seems to have assumed that our concepts were (rather faint) images in our minds with a specific introspectible content which, presumably, determined their application. This is evidently a tempting gloss on the natural view as so far described. (I have deliberately described it more vaguely in terms of the involvement of a certain subjective or mental state (not necessarily including imagery or picturing of any kind).) The *imagist* account or model of meaning would be especially tempting for an empiricist philosopher who supposed that it must be possible to explicate any justified claims to knowledge in terms of introspectible states of mind.

As is well known by now, among the other things Wittgenstein attacks are imagist accounts of concepts or meanings of the kind the classical empiricists entertained. The attack invokes considerations like the following. A mental image or picture of a fuzzy red patch, say, can be 'applied' in infinitely many ways. Thus suppose I associate such a patch, now, with the sound I utter, 'red'. It hardly seems that this association determines anything about how I am to use 'red' in the future. If anything is determined, what it is will depend, intuitively, on how I *take* the red patch. In other words, what is determined will depend on how I interpret the patch, on the sense, so to speak, that I give to it. A red patch hardly seems adequate in itself to determine anything about the future. The same may be said for verbal rule formulations, which by themselves are just strings of 'meaningless' symbols. Such a formulation or 'rule' cannot determine the correctness of future uses of a word. Obviously, if a similar formulation is invoked to provide an 'interpretation' of the original, the problem of *its* application or interpretation will arise in the same way. Such 'rules' then, seem not after all to provide any way of determining whether a word is used in accordance with them, or whether things are sorted in accordance with them. It is ultimately unclear, given this version of the natural view, what 'in accordance with them' could *mean*.

Meanwhile, the multiple rules point noted earlier suggests that nothing is determined about other cases by a given bit of *ostension*, such as one's saying 'red' while pointing to this book. As already indicated, we cannot say that what is determined is that all and only things *relevantly similar* may be referred to as 'red'. For when the question becomes 'what counts as relevantly similar?' or 'what determines what is relevantly similar?', it is clear that relevant similarity cannot be determined simply by the fact that the sound (or word) 'red' is correctly said of this particular thing.[39]

In his exposition of Wittgenstein's views, Kripke carefully develops the example of someone whom we take at the beginning of the story to have added various pairs of numbers over a period of time. Suppose this person has said 'One plus two is three' and so on, re-using the word 'plus' each time. Now, he has never said (for example) 'Fifty-six plus forty-three is. . .'. The question then arises: is there anything about how it has been with him personally which determines what the answer *should* be in *this* case if he is to accord with the meaning he gave to 'plus' in the past? It begins to look as if it would be necessary for him to have done every conceivable sum in the past in order that the answer already be determined for any arbitrarily chosen pair of numbers now. But by hypothesis he has not already done so, at least not in the way the sums he clearly has done were done. Wittgenstein suggests that there is an inclination to say that 'it is as if we could grasp the whole use of the word in a flash', regarding what happens when one grasps a sense (sec. 191 ff.). *Could* the 'whole use' really be present somehow?

If we consider this question, one possibility that falls out is that the infinite table of the addition function is somehow surveyed at a glance on a given occasion. That is, every possible sum is laid out before us. The trouble with this supposition is twofold. First, it seems false to the facts. Our mental imagery, at any rate, is not *that* detailed. It is not even clear that it could be. Is it intelligible, even, to think of our surveying an infinite table in an instant? (Wittgenstein says of 'grasping the whole use of a word in a flash': 'But have you a model for this? No'. (sec. 191)) Second, even if this were intelligible, would we not just be faced with the red patch problem again? We would, surely, if we construed the idea of surveying the infinite table of the addition function as the idea of surveying an infinitely detailed mental image. What is one to do with this 'enormous' imagined table? How, in other words, is one to take it, to interpret it?

Another possibility regarding our grasp of the 'whole use' is to refuse to appeal to mental imagery, but at the same time to insist that there is a *unique kind of mental state or act*, the grasping of a sense, which simply does have as a consequence that once this act has been performed, how I ought to go on in a potentially infinite number of future cases is determined. I shall refer to this as the 'primitive state' account of meaning.[40] It may be objected to this that it has the air of stamping one's foot. 'Have you a model for this?' The question seems very apposite here. The nature of the supposed state is 'left completely mysterious' (Kripke, p. 52).

What I have called the infinity thesis, which was clearly a problem for the imagist account, may appear to present an insuperable obstacle to *any* account of meaning as a mental state, and thus to challenge the primitive state account also. How can any 'finite state of a finite mind' be what the state of meaning is supposed to be? How can it be determined for the infinity of possible addition problems, what counts as their 'sum'? How can it be determined for the infinity of actual and possible things, which of them are 'red'?[41] I return to this issue later, and to the primitive state account, in my comments on the sceptical argument.

As I have noted, Kripke does not develop the argument in the light of an initial characterization of our intuitive conception of meaning such as the one I have presented here. If one accepts my initial characterization, one does not need to consider certain possible suggestions about meaning. Thus I suppose someone might try positing some form of *unconscious* encompassing of all possible cases given that we apparently do not have all the cases to which a term applies consciously in mind. Among other things, this hypothesis ignores a salient feature of the natural view as that has been characterized here. On that view, one's *experience of meaning* is crucial to one's meaning anything, and it is by virtue of this experience that one knows what one means. These aspects of the natural view seem to rule out our attempting to spell out that view in terms of facts about a speaker which lie outside his consciousness. The idea that to mean something is to be disposed to behave in certain ways, therefore, also need not be considered.[42]

Let me now summarize the import of the sceptical argument Kripke presents for the natural view as I have characterized it. On that view, to use a word in a certain sense involves having an experience by virtue of which one grasps a particular concept, and knows that one does. Meanwhile, a given concept is such that it determines for all possible cases whether they fall under it or not. That is, it is a *rule* with an infinity of implications. According to the sceptical argument, there neither is nor could be a subjective experience (or, indeed, an objective state of the speaker) of the kind called for. The conclusion seems to be that there is no such thing as language or thought. This does indeed look like a radical sceptical problem.

As Kripke points out, there are striking parallels between Hume's scepticism and Wittgenstein's, as Kripke reads him (pp. 62–4). Consider one standard way of seeing what Hume is up to on the issue of natural necessity. Hume notes that we have (or seem to have) a notion of *natural necessity* which we apply to the physical world. Thus when we say that the billiard cue *caused* the billiard ball to shift position, we imply that there was some necessary connection between the action of the cue and the movement of the ball. But, Hume argues, all we actually perceive (the content of our subjective impressions) is a series of 'frames' in which the cue and the ball are in successively different positions. We see no necessity. So the content of our experience does not justify us in talk of natural necessity. Indeed, there is arguably an incoherence in the complex notion of 'natural necessity'. If some such account of Hume is right, the parallelism so far with Wittgenstein is quite exact. Both stress that there is nothing in our experience (in Hume's case, of the physical, external world, in Wittgenstein's, within our inner, mental life in particular) which justifies the application of a given conception (in Hume's case, causation viewed as natural necessity, in Wittgenstein's, concept possession and language use on the natural view). Indeed, that conception is arguably incoherent. (Wittgenstein: how could the contents of our inner life determine for us what is correct and incorrect in a potentially infinite range of cases? We have no model for this. Hume: The only model of necessary connection we have is the model of connection between propositions of the intellect in so far as one is inferable from the other. This model is inapplicable to occurrences in nature.)

Now both Hume and Wittgenstein, as Kripke notes, attempt to go further than express scepticism about the instantiation of a conception we seem to operate with. Both engage in a kind of philosophic therapy. Each attempts to delineate the context out of which the offending conception arose. And each then makes suggestions about the proper approach to the observable phenomena connected with the conception (our regular utterances of certain sounds and marks and the subjective phenomena associated with them; the regularities in the natural world).[43] Before considering whether the natural view can be defended against the sceptical considerations noted, I shall first complete my brief survey of Wittgenstein-as-interpreted-by-Kripke, turning now to Wittgenstein's positive approach to language.

4.3 The language game with 'meaning'

Suppose one's conclusion is that no one ever means or thinks anything. This seems to be a more than preposterous conclusion. It seems to be self-defeating, something that one cannot intelligibly express as a conclusion. How can one conclude anything, if one cannot mean or think anything at all?

If we cannot come to this conclusion, how can we avoid it?[44] Obviously one way is to reject what I have called the natural view of meaning. In particular, we can try to resist assuming that there is such a thing as meaning as characterized by the natural view. We have left certain phenomena of everyday life. Quite unreflective people say things like 'What do you mean by "serendipity" ?' and so on. Let us take it that such references to what people 'mean' and so on may be quite in order. We must assume that their being in order cannot be a function of the truth of the natural view of meaning. So we now have the question – what *is* it a function of?

Wittgenstein's approach to this question is to tell us to look and see how the 'language game' we play with words like 'meaning', 'means', 'understands', 'language', and so on, works. (In what follows I shall sometimes refer to this language game as 'the "meaning" game' for short.) Ask: in what contexts are utterances containing these terms standardly considered acceptable or unacceptable by the participants in the game? For example, when would we allow that it is proper to say of someone that he knows what a given word means?

This programme is, in effect, that of considering what Kripke calls 'assertability conditions'. We are to look not for the truth conditions of our sentences, but for the conditions under which they may properly be asserted. This programme provides a context for locutions like 'Here perhaps one really would say . . .' which are typical of Wittgenstein, and are echoed unexplained in Winch's text.[45] There is no question that Wittgenstein talks a great deal about what we *say*, stressing that we do in fact use certain words in certain contexts. This suggests a clear wish to stick as far as possible to what is said when, as opposed to what is meant and what is (correlatively) true.

One kind of context that Wittgenstein focuses on is teaching the meaning of a word or sentence to someone else. In certain cases the language learner's ability to 'go on' spontaneously in his overt use of the term as the teacher does is crucial. It is when and only when the pupil manifests this ability that the teacher may appropriately say 'You've got it!' Here again we have a condition of congruent behaviour (with spontaneity). But here it is presented as a necessary and sufficient *assertability* condition for a certain utterance, not as a logically necessary and sufficient condition for the truth of the utterance. Presented as such, it seems less open to question.

Asked what enables us to get the 'meaning' game started, one who accepts the natural view can answer along the following lines. Individual humans have the capacity to grasp concepts (as this is explicated by the natural view) and to associate them with terms. Moreover, concepts are shareable: different individuals can grasp the same concept. Given that people have these capacities, it is natural enough that they should recognize them in one another, and develop terms to refer to them ('He means . .'; 'I know what courage is . .'; 'We mean the same by. . .'). Knowledge that someone means what you do by a term can clearly be very useful. For example, if Shiela knows that Jerry has grasped a certain concept which she too possesses and that he associates it with the term 'shell', she can with some confidence rely on his getting what she wants when she says, imperiously, 'Shell!'[46] If we abandon the natural view as untenable, however, we cannot explain how the 'meaning' game is possible in any such way.[47]

According to Wittgenstein, what makes language games in general possible is the fact that there are natural human responses to certain stimuli. Consider first an example that does

106

not involve words. In order that a pointing finger can do its work, people must react to it by looking in the direction of the line from wrist to fingertip, not the other way round. Wittgenstein suggests that this is indeed a natural human reaction. (See sec. 185.) It turns out that this kind of fact alone has enormous practical consequences.

Suppose it could be brought about that people acted similarly in response to particular sounds or marks, such as the marks 'Keep off'. Evidently we would have a user-friendly instrument of inestimable practical value. With great economy of effort and time, we could get people to do things, alter their expectations, and so on. We could say 'Run that way' as well as 'Go that way' and have an importantly different result.[48] We could get many different people to act similarly in relation to a single small stimulus. And this is what we do. We can all agree that this is so, whether or not we accept the natural view of meaning.[49]

Given that we reject the natural view, the above considerations suggest that it is ultimately the agreement in reactions among human beings that allows for language games in general. That is, it is the fact that, given similar training, human beings react behaviourally in similar ways to sounds, marks, and so on. Our practical need to influence one another in certain ways is one thing that motivates our participation in language games in general.

Let us now turn to the 'meaning' game in particular. One of Wittgenstein's central concerns in developing an account of this game is properly to locate the role of the subjective dimension of our linguistic lives within it. He is keenly aware of how easy it is to assume that *meaning something by a word* is a 'mental process', something that happens 'in the sphere of the mind'. He clearly has a strong tendency to think this way himself. He acknowledges that there are subjective experiences typically associated with the situations where we grant that people mean something by what they say. Meanwhile, he insists that 'meaning it' is not something 'in the sphere of the mind'.

This denial is backed up by appeal to considerations about the role of such locutions as 'But I meant. . .' in our lives. For example, usually the blank in such a locution will be filled in with another word: 'But I meant *green* by "rot" '. I can be seen as indicating something like this: to go on in the use of 'rot' as I was doing, you must go on as you would with 'green', not as you would with 'red' or whatever. Wittgenstein's thrust is that we do not have to see talk of what I meant and the like as references to a subjective experience associated with my use of a word.

Wittgenstein does not say that our experiences of meaning, the

107

sense of having suddenly 'got it' and so on, play no role in the 'meaning' game. My having these experiences can serve me and others as a useful sign that I have indeed got it. In the right context, my 'Got it!' experience may, indeed, fulfil a sufficient condition for my quite properly asserting 'Got it!' or 'Now I know how to go on!' But to accept this is not to accept that my 'Got it!' experience is the final court of appeal with respect to whether or not I 'really have got it'. Nor is it to accept that my 'really getting it' is even partially *constituted by* my sense that I have got it. It should be stressed that, as Kripke reads Wittgenstein, *Wittgenstein is not trying to give a positive account of what constitutes meaning.* His positive approach involves him in considering assertability conditions, as opposed to truth conditions. He considers when utterances involving the terms 'meaning' and the like are found acceptable by those playing the 'meaning' game.

Just as he is concerned to place subjective phenomena in the 'meaning' game, Wittgenstein pays great attention to the role of *normative* terms in this game. In expressing his approach to our use of such terms ('correct', 'incorrect', 'right', 'wrong', and so on) he often alludes to cases of 'continuing a series' of numbers, a type of case around which, as we have seen, Winch built much of his discussion. Here is an example from Wittgenstein: 'let us suppose that, after some efforts on the teacher's part, he continues the series [of natural numbers] correctly, that is, as we do it. So now we can say he has mastered the system' (sec. 145).

If we extrapolate from this to the case of 'using a word in a certain sense' or 'meaning something' by it, two general assertability conditions suggest themselves. (They also find expression elsewhere.) First, if the sentence 'He is using a word in a certain sense' is assertable, then the sentence 'There is a correct (and an incorrect) way to go on in relation to what he does' is assertable also. (Cf. Wittgenstein, sec. 185.) Call this the 'evaluability' condition. It is, if you like, the assertability conditions analogue of a thesis I have characterized as part of our intuitive conception of language use: the rule thesis. Second, one can be said to 'go on correctly' in one's use of a term if and only if one can be said to go on 'as we do'. 'As we do' appears ultimately to be the natural human way of going on in the relevant context. 'Continuations' that we can all learn to match spontaneously and noncollusively are the ones we count as 'correct'. In other words, we take approving assertions of 'rightness', and so on to be in place when and only when someone's practice conforms to the standard of 'human agreement'. (Cf. Wittgenstein, secs. 224 and 241.) Call this, then, the condition of 'human agreement'.

In Wittgenstein's picture of things, then, the ability of humans as a species to react similarly to verbal stimuli does not only underpin the possibility of successful language games in general. It also grounds the specifics of the language game with 'meaning'. We should not be misled by the way we talk into holding the mistaken view (as Wittgenstein sees it) that in using a word in a certain sense one *mentally grasps something* (a 'rule', 'concept', or 'sense') which itself dictates *how one is to go on* in indefinitely many cases. Rather, when someone uses a word as we all do, we say that he goes on 'correctly'. What about our acceptance of conditionals about 'concept grasp' such as: 'If Lucy has grasped the concept of addition, it will be proper for her to say "120" if asked for "68+52"'? According to Wittgenstein, in making such assertions we commit ourselves to behave in certain ways should Lucy not say '120' in the circumstances envisaged. Roughly, we commit ourselves to accepting that some doubt has been raised over whether it can indeed be asserted that 'Lucy has grasped the concept of addition.' For at least in this case, she has failed to go on as we do. (See Kripke, pp. 94–5 especially.)

Wittgenstein stresses that the 'meaning' game is of immense practical importance. If I can assert 'Joey knows what "five" means', I can go ahead and use the sign 'five' with perfect confidence in interactions with him. I can ask him to 'Please bring me five apples from the garden' and rely on his bringing what I need. It is this practical importance which presumably explains why the 'meaning' game is played.

Let me now refer back to two things that appear to be possible intuitively: a pure sensation term and a congenital Crusoe. What does Wittgenstein have to say about these?

By a 'pure sensation term' I mean (as usual) a term for a sensation quality whose presence has no distinctive behavioural correlates accessible to ordinary observers. On the basis of certain key passages Kripke tentatively concludes that Wittgenstein took a strong position on this issue: within our 'meaning' game no ascription of a pure sensation term is acceptable.[50] At the same time, he makes the following points. Even supposing that Wittgenstein did take this strong position, a weaker view would be more consonant with our actual experience and practice.[51] And there is a weaker position available that respects a condition that Wittgenstein stresses, the condition that it cannot be said that whatever a given user of a term calls 'right' is thereby right, period.[52] Kripke hazards that it is possible that Wittgenstein's own statements on the topic of pure sensation terms were intended as expressions of this weaker position. The exegetical situation, then, is somewhat complex. There is also the question whether Wittgenstein in fact had some reason to prefer the strong position on pure sensation terms, given that a weaker position is consonant with at least one important aspect of his general position on what is assertable.

Let me briefly argue that one can see why someone taking Wittgenstein's general approach would be inclined to endorse both of two general assertability conditions that together apparently lead to the strong position on pure sensation terms. I have in mind the evaluability and the human agreement conditions noted earlier.

According to the evaluability condition, 'Penny is using "rog" in a certain sense' is assertable only if 'There is a correct and incorrect way for Penny to go on in her use of "rog" ' is assertable. According to the condition of human agreement, 'Penny is using "rog" correctly' is only assertable if 'Penny uses "rog" as we all do' is assertable. The condition of human agreement in effect ties genuine rule-following *in a given case* to doing as we all do *in that case* (or to doing what we all would do once we had grasped the use of the term in question). Thus it supplies a unitary standard for all correctness judgments. This is surely an attractive feature of this condition. But if we accept it and the evaluability condition together, it seems to follow that 'Penny is using "rog", a pure sensation term' is not assertable. For at least in so far as we maintain the character of ordinary observers, and other relevant circumstances remain unchanged, no one can ever be in a position to assert that *she goes on as we all do* in her use of any putative pure sensation term. Penny herself is in the same position as everyone else. The reason is simple: our spontaneous and noncollusive uses of the term cannot be observed to tally.[53] It seems that they would have to be so observed, in order that anyone could justifiably assert precisely and categorically that Penny uses the term as we all do.[54] But if we cannot do this, then we cannot say that there is a 'right' and 'wrong' to what she does. And so we cannot talk about the 'sense' her putative pure sensation term has. This particular line of reasoning, then, seems to lead to the strong conclusion that our 'meaning' game does not allow us to say of anyone that he has a pure sensation term in his linguistic repertoire.

In any case, let us assume, as Kripke tentatively does, that Wittgenstein himself did reach this strong conclusion. At one point he writes: 'An "inner process" stands in need of outward criteria' (sec. 580). What precisely are *criteria*? For present purposes, it will suffice to say that the idea of outward criteria is, roughly, the idea of behavioural correlates by reference to which an ordinary observer can judge if the user of a term for a particular 'inner process' is inclined to go on as we do, and so can be said to have 'mastered a rule' for the use of this term. If there must be such criteria for *any* genuine 'inner process' term, then it seems that there cannot be a genuine pure sensation term as defined here. As I have argued, it is hard to see how anyone could check that its user goes on as we do.

In the case of our sensation word 'pain' in English, for instance, there are indeed public occurrences which serve an important function in teaching the meaning of the word, and ascribing understanding of it. A child cries and we say 'Where's the pain?' Thus we teach the word in the context of observable behaviour. It is apparently part of the language game that the child may properly say 'I'm in pain', without crying. But we would doubt that the child really knew what 'pain' meant if he saw another clasping his bleeding knee and crying and said 'As far as I can see, he is not in pain'. Thus it can be argued that the crucial assertability condition for 'He knows what "pain" means' in English is that we see that he is inclined to 'go on' as we all observably do with respect to ascriptions of 'pain'. And it seems that we must deny him such knowledge if he denies someone is in pain when certain public occurrences occur. Precisely what implications these facts have for the possibility of a pure sensation term in general is another matter. (I say more later about how such facts can be accepted and explained outside the framework of Wittgenstein's approach to language and linguistic normativity.)

This is all I shall say for now about Wittgenstein's views on 'private languages' in the sense of terms for sensations lacking public correlates, whose use can therefore not be checked against that of others. Let me now turn to the question of 'private languages' in the sense of languages possessed by asocial beings.

In Winch's interpretation of Wittgenstein, not only was a pure sensation term logically impossible (and hence presumably no one should be asserted to have one) but all language users must have 'had experience of human society' as a matter of logic. Hence a congenital Crusoe was logically impossible. Presumably one could never then legitimately assert of an ever solitary islander observed from afar 'Look, a congenital Crusoe with a language!'

Crusoe fares better at the hands of Kripke's Wittgenstein. Let me describe Crusoe's fate as I understand it. One who accepts Wittgenstein's account of the standard assertability conditions for language possession would say that in order legitimately to assert that a certain congenital Crusoe has a language, we must first ascertain that his reactions observably tally with ours in the right way. At this point we must simply decide whether or not to play our 'meaning' game with respect to him. Are we to treat him as 'one of us' in this respect? (With this in mind, Kripke writes of our 'taking him into our community', p. 110.) Assuming that the decision to do so can be legitimate, then the assertion 'Look! A congenital Crusoe with a language!' is not ruled out by the nature of our 'meaning' game.[55]

4.4 Comments on the scepticism

Does the sceptical argument force us to deny that there is such a thing as meaning as characterized by the natural view? Even after hearing the argument one may still be strongly inclined to say: But surely there must be something to the natural view?[56] One may even be inclined to take a Kantian attitude to the notion of meaning as characterized by the natural view. That is, one may feel that if in practice we were to try to do without the *assumption* of meaning as characterized by the natural view, our intellectual hold on the world would collapse. I shall not try to develop an argument for this conclusion here. I shall clear the ground for it, however, by arguing that the impact of the sceptical argument is not as devastating as it may first appear.

Reviewing the sceptical argument we recall that it raises two important problems. The first may be dubbed *the infinity problem*. The natural view seems to require that with a single momentary mental act we encompass the infinite in a certain way: it is determined how we should go on for an infinity of possible cases. But it is not clear how this could be achieved: *our minds are finite*. The second problem may be summarized as follows: consider any introspectible state I am in at a given time. *This* could not have consequences regarding how one is to go on. For it is open to interpretation, and can be interpreted any way you like. So it is not a rule. The problem here could be dubbed: *the impotence of introspectibilia*.

Let us now return to what I have called the primitive state account of meaning. According to this account, when one means something by a word one is in a unique type of subjective state. The account does not claim that in order to mean addition by 'plus', say, one must conjure up an image of the infinite table of the addition function. Somehow, though, one is supposed to grasp or encompass the concept of addition when in this state.

I believe that the natural view as described so far can and should be characterized further as a version of the primitive state account of meaning. In other words, our intuitive conception of meaning is a version of the primitive state account. I shall now argue that

112

the primitive state account is capable of resisting the sceptical attack. Let us first consider whether the primitive state account can be conclusively refuted by reference to the mind's finitude.

That there is a genuine infinity problem in this context is not completely clear. The question of whether the mind is finite in such a way as to make the primitive state account inconsistent does not seem to admit of a clearly negative answer. It may be true that our brains cannot physically contain an actual infinity of discrete particles, and that such an infinity of particles would be required for the physical encoding of an infinite set of ordered triples, say, as in the case of the table of the addition function. The connection of this with the issue at hand is not immediately apparent. For one thing, its connection with what our minds can or cannot do is not obvious. From a conceptual point of view, the mind itself is neither spatially finite nor spatially infinite, for it does not obviously itself take spatial predicates at all.

Does temporal finitude present a problem? We supposedly grasp a particular concept at a given moment in time. Consider the concept of addition. Would it be logically possible to review every possible sum in a single moment, one sum at a time? Some have argued that it is logically impossible to review an infinity of items in a finite amount of time, but this has been disputed.[57] Posssibly, then, we could perform some such review in a single moment. But it may seem unlikely that we do, and it may appear not to be quite what we want here. Grasping the concept of addition, for instance, may seem to be a different matter from mentally reviewing every possible sum. We seem to be left, then, with the following possibility, that grasping a concept is grasping or encompassing an infinite abstract object in a way that does not consist of such a review. Is this to be left with nothing, or with nothing intelligible?[58] From a logical point of view it seems possible that there are ways of encompassing infinite abstract objects which are unique to the mind (and to abstract objects). While it is clear what those ways cannot be like, it is not clear that there cannot be such ways.[59] It seems, then, that the primitive state account can avoid the infinity problem. Let us leave it at that, for now.

What, next, of the impotence of introspectibilia? The primitive state account seems well set up to avoid the problems of imagism. In particular, it does not claim that in meaning addition by 'plus', say, one pays attention to an image which dictates how one is to go on. What Kripke says, however, suggests that there may yet be a problem for this account which is somewhat analogous to that of the impotence of introspectibilia: can we conceive of any state of our minds which is not open to a variety of possible

113

interpretations?[60] Let us call this the problem of *interpretability*. It is a general problem not specifically about introspectible states, but about any subjective state whatsoever. (For the point that there is a real distinction between introspectible and subjective states in general see below.) We may take this problem in terms of normativity: will there not be a variety of ways of 'following' any such state, of according with its dictates, and so on? Does it make sense, then, to talk of its dictates at all?

It is not clear that such questions can be used to invalidate the most intuitively acceptable version of the primitive state account. For intuitively speaking, while the act of meaning *involves* a subjective state, it is not a matter of regarding any state of one's own mind as constituting a rule. Let us henceforth take the primitive state account accordingly.

The Wittgensteinian considerations expounded by Kripke do seem to show that a subjective state of meaning such-and-such could not be such that we can tell what we are to do by reflecting upon its introspectible, qualitative nature. A particular subjective state of our minds considered introspectively could function as a sign, but signs are 'dead'.[61] They stand in need of interpretation. But this does not seem to run counter to intuition regarding the state or act of meaning. Intuitively speaking, the subjective state involved in the act of meaning is not itself a rule. It is not my subjective state which I follow. From this point of view, it is not clear why the fact that there is a problem about how to interpret or follow any subjective state (a problem that no *rule* should have) should be worrying.

It may be queried whether the natural view as I characterized it earlier does not, after all, involve appeal to the 'following' of some introspected state. This is not so. It was a part of the natural view as characterized earlier that to mean something I must be in some subjective state, and that, by virtue of being in that state, I must know what concept I grasp or what I mean. But this does not entail that what concept I grasp is determinable by considering the introspectible quality of my state. Though I must be in some sense aware of my subjective state (that is what it is for a state to be subjective), such awareness is even compatible with my state's not being introspectible in the sense of having a qualitative character that can be reflected upon. In other words, my state may not give a 'what it is like' result when I try to attend to it. It could be that the more one tries to focus on what one's act of meaning is subjectively *like*, the less one is engaged in the act of meaning. (Compare: taking careful aim at a target versus introspecting what it is like to take careful aim at a target.)

114

Let me sum up what I have been arguing concerning the general problem of interpretability. The fact that introspected states, or even subjective states period, cannot *constitute rules* does not obviously refute anything that the natural view supposes.

I note that Kripke remarks:

> it remains mysterious exactly how the existence of any past finite state of my mind could entail that, if I wish to accord with it, and remember the state, and do not miscalculate, I must give a determinate answer to an arbitrarily large addition problem. (p. 53)

Now in so far as the impotence of introspectibilia is concerned, it seems that one can argue something stronger. One can argue for impossibility rather than mystery. If by 'past finite state of my mind' we understand 'the introspectible character my state then had' it is arguably impossible for my past state to have the implications alleged for it. But proponents of the natural view need not contend that the introspectible character of any subjective state of my mind as such, when recalled in memory, has implications for what I should do. As I have just argued, according to that view, though my acts of meaning do have a subjective component, it is not by introspecting these acts, or reflecting upon them phenomenologically, that we mean. Recalling what I meant cannot, then, be simply a matter of recalling how it was with me phenomenologically, if that is any part of it at all. If I recall what I meant, if for instance I recall that I then meant by 'plus' what I now mean by 'plus', then I recall that I was in a particular state of the special kind in question, that is, a state in which I grasped a particular concept. Given that this was so, there will have been an infinity of implications regarding how I should go on. There is no obvious ground here for claiming impossibility by virtue of the impotence of introspectibilia or the general problem of interpretability. If there is a crucial difficulty for the natural view, it must be found elsewhere.

So far, then, I have argued that meaning according to the natural view has not been proved impossible for a human mind. On the one hand, it is not obvious that human minds are finite in some sense which obviously rules out their grasping or encompassing infinite abstract objects in some way. On the other hand, according to the natural view, meaning something does not involve one's attempting to follow or interpret a subjective state of one's own.

Let us now consider further the precise content of the natural view. According to this view, an infinity of normative implications ensue upon my mental act of meaning or concept grasp. It now appears that in order to allow for the coherence of this root idea, it needs to be articulated or developed further as follows. To grasp a concept is to grasp a special kind of object, an abstract object with an infinity of normative implications (which we may then think of as an infinite object). It is of the nature of this special kind of object to be a rule.

Other considerations, in any case, suggest this articulation of the natural view. Familiar ways of speaking suggest that concept grasp is indeed conceived of as grasp of an object of a certain kind. I have in mind not only the rather sophisticated language of 'concept grasp' that I have repeatedly used here, but more garden-variety remarks such as 'Do you get the idea?' 'Yes, of course.' It is almost impossible not to fall into speaking in this way, that is, to avoid treating concepts as objects. Meanwhile, the intuitively plausible meaning-shareability condition implies that concepts are not particular subjective states of persons, and it is clear from an intuitive point of view that they are not conceived of as physical objects or as in principle accessible to the senses. (Hence the extreme bizarreness of the philosopher G. E. Moore's reported nightmare in which he could not distinguish propositions (roughly, sentence-meanings) from tables (of the type made of wood and so on).)

Be that as it may, it certainly looks as if one who desires a philosophically tenable version of the natural view that retains all the aspects noted, or even the central rule and infinity theses alone, must take the act of meaning to involve grasp of an abstract objective particular, a concept, something which is by its nature a rule. So let us now continue with the explicit assumption that the natural view involves this conception.

At this point we seem to have reached a form of platonism. By 'platonism' I mean precisely the view that in meaning something by a word one expresses grasp of an abstract objective particular, a concept or rule. A question I have heard is: given that platonism is unacceptable, what account are we to give of meaning? There is little doubt that Wittgenstein thought along these lines (though see below). Empiricist philosophers such as Hume attempted to reduce the act of grasping a concept to the act of entertaining an image, where image was substituted for concept. Wittgenstein rightly denigrated this fudge. Images do not have the right properties to be concepts – they can only be signs. The entertaining of signs cannot constitute meaning.

As is now apparent, the very question 'Given that platonism is unacceptable, what account are we to give of meaning?' is problematic. Suppose that platonism is indeed part of the natural view of meaning. Suppose, further, that we (naturally) understand the term 'meaning' in the phrase 'an account of meaning' according to the natural view. Finally suppose that an account of meaning is understood to be a definition or a set of logically necessary and sufficient conditions. Given all these things it seems that there can be no acceptable answer to the question. If an account of *something* is given, it will not be an account of *meaning*. (Evidently, on Kripke's view, Wittgenstein's own positive views on meaning are *not* intended to constitute an 'account of meaning' of the problematic kind in question.)

In any case, let us briefly consider the question of platonism: can Wittgensteinian considerations be used to reject it? Kripke considers this question very briefly (pp. 53–4) in relation to platonism about mathematics, with reference to the views of Frege.[62] He suggests that Wittgenstein's sceptical problem is a problem here too: 'it arises precisely in the question how the existence in my mind of any mental entity or idea can *constitute* "grasping" any particular sense rather than another'. Can this idea not be interpreted in a multiplicity of ways (p. 54)? But he also says something which suggests that platonism is not open to the central Wittgensteinian moves (problems of interpretability, infinity). 'For Wittgenstein, platonism is largely an unhelpful *evasion* of the problem of how our finite minds can give rules that are supposed to apply to an infinity of cases' (p. 54; my stress). This is the more obviously apt verdict for the Wittgensteinian. The platonist as he has been characterized here, at least, does not claim that any subjective state of a person's mind can constitute, or partly constitute a rule or concept, a doctrine clearly at risk from the interpretability problem. Rather, the platonist takes a route that the Wittgensteinian is hardly willing to consider. For his account of meaning, the platonist not only goes beyond the body, but beyond the mind as well.

Now though Wittgenstein (and others) might find platonism unhelpful, possibly repellent, is it incoherent, does it involve a logical impossibility? Must we accept that Wittgenstein's sceptical argument renders the natural view of meaning *senseless*? I have already argued in effect that this is by no means clear. And as long as the view is not senseless or incoherent, the possibility of providing at least a Kantian defence remains open.

We might ask the platonist: have you a model for this? That is, roughly, is there a familar type of structure that might be appealed to as a way of making the special state of concept grasp easier to envisage? I would argue that there is indeed a model that the platonist can appeal to. This is a model in which my mental state when I mean something is a mode of *perception* of meaning or of a concept.[63]

Consider in this connection the way we think of the perception of physical objects, of objects in space 'outside the mind'. Roughly, it goes like this. When I perceive a tree, I am in a certain mental state. Moreover, when I introspect or focus on what it is like for me to be perceiving a tree, my state has a very specific content. Meanwhile, we do not consider that a mere mental state of mine can constitute a tree (or even partly constitute a tree). Rather, my mental state partly constitutes, quite precisely, my perceiving a tree. We hold that the tree has the power to generate indefinitely many tree-impressions in the right circumstances. This certainly is not something we hold to be true of a given impression of a tree. It would be rash to do so, since it is surely absurd to suppose that someone's personal temporary impression of a tree, a sensory state which can be considered introspectively, has any such power. In some sense it is true that neither this temporary impression of a tree, nor any finite series of similar impressions in the past, logically warrants my positing something outside me which is of such a kind that it can generate an in principle infinite set of similar impressions in the future. None the less, we persistently claim to perceive trees and other such objects, going far beyond what our impressions alone, considered in themselves, logically warrant.

As is well known, there is the possibility of philosophical scepticism here. 'All I have' is my mental state, my temporary impression of a tree. How can I be sure I perceive a tree rather than that I simply have the impression that I do? I can be sure, by introspection, that I have the impression, not that there is something 'out there' that it is an impression of.

The tree problem was of course raised most forcefully by Hume in his scepticism about the existence of enduring external objects, the putative providers of impressions. In the Humean view, acceptance of the natural view of externality and belief in external objects is philosophically unwarranted. It seems, however, that we keep 'slipping into' the original concept of externality: we regard ourselves as contemplating external objects. We consider the objects as (in part) responsible for our sensory states, but not identical with them. Kant argued, roughly, that we cannot get any grip on our subjective experience at all if we do not apply the category of external object within our experience, if we do not see ourselves as perceiving external objects through our sensory states. It is thus, after all, philosophically legitimate to apply the category – since this is required if our experience is to make any sense.

It is arguable, then, that there is a model which is appropriate to the natural view of meaning. It is the model of our perception of external objects – spatially located objects outside the mind.

This model has certain features which are clearly relevant to a model of meaning. First, it involves a relation between a subjective state or states, and an independent object, an object which exists when the subjective state does not, and to which the subjective states of many different persons, and the same person at different times, can stand in the same relation. Second, we hold ourselves to perceive objects in space, and to know that we do, in part by virtue of, or through, being in the relevant subjective state.[64] Third, we do not think that the object is constituted by the subjective state. The object has its own qualities. Finally, the object has qualities which are importantly distinct in kind from those of our subjective states. Thus the existence of the object has an infinite number of implications regarding how our future experiences will go. A sensory state with a particular phenomenological quality has no such implications in itself. (This assumption forces us, of course, to distinguish object from impression of object.)

Now both the Wittgensteinian considerations presented by Kripke and other considerations suggest some ways in which one might try to throw doubt upon the idea that in the act of meaning we perceive senses or concepts. I do not see that any of the problems are clearly devastating, however.

Let us leave aside questions of how we could be in touch with abstract objects of the relevant type. (I suspect the honest answer here has to be 'who knows?' rather than 'it's impossible'.) One thing that might be argued is that the results of our attempts to introspect the mental states involved in the act of meaning do not show that there is indeed a 'complete' concept out there (in platonic space) or indeed, any concept out there at all. In so far as this is correct, however, it does not in itself prove any internal incoherence or logical difficulty in the idea that concepts *are* perceived, or even that they are perceived whole.

With respect to any appeal to the meagreness of the 'givens' of introspection in this area, the following points may be noted. On the one hand, it is not clear that we should expect that any aspect of an act of meaning can be observed in introspection. Recall the analogy with observing what it is like to take careful aim at a target. Taking such aim has a crucial subjective component, as meaning does on the natural view. One cannot be taking careful aim at a particular target unless one is in a fairly specific conscious mental state. Now we can be said to know what it is like to be in that state, in a sense, just by virtue of being in it. But there is also a sense in which it is impossible to know what it is like to be in that particular state. For it is impossible to focus on or observe the state in question directly. (The act of observation causes the state to cease. You cannot be taking careful aim at a target if your attention is elsewhere.) A subjective state of meaning could have the same type of inaccessibility to introspection, where introspection involves more than mere 'experiencing'. An attempt to focus on 'what it is like to mean' may entail that one no longer means. Whatever is observed, it is not an aspect of *meaning*. If *this* were true of meaning, it would not show meaning could not have a crucial subjective component, a component without which it could not occur, just like aiming carefully at a target.

On the other hand, in so far as we *can* introspectively observe what it is like to mean such-and-such, it is not clear that we should be worried by the fact that the introspected nature of states of meaning does not seem to provide an adequate basis for knowing that we perceive a particular concept. For its introspected aspect is at least not constitutive of the act of meaning. This point may be made more clearly in relation to acts of perception of physical objects. I may 'step back' and consider the question: what is it like (from the point of view of the introspectible quality of my state) to observe a room? Then I start observing what it is like to observe a room. Even if there is a sense in which I can indeed observe this (I can presumably have a good idea of what sensory state I was in when I was simply observing the room) what I observe is not the act of observing the room itself, certainly not the act of wholly focusing on the room. Once again, there is a kind of recalcitrance to observation of the phenomenon that is really in question.

With respect to our intuitive conception of perceptual knowledge in general, it can be argued that we do not think such knowledge must involve our having 'evidence of our senses' such that a description of an introspectible 'sensory given' logically entails that the item in question is perceived. There seems to be no good reason to insist that concept perception must involve our having such evidence.

None the less, a possible objection to the idea that grasp of meanings or concepts could be analogous to physical object perception runs as follows. Standardly the whole of an object such as a tree is not perceived when I see it at a certain time from a certain perspective. Meanwhile, it is part of the natural view that when I use a word in a certain sense at a certain time, I know precisely what I mean. That is, I already know that by 'plus' I mean the addition function and not some other related but distinct function, say, the *quaddition* function, according to which numbers less than 57 are to be added to each other, while the result of quadding all other numbers is 5. (The idea of 'quaddition' is Kripke's; see his p. 9.) This knowledge cannot be thought of as explicit or present in detail of which one is conscious. However, it is supposedly knowledge that we have by virtue of whatever goes on in our minds, at a time, when we mean. Hence it seems that the model of perception at issue here must allow us, while perceiving an object which is distinct from our sensory state, at the same time to perceive the *whole* object, so that it can be known to us in its entirety.

There are various ways of responding to this objection. It could be noted that we usually feel comfortable enough saying that we see *a tree*, rather than a part of a tree. However, it is undeniable that there is something to the point that standardly we do not see every part of a tree at once. The problem, presumably, could be posed thus: the analogy with perception of physical objects can only get us outside the area of Wittgensteinian difficulties if we can allow that a whole concept could be perceived.

In response to this, we might first query whether it is not possible to perceive the whole of something physical, whether or not this frequently happens. Can one not perceive a whole *sound*? True, there will be different, indeed infinitely many *perspectives* on the sound, as there will be infinitely many possible perspectives on a tree. But from each perspective, the whole sound is perceived. Again, might one not see the whole of a transparent object, such as a glass marble?

Whether or not we can find cases of the sensory perception of whole physical objects, it is surely not unreasonable to propose that concept perception need not parallel standard cases of physical object perception in all ways. We usually do not see all the detail of a tree because we perceive a tree from a particular spatial location and cannot see all around the tree, given the limits of our perspective. But there is no obvious analogue in concept perception with the limits of perception due to the perceiver's location in space. Again, we might have trouble with the idea of perceiving a tree 'in its entirety' in so far as even if we can see its whole outer surface, there remains its inner constitution. But concepts have no physical density. The kinds of incompleteness of perceptual knowledge at issue here, then, depend on special features of physical object perception which we would not expect to be present in concept perception. It cannot thus be used to bolster an attack on the idea that there is something which could be called concept perception.

What is most important about the model of perception of physical objects in this context is the idea that there is a relation (perception) which has the following properties. First, I am in a certain subjective state when I perceive the object, but the object is distinct from the state. Second, I can consider in introspection what it is like 'inside me' when I perceive the object. That is, I can consider what my sensory state is like qualitatively. But to do this is not to consider what the object itself is like. Third, others can perceive numerically the same object, though their sensory impression of it will be numerically different from mine, and may also be be qualitatively different from mine.

The question of how we can perceive an object, namely a concept, which has an infinite number of implications for correct use or a determinate range of application (including a determinate'range of borderline cases, maybe) has to be a very special question. For it is a question specifically about a special type of object, something which is clearly *sui generis*. It is not clear that objections in terms of aspects of the perception of physical objects which are special effects of their physicality can be to the point. At this point the proper attitude to the idea that we could perceive whole concepts and know that we do on the basis of our subjective state may be agnosticism.[65]

Kant may be seen as arguing, roughly, that in the case of our presumed knowledge of causation and the world of physical objects, we are right to make and to accept claims to knowledge, logical insufficiency of the 'evidence of our senses' notwithstanding. Kant did not just state that we were right (as we assume), but famously gave a 'transcendental argument' for our rightness: our having any coherent course of experience, our having any means of tracking the course of our sensory states themselves, and hence our own inner histories, depends upon our taking it that we have such knowledge.

In conclusion, then, I suggest that the indubitable power of Wittgenstein's argument is to have shown that *what we are aware of in introspection* cannot be regarded as itself a rule or, more relevantly, a concept. This goes for any conceivable mental state, however large or vague or complicated the qualities involved. This is well worth showing, given the naturalness of the opposite view as evidenced by imagist philosophies of meaning as well as in 'verbal formulation' views of what it is to grasp a rule. In short, introspectible states can only constitute signs, not rules. As I have argued, platonism invokes a model of meaning in which mental states themselves are neither signs nor rules but rather states of perception of concepts. Concepts, meanwhile, *are* rules. Questions of the adequacy of the introspectible aspects of such states as bases for knowledge of concepts can indeed be raised, as can questions as to how such states can in any case do the job supposed of them, but they do not obviously show that platonism is incoherent or even that we cannot have confidence that we

122

mean what we say in the way that the natural view supposes.

I do not say that there is nothing 'mysterious' about the natural view when it is spelled out platonistically. Probably any phenomenon that is *sui generis* is by that very token mysterious. To some degree it is unlike anything else. But I take the charge of mystery, noted in this connection by Kripke and endorsed by many, to be far weaker than the charge of incoherence, inconsistency, or unintelligibility.[66]

Platonism has also been tagged with the (intendedly derogatory) label 'mystical'. Possibly this tag can be interpreted in terms of the way platonism goes beyond experience. But then each of us is involved in mysticism every time we go to the supermarket, every time we reach for our coffee cup. That seems, at least, to be the lesson of both Hume and Kant. Or perhaps it all depends, in the final reckoning, on whether a platonic conception of the grasp of concepts is, after all, a category in the Kantian sense, on whether or not it is incumbent upon us to accept this conception (whether we acknowledge it or not) if we are to make sense of anything. Perhaps a view should only be tagged as mystical if it is not a view we *must* hold.

Much of the deepest philosophy to date has been a matter of uncovering categories in the Kantian sense, and it is part of the genuine pain of such philosophical discovery that it sets a wish to take no risks in our beliefs and hence to root our beliefs absolutely firmly in experience (a wish for utter certainty) against a need to make something of that very experience. A test of whether we are faced with scepticism about a category in the sense in question would appear to be the test of inducing something close, phenomenologically, to madness or terror when the argument is taken seriously. I think that scepticism about meaning on the natural view, like scepticism about external objects, is of this sort. Its power cannot be ignored and it would be intellectually dishonest – though comforting – to think that it did not need to be faced. However, and rather paradoxically, if it is indeed an argument about a category, we, as beings engaged in the attempt at science in a broad sense, cannot ultimately reject what it shows to be close to a matter of faith. What I have argued very sketchily here is that the natural view has not obviously been shown to be incoherent, and that real problems that may be associated with it are quite parallel to those in another area where Kant has forcefully argued that the view in question (that we perceive external objects) cannot be and hence need not be given up.

This is as far as I shall go regarding what I have called the natural view of meaning here. Evidently I feel that in spite of the powerful Wittgensteinian scepticism outlined by Kripke, and a different, but related scepticism about perceptual knowledge broadly speaking, it is still philosophically respectable to hold the natural view of concept possession and intentions, interpreted platonistically.[67] It may even be incumbent upon us to do so: whether we like it or not, this may be the only view we can live with.

4.5 Comments on the positive approach to language

The general idea of looking closely at 'language games' is not obviously in conflict with the natural view of meaning. Wittgenstein asks us to 'look for the use' of terms. It would seem that we could adopt this general approach while continuing to maintain the natural view and to think without qualms in terms of the family: meaning, truth, truth conditions of sentences, logically necessary conditions of application of a term, logically sufficient conditions, analysis of concepts, and so on, in ways corresponding to the natural view. For at least in advance of confrontation with the sceptical argument, and conviction that it is right, it is not obvious that we need restrict ourselves to 'assertability conditions'.

It seems that the territory of such conditions, and that of our semantic and logical notions, is simply different. Thus it may be that 'Jemima has grasped a concept' is not properly assertable if as far as we can tell she is collecting objects into a pile at random. Meanwhile we can argue that it is still logically possible that Jemima has grasped a concept and is systematically putting together things that fall under it. Thus it looks as if the results of a general search for assertability conditions need not conflict in any way with implications of the natural view. Indeed, one would not expect any conflict here. After all, we are just to describe how it is with our use of words. One would hope and expect that this would not conflict with our intuitive conception of meaning.

In the next section, I shall consider the implications for the intentionalist programme of an exclusive concern with assertability conditions. In this section, I want to focus on the fact that there is some evidence that Wittgenstein's own views about what is assertable conflict with our actual use of terms. I shall argue that in so far as they do so conflict, this may be traceable to his rejection of the natural view.

As noted earlier, there is some evidence that Wittgenstein believes it to be impossible in principle ever justifiably to assert that someone's language – one's own or another's – includes a pure sensation term. Let us consider one of the most famous passages that concerns this issue. In the context of a discussion in which it is supposed that 'I didn't have natural expression for the sensation, but only had the sensation' (sec. 256), Wittgenstein famously writes as follows:

> Let us imagine the following case. I want to keep a diary about the recurrence of a certain sensation. To this end I associate with it the sign 'S'. . . . I impress on myself the connection between the sign and the sensation. – But 'I impress it upon myself' can only mean: this process brings it about that I remember the connexion *right* in the future. But in the present case I have no criterion of correctness. One would like to say: whatever is going to seem right to me is right. And that only means that here we can't talk about 'right'. (sec. 258)

A natural response here would be: but wouldn't we quite happily talk about 'right' here? Wittgenstein appears to have reached an interesting, indeed a provocative philosophical conclusion. It is not clear that the constraint of 'leaving everything as it is' really leaves room for a conclusion with this kind of interest. It appears to involve more than simple natural history, more than a simple demonstration of how we use words.

Kripke points out that as an empirical fact there are sensations without the kind of natural behavioural correlate that would enable anyone else to figure out that one has them (p. 103, fn. 83). And if we look at how we actually use language, we find people saying things like this: 'I have a funny kind of sensation in my toe which I can't quite describe . . . there it is again. Maybe I'm confused since there's no obvious physical change that goes with it. But . . . there it is again.' Suppose Sue has just said this. It would be in no way bizarre for her to go on: 'I call this kind of sensation a "wuzzy" sensation.' If asked 'What is it like?' Sue may have no answer. She might manage various analogies, but it could still be impossible for someone else to feel any confidence that he knew what quality was being talked about.[68] Surely we would not conclude from all this that Sue used 'wuzzy' in no sense at all? In the terms of this discussion, we would conclude, rather, that Sue had a pure sensation term in her repertoire.[69]

As Kripke makes clear, the idea of an 'uncorrelated' sensation cannot be characterized as 'bizarre' or as a far-fetched philosophical counterexample. Contrary to his own expressed conception of philosophy, Wittgenstein's approach to language may, then, have led him to deny something that 'everyone admits'. It can be argued that the rejection of the natural view even *as our natural view* would be an important stimulus to denying that the 'meaning' game allows us to accept the possibility of a pure sensation term. Let me explain.

In the section from which I last quoted, Wittgenstein refers to the idea that one can give oneself a 'sort of ostensive definition' for term 'S' by 'impressing on oneself' the connection between 'S' and the recurrent sensation in question. And he writes '"I impress it upon myself" can only mean: this process brings it about that I remember the connection *right* in the future.' However, that is not what it would be taken to mean, given our intuitive understanding of what meaning is. For one thing, it would not necessarily be connected so immediately to memory or even to the future. It would mean something like: I determine that 'S' *is the name of* this type of sensation. This construal, of course, uses an unanalysed term relating to semantics ('is the name of'). We would at the same time understand that it was the fact that this sign had been stipulated to refer to this type of sensation (and hence associated with one particular sense rather than another) that would make what I did later right or wrong (presuming I wished to accord with my past stipulation).

In this crucial passage Wittgenstein appears at one and the same time to reject the natural view himself and ('this can only mean') to reject it in the name of an imagined speaker of his language. (The second form of rejection would naturally occur to one who preferred a supposed error to lie in philosophic rather than everyday understanding.) This could make it easier for him to overlook the fact that we actually seem willing to allow that people can name sensations without outward manifestations.

Wittgenstein's rejection of the natural view of what meaning is has left him with a number of central kinds of judgments, in particular 'normative' judgments, which cannot now be accounted for in a certain way. So how might they be accounted for? Don't think, look at how we use language. Given a certain amount of looking, one may apparently decide that it is our natural tendency as human beings observably to 'go on the same' which allows us to make our judgments of normativity. In particular, one may decide that in order for there to be a 'right' way to go on, a person must go on 'as we do'. An outright rejection of pure sensation terms, then, is a natural consequence of a certain set of conclusions about normativity in general. If one accepted the natural view, one would not start out on the road that can lead to this conclusion. Thus the rejection of pure sensation terms can be seen as a natural outcome of reasoning with the sceptical argument as a premise. Meanwhile, the unsatisfactory nature of this rejection from the point of view of our actual linguistic practice is surely a point against

126

Wittgenstein's argumentation as a whole. Precisely where one chooses to locate the error is, of course, another matter. My main point here is that rejection of the natural view, and a concomitant tendency to reject it even as our natural view, has a way of leading to consequences that do conflict with our actual linguistic practice.

At one point Wittgenstein asks: 'Is what we call "obeying a rule" something that it would be possible for only *one* man to do, and to do only *once* in his life?' (sec. 199). The question is rhetorical and Wittgenstein intends a negative answer. But why? Here is another denial that seems to be in conflict with what one is likely to think off the cuff. Would it not be possible for a single thinking being to be created for just an instant of life, to see a beautiful sunset, and to think: 'Ah, beautiful!' If someone asserted that this had in fact happened, should we be bound to laugh him out of court as having violated the assertability conditions associated with our language game? If rejection of such an assertion is a result of Wittgenstein's picture of linguistic normativity, if it is something that falls out from that picture, then once again there is some reason to conclude that something is wrong with that picture.

One suspect, again, is the rejection of the idea that what I have called the natural view is indeed our intuitive conception of meaning. If this view contains some error, it is not a philosophical error, it is apparently an error of those who play the 'meaning' game. Wittgenstein suggests that he has no problem with our playing this game, and, indeed, that it would be wrong of him to reject any aspect of it. He wants, rather, to point out some metaphysical mistakes people get into when they turn from living their lives to being philosophers. But it can be argued that these mistakes are embedded in the 'meaning' game, and that we are all metaphysicians, in that our language game presupposes a certain metaphysics of concepts and concept grasp. Destroy or reject the metaphysics and the game in its full richness is abandoned. (Some, of course, have become inured to accepting the impossibility claims considered in this section, by virtue of their reading of Wittgenstein. The game that such people now play is doubtless somewhat different from that of the rest of us.)[70]

In sum, certain details of Wittgenstein's positive views (or, more tentatively, views he can appear to have) are far from obviously acceptable. That is, they seem to stray rather far from what the unsuspecting person would say or hear without fright. They seem to draw the boundaries of the 'meaning' game too tightly. Built into the game there appears to be an approach to linguistic normativity that is different from the general approach suggested by Wittgenstein, according to which no criterion of correctness can be found 'in the sphere of the mind' broadly speaking.

I believe that there is *something* clear and important to be said about the impossibility of a pure sensation term, and about the necessity for behavioural criteria. I shall turn to it shortly. It really goes beyond Wittgenstein, and takes us in a different direction. It may, however, help to explain why some of his 'deviant' conclusions (from the point of view of our language game) have seemed reasonable to many, even to Wittgenstein himself. Something very like these conclusions are the valid conclusions of a different argument. First, however, I must turn directly to the relevance of Kripke's Wittgenstein to the intentionalist programme.

5 THE INTENTIONALIST PROGRAMME

5.1 The analytical issue

According to the intentionalist programme, an adequate explication of the everyday concept of a human social group will appeal to the intentional or meaningful behaviour of human beings. This supposes that the concept of intention is logically independent of the concept of a social group. Is there anything in the arguments considered that shows this programme must be abandoned?

I have argued that according to our intuitive conception of concept possession and language use, the 'standard of correctness' involved in someone's grasp of a concept has nothing to do with an individual's relations with his fellows. Consideration of the sceptical argument Kripke details on Wittgenstein's behalf involved further clarification of the implications of the natural view. I have argued that, in spite of the power of the sceptical argument, the intuitive conception of concept possession is logically coherent and, more generally, philosophically tenable. In sum, no compelling reason has been derived from the investigation of our intuitive conception of concept possession for abandoning either intentions or the intentionalist programme.

5.2 The intentionalist programme and the assertability conditions approach

As an adjunct to the defence of intentionalism just summarized, it is appropriate to enquire whether a form of intentionalism could be sustained if, bowing to the sceptical argument, one adopted an assertability conditions approach to our 'language games'. What, then, are the implications for the intentionalist programme of an assertability conditions approach in general and of Wittgenstein's particular working out of such an approach?

An assertability conditions approach in general stands in opposition to the approach of the intentionalist programme, in so far as the latter is concerned with questions of logical constitution or conceptual analysis as opposed to assertability conditions. But it is not clear that these two approaches are opposed in any stronger sense than that of being different: in principle it seems one could ask both types of question within a given domain.[71]

Meanwhile, an assertability approach as such poses no obvious threat to the general premise of the intentionalist programme with respect to the priority of intentional states over society. The general assertability conditions approach would have us search for the conditions under which we would assert people had intentions, and, as a possibly distinct enterprise, for the conditions under which we would assert that they were members of societies. Now, on the face of it the assertability conditions for intention and the like do not presuppose fulfilment of those for membership in a society. If they did, we would never have to bother to investigate the conceptual and linguistic capacities of feral children or human infants who were known to have developed from birth in isolation from any society. Again, it looks as if we could have sufficient grounds for asserting that a lone human being, observed from a distance, had the concept of a tree, say, or, had a language, without yet having grounds for asserting that he was or ever had been a member of any society.

In his exposition of Wittgenstein's positive views on the 'meaning' game Kripke frequently uses the term 'community'. And the language game *we* play, in playing the 'meaning' game in English, is a game we play within one or many actual communities. But what, in essence, is the ultimate basis envisaged for our game by Wittgenstein? In brief, the confluence of natural reactions *within the species homo sapiens* to certain gestures and procedures. More briefly, our naturally homogeneous life-form. But intuitively speaking we are not members of a society simply by virtue of species membership. None of the various attempts to define a human collectivity, community, or society, has gone as far as that. Again, from the point of view of intuition, that someone goes on as we all do, that we react as he does, does not seem to make us into a society, or a community, or any genuine collectivity, so far. As Weber rightly suggested, given only a number of people who all reacted similarly to the same stimuli we would not say that anything social (in particular, any action properly called 'social' action) was yet involved. So the most basic or primitive underpinning of our 'meaning' game is not 'society' in any intuitive sense, even if it *is* our homogeneous species-nature resulting in tallying responses and continuations from an initial segment of ostensions.

Consider the decision to say of someone isolated from us on an island that he 'means' something by a word, having observed that he continues using it 'as we do'. Wittgenstein might characterize this as 'taking him into our community'. (The phrase is Kripke's, p. 110, also referred to above.) This may be a natural way to put the point intended. To speak of someone as 'meaning', and of 'intending', 'going on wrong', and so on, is to treat him as we treat one another. It is to take a certain attitude towards him, not (according to Wittgenstein) a matter of hypothesizing that he is in some special mental state. However, our willingness to treat someone in these ways is surely not enough in itself to make it literally true or, indeed, assertable that the person in question is a fully fledged member of any social group or community. Surely our reasonably deciding to say of someone we observe from a distance 'He means *tree* by "zwog"', 'He obviously intended to use this as firewood', and the like, does not itself entitle us to assert that he is a member of our group or society, or of any?

It is true that Wittgenstein's positive approach to language and concept possession is to 'look at the use' in our own linguistic practice of such utterances as 'Cheryl is thinking about Peter', and so on. At the same time, however, it seems that these utterances could in principle be part of an individual's personal linguistic practice, a practice arrived at independently of anyone else. We could look at his use of the utterances. If his practice or custom was like ours, we would find that the assertability conditions within it were the same as ours. My point is that the fact that our 'meaning' game is in fact anchored, so to speak, in an actual community (or in many actual communities) is not obviously crucial to one's understanding of the components of the game. (That is not to deny, of course, that a major stimulus to playing the 'meaning' game is the constant commerce with others that is typical of group life.)

In sum, there appears to be nothing in an assertability conditions approach in general, or in Wittgenstein's own working out of such an approach, that shows an assertability conditions version of the intentionalist programme is flawed by some analogue of initial circularity. In particular, it appears that the assertability conditions for 'Emma has manifested certain intentions' may be satisfied without the assertability conditions for 'Emma is the fully fledged member of a social group' being satisfied. As far as one can tell, it may be that the assertability of 'Emma has manifested certain intentions' is a precondition of the assertability of 'Emma is a fully fledged group member'. I conclude that the various Wittgensteinian positions considered in this chapter do not show that one must reject out of hand the intentionalist programme, or its assertability conditions analogue.

5.3 A final note on the intentionalist programme

My main aim in this chapter has been to defend the intentionalist programme against a specific objection by arguing for the logical independence of intentions from society. In the next chapter, I hope to show that the concept of a human social group can indeed be explicated in terms of human thoughts and intentions. In this concluding note I aim to forestall a possible worry about the general plausibility of such an explication.

Given the observation that in order to develop normally human infants appear to require close contact with other, mature humans, it might be supposed that human thought is only awakened in the context of pre-existing social bonds. It might then seem that an account of human social groups that made thought and intention a requirement for group membership could not be correct. For it may appear that we are willing to grant infants group membership before they can think.

This worry rests on assumptions about delicate issues regarding which all the facts are doubtless not yet known. But the following points should help to clear the ground for an intentionalist account of social groups.

First, let us suppose for the sake of argument that an infant will not get to think at all without prior close contact with other humans. Still, the concept of 'close contact' is a broad one, as is the similar notion of 'interaction'. In so far as the infant cannot yet think or intend while the necessary contact takes place, we may well feel that this contact does not yet involve the infant and its nurturer in being the fully fledged members of a two-person social group. To go so far as to talk of a 'social bond', at this stage, then, will be to go too far, if such talk implies the existence of a social group. (We can of course imagine that once an infant's ability for thought and volition is awakened somehow, it may quite quickly avail itself of an ability to form a social unit or group. In principle the thoughts requisite for such social bonding could be among the earliest awakened in the human infant.) Secondly, the very young human infant is surely quite opaque to us. It is therefore doubtful that we should attempt to clarify our concept of a human social group by reference to infant–adult dyads and the like. Matters are not made easier by the fact that people tend to treat infants as if their behaviour is less instinctual than it is. (The infant smiles and someone says 'See! He likes you!', and so on.)

The main point I want to stress in connection with the current query is that we need first to articulate an account of a human collectivity *using the least ambiguous data*. If the account turns out to be intentionalist, and it is indeed a fact that infants cannot form intentions before they experience some form of human contact, then we will have reason to accept that infants cannot be fully fledged group members before experiencing human contact of a sort in which they do not yet participate as fully fledged group members. This would not seem to be a worrying outcome, should it arise.

6 GROUP LANGUAGES

6.1 Introduction

In my defence of intentionalism I have argued that our concept of thought and language in general is such that even an individual forever isolated from others could, in principle, think and use a language. I have argued, if you like, that our basic notion of thought and language in no way involves a community or society of language users. Now I noted earlier that someone might be inclined to assume the social nature of all language because of facts about languages like English. English, it might be said, is hardly a 'privately owned' language. It is 'the language of the people of England' and of other peoples.[72] It is a superb instrument of communication. Such a language, the language of a group, surely cannot be a mere sum or a kind of average of idiolects, a phenomenon resulting from the lucky coincidence of 'privately owned' languages? I agree with this point about the languages of groups. At the same time I believe there is a radical distinction in principle between the notion of a group's language and the notion of a single individual's language, both of which notions are perfectly coherent.

In the concluding sections of this chapter I offer a rough explication of the concept of a group's language. This notion uses the basic semantic notions needed to characterize an idiolect. But it is not the notion of a sum of idiolects. And it can be shown that a group's language better facilitates communication among humans than a mere coincidence of idiolects could ever do. When the content of this notion has been clarified somewhat, it will be clear that its existence and the existence of group languages lend no support to the idea that language use in general logically requires group membership. More generally, the existence of this concept goes no way to show that the concept of language use in general involves the notion of a group in some way or other. The concept of a group's language is of particular interest in the context of this book, for it introduces an undoubtedly social phenomenon.

In the context of a discussion of Wittgenstein's work, the concept of a group's language as explicated here has one particularly interesting feature. One can show that *for a group's language* 'an inner process stands in need of outward criteria'. As I shall explain, the precise sense of 'criteria' at issue has important similarities to the sense in which it was used by Wittgenstein. This may or may not help to throw any light on Wittgenstein's own intentions. But it is certainly worth pointing out. For here, once again, is a situation where a highly controversial doctrine (the claim that for any language whatsoever inner processes require outward criteria) could gain acceptance in part because of its close resemblance to a relatively uncontroversial one (the parallel claim for group languages). (The earlier case I have in mind is, of course, the possible confusion of the innocuous meaning-shareability condition with a strong meaning-identifiability condition.)[73] Before proceeding to the account of a group's language, let me say a little more about 'criteria'.

6.2 'Criteria'

As interpreted by Kripke, Wittgenstein arrives at his claim that outward criteria are needed for inner processes in following out his 'assertability conditions' approach to language. I shall in no way dispute this interpretation in what follows. Meanwhile, it is apposite at this point to refer to some other discussions of Wittgenstein on criteria.

There has been much debate over Wittgenstein's conception of a 'criterion'. People have asked: what precisely are 'criteria'?[74] This has not been found easy to decide. Meanwhile, the following points have been stressed. Given Wittgenstein's conception of a criterion, the presence of the or a criterion for pain, say, is never *logically sufficient* for the presence of pain itself. Yet the relationship of the criterion to the inner process is not just that of empirical evidence for the presence of the process. The notion of a criterion is, apparently, stronger than that. The flavour of these points taken together might be summed up somewhat opaquely thus: in relation to an inner process term, an outward criterion for an inner state is *meaning-determining, but not quite.*

In my discussion so far I have taken a negative stance to the notion that an inner process term requires an outward criterion even in the weak sense of 'outer correlate'. Given our intuitive concept of language use in general, no outward criterion seems to be necessary in order for there to be a genuine inner process term. In what follows I shall be more positive about outward criteria. Moreover, I shall take an outward criterion in the strong sense, as something that is meaning-determining, but not quite. I shall argue that there is *a* doctrine of outward criteria in this sense which is quite plausible. This is not a doctrine about languages in general, but about the language of a group. Though I have no desire to press this issue, it seems possible that Wittgenstein was aware of the facts about outward criteria but misplaced their basis. For his own sceptical and complex reasons he connected them with thought and language as such. The outward criteria doctrine I shall propose, meanwhile, fits happily together with the natural view of language use in general as I have characterized it here. It is quite consistent with a platonist account of meaning.

In what follows, then, I shall make no attempt to avoid any of the assumptions of the natural view. In particular, I shall not attempt to avoid ways of talking that might appear to suggest a broadly platonist approach to language and meaning in general. I have, after all, argued that such an approach is philosophically tenable. At the same time, I shall make no special attempt to incorporate explicitly platonist elements into what I say. I shall simply write in those ways that seem appropriate. Within this framework, I shall explain how a doctrine of the necessity of outward criteria in the sense now at issue can be maintained. To clear the ground, I first argue briefly that one line of argument for the necessity of outward criteria which may seem attractive is not adequate.

It may be thought that there is a compelling doctrine of outward criteria concerning the conditions for linguistic communication, as opposed to the conditions for language possession as such. There is a well known passage in *Philosophical Investigations* in which the prefix 'If language is to be a means of communication . . .' is not usually stressed.[75] Perhaps it is generally ignored because people assume that all language, as such, is a means of communication. In any case, let us consider whether linguistic communication in general requires outward criteria in the sense at issue here.

In order for what I earlier called *communication in the thin sense* to take place between two people by means of language, each person must, in a sense, have the same language. At the least, on a given occasion each must interpret a given string of words in the same way. But it appears that people could fulfil this necessary condition for communication in the thin sense, without knowing that they do, and, indeed, without having any means of knowing. Thus for this minimal type of communication no behavioural correlate of any kind seems necessary.

Now, if two people have no means of knowing that they are likely to interpret a given string in the same way on a given occasion, it does appear that they will not then be in a position to engage in what I have called *seriously intended* communication.[76] Obviously if one's central concern were the conditions for seriously intended communication as opposed to language use as such, the scope of one's argument would be seriously restricted. Meanwhile, it does not appear that seriously intended communication requires criteria in the sense at issue here. Jack could have reason to think Jill will interpret his words as he does under a variety of circumstances. He could have such a reason merely if he has reason to suppose that Jill has reason to suppose that he means such-and-such. In brief, it does not appear that seriously intended communication requires criteria as opposed to evidence for meaning.

It is now time to bring forward the concept of what I shall call, for short, a *group language*. This provides a framework into which an outward criteria doctrine fits very well. I believe that this concept has not been clearly seen and articulated previously, though those stressing the role of the community and of convention in Wittgenstein's account of language, as well as those stressing his concern with communication of some kind, may have been working in terms of some background sense of its nature. This would not be surprising, since I take it to be a concept in terms of which most of us in fact operate most of the time.

6.3 Group languages

My account of a group language here will be rough. More precision will be derivable from the detailed discussion of the nature of collectivity concepts in the following chapters.

Suppose we are a set of agents who are 'linguistically free' in the following sense. We are capable of associating any of an infinite variety of sounds and marks with a given sense. Suppose also that each of us desires that when any one of us utters some sound in the presence of another, the other will assign the same interpretation to the sound that the utterer assigns to it. (No one cares in principle what people do when they are alone, writing up diaries or notes to themselves, or whether anyone else could interpret what they say to themselves in silent monologues.) Let us assume that we have been able to express to each other, perhaps through some primitive mechanism of gesture, our shared desire. This mutual expression of desire has eventuated in a joint project: we jointly seek to bring about the state of affairs desired by all.[77]

How can we best achieve our aim? Given that there are no natural primitive ways of referring to some particular thing that we need to refer to, it seems that we should agree upon a particular sign as the sign for that thing. I shall shortly consider how we might do this, and what it would entail. But let us first reflect for a moment upon what it would be like if, as we all realize, there has been no agreement on terms. Feeling perfectly free to do so, each person has invented words of his own, and uses these when attempting to communicate with others. Call this a situation of *linguistic anarchy*.

As is well known, it is hard for a set of people all speaking different languages to build a tower to heaven, or to achieve anything very much together. Consider some of the difficulties of those in a situation of linguistic anarchy. Suppose that, as we all realize, each of us has individually chosen a word of his own with which to refer to stamps. Then, if I wish to ask you if you have a stamp, I know I have to find out what your word for stamp is. Or I could try to teach you mine. Now, if there are stamps in the vicinity, this may not take long. If there are not, it will take longer. But even when there are stamps to point to, teaching my meaning or learning yours may take a while. For ostension can be very ambiguous.

Moreover, in a situation of real linguistic anarchy things are very widely open. Maybe I used 'glupp' in the sense of stamp, yesterday, but who says what I am to mean tomorrow? Why shouldn't I, if I choose, change my meanings? As far as I am concerned personally, I am entitled to switch from day to day. There is nothing obvious in the nature of language as such which prevents a speaker from making different sound–sense connections on different occasions. In so far as this is understood, I will realize that my learning what you mean now, in so far as I can pin this down relatively quickly, will not necessarily help me tomorrow. When I meet you tomorrow, then, I will not feel fully confident that you will still interpret 'plibb' as stamp, or whatever it was you did yesterday. Life among the linguistic anarchists looks as if it could be an exhausting business. More could be said, but these considerations show that linguistically free agents in a situation of linguistic anarchy are likely to encounter serious problems.[78]

How, then, might a set of linguistically free agents ensure that they have smooth and successful verbal interactions? As I have suggested, it would be good if they could agree on signs for particular things. Spelling this out a little, it would be good if they could agree upon what is to mean what in *their language*. Let them create a group language, a language that each can individually regard as 'our' language. (I leave till the next chapter the attempt to clarify the notion of 'us' implicit in this suggestion.) Taking the above at face value, one might well ask: how, roughly, could this be done? And how precisely would it help?

As should be clear by now, the lack of existing signs with agreed-upon meanings does not have to doom the enterprise of setting up a group language to failure. If we are lucky, among the gestures and sounds that we all happen to take in the same way, will be gestures and sounds sufficient for us to reach an adequate understanding about what is to mean what. Clearly a benign creator of a set of linguistically free agents would do well to ensure that this was so.[79]

Putting this issue aside, one can see that it is in any case not a trivial matter for a set of people to agree on the meaning a given term is to have. Intuitively the case differs radically from that of an individual deciding to stipulate a sound–sense link. One may allow that the individual in question can simply decide that a certain word is to express a given concept or sense. But a joint decision about such a thing must take a more subtle route. I cannot physically point directly at the concept or sense I wish our word to express, and ask for your agreement. I need to find some indirect way of indicating the sense in question. I suggest that after we have gone through the procedure outlined below we may reasonably take it that we have indicated the relevant sense to each other, and in so doing agreed on a particular sense for the term at issue.

One thing someone can do in order to help bring about an agreement that, say, 'blue' means *blue* in our language, is to point at some blue thing and (if we have no other words yet agreed upon) simply utter 'blue'. In other words, ostension is an obvious tool. Ostension cannot fully determine meaning, as we know. However, we can start to pin things down if we can agree that, in a certain context, *the concept a given term expresses applies to this thing.* Agreement on an ostension can be read as an agreement on a judgment of the above form. More precisely, it can be read as a joint *stipulation* regarding what concept the word in question expresses. Agreeing on an ostension can thus be construed as agreeing on a judgment with a special, definitional status.[80] It will, that is, serve partially to fix the meaning of the term involved. Clearly we cannot rely on a verbal definition of the standard type until we are confident that we all assign the same meanings to the definiens.[81] In sum ostension will surely play a quite crucial role in determining the nature of a group's language. A given agreed-upon ostension will partially fix the meaning of a term for the group. Thus there is a sense in which it is (partially) meaning-determining.

In order for the process of 'agreeing on ostensions' to work, it is evident that certain unagreed but manifestly shared understandings must exist. For instance, to refer to a now familiar example, we must all naturally interpret the 'direction' of a pointing finger in the same way, and that we do so must be clear to all. We must all, indeed, 'get the point' of the whole procedure. And we must understand that achievement of the definitional aim of an agreed-upon ostension depends on the satisfaction of certain conditions. For example, it is presumably necessary that we in fact point to what we appear to be pointing to (a physical object seen in normal daylight, say). If it turns out that what was in front of us was a mirage rather than, as we naturally assumed, a real pond, we will not be committed to the stipulation that the word 'pond' is applied literally to pond-mirages.

A *series* of agreed-upon ostensions will obviously help adequately to pin down the meaning. How far, it may be asked, need we go? To be sure, from a philosophical or 'in principle' point of view we could agree on a million cases of 'blueness', say, yet there still be infinitely many potential candidate concepts at issue. None the less in a given group of human beings with initially similar backgrounds, it is surely reasonable to assume that something like the following is so as a matter of fact: if we have made sufficient agreements on particular cases for our subsequent noncollusive use of a word to be congruent, then we have indeed individually latched on to the same concept. Given that our project is to home in on a given meaning as well as we can, then, the definitional or meaning-determining agreements should go on until disparities in the application of a term no longer occur. Let us suppose that each of us has reasonably concluded on such a basis that blueness is the concept at issue. At roughly this point we can be said to have agreed that 'blue' means *blue*. In other words, our group language now involves the element: 'blue' means *blue*.

Given the above considerations, one can argue that the core of a group language will be precisely the set of agreed-upon ostensions by virtue of which we manage to agree on the meanings of the various terms in our language.

So far I have not mentioned sensation terms or 'outward criteria'. But now consider the case of the group faced with a decision on sensation terms. Here there is no possibility of performing an ostension strictly speaking. Though I can focus on my own sensation of pain, I cannot point it out to you, expecting you to be aware of what I am myself focusing on. (Of course I can say 'It's in my foot', but that does not bring any specific type of phenomenological quality into focus.) Meanwhile, given that we have sensations and the like that are important to us, we will feel the need of some way of referring to them in our interpersonal discourse. So we need some way to agree that it will be pain that is referred to by 'pain' or whatever. As Wittgenstein stressed, pain and other of our important sensations have natural behavioural manifestations. We utter sighs of pleasure, howls of pain. Specific taste sensations are correlated with the ingestion of particular substances. And so on. Nothing is more obvious and natural, then, than to try to fix the meaning of a sensation term by concentrating on such natural behavioural correlates, perhaps including some pointed reference to context. For the closest we can come to fixing such meanings by interpersonal agreement is by reference to such public phenomena.

What will be the result of using behavioural manifestations to help fix meanings in these cases? Ostensions of behaviour here clearly cannot be construed in exactly the same way as ostensions of public phenomena intended to fix the meaning of terms with public referents. If for terms of the latter kind we understand as our definitional judgment form, roughly, 'The concept that term "T" expresses *applies to this*', we need something weaker for sensation terms. Something like: 'The concept that term "T" expresses *standardly applies* to a person who behaves thus.'

One can see how, if 'pain' is introduced into our language in some such way, then the paradigmatic behavioural manifestations used to pin down its meaning may be judged to provide more than mere evidence that the term 'pain' applies. One can see why, if someone were to deny another was in pain, given the right behaviour plus context we might feel justified in saying 'If she doesn't accept that he is in pain now, she can't know what *pain* is (or, what "pain" means).' At the same time, however, given that it is the concept of pain that the term 'pain' expresses, clearly we must accept that the behaviour does not *entail* that there is pain: it is not logically sufficient for pain. In contrast, in the case of truly meaning-determining ostensions, the presence of the phenomenon by reference to which meaning has been determined is logically sufficient for the truth of the relevant assertion.

The conclusion of the above considerations on sensation terms for group languages can now be summed up as follows: an inner process term may be successfully introduced into a group's language by reference to outward criteria. Such criteria will be meaning-determining – but not quite.[82]

6.4 Group languages and pure sensation terms

Can there be a pure sensation term possessed by a group? Given that ostension and quasi-ostension through criteria are the basic means of agreeing on meanings for our terms, it seems to fall out that the answer is no. That is, there is no way adequately to fix the meaning of a term for a new kind of sensation without some observable behavioural correlate. Possibly the other members of a group can let Jones tell them 'wuzzy' is a sensation quality, given that 'sensation' is already a term in their language, and can say things like 'Jones, are you feeling wuzzy?' But in such cases they have to let Jones's say-so be the *sole* 'criterion' for the applicability of 'has a wuzzy sensation' to him. This is close to the situation of linguistic anarchy, Jones being, as Plato might say, the lawgiver here. Everyone has to admit: 'In "our" language, "wuzzy" means what Jones has decided it shall mean.' This seems close to saying ' "Wuzzy" is not a term of *our* language.'

In this connection someone might allude to the idea of a 'division of linguistic labour'. (The phrase is due to Hilary Putnam.)[83] Let us briefly consider some kinds of 'division of labour' that may occur in connection with group languages. First and foremost, in what I take to be the central or paradigm case of a group language, there is a *sharing* of labour, in so far as everyone is involved in the process of fixing meaning. In the context of this paradigm the following can presumably happen. I am a newcomer in a certain group. I hear people using the word 'squobb'. For instance, someone says 'There's a squobb in Jan's garden.' I presume that the group has accepted certain ostensions as fixing the meaning of 'squobb'. I want to use 'squobb' 'as we all do'. So I will seek to use it in its established meaning. In such cases another type of 'division of labour' takes place. Others have done all the work. I am ready to defer to their decisions.

It may be that certain terms can reasonably be said to be part of 'our' language even though fairly few of us have been party to the central type of agreement. Thus it may be reasonable to allow that scientific terms like 'quark' and 'gluon' are terms of 'our' language even though most of us have no idea what they mean. Perhaps in such cases we can be said to have granted certain individuals or groups the authority to make linguistic decisions for all of us. The issue then becomes how far this sort of 'division of linguistic labour' can go before it seems to make nonsense of the idea that something is a genuine part of our language.

Before going into this further, consider the situation of group members who know little about a term except that it has some meaning or other in the group. (This can perhaps be so in circumstances such as those just envisaged.) They may sometimes utter the term in company, expecting others to interpret it appropriately, but not associating it with any very specific interpretation themselves. Thus Melanie may say: 'I gather Sam likes emoting' without having a clue as to what 'emoting' is, or even whether the term 'emoting' is a noun or a verb. This type of case itself suggests that we need to make a distinction between the components of a given individual's idiolect, his own language, and the components of the language of his group. Consider that in the case just envisaged, there need be little reason to deny that the term 'emoting' is part of the group's language. The case seems different when we turn to Melanie. It is surely doubtful whether she can be said to use the term in any particular sense. (To do so is clearly rather different from using it with the intention that it be taken as if it were meant appropriately, however that is.) It may then seem reasonable to say that 'emoting' is not part of *her* language. Surely one could not be said to have a language of one's own if one did not grasp for oneself, so to speak, the meaning of *some* terms. Imagine that you utter to yourself sentences in which *all* of the words are such that you implicitly defer to some authority with respect to what they mean or refer to. Surely you do not understand any of these sentences? Can *this* be *your* language? But then why consider that a single term that you fail to understand can properly be said to be part of *your* language?

Now it may seem counterintuitive to deny that English is one's language on the grounds that one does not understand all the terms in English. Surely English is *my* language and I do *not* fully understand all its terms? This indicates that there are two rather distinct ways of construing the phrase 'my language'. When I say that English is my language, the relevant notion of 'my' language

141

appears to be explicable in terms of my membership in a group with a certain language, and my general intention to conform to the agreements that fix that language, in so far as I can. Then it is easier to see how I could have various blind spots with respect to 'my' language. The notion of my own idiolect, of my own personal language, in so far as one is naturally constructed, would appear to leave less room for the possibility of a term that I do not myself understand.[84]

Let us now ask once again: can a group have a pure sensation term? Could a particular group member introduce such a term into the group's language, making it a part of that language? In the central cases of a group's term, the members have together agreed that certain ostensions fix or quasi-fix the meanings of the terms. We have seen that within this framework it may be that certain terms can reasonably be said to be terms of 'our' language even though not all or even most of us have been party to an agreement on its meaning.

Now, in so far as the idea of granting lawgiver status to a single individual with respect to a group language is acceptable, it might seem that the idea of a pure sensation term as part of a group language must be acceptable too. However, this case has a special feature. Here the group members are very far removed from an agreement to the effect that the term in question means *such-and-such*. For in this case there is, by hypothesis, no possibility of their convening to establish in the usual way that *such-and-such* is what the term means. For, by hypothesis, there are no properly discriminative behavioural correlates to be appealed to. There is reason to argue, then, that a pure sensaton term cannot be a fully-fledged part of a *group*'s language. Thus a strong outward criteria doctrine (the impossibility of *any* term for an 'inner' process lacking outer correlates) finds a home in the domain of a group's language.

6.5 Further remarks on group languages

Consider now a simple situation in which communication is desired. Tim and Fay are members of a group (possibly the dyad constituted by the two of them) in which the meaning of the term 'jeeb' has been agreed upon in the usual way. They understand that 'In our language, "jeeb" means . . .' or, ' "Jeeb" means . . . among us.' I take it that, roughly, each member will thereby understand that all else being equal it is incumbent upon him as a group member to interpret 'jeeb' in accordance with the meaning-determining ostensions, at least when he is among group members. (I say more in the chapters that follow about how claims about 'us' of the sort in question are understood, and about how the acknowledgement of certain facts about us entails the acceptance that one has certain obligations.) Now suppose that Fay wishes to ask Tim for a jeeb (as she understands the term 'jeeb'). She can now, surely, say 'Have you a jeeb?' with the best possible assurance that Tim will understand her utterance as she herself does. Against the background of an existing group language, they will achieve what they most need to achieve in the matter of communication smoothly and well.

Maximally efficient interpersonal discourse among linguistically free agents, then, can be argued to require a group language. In a group language terms are associated with given meanings by interpersonal agreement. The available methods (which do not, of course, fully determine meaning) are ostension in physical space, perceivable by all members of the group, and the quasi-ostension possible for psychic phenomena with interpersonally perceivable, ostensible correlates. It is a corollary of this that a 'pure' sensation term cannot be a fully-fledged part of a group language. It is *not* a corollary of this that no individual can have a term in his language referring to a sensation without a behavioural correlate.

Now it seems to follow from what I have said that linguistically free rational agents, living together, and needing to communicate with each other, can be expected to develop group gestural (including verbal) languages. Can they be expected, also, individually to have languages of their own? If so, what may we expect these languages to be like, and how will they relate to the group language? I suggest that, on the one hand, individual languages or signalling systems are prior in an important sense to group languages. On the other hand, group languages will influence the form of individual languages.

Let us momentarily recall how different, intuitively, is the language of an individual from a group language. The language of an individual need not be bound up with a system of joint decisions about which judgments using its terms are correct and which are not: such a language need not be bound up with ostension and criteria. As long as I can associate terms with concepts, that is sufficient to set up the semantics for my language.[85] It seems, then, that in an individual language there can be pure sensation terms. No outer correlate of any sort is required to set up the language.

In this connection consider Wittgenstein's idea that the utterance 'I am in pain' can be seen as replacing a cry of pain (sec. 244). What of the status of the cry of pain itself? I do not know whether it is plausible to regard the human infant who cries when in pain as expressing a thought in an innate or instinctive language. On the other hand, it is fairly clear that crying when in pain is a matter of instinct in the human being, and that the 'meaning' of crying is instinctively recognized by other humans. As a child develops, it realizes that it can use crying to produce a certain reaction in others – to provoke attempts to come to its aid, in particular. It is not obvious that there needs to be a group language in which crying is a gesture with an agreed upon meaning. The 'crying game' would probably work quite well without any such agreement, given its instinctual underpinnings. Then the general and effective practice of crying when wishing to signal distress and provoke aid could be seen as involving a meshing set of individual signalling systems, sufficient, given its underpinnings, to enable smooth communication. Meanwhile, since the human species does not have a unique set of reactions to all the things it needs to signal and talk about, it will be rational to form group languages.

Such formation seems in itself to depend on communication at a more primitive, individual level. Our meshing, individual languages enable us to perform the ostensions that are the foundation of group languages. Meanwhile, once a group language has been formed, it is to be expected that people will economize and make it their own. That is, their own language will conform to the agreements which, in a sense, constitute the group language. They will find it so natural to associate a meaning that fits the group agreements to a given term, that they may think themselves incapable of using that term in a different sense. Perhaps they really will be so incapable, at least without a certain degree of practice. They will also teach their children the group language in terms of which they express their own thinking. Thus they will correct children who are going on wrong in their use of terms – wrong from the point of view of the group agreements. They know that if allowed to develop an idiosyncratic language of his own the child will have enormous difficulties communicating to others in the group. None of this, meanwhile, goes to show that an individual cannot independently use a term in some new and idiosyncratic way, or associate some new and idiosyncratic sense with an old term. Social conventions and joint decisions about how to use a term are important aspects of the social use of language. But this does not show that language as such has a social nature.

The following points about group languages should be stressed. A 'group language' as I am using the term is not identical by definition (a) with a language that all members of a group individually use as their own language, or a 'shared' language in that thin sense; or (b) with a language having publicly accessible 'outward criteria' for inner process terms. Given what a group language is, it can be argued to be a *theorem* that group languages need such criteria.[86]

The notion of a group language is evidently of some richness and interest. It is quite striking how well and uncontroversially at least one famous and controversial Wittgensteinian claim concerning languages as such applies in the context of group languages in particular. Meanwhile, its relationship to Wittgensteinian views is not the only claim that the concept of a group language has on our attention. It must surely be considered a key concept for the philosophy of language in general, and in this capacity it deserves more attention than I can give it here. In addition, it is an important collectivity concept. As such, it has only been given a rough explication in this chapter. The following chapters will help to amplify this sketch. For it will be their primary business to bring the special nature of our collectivity concepts in general into sharper focus.

IV

SOCIAL GROUPS: A SIMMELIAN VIEW

1 INTRODUCTION: SIMMEL'S STATEMENT

1.1 Simmel's statement

It is now time to present a positive view on the everyday concept of a social group. I approach that task with some hesitancy. Still, there is a positive account of the nature of social groups that I find attractive, illuminating, and consequential.

I could call up many names in support of something like the view of social groups that I shall propose here. I shall give references to authors with related views at various points in the main text of this chapter and in the notes; I do not claim that they will be exhaustive. At the outset, however, I should single out the sociologist Georg Simmel as an inspiration and an ally. I refer in particular to his essay 'How is society possible?', first published in 1908.[1] With this I must immediately warn the reader that I shall not try to do justice to the details of Simmel's delicate and complex discussion in that essay. Nor do I want to ascribe to him the details of my own latter-day views on this matter.

As far as I am concerned, Simmel's most provocative statement on the nature or conditions of existence of society is the following. According to Simmel, a society is an 'objective unit' of a special kind:

the consciousness of constituting with the others a unity is actually all there is to this unity. (p. 75)

Simmel's claim suggests three plausible general ideas about social groups constituted by humans. First, that social groups are real phenomena, as opposed to fictions or illusions of some kind. Second, that the core or essence of a social group is to be found in a specific mental state common to group members. Third, that

146

the mental state in question involves the conception of the people concerned as linked by a certain special tie.

In what follows I shall develop an account which can be seen as having some affinity with Simmel's claim while avoiding the pitfalls some developments would fall into.

One way of formulating my account runs as follows:

Human beings X, Y, and Z constitute a collectivity (social group) if and only if each correctly thinks of himself and the others, taken together, as 'us*' or 'we*'.

This way of formulating the account uses a particular interpretation of the first person plural pronoun in English. I have put asterisks in the above formulation because my main aim in this chapter is to present a particular account of social groups, whether or not I have given a correct account of one sense of the English 'we'. However, I believe there is a central sense of 'we' in English in terms of which it makes good sense to define social groups. The sense I have in mind will be explicated with care in what follows.

Before plunging into the details of and justification for my own account, I note some other accounts of social groups which might be derived from Simmel's statement, and indicate why I find them problematic. Thus I will, in effect, note certain desiderata for an acceptable 'Simmelian' account of social groups (which these accounts do not meet), and explain why I believe my own Simmelian account of social groups is preferable to the accounts considered.

1.2 Two problematic versions of Simmel's statement

Simmel's own way of putting his point is provocative, and could induce a too hasty rejection of what I take to be a fruitful general line of thought. He might be thought to be claiming that a social group is wholly constituted by people knowing *that they form a social group* with certain others. To this, as it stands, it could be objected that generally speaking knowledge of the existence of an X cannot be a necessary precondition of the existence of an X; the latter, on the contrary, is a necessary precondition of the former. Possibly an account of social groups can be given in terms of something which must be known by the people who are to be counted members of a given group. The account just noted, however, is unacceptable on quite general logical grounds.

We do no better if we replace 'knowing that' by 'believing that' in the above account, thus construing Simmel as saying that social groups are wholly constituted by people believing that they form a social group with certain others. For Simmel's theory would then entail that two people together constitute a social group if and only if each believes that they do. Meanwhile, it can be proved that if a person accepts the theory and has certain rigorous standards of evidence, then he will never be a member of a two-person social group.

Thus suppose Lily accepts the theory and determines not to believe that any two people form a social group unless she knows that the conditions stated are satisfied. Lily's belief that she and Rose form a social group will not, then, precede Lily's investigation of whether they do indeed form a social group. But then, by hypothesis, her investigation cannot reveal that she has the belief. Nor, evidently, will she proceed to form it on the basis of her investigation. But then according to the theory she cannot constitute a social group with Rose. People like Lily, then, who know the theory, cannot form dyadic social groups.

A proponent of the theory might try to defend it by saying that real people are not like Lily. This defence of the theory would be inadequate, however. One needs to show that people like Lily would be radically misguided in some way we would not expect of the kind of people who help to constitute social groups. Once again, an account of social groups in terms of what a set of people believe could be viable. There are good grounds for rejecting this particular version, however.

One might proffer the view that *all there is* to a collectivity in the everyday sense is people's beliefs that they form collectivities, if one's aim was to argue that in reality there is no such thing as a collectivity – that we are simply under the illusion, or have adopted the fiction, that there is. There are hints of such a view in Max Weber. I have also heard it advanced more recently in discussion. Simmel, however, asserts that society is an 'objective unit'. This assertion looks like a claim to real existence.

1.3 The Simmelian schema

In spite of the possibility of a paradoxical construal of Simmel's characterization of a social group in terms of people's knowledge or belief that they constitute such a group, it is possible and perhaps more natural to take it in terms of the following more general idea, which I shall call the *Simmelian schema* for social groups:

a social group's existence is basically a matter of the members of a set of people being conscious that they are linked by a certain special tie.

Some immediate comments on the way I am taking this rough schema may be helpful. They are not intended to explain the specifics of my own version of the schema, which will take some while to detail.[2]

First, someone might wonder whether I interpret the schema as saying that *every* member must be conscious that *every* member is linked to *every* other member by a certain special tie? I take it that although it will not hurt the claims of a set of people to be a social group if they fulfil this strong condition, a development of the schema could be capacious enough to count as social groups some sets of people in which it is only true that, say, almost all members are conscious that almost all members are linked in whatever relevant way. One way in which this sort of thing could happen is that a core set, in which every member is indeed involved in the relevant ways, deem that certain others (say their infant children) will count as if they too were members of the core set, even though they lack the right kind of mental competence really to be members. In developing a version of the Simmelian schema, I shall write as if *each* member of a given human population must be conscious of certain facts about *all* members of the population, in order that they form a social group. In so far as I do this, the account may be regarded as an account of a paradigm or 'ideal' case, along the lines of Weber's ideal types.

Next, I take the idea to be that each of a set of people must view the others as linked to him, and to each other, by a single common tie. It is not enough that each one views each one as linked to every other in some way, but not in the same way. Again, the idea is that one and the same special tie is at issue, is what makes any set of people a social group.

For the most part I shall write as if consciousness of facts about particular individuals is at issue. Though I develop my account in those terms, it can be modified to allow for groups in which a given member does not know of every other member as an individual. Large populations tend to be of this kind.

Regarding what might constitute the special tie in question, two clear negative points can be made at once. Consider some set of randomly chosen people, say Shirley Williams, W. V. O. Quine, and Brigitte Bardot. Assume for the sake of argument that each one knows of the other two, and that each one knows that the three of them are the sole members of a certain set (in the logician's sense), namely, the set whose sole members are

Shirley Williams, W. V. O. Quine, and Brigitte Bardot. Do they form a social group? As I noted earlier, I take it as obvious at the outset that mere membership in the same set (in the logician's sense) is not enough to make people into a social group in the sense I am pursuing here. It seems equally obvious that *consciousness that* one forms such a set with certain others is not sufficient for the existence of a social group. Indeed, intuitively, consciousness that one is 'linked' to certain others in this way is hardly consciousness of some 'special tie'.

Again, as previously noted, I take it that being the only persons with a certain quality does not in general make people into a social group. (Consider the current population of red-haired people.) Similarly, consciousness that one possesses qualities in common with the sole other possessors of that quality seems quite insufficient in general to produce a social group.[3] The question of how the Simmelian schema may best be fleshed out remains.

There are some notions in the literature that I take to be insufficient for an adequate development of the Simmelian schema. Each of these, which may be *appropriate* to the conception of social groups I am proposing here, appear as they stand to be either too general or in need of further development. Let me explain.

In the statement quoted earlier, Simmel wrote of 'consciousness of unity'. Consider now the notion of a unit. It seems that almost anything can be *perceived as* a unit.[4] For instance, I may think of my office desk and the chair I use with it as a unit. I could think of my desk at home and the desk in my office as a unit. I could give this pair of objects a name, for instance, and make assertions about it, and act in terms of it (to preserve it, say, or to bring its parts closer together). This line of thought suggests that the category of unit-hood involves no interesting restrictions, that is, anyone is justified in thinking of anything as a unit. Given that the category of unit-hood is so thin, one might feel that 'to be conscious of being a unit' would best be regarded as equivalent to 'to perceive as a unit'.

Suppose, then, that we were to slot into the Simmelian schema for social groups 'perceiving the members of the set as a unit'. This seems far from capturing our intuitive concept of a social group. For suppose that as it happens I regard myself and the people with me in a certain railway carriage as a unit, and each of them regards the same people likewise. I do not think that we have been given sufficient reason to think that these people form a social group. One reason surely is that 'regards as a unit' is terribly vague. How precisely do they regard themselves?

Perhaps they would put on their lists of 'things in the world' both themselves individually and the thing whose parts are the people in this carriage. Would this be enough to make them a social group? I would say not.[5]

Simmel also speaks of the 'knowledge of determining others and being determined by them'. As far as this goes, however, and I cannot claim to be certain of its import as far as Simmel was concerned, it too seems either too general or else too vague to be helpful in the definition of a social group without further clarification or specificity.

The same may be said for references to a feeling on the part of the people concerned that they 'belong together'. It is in terms of such a feeling that Weber defines his concept of a 'communal' social relationship (*Vergemeinschaftung*): this is a relationship in which the 'orientation of social action' is based on the 'subjective feeling of the parties, whether affectual or traditional, that they belong together' (1964, p. 136). This feeling has been referred to by others also.[6] As Weber himself says, his 'concept of communal relationship has been intentionally defined in very general terms and hence includes a very heterogeneous group of phenomena' (p. 137). We need to ask what it is for people to belong together. Do the components of any *unit* belong together? If so, the notion of belonging together seems too general to be useful in the project of saying what a social group is. If something less general is intended by the reference to belonging together, it needs to be specified.[7]

Going back to the notion of a unit in general, it might be urged that we consider the possibility that group members must realize that they form a *natural* unit. Here, 'natural' does not mean 'found in nature, as opposed to man-made or artificial', but rather something like 'having components which hang together naturally'.

It is not an easy matter to clarify the concept of a natural unit. Presumably what we think of as *organisms* will be natural units if any are. Perhaps machines like clocks and cars are. Let us in any case take organisms (amoebae, spiders, frogs, elephants, etc.) and machines as paradigm cases of natural units. What, then, of social groups? Presumably, only if those populations which are social groups *are* natural units is it plausible to suggest, as one's version of the Simmelian schema, that the realization that they form a natural unit is what makes people into a group.

The question that needs answering in the light of the Simmelian schema is, specifically, whether it is plausible to suppose that (a) the people who are members of social groups always constitute natural units, (b) their constituting natural units is independent of their being social groups, and (c) their being social groups is a simple function of their perception that they already constitute natural units. Only if these conditions are satisfied could it be that their being a group resulted from their perception that they constituted a natural unit.

Clearly the idea of a social group as some sort of natural unit is a gesture away from the spare and rather empty notion of unity, and the other rather vague notions considered in this section. We do need to get away from those if possible. None the less the three conditions noted above are prima facie not very plausible. It is rarely very natural to see sets of mature human beings as constituting machines or organisms, but in so far as it ever is, this is mostly when they can already be counted as collectivities, and members' acts reflect their group membership. (One might think here of the behaviour of a basketball team on the court, say.)

I see it as a merit of the Simmelian schema that it suggests to us that, first, human group membership is a function of the ideas and beliefs of humans regarding their situation, and, second, that if human groups sometimes look as if they are organisms or machines, the existence of such phenomena does not occur independently of the beliefs and ideas of human beings.[8]

1.4 A Simmelian account of social groups

As I have indicated, one way of formulating my own specification of the Simmelian schema is as follows:

> each one of a certain set of persons must correctly view each one of their number, including himself, as 'one of us*'.

Putting this slightly differently:

> each of a certain set of persons must correctly view himself and the rest, taken together, as 'us*' or 'we*'.

Some delicacy will be needed in order to make clear the precise import of and justification for this proposal. There is obviously the following question of elucidation. What is it correctly to view certain persons, including oneself, as 'us*' or 'we*'?

As indicated earlier, I use the technical term 'we*' because I believe that the sense I shall stipulate for this term is identical to a central sense of the pronoun 'we' in English. Indeed, I shall lead up to my specification of the technical notion in question by arguing for a particular sense of the English pronoun 'we'.[9] The accuracy of my account of groups does not ultimately depend on there being an identity between 'we*' and a central sense of 'we', but such an identity would surely support it.

The first person plural pronoun has received little attention in recent analytic philosophy.[10] Questions about the first person singular pronoun, on the other hand, have long provoked philosophers from Descartes to the present.[11] As is well known, the first person singular pronoun has often been seen as having something special and deep about it, to raise important questions which cannot be answered easily.[12]

Since the issue here is 'we' and 'we'-thoughts or, more specifically, the kind of 'we'-thoughts which might be constitutive of social groups, and since the territory of 'I' and of *the I* (or self) is still a matter of controversy, it is best here to forage directly within the territory of our use of 'we'. Possibly consideration of 'we' can throw some light on 'I'.

I shall suggest that the vernacular English pronoun 'we' has a central somewhat narrow sense. There are some interesting and precisely specifiable constraints on the appropriate use of 'we' in this sense. In addition there is the possibility of using this term rather loosely, or of an additional wide sense

I speak of 'explicating sense' and of 'conditions of appropriateness of use' rather indiscriminately and vaguely. Possibly the technical notion needed is that of presupposition. In any case the main idea is that according to the rules of English one who uses the pronoun 'we' in a certain central sense is subject to certain constraints. There are conditions under which 'we' is not appropriately used. Knowing what these constraints are is part of understanding what the English word 'we' means. Thinking a 'we'-thought is thinking in terms of a concept whose application is subject to the constraints in question.

Suppose that I am wrong about the English pronoun 'we'. (Perhaps the evidence I shall cite can be interpreted differently.) I will still have delineated a set of possible constraints on the use of a pronoun in a language. I will at the same time have characterized a concept. I believe that the concept in question is integral to the thought, action, and social life of human beings, whether or not it is clearly represented in language

The central sense I claim for 'we' is roughly as follows:

> 'We' refers to a set of people each of whom shares, with
> oneself, in some action, belief, attitude, or other such
> attribute, that is, in some traditionally so-called 'mental'
> attribute.

I shall explain and develop this rough description with some care.[13]

2 ON SHARING IN AN ACTION

2.1 Doing things together in the strong sense

Let me set the stage for my discussion of the semantics of 'we' by attempting to clarify somewhat the strong notion of sharing in an action that I have in mind. (I shall concentrate on action as opposed to belief or attitude in this exposition. In subsequent chapters I have more to say on the issue of belief and attitude.) The fact that X and Y share in an action, in the sense I have in mind, is not the same as the fact that what is going on can be described in a sentence of the form 'X and Y are doing A' (such as 'X and Y are shopping' or 'X and Y are playing tennis'). Let me take the homely example of shopping, and note how different types of cases fall under the same linguistic description.

Suppose someone tells me 'Ralph and Alice are shopping for clothes'. A variety of situations could be at issue. First, Alice could be in one store buying a dress, while Ralph is in a store five miles distant, buying a suit. Or Alice and Ralph may both be in the same store, each one buying what he or she individually needs. Her shopping is being carried out quite independently of his. In both of these cases, it might be said that Ralph and Alice will not be shopping for clothes *together*. In these cases it *would* be natural to say: 'Ralph and Alice are both shopping for clothes'. Finally, they may be doing something we really would think of as shopping for clothes together. He may sit near by while she looks at dresses, may make suggestions and comments, and may be consulted carefully before the final purchase is made. There might be some dialogue like this: 'Well, so is this definitely the one?'; 'Sure, I'd say so. What do you think?'; 'Yes, I think I agree.'; 'Good, so that's it.'

The main point I want to make in relation to the possible situations covered by a statement like 'Ralph and Alice are shopping for clothes' is that the third case, as described, has a very different flavour from either of the first two, as they have been described, and it is the third kind of case that I want to focus on.

I should note that, to confuse things further, the sentence form 'X and Y are doing A together' is susceptible of a weak intepretation in which what I call *sharing in an action* is not involved. For instance, to say that Fred and Martha are sitting together in the auditorium may not be to say more than 'Fred is sitting by (next to) Martha.' Presumably 'shopping together' also has this weak interpretation, but on its most natural construal 'X and Y are shopping together' is not, or not simply, a matter of individually shopping while in physical proximity. It is this construal that I take to be correlative to the notion of sharing in an action that I wish to elucidate. To refer once again to the case of sitting together, when one says that some people are sitting together, or that one is sitting *with* the other, one may have something more than spatio-temporal contiguity in mind – something naturally describable as a *shared* or *joint* action. When wishing to be especially careful, I shall, in what follows, write of *the strong sense* of sentences of the form 'X and Y are doing A together', when construing this sentence as referring to a shared or joint action. Similarly, I shall write of the strong sense of 'X and Y are doing A'. Meanwhile, unless the context indicates otherwise, I should in general automatically be read as using sentences of these forms in the strong sense.

2.2 *Partners, not just participants*

In general, that X and Y do A together does not entail that each person, considered in isolation from the other, does something that would count as his doing A independently of the other. This is true even for an action A which can be performed without a 'partner', as opposed to actions, like playing tennis, which involve two or more participants as a matter of logic. (I am taking it that it cannot be true that I played tennis unless somebody else played tennis with me.)[14] Let us concentrate initially on actions which an individual can perform without a partner. In such cases doing A may involve performing related actions (or 'subroutines') x,y, and z. Thus 'investigating the matter fully' may involve interviewing witnesses, photographing the scene of the crime, and so on. If two people are doing A together, it is possible that the necessary chores be divided up and that neither alone will be doing enough to count as doing A independently.

As already indicated, another negative point to be made is that X's doing A together with Y is not in general *entailed by* each one's doing A separately, even given the extra condition that X and Y do A in close physical proximity. I noted that this was intuitively true for shopping together and even for sitting together (in the strong sense). One might also cite, harking back to my discussion of Weber, picking mushrooms together, going for a walk together, and travelling together, all of which can be joint actions, and would normally be thought of as such.

In searching for some plausible positive conditions on joint

155

action, it seems sensible to look for clues by considering the particular kinds of things that happen when people do things together. Let us consider the case of travelling together. If two people are travelling together, then usually a lot of things will go on which have no counterparts when people are travelling alone, albeit along the same route. For instance, one will look out for the other, make sure the other does not fall behind, probably talk to the other, and so on. I find it plausible to conjecture that when people travel together, they are doing something on a par with playing tennis, in that they are doing something which requires a partner. I use the term 'partner' advisedly here. The claim that they are doing something which requires more than one 'participant' is likely to be construed rather weakly, making my point here appear weaker than intended.

Consider the conditions under which a person is properly deemed to *zigg*. By (my) definition, if X *ziggs*, then X cleans his teeth while, in the very same house, there is someone else, Y, who cleans her teeth also. It is true of zigging, then, that one cannot zigg on one's own, or without the participation (in some weak sense) of another agent. Now it is possible for someone to zigg deliberately. That is, he deliberately brings it about that he cleans his teeth while someone else in the house is cleaning hers. Two people could even deliberately zigg, in relation to each other, each expecting the other to be engaged in teeth-cleaning at a certain time, and hence cleaning his own teeth at that time. Meanwhile it is obviously perfectly possible that two or more people zigg entirely by accident. They really do zigg, none the less.

Now it is apparent, I would say, that travelling together 'takes two' in more than this sense. Both participants have to be involved in travelling together, if they are to travel together, in a way in which neither participant in an act of zigging has to be involved. One way of putting this is that they must be partners, and not just both be participants in the act of travelling together. I shall say more shortly about what I take the relevant kind of partnering to be like.

What people travelling together are doing could be given a name of its own, such as 'co-travelling'. Generalizing, I conjecture that when people *do A together* (in the strong sense) there is always some available action-description A' (possibly A = A'), such that they may truly be described as doing A', where it is impossible for a person to do A' without a partner.

I shall refer to any kind of action like 'co-travelling' and playing tennis, which 'takes' two or more partners, as a 'necessarily partnered' action. I couched my discussion originally in terms of shopping. Shopping is not a necessarily partnered action, but people can shop together, and when they do, it is possible – I have conjectured – to think of them as co-shopping, where co-shopping is a necessarily partnered action.[15] Bearing all this in mind, how might one attempt a general account of joint action?

2.3 On the goals of shared action.

Consideration of what happens when people travel together may suggest that the following is a condition on travelling together in the strong sense: X must have as a goal that he travels from A to B, that Y travels from A to B, and that they do so in one another's company; and similarly for Y. Evidently if someone, X, does want to travel in Y's company, things like the following will happen. Failing special preliminaries or background, if Y suddenly bids X farewell and moves to another railway carriage, X will be perturbed. If Y starts lagging behind, X will want to do something about it, and will perhaps slacken his own pace, or ask Y if anything is wrong. I have already observed that these are indeed things of a kind that we expect to happen when people travel together in the strong sense.

One might then try generalizing the above condition as follows. For any action, A, such that it is possible for a single person to do A alone, in order for X and Y to do A together in the strong sense, each must have the goal that both X and Y do A and that they do so in one another's company.

This condition is not *sufficient*, even for the original case of travelling. With respect to that case, one can imagine examples in which it is fulfilled, but which would be a travesty of genuine travelling together. For example: Jill sees Jack on the platform at Oxford station and desires to travel in his company. She walks up to him and engages him in conversation. When the train comes, Jill follows Jack into one of the carriages, and the following dialogue ensues: 'Is it all right if I sit here?' (says Jill). 'Sure,' says Jack, without great warmth. They sit, and Jill engages Jack in further conversation, remaining in the seat next to him till the end of the line in London. Looking at things now from Jack's point of view, we find that when Jill came up to him he was secretly thrilled but did not show it, having reasons not to express these feelings. However, while chatting to Jill on the station platform he desires very much that he will be able to go on talking to her all the way to London, if she is going that far. He says nothing about this, but deliberately looks for a seat where she can sit next to him if she chooses. Of course, he makes no show of *expecting* her to sit there. Somewhat nervous of his own hopes, plans, desires, and intentions, if anything he betrays only their opposite. Under such circumstances both Jill and Jack individually espouse the goal that they travel to London in one another's company. But they do not count as travelling together in the strong sense, even though each has this goal and it is indeed fulfilled.

If anyone's intuitions need further help here, consider the following. One can imagine that Tim, a colleague of Jack's, spots him on the train. Tim and Jack need to discuss some business as soon as possible. Tim notices that Jack is exchanging words with Jill and wonders if they are together, which would make his asking Jack to move so they can discuss business less appropriate. He approaches Jack and Jill and asks Jack: 'Are you two travelling together?' Jack could surely reply quite truthfully: 'No, we were just chatting'. At no point in the story so far need it have happened that Jill and Jack came to be travelling together. Certainly each one's having the goal in question was not enough.

The condition under consideration, then, is not sufficient to produce a joint action. Nor is it a necessary condition in general. I noted earlier that, for many standard English action terms, two people can do A together, while neither is doing enough to count as doing A himself, when considered in isolation. This can be the case when people shop together, when they together investigate the matter fully, and so on. But if neither of the parties need count as doing A when considered in isolation, it surely cannot be a necessary condition on doing A together, in general, that the goal of each be that each acts in such a way as to count as doing A when so considered. Yet this is the import of the proposal we are considering.

Even if it is put forward only as a necessary condition on cases like that of travelling together, to which it may seem well tailored, the proposed condition may best be construed behaviourally. Let me explain. At a minimum, in order to perform some action A by oneself, one generally has to fulfil some behavioural condition. However much one wants to be eating an apple, and tries to, one is not performing the act of eating an apple unless one's behavioural relation to some apple is appropriate. One way in which an individual who is buying something with another may fail to count as himself buying anything when considered in isolation is in a broadly speaking behavioural way. He sits and watches while someone else hands over the cash, say. He himself could not count as buying anything if this is all he does. Meanwhile, an individual who is travelling together with another will generally count as travelling, behaviourally speaking, when considered in isolation. It is true that he will be engaging in some behaviour which is bizarre for one travelling alone (there will be much behaviour aimed at keeping close to one other party). But enough will be done behaviourally for this person to count as travelling, all else being equal. Meanwhile, the putative condition on shared action itself suggests that there is something to distinguish the canonical *state of mind* of one travelling with another from that of one travelling by himself. I would agree that this is so. My own views on the difference will emerge in due course. If this is right as a general claim, however, it looks as if the proposed condition may be least misleading if it is interpreted in purely behavioural terms.

What may be referred to as the minimal case of two people travelling together involves each one in *seeing himself* as travelling (in some sense) to place P *in the other's company*. Meanwhile, the minimal case of one person travelling to P alone simply involves his seeing himself as travelling (in some sense) to P. One might prefer, then, to amend the proposed condition in relation to travelling together, as follows: each one's goal must be that X and Y behave in such a way that each counts from a behavioural point of view as travelling, and does so while in the other's company. Putting things this way avoids the mistaken idea that X's goal is properly specified as the goal that he and Y each fulfil the mental and behavioural conditions for a minimal case of travelling on his own.

Even in its weakened, 'behavioural' version, the proposed condition is not a necessary condition on shared action in general, by reason of facts already cited. There are cases of sharing in an action that each is capable of performing on his own, like shopping, that are not plausibly thought of as cases in which the parties desire that each, behaviourally at least, count as performing that action when considered in isolation.

What of some more general condition along these lines? To cope with the case of shopping together one might suggest that what is necessary is that, when two or more people do some action A together, each has the goal that each one achieves, behaviourally speaking, at least some proper *part* of what would constitute one person's doing A, while they are in another's company, in such a way that all necessary behavioural tasks are done. This might work for the case of shopping together. However, as it stands it does not cope felicitously with the case of travelling together, walking together, and so on, for in these cases each person must achieve the whole, behaviourally speaking, of what one person does when performing the action in question alone.

More importantly, it does not cope with cases like the

following: Ted and Carol are looking after Jo's baby; Ted and Carol are taking care of the firm's accounts. It seems that, on the one hand, these can be construed as cases of two people's sharing in an action. On the other hand, *the most natural description of the goal in question seems not to involve either agent directly.* In one case, the goal is that Jo's baby be cared for, in the other, that certain accounts be properly maintained.

With respect to the specific idea of being in one another's company, it seems that (in the first case) the goal in question could be achieved by Ted's staying home with the baby and Carol's going to the cinema. Even when the goal is indeed achieved in this way, Ted and Carol could still count as looking after the baby together. Imagine that they had carefully discussed whether Ted could manage alone and decided that Carol might as well go to see the film she wanted to see. Though I do not want to focus on this now, what seems to be important is something like this: Ted and Carol regard Carol as jointly responsible with Ted for the care of the baby, and each acts appropriately. When roughly this is so, it seems that we can still count Carol as looking after the baby with Ted. As always, matters are linguistically a little complex. Carol could say to a friend she meets at the cinema, 'Ted is looking after the baby while I'm here.' But it seems that there is a sense in which she can also honestly say that she and Ted are looking after the baby together. Similarly for the accounts case. These cases, then, present a contrast to those of eating, sleeping, walking, travelling, sitting, and even shopping together, where the goal is that two or more people do something in relatively close proximity.

Evidently, one may be tempted to elide different sorts of cases because of the ambiguity of 'together' noted earlier. The phrase 'travelling together' and the like, when referring to a joint action, also refer to an action involving the goal of doing something in relatively close proximity. However 'looking after the accounts together' does not. The Ted and Carol cases, then, suggest that, contrary to what might be thought by extrapolating from one set of cases, *it is not necessary to joint or shared action that each person involved has as a goal some state of affairs involving both himself and the other parties.*

It might be objected that even if physical proximity is not involved in the Ted and Carol cases, each participant must espouse a goal which involves both parties. In the baby case, that goal is that the baby be taken care of *by Ted and Carol.* I do not think this is quite right. As will emerge shortly, I do believe that the following is correct: each of the parties must understand that something is being done *by them.* 'By so and so' is most naturally seen not as part of the characterization of a goal, but rather as a characterization of *who is to aim* at some goal, indeed, one might say, of *whose goal* it is. The conclusion of this section, then, seems to stand.

2.4 Towards a model of shared action: joining forces

So far ground has been cleared but no necessary condition on shared action has been found. Suppose we start again and ask how might the case of Jack and Jill, described in the last subsection, be converted into a case of travelling together?

Here are two ways. Jill might have asked Jack if he was going all the way to London and then asked 'Shall we travel together?' Jack might have replied: 'Yes, that's a fine idea.' Or there might have been no explicit acceptance of the idea of travelling together. Jill might have exclaimed: 'Jack! How wonderful! Are you going all the way to London? Marvellous!' Jack (smiling with delight): 'I can't wait to hear all your news! If we get separated when people are getting on the train, don't worry, I'll save you a place.' Here it seems clear enough that, as they proceeded on their way, these people would count, and know they counted, as travelling together.

Now, how might we spell out what has been achieved in these new scenarios? More particularly, what precisely is it that allows Jack and Jill to travel together, that, as one might put it, sets Jack and Jill up to travel together? I say 'sets them up' because, possibly, even after one of these scenes has occurred, their journey together might be thought of as not yet having begun. Still, once one of these scenes has occurred, all that seems necessary, if anything, for them to be travelling together, is that when it becomes appropriate each one begins to act appropriately, helping the other onto the train, making sure they keep close to each other, and so on. I say more about the conditions on actual joint action below.

An obvious first thought is that what is crucial to the generation of genuine travelling together is an agreement between the parties. This idea, however, obviously raises further questions. Though the first case does involve an explicit agreement, the second does not. Meanwhile, the notion of a 'tacit agreement' requires careful handling. Rather than pursuing the question of whether there needs to be anything that would naturally be called an agreement, I shall tentatively accept a different and somewhat weaker hypothesis, that is, that one who is set up to travel with another must have *made certain things clear* to his opposite number. I want now to move on to the question of *what* each must make clear to the other.

On the basis of what was said in the last subsection about the case of travelling together specifically, it might be suggested that in this case each of the parties must make clear to the other that his goal is that he proceed to London in the company of the other. In so far as this is all that is made clear, however, I do not think what is needed for joint action has been conveyed. An explicit statement from each one that he desires to travel in the other's company may be enough in practice to set them up to travel together. But we are trying to spell out in detail the content of an understanding which will, of course, often be implicit. What is stated explicitly may well not be enough to determine this content.

It is worth saying more, if only sketchily, about the insufficiency of the mutual declaration of the personal goal that Jack travel in Jill's company. If each has made clear that he or she individually has this goal, then we are further ahead than we were when each kept his personal goal secret from the other. But still, at this point each one knows only that both individually have a certain goal. Were they to go no further in their assumptions about each other, each might still feel obliged to attempt to fulfil the goal in question independently. For instance, when Jack finds two seats on the train, it would not be completely bizarre for him to wait hopefully for Jill to reach him before anyone else does, rather than getting her attention and urging her to come quickly. In short, he may feel he has no right to interfere or involve himself in *her* progress towards the goal in question, even though it is a goal both have, a goal they share, in a weak sense, and, indeed, given that it is *common knowledge* between them that they both have this goal. (I say more shortly about the notion of 'common knowledge'. Roughly, the idea is that the fact that both have the goal in question is completely out in the open with respect to the two of them, and they realize this.)

Someone might object here that surely Jack does have a moral right, indeed he has a moral duty, to help Jill achieve her goal, in this case, given that it will be so easy for him to do so. Perhaps this is so. But suppose Jack is quite amoral. Even so, if they were really travelling together, this failure on his part would be bizarre. Otherwise it would not be. This suggests that *genuine travelling together involves rights and duties that are something other than moral rights and duties*, a point to which I shall return.

The same goes for prudential considerations. It will obviously be prudent of Jack to help Jill fulfil her goal, in so far as his own goal will not be fulfilled unless hers is also. But Jack may be an imprudent fellow. Or he may feel that one oversteps the limits of acceptable prudence if one acts to influence another's behaviour in order to help oneself. Given that he thinks this way, it will not be bizarre for him to do what he can by himself to travel in Jill's company without attempting to influence her behaviour in any way. If they were travelling together, meanwhile, it would be bizarre.

Similar things can be said even if what is mutually declared is a lot more complex. For instance, Jack might say: 'This is my goal, and I intend to do whatever I can to reach it, monitoring all the while what you are doing, so I can be as effective as possible in bringing my goal about'. Jill might make a similar avowal. It will then be clear to both that, if Jack finds a seat for two he will signal to Jill that he has done so, since he can rely on this signal having the effect he desires, given his knowledge of her intention to reach her own goal as best she can. But even in this case the right kinds of *entitlements* and *duties* do not seem to have been created. Motives of prudence, altruism, morality generally, could motivate each person to urge on and help the other to reach her own goal and hence to reach his own. But in my view none of this properly captures the flavour of travelling together in the strong sense.

I suggest, as a first approximation to a full characterization, that each party to a genuine act of travelling together must have made it clear to the other that he is willing to *join forces* with the other in accepting the goal that they travel in one another's company. Can one say more about the notion of 'joining forces'? There are various other ways in which one might express the point here, but none of them seems to constitute an analysis or breaking down of the notion. Thus I might have said that each must make clear his willingness that the goal in question be accepted *by himself and the other, jointly*. Or his willingness to be *jointly responsible* with the other for achieving the goal. Putting it in somewhat technical terminology, one might say that each must manifest his willingness to constitute with the other a *plural subject* of the goal that they travel in one another's company. There are further alternative ways of capturing what must be expressed, but let us stop with these for the time being.

Given that such attitudes on both sides have been made clear, a foundation has been laid for each person to *pursue the goal that he and the other travel from A to B* and to do so *in his capacity as the constituent of a plural subject of* that goal. When someone does this, it seems to be true that both the intended goal and, most importantly, *the intended subject* of the goal is distinct from the goal and subject intended when he travels alone. For, when one travels alone, one's goal is one's own movement from A to B, and this is one's *personal* goal.

In so far as this is right, then it bears on the question whether, in order for joint action to take place, each party to the action must himself espouse some goal or other. Perhaps in some sense this must be so. But to join forces in accepting some goal is, in effect, to accept that goal as a joint goal. It is not in itself directly to accept that goal as one's own. Hence there is reason to answer that question in the negative. In so far as those who have joined forces to do something will *personally make an effort* to reach the relevant goal, one might feel justified in saying that reaching that joint goal will be their personal goal. But I suggest that the fundamental condition on joint action is best not put in terms of what their personal goal must be, but rather in terms of what they must be trying to bring about *in so far as they are members of a particular plural subject.* I shall not dwell further on this particular aspect of the matter in this chapter, but I shall return to it later.[16]

Here, then, is rather a deep way in which going for a walk alone, for instance, is different at the level of intention from going for a walk with another person. (This distinction presumably applies to all cases of joint action, including the Ted and Carol cases noted earlier.) The goal of any joint action is seen by the participants as the goal of a plural subject. Meanwhile, the goal of an action one performs on one's own, independently of others, is seen as the goal of oneself, a singular subject one might say. More will eventually be said in clarification of these remarks. For now the general idea of what I see as the core of shared action should be clear. A participant in a shared action acts in his capacity as the member of a plural subject of the goal of the action. He will count as the member of such a plural subject when, at a minimum, and roughly, he and others have expressed to each other their willingness jointly to accept the goal in question now. They will then count as jointly accepting it, and hence as constituting the plural subject of that goal.

2.5 *Further considerations on the model of joint action*

I have been discussing a concept of doing something together in the strong sense, which I take to be part of a conceptual scheme inherent in vernacular speech. This notion posits as necessary a special intentional or 'inner' component in joint action. Thus no behaviour on behalf of the parties, however appropriate, can be considered sufficient in itself for joint action. It is even true that

'X and Y do A together at time t' entails, but is not equivalent to, 'X and Y are in spatial locations and positions appropriate to doing A jointly at t, and A intentionally does something the performance of which involves him in doing his behavioural part in jointly doing A at t, and B does likewise.' All onlookers might be fooled, but even these conditions, though necessary, are not sufficient logically speaking.

Someone might, I suppose, object to these claims as follows: imagine that you see two people, a man and a woman, say, on a dance floor. He has his arm around her waist; they expertly perform the steps of a waltz. Surely the fact that they are dancing together can be obvious, even to one without access to the thoughts of the parties concerned? So how can the fact of their dancing together be in any way dependent on their thinking any particular thoughts?

I would reply that our full-blooded action concepts are in general complex: they refer to a species of overt behaviour on the one hand, and to intentions and other subjective phenomena on the other. Sometimes they may seem to be clearly applicable when the behaviour looks right. (Perhaps due to a natural assumption of appropriate intention.) It may then seem that they are used without any subjective reference at all. Look, one might say, those people just *are* dancing together; that man just *is* chopping wood. It does not matter what any of them are thinking, that's what they are *actually doing*. At this point the notion of what someone is (actually) doing may seem to be entirely behavioural. However, knowledge of intention can lead us to revise our view, and I submit that in general if the intention does not 'fit' the behaviour we will be inclined either not to know what to say, or to say that the apparent action is not in fact occurring – no action is occurring – or to sense that we are indeed now operating with a revised concept, with a purely behavioural concept. Thus consider our waltzing couple. Unbeknownst to the observer, she is moving automatically, while her mind is a complete blank. Are they waltzing together? Are they doing anything together? Is *she* doing anything at all? That she is, is not obvious to me, except in the sense in which mere physical movements are doings.[17]

Discussion of the waltzers allows me to clarify further what I have been doing here. I have not been asking 'under what conditions from a physical point of view are people doing things together?', for instance 'under what physical circumstances may people be said to be dancing together?' but rather 'what thoughts or conceptions must be involved in order for people to count as (intentionally) dancing together? Or, given that the behaviour is appropriate, what inner conditions make this a case of the parties (intentionally) dancing together?'

Possibly it may be objected that, more specifically, it cannot be a requirement of doing something together that the parties accept that they are the components of a plural subject of action. A case of 'unwilling participation' like the following might be cited.

Suppose that at a dance a man rushes up to a woman, pulls her on to the dance floor, and starts dancing with her, as we might say. He attempts to lead her in a waltz. She is unclear at first what is going on, then whether she wants to dance with him; she is pulled unwillingly and manœuvered around the floor unwillingly, half resisting, half letting herself be moved. After a moment or two, though, let us say she relaxes into the dance and no longer sees herself as struggling, but as dancing with the man. The point of such an example would be, presumably, to suggest that dancing together can occur prior to any acceptance on the parts of the participants that they are acting as constituents of a plural subject, or have joined forces in order to dance. It may also be intended to suggest that the sense that one is part of a plural subject is something that tends to occur (inessentially if pleasantly) as a result of doing things together.[18] The example given, however, does not really prove either claim. For first we have to decide at what point these two really are dancing together. Are two people dancing together if one is trying to get out of it, possibly pulling away, saying, 'look, no really, I don't want to do this'?

Consider an analogue in the case of the action of a single person. One might think of someone whose hand, say, was being forced to write a note. Someone else was moving his hand, though he himself was knowingly 'going through the motions' of writing. *Was* he himself writing a note? Our action concepts are such that here we might want to say: well, on the one hand he does write something. The physical conditions for the action are satisfied. On the other hand he does not, because he has no intention to write anything. His movements are completely coerced; it is not his own intention that they be the way they are. So it seems that we might, using the action concept in the full (not-merely-behavioural) sense, justify the idea that this man is not writing a note. Analogously we can justify saying that the woman forced to dance is not dancing with the man, since she has no intention of dancing with him, and the bodily movements that might lead one to say that she is dancing with him are in large part coerced and not voluntary. One might say that just as our action concepts, or our fullest action concepts, are voluntaristic, so are our concepts of joint action. If the woman is not really dancing with the man until she relaxes into the dance with him, throws herself into it, as we might say, then this kind of example does not show that dancing with can precede one's joining forces with one's partner. As examples additional to that of the woman forced to dance, one might cite the uglier case of rape, and the altogether innocuous case of two people walking along a path side by side, or nearly so, but not together in the strong sense.

It is now time to sum up my discussion of sharing in an action in the strong sense at issue here. In order for X and Y to be doing A together, some condition of behavioural appropriateness must presumably hold, but both X and Y must also have a special kind of conception of what is going on. Crucially, each must intentionally act in his/her capacity as a constituent of a plural subject of a certain goal, a subject whose other constituent is the other person in question.

One might wonder why we should have or use the concept of a shared action in the strong sense. There is reason to think we have it because we need to use it. It seems reasonable to conjecture that the best way to get humans to do things together from the behavioural point of view, to dance and walk and talk and so on in a meshing and harmonious way, is to have them see themselves as parts of a plural subject or as joining forces, to see themselves no longer as, or as entirely, independent individuals. To put it crudely, if a benevolent creator were to make a set of rational agents like human beings, she would be wise to give them an innate concept of a plural subject. If this is the best way, or one highly efficient way, to create human harmonies, it should not be surprising that we have this conception and do things in terms of it.

In my view, then, the concept of a shared action in the strong sense is both one we have, and one which is everywhere embodied in what we do. For one shares in actions, in this sense, by virtue of offering to instantiate this concept together with certain others, who offer one the same thing. The key to the notion of a shared action is that of the plural subject of a goal. I shall say more about this key notion in what follows.

3 'WE'

3.1 Introduction

I now turn to direct discussion of the pronoun 'we' and what I take to be its central sense. In the context of this book, 'we' is of interest not only as a means of further fleshing out and justifying my account of social groups, but also for its own sake. The first person plural pronoun is of obvious relevance to anyone concerned with the everyday concepts applied in the context of human social life.

By the end of this section, the core of my account of social groups will, in effect, have been fully delineated. As already noted, in my view the, or at least a, central sense of 'we' is as follows.

'We' refers to a set of people each of whom shares, with oneself, in some action, belief, attitude, or other such attribute.

To put it another way now, my idea is that 'we' is used to refer to a plural subject. Clearly, if there is a central sense of 'we' this will help to establish the centrality in everyday life of the conceptual scheme of plural subjects. (The centrality of the latter does not *require* that there be such a sense.)

3.2 A linguistic note

In the previous section I wrote of the ambiguity, in effect, of sentences involving conjunctive noun phrases like 'Ralph and Alice'. (See section 2.1 above.) Sentences involving 'we' can be similarly ambiguous. Thus consider the mini-dialogue: 'What are you and Margaret going to do this afternoon?' 'We're going to play tennis'. The questioner might not yet be sure whether the person questioned is going to play tennis with Margaret or with someone else. Again, if the answer is 'We're going shopping' it will not be obvious whether they are going together or on separate expeditions. Such ambiguous 'we'-sentences, like those with conjunctive noun phrases, can be disambiguated by the explict use of the 'we . . . both' or 'we . . . together' construction.

All that can be concluded from the 'we . . . both' use of 'we', however, is more or less what has already been said: 'we' plus a verb of action does not entail that the people referred to in this particular use of 'we' are sharers of the action in question. My boldest claim about 'we' can accommodate this conclusion, and be put in terms of it. The claim is that some sentence using the 'we . . . together' construction is true of those to whom 'we' in the central sense applies. This would not prevent 'we' from being used in this sense in the 'we . . . both' construction.[19]

168

3.3 'We', action, and social groups

I do not claim that the pronoun 'we' only refers to people who share in *action*. Some might feel inclined to question this for the following reason. On the one hand, when people are doing things together (whatever precisely this amounts to) it seems indisputable that they can refer to themselves as 'us'. On the other hand, that there is an intelligible parallel conception of 'believing together' and so on might be doubted. This suggests the stronger condition that people must be *doing something together* at the time 'we' is used.

I agree that whenever a set of people are engaged in some activity together – playing tennis, chatting, shopping, fencing, dancing, or whatever – then members of the set can appropriately refer to themselves, together with the others, as 'we'. But I would argue that actually *doing* something in the narrow sense at issue here cannot be a necessary condition for the appropriateness of 'we'.

It seems that in order to proceed with proper confidence to do things together, people must already justifiably see themselves as 'us' or 'we'. It is not our dancing together, say, which 'creates' or is a precondition for the appropriateness of 'we'. Rather, it is the perceived appropriateness of 'we' which makes our dancing together possible. Our dancing together must come after, or at least depend for its occurrence on, the assurance that we are 'we', rather than vice versa. Our actually dancing together may of course confirm our sense that we are 'we' in various ways.

I argued above that in order that people may set out with proper confidence to do something with certain others, they must already justifiably see themselves in a certain special way, namely as parts of a plural subject of the relevant goal. Questions about the use of the pronoun 'we' were not being debated there. I have not yet, of course, argued for a tight relation between 'we' and plural subjects. But the symmetry of structure of the two independently plausible ideas noted here already suggests it; in other words, it provides, in itself, *an* argument for it.

Those who form the plural subject of a goal, whether or not they are actually engaged in joint action, can be thought of as already set up to share in the correlative action. So it might be conjectured that 'we' is appropriately used not only of those actually engaged in joint action but also of those set up to share in such an action by virtue of sharing a goal. Someone might, I imagine, demur. Can people share a goal in advance of actually sharing in an action? If these two things cannot be distinct in time, then in practice 'we' will only apply when people are actually sharing in some action. So it will be rather pointless to state that it also applies when people only share a goal.

Here is an example apropos of the last query. Consider how people might come to have a conversation. You see this person (in the kitchen, say) and notice that he is deep in thought. You say 'Do you have a minute?' He does not respond. Since in fact you feel it is important to discuss a particular issue, you say. 'Did you hear? I need to talk to you'. This time he does hear. He looks you full in the face with every appearance of being on full alert. Confirming this impression, he says 'Yes. What is it?' Now you are finally set up for a conversation of sorts. You have jointly accepted the goal of your having a conversation now. The two of you are – to put it generally – set up to share in the action of a conversation. Actual conversing will, of course, follow swiftly in most circumstances. However, before anyone speaks it is not altogether natural to say that the participants are conversing. An earlier case may be mentioned in contrast. Recall the case of Jack and Jill agreeing to travel together, having met on the station platform. There, in so far as being on the platform is itself already part of travelling, the participants may be regarded as having put themselves instantly *in medias res* by virtue of their agreement to travel together. Once this agreement is made they are travelling together, now.

In the example of the conversation the satisfaction of conditions on having a joint goal can plausibly be claimed to antedate the actual conversation. So being set up to share an action and actually sharing in that action can be temporally distinct, and the first can antedate the second. Meanwhile it is doubtful whether the second can antedate the first.

In order to drive a wedge between 'we' and actual joint action we need not, in fact, attend to the kind of fine-grained detail to which I have just been alluding. There is surely at least one other kind of relation to action that those who properly refer to themselves as 'we' may have. Consider a married couple. The members of such a couple tend to think of each other as 'we' over the course of their life together. Without enquiring precisely why this is, we can note that such people can be said to have been set up, when a certain ceremony takes place, to share in various kinds of action, in certain circumstances, throughout their lives. At the same time, it is surely wrong to think of them as either continuously sharing in the relevant actions or even possessing the related goals of action at the time they are set up for such action in the way noted. Thus, for example, for them jointly to

170

accept the goal of having a particular conversation special conditions must obtain, conditions that the marriage ceremony alone does not satisfy. It looks as if we could use some understanding of the conditions under which people get set up for action in this 'advance' fashion, for it looks as if these, also, may be sufficient conditions for the use of 'we'. This is something that I hope to achieve later in this section.

I have now noted two kinds of situation which look as if they may be sufficient for 'we', neither of which involves what would naturally be construed as joint *action* as such. I take this to be a good result from the point of view of using 'we' in an analysis of social groups, in spite of some apparently contrary assumptions in the literature.

There is some tendency among writers on the nature of social groups (Rawls, for instance, in his discussion of 'social union' in *A Theory of Justice*) to see the existence of a social group as requiring co-operative action in relation to a shared purpose (Rawls writes of a 'shared final end'). That is, a social group is more or less assumed to be definable as a set of people who acknowledge a common purpose and are seeking to achieve it together. I find this idea rather suspicious without further explanation. (In what follows I shall construe 'shared purpose', 'common end' and so on as the purposes or ends of plural subjects. To my knowledge the authors I am referring to have not articulated their concept of a shared or common end in this way. To my knowledge they do not articulate it at all. In any case I am discussing a tendency that various authors have manifested in different ways, and not attempting anything like critical exegesis at this point.)

It does not seem to be obviously true of all cases of social groups (including what are admitted to be social groups by these authors) that their members must have some acknowledged shared purpose or purposes that they are currently engaged in pursuing together. For example, families, in particular nuclear families residing in one home, are normally assumed to be social groups of a small but paradigmatic kind. Now perhaps some particular families are and some are not qualified to count as paradigm cases of social groups. But assuming that most do so count, it seems wrong to think of these families as in any obvious way sharing and pursuing a common purpose or purposes.

Like most people, I suspect, I am unaware of any particular purpose or purposes shared by the members of the family in which I grew up. We did do things together, for instance we might go somewhere together; we fairly regularly ate together, and so on. But such temporary if regular sharing in action does not seem enough to entail a common purpose of the kind in question. It is true that we lived together, that is, we lived under the same roof. Could families of the same sort plausibly be thought of as having such living together as their shared purpose? I think it is far more natural to say of family members that they just take it that they do live together. In some special cases there may be a conscious desire to keep the family together, in the sense that no one has to live elsewhere due to cramped living quarters, say, or financial hardship. But in many clear cases of families I suspect that there are just a lot of shared assumptions about what it is natural and right and proper to do, and little in the way of a shared purpose. Meanwhile, the family *is* the family – 'us'.

It may be pointed out that there are deeper senses of 'living together' such as the one at issue, say, in Aristotle's discussion of friendship in the *Nichomachean Ethics*. Aristotle characterizes living together as a 'sharing of conversation and thought'.[20] Ideally, we might think, the members of families will have living together in some such sense as their aim. Though this aim may be shared by the members of many families, it is by no means clear that it characterizes all clear cases of families.[21] The same goes for another attractive aim: the good of all.[22] Quite generally, it is not clear that all families have some shared underlying *aim*.

Another type of case is found in John Updike's short story 'Minutes of the last meeting'. Here we find a committee whose purpose is much in dispute. Though there is some sense of why the committee was set up in the first place, its original purpose is now obsolete. Yet the committee endures. It begins to seem somewhat dangerous to enquire too far into the purposes or purpose of the committee, in case it should transpire that it has no charge, and thus has no reason to exist. However, as one member suddenly observes, it may not matter if the committee has no charge, since the members keep attending committee meetings, they seem to get something out of it, and 'we love each other'. Whether or not the members enjoy being members and whether or not each one personally attends meetings out of love for his fellows is surely irrelevant with respect to whether or not the committee itself really has a charge. It seems fairly clear that the members of this committee are members of a group which will continue to flourish for a long time. Why they should count as the members of a group needs to be determined. However, it is by no means clear that the reason is that its members have a shared goal.

There is, of course, a well-known doctrine in sociology, namely 'functionalism', which (to give a crude summary) has it that all societies (and smaller social groups?) have a goal or end-state, namely, the perpetuation of their own existence, and particular institutions or other phenomena within a given society can fruitfully be investigated in relation to their promotion or frustration of this goal. If an institution, say polygamy, has a clear role in promoting the smooth running of the complex of institutions into which it fits, it can be seen as flourishing in part because of its beneficial role in the system as a whole. Even the existence of crime may have its socially beneficial aspects in the long run (as Durkheim, for instance, argued). Sociological functionalism as characterized here is a doctrine about how to understand particular social facts. It is not intended as a doctrine about what is meant by the term 'a society', or about how societies or social groups are to be individuated in the first place. It is an empirical theory, rather, of great generality, about why particular social institutions survive within particular societies. In so far as sociological functionalism supposes itself to be dealing with goals or end-states not necessarily accepted by any individual human being, it is not really relevant to the view that some are inclined to hold, that the members of social groups must have a common purpose which, if not explicitly avowed and stated, is at least implicit in conscious intentions and conceptions.[23]

Of course some kinds of groups do have explicit common purposes, which are actively pursued. The members of CREEP (the Committee to Reelect the President) in 1972 obviously had at least one explicit common purpose. People might organize an evening meeting explicitly for the purpose of discussing an important recent political event. Tennis clubs and golf clubs and churches and synagogues and so on all more or less avow a unique common purpose, whatever other important functions they may in fact serve – facilitation of business or political contacts, say, the making of personal friends, a way of whiling away the painful times when the office is closed. As is indicated by a variety of examples, however, it badly needs arguing that all groups are like these. That this is so is false on the face of it. One reason it may be assumed by some writers is that they are unclear as to what could justify thinking of certain people as a group in the absence of a shared purpose. They may sense that a shared purpose is sufficient, but not have a clear sense of why that is, nor a clear sense, therefore, of how anything else could make a group out of a set of persons. I hope that what I have written in this book so far, and what follows now, will help to remedy this situation.

3.4 Some basic constraints on the use of 'we'

I have argued that 'we' does not only apply to those sharing in an action. It applies also at least to those who are set up to share in an action in a certain way. This could be, of course, because 'we' always has a very capacious sense. It could be that a speaker could always use 'we' with complete propriety, to refer to himself and whoever else he happened to have in mind. Let me now argue for the view that there is a strong sense of 'we' whose semantics is characterizable thus: 'we' refers to a plural subject.

Let me first run briefly through some rather obvious constraints on the use of 'we' in general. (I am in all this disregarding the special case of the 'monarchic' or 'royal' 'we'.)

First, there is a *self-inclusion constraint*: the thinker/speaker is always included in the referent of 'we'. Second, there is a *multiplicity constraint*: 'we' indicates that more than one person is being referred to. (It could be queried whether or not 'we' ever refers to particular people, strictly speaking, rather than to a complex phenomenon consisting of persons possessing certain specific properties, persons conceived of and conceiving in certain ways. Some casualness about this will not matter at this point.)

A parochial fact about English is that it does not have words to distinguish the case where the person addressed (if there is one) is included in the referent of 'we' from the case where he or she is not included. That is, English does not have both an inclusive and exclusive 'we'. We seem to rely on the context to indicate the precise referent.[24] In some languages this distinction is marked by two different words. In any case, it seems to be true quite generally that if 'we' is appropriately used at all, then there must be at least one other person whom the speaker *could* appropriately address with an inclusive 'we'.[25]

The notion of a person, used above, is not entirely perspicuous. So let me briefly argue next for a specific feature which is required in the 'components' of any 'we'. Imagine that a man were to gesture at his chair and say to a friend 'Well, so here we are in Princeton at last'. 'We?' says the puzzled friend. 'My chair and I' he replies. The friend would reasonably conclude, I suggest, that the man has forgotten what 'we' means, somehow, or he believes that his chair is animate, or his use of language is whimsical and playful, not serious and literal. In the light of the bizarreness of this man's use of 'we' it is arguable that 'we', properly and literally used as a plural pronoun, presupposes that all the parties intended to fall under the pronoun are animate. I conclude, then, that the multiplicity constraint refers at least to a

174

multiplicity of animate beings. (Call this the *animacy constraint*.)

Animacy is a rather basic and obvious constraint. We might wish to investigate some related issues. For instance, is knowledge that one is animate another requirement? Rather than dwelling on such issues now, however, I shall turn to another obvious and basic constraint. I shall then look at some examples in which the beings involved are all normal human beings with whatever capacities these have, and see what seems to be required, in addition to animacy, in the 'components' of a proper referent of 'we'. One can then work back to the conditions for the satisfaction of these conditions, if one wishes.

A final rather basic constraint on the appropriateness of using the term 'we' seems to be that one must be able to specify at least roughly which others one intends to include in the referent of 'we' (call this the *specified range constraint*). In practice, hearers may often be able to 'disambiguate' the pronoun in this respect by reference to the context, that is, the intended referent may be clear enough without explanation. But it seems that there must *be* an intended referent. If one of my guests says 'We have to leave now' I do not expect her to be completely vague about who the others might be.

3.5 Some cases and an hypothesis

Now even when the above basic constraints are satisfied, it seems that 'we' can be used inappropriately, though sincerely.

(i) The restaurant case

Here is an example, based on an actual situation, in which someone's use of 'we' is seen as inappropriate. (I shall refer to this case in what follows as 'the restaurant case'.)

A group of people are eating together in a restaurant at the conclusion of an academic conference. Two of their number, Tony and Celia, are engaged to be married. The restaurant is famous for its sweet pastries, and at one point Tony asks Celia 'Shall we share a pastry?' Celia nods agreement. Then one of the other men, Bernard, turns to Sylvia, who is sitting on his right, and whom he hardly knows, and asks 'Shall *we* share a pastry?' She finds his use of 'we' inappropriate. (In fact one could say that she resents it; she finds it presumptuous.) She tries to show this by replying: 'I'm willing to share something with you, yes.'

I am going to assume that Sylvia's sense of inappropriateness is justified. Let me look at some hypotheses as to what might justify the sense of inappropriateness.

It is perhaps worth stressing at the outset that in my description of the case it is *the use of 'we'* by Bernard in this context which is judged to be inappropriate. When I have brought up this case in discussion, various people have commented that what is really judged inappropriate is the idea that Sylvia and Bernard engage in the especially intimate act of sharing a pastry, and not Bernard's use of the pronoun 'we'. Perhaps these people assumed that Sylvia must be wrong about where the inappropriateness she senses actually lies. However, I want to credit her with being right. One might feel that, in any case, sharing a pastry by splitting it and putting each half on a separate plate is in itself hardly an especially intimate act.[26]

It might be suggested that it is Bernard's use of 'we' in this particular context, where someone has just used the pronoun to refer to himself and his fiancée, that causes the problem. Sylvia could be taking Bernard's use of 'we', in this context, to imply that he and she are romantically involved, like Tony and Celia. Such an implication could explain her sense of presumption. I shall not accept this suggestion. In reply to it let me clarify further the nature of Sylvia's actual response. She sensed that the inappropriateness of Bernard's use of 'we' lay in the semantics of 'we' itself.

It will not do, I think, to suggest that 'we' in English actually *connotes* or *presupposes* the existence of romantic intimacy between the parties referred to, though its use in a particular context could appear to carry an allusion to such intimacy. Consider a second version of the restaurant case, in which Bernard and Sylvia both have good and obvious reasons not to become romantically involved, but are quite good friends. In this context it is quite likely that Sylvia would not find Bernard's use of 'we' inappropriate, even though we can assume that the presumption of an actual or practically possible romance would have been inappropriate. I do think it possible to argue that there is a degree of something we could call intimacy whenever 'we', in the sense in question, is appropriate. I do not think, however, that it is the sort of intimacy I have vaguely characterized here as 'romantic'.

Given that 'we' does not connote or presuppose that the people referred to are romantically linked, and that in the present context an implication of such linkage is not what is at issue, let us consider what standing presuppositions of 'we' Bernard might have ignored in the (original) restaurant case.

What else could have caused a problem of inappropriateness?

One possibility is that Sylvia has not manifested any willingness ever to do anything with Bernard in particular, to share in any action with him alone. Though someone might object that she surely has, by sitting with him and the rest at table, manifested a willingness to do various things such as talk to him, it is in fact often understood in such gatherings that the conversation is to be general. One person's drawing another aside for a private conversation may be presumed unacceptable. Questions about sharing pastry may be raised in a rather public way, out in front of the whole group, so to speak, not as private asides. So Sylvia's presence at this table need not prove that she has manifested any willingness to do anything with any given member of the party, that is, where they two constitute the sole participants in the action. For now, let us keep in reserve the conjecture that as long as Sylvia had manifested a willingness to do things of some kind with Bernard, his use of 'we' in this context would have been appropriate.

Another possibility, another fact which could equally well account for the sense of inappropriateness, is that Sylvia has on no occasion manifested a willingness to do things of some relevant sort with Bernard. For instance, she has not manifested a willingness to do anything implying friendship. Given that this is so, we may take it that it is not the case that she has *in effect* manifested her willingness to share a pastry. That could be the problem. A third possibility is that she has not directly shown herself willing to engage in the particular joint or shared action proposed, the sharing of a pastry.

Of these three possibilities, the third seems too specific. Presumably, Celia may never have directly indicated to her fiancé Tony that she was willing to share a pastry with him, but his saying to her 'Shall we share a pastry?' is in no way untoward. There remain the first and second suggestions above.

One could presumably adjudicate between these two by asking whether 'we' can indeed be appropriate if one type of shared action is being mooted for a certain set of people, while it would be inappropriate if a different type of action were suggested for the very same people at the same time. There is reason to think this is so.

(ii) *The* Shoot the Pianist *case*

Consider the following case. At a meeting of the History Department at Exx University, Mary and Maureen have agreed to take charge of the journals section of the departmental library.

Maureen and Mary have otherwise had little to do with each other; they teach on different days and their offices are on different floors. As the meeting breaks up, Maureen says to Mary 'When shall we meet to discuss the journals situation?' Quite likely, this use of 'we' would seem entirely appropriate. They have, after all, publicly agreed to share in looking after the journals. So Maureen's use of 'we' here does not violate any possible condition that someone included in one's referent for 'we' must have manifested willingness to share in actions of the type in question. However, suppose Maureen had said 'Shall we go and see *Shoot the Pianist* at the College Theatre tonight?' This use of 'we' might well be deemed inappropriate. Would there really be inappropriateness in the use of 'we', though, rather than in the particular action suggested? In my view a good case can be made for the inappropriateness of 'we' as such. For suppose Maureen had said: 'Would you like to come with me to see *Shoot the Pianist* tonight?' I suspect this would seem less presumptuous. The issues here are, clearly, delicate, and I do not want to rest too much on any one example.

There is a complicating factor which I shall return to again: 'we' may often be used *tendentiously*, as one might put it. That is, it may be used as if it is already entirely appropriate, when it is not. Someone could use it in this way in an effort to bring the conditions for its appropriateness into being; and it could be an effective tool in such a project. What I am trying to get at here is the conditions of appropriateness for a full-blooded but *non-tendentious* use of 'we'. (It would be odd to speak of 'conditions of appropriateness' for a tendentious 'we'. In so far as we are talking about semantic conditions, these will be the same as for a full-blooded 'we'. A tendentious 'we' is by definition inappropriate, though it may have its intended effect.)

One can also distinguish an *initiatory* use of 'we', which is not properly characterized as tendentious. One who says 'Shall we dance?' will not necessarily seem to be taking it for granted that the conditions of appropriateness for 'we' are already satisfied. Rather, he may be seen as requesting that the other party join with him in satisfying those conditions in a certain way. I discuss the idea of an initiatory use of 'we' when I come to the issue of group formation. (I take it that Sylvia did not see Bernard's use of 'we' as initiatory (and even so as inappropriate).)

The *Shoot the Pianist* case tends to support the view that if someone says 'Shall we do A?' when doing A does not at least fall into a particular class of actions the people referred to have shown they are prepared to share in, then a full-blooded 'we' is inappropriate. It will not be sufficient that they have shown that they are prepared to share in some apparently different type of action. In other words, the first suggestion regarding the inappropriateness of Bernard's use of 'we' in the original restaurant case seems to have been refuted.

A third version of the restaurant case itself provides further evidence against the first suggestion. Suppose that, in a third version of this case, Sylvia had indeed muttered some private aside to Bernard at some point in the dinner. In other words, she had effectively shown that she was prepared to exchange a few words with him alone. Even given this background, it would not necessarily be untoward for her to find Bernard's 'Shall we share a pastry?' inappropriate. For it is natural enough to think of a brief private aside as a kind of enterprise with few if any connotations regarding preparedness for other joint activities. This is particularly clearly so if a given exchange was provoked by special circumstances, as such exchanges often are. Similarly, strangers who, passing each other on a country road, exchange 'Nice day!' and 'Yes indeed!' do not feel they have manifested preparedness for other kinds of interaction, even for further talk.

Let me now sum up the gist of this section so far. We have seen that there is support for the view that a full-blooded 'we' is inappropriately used in questions of the form 'Shall we do A together (with each other)?' if doing A does not fall into a range of actions that the people referred to have shown they are prepared to perform together. Thus there is reason to examine the following positive hypothesis: *appropriate full-blooded use of 'we' in 'Shall we do A?' requires that each of the people referred to has in effect expressed to the others his willingness to share with the others in doing A, in circumstances of the type at issue.*

A subtle but important clarification of the intended import of this hypothesis may be noted briefly here. It relates to an ambiguity in 'sharing with the others in an action'. I should say that I shall construe the current hypothesis, and developments of it in the next subsection, as follows: the presupposition is that each has expressed willingness to share in an action (or actions) jointly with all of the people referred to, as opposed to willingness to share in an action jointly with any proper subset of the people concerned.

This is in fact not as restrictive as it may first appear. Suppose that Kathy, Edith, and Bob agree to form this year's departmental library committee. If when leaving the meeting room Kathy had said to Bob something like: 'Shall we meet to discuss the materials on Asia Minor before Edith returns from her conference?' this might well seem quite appropriate. Presumably in the circumstances agreeing to form the library committee with the two others could have been assumed to signal a willingness to talk with any single other of the two about library affairs where necessary to the business of the committee. More generally, it is reasonable to assume that in many circumstances willingness to do certain things with any member of a given set of people can be assumed to have been expressed implicitly on the basis of more explicit acceptance that all members are to share in a certain activity.

3.6 Some checks on the hypothesis

Let us backtrack a little now, and consider whether the hypothesis arrived at in the last section may be too strong. It involves two important components: willingness to share in a certain action, and the (in effect) expression of such willingness. Could it be the willingness to share in certain actions, rather than the manifestation of this willingness, which is crucial? In the original restaurant case, perhaps Bernard's use of 'we' was inappropriate because he had been wrong about Sylvia's state of mind, rather than because she had failed to manifest how she felt. Perhaps in the *Shoot the Pianist* case we assume (given the information that we have) that Mary is not prepared to socialize with Maureen, and 'Shall we go. . .' is inappropriate for that reason.

In favour of this view, someone might ask us to consider a fourth version of the restaurant case. We stipulate that Sylvia finds Bernard very congenial and would love to be a friend of his. Being rather shy, she has not, however, given any indication of this. Imagine now that he asks: 'Shall *we* share a pastry?' In such a situation she is unlikely to force him back to 'you' and 'I'. She would say, rather, 'Yes, let's.'

The likelihood of an 'accepting' reply in this context does not prove, however, that Bernard would have been correct to use a full-blooded 'we' just in case he and Sylvia were in fact both willing to engage in the relevant type of joint action.

This case could be one best described as involving a tendentious 'we' which is *met*. That is, Bernard could be, and be known to be, using 'we' in a full-blooded way when this is not strictly speaking appropriate. It could also be understood that if Sylvia *accepts* that 'we' can be said of them here, she thereby makes it appropriate – but only after the fact of Bernard's tendentious use.

In this version of the restaurant case, just as Sylvia is likely to be glad that Bernard spoke of them both as 'we', and not to be inclined to object to his mode of address, she is also likely to be *surprised* by it, albeit pleasantly. One possible source of such surprise is that, in the circumstances, 'we' was not yet properly said of them, in spite of their actual mutual interest in joint action.

To continue the discussion in slightly more formal terms, let me first formulate hypothesis H1:

> The full-blooded 'we' in 'Shall we do A?' is correctly used by X in relation to X, Y, and Z if and only if each of X, Y, and Z is willing to share in some action or range of actions with X,Y,and Z, in circumstances of the type at issue.

This represents the hypothesis we have been considering in relation to the fourth restaurant case – that the mere fact of general willingness to participate in joint actions ensures the appropriateness of 'we'.

Now, if H1 were right, it could be that X's use of 'we' with respect to herself, Y, and Z, was correct, even though she had no evidence for their views. This would be so, according to H1, as long as each of the three was in fact prepared to share in some particular range of actions with the others. No one need have any clues as to the attitudes and views of the rest on any matter whatsoever, in order for their personal use of 'we' to be correct. Can this be right?

Now the following thought may complicate our appreciation of the situation. Even according to H1, it could be that it would be *irresponsible* of X to think of herself, Y, and Z, as 'us' in the absence of any evidence as to their attitudes. For given her understanding of H1, she knows that 'we' is only correctly ascribed if the others are willing to perform some joint action with her. So her saying 'we' of them in the absence of any relevant evidence about them is what we might call *epistemically* irresponsible. What needs to be decided is whether it is also in some sense semantically or conceptually irresponsible. For instance, does it violate any semantic presuppositions of the use of 'we'? If H1 is correct, it is hard to see how it could. Yet my sense is that it does.

Perhaps the distinction between epistemic and semantic irresponsibility merits some attention, to clarify matters further.

Suppose I use the English term 'brother' in its central, standard sense of *male sibling*. I see a man chatting to you in a lively way. He could perhaps be your brother, though he does not look much like you. I think: her brother does not look much like her. This thought, one may suppose, is epistemically irresponsible. That he is male certainly does not prove that he is anyone's male sibling;

that he is talking to you is hardly evidence that he is *your* male sibling. However, nothing about the facts of which I am aware make it logically impossible for him to be your brother. He *could be* your brother; I might be right about that. What I know, in other words, does not rule out the applicability of the term 'your brother' on *semantic* grounds. My belief that the person talking to you was a woman dressed as a man would, in contrast, rule out the applicability of the term 'brother' to this person. (There could be circumstances in which I had reason to *refer to* someone as 'your brother' while knowing facts which entailed that he could not in fact be your brother. Such uses could not intelligibly be literally meant.)

Going back to my quarry, 'we', the question is whether X is more than epistemically irresponsible in referring to herself, Y, and Z, as 'we', when she has no evidence of their views about her or each other. As I have indicated, I am inclined to think that this is more than epistemically irresponsible. Use of a 'full-blooded' 'we' in such a circumstance would, I think, 'ring false', would strike one as hollow. It seems to *connote* something which is clearly lacking. So much for my intuitions on hypothesis H1.

It may now appear that what is needed to complement H1 is a condition which stipulates simply that each one is aware of the other's attitudes. We might first consider hypothesis H2, which is H1 with the addition that *each one must be aware of the others' willingness to act jointly*. I believe that H2 is also inadequate.

Consider a fifth version of the restaurant case. Imagine that a friend of Bernard's has secretly told Sylvia that Bernard would like to know her better. At the same time, a friend of Sylvia's has secretly told Bernard that Sylvia would like to strike up a friendship with him. Relying on this fact, he addresses Sylvia in the way I have described. Here I do not find a full-blooded, literal use of 'we' in place yet. Bernard is now fairly sure that his use of 'we' will be accepted and endorsed, yet – so my sense of things goes – its full-blooded use here is still semantically inappropriate. Bernard's use of 'we', one might say, can still only be tendentious.

At this point it is natural to venture hypothesis H3. This is H2 plus the idea that each one is aware of each one's willingness by virtue of each one's *expression* of his willingness to the others. I thus reinstate an 'expression' condition which was envisaged earlier.

> In saying 'Shall we do A?' X may use the full-blooded 'we' with regard to himself, Y, and Z, if and only if each of X, Y, and Z is willing to share in doing A with the others in circumstances of the type at issue, and each one knows this as a

result of each one's having, in effect, expressed this willingness to each of the others.

This hypothesis is roughly what I shall end up with. Before developing it further, however, one final aspect needs defence. I am envisaging quite a rich semantics for 'we'. Its two distinct components may be called the *expression* and the *expressed* components. It could be questioned whether we need the latter: is actual willingness to share in an action necessary? Or is all that is required an *expression* of willingness (which could be insincere)? In other words, could it be that 'we' connotes something like: all these people have given some expression of willingness to share in an action (and each one knows this)?

Quite generally, from a speaker's or knower's point of view, the fact that they have knowledge as opposed to belief is never a subjectively relevant fact. That is, I am neither epistemically nor semantically irresponsible in saying that p, if, as far as I can tell, the conditions under which p is true obtain. Thus there is a sense in which someone can appropriately apply a term when the semantic conditions for its applicability are not fulfilled. Let us say that his use is then *epistemically appropriate*. Meanwhile there is obviously a sense in which his application of the term is not then appropriate: the term in question does not in fact apply. Let us say that his use is *semantically inappropriate. In discussing the question of when 'we' is appropriately used I mean to be discussing semantic appropriateness*. With this clearly in mind let us turn to the question of the sufficiency of the expression condition.

It is reasonable to propose that generally speaking one will be deemed to use 'we' with epistemic appropriateness if one has good evidence that the expression condition holds. Meanwhile, good evidence for the fulfilment of the expression condition is also, generally speaking, good evidence for the fulfilment of the expressed condition. Hence the truth of the proposal about epistemic appropriateness does not settle the matter as to what 'we' means or connotes. In particular, it is compatible with the expressed condition. Argument on such issues is not easy. Let me offer a few points in favour of the expressed condition.

To begin, I presume that genuine willingness to share in an action often underlies expressions of willingness. I presume, in other words, that the following phenomenon is quite standard: there are expressions of genuine willingness. It would not be untoward if the semantics of 'we' reflected the existence of this phenomenon, that is, if it reflected a way things standardly are. Further, this is an important way things standardly are. It is certainly important to each of us that we can sometimes rely on certain others to share in the relevant action when the time comes. For this reason there seems to be less point in thinking in terms of sets of people who have expressed willingness to do certain things with us, but possibly mendaciously or insincerely, than in thinking in terms of those who have expressed a genuine willingness to join us.

In this connection one might wonder why the *expression* of willingness should be important to us. One possibility is that we are concerned here with a psychological state that is only brought into a reliably robust state by being expressed. It may be easy for me to say to myself that I am willing to fly to Paris with you or to marry you when I am not likely to have my willingness put to the test. One condition making such testing less likely is my never having expressed such willingness to you. Perhaps I can be genuinely willing to do these things with you even though I have never expressed my willingness. One can grant this while accepting that my willingness may well not be very robust if I have never got past the point of expressing it. It could be that I would find myself freezing up if I tried to express it. In this case it is not very hardy. (A case which may be fairly common is that of someone who erroneously thinks he or she is about to utter (and complete) a proposal of marriage.)

Given that the stability or robustness of each one's individual willingness to share an action is important, then, a semantic lawgiver could reasonably insist that I not count as part of a 'we' unless I have expressed my willingness to all. I must take it out of my private world and put it out in the open. There are reasons, then, why 'we' should have precisely the semantics I conjecture for it here.

Finally, here is a thought-experiment in favour of a condition requiring actual willingness. Suppose that in my company you have enthusiastically expressed willingness to partner me at chess sometime. Later a mutual friend tells me how embarrassed you were to have been confronted with this issue and how ashamed you are of having deceptively expressed willingness to play with me. In fact, you have said to our friend, if I were to ask you to play chess you would have to refuse. You simply could not face the embarrassment it would cause you. Knowing all these things, I suggest that it would be odd of me to say to you 'Shall we play chess?' Now of course it would be odd for many reasons. But I suggest that part of the oddness would be its semantic irresponsibility: I know you are not prepared to play chess with me and thus I know that the conditions for a proper use of 'we' here are not satisfied.

3.7 Refining the hypothesis

I have arrived, then, at the following hypothesis (H3).

> In saying 'Shall we do A?' X may use the full-blooded 'we'
> with regard to himself, Y, and Z, if and only if each of X, Y,
> and Z is willing to share in doing A with the others in
> circumstances of the type at issue, and each one knows this as a
> result of each one's having, in effect, expressed this willingness
> to each of the others.

This now requires further articulation and expansion.

(i) Quasi-readiness

Enemy troops can be heard advancing through the woods. The
partisans pick up their weapons. They exchange glances. One
says to the others: 'Well, we're ready.' From this scene we can
abstract a concept of *joint readiness*. I propose that we can best
sum up the conditions of appropriateness for 'Shall we do A?' in
terms of this concept, which first needs a more careful
introduction.

Consider what it is to be ready to do A oneself (where a joint
action is not in question). To be ready to do A oneself is not
necessarily to be about to do A, or to be poised to do A, where
one's doing A is immediately imminent. I may be ready to be
pleasant to any one of my friends, even though I am not about to
see or speak to any of them. Their still being my friends demands
(on some views of friendship, anyway) that I am ready to be
pleasant to them if and when I see them. It does not entail that I
am to be in contact with any of them ever again. I may not, then,
be about to be pleasant to them, though I am ready, or in a state
of readiness, to be pleasant to them. Being ready to do A is,
meanwhile, a more active matter than merely approving of the
idea that one do A when appropriate. It could be described as
having 'set oneself up' to do A if and when the appropriate time
comes. Readiness to do A oneself involves, intuitively, a state or
disposition of the will, a kind of engagement to act when the
appropriate conditions obtain, rather than (or rather than only) a
kind of thought or attitude regarding one's so acting.

So much for readiness to do A oneself. What is it, however,
that one must manifest in the case in point, when one manifests
readiness to do A *jointly* with certain others? It is presumably not
the case that one must manifest readiness to strive for the
relevant end by oneself. For doing A jointly with others, as I

argued in the previous section of this chapter, requires that the people involved *together* perform the action. So, should one manifest readiness to do A together with the others? Though I think this is right, it could do with some unpacking from the point of view of precision.

Now, it is by no means inconsequential that I cannot do A jointly with certain others unless they do A jointly with me. For, as a result, there seems to be a sense in which I cannot, independently of others, be *ready* to play tennis, for instance, in the sense in which I can be ready to be pleasant to my friends. In the latter case, the only relevant state of will is mine: in the former this is not so. If, however, it is impossible by one's own efforts to be ready to act jointly, it presumably cannot be required that one manifest readiness of this specific kind.

What, then, can be required in this area ? Consider the sort of thing one sometimes says. Asked by one's spouse, for example, if one is ready to go for a projected walk, one says 'I'm ready if you are.' (Or, perhaps, 'I'm ready when you are.') This familiar, humdrum type of statement suggests the possibility of a somewhat complex state of affairs, if it does not connote one. The situation to which the speaker refers may be as follows:

(1) Independently of you, I am in a certain state with respect to my will. Call this state *quasi-readiness*.

(2) In order for the required state of readiness for the relevant joint action to be reached, it is necessary that you too be quasi-ready.

(3) At that point, in so far as the state of our wills is concerned, we will be *jointly ready*.

(4) Only then will each of us personally *participate in joint readiness*.

The set of points (1) to (4) seems to characterize the situation of those who are, as far as is in their own power, 'ready' to share in a certain action in certain circumstances. Assuming that this is so, I now partially reformulate hypothesis H3 in terms of quasi-readiness as follows (H3'):

In saying 'Shall we do A?' X may use the full-blooded 'we' with regard to X, Y, and Z, only if each one is quasi-ready to perform A with the others . . .

(ii) Common knowledge

H3' does not claim to give sufficient conditions for the

appropriate use of 'we' in the full-blooded, non-tendentious sense, but only to spell out a crucial necessary condition. This is a condition concerning the volitional states of the persons involved. As became evident earlier, it is not enough for the parties concerned to be in the required volitional states. It seems that, in addition, each one must at least know that each one is in the relevant volitional state, and know that they are, not just anyhow, but via something like each one's manifesting his quasi-readiness to each of the others. This may suggest that we move, finally, to H3'':

> In saying 'Shall we do A?' X may use 'we' in its full-blooded sense with regard to X,Y, and Z if and only if each of X, Y, and Z knows that he and the others are individually quasi-ready to share in doing A, and they know this on the basis of each one's having expressed his quasi-readiness to each of the others.

This does not seem to be quite right, however. Consider the following case.

Angela knows that Charles is quasi-ready to go on vacation trips with her and Basil, since he has made this abundantly clear to her. She is in the same position regarding Basil. In sum, she knows that she herself, Charles, and Basil are all quasi-ready to go on vacation trips together. She also knows that each of them knows this. For she has observed that each has openly expressed his readiness to each of the others individually, and the person addressed has clearly received the message. Thus Angela knows that the condition postulated by H3'' is satisfied. Does she know enough appropriately to use 'we' in its full sense of herself, Charles, and Basil?

Consider what may be missing. Angela may have no idea whether Basil knows of her knowledge of his knowledge of their common quasi-readiness. For instance, Basil may have mentioned it quite secretly, as he thought, to Charles, quite unaware that Angela had overheard them. He did not realize that she was just outside the door. As far as Angela knows, her use of the first person plural pronoun could come as a surprise to any one of them if, when they happen to find themselves together, she says 'How about our going to France this summer?' for example. This suggests that her use of 'we' will not yet be fully justified or appropriate.

Let us consider what may be needed to eliminate the possibility of an element of surprise at Angela's use of 'we'. Suppose that Angela and the others have converged for lunch at a cafeteria table. She says: 'How many of you people would like to come with me on a vacation trip this year, if it can be arranged?' Suppose that they both enthusiastically say they would. Each one's expression of quasi-readiness for the shared action is thus made entirely overtly, in the presence of all. I take it that if Angela then said, 'Would we best go to France or to Italy?' her use of 'we' would be quite unexceptionable.

How is one to spell out what has been achieved in this case? It can surely be said that each one will now know that each of them is quasi-ready for joint action. It can surely also be said that each will know that each one has this knowledge. But actually something more, and something deeper, seems to have been achieved.

A number of philosophers, beginning with David Lewis and Stephen Schiffer, have tried to describe cases like this. A considerable literature has arisen on what has come to be called (following Lewis) 'common knowledge'.[27] The 'discovery' of common knowledge is one of the most exciting discoveries of recent years. The best way to describe or define 'common knowledge', however, is still somewhat moot.

Let me now describe what I think is most importantly at issue in the cafeteria case. In accordance with tradition, I shall call what I describe 'common knowledge'. What I say is both tentative and somewhat rough. None the less the discussion will be fairly complicated, since a number of technical terms will be introduced. In spite of this, the general idea should be clear enough from a quick perusal.

Situations like the encounter in the cafeteria involve a set of human beings in a special perceptual relation to each other and to a fact such as the fact that each has expressed quasi-readiness to share in some action. I shall call such situations 'paradigm situations of common knowledge'. Their important general features include the following, for any participants A, B, and C. (Any number of persons greater than one could in principle be involved, given the feasible limits of perception.)

(1) A, B, C are normal human beings. In particular they have normal perceptual organs functioning normally, and they have normal reasoning capacities.

(2) A, B, C have similar conceptual equipment. In particular, they have the concepts they need in order to fulfil the other conditions.

(3) A, B, and C perceive each other.

(4) A, B, and C perceive that (1) and (2).

(5) p. (For instance, each has expressed quasi-readiness to share in action A.)

(6) A, B, and C perceive that p

(7) A, B, and C perceive each other perceiving that p.

Now let me introduce a technical concept of my own. The *smooth reasoner counterpart* of a person, X, is, roughly, a being otherwise like X, but whose reasoning is untramelled by limits of time, memory capacity, and perseverance. Otherwise its perceptual and conceptual equipment and background assumptions are the same as X's. X's smooth reasoner counterpart represents, roughly, the power of the principles of inference that X has grasped.

Let us assume that X himself is disposed to reason in accordance with these principles on the basis of any evidence of which he is aware, except in so far as lack of time, memory, and concentration prevent this. We can then take it that his smooth reasoner counterpart *will infer* that p from evidence E, where, roughly, X would infer that p on evidence E (plus any given background assumption) given none of the usual distractions and human limitations.[28]

Suppose now that persons A, B, and C, are in situation S, which has properties (1) to (7) above, in relation to the fact that each of A, B, and C has expressed quasi-readiness to share in a certain action. Next, consider the situation S'. We stipulate that S' is like S, except that A, B, and C are replaced by their smooth reasoner counterparts A', B', and C'. Premises corresponding to (1) to (7) above are true of A', B', and C'. The only premise we need to change in content is (1), which becomes: (1') A', B', and C' resemble normal human beings in that they have the normal human perceptual organs functioning normally. We also need to add, as an assumption: (8') A', B', and C' perceive that they are all smooth reasoners. That is, they perceive that they will all reason their way to whatever conclusion is warranted by the evidence, untramelled by limitations of time, and so on. (We assume that the fact that one is a smooth reasoner is directly perceivable – it shows on one's face.)

A neat account of the crucial feature of S' uses some set theory, but those with no set theory should get the idea.

First, as most discussions of common knowledge imply, S' is such that:

(Z(1)) Each one of A', B', and C' has expressed his quasi-readiness to travel together with the others.
(Z(2)) A', B', and C' will infer that Z(1).

(Z(3)) A', B', and C' will infer that Z(2).
And so on, ad infinitum.

Call this property $Z(\omega)$. 'Common knowledge' is standardly defined in terms of the infinite chain of knowledge corresponding to $Z(\omega)$, and stops there.[29] However, there appears to be no good reason for stopping at one level of infinity. If knowledge can already go 'so far', there seems no reason not to go further.

If we ourselves can see that the property $Z(\omega)$ obtains in S', then presumably the smooth reasoner counterpart of a normal adult human being who finds himself in S' will be able to infer that $Z(\omega)$ obtains. But this is stronger than any of the individual inferences contained in $Z(\omega)$ and ought to be recorded separately. Hence:

(Z(ω+1)) A', B', and C' will infer $Z(\omega)$.

But if we draw this conclusion, so can A', B', and C'. Hence:

(Z (ω+2)) A', B', and C' will infer that $Z(\omega+1)$.

And similarly, for all finite n:

(Z(ω)+n) A', B', and C' will infer that $Z(\omega+(n-1))$.

But then, we can summarize all these properties in:

(Z(ω+ω)) A', B', and C' will infer all the $Z(\omega+n)$.

But once again, since *we* can know $Z(\omega+\omega)$, so can A', B', C'. So the process starts again, giving properties $Z(\omega+\omega+1)$, $Z(\omega+\omega+2)$, etc., summed up in a property $Z(\omega+\omega+\omega)$. And so on. Nor does the process stop at $Z(\omega)$, $Z(\omega+\omega)$, $Z(\omega+\omega+\omega)$, and all these. After all of them, there is a property

(Z(ω^2)) A', B', and C' will infer that all of $Z(\omega)$, $Z(\omega+\omega)$,
and so on, obtain.

Then the process goes on again, since A', B', and C' will infer that $Z(\omega^2)$.

The reader familiar with set theory will see that we can formulate an appropriate property $Z(\alpha)$ for every 'ordinal number' α. In a situation of the kind in question, there seems to be no reason not to conclude that *all* the $Z(\alpha)$ ought to obtain.[30] Readers unfamiliar with set theory may not be able to set out the matter as rigorously, but they should be able to get the rough idea: in some sense, there is 'no limit' to the iteration of the intuitive idea. Apparently, then, S' has a rather fabulous property: all the $Z(\alpha)$ obtain in relation to the participants. Call this property of a situation, property $Z(\alpha)$.

I shall say that the fact that p is *open** *to* persons A, B, and C in a situation S if and only if the situation S' in which A, B, and C are replaced by their smooth reasoner counterparts has the analogue of property $Z(\alpha)$ with respect to those counterparts and the fact that p.

I am going to suppose that human beings generally possess the concept of openness*, and that this is effectively known by all adult humans. I find this assumption plausible. If something like it is *not* true, I do not see how adequately to characterize situations like the cafeteria case. Locutions like 'Everything is out in the open' may reflect a grasp of the concept of openness* and exemplify its application to a concrete case. It is also clear that the concept of openness* can be explicated in its essentials to someone without great mathematical sophistication. Let me say, finally, that I do not find it surprising that the content of an everyday concept appears to be extremely rich and fine-grained. It would be odd to find anyone capable of grasping detailed and fine-grained explicit definitions, if humans generally lacked the capacity to grasp such concepts at a different, implicit, or tacit level. Ultimately the same capacity surely has to be at issue in grasp of explicit definitions or of concepts at a more tacit level.

I can now describe a crucial general feature of paradigm situations of common knowledge. (This can be derived from the basic features (1) to (7) noted above, in particular given the premise that the participants have normal human reasoning capacities.)

(8) The fact that p is open* to A, B, and C.

It will also be the case that

(9) A, B, and C have the concept of openness*.

And

(10) A, B, and C know that (9).

Now it seems reasonable to suppose that if someone has the concept of openness* and p is open* to him and certain others, then (other things being equal) he will know that it is. He will realize or perceive or notice the openness*.[31] Hence the last central feature in this list may be expected, in general, when the others are present:

(11) A, B, and C perceive that (8), that is, they perceive that the fact that p is open* among them.

Conditions (1) to (11), then, complete my account of a *paradigm situation of common knowledge* involving A, B, C, and the fact that p.[32] I shall say that *it is common knowledge among A, B, and C that p*, when they are in a paradigm situation of common knowledge with respect to p.

Can common knowledge as characterized so far be a common or garden phenomenon? I agree that either common knowledge as characterized so far is very common, or the account is wrong. For I presume that the phenomenon in question is ubiquitous. As far as I can tell, however, there is nothing in the account which shows that common knowledge can only occur in an epistemological greenhouse.

Now let me spell out some apparent further features of a typical paradigm situation of common knowledge.

(1) First, if we are dealing with normal mature humans, one can argue that those in a typical paradigm situation of common knowledge not only know that p is open* among them (which they do by definition) but also know that this is so. Lewis and others have attempted to articulate a feature of actual common knowledge situations, one that is especially obvious in typical paradigm situations, that will guarantee this result. (See below, p. 195.) Aside from such formal arguments, informal reflection on such paradigm situations as the cafeteria case, using considerations such as I have used to support knowledge of openness*, seems to support knowledge of such knowledge. Hence I shall regard it as a standard (though not a defining) feature of paradigm situations of common knowledge that *the existence of common knowledge is known to the participants.*

(2) By an extension of the reasoning involved in (1) above, we can argue that it will be known to the participants that the common knowledge is known to each of them. How far, though, can we go with these iterations? There is surely no danger of a vicious infinite regress here. We can go on as far as is reasonable, given the human capacity for knowledge.

(3) *If* one allows that X *knows* that p if, roughly, X would infer that p given sufficient time, attention, memory capacity, etc., it seems that if there is a paradigm situation of common knowledge, the conditions laid down in a standard account of common knowledge are fulfilled. This is an account in terms of the infinite series beginning: p, X knows that p, Y knows that p, X knows that Y knows that p, Y knows that X knows that p. Indeed, the conditions laid down in a stronger account in which the existence of the first series is known, known to be known, and so on, will be fulfilled. And so on.

I prefer an account in terms of knowledge of openness*.

Probably the main reason is that I think it captures better the flavour of the situations in question, such as the cafeteria case. For these involve, I would argue, a *sense of openness**, albeit an inarticulate sense.

It also avoids some objections in terms of the capacity of our minds. Apart from the problems of distracting 'noise' in our systems, people have cited the fact that we seem incapable of explicitly entertaining very 'long' or 'complex' propositions. Hence, how can we properly be said to know that they are true?[33] I am not entirely sure how well defined the notion of a long or complex proposition is, as opposed to a long or complex sentence. This is one reason that the force of these objections is not entirely clear to me. In any case, I am not committed to the idea that anyone ever has to think explicitly that, say, A knows that B knows that A knows that B knows that A knows that . . . where there are five hundred more 'knows that' clauses before we get to 'knows that p'.

The force of objections in terms of our capacity for entertaining 'long and complex propositions' is in any case weak, if we take these other accounts of common knowledge to use a strongly counterfactual account of knowledge (X knows that p if he would infer that p, given some things were true of him which are not, such as increased time available, a better memory). As I have indicated, such accounts may best be construed as saying, roughly, that X knows that p if the principles of inference he grasps lead to p, given the evidence available to X.[34] On the other hand, given that the account of knowledge involves suppositions sufficiently contrary to fact, it is unclear how very long chains of 'knowings about knowings' can be of much relevance to what anybody does or thinks. It seems it could only be relevant if people somehow know that they have this 'knowledge'.[35] It is not necessary for me to take a stand on the relevant questions about the definition of knowledge here. Suffice it to say that the only knowledge I posit here is knowledge no one would reasonably doubt could be made explicit fairly easily by a mature adult human. I posit, of course, that what one knows involves a grasp of the 'fabulous' power of our principles of inference. As indicated, I do not believe that any objection in terms of the 'complexity' of the thought is germane here.

(4) Pretheoretically it seems that in a paradigm situation of common knowledge one will feel free to act in the light of the commonly known fact among other participants. For example, he will feel licenced to take the kettle off the stove if it is common knowledge among those present that the kettle is whistling

loudly. What this 'freedom' and 'licence' seem to amount to quite generally is this: he can rely on *no one's being taken by surprise* if he acts on the assumption that the fact in question obtains. As its context in my own discussion suggests, in seeking an account of common knowledge one is in part seeking an account of a phenomenon such that, for a given proposition p, acts which are premised on the belief or assumption that p will surprise no one if this phenomenon is present.

Can one articulate an explanation of the view that one can rely on a lack of surprise in paradigm situations of common knowledge? A rough explanation may be given as follows. It is a particular kind of surprise that is avoided. Surprise which would be expressed in terms like these: 'I didn't realize he knew the kettle was whistling'; and 'I didn't realize that he knew that I knew that the kettle was whistling', and so on. Presumably the 'and so ons' in this case go no further than a human being can reasonably be expected to think. Now, given my account of them, paradigm situations of common knowledge are clearly apt to ground inferences, for each participant, that cover all the cases of 'He knows that p'; 'He knows that I know that p'; and so on, that can be thought. Given the relatively few levels of knowledge at issue, one may presume that all levels a given person is likely to encompass at all in thought will have been encompassed already, along with the rest of the common knowledge conditions. Hence each one will indeed realize that each one knows the kettle is whistling, and so on. This would obviate any surprise once the act premised on the fact that p occurred. And each party will normally know this is so.

In sum, paradigm situations of common knowledge in my sense, then, may be expected to have the *presupposition-licencing* or *surprise-avoiding* nature of situations of common knowledge, which is evident pretheoretically. In what follows I shall accordingly make the following assumptions. (a) If it is common knowledge that p among persons A, B, and C, then (all else being equal) no one will be surprised if one of their number acts on the assumption that p. (b) Consistently with this, and, again, all else being equal, no one will feel justified, among the persons concerned, in publicly questioning whether p, doubting whether p, or denying that p or that any obvious part of p holds. Common knowledge is a potent conversational force.[36]

I have so far characterized common knowledge in relation to a special, important class of cases, those where the participants are in direct perceptual reach of one another. (The cafeteria case that we have been concerned with is of this type.) A generalized definition of common knowledge can be derived from the one I have given as follows.

> It is *common knowledge among A, B, and C that p*, if and only if (by definition) (1) the fact that p is open* to A, B, and C, and (2) A, B, and C have noticed this.

I am going to assume that, in practice, whenever common knowledge in my sense occurs, there is always a specific underlying type of situation from which it derives, such that: *when it is common knowledge among A, B, and C that p, then A, B, and C know this, know that they know this, and so on* as far as human beings can travel. (See Lewis, 1969, pp. 60–1, for an explicit description of how inferences of the type I am assuming can be derived. See also Schiffer, 1972; Heal, 1978.) I shall not commit myself here to any specific account of the underlying situation, but assume that this situation will resemble those in the analyses cited.

I now return to the cafeteria, where Angela, Basil and Charles have been patiently waiting. I noted that in the situation at the table, once Basil, Charles and Angela have all expressed their quasi-readiness to travel with one another, Angela's asking about where 'we' should go would cause no surprise. It now looks as if we can attribute the absence of surprise to the existence of common knowledge as I have defined this. Common knowledge is, I contend, a common or garden phenomenon. Moreover, it is not clear that anything else of this sort could have excluded surprise so effectively. I shall now take it that common knowledge of mutually expressed quasi-readiness was a necessary condition for Angela's appropriate use of 'we'.

Notice that what this implies is not simply that Angela herself must notice the openness* of the expressions of quasi-readiness. If there is to be common knowledge of these expressions, then by definition *everyone* must notice their openness*. Thus everyone must notice the openness* prior to any one person's appropriate use of the full-blooded 'we'. Hence, a justified 'we' user here must know that everyone else has noted the openness*. That is, he must *know that there is common knowledge*. I see no problem with this. For remember that I am assuming that where there *is* common knowledge that p, the parties to it *know* that there is.

Let me now consider whether common knowledge of expressed quasi-readiness may not only be necessary, but also sufficient for Angela's use of the full-blooded 'we'. Consider the following. One might think that there is a sense in which 'we' cannot be used appropriately *by one person alone*. To put it vividly, 'we' can only properly be said in a chorus (by all of us together). This is an attractive suggestion, making a nice parallel between 'we' and 'I'.[37] What difference would the idea that in some sense 'we' can only properly be said by a chorus make to the account of the semantics of 'we' that one might want to give? It would be good if the necessary and sufficient condition for a given person's use of 'we' would at the same time legitimate the relevant others' use also. It would also be good if everyone could be expected to know that these conditions held when they did. Then one might feel no explicit chorus would be necessary. We could presume the endorsement of any one person's legitimate use of 'we'.

It turns out (rather wonderfully) that the proposed sufficient condition of common knowledge of expressed quasi-readiness has the desired features. For suppose that this is known by all to be sufficient for 'we' on the part of each. Then, whenever X uses 'we' appropriately, everyone else is licenced to do so, and everyone knows this (given the nature of common knowledge).

If my 'common knowledge' condition, then, is sufficient for Angela's use of the full-blooded 'we' to be appropriate, in so far as a single person's use can be, it is also sufficient for everyone else's full-blooded 'we' to be appropriate. If she is justified in saying 'we', so are all the relevant others. In effect, her use of 'we', of the others, is only proper when they may say 'we' also. A solo use is only appropriate when a chorus is also.

Suppose that common knowledge of expressed quasi-readiness is indeed logically sufficient for an appropriate use of 'we' by an individual in Angela's situation. Imagine that we are in the cafeteria before Angela uses 'we', but after common knowledge of expressed quasi-readiness has been established. We will predict that Angela's use of 'we' in the cafeteria case *will be endorsed* by all. Certainly, no one will question it. No one has any grounds in terms of which to question it. More, given that they all understand the semantics of 'we', all will understand that they too may speak similarly. Indeed, they are obligated to endorse such speech on the part of any of their number, and will realize this. When they hear her saying 'we' they will not think 'we?', but rather, 'ah, yes, we'. Observers knowing the (proposed) semantics of 'we' can predict this, so can Angela, and so can everyone else in the situation. This prediction gives the right results, intuitively. This gives some support to the idea that we have arrived at a sufficient condition for the use of 'we' in a particular context. I believe that, to all intents and purposes, we have. Before officially presenting that condition, there are a few more things to cover.

I want to add two wrinkles without much argument. Both appear to be implicit in my description of the cafeteria case. First, each person's expression of quasi-readiness must be one he intended to give and gave in part by virtue of having that intention. Thus it is not, for example, a reflex movement which expresses his quasi-readiness. Second, let us say that someone expresses his quasi-readiness *openly** if and only if he intends his expression to be open* to all. I take it that we presume, when we take expressions of quasi-readiness to licence 'we', that not only were these expressions in fact open* to all relevant parties, but that they were intended to be. I shall assume, then, that what is required is common knowledge that a meshing set of *intentional* expressions of quasi-readiness have been *made openly**. So as not to complicate my discussion unnecessarily, in what follows I shall generally take these two wrinkles as read.

(iii) Joint readiness

I can now stop talking about 'quasi-readiness'. I shall take it that common knowledge among X, Y, and Z of their mutually expressed quasi-readiness to share in action A in C entails the actual *joint readiness* of X, Y, and Z, taken together, so to act. Nothing more is needed before all can be sure that *it is appropriate to begin acting on the presumption of joint readiness*. I shall take it, then, that

> a set of persons are jointly ready to share in action A in
> circumstances C if and only if it is common knowledge among
> them that they have mutually expressed their quasi-readiness
> so to share.

If 'in circumstances C' is replaced by 'here and now' joint readiness to share in action A will presumably amount to current joint espousal of the relevant goal. Each will then immediately be obligated to engage in whatever behaviour on his part seems called for.[38] A *joint action* will occur if and only if each of X, Y, and Z acts *in the light of their joint espousal of the goal in question*, in such a way that the goal is achieved. I say more on the nature of joint action in my concluding chapter.

Joint readiness in general does not entail joint espousal of a goal now, nor entail that it is now in order for each person concerned to act appropriately to the current joint espousal of some goal. If we are jointly ready to attack the enemy if the enemy attacks, then we will individually act to promote the joint goal of attacking the enemy only at the time the enemy is perceived to attack. This is what our joint readiness obliges us, individually, to do.

(iv) A pool of wills

One might say that one who expresses quasi-readiness to do A in

C in effect *volunteers his will* for a pool of wills to be set up so that in certain circumstances, that pool will be dedicated to a certain end.[39] His understanding is that *just in case his so volunteering is matched* by that of the relevant others, etc., *the pool will be so set up.* This formulation is strongly reminiscent of Rousseau's *Social Contract*: 'since men cannot engender new forces, but merely unite and direct existing ones, they...form by aggregation a sum of forces, so that their forces are directed by a single moving power and made to act in concert.'[40]

Another way of describing the situation is that each person expresses a *conditional commitment.* In the case of joint readiness, the conditional commitment is to the joint espousal of certain goals, and appropriate action, when the time comes. Each one's understanding is that when the set of open* conditional commitments is common knowledge, these people will be *jointly committed* to do A together when the time comes, or whatever. (No one will be individually committed to anything independently of the others.) Each party to the joint commitment will have certain ensuing entitlements and obligations.

The above formulation and the previous 'pool of wills' formulation can be run together to give what is perhaps the most perspicuous of the three. The expression of quasi-readiness involves *a conditional commitment of one's will*, made with the understanding that if and only if it is common knowledge that the relevant others have expressed similar commitments, the wills in question are unconditionally and jointly committed. In the case of readiness for an action in given circumstances, the wills are together committed or dedicated to the pursuit of the goal in question in the circumstances.

More will be said about the force of these formulations later. At this point, let me simply say that if we go as deeply as possible into the explication of vernacular notions like that of doing things together, it seems that formulations like this will eventually be reached.

In the case of action it has been useful to distinguish a distinct state of 'joint readiness' for action when the time comes, as opposed to the current joint acceptance or pursuit of a goal. In the case of shared belief and attitude, time and circumstance indexing do not seem to be appropriate. Hence a distinct state of joint readiness will not be distinguished for these cases. My account of shared beliefs and the like has not yet been presented, but the general idea of *conditional commitment of the will* applies to them also.

Yet another way of putting things, which I take to be implied by the above, is that the expression of quasi-readiness is

198

tantamount to the expression of willingness to be jointly responsible with certain others for the doing of certain things when the time comes. Again the thought involved here will include an understanding that one will indeed be jointly responsible for performing the relevant joint action with those others, provided only that all have openly matched one's expression of willingness in a situation of common knowledge.

The expression of quasi-readiness, then, turns out to be a complex kind of expression, involving an understanding that one conditionally commits one's own will in a certain way, and that it will indeed be so committed, under certain circumstances not at one's own disposal. That is, the circumstances in which it is common knowledge that all concerned have expressed their own quasi-readiness.

(v) The refined hypothesis

I conclude that there is reason to accept H4:

> A person X's full-blooded use of 'we' in 'Shall we do A?' with respect to Y, Z, and himself, is appropriate if and only if it expresses his recognition of the fact that he and the others are jointly ready to share in doing A in relevant circumstances.

For the purposes of this hypothesis it is assumed that people are jointly ready if and only if it is common knowledge among them that each has openly* manifested to all his quasi-readiness to share some action in the circumstances in question.

3.8 Plural subjects

When I discussed the concept of sharing in an action, prior to discussing the semantics of 'we', I introduced the technical term 'plural subject'. I noted then that a condition on shared or joint action seemed to be that each must make clear his willingness to accept a certain goal jointly with certain others. I then rephrased this with what seemed like an appropriate technical terminology: each must manifest willingness to constitute with the other a *plural subject* of the relevant goal. I have not used this phrase yet in the course of my discussion of 'we'. It is now time to reintroduce it. For it can enable us to give a compact general account of the semantics of 'we'.

Construing 'action' very broadly, the label 'plural subject' seems appropriate to all the cases of *joint* action so far considered. Thus we can say that those who currently jointly accept a goal (such as those on the verge of starting a conversation) constitute the plural subject of the goal, even if they have not yet started to act in terms of it. *A fortiori*, those currently engaged in (joint) pursuit of a joint goal constitute a plural subject. (Example: those travelling together, each keeping an eye on the other so as to reach their goal more effectively.) Finally, those who are jointly ready to do something together in certain circumstances constitute a plural subject if the others do. The intuitive notion of *joining forces* is surely as apposite here as it is for the case of joint acceptance of a goal.

As I have argued, joint readiness can be described as involving a pool of wills constituted in a specific way in relation to what may happen. Such a description is apposite also for the joint acceptance of a goal now. Evidently plural subjecthood in general is a matter of there being a plurality of wills dedicated to something. It also appears that, quite generally, *to become the member of a plural subject of some kind one must openly* express one's willingness to do so* with certain others. And it must be common knowledge among the parties that one has done this. The case I have discussed so far in the greatest detail is in effect the case of a *plural subject of readiness* jointly to accept a certain goal when the time comes. Instead of speaking of 'quasi readiness' we can now say that to be jointly ready to do A in C, people must *express their willingness to be part of a plural subject of* readiness. Similarly, we could speak of the quasi-acceptance of a goal, or of willingness to be part of the plural subject of a goal.

3.9 On the referent of 'we'

What, then, of the semantics of 'we'? I have argued that there is a sense of 'we' such that it refers, for example, to those who currently jointly accept a certain goal, and to those who are jointly ready for something. In other words, it can be used whenever people constitute plural subjects of two distinct kinds. This consideration strongly suggests, if it does not prove, the general hypothesis H5:

> There is a central sense of 'we' such that 'we' refers to a plural subject.

We can leave aside for now any detailed discussion of the range of possible properties of plural subjects. But since I believe that these cover beliefs and attitudes in general as well as actions (and the special attitude of 'readiness') my hypothesis about 'we' here in effect includes a reference to these, specifically. (I attempt to justify my belief in the following chapters.) Thus another way of putting H5 is as follows:

'We' refers to a set of people each of whom shares with oneself in some action, belief, attitude, or other such attribute.

It is important to note that 'shares' is understood in a strong sense, such that those who share in an action, and so on, constitute the plural subject of the action. This is clearly an importantly different, much richer and more subtle sense than that according to which we share in an action, belief, or whatever, if we all personally perform that action, have that belief, and so on.[41]

Further considerations which support H5 will be adduced in later discussion, in particular in a discussion of the role of 'we' statements in practical reasoning, in the final chapter. For now, I shall stop arguing in support of H5.

Waiving issues about the precise semantics of English, it is clear that H5 provides conditions on the appropriateness of an important type of *thought*, a type of thought in terms of which a social group might plausibly be defined along Simmelian lines. This may be called a 'we'-thought. The question of what thoughts and experiences are possible in the absence of a given linguistic item is an important one. It can hardly be doubted, however, that there are ways of thinking, feeling, and experiencing which cannot be captured exactly by any existing compact description.[42] In what follows I shall use the term 'we*' rather than 'we', to avoid confusion and any contentiousness about my account of 'we'. I hereby stipulate that 'we*' is appropriately uttered under the conditions hypothesized for the English 'we' in H5. I shall, similarly, refer to the correlative kinds of thoughts as 'we*-thoughts', the asterisk indicating that the pronoun in question is to be interpreted as 'we' is interpreted in H5.

One rightly views oneself and certain others as 'we*', or rightly has a we*-thought about them, then, if and only if one appropriately sees these persons and oneself as constituting a plural subject. For example, one observes that it is common knowledge that each has openly* expressed quasi-readiness to share in action A next week, and one knows that this is a logically sufficient condition for joint readiness to share in A. Thus one knows that the people in question constitute a *plural subject* of readiness. Hence, one views these people as 'us*'.

Now, given that someone has indeed openly* expressed quasi-readiness, then we can take it that he has a grasp of the connected concepts of quasi-readiness and joint readiness. He knows, in particular, that if certain people have openly* expressed their quasi-readiness to do A together and this is common knowledge between them, then they are jointly ready to do A. It follows that if he and any others are jointly ready for something he will know that they are. For in common knowledge situations the participants know that there is common knowledge. Hence whenever the condition necessary and sufficient for joint readiness is fulfilled, each participant will know that it is. Each will know that they are jointly ready. More generally, one can conclude that, first, *one will view oneself as a member of a plural subject if one is indeed such a member.* Second, *if there is a plural subject its component persons will all have we*-thoughts which refer to it.* And, third, *if one has a term for 'we*' one will see that it is justified when it is.*

This result implies that if one is inclined in this general direction, there is not really much to choose between defining a social group in terms of a set of persons having correct we*-thoughts (as in the earliest formulation I gave) and defining one in terms of a plural subject as this has been explicated. These conditions are distinct, but they are so tightly connected that they will always give the same result. If one takes the basic condition on collectivity-hood, then, to be plural subjecthood, one will in effect accept that an appropriate we*-thought is a necessary and sufficient condition, also.

3.10 'We*' and common knowledge

Before leaving the semantics of 'we', or, more guardedly, 'we*', I should like to make a point about the relation between appropriateness conditions for 'we*' and common knowledge in general. It could seem plausible to suppose that common knowledge of anything whatever automatically justifies a use of 'we*'. Is there not something 'we*' know, it may be queried. If so, then 'we*' has a referent. My account of 'we*' implies that common knowledge alone is not enough to produce a 'we*' in the sense at issue. From a logical point of view, common knowledge can exist though there is no plural subject.

Let us briefly consider a concrete case, which will exemplify how common knowledge as defined here can be present and much else be lacking. Janet strolls in Magnolia Park past two boys, David and Joshua, who are playing together. It could be common knowledge among Janet, David, and Joshua, that she is strolling past them. She would not, then, expect a startled jump from either one if she started to address them. (She might get one, but not because they did not realize she was there at all, or did not realize that she knew they were there, and so on.) But it is hard to argue that Joshua, David, and Janet form a plural subject at this point. There have been no expressions of willingness to share in any actions, or anything similar. Should Janet address them with, say, 'Which way to Cedar Lane?' and they reply in chorus, things immediately change. Now there is a plural subject by reason of facts other than the mere existence of common knowledge among the three. The three have engaged in a verbal interchange of the right type, involving everyone in playing an appropriate role so that there be an answered question.

Common knowledge is one thing, then, and plural subjects are another. Common knowledge does not automatically give rise to plural subjecthood, though it is a requirement of plural subjecthood. For plural subjecthood, people must 'get together' in a way other than the special mesh produced by common knowledge.

The question of when it is proper to claim that *we* know something is an interesting issue. I shall touch on it briefly in the course of my discussion of group belief. For now suffice it to say that 'we*' in 'we* know' or with any other predicate is not licensed just by virtue of common knowledge as that has been defined here. This suggests, of course, that there is a unique type of knowledge which could be *called* 'common knowledge' such that we have this knowledge *when we* know something*. This seems right. My main point here is that this phenomenon is distinct from the phenomenon of common knowledge as defined here.

Many writers on social phenomena have rightly stressed the importance of what I have been calling common knowledge here.[43] For reasons just indicated, however, the recent focus on common knowledge could have had something of an unfortunate effect on our understanding of social processes. (Amid rather general excitement Charles Taylor expressed scepticism about common knowledge in a number of places.)[44] Though understanding the nature of common knowledge is crucial to the understanding of human social life, it is evidently not the last word on social reality. Indeed, as I shall argue, it is not clear that common knowledge in itself is a matter of *social* reality at all.

4 SOCIAL GROUPS

4.1 Social groups as plural subjects

I am now in a position to present my own account of social groups. In brief, in my view a set of people constitute a social group if and only if they constitute a plural subject. Before proceeding to discuss some implications of my account, it may be useful to review the course of discussion in this chapter so far.

I have been developing a version of Simmel's idea that a social group is a set of people who are conscious that they are linked by a certain special tie. This version is in terms of what I take to be a central sense of the English pronoun 'we': human beings X, Y, Z, constitute a collectivity (social group) if and only if each appropriately thinks of himself and the others as 'us' or 'we'. 'We' in this sense refers to a set of people each of whom *shares with oneself* in some action, belief, attitude, or similar attribute.

In section 2 of the chapter I examined the vernacular notion of sharing in an action. In subsection 2.4 an hypothesis was sketched. In order that two people share in an action each must have made clear to the other that he is willing to join forces with him in accepting the relevant goal. The technical term 'plural subject' was first introduced here. The hypothesis became: each must manifest his willingness to constitute with the other a plural subject of the goal in question. When each has done so, the foundation is laid for each person to act in his capacity as the constituent of a plural subject of the relevant goal.

In section 3 I presented considerations in favour of the idea that there is a central sense of the English pronoun 'we' in which 'we' refers to a plural subject of some kind. This confirms the importance of the plural subject notion. In subsections 3.5, 3.6, and 3.7, I argued that there is a sense of 'we' such that it is inappropriate to say something of the form 'Shall we do action A' unless each of the people concerned has manifested what I dubbed his *quasi-readiness* to share in action A when the right circumstances obtain. When all have manifested this and this is common knowledge, then the parties are *jointly ready* to share in action A in the proper circumstances. But what precisely is it to manifest quasi-readiness? And what, really, is joint readiness? To illuminate these notions further I turned (3.7, sec. iv) to an image of a kind used by Rousseau: in manifesting quasi-readiness each volunteers his will for a 'pool' of wills dedicated to the acceptance of a certain end under certain circumstances. Each understands that when his so volunteering is matched by that of the others, and this is common knowledge, the pool is set up. The wills are now jointly dedicated in the relevant way. Another way of putting this important point is that each expresses a *conditional commitment* of his will, understanding that only if the others express similar commitments are all of the wills jointly committed to accept a certain goal when the time comes. There must also be common knowledge of the individual conditional commitments in order that the joint commitment, with its attendant obligations on individuals, obtain. The general concept of a plural subject subsumes these ways of putting things: we may say that for a set of persons to be jointly *ready* each must openly* express his willingness to be part of a *plural subject of readiness*.

The technical term 'we*' was stipulated to refer to a plural subject. To become the member of a plural subject one must openly* express one's willingness to do so, and it must be common knowledge among those concerned that each of them has done this. A number of plural subject concepts are available. I leave careful discussion of some of these till the following chapters.

Some important aspects of the concept of a plural subject should be stressed. Consider again the complex *logically necessary and sufficient condition* for the existence of a plural subject. This is (to repeat) that a set of persons with the concept of a plural subject must have openly* mutually expressed their willingness to be members of such a subject, and this is common knowledge. This means that only those with the concept of a plural subject can help to constitute such a subject. It also means that those who constitute a plural subject know that they do, and will thus think of themselves as *us**. So, as I have noted, if one takes the basic condition on collectivity-hood to be plural subject-hood, one will accept that an appropriate we*-thought is a necessary and sufficient condition also. (An appropriate we*-thought is not a necessary *precondition*, of course.)

One nice result of an account of social groups in terms of plural subjects will be that groups always have a kind of 'self-knowledge'. That is, the members of any group (plural subject) will all properly think of themselves as 'us*'. (This is not to claim that the members of any group must have a term for 'we*' in a group language or in their various idiolects. I do not mean to presuppose a view on the relation of thoughts about things to labels for them.)

I opt, then, for plural subjecthood as the core condition on collectivity existence. A social group is a plural subject. It has taken some time to explain the fine structure and general nature of the notions central to my account of social groups. More will be said in subsequent chapters. The elaboration and defence of the account of social groups that follows here will be relatively brief. A number of important aspects of the account will be noted. There is not room here to discuss any of them in the depth they deserve. I begin with some general comments on the account.

(1) The idea that social groups are subjects of action and cognition clearly accords with one way in which collectivities are commonly spoken and thought about: we say that Russia invaded Czechoslovakia, Britain devalued the pound, this tribe does not like strangers, this group craves freedom of the press, we are going to France this summer, and so on and on. Of course, exactly how social groups collect particular kinds of attribute is an important issue that has not been resolved here.

One special case may usefully be referred to at once. Often we ascribe an action to a group as a whole when most group members are not directly involved. For instance, in at least two of the above examples what really happens is that a special person or group makes a certain decision and organizes the carrying out of a certain action. All Russians did not share in the act of invading Czechoslovakia in the simple way in which you and I may share in the act of travelling together. Most Russians did not take part in the invasion. Many may not even have heard about it. This is even more obviously true for so-called covert operations that a particular country may engage in. Meanwhile, in order for us to feel comfortable with the idea that a certain group invaded Czechoslovakia, there surely must be a sense in which whoever organized the invasion, and whoever took part in it, was the authorized representative of the group as a whole. In order for that to be so, something like this must be true: members of the group jointly accept that certain decisions of a certain few are to count as our* decisions. Something like that often is true and it seems that in such situations, at least, we can reasonably allow that the group itself has made the decision or performed the act in question.[45]

There may be some cases in which the individual members of a certain population do the bidding of some individual or small group of individuals out of fear and nothing else. Anyone (observers, individual members of the population) could give the population as a whole a name, say, 'the Fearful'. They might think of the feared individual as the 'ruler', 'leader', or 'governor.' If the ruler 'orders' all young male members of the Fearful into battle, and each one complies, we might find ourselves saying that 'the Fearful are at war'. Yet there are surely circumstances in which the Fearful, as so far described, would not constitute a social group or collectivity at all. If it was wrong to think in terms of a genuine collectivity here, then, *a fortiori*, it would be wrong to think of this collectivity as acting, through representatives or in any other way. In this case, then, our using language expressive of concepts relating to groups would be at best misleading, and at worst would embody a mistake.

In the above rough account of the acts and decisions of representatives, I have appealed to the idea of a group as a whole accepting that one thing is to count as something else. A certain individual's or small group's deciding is to count as our* deciding, and so on. This involves, one might feel, a group belief and indeed a group belief of a rather special kind, which might naturally be called a convention. I shall discuss group beliefs and social conventions in more detail in the next two chapters.

In this chapter I have concentrated on the idea of a shared action (and shared readiness for action). It is clear that there is an important concept of shared action which is not a matter of the acts of special representatives, be these individuals or small groups. This is what I have tried to spell out here. For it seems to me that this is the basic case of shared or collective action, just as the parallel case for belief is the basic case for belief. As I have just indicated, the possibility of action through special representatives appears to rest on the possibility of beliefs or conventions of a group as a whole, as opposed to actions of a group as a whole. A thorough understanding of action through special representatives must therefore await consideration of collective beliefs. I can say in advance, however, that in my view a plausible account of group action through the acts of special representatives will not generate any objections to my general account of social groups.

(2) It should be clear that my account of social groups does not entail that every group is *currently pursuing some goal*, or, in that sense, *has goals*. In other words, plural subjects are involved in things other than shared action in a narrow sense. This is shown by the plural subjecthood of those who are jointly ready for action. When people are group members by virtue of joint readiness for action a particular time or circumstance index is involved; the time may be other than now, the circumstances may not currently obtain. For example, I may be quasi-ready to travel with you sometime, but not immediately. It may be understood that a period in which it is appropriate for me to take a vacation from work must come up. Thus it may come about that what *we* are ready to do is to go on vacation as soon as I have a vacation

period. Or we may be ready to chat to each other in the department corridor whenever one of us feels like it, unless someone is late for a class. Our being ready to talk should we meet in the department corridor, and the like, would not naturally be described as a matter of our having a current goal. Even our being ready to dance the next waltz together does not seem to involve our jointly pursuing any end, though we shall do soon.

There are some special cases in which the existence of a joint goal may be implied by readiness to undertake a certain joint action at some future time. Thus it could be argued that if we are ready jointly to repel any aliens who try to enter our island, then we surely have a current goal of keeping the island free from aliens. The basis of the argument would presumably be that one who expresses quasi-readiness to repel any alien intruders in effect expresses a readiness jointly to accept, now, the goal of keeping the island free from aliens. Such an argument has some plausibility for this case. But it is not plausible that in general joint acceptance of a specific current goal is implied in joint readiness to act in a certain way at certain times or in certain circumstances.

Waiving further discussion of this issue, the point about my account of groups not entailing that all groups have joint goals should be clear from other considerations. Though I have not yet given an account of the specifics of collective or joint belief, it should be intuitively clear that a joint belief does not necessarily imply a joint goal. For example, it may be our belief that both you and I are well-meaning people. It is not apparent that we must jointly espouse some goal just because we believe this. In my view, plural subjecthood and hence group existence can in principle arise on the basis of a joint belief as well as preparedness for joint action. As I indicated earlier, the result that groups do not as a matter of logic have to have shared goals or ends is a desirable one for an account of the nature of groups in general.

(3) This is an appropriate place to focus on another aspect of my account which could seem surprising at first. On my view, even when what makes people into a group is their joint readiness to act in certain ways at certain times, a group can forever be *inactive*. In other words, such acts as the members are ready to share in may never take place; the individual members may never act on the basis of their knowledge that all are ready for a certain joint action, each playing some part in achieving the relevant goal. According to me, all that is necessary in order that people form a group is that they share in an action, belief, attitude, or some attribute. Joint

readiness for action is one such attribute. This is all that is necessary, and according to me, it is sufficient. Hence no action on the basis of joint readiness is necessary in addition in order that a group be constituted. I do not find this counterintuitive. However, some related points may be noted.

A sense that certain people have indeed manifested quasi-readiness to engage in a certain joint action on relevant occasions may in some cases not be properly confirmed until the relevant circumstances have obtained many times and people have acted appropriately. When nothing is explicit, this will tend to be so. An explicit discussion among trusted friends, however, could be quite sufficient clearly to create a state of joint readiness with no need for proof through action. At the same time, even regular participation in joint action on a certain type of occasion may not be enough to ground a sense that two people are indeed quasi-ready to participate whenever these circumstances obtain. Each may have a strong sense that what happens happens on an *ad hoc* basis. (Two people may have gone for a walk ten times after a certain seminar has ended, but each still feels it is appropriate to enquire into the other's readiness for a walk as if *de novo* when the current seminar ends.)

Certainly someone's failure to act appropriately on a given type of occasion could lead one to doubt whether he ever was quasi-ready to do certain things jointly on such occasions. Perhaps one misconstrued his original intention. But perhaps he has forgotten the original exchange of open* expressions of quasi-readiness, or forgotten the details of what the joint readiness was readiness for. In any of these cases, one can hardly rely on him to carry out the obligations correlated with the relevant state of joint readiness.

This suggests some rather subtle questions about when states of joint readiness, once established, can cease to be. Apart from the death of one of the parties, or an explicit agreement to desist, what might do it? If one participant has forgotten what occurred between the parties, or forgotten the details, does the state of joint readiness cease?

It may seem startling to suppose one could lose a set of obligations by forgetting that one had them. And those who become jointly ready become obliged, in some sense, to act accordingly. At the same time, it seems that something like this is right. Suppose someone's brain has been tampered with, and he no longer recalls, or ever could recall, that he agreed to meet me for lunch every Thursday this month. We could say: since he agreed, he is obligated to turn up by virtue of his agreement. Something like this could be true in law. But this could be for special reasons having to do with the function of law. In any case, surely it is odd to think of this person as any longer a participant in joint readiness. I have a sense that everyone involved has to be continuously active in some relevant way, in order for this state to persist. The man whose brain was tampered with was a participant, and perhaps he can be brought to believe this, and hence to re-establish his participation. But that he is still such a participant seems hard to accept.

A parallel here might be a personal decision to do something. Suppose I decide to go shopping tomorrow. It could be argued that I now have an overriding reason to go shopping, provided that no new considerations force me to rethink things. But suppose I forget all about my decision. Suppose indeed that all traces of it are excised from my brain. Does the fact that I once made this decision provide me with an overriding reason for acting now? If someone tells me that I decided, or I discover that I did from my diary, this seems different from my continuously recalling or in some substantial way holding on to my decision. It seems that only if I consciously repossess, or re-establish my past decision, could I have the same sort of reason for action that I had in the past. Joint readiness could be like a decision so conceived in that if a single participant loses hold of the situation between the parties, the state of joint readiness ceases, and needs to be re-established somehow.

New knowledge that the relevant joint action is impossible *will* presumably destroy joint readiness for action. Suppose that after some discussion at Zoltan's house each of us has expressed our quasi-readiness to act in concert to destroy the regime. We plan to meet at Zoltan's in three weeks' time for further discussion. Shortly after this, the government increases the powers of the already ruthless secret police, Zoltan is arrested for talking to a tourist, and we have no chance now of getting together to make plans or to carry out any joint action. It seems that we are unlikely to maintain our readiness to act jointly to overthrow the regime, under such circumstances.

It is important to see that even when the relevant joint actions can never *in fact* take place, the group may not regard the situation as completely hopeless, and could remain ready for action. Thus it could be that whenever they meet at the market or on the street those who originally got together at Zoltan's house whisper to each other 'We're going to make it somehow'. In such a case it seems that they could still be ready for joint action. The content of their exchanges could change over time: 'Will we ever get together?' 'Will Zoltan ever be released?' 'I don't think so.' Once it gets down to this, then it becomes dubious whether they are ready for action any more. If they are not, they cannot remain a group by virtue of such readiness. They could still remain a group even in this situation, for they could jointly maintain a *credo*. Presumably as long as members go on encountering each other, and perhaps even if they don't, they could jointly maintain the view that the government should be overthrown.

A group could be inactive, clearly, for reasons other than antagonistic action on the part of others. There may be no fires for the Willington Firefighters to fight. The Ethics Committee may not meet because no complaints have been filed. Here it is a simple matter of the relevant circumstances not arising. Yet there may be every reason to believe in such cases that the people in question remain in a state of joint readiness for action. They may actually hope, individually, and collectively, that the circumstances will not arise. This need in no way detract from their joint readiness.

These results on groups, stemming from my account, accord with my own pretheoretical intuitions. Inactive groups are possible. Some will be ready for action but prevented from acting by the deliberate action of outsiders. Some will only be groups by virtue of more passive attributes such as a credo as opposed to action or readiness for action. Some may be jointly ready to act in circumstances which never arise. At the same time, joint readiness can be destroyed in certain special circumstances, just as groups can, even though the individual participants survive.

(4) Consider again the case of the politically suppressed group which maintains its readiness to plan revolt. Even when all that is going on is whispering in corners, there is what might be thought of as a special kind of force in the world, albeit one which may prove impotent in the end. Each of a number of people is quasi-ready for joint action; each has expressed his quasi-readiness in such a way that it is common knowledge that all are quasi-ready. They are jointly ready for joint action. At that point there is what I have referred to as a 'pool of wills' dedicated to the pursuit of a certain end when circumstances are right. If circumstances are ever right, then these wills will be directed at that end, as if they belonged to a single person. That is, the coherence of the behaviour which is their output will approximate in coherence to the output of the will of a single person acting in pursuit of a goal of his own. These last two points show how heavily group existence, in my view, is a function of the states of mind of individual persons, and of common knowledge of these states. I say more about this aspect of my view later. Given that we are

concerned with human groups, I do not find it counterintuitive.

(5) I now turn to a modification that needs to be made to my account of social groups. As I have made clear, a common knowledge condition is an integral part of my account of plural subjects, and hence of groups. So far common knowledge has been defined in such a way that only those who at least know of each other can be parties to common knowledge. (Thus X, Y, and Z, say, must have noticed that certain things were true of X, Y, Z.) But from an intuitive point of view, there can be social groups in which the members do not all know each other, or even know *of* each other as individuals. Even huge nation-states may be thought of as collectivities. Locutions such as 'we British' or 'we Americans' are common, and Americans may be supposed willing to do certain things together like participate in a democratic system of elections. None the less, it is clear that no American knows of all the others individually. Now, the thought that the citizens of the United States are members of a single collectivity or social group may be a false one, something of a convenient myth, perhaps. Probably such huge nation states are not paradigm cases of such collectivities. None the less, the problem of lack of acquaintance with particular individuals is not unique to such huge states; and this aspect of the United States cannot count against its true collectivity-hood.

What can be the case in populations where not everybody knows of everybody else is something like this. Each of a set of persons with a certain property (living on a certain island, say) has evidence from which they can infer that all such people have openly* manifested quasi-readiness to join in certain kinds of action with other members of the population. For example, people on the island come regularly to fish at a certain creek. One day someone begins building a stone tower, and those around at the time join in happily. Later a different set turn up, together with a few of the original group. Everyone spontaneously helps to make the tower higher. If this sort of thing kept happening, it could presumably soon be open* to all on the island that all had openly* expressed quasi-readiness to join in building a high tower by the creek, and all would realize this. For all have directly observed an apparently representative subset of the population openly* manifesting quasi-readiness.

I take it that the account of social groups I have given can and should be modified to include such cases. The basic change needed is to introduce and use the notion of *common knowledge in a population*:

It is *common knowledge in a population P that q*, if and only if the fact that q is open* to everyone in P, and everyone in P has noticed this.

By definition, the fact that q is *open* to everyone in P* if and only if (1) q; (2) the smooth reasoner counterpart of each member of P would infer that q; (3) the smooth reasoner counterpart of each member of P would infer that (2), and so on. (For the extent of 'and so on' see the long discussion of openness* above.)

We can now allow that a plural subject will exist if it is common knowledge in a certain population P that everyone in P has openly* expressed willingness to be part of a particular plural subject. (I discuss the notion of population common knowledge further in the next chapter.)

(6) My final comment here concerns the nature of the understandings of group members, and the possibility of radical misunderstanding of the intended content of plural subjecthood. Consider again joint readiness to share in some action at a certain time or in certain circumstances.

The parties' understanding of the restrictions on time and circumstances and on the nature of the action in question may be very vague or general. For example, it could be understood that certain people will meet 'every so often' when no one has a very clear idea yet of how often 'every so often' is. People may wonder whether their own personal interpretations of this phrase would be jointly accepted. Again, Americans may all be manifestly prepared to defend, with others, what they take to be valuable about their country. But what is deemed to be valuable, or genuine defence, may differ quite radically among them.

The understandings about the circumstances or the action involved may use vague generalizations on the basis of ostension and example. Thus they could involve a sense that 'this is the sort of thing we might do together' and 'that is not'. The people concerned might be hard put to it to advance descriptions of the kinds of action in question. In such cases it is quite likely that details will have to be negotiated later.

Attempts at further definition could cause the parties to fall out and the group to disband. You and I may agree to 'keep in touch'. Once I realize that you are thinking of our getting together about every six months, whereas I would like to see you every two weeks or so, I may decide to end our understanding altogether.

In sum, my account of social groups should be taken to demand only that some rough general type of action or cognition must be understood to be in question on all sides.

There is plenty of room for misunderstanding in the contexts where a plural subject might be generated. Bill's slap on the arm may be intended to initiate a friendship, but Joe may take it as an hostile act, reacting inappropriately with a belligerent punch. So far Joe and Bill seem to have created a mess rather than a plural subject. In the least messy cases the content of each one's quasi-readiness will be adequately expressed and recognized and it will be clear and evident what each party is quasi-ready for.

The following subsections contain relatively brief comments on further aspects of my account of social groups. I discuss, in the following order, the relation of communication to social groups and group formation, the identity of groups over time, the relation of my account to the statement from Simmel from which I started, some possible objections and my replies, and the importance of social groups in my sense. Further aspects and implications of the account will be discussed later, in particular in the concluding chapter.

4.2 Social groups, communication, and group formation

Human interactions and specifically interpersonal communication appear to be needed in order to bring human collectivities into being. It may then be assumed that collectivities are secondary social phenomena: they must share the field with social interactions, especially with communicative acts, which are distinctive kinds of social things, not themselves presupposing the existence of societies or collectivities. This brings us, in effect, to the question of group formation, and, in particular, to the question whether communication has to play some role. It also raises the question of the social nature of communicative acts.

As is clear from my discussion in the last chapter, some very broad definitions of communication can be given for certain purposes. Meanwhile, if we take terms like: converse, discuss a problem, talk to, or talk with, we are dealing with the most typical forms of human communication. At the same time, we are arguably already dealing with social groups, albeit ephemeral and small ones. A conversation between two people requires that each one does his part as hearer or listener as the case may be. I cannot tell you something if you are not ready to listen to what I say. You *can* listen to what I say without my telling you something – I might be soliloquizing or talking to a third party, unaware of you. Thus communication of a sort can take place between A and B without their participating in any joint action or forming a social group. But in the standard case in which A tells B something, both have to do their bit; it will hardly make sense for anyone to go on talking 'at' anyone else for very long, if that other person has manifested no willingness to act as 'hearer'. In short, I suggest that A and B need to be in a position appropriately to think of themselves as 'us*' in order for A intelligibly to set out to tell B something.

There are, of course, various kinds of groups, and social scientists have historically tended to concentrate on large and persisting ones, from whole societies, to smaller groups within them like political parties and religious organizations. Discussions between individuals will, I presume, often play a role in bringing such groups into being. This does not refute the idea that all these discussions themselves are, individually, collectivity-involving, even though the collectivity itself is emphemeral and small.[46]

But, it may be queried, how do people get set up to converse or discuss matters, in short to communicate in the typical ways of the mature, socialized human beings we are familiar with? This question may seem pertinent here because it could appear that a form of communication must be involved at *some* level in the generation of social groups, including ephemeral conversational groups. Perhaps this is so, if we take the notion of communication broadly enough.

By way of clarification, I should stress that on my Simmelian account of social groups it is not required that anyone *say* to anyone else that they are quasi-ready to converse, say. The condition stated is relatively weak: it is just that each must have manifested quasi-readiness openly*. Must we none the less concede that a 'primordial' expressor of quasi-readiness and the like must intend to communicate with the others concerned, or, when his expression is seen for what it is, does communicate something to the others? This clearly depends on what we think communication is, in particular on whether it is seen as necessarily involving joint action or not. Only if it is not, could a primordial expressor of quasi-readiness intelligibly *intend* to communicate his quasi-readiness. For I take it that one cannot do one's part in a *joint* action unless one's opposite numbers have already participated in creating the conditions for its possibility.

It is most natural to describe the situation of a primordial expressor of quasi-readiness as follows: he does something which he *hopes* will have a certain effect on observers. If he plays his cards right, he will have that effect: his quasi-readiness to converse, say, will be perceived, and the perceiver can then convert it, by his own expressive action, to participation in joint readiness, so that actual conversation can take place.

There's little point in fussing over how one uses the busy term 'communication', but it is important to see how different the process of getting set up to perform a joint action is from setting out jointly to perform an action. One who has not yet had his expressed quasi-readiness met is 'out on a limb', in a sort of no man's land.[47]

Are intentional acts of communication in the thin sense intuitively social phenomena? More specifically, would one naturally describe as a social phenomenon the act of voluntarily and deliberately expressing one's quasi-readiness openly*, so another can perceive it and respond accordingly? Such acts are, one could say, the foundation of all sociality. They are indeed other-oriented actions. The others are seen quite specifically as agents, as possessors of will and ideas. This crucial type of act, then, involves action which is social in Weber's sense. However, we have already seen that it is not clear how 'social', intuitively, action social in Weber's sense is as a genus. It is true that, if I am right, initiatory and 'clinching' expressions of quasi-readiness have such a close relationship to the formation of those paradigmatic social phenomena, social groups, that they might well be thought of as social phenomena in an extended or derivative sense. Yet in being only a means by which collectivities arise, these expressive movements, the perception of them, and reactions back, up to the point where all this is common knowledge, are less obviously candidates as paradigms of the social. In the end, we have here a matter of categorizing or labelling two kinds of phenomena whose nature and relations to each other should be fairly clear by now. I leave till the final chapter further consideration of how social phenomena in general might best be characterized.

Let me now summarize and expand a little on what has emerged regarding the process of group formation. It is obvious that many groups are set up by means of talk in a group's language. As I have already indicated, the English pronoun 'we' may often be used for this purpose.

One basic procedure is as follows. In using 'we' I may be making manifest my personal quasi-readiness to engage in some kind of joint project with you. Thus I might say 'How about our taking a walk tomorrow afternoon?' and so on. I may do so without any certainty that you are similarly minded, and certainly without your having expressed to me such readiness on your part. My use of 'we' in this case may be what I have called *initiatory*. It may be quite clear that it is not presumptuous, in the sense that it does not presuppose that you are already willing, or that you have already expressed willingness. It will not then best be referred to as 'tendentious', which has overtones of presumption.

(That is not to deny that sometimes one or more of these presumptions are indeed present when 'we' is used in what is basically an initiatory way, intended to create a group or plural subject.) You, seeing from my use of 'we' that I am willing to play my part in joint action, may then manifestly accept my 'we', thus implicitly expressing your own willingness to play your part. 'Yes, let's.' Let us call this the 'closing "we"'. It will now be obvious to both that each of us is justified in referring to us as 'us'. Indeed, the closing 'we' can function as a full-blooded use of 'we' at the same time. (In the case of two persons this will be so. If there are ten people involved, then it is possible that only one's closing 'we' can be a full-blooded one.)

One person's use of an initiatory 'we' may be met by a closing action, rather than with words. Thus after I say 'Shall we dance?' you might simply begin to dance with me at the edge of the dance floor, thereby both manifesting your willingness to dance with me, and at the same time beginning to participate in the joint action itself. The pronoun 'we', then, can be an effective tool in the project of group formation. (As the story of Bernard and Sylvia showed, it can also fail to produce the desired effect.)

There can be no group language – no 'our* language' – prior to the existence of 'us*'. One of the standard mechanisms for bringing a group into being, then, the utilization of a group's language (by using 'we' or by having a discussion or whatever) requires a preformed group. This does not lead to any paradox. As I argued in the last chapter, in order to set up a group language, no group language is needed. I can now be a little more precise about what is needed: it is the communication on each person's part of his quasi-readiness jointly to accept that a certain sound has a certain sense. The preconditions for this do not include an existing group language in the sense at issue.[48]

One way of getting one's quasi-readiness across is by deeds rather than words. I have already mentioned that an initiatory use of 'we' could be met by a closing *action*. It seems equally possible that both the initiatory and the closing expressions use actions rather than words. Instead of asking you to dance, I might simply make as if to start dancing with you. If you proceed accordingly, then we are dancing together. Much courtship behaviour proceeds in this tacit fashion. Thus Odette silently tilts her face up towards Swann's, showing she wishes them to kiss.

At this point it is appropriate to stress a crucial, though 'minute' phenomenon of social life, the phenomenon that I shall label 'mutual recognition'. Let me first give a humdrum example from everyday life. I shall refer to it as the Merton Street Library case, since it happened in that library one summer. I was sitting at a table in the library, looking down at a book. I noticed that someone else had come to my table and had sat down opposite me. I took it that it was now common knowledge between this barely seen person and myself that he and I were sitting at this very table. However, we had not yet acknowledged each other's presence in any way. At a certain point, I looked up, and looked somewhat fixedly at him, until he too looked up. I caught his eye (as we say); we looked at each other. I nodded and smiled briefly; he did also. We then returned to our respective concerns and had no further interactions.

In my view, in this case, a small group had been formed as a result of the process of mutual recognition. This group had something like the following feature. Each of us had manifested our willingness jointly to accept that he and I were there at the table. It thus became proper to refer to the two of us as 'us' in the full sense. (I take it that this was not proper, and we did not form any sort of collectivity, at the point where (if I am right) there was common knowledge between myself and this person that we were each sitting at the table.)

Mutual recognition may be the basic mechanism which underlies the formation of more complex, enduring groups.[49] Once mutual recognition is achieved, an appropriate environment for attempts at pointing something out and agreeing on a label for it, for instance, has been created. Hence mutual recognition provides a framework for the creation of a group language.

In the Merton Street Library case, each person nods and smiles. This, it may be argued, is a *conventional* way of acknowledging a person, or setting oneself up jointly to acknowledge co-presence. Meanwhile, as I shall later stress, it is natural to presume that the existence of a social convention requires the existence of a group whose convention it is. There are many conventional ways of connecting with others, as one might put it, and of course this would not be surprising. However, I see no reason in principle why such ways have to be conventional. What one needs is some way of attracting the other person's attention, and then, or at the same time, engaging in whatever behaviour will communicate willingness jointly to acknowledge co-presence. It is not obvious that the only means of doing this will depend on social convention.

In some cases, there may be none. There may be no ways I can connect with a Martian, for example, in the relevant way. There may be some asocial rational beings, who lack the concept of a plural subject. It seems reasonable to suppose that there may sometimes be practical or psychological constraints on 'we*' formation or tentatives, and some situations in which these things are overwhelmingly natural. When there is no pre-existing larger group with 'mutual acknowledgement' conventions, such tentatives may tend to be limited from a rational point of view by the presence or absence of something we might call 'consciousness of kind'. If I sense that a lion's psychology, or a bird's, or a tortoise's, is completely opaque to me, then I will not seriously attempt to get together with that lion, bird, or tortoise, in the group-forming way. Similarly, if I know that someone is in a catatonic trance, I will probably not think it worth attempting to say hello to him. (I might do so, of course, if I hold the view that he is not completely unconscious of his environment, and might be helped to come out of his trance by a communicative attempt.)

The point about consciousness of kind deserves a moment's further comment. In connection with Wittgenstein's view I observed that the possession of similar natural reactions or a similar psychological nature is intuitively distinct from membership in the same society or social group. Hence there is no problem in the claim that perception of a common nature may be a prerequisite for the intelligibility of the expressions collectivity existence depends on.

If I am right about the general way in which groups come into being 'at the logical end', then any further existence conditions on collectivities in terms of things like physical proximity, noting similar properties, perceptual awareness of each other's presence, and so on, will be a function of their contribution to the emergence of plural subjecthood.

4.3 The identity of groups over time

All that has been proposed at this point is a condition necessary to, and sufficient for, the existence of a social group at a given time. Nothing has been said about the way in which a given group can change over time. There is little doubt that from the point of view of our everyday concept of a social group, groups can change in various ways. In particular, they can change their membership. New members can join up after the group is first formed; founding and later members can drop out. In addition, we seem to allow for changes in the character of groups, in their dispositions, aims, beliefs and attitudes, just as we allow for such changes in an individual person. Precisely when we say a group has changed and when we say it has ceased to exist is a matter for detailed investigation. I shall not attempt this here. I shall indicate briefly, through an example, how it could seem reasonable to say of a social group in the sense articulated here that it has changed in membership or character.

Suppose I am walking along in the woods when I run into an acquaintance and we decide to walk together for a while. After a time, we run into someone known to both. He asks 'May I join you?' We graciously agree, and the three of us continue along our path. Under these conditions it may seem correct to say that a certain group has incorporated a new member, rather than to say that one group has gone out of existence and another come into being. In the terms of my account of social groups, one can describe the situation thus: initially two people were jointly pursuing a certain goal, that goal implicit in their going for a walk together. Next, a third party expressed his willingness jointly to accept a closely related goal. The original two then met his expression in such a way that the three of them may now pursue the new goal together. It seems natural enough in this case to say that the new member has, in effect, added his will to a given pool of wills.

It seems that the group of three walkers could change its character. For instance, I might decide that I would like to run for a while rather than walk. I say to the others 'Shall we run for a bit?' They agree. It would be natural enough under these circumstances for me to say that, for instance, 'We walked for a while but then we decided to run, and we ran for twenty minutes.' These things indicate a presumed identity of 'us'. In terms of my account of social groups, an already formed plural subject or pool of wills, formed to pursue a particular goal, accepts a new goal.

In so far as, in both of the cases so far considered, we have intuitively a continuity of group identity, then according to my account of groups this intuition could be based on the notion of continuity in a given pool of wills. Under certain circumstances, new wills may be added to a given pool; under certain other circumstances, the force of an existing pool is redirected at a new goal.

An important complicating factor in considering how groups are to be identified, and identified over time, is the consideration that, intuitively speaking, a given person can be a member of several different groups at once. In principle, indeed, a given set of individuals could constitute two different groups at once. For example, suppose that the three people walking together through the woods in the above example are also the sole members of the local play-reading society. We are not walking along together *qua* members of that society, it may be said. After all, when the third person joined the first two, all may have been perfectly cognizant of the fact of their membership of the play-reading society, yet it was still necessary for him to ask if he could join us on our walk. Had we two been sitting at our regular play-reading venue on the relevant evening, he would not have thought it relevant so to enquire. Meanwhile, it may not be at all clear that *qua* walkers in the wood it is appropriate for us to discuss plays, as it would be clear were we at Molly's house on a Wednesday evening. Thus it may be appropriate for me to say something like: 'Do you people feel like talking about plays?' in order to clarify the situation in *this* group. If the answer is affirmative, this group may be deemed to have taken on a new property.

The foregoing considerations imply a fairly complex situation in relation to group identity. Tom, Dick, and Harry can form a walking party, and a new social group, at a certain time. In terms of my theory, they can have pooled their wills in relation to a given end. However, they will not thereby have pooled their wills in relation to other ends, except those necessarily reached in fulfilment of the first one. Unless they go through something like the original process of group formation – affirmation of an additional joint goal, or a substitute, seen as such – then they will continue to have this original end. These very people may already have pooled their wills or contracted their wills, so to speak, in pursuit of a quite distinct end, in relation to a distinct set of circumstances. But this need not mean that the end of walking together is now an end of that other, previously formed group. Presumably the underlying reason has to do with the understandings everyone has about what is going on.

When we meet in the woods, we are not in the right circumstances to act *qua* members of the play-reading group. We are members of that group, but not acting as such. We only act as such, and are understood to act as such, in a particular restricted set of circumstances. Perhaps for this reason what we agree on here is understood to have no bearing on the play-reading group and *its* properties. The three of us can create a new group, and acting as members of that group, allow that group to change its character; acting as members of the new group we can co-opt new members into the new group, without co-opting them into the old.

In conclusion, I suggest that our pretheoretical intuitions on group identity and change over time, and also our intuitions on the nature and possibility of coextensive groups, do not present any obvious obstacle to my account of social groups. My account appears able to accomodate them, and at the same time to suggest a particular line of interpretation for them.

4.4 Unity and consciousness of unity

Does my version of what I have called the Simmelian schema, as developed so far, support Simmel's idea that 'consciousness of constituting with the others a unity is all there is to this unity'? I recall that it is possible to see this as an unfulfilable claim: generally, how could the existence of an X depend on anyone's consciousness that there is an X? The possibility of the latter appears to depend on the former.

Simmel himself at one point suggests that something other than the *cognition* that there is a unit may be at the base of a collectivity.[50] So it is, at any rate, in the account that I have given.

According to that version of the Simmelian schema, social groups are plural subjects. When the notion of a plural subject is examined, it appears that the ultimate foundation of a collectivity could be described as each person's volunteering (possibly in the face of considerable compulsion) to share in something with certain others. As one might put it, each must think 'we*-for-my-part' with respect to some action, belief, or attitude. But it needs to be stressed that this 'thinking' is not a matter of cognition, or relation to external facts, as belief and knowledge are; rather, it is a matter of will, of one's personal decision.

As noted earlier, one way of putting what has to go on is this. Each one expresses, in effect, a conditional commitment of his will. This commitment is understood to have the following status. If I express this commitment, then, provided you (openly*, etc.) 'match' it with a similar commitment of your own, these wills are jointly committed. In other words, our wills are now properly regarded by both of us as constituting a pool of wills dedicated to whatever enterprise is in question.

According to my account of social groups, then, the basic condition on social group existence involves everyone in volunteering his part in a certain special kind of unity: a unity of wills. Let us call this the *willed unity condition*. (Less attractively but perhaps more perspicuously this might be called the 'willed unity-of-wills' condition.) If we were to construe 'consciousness of constituting with the others a unity' in terms of one's personal contribution to the willed unity condition, that is, as 'willingness to constitute with the others a unity', then one could agree – albeit stretching a point – that such consciousness is 'all there is' to this unity. For it is the basic building block, so to speak, of the social unit: this is 'all that' underlies the existence of the unit constituted by the individuals concerned.

In addition to the basic willed-unity condition, I have of course included further conditions on the existence of a social group. There is what might be called the *expression condition* (each must have manifested his willingness for unity openly* to the others) and the *common knowledge condition* (this manifestation of willingness must be common knowledge).

Among other things, then, I stipulate that it must be common knowledge that the willed-unity condition is satisfied, on the basis of the satisfaction of the expression condition. I could, therefore, be seen as stipulating that there be 'consciousness of unity' in the following sense. The satisfaction of the willed unity condition already produces a unit of sorts, a meshing set of 'we*-for-my-part' thoughts on the part of each person concerned. Thus on my view knowledge of a type of unity is necessary for the existence of the complex kind of unit at issue – a social unit or group. I should stress that the knowledge at issue here is of a type of unity which is still not the unity or existence of a social unit itself. I have not said anything of the form: the existence of a thing of type x (a social group) is a matter of knowledge that there is a thing of type x. What I have said rather is that (roughly) knowledge that there is a y is what makes an x. There is nothing paradoxical or otherwise logically unacceptable in this.

Finally, I note that a corollary of my account of social groups is what may be called the *recognition corollary*: all of the members will recognize that the group exists, when it does. Alternatively, all will think of these people as 'us*'. This does imply that if there is a social group with its special kind of unity there will be consciousness of precisely this unity among the members. However, it is part of the structure of my account that this consciousness is not constitutive of the collectivity, or a prerequisite of collectivity existence. Rather, it is a function of the independent existence of a collectivity. Once again, then, my particular version of Simmel's schema appears to be logically sound.

4.5 On feelings of unity

It should be clear that my account of when 'we*' is appropriate, and of when there is a collectivity, does not appeal to 'mere' *feelings*. I noted earlier that Weber defined 'communal relations' in terms of orientation to a 'subjective feeling of the parties . . . that they belong together'. Probably feelings appropriately described in this way could be present without the presence of the grounds for 'we*' that I have proposed. It is probable that such feelings, perhaps associated with quite a vague cognitive content, often impel people to seek to share in some or other action with each other, and hence to create the grounds for 'we*' as I elaborate them. It is also probable that deep feelings of sympathy and of belonging together can arise as a result of sharing in an action in the sense I have been concerned with.

This last remark may recall Ludwig Von Mises' idea that such feelings are the fruits of what he calls 'social co-operation'. Meanwhile, Von Mises denies any constitutive role to such feelings – social co-operation is not to be defined in terms of them. Though I do not want to give such feelings (or merely such feelings) the role of constituting collectivities, I suspect that I take them to have a closer relation to the existence of collectivities than Von Mises takes them to have to social co-operation. As I have just noted, there is obviously sense to be made of the idea that, on my account of social groups, the members of social groups constitute a unity of a complex sort. It would therefore not be surprising if engaging in joint action, as I have elucidated that here, may produce experiences which people feel moved to describe in terms of their belonging together, their being 'at one', and so on.

Two familiar contexts in which such feelings of unity can be very pronounced are sexual relations and dancing. Neither of these need involve the feeling mentioned, and the relevant kinds of behaviours need not involve the cognitions necessary for joint action. But many cases of both activities involve both these cognitions and these feelings. It is interesting that in both of these cases it may come about that neither party has a clear consciousness of him- or herself as a distinct centre of volition. One may experience oneself part of a flowing, wordless, harmonious system, in which one's movements seem 'called for' by the movements of the other. At such points one may seem to have moved close to the mode of social life of some non human creatures.[51]

There are other examples of the kind of experience at issue here, though perhaps those already mentioned are the most striking examples. People can also 'lose themselves' and be 'carried away' in conversations and discussions, 'selflessly' participating in the argument, not in any way reckoning on how what they say will reflect on themselves or, indeed, will affect the other participants personally. (In so far as such losing of oneself is pleasant and tends to happen in a relaxed conversation, this could be a strong motivation to seek out in friendship like-minded people, or at least those one is not likely to offend when not calculating the effects of one's utterances.)

Participation in many sports will have to some degree the experiential qualities of 'oneness'; this includes even the relation between antagonists. Thus in a football game the members of one side may act as one and feel that they do, but the two teams may do so also. Once a member of 'the other side' gets the ball, your side automatically changes its formation. This is called for by what he (as a member of that team) has done. Thus one plays not just against someone but with them too.

All of the activities mentioned so far can seem to have a great beauty to the participants, for reasons other than the experience of pleasurable personal sensations, or the sense of personal mastery of an activity. Words such as 'merging together', 'fusion', 'harmony', 'union', 'communion' are in place. In all these cases it is evident that the sense of being a part of something other (and 'greater') than oneself and other than the other is to some extent present: together you make a new thing, you are, individually, the components of something. Such feelings, I would argue, can be more than mere 'subjective feelings'. They have an objective basis in so far as they are based on the fact that one is part of a plural subject of action.

The words just cited ('union' and so on) have seemed particularly in place in descriptions of romantic love and the aim of marriage. Though I cannot develop this theme here, it seems that there is a conception of marriage which involves the idea of a particular kind of plural subject, a plural subject with a specific primary goal: something like the well-being of both parties equally. Such a conception has often been expressed in terms which may seem perplexing or mysterious. I hope that my discussion of plural subjects in general may turn out to be of help in demystifying such statements without improperly bowdlerizing them.[52]

4.6 Objections and replies

Is the account of social groups proposed here acceptable? In this section I shall consider some possible objections. Let me first summarize what I take to be the criteria by which the account may appropriately be judged. There are several. One is whether intuitions on the existing meaning of 'social group' and other relevant terms are effectively articulated. Another is whether we now have the most plausible principle to cover a generally acceptable list of types of collectivity. Finally there is the question whether a concept which picks out an important, distinctive, actual phenomenon has been delineated. Intuitions on meaning may vary between so-called 'speakers of the same language'. In so far as my personal reactions over the use of 'social group' differ from yours, it may be that there is no unique interpretation of the English term 'social group'. Luckily, capturing 'the' meaning of 'social group' is the least important criterion. I take the second to be more important, though it is always possible that different people extrapolate somewhat differently from a given list of examples of types of collectivity. The final issue is at least as important and has to do not with existing meanings or *de facto* projections or continuations from an initial list, but rather with how things are. It relates in this case to a possible projection from agreed cases, and asks: is it revealing of reality? Does it show us a good way of 'carving nature'? Does it enable us to carve nature at the joints?

Supposing that one has proposed a particular account of social groups, then, there is always the question: are there social groups in the sense in question, and are they important phenomena? If the answer is positive, then the search for an existing 'intuitive principle' has been useful heuristically, though of course if the actual intuitive principle behind our list of groups or our term 'social group' has been missed, something important may well have escaped notice. For that reason, it is always worth considering whether or not a purported analysis of an existing concept or meaning does succeed as such, even given its success in latching on to something which clearly is important.

With these remarks in mind, I address some objections that might be levelled at my account. The first two, and the fourth, involve specific examples intended to show that my account is too narrow. The third involves the claim that it is too broad. (It could, of course, be both too narrow and too broad, in different respects.)

(i) Economic classes

One possible objection runs as follows: an account of social groups which makes consciousness of oneself and certain others as 'us*' essential to social groups leaves out economic classes such as those of workers and of capitalists in many societies. Such classes, the objection may run, are obviously social groups. If valid this objection would stand against any version of Simmel's schema, not only against my own.[53]

To put things rather generally at first, suppose a proposed account of social groups leaves out certain kinds of population, and suppose that such populations are socially important in some way. For instance their existence within a society and the features they possess are of great relevance to our evaluation of the society and/or to the way it functions. There are clearly two ways to go given that this is the case. We could insist that these populations be classified as social groups, and the proposed account thus amended or abandoned, or allow that they are an important type of population which is not a social group.

How might this decision be made? One way is, obviously, to consider intuitions about the existing meaning. Would all populations of the kind in question naturally be referred to as collectivities or social groups? Again, are the classes of wage-earner or capitalist, say, intuitively of a piece with families, armies, discussion groups?

Let us now consider economic classes in these terms. It is worth noting that such classes do not tend to appear on the lists of cases of social systems, social groups, and such given by the social scientists I have read. Conceivably this is due to some bias of capitalistic academics. I am not in a position to substantiate a view on this, though it is not immediately obvious what political gain there could be in denying that economic classes are always social groups.[54] Suffice it to say that they do not generally in fact appear on such lists.

To go into the question of intuition briefly, my own reaction is that economic classes are not *as such* social groups, though they may be so in particular cases. (My intuition here is of course a function both of my sense of what makes something a social group and my sense of what makes something an economic class.) The call in the *Communist Manifesto* urging that 'workers of the world unite!' can be seen as intended to be a collectivity-creating catalyst rather than an appeal to an already existing collectivity. I suspect that as an *empirical* matter economic classes or groups are not always in fact social groups; that is, our intuitive concept of a social group would not apply to all actual economic classes. My Simmelian model of a social group, then, accords with my sense that the concept of an economic class is not such that economic classes are always social groups.

Perhaps the objector may continue that though economic classes are indeed not social groups in the Simmelian sense, it seems to him that they are social groups none the less. Let us consider what intuitive principles could be at issue in this person's case.

Objections to accounts of social groups which leave out economic classes in particular could be based on the view that since an influential social theory, namely Marxism, places great importance on such classes, they are clearly classes or groups of a social sort. Alternatively, and with less deference to authority, the idea may be that the existence and nature of these classes in fact strongly influences the way things are in a given society, thus their existence within a society and the features they possess are relevant to our understanding of how the society functions or indeed of how particular members of that society function. The implicit notion of a social group at issue, then, could be one of the following: population of a kind credited with importance by Karl Marx; population credited with importance by some major social theorist; population of a kind with an important effect on societies. Alternatively, the notion could involve a disjunction of some or all of the above conceptions, or some very capacious conception like 'population of persons with some feature in common'. It is worth pointing out that each of these conceptions clearly runs the risk of not cutting nature at the joints, of lumping together phenomena which are quite significantly different, and not very significantly the same. (The conceptions noted are obviously very different from each other and may be expected to give different results with respect to which populations are social groups.)

A further possible 'intuitive principle' should also be mentioned. With respect to economic classes in particular, one reason they could be held to *be* social groups is that they may be, or be believed to be, very *apt to become* such groups. It may be thought not only that they are likely candidates to turn into social groups, but that they *ought* to become social groups, from the point of view of the personal interests of their members, of the class as a whole, of the whole society in which they are located , of the progressive development of the world-spirit, or whatever. When Marx and Engels urged the workers of the world to unite, in the *Manifesto*, the message behind the call to unify was that workers should set themselves up to *act jointly* in throwing off the capitalist yoke. The authors of the manifesto obviously felt that the workers *ought* to unite in order to lose their chains.

Now, quite generally, one may sometimes be tempted to call some thing, T, an X if it is likely to become an X or if you think it ought to be an X.[55] However, if one realizes that this is why one is saying that T is an X, one will realize at the same time that one does not believe that T, is, as it stands, literally an X. Obviously, from a theoretical point of view the idea that it is in the interests of the members of economic classes to join forces and hence become social groups must be distinguished from the view that they are already and always social groups. These two views cannot intelligibly be held at the same time.

So much for some of the intuitive principles which could underlie the conviction that economic classes as such were social groups, principles which might inform someone's judgments that a certain phenomenon or type of phenomenon was a social group. Whether one of them is your intuitive principle or not, there is not much point in the long run battling over which is 'right'. We may just have different idiolects regarding the term 'social group', or you may make different extrapolations from the cases. These principles can also be viewed, as can my Simmelian model, as proposed standards for judging how the term 'social group' should be used as a technical term, or in order to make it useful rather than vague and uninformative. How might we choose between principles if this is the issue?

It is clear that importantly different kinds of population are of interest to us, and have their effects within human societies. Marx himself distinguished between classes conscious of themselves, and those not *(Klasse für sich* and *Klasse an sich)*.[56] Given, then, that some populations fit my Simmelian model, and given that being a group of the type in question is an important feature of a population,[57] there seems to be some reason to give such populations a special label and to think of economic classes, in so far as they do not fit the model, in other terms. Meanwhile, there are good reasons for giving my 'Simmel groups' the label 'social group'. I believe that they possess a salient feature of those phenomena we standardly call social groups. Further, if we look to etymology for a moment, and consider the Latin '*socius*', usually translated *ally*, we see how very apt it is to call my Simmel groups[58] *social* groups. For those who share in an action, even a single action lasting a short time, are clearly allies of a kind, allies in performing the action in question. Whereas those who would do well to join forces but have not, cannot yet be said to be allies, or allied. (Reference to people as 'natural allies' implies, I take it, only that it would be natural or proper for them to join forces if they have not already done so.) I suggest therefore that if we are to choose, it be the economic classes, as such, which fail to get the label in question. They do not tend to appear in lists of paradigm types of social group, and the members of a given economic class may never ally with each other, even though it would be a good thing if they did.

To sum up my discussion of the economic classes objection: economic classes are not always social groups intuitively, at least according to me. That they may not be plural subjects in the sense I have defined does not, then, in my view count against my account of groups as plural subjects. Economic classes will, of course, count as social groups given some alternative accounts of such groups which could be adopted; these accounts, however, do not seem to make the notion of a social group a very useful one theoretically. Nor do economic classes as such tend to be included in standard lists representing what social scientists take to be social groups. Finally, the label 'social group' seems especially apt for populations which are plural subjects. There is, in sum, reason to argue that if plural subjects are labelled 'social groups', economic classes in general should not be, irrespective of the matter of intuition on meaning or personal extrapolations from lists.

(ii) Organizations

It may be thought that some classic dichotomies of theoretical sociology can be made to yield an objection. I have in mind Tönnies' famous distinction between *Gemeinschaft* and *Gesellschaft* (usually translated as 'community' and 'society'), which is echoed in Weber's distinction between communal and associative relationships Examples of the latter are the relationships which occur in business, as opposed to familial relationships, say. Taking a cue from this example, it might be argued that typical cases of business organizations, like the firm, for instance, will not fit my Simmelian model. But, it may be said, they are still social groups.

I shall not attempt any exegesis of Tönnies or others with similar views here, but I do want to look at the particular case of organizations. First, must members of organizations think of themselves as 'us*'? If not, what follows from this?

Consider the following example.[59] Suppose we have an organization, say the firm of Biggs and Boggs. We can speak of members of the organization, and people doing their bit in the organization. Perhaps it seems obvious that we have a social group here. Say that the firm of Biggs and Boggs consists of a factory producing shoes and a central office which deals with administration. It seems that in principle, though at first human beings deal with the paperwork and shoemaking, there could come a point when everything is done by computers and automata. The making of shoes could be ordered, and shoes made and sent out without any human intervention at all. Presuming that the automata do not have genuine thoughts, they will not see themselves as 'us*'.

On the basis of this story someone might try to argue that there could be an organization or firm among whose participants there were no 'we*' thoughts, so there could be a social group in which there are no such thoughts. There are various assumptions one might question here. Possibly the automated firm does not count as a social group even though the non-automated one does. But having noted this interesting type of example, I want to focus on a less extreme, more currently realistic, and less pleasant one (except from the point of view of human unemployment) which does not get rid of human beings altogether.

Suppose that, in its original form, the Biggs and Boggs organization is enormous, and its purpose unclear to most employees. People are told what to do without being told about the purposes of the firm. Many are assigned to offices where they work alone. The general sense in everyone's mind is: I work in this office, I don't have a clear picture of what goes on elsewhere; sometimes I wonder if I am the only person here; for all I know everything I do is thrown in the garbage dump. There is, in sum, a Kafkaesque sense of disconnection in everyone's mind: who knows what this is all about, and who these people I occasionally see are? No one thinks in terms of sharing in any joint effort, or of having anything in common with the others except that they work in close geographical proximity. But for all that, is this not a firm? Let us suppose that, in fact, the set-up is such that Biggs and Boggs produces more shoes than any other firm in the world; the company won a Presidential award for productivity. Everyone who acts as a judge of these things thinks that this is a great organization, though no one has looked into the subjective satisfactions or intentional states of the workers on the job.

Is this – or some such case – a good counterexample to my Simmelian account? My feeling here is that once the details of this particular organization are spelled out, it is not intuitively that clear that it is a social group or human collectivity. Thus my intuitions on this case do not find it a counterexample to my Simmelian model.

Now it might be objected that people do in fact put organizations on lists of paradigm cases of social groups. However, it is important to realize that the reason that certain types of population or set-up find their way onto a list of types of social group may have to do with what typical or egregious examples of the type are like, or indeed may have to do with mistaken views of what such examples are like. This means that such lists, while inevitably used and useful in setting out to investigate the concept of a collectivity, must be used with caution. Clearly, in some organizations there is a clear sense of what is being achieved by the firm and that it is being achieved by the efforts of all. There are firms in which it would be natural enough for members overall to refer to what 'we' do in referring to the organization. I could argue, therefore, that it is this aspect of some organizations and firms which could lead organizations in general to be put on some lists of social groups.

231

It is worth noting that Weber expressly points out that in many of the cases which he calls associative relationships a 'communal' element creeps in. So his dichotomy is not that rigid, and he clearly feels that human beings have a tendency to develop communal relationships in every context of interaction. Thus, there seems to be good reason to choose to define a social group in terms of a 'communal' element which has a wide range and doubtless has its practical effects, irrespective of intuitions on existing concepts and meanings.

(iii) Ephemera

A different type of objection comes from a different quarter: are not some set-ups social groups on my Simmelian model which are not so intuitively? Is not my account of social groups, in other words, too broad? A couple of people chatting in the library, even a couple of people who have simply *acknowledged one another* in the library, might count as a social group on my interpretation. Most paradigm cases, it may be argued, are less ephemeral. Why should these count as in the same class?

One answer to this is that people's lists do vary, but most social scientists are happy to acknowledge the existence of so-called 'small groups'; sometimes particular types of small groups are picked out as special and given special labels, like 'face-to-face group' and 'primary group'. Erving Goffman and others have put 'conversational groups' on a list of social groups or social systems. Clearly, within the populations that fit the Simmelian model, we can make important distinctions. For instance, we can distinguish ephemeral groups from lasting groups; small, intimate groups, from large groups where the members are not known to each other; groups which have few attributes and groups with rich tapestries of tradition and convention. Groups of these different types may be expected to have further differences between them.

My own sense is that the ephemeral, two-person group is far from being an unimportant curiosity, an 'end-of-the-spectrum case' one just might mention for completeness, but might just as well ignore. It is, rather, a fundamentally important case, which it would be more than arbitrary to ignore. As I have indicated above, it is can be argued quite plausibly that these are the cases that spawn all the others; the little groups are causally crucial for the beginning and life and change of larger groups and societies.

(iv) Complex groups

The following kind of case is familiar. Someone joins a club knowing little about its aims and ideology. This person is henceforth counted a genuine member of the club. Can my view of groups accommodate such cases?

Note that in such a case, we assume that there already is a club with a purpose, ideology, or whatever, and that it is possible at this point for individuals to 'join the club' by going through certain procedures which do not acquaint them with this purpose. That *this* is so we take to be part of accepted club procedure. Thus we are clearly dealing with a sophisticated type of case. Meanwhile, note that the 'ignorant member' in such a case is not so far removed from those who participate in the relevant joint action in the fullest way. Suppose that Diana joins the Arrow club without knowing the club's purpose. It is true that she is not yet in a position fully to participate in the pursuit of this aim. None the less, we may presumably take her joining of the club as an expression of her willingness jointly to pursue with the other members whatever as yet undiscovered purpose the club has. Further, we may take it that on discovering that purpose she will, all else being equal, be fully involved in the joint pursuit of it.

Observation of this type of case helps me to spell out my main aim in developing an account of social groups here. This has been to isolate the phenomenon which is central to collectivity existence as intuitively conceived. This, I argue, is the phenomenon of plural subjecthood. Of course there are many different ways in which human beings relate to each other. My main claim is that when there is no fully-fledged plural subject, then there is no collectivity.

Meanwhile, I can allow that there are some complex cases. Plural subjects proper can develop along a variety of lines. For instance, a plural subject may adopt a name; it may develop a sense of specialness and a desire for exclusivity: 'We don't want anyone else in on this, unless we all really like her'. Or it may have a sense of need for more members. For such reasons the existing members may establish rules that determine who may become a member. The possibility of such entry rules allows for complex cases. The rules can in principle be so capacious as to allow those lacking the ability to be members of the initial plural subject to be considered members none the less. Thus infants can be thought of as 'members of the tribe', though they have no conception of the tribe as a whole. Similarly, an adult may know nothing of the tribe but still be a member according to the group's rules.

In Chapter VI I discuss the important notion of a group fiat. The possibility of group fiats enables a group to make its own rules, including rules regarded as 'constitutional' and entry rules.

This enables the phenomena to become more and more complex. Earlier in this chapter, I mentioned the possibility that a group set up representatives certain of whose decisions are to count as the group's decisions. Later (in Chapter VI) I focus briefly on the case of lawgivers. It is clear that there are very important, complex phenomena to be investigated in this area. I shall not attempt any lengthy discussion of them here. I believe that discussion and understanding of the concept of a plural subject must come first.

4.7 The importance of social groups

Though offered as an account of the intuitive conception of a social group, what may be most important about the account of 'social groups' given here is that it characterizes a special kind of phenomenon, in which human beings see themselves and certain others in a special light – as the components of a plural subject.

In talking of 'society', 'social groups', and in using other terms for collectivities, people may well be aware of and somewhat constrained by their awareness of this phenomenon. As with any term, however, it would not be surprising if we tended to talk of social groups rather loosely. As I indicated when raising this issue at the outset, we tend to rely on a list of types of group to indicate what we mean by a social group: families, tribes, clubs, conversationalists, literary societies, political parties. What, however, is a family? And are all families social groups – do all individual cases of families deserve a place on a list of social groups? It is obvious that not all biological families form social groups in any intuitive sense. But even if we limit ourselves to families in which two parents have brought up their biological children, we find that these may now have rather limited connections with each other: there may be a 'black sheep' who has severed connections with the rest, for instance.

As Max Weber often insisted when presenting his 'fundamental concepts of sociology', reality, perhaps in particular social reality, is complex, and one can find all sorts of variations and complications of the possible phenomena. In picking out a particular phenomenon, and calling that the phenomenon of collectivity-hood, I mean to manifest no disrespect for the facts, for the mess and the individuality of real human relations. Rather, I mean to stress that this phenomenon seems worth calling the phenomenon of collectivity-hood if any does, and it seems to be a phenomenon of importance, worth picking out by some label or other. What our words mean, or were intended to

direct our attention to, is an interesting question; what phenomena of note the world contains is another interesting question. I
believe that a study of the former can lead us to some of the
latter – though doubtless not all. In any case, the results of an
inquiry into meanings can and should also be judged in relation
to the question: has an important, real phenomenon been
characterized here?

I have dropped a number of hints about the importance of
social groups in my technical sense. It seems that social groups in
my sense are ubiquitous, and it is by forming small and simple
ones in brief encounters, in conversations and arguments and
discussions, that we come to form more and more complex
structures, some of which are social groups in the same sense, or
at least have such a group at their core, others of which may not
be (the automated version of Biggs and Boggs).

I suggest that the concept of a social group delineated here is
important because it picks out an ubiquitous real phenomenon
which has widespread and major consequences. Some of these
consequences are behavioural – human beings behave in new
ways by virtue of being group members. For instance, they do
their parts in the relevant joint action when appropriate. There
are also subjective consequences. These are hardly trivial. In
discussions of human psychology and social life one often hears
of the importance of a sense of intimacy with others (particularly
spouses) and of the way in which actively 'doing things together'
and 'sharing' things can help to produce such a sense.[60] I take this
as an indication that social groups in my sense are implicitly
understood to be psychologically important. In fact I suspect that
membership in a social group in my sense, and simply
that – without the performance of related actions – can have a
profound effect on psychological health. I conjecture that much
of what we call 'loneliness' is a sense of group-lessness in
precisely this sense. As is well known, it is not plausibly thought
of as a sense of being physically isolated.

As will emerge later, group membership in my sense provides a
way of thinking which can enable individuals to break through
dilemmas of rationality in 'game-theoretic' situations of certain
types. Finally, social groups in my sense may be judged (and
actually be) of considerable intrinsic value in themselves. A
group is often judged much like an individual: we prefer that the
group survive than that it disband. Ideas like those of 'organic
unity' and 'organized complexity', which have been taken to
connote intrinsically valuable properties, seem well applicable to
groups in my sense. Plural subjects are unified, complex entities.
Perhaps this is one reason we value groups as such, and things

are done 'for the sake of the marriage' for instance, as well as for the sake of the individuals involved.

As yet, I have hardly touched on the interesting specific properties groups in my sense can have. Some of these properties can influence individual lives enormously, not always for the good.

The next two chapters focus on the debated issues of the nature of collective beliefs and social conventions without presupposing the conclusions of this chapter. In particular, I shall not assume at the outset that these are plural subject phenomena. By making a fresh start in this way, I can derive a degree of independent support for the idea that social groups are plural subjects and, more generally, that plural subject concepts are central to our everyday understanding of social life. For after considering carefully the merits and demerits of a number of alternative accounts, I conclude that according to our everyday conceptions these phenomena are indeed a function of the existence of plural subjects.

V

AFTER DURKHEIM: CONCERNING COLLECTIVE BELIEF

1 INTRODUCTION

1.1 A puzzle about collective belief

The number of members, the duration, and the particular membership of a social group are clearly important facts about it, but there is nothing obviously problematic or intriguing about these features. Populations which are not social groups, including populations of randomly chosen individuals, also have a particular size and duration, and contain particular individuals as members. Our ascription of such properties to social groups does not in itself suggest that they are particularly impressive or unusual entities. Other ascriptions are more intriguing. In this chapter I focus on our tendency to talk about the *beliefs* of groups.

The idea that social groups can have beliefs appears to be part of our everyday conceptual scheme, yet at the same time it may appear puzzling or even preposterous. A careful investigation of the idea of a collective or group belief seems called for. In this chapter I develop an account of a group's beliefs. I shall not presuppose at the outset the accuracy of the account of social groups developed in the previous chapter. It turns out, meanwhile, that my arguments here strongly suggest such an account. So they provide a degree of independent support for it.

That our everyday conceptual scheme does contain the idea that groups have beliefs, opinions, and other such properties is evidenced by familiar forms of language. We say things like: 'In the opinion of our board of directors, the adoption of such a policy would be a disaster'; 'Our group thinks that we should not accept the offer'; 'This nation knows that war is never without cost to the victor', and so on. (I shall call these *group belief* or *collective belief* statements.) Meanwhile, the idea that a social

237

group can have beliefs may seem ridiculous on the face of it.

The thought that groups cannot believe anything could be an inference from the conjunction of two theses, both quite plausible, if hard to formulate precisely. One thesis concerns the concept of belief: in order for the English predicate '. . . believes' to apply to something, that thing would have to have a mind. I shall call this thesis *psychologism about belief.* On behalf of this thesis it might be argued that a belief is, by definition, an attitude to a proposition (a 'propositional attitude'), so that something with a belief must be capable of somehow envisaging propositions and having attitudes towards them (in this case, the attitude is something like: taking them to be true). Meanwhile, it may be claimed, only a being with a mind – whatever precisely that is – can either have attitudes or entertain propositions, which involves grasping concepts. The second thesis, which I shall call *anti-psychologism about social groups*, claims that social groups do not have minds. The plausibility of this thesis may not seem to need arguing though what precisely it is to have a mind is a deep and difficult issue. Clearly enough, if these two theses are correct, and use terms in the same sense, then social groups cannot believe anything. The concept of belief will not apply to social groups. All claims to the effect that a certain group has a certain belief will be false.

Two quite plausible theses, then, generate a puzzle concerning our group belief statements. What are we to make of them? Can something be made of the notion that groups have beliefs, after all?

1.2 Possibilities of meaning and truth

Let us consider some possibilities regarding the meaning and truth of everyday group belief statements. It is possible that these statements are simple falsehoods: they embody or presuppose the view that to have a belief you must have a mind of your own, and they ascribe beliefs to entities which obviously do not have minds of their own. It would be good not to have to write off our group belief statements as simple falsehoods of this kind. If they were like this, one would certainly want to know how such obvious falsehoods could be enunciated and accepted over and over again. A similar question would arise for the related but more subtle possibility that group belief talk involves a sort of fiction or pretence, that in talking this way we pretend or imagine that social groups have minds of their own, and ascribe beliefs to them.[1]

After Durkheim: concerning collective belief

We need to distinguish two types of question concerning our talk about group belief. One concerns motivation. What motivates this way of talking? What might a speaker have to gain from it? Motives for mouthing the falsehood or adopting the fiction that a group is or has a mind can easily be found. Political leaders and rhetoricians in general could effectively intimidate or encourage by getting people to think in terms of a powerful spirit to whose views and attitudes they should defer. Try explicitly giving such an interpretation to such statements as 'The United States intends to defend its own vital interests'; 'Management is completely opposed to a salary raise'. The potential influence of belief in the specific views of a great spirit need hardly be stressed.

There are important prior questions which are not concerned with motivation. What situations do we have in mind when we speak about group beliefs? Which phenomena would most appropriately be characterized as involving a group's belief? The questions I shall focus on here are of this type. They are semantic questions, broadly speaking. Until the semantics of collective belief statements has been settled, questions of motivation are premature: until we know what we are saying, we cannot properly investigate the question of why we are moved to say it. Indeed, once we know what we are saying, why we say it may be obvious.

Our group belief statements need involve neither simple falsehoods nor fictions of group mentality. It is possible that they will cease to be problematic once their meaning is spelled out.

One common view of collective belief statements falls under this rubric. According to this view, statements of the form 'Group G believes that p' are equivalent in meaning to statements of the form 'all or at least most members of G believe that p'. On this sort of analysis the ascription of a belief to a group is not to be understood as if it paralleled the ascription of a belief to a human individual. It is tempting to say that the belief that p is not really ascribed to a group at all on this sort of analysis, but rather to certain individual people. The existence of a group 'belief that p' is on this view a function simply of the existence of a certain set of *correlative individual beliefs*, that is, beliefs held by individual persons to the effect *that p*. There is not even an ostensible challenge here either to psychologism about belief, or to anti-psychologism about groups. This, of course, may seem to be a clear advantage of such an analysis of everyday talk. I shall discuss this analysis further shortly.

Another candidate analysis may usefully be noted here. In practice group belief statements may be made when some special

239

subgroup within the group in question believes the relevant proposition. Thus a politician may say 'The United States believes it is time to sign a non-aggression pact with Sri Lanka' when what he knows is that the United States government believes this. (He may also know that most citizens of the United States have never heard of Sri Lanka.) That this kind of thing happens may suggest the following analysis: to say that group G believes that p is to say that some special small group within group G believes that p. There are a number of immediately obvious problems with this view, however.

First, the case this analysis derives from is a somewhat special and complex case. Second, in order to clarify it fully we need an account of what makes the smaller group special in the appropriate way. This is likely to be some type of collective belief or other collective property. Third, the analysis makes use of the notion of the belief of a group, albeit of a small group within the larger group concerned. It can be reapplied to itself, but this leads to an infinite regress. Meanwhile, it is not at all plausible to suggest that 'in the final analysis' the belief in question is always being ascribed to a single person who is a member of the 'core' group, with some fact about his status, perhaps, alluded to implicitly. For often when the kind of analysis suggested here is most plausible, it is precisely a smaller group (government, management, parents) as opposed to an individual (absolute monarch) which is presumed to have the belief ostensibly ascribed to the larger group in question (nation, firm, family). I conclude that a hypothesis of implicit reference to the correlative belief of special individual or subgroup is unacceptable as a general account, for the reasons mentioned. (I shall consider the cases which suggest such an account later.)

Finally there is the possibility that group belief statements are metaphorical. The idea of metaphor is not an entirely easy one. Let us suppose that one speaks metaphorically under roughly the following conditions. One uses words in a certain sense to make a statement which is false. One does this to signal that the situation referred to is strongly analogous to one in which these words would say something true. (Compare: 'She flew into his arms.') Given the complexity of the situation, we may not want to say that what is said is false without qualification. We might prefer to say that though it is literally false, it is entirely appropriate as metaphor, even true 'metaphorically speaking'.

A term's supposedly 'metaphorical' application in a certain situation may seem altogether natural. If so, we should ask why this is. Perhaps we are faced with two rather different phenomena (the beliefs of individuals and the beliefs of groups, say) to both of which the term applies literally, after all. Thus a careful consideration of the conditions under which group belief statements are in place could lead us to revise our views on belief. We could become less hospitable to psychologism, more open to the idea that groups can have beliefs, literally speaking. Alternatively, a more general concept than that of belief may emerge, applicable to two phenomena that are importantly similar, but can only be linked by metaphor, using the limited concepts we have.

It should now be clear that group belief statements do not have to be seen as plain, blatant falsehoods or wild fictions, and that they merit an unprejudiced consideration in their own right. It is not obvious that scientific discourse should eschew them, as might be thought at first blush. Meanwhile, an abstract note of semantic possibilities cannot decide the issue.

What actual phenomena, then, are the collective belief statements of everyday life intended to pick out? Which if any among the phenomena of human social life would be most aptly referred to by such locutions? What is a collective belief?

1.3 Two views of collective beliefs: summativism and anti-correlativism

One important issue is the following: is a *summative* account of collective beliefs the most plausible one? I take the term 'summative' from Anthony Quinton, who introduces it thus:

> In some cases, which may be called summative, statements about social objects are equivalent to statements otherwise the same that refer explicitly, if at some level of generality, to individual people. To say that the French middle class is thrifty is to say that most French middle class people are. (1975, p. 9)

I shall use Quinton's term in a broader sense. By a 'summative' account I mean one which holds that for a group G to believe that p it is *logically necessary* that most members of G believe that p. According to one simple type of summative view, which Quinton apparently accepts in the paper from which I quote, in order for a group G to believe that p it is both necessary and sufficient logically that most members of G believe that p. (Quinton himself puts the point linguistically.)

> We do, of course, speak freely of the mental properties and acts of a group in the way we do of individual people. Groups are said to have beliefs, emotions, and attitudes and to take

decisions and make promises. But these ways of speaking are plainly metaphorical. To ascribe mental predicates to a group is always an indirect way of ascribing such predicates to its members. With such mental states as beliefs and attitudes, the ascriptions are of what I have called a summative kind. To say that the industrial working class is determined to resist anti-trade union laws is to say that all or most industrial workers are so minded. (ibid., p. 17)

What considerations might lead someone to hold the simple summative view just described ? First, there are the two plausible theses of psychologism about beliefs and anti-psychologism about social groups. Given acceptance of these, one may feel that in order to find the 'on the ground' phenomena that we are alluding to when we are talk about the beliefs of groups, we must look to the minds of the individual members of the group in question. Second, many predicates that are applied to groups are not applicable to individuals (an example from Quinton: 'is hierarchically organized'). Meanwhile, 'believes' does literally apply to individual persons. It may thus be tempting to suppose that what is apparently the ascription of a belief to a *group*, is really no such thing, but is rather a way of implicitly ascribing a belief to the individual members of the group.

A semantic form of individualism might also underlie this view. One might hope or expect that statements about groups are ultimately analysable into statements about the individuals who are members of 'collections' or mere sets of individuals. Given that some predicates of groups (for instance, 'is hierarchically arranged') will need careful unpacking and reference to predicates of individuals other than the original predicate, the semantic individualist might assume that at least 'believes' and other mental predicates like those ascribing attitudes and feelings, can be dealt with quite simply, as in the simple summative view.[2]

The possible influence of normative views may also be mentioned. One's view that a 'group belief' is a widely held belief could reflect a sense that if there is a majority view on any matter, then the belief of the group, whatever that is, *should* reflect it.[3]

Though certain background assumptions or programmes may facilitate its acceptance, one cannot say a priori that a summative view of collective belief statements must be correct. Though psychologism about belief and anti-psychologism about groups are both plausible assumptions, it simply does not follow from them, nor is it otherwise obvious that sentences like 'Our group believes Jones is wrong for the job' are standardly intended according to the summative view, or must be, if it is to refer to actual phenomena.

Nor is it even obvious that some form of *correlativism* must be correct. A correlativist, as I shall use the term, holds that a collective belief that p requires that at least some member or members of G believe that p. To hold a summative view is, of course, to espouse a form of correlativism. Other forms are possible. One such form, in terms of the beliefs of authoritative individuals, was alluded to earlier.

In the critical sections of this chapter I shall concentrate on the problems with various forms of summativism because of its prevalence and evident initial plausibility. It is clear to me that a form of summativism is often what comes to mind when the nature of collective beliefs is mooted. I shall myself argue in favour of a non-correlativist account of group belief. I am in particularly good company in this respect. One of the founders of sociology, Emile Durkheim, inclined towards an account of collective beliefs that is neither summative nor correlativist. I argue on behalf of this view of Durkheim in the next section, since others have seen different things in what he says. In discussing Durkheim I shall not try to give an unassailable account of the controversial text I shall focus on. I shall, rather, draw out of this complicated and sometimes confusing material certain broad and central ideas which can be seen as signposts to a non-correlativist account of collective belief. That Durkheim's text, interpreted in a certain way, coheres with conclusions arrived at independently, provides a form of support for the interpretation. It also provides a form of indirect support to those conclusions. (Readers wanting to concentrate on the issues could omit this interpretive section without losing the thread of my argument in this chapter.)

2 DURKHEIM ON SOCIAL FACTS: SOME SALIENT FEATURES OF THE *RULES* DISCUSSION

2.1 Durkheim's project

In a number of places, in particular in his famous treatise *The Rules of Sociological Method*, Durkheim insisted on the existence of a special range of phenomena which he labelled *'faits sociaux'* or, according to the usual translation, 'social facts'.[4]

Durkheim was concerned to demarcate the realm of sociology. This, in his view, was to demarcate the realm of social science as a whole. He wished to do this by reference to one clearly specified kind of phenomenon. Thus:

> We must accurately distinguish social facts and show what it is that gives them their identity, if we are to avoid reducing sociology to nothing but a conventional label applied to an incoherent collection of disparate disciplines. (1900, pp. 127–8; tr. from Giddens (ed.), 1976, p. 52)

So far his project is not so obviously distinct from Weber's implicit project in defining 'social action'. It is important, however, that Durkheim was not working within the constraint Weber imposed on himself, that of giving an account of social science in terms of a kind of action performed by individual people. Part of Durkheim's motivation, rather, entailed that he would shy away from any such constraint, espousing rather a conflicting one. For he wished to show that there clearly was room for a science of the social distinct from the already existing sciences of individual psychology and of biology. Evidently, many would agree that if the subject matter of a science was the actions of individuals, this science would be part of individual psychology. Not unexpectedly, then, Durkheim does not choose a type of human action as the central social phenomenon. Rather, he focuses attention on *collective ways* of acting, thinking, and feeling.

2.2 The definitions

It is common and natural to focus an account of Durkheim's concept of a social fact on the so-called 'definitions' in the *Rules*. These definitions have been much criticized in the literature, with accusations ranging from ambiguity and unclarity to plain unintelligibility. There are good reasons, meanwhile, not to take these definitions as expressing Durkheim's basic conception of a social fact, even at the time he wrote them. He himself characterized them later as 'preliminary', and as attempts to tell the practising sociologist by what *perceptible signs* he might be led to particular social facts in particular societies. None the less it will be useful to start by considering these well-known definitions.

Chapter I of the *Rules* is entitled 'What is a social fact?' At the end of this chapter Durkheim presents what looks like an answer to the question in the title: two alternative ways of defining 'social fact'.

A social fact is any way of acting, whether fixed or not, capable of exerting over the individual an external constraint; or: which is general over the whole of a given society, whilst having an existence of its own, independent of its individual manifestations. (p. 59)

I note that in both definitions a social fact is said to be a *way of acting*. I take it that 'acting' here is short for – perhaps seen as the genus involved in – what throughout his discussion in Chapter I Durkheim tends to refer to as ways of acting, thinking, and feeling. I shall similarly write of 'acting' alone, for short, in much of what follows. Again following Durkheim, I shall also refer to the ways of acting which are social facts according to Durkheim as *collective* practices; and, when wishing to be more specific, as collective practices, beliefs, attitudes.

Let us start with the first definition. A social fact is said here to be any way of acting 'capable of exercising on the individual an external constraint'.[5]

What did Durkheim have in mind when he connected social facts with external constraint? As critics have commented, the examples Durkheim gives on this subject are confusingly varied. None the less it is possible to isolate at least one general, central thought, by concentrating on some of the key points of Durkheim's discussion of constraint.

Durkheim introduces the idea of the 'coercive power' of social facts in a paragraph early in Chapter I. He explains that social facts are ways of acting such that, if a member of a group acts in one of these ways 'of his own free will', then the coercive power of the social fact is 'not felt, or hardly felt at all' (p. 51). However, as soon as someone attempts to act contrary to one of these ways, then he will feel their 'constraining power' (p. 52).

In this paragraph, Durkheim gives a number of examples of the operation of external coercion which have been criticized for their apparent heterogeneity. Durkheim himself is evidently aware of some differences. Thus first he notes how contravention of law, moral rules, and 'ordinary convention', are followed by punishment in the first cases and the unpleasant experience of ridicule in the last. He goes on:

> In other cases, although it may be indirect, constraint is no less effective. I am not forced to speak French with my compatriots, nor to use the legal currency, but it is impossible for me to do otherwise. If I tried to escape the necessity, my attempt would fail miserably. (p. 51)

It has been argued that in the 'other cases' mentioned we are dealing with a different sense of 'constraint' from before; in these cases we are dealing, to quote Steven Lukes, with 'the need to follow certain rules or procedures to carry out certain activities successfully' (1982, p. 4). The same may be said for using contemporary modes of production, another example Durkheim cites in the same paragraph. Meanwhile, in the cases of law, morals, and convention, 'sanctions are brought to bear' by others on the deviant or would-be deviant. Certainly, Durkheim's reference to 'miserable failure' suggests he is, in effect, describing a different type of coercion here.

It is worth noting, however, that speaking that particular language which is the language of one's community, French, say, and using that currency that one's fellows use, say the French franc, are likely in practice to be ways of acting protected by the sanctions associated with social conventions, such as ridicule. This may occur even when no one's immediate projects stand to fail. Thus someone might express annoyance to a friend for speaking to him in Yiddish at High Table in All Souls' College, even though he understood perfectly what was meant, and it was meant only for him. He might feel that use of a language other than English was a breach of etiquette, and should not have occurred.

It is, clear, of course, that the overall effect on one's life of not doing these things, given generally prevailing conformity, will be rather special. Failure to dress as others do may do no more than attract others' disapproval. (Which is, of course, quite a lot.) On the other hand, speaking a language that is not commonly spoken will most likely involve further grave consequences such as being misunderstood, failing to elicit vital information by questioning, and so on. These further consequences are so grave that their occurrence will likely be a disaster overshadowing any that social disapprobation could inflict. Similar things can be said about the use of legal currency and the prevailing mode of production. None the less, there is reason to maintain that some one kind of coercion is involved in all the cases considered here, whether or not Durkheim locates the type correctly in the paragraph last quoted.[6]

Now, Durkheim at one point uses lively anthropomorphic language, saying that 'the rules of law react against me'. In reality the punishment when one breaks the law is imposed by human beings by virtue of the nature of law, and similarly for established morality and convention. Durkheim also writes repeatedly of the collective practices as having 'coercive power'. It looks, then, as if his basic thought may be that certain ways of acting are *of such a kind* that when someone deviates from them his punishment is deemed appropriate. The basic thought behind the reference to coercion, in other words, could be a thought about an *as yet unspecified special status* which certain ways of acting have. This would make the reference to coercion relatively peripheral to Durkheim's thought here, in the sense that it was derived from something more basic.

This idea is confirmed to some extent if we look at some of Durkheim's own later thoughts in the preface to the second edition. (Clearly, a change of mind could be involved.) There he tries to reformulate his position on constraint, and this involves an attempt further to characterize social facts themselves. Here the key ideas are 'prestige', 'externality', and 'reality'. Durkheim agrees that the coercive power of social facts is analogous to that of one's physical environment, inasmuch as people are 'forced to adapt' to both. However,

> The pressure exerted by one or several bodies on other bodies or even on other wills should not be confused with that which the group consciousness exercises on the consciousness of its members. *What is exclusively peculiar to social constraint is that it stems . . . from the prestige with which certain representations are endowed.* (p. 44; my stress)

Like the physical environment, however, and contrary to personal habits, 'social beliefs and practices act upon us from the outside' and are 'real' (ibid.); 'they are things which have their own existence' (p. 45).

The last phrase echoes part of Durkheim's second alternative definition of a social fact. Let us now consider that definition, and its own mysteries. Here two features are ascribed to a way of acting which is a social fact: generality 'over the whole of a given society' and 'existence in its own right, independent of its individual manifestations'. Now the reference to generality may appear to show that Durkheim endorsed a form of summative view. If a way of acting is 'general over the whole of a given society' that looks as if it is a way generally conformed to by the individual members. Yet at the same time a social fact exists, according to Durkheim, independently of its individual manifestations. The characterization in terms of independence may appear to be in conflict with that in terms of generality; it suggests that the existence of a particular collective way of acting is *not* a function of that way of acting's being generally conformed to, though it may happen to be generally conformed to. Is the above construal of independence simply wrong, so there is not even the appearance of a problem here? Or can it be argued that, say, generality is considered less crucial to social fact-hood than independence?

Durkheim's text supplies material to support relegating generality to a secondary position; it also supplies some material for a different interpretation of independence. Some writers have favoured the latter approach. I shall pursue the former. First, I address the status of 'generality'.

There is reason to think that generality is not part of Durkheim's core conception of what a social fact is, in spite of its appearance in his second 'definition'. At many points in his discussion he downplays its importance. Thus we read:

> It is not the fact that they are general that can serve to characterize sociological phenomena. Thoughts to be found in the consciousness of each individual . . . are not for this reason social facts. If some have been content with using this characteristic in order to define them it is because they have been confused, wrongly, with what might be termed their individual incarnations. What constitutes social facts are the beliefs, tendencies and practices of the group taken collectively. But the forms that these collective states may assume when they are 'refracted' through individuals are things of a different kind. (p. 54)

This may seem to settle the matter against generality as a way of defining social facts.

In one place, Durkheim cites and appears to concede the claim that a phenomenon 'can only be collective if it is common to all the members of a society, or at least to a majority, and consequently, if it is general' (p. 56). However, he goes on to make statements which once again impugn the status of generality as a truly defining characteristic as firmly as in the earlier quotation.

> If it is general, it is because it is collective (that is, more or less obligatory); but it is very far from being collective because it is general. It is a condition of the group repeated in individuals because it imposes itself upon them. It is in each part because it is in the whole, but far from being in the whole because it is in the parts.

In other words, generality may flow from or be a result of collectivity, but it is not part of collectivity as such.

So why is generality in the final definition? I suggest that, as Durkheim himself later argued, in giving this definition Durkheim was largely intent on noting ways in which social facts may be discovered by the sociologist. After all, he is writing a treatise on method (unlike me) and that is his primary focus. What I take to be his basic underlying conception of a social fact is expressed somewhere early in the chapter (to which I shall shortly come). But in giving his definitions Durkheim is already largely concerned with methodology. There is a bit of a mix in the preamble to the definitions of 'how to recognize' and 'how to define' or 'how to characterize in terms of essential features'. Meanwhile, Durkheim clearly wants to stress two main *ways of recognizing* social facts: constraint and generality, and he incorporates a reference to these into his so-called definitions.[7]

I have suggested that from our discussion of the two definitions we take the following to be constitutive characteristics of social facts for Durkheim: social facts are ways of acting with a special status, which involves their having a special prestige within a group; these ways 'exist in their own right, independently of their individual manifestations'. General conformity and the imposition of sanctions for nonconformity are probable concomitants rather than constitutive elements of social facts. It is now time for me to note what I take to be Durkheim's basic or underlying conception of a social fact.

2.3 Durkheim's basic conception of a social fact

In the second edition preface Durkheim denied that in giving his two definitions he was attempting to delimit the field of sociology by means of an all-embracing intuitive principle (*'intuition exhaustive'*, 1968, p. xx). It is obviously somewhat dangerous for anyone else to try to delimit the intuitive principle with which Durkheim himself was operating. None the less, he himself does give expression to what can be thought of as a fundamental, if highly abstract, intuitive principle in Chapter 1 of the *Rules*.

Speaking of the ways of acting he has in mind, Durkheim writes:

> to them must be exclusively assigned the term *social*. It is appropriate, since it is clear that, not having the individual as their substratum, they can have none other than society, either political society in its entirety or one of the partial groups that it includes – religious denominations, political and literary schools, occupational corporations, etc. Moreover it is for such as these alone that the term is fitting, for the word 'social' has the sole meaning of designating those phenomena which fall into none of the categories of facts already constituted and labelled. (p. 52)

In the quoted passage Durkheim is apparently expressing the view that a truly social phenomenon is one whose 'substrate' is a social group. More precisely, he argues that, first, ways of acting whose 'substrate' is a social group are *aptly* called social; second, he argues that they alone are properly called 'social' in so far as this term designates a separate category.[8]

I shall take Durkheim's *basic, intuitive conception* of a social fact, then, to be the conception of *a way of acting whose substrate is a social group*. (Such a group need not, as is clear, be a fully-fledged society or embrace all aspects of its members' lives.) Another way of expressing this conception is in terms of a relation I shall call *inherence*. (If X is the substrate of Y, then as a matter of logic, Y inheres in X.) Durkheim uses various terms for this relation in the second edition preface: *résider dans, être situé dans, s'incarner dans, être dans, avoir pour siège*. So Durkheim's conception may be put this way: a social fact is a phenomenon which *inheres in* a social group. It would be helpful to have this characterization spelled out more fully.

2.4 The full conception

In a passage in the second edition preface the conception of inherence in society is connected with the notion of production by society. Durkheim also characterizes society in a telling way in this passage. Finally, his remarks are connected to a notion of independence of or externality to 'individual consciousnesses'.

> If, as is granted, this *sui generis* synthesis which constitutes every society gives rise to new phenomena, different from those which occur in consciousnesses in isolation, one is forced to admit that these specific facts reside in the society itself that produces them, and not in its parts, that is to say, its members. In this sense therefore they lie outside individual consciousnesses (*consciences individuelles*) considered as such. (My translation of Durkheim, 1968, pp. xvi-xvii)

This occurs in the context of some provocative biological and chemical analogies, and it is not crystal clear.[9] None the less, what Durkheim says, both here and in some other places, strongly suggests the following theses. Though still highly abstract, they constitute in effect an expanded version of the basic conception.

(1) *The synthesis thesis.* First, there is a thesis about social groups: social groups are syntheses *sui generis*. In the human case, they involve a unique kind of synthesis of individual human beings. (2) *The productiveness of society thesis.* A social group as such gives rise to collective ways of acting, thinking, and feeling.

(3) *The newness thesis.* Collective 'ways' are 'new' phenomena. In particular, they are of a genus different from that of the ways of individual human beings. For example, collective beliefs are phenomena of a genus different from that of the beliefs of individual humans. (4) Given all these things, one must infer *The inherence thesis.* Collective ways *inhere in* social groups; they have a group as *substrate.* (More on the central notion of inherence below.)

For purposes of the discussion here, I shall regard the above four theses as expressing, albeit in relatively obscure language, Durkheim's *full conception* of a social fact. I shall take it that they characterize the features Durkheim saw (in 1901) as essential to social facts, however they might occur, or be recognized, in actual instances.

2.5 Externality and inherence

It would be well to say some more about the relation of inherence. In so doing light may be shed on Durkheim's reference to social facts as 'external' to individuals.

Recall first that, as I argued above, Durkheim inclined to the view that the *collectivity* of a given practice was logically independent of the *generality* of that practice within the population in question. Now Durkheim also makes what look like far stronger statements, as when he writes of social facts 'lying outside individual consciousnesses considered as such'. This kind of statement has been strongly criticized.

> Social facts, Durkheim wrote, exist 'outside individual *con-sciences*'. Durkheim here perpetrated an important ambiguity. . . . Social facts could be 'external' to any given individual, or else to all individuals in a given society or group: to speak of them as 'outside individual consciences' leaves both interpretations open. He obviously meant the former, but he frequently used forms of expression which implied the latter. (Lukes, 1973), pp. 11–12)

(Lukes continues: 'In claiming that social facts (and in particular *representations collectives*) are external to individuals, Durkheim should have said that they are both external to and internal to (that is, internalized by) any given individual; and that they are only external to all existing individuals in so far as they have been culturally transmitted to them from the past'.)

Now given the obscurity, and, as Lukes accepts, diverse tendencies within Durkheim's text, it is hard to say what he really meant or should have said. However, the passage from Durkheim most recently quoted suggests a reading of him in which the ambiguity noted by Lukes is not what is at issue.

This reading invokes the notion of *inherence* alluded to in the last section here. According to Durkheim social phenomena in general inhere in social groups as opposed to the individuals who are their members.

Let me now say more about the notion of inherence in a social group as I understand it. Recall that Durkheim conceives of a social group as a special kind of synthesis. The 'elements' involved in the synthesis are individual human beings; by associating with each other in certain ways, and only thus, these come to constitute a social group, an entity of a special kind. When *and only when* they have formed a social group a certain special type of phenomenon can occur among them. For this type of phenomenon is 'new'. I take it that by this Durkheim implies that a social group as such is, crucially, not just a cause but a *causal prerequisite* for the occurrence of these phenomena. Given these facts we say that these phenomena inhere in the group, as opposed to the individual human beings who are its members.

A simple analogy from the physical realm may be helpful in connection with these ideas. Imagine a set of iron filings. In order that the filings-in-combination have certain special properties, they must combine in special ways, forming, in effect, entities of special kinds. Thus, only if they are combined (somehow) to form a wheel, or roughly circular form, will the filings-in-combination have the property of rollability, and the phenomenon of rolling be observed. It looks as if we might say, along Durkheimian lines, that the phenomenon of rolling inheres in the wheel (which itself is a combination of filings) rather than in the filings themselves.

Now, to inhere in a social group is, evidently, to inhere in something constituted by individual human beings in association. Hence in a sense no phenomenon inhering in a social group is *totally independent* of individual human beings. However, it is proper and perspicuous to insist that a special and significant relation to a group is involved here, if it is the case that the existence of any phenomena of this type is causally dependent upon individuals being 'synthesized' in precisely the relevant special way.

In the passage most recently quoted, Durkheim explicitly links his claim that social facts exist outside individual consciousnesses to the claim that they inhere in social groups. 'In this sense, therefore, they lie outside . . .' – that is, in the sense that they inhere in social groups. And one can surely see that, given that social facts inhere in social groups in the sense explained, someone might want to say that – in a sense – these phenomena exist outside, or externally to, the associated individuals and their consciousnesses. For they are located, so to speak, precisely in individuals-in-association, that is, in the group, rather than in individuals, period.

It is worth stressing on Durkheim's behalf that in the passage most recently quoted he is careful and delicate in his phraseology. He says precisely that 'in this sense' social facts lie outside of individual consciousnesses 'considered as such'. Not altogether and in every sense outside. Durkheim did not dispute that individual human consciousnesses – human beings and their mental states – are the stuff out of which social groups are made. No facts about collectivities are totally independent of them.[10] But social facts are immediately dependent on individual consciousnesses or persons only in so far as they are 'combined' to form social groups.

2.6 Durkheim and collective beliefs

Let me now focus on Durkheim's ideas about collective beliefs in particular. Durkheim evidently thinks that the world is such that there is a point in speaking of the collectivity of a certain belief. What point, then? In spite of his language on occasion, it is doubtful whether he would have accepted that a society had subjective states of its own. He speaks of collective beliefs and attitudes as 'new' phenomena, different from those which occur in isolated minds, or in 'consciousnesses in isolation'. This can be taken to imply that the phenomena he refers to as collective beliefs are in some important sense not of the same kind as the beliefs of individual human beings. At the same time, the phenomena are such that the term 'collective belief' or 'the belief of the group' are appropriate to them.

Now, as I have argued, Durkheim holds that to speak of the collectivity of a belief is not to allude to the generality of that belief. In short, he was not a summative theorist. More strongly, one can argue that he was not a correlativist of any sort. For one can understand the view that collective beliefs are 'independent of their individual manifestations' as implying that the collectivity of a certain belief is logically independent of correlative individual beliefs altogether. It is precisely the belief, not of any of the individuals concerned, but of the group itself. Finally, Durkheim evidently wants to say both that collective beliefs are beliefs of a group as such, and that they are such that phenomena of their type can only occur when there are groups. These phenomena are, one might say, essentially group-involving.

In sum, two central ideas which can be gleaned from Durkheim's text are: (1) The existence of a group belief that p is logically independent of the correlative individual beliefs. (2) The phenomenon of group belief is a phenomenon of a special kind, such that a special kind of synthesis of individuals is required (synthesis into a social group) in order for it to arise.

Now nothing that has been said so far has told us much about what collective beliefs are like. We have heard something of what they are not, and have been given abstract characterizations of them, some not entirely pellucid. One who has got so far may still feel quite unconvinced by the theses I have drawn from Durkheim. What are the new phenomena in question? Is it not the case that, conceptually speaking, the best and most appropriate candidate for the fact of collective belief that p is a widespread belief that p? Leaving Durkheim, I turn to this last issue. By the end of the chapter, I believe I shall have described the phenomenon which is intuitively most apt for the label 'collective belief'. It is a phenomenon to which his full conception of a social fact in general applies, as do the two claims about collective beliefs just noted.

3 ASSESSING ACCOUNTS OF COLLECTIVE BELIEFS: SOME TESTS

3.1 A variety of accounts

In what follows I discuss four accounts of collective belief. I argue in favour of one of these, but spend some time on prior discussion and evaluation of the others.

I discuss accounts other than the one I prefer for a number of reasons. For one, the other accounts I discuss have at least some plausibility as accounts of collective belief. Two of them are natural developments from the first, and the first, which I call the simple summative view, is an account that many people suppose must be correct. Further, these accounts describe important types of phenomena. In the case of the two developments from the simple summative view, these could easily be overlooked because of their rather subtle nature.

My own preferred account is most likely to be of value as drawing attention to an important phenomenon whose possibility, not to speak of its actual existence, may easily be overlooked, particularly if one's thinking has come to be cast in a certain type of individualistic mode. The search for a most appropriate object

254

for the label 'collective belief' or 'belief of a group' is ultimately of interest because of the possibility of such results.

Finally, the different phenomena which might attract the label 'the belief of a group' are importantly different from one another, and the nature of the relationship between them is of interest. It is therefore worth describing each one with some care, so as best to compare them. (If the reader prefers to go straight to my own view, described in section 7, below (p. 288 *et seq.*), I recommend that the rest of this section be read first.)

3.2 *Criteria of assessment*

I shall use the following tests as a way of arriving at a most appropriate object for the label 'collective belief'. The criteria or tests are twofold.

First, I shall appeal to linguistic intuition on sentences like: 'The University's research board believes that women are more creative than men', or 'This party believes that capitalism untrammelled will lead to happiness for all'. I shall occasionally refer to such sentences as 'the test sentences'. I shall ask, of certain candidates: would we properly or appropriately say things like this if these were the facts? Would this locution be clearly and squarely in place? If the answer is negative, or even unclear, this will – I propose – suggest that we have not yet latched on to a type of phenomenon which is well described as the belief of a group. Less strongly, it will suggest that there are phenomena of some other sort which are better placed in this respect.

In the example test sentences given so far, the subject term involves what everyone will agree is a collectivity concept. In discussion I sometimes also include sentences of a different form, such as 'We think drunken drivers should lose their licences' and 'The Russians think that vodka is life-enhancing.' All the sentences must be viewed with caution. The last type in particular may be ambiguous, or very capacious in meaning, or at least often used loosely to mean, say, what the simplest summative view says it means. For this reason I shall concentrate on the sentences involving collectivity terms.

As a second type of test, I shall appeal to intuition on the phrases: 'the belief of a group' and 'a collective belief'. I shall occasionally refer to these phrases as 'the test phrases'. In connection with them I ask: does the phenomenon in question seem aptly to be referred to as the *belief of a group*? Does it seem *very* apt to be so labelled? How much so in relation to other phenomena?

In connection with this test I shall ask some more specific

questions also. The first will recall my discussion of Durkheim. It seems reasonable to suppose, in advance of inquiry, that a phenomenon very apt to be called the *belief of a group* would be a phenomenon which essentially involved a collectivity. The fact that the people involved formed a group would be crucial to the existence of the phenomenon in question.[11]

This is a plausible idea if one takes a group to be a special kind of thing, as Durkheim does. It would then seem reasonable to suppose that any phenomenon aptly called the belief of a group will involve something of the special kind in question. At least against these background assumptions, which I take to be plausible, it is worth asking: is this phenomenon essentially collectivity-involving?

In what follows I shall assume the following account of a phenomenon's being 'essentially collectivity-involving'. Suppose we have an account of collective belief of one of these forms: 'There's a collective belief if and only if there are some people who form a group G, and G has feature F' or 'There's a collective belief if and only if all members of group G have quality Q'. Then we may say that a collective belief is essentially collectivity-involving on this account if a population P could not have feature F, or all members of P have quality Q, without it thereby being true that P was a social group. The intuitive idea could be put thus: giving a population which was not already a social group a belief of its own makes it a social group. Or: the 'population analogue' of a group's belief *is* a group's belief. So a phenomenon which is essentially collectivity-involving in this sense could be deemed a collectivity-creating phenomenon.

It would be quite demanding to insist that an acceptable account of collective beliefs must entail that such beliefs are essentially collectivity-involving in the sense defined. I do not set up any such criterion in advance. None the less if a phenomenon does meet this strong 'requirement' it would for that reason be a good candidate for the status of the belief of a group, other things being equal.

Another question that I shall ask, relating to the aptness of talking of a group belief, is less precise and implies a less stringent criterion. Is there any obvious point in talking about a group's beliefs, on the account in question? Is there, in particular, a clear contrast between 'the group believes that p' and 'the members believe that p'? If not, this certainly suggests that the phenomenon in question is not essentially group-involving. But collectivity-involvement is not the only possible factor which could make for such a contrast, as we shall see.

Again, in so far as there is one, how strong is the contrast? The clearer the distinction between the phenomenon alleged to be a belief of a group, and the phenomenon of the members believing that p, the more apt it will be (all else being equal) to be picked out as a distinct phenomenon worthy of the label.

I should stress that I take the second battery of tests as important supplements to the first. The test sentences may be susceptible of fairly weak interpretations, or seem to be appropriate enough in a variety of situations. Once we find a phenomenon which passes the other tests in a clearer manner than the others, it should become clear that sentences such as 'Our group endorses Mondale' are especially appropriate to it. Thus I hope and indeed expect that readers who are at first inclined to accept an account of collective belief that I reject, will come to agree with me in the light of the discussion as a whole.

4 THE SIMPLE SUMMATIVE ACCOUNT

I now turn to the simple summative account of collective belief. This has been trenchantly espoused by Quinton, as an account of what we mean when we talk about the beliefs of groups. On this account, a group G believes that p if and only if most of its members believe that p. Though more inclined to some more complex summative view, Ernest Gellner also at one point contemplates the simple account:[12]

> In as far as the proposition used as an example ['The committee decided to appoint Jones' – M.G.] is only a generalization of the form 'All members of the committee . . .'.

Gellner and Quinton are certainly representative of many.

Some motivations for holding a form of summative view were noted earlier. The simple summative account is the most straightforward, simple account of this type. Let me now consider it in the light of the tests mentioned above.

Suppose an anthropologist were to write:[13]

> The Zuni tribe believes that the north is the region of force and destruction.

I think that no one who heard this would expect the writer to say he intended to refer to the following situation (which I dub the *secrecy situation*).

> Each member of the tribe believes that the north is the region of force and destruction, but at the same time is afraid to tell anyone else that he believes this; he is afraid that the others will mock him, having no reason to think that they believe it.

Such an 'explanation' might well, I suggest, be taken as throwing doubt on the original statement.

Now this suggests that when we ascribe a belief to a group we are not simply saying that most members of the group have the belief in question. That is, it is at least not logically sufficient for a group belief that p that most group members believe that p.

Consider also the sentence 'We believe that p'. Presumably, on the basis of a belief that he alone of his tribe believes that p, a Zuni will not deem 'We believe that p' appropriate. Moreover, were he apprised of the fact that the secrecy situation obtained, I suggest that he would be unlikely to utter the Zuni equivalent of 'Ah, so we believe that p. To think I had no idea!'. He might, of course, say 'So *we all* believe that p. I had no idea!' Or: 'So *all of us* believe that p'. But 'we all' and 'all of us' are distinct from 'we' and, in contrast to 'we', are explicitly summative.

It can be argued, then, that the simple summative account is in some trouble when matched up against our natural understanding of the test sentences.

Turning to the test phrases, my sense is that a set of actual, but secret or unrevealed beliefs would not be enough to constitute something we would naturally call the belief of a group. At the least, it does not seem to constitute the belief of a group in any but a very weak sense.

To consider two more specific tests. The phenomenon involved when most people in a certain group believe that p is not in itself essentially collectivity-involving. That is, the phenomenon of a set of people most of whom believe that p, is one which can occur when those people do not together form a collectivity. Take any random collection of adult humans; presumably most of them believe individually that fire burns. This does not make them into a social group, intuitively speaking. Indeed, one might well judge that there is nothing *social* about each of a set of people believing the same thing. (Poignantly so: X and Y might have all their carefully considered beliefs in common, yet never know it; were they only to find this out, they might become firm friends.)

Again, given that the people most of whom believe that p do form a group, it does not follow that their mostly believing that p bears any important relation to that fact. It is true that faced with any unusual view that is widespread throughout a given group, we will tend to presume that the fact that this view is widespread is the result of some further fact about the group. But this presumption is an empirical hypothesis. I say more to this effect later. At this point someone might want to suggest some type of causal account of group belief, for instance, that a group belief is a widespread belief caused by some property of the group in question. I discuss one possible account of this type later in this chapter. However, the simple summative view involves no causal elements.

Turning to another test, the simple summative account hardly provides a meaty contrast between the belief of the group on the one hand and the correlative beliefs of the members. None the less it might be argued that even according to the simple summative view there is a point to talking about the belief of a group. Sometimes we want to look at the members of a group 'taken collectively', to look at it 'as a whole' and consider which beliefs are highly prevalent among the members. So, on the summative view, the point of characterizing 'what the Zuni believe' or saying that groups believe things, is whatever point there is in picking out the fact that there are widespread general beliefs in certain populations.

One reason for doing such a thing, it might be added, is that a widespread and somewhat peculiar belief within a group may indicate that the group has further special features. Even a secret but widespread belief might, if sufficiently idiosyncratic, lead to important further investigations into the nature of the group; it should surely pique the investigator's curiosity. There is no need for me to dispute such contentions. The question remains whether some phenomenon other than a widespread belief as such might have a better title to the label 'belief of a group'. The simple summative account purports to characterize the phenomenon most worthy of that label.

In closing this section, I note that the simple summative account violates a principle with some intuitive appeal, which has not yet been mentioned. It might be proposed that it will not be the case that a group G believes that p, unless the members of G know that G believes that p. (Call this principle *the members' knowledge principle*.) As the secrecy situation makes plain, on the simple summative view there can in principle be a clear case of a collective belief whose existence is unknown to the members of the relevant group.

Someone might counter that the proposed 'intuitive principle' is unacceptable, because an individual person, after all, may be said to believe that p even though he does not know that he believes that p. It may take fifteen years of psychoanalysis for a person to recognize that he has certain 'secret' or repressed beliefs.

It is true that we allow that someone may not easily realize that he has certain beliefs. However, in the clearest cases in which we say someone believes something the belief is not buried that deep. Though the question of how we access our beliefs is hardly easy, and the same goes for what a belief is, we should surely not take as our paradigm a repressed belief or, more generally, a belief whose possessor does not acknowledge it given a certain amount of sincere reflection.[14] It is therefore not obviously unreasonable to prefer a model of collective belief such that collective beliefs are known or at least fairly accessible to the group members.

The strict analogy with paradigm cases of the beliefs of individuals requires that *the group itself* know or could easily come to know of its belief. That this should be so seems plausible. A test based on this constraint, however, can hardly be applied until we know what it is for a group to believe something. Meanwhile, it seems independently plausible to suppose that a group's belief should be accessible to the individual members, whatever the relation of their personal knowledge to the group's knowledge may be.

5 A SECOND SUMMATIVE ACCOUNT: ADDING COMMON KNOWLEDGE

5.1 Introduction

Given the above considerations, one may still feel convinced that the 'core' phenomenon of a collective belief that p must be the widespread belief that p within a group. One might then ask what seems to be the basic problem in the secrecy situation.

In the example given above, people deliberately keep their beliefs secret. It is plausible to argue, however, that the force of the example does not stem specifically from the deliberate secrecy, but rather from the fact that no one knows of anyone else's belief. So we might take it that we should add to the simple summative view the requirement that everyone in the group should know that the belief in question is widespread. This does not seem to be enough, however.

Suppose that everyone knows that the others believe that p (perhaps because each one has confided in each other) but each one thinks that he alone has this knowledge (he thinks that he alone has been chosen as confidant). This situation does little better in relation to the test sentences and test phrases than the secrecy situation did. And there is no obvious stopping place in the chain. What if everyone knows that everyone knows about a certain widespread belief, but each one thinks that he alone has this knowledge? It may become hard to imagine circumstances in which this is so, but it may also seem that one had better rule out this *kind* of thing entirely. (Compare David Lewis, 1969, p. 59:

'the cases become more and more unlikely, but no less deserving of exclusion'.)

What seems to be the general problem here? One aspect of the situation recalls the members' knowledge principle mentioned earlier. Just as a generalized belief need not be known to all, so it may not be known to all that a generalized belief is known to all, and so on. So if a collective belief is defined in terms of some finite number of levels of knowledge, it always remains possible in principle that the members of the group have a collective belief in that sense but neither know it nor could come to know it given a little reflection. Hence the plausible members' knowledge principle is not satisfied.

Another aspect of an account in terms of a finite number of levels, however high, is that it may not seem to capture properly the flavour of the sort of situation one sees as paradigmatic. What, we might ask, would be the opposite, so to speak, of the secrecy situation? Presumably something like the following. The members of the tribe mingle regularly in the market place. People often loudly express to others their personal belief that the north is the region of force and destruction. Now the epistemic situation here does not seem to be captured by saying simply that all know that all have the belief; nor by saying that all know this, also; and so on, even for quite high orders of knowledge about knowledge. Evidently, we should try carefully to characterize what this sort of situation is like.

The obvious way to amend the simple summative account is by using a technical notion of 'common knowledge' along the lines of David Lewis and others. A notion of this type was introduced in the last chapter, for use in a different context. Evidently, addition of a common knowledge component brings into the discussion of collective belief an important aspect of human life which is not part of the explicit conceptual repertoire of classic sociologists such as Durkheim and Weber. In the next two sections I develop an appropriate summative account of collective belief. I then assess it in the usual way.

5.2 Population common knowledge

In the last chapter I introduced the definition: it is *common knowledge in a population P that q* if and only if q is *open** to everyone in P and everyone in P has noticed this. (The fact that q is *open** to everyone in P if and only if the situation is such that (1) q; (2) the smooth reasoner counterpart of each member of P would infer that q; (3) the smooth reasoner counterpart of each member of P would infer that (2), and so on.) I shall say that it is *population common knowledge* that q, in population P, when it is common knowledge in P that q.

A few notes on the phenomenon of population common knowledge are in order. First, what is a *population*? I shall take it that any condition on people, including conditions stipulating particular people as members, defines a population of people. Thus 'Tom, Dick, and Algernon', 'those who have walked on the moon', 'the Nuer', 'the Russians', and so on, define populations.

Two population-defining conditions may be true of exactly the same people. Meanwhile, it is of some importance to note that even when this is so it may be population common knowledge that p among those satisfying condition C1, but not population common knowledge that p among those satisfying condition C2. Thus, in the sense defined above, it may be population common knowledge among, say, the Transylvanian spies in London, though not among those seated around this dinner table, that the Transylvanians plan to tap the phone of a certain Conservative Member of Parliament. For secrecy may be so great that Transylvanian spies are not even known to one another, and thus the assembled company are not aware that they comprise precisely the Transylvanian spies. Then, if in the definition of population common knowledge just given we replace 'members of P' by 'the Transylvanian spies in London', all the conditions will be satisfied. On the other hand, if we replace 'members of P' by 'those seated at the dinner table' or 'Kim, Don, Tony, etc.' conditions (1) and (2) in the definition will still be satisfied, but none of the other conditions will be.

It seems natural to say that having or lacking population common knowledge is a property of the population in question. Meanwhile, the combination of the ideas that (1) any condition on people defines a population, (2) coextensive populations may differ with respect to their common knowledge, and (3) having common knowledge is a property of the population in question, implies that two conditions may be be true of exactly the same people but determine different populations. Given these assumptions, then, a population is not merely the set of its members.[15]

Finally, a note on what might be called 'recognitional capacity' is in order. The existence of population common knowledge as defined here does not imply that the members of the population can recognize each other as members of the population, except in so far as this capacity is implied by their having the concept of the population in question. This is worth comment since the discussions of both Lewis and Schiffer include remarks which suggest the contrary.[16] Whereas population common knowledge, where it exists, is an important phenomenon, it is by no means so powerful that it gives people special powers of perception they might not otherwise have. Let me justify and clarify my own position briefly.

From the existence of population common knowledge in P, as defined, it follows that each member of P has the concept of a member of P. Does it follow that members of P are able to recognize other members of P? I would say not, but one can be more specific than this.

Membership in a population need carry with it no external marks on the basis of which members may reliably be recognized. So if one is thinking of recognition by external appearance, people could be parties to population common knowledge yet be unable to recognize each other in *this* way. Nor need they be able generally to recognize each other in practice on the basis of conversation, observation of behaviour, and so on. Imagine cases involving a group of spies. Such a group may, surely, have items of population common knowledge. It may be common knowledge in the spy division that each spy believes that to be detected in the course of duty – to be recognized – is worse than committing murder (in the course of duty). But, as we know, a spy is pretty much always on duty. It may be that each member of the spy division is so good at his job, he manages to fool the members of his own division whenever they encounter each other. Evidently merely having the concept of a member of P does not entail the ability to tell by external marks, or the ability in practice to find out, who are the members of P around one.

One might wonder how population common knowledge could ever become established if members could not recognize one another on the basis of observation. Clearly in many cases of population common knowledge people will perceive certain others to be members of P, and note some further facts about them. But it does not follow from the definition of population common knowledge that this is the way things must come about. One alternative mechanism is exemplified by, say, the appearance of a booming voice from heaven with an indubitably authentic ring which says 'Everyone on this island fears me.' A coded letter mailed to each member of the spy division and saying that it has been so mailed could also do the trick. Even where the population common knowledge is generated in the first instance by people noting things about people who are perceptibly members of the population this does not mean that once the knowledge is established, one will thereby be able to continue to recognize such people for what they are. When observant Jews went underground in Spain, they may not have been able to recognize each other, yet there may have been many things which continued to be population common knowledge among them. It seems then that there is nothing about the nature of population common knowledge as such which entails that members of the population can currently recognize one another.

5.3 A common knowledge account of collective belief

Given the notion of population common knowledge, we can give the following 'common knowledge' account of collective belief:

a group G believes that p if and only if (1) most members of G believe that p, and (2) it is population common knowledge in G that (1).

I should address two aspects of this account which might be questioned.

(i) The scope of common knowledge

Recall that population common knowledge is defined in terms of what *everybody* in a certain population has noticed. So this account of collective belief implies that *everyone in group G* must participate in population common knowledge with respect to G. This may appear to raise a problem for an account of the belief of a social group in general.

Let us assume that normal adult members of human groups can fulfil the conditions on population common knowledge.[17] What, though, of young children and adults of very low intelligence? It is plausible to suppose that they will not be capable of participating in population common knowledge that a certain belief is general in a given group. This suggests that we should not require that *everyone* in G must participate in the population common knowledge. There are other grounds for this suggestion also. Evidently people other than those intellectually incapable of being parties to population common knowledge in a social group may fail to be parties to it. For instance, suppose one Zuni member goes to Oxford University and while there ceases to believe that the north is the region of force and destruction. Assume that he, together with all his kinsmen, believed that before. He then returns home to his tribe, and stays home most of the time. He hears no one express the old belief about the north, and comes to believe that no one has that belief any more. He is, then, no longer party to the relevant common knowledge.

One particular type of move in relation to this issue will not do. David Lewis argues (in a different but related context) that we can ensure that a universally quantified condition of population common knowledge obtains in a population by using the following device: 'anyone who might be called an exception might better be excluded from P' *(Convention*, p. 77). This looks like a suggestion to use the common knowledge condition to specify the population in question.[18] But this kind of move has to be out of place given the type of conception of population common knowledge at issue here. In order to participate in population common knowledge, members of population P must themselves notice that some fact is open* *to everyone in P*. It is therefore a requirement of such a definition of common knowledge that *the population be specifiable antecedently to and independently of the fulfilment of the common knowledge condition*.

Let us look at the implications of the case of the Oxfordian Zuni for one more moment. What I have imagined is that he returns home and does not go to the market place, which is where people loudly express their views about the north. This implied that he could fail to realize that most people believe that the north is the region of force. We might also take it that those Zuni who do frequent the market place understand that if any of their number does not do so, he or she will not know about most people's belief about the north. Thus what people actually notice is not that the general belief about the north is open* to *all*, but that it is open* to those who frequent the market place, which we may assume is the vast majority of members of the tribe. Given the way things are in actual groups, then, there is a case for amending the present account of collective belief so that it is not only unnecessary for everyone in G to believe that p, but also unnecessary for all to notice that the general belief that p is open* to all.[19]

Meanwhile, there are circumstances in which the present strong conditions hold. In particular, one would expect them to hold in small groups of intelligent adults, where there is much interaction between the parties and where evidence is easily and obviously available to all that a certain belief is general throughout the group. In larger and more complex groups, the strong conditions become less realistic.

At this point in our discussion we could go either way. We could amend the account as indicated or stick with a less realistic, more 'ideal' account. A reason for doing the latter is that it is of some interest to discover what follows, intuitively, from the fulfilment of the more stringent conditions. We might then think of ourselves as investigating a paradigm case of collective belief.

For the purposes of discussion here, I shall stick with what we have. My argument as a whole will show that whichever alternative the summative theorist were to choose, he would not have characterized the phenomenon most apt for the label 'collective belief'. For even in the 'ideal' case, we do not get a phenomenon with this character.

(ii) Population versus individual common knowledge

I argued above that population common knowledge did not entail that members of the population could recognize each other as members of that population. It is also true that given that there is population common knowledge, members of the population need have no very clear idea of who the members of the population are. A member of a university class of 1925, for example, may have lost track of his classmates, and have little idea of who the survivors are. None the less it could be population common knowledge in this group that, say, they have a class mascot called 'Sooty'.

We can contrast population common knowledge with what I shall now call *individual common knowledge*. This may seem to be of greater practical importance than population common knowledge. An account of it was, in effect, given in the last chapter. I shall say that individuals X, Y, Z, *commonly know* that p if and only if the fact that p is open* to each of the individuals X, Y, and Z, and each of X, Y, and Z have noticed this. I shall say that it is *individual common knowledge in a population P that p*, if and only if the members of P are individuals X, Y, Z (or whoever) and X, Y, and Z commonly know that p, according to the above definition. Clearly there can be imperfect cases of individual common knowledge in a population such that not absolutely everybody is involved.

Individual common knowledge in a population will clearly be an important phenomenon if it occurs, and something like it surely does often occur, though it will be less likely to occur the larger a population grows.

Now it may reasonably be asked why the summative theorist should use the notion of population common knowledge in preference to that of individual common knowledge. One simple reason for not defining a collective belief wholly in terms of individual common knowledge in a population is that this phenomenon requires that every (or almost every) member of the population in question knows of every other member. But this will not be true of the members of many largish groups. Obviously, the account of collective belief will be simplest if it refers to only one type of common knowledge.

It does seem possible to argue for an account wholly in terms of population common knowledge. Consider the following example. Let us assume that the army of a small country, Wye, has been severely depleted by the enemy. Three men, A, B, and C, are in fact the sole surviving members of the army. Each knows that he is a member of the army, but when he meets the others at a political meeting one day, he does not realize that they are fellow members. Now suppose that those present begin speculating about the problems of the Wye army. One of the guests, D, an experienced and trustworthy politician, says 'I know for a fact that most Wye soldiers think discipline is of no importance.' Let us now assume that it is individual common knowledge in P, where P is the Wye army, that most Wye soldiers think discipline is of no importance. For (i) A, B, and C commonly know that most Wye soldiers think this, and (ii) A, B, and C are the only surviving Wye soldiers. Now it does not follow from this that it is *population* common knowledge among Wye soldiers that they mostly think discipline is of no importance. Assume it is not. Assume that as far as A knows, he alone of his fellow soldiers knows that most of them hold this view. For he thinks he is the only such soldier who has received D's information. He also believes, meanwhile, that he is not the only surviving soldier. Assume that the same goes for B and C: each thinks *he* is the only Wye soldier who has received D's information, and so on.

Now it seems to me that the above case is a particularly unpersuasive candidate for the description of a group belief. That is, it does not seem to bear out the claim that *the Wye army* thinks discipline is of no importance.

In spite of the *individual* common knowledge within the Wye army, this case is quite close to the cases it was deemed desirable to rule out at the beginning of this section. For in this case, even though it is true that the members of P, the Wye army, all know that most members of P think discipline is of no importance, they do not know that most members of P have any access to that fact.

It seems, then, that the summative theorist should stick with the notion of population common knowledge as opposed to individual common knowledge.

5.4 Assessment: (1) Situations of personal confession

Our new account rules out the secrecy situation and certain analogous ones as intended. It also, evidently, describes a phenomenon which would be important where it occurred. Let us now assess it as an account of collective belief.

I first consider how it measures up against the test sentences. I shall do so by reference to a small-scale imaginary example involving a group therapy session; I shall call the type of situation involved a *personal confession* situation. Five women regularly meet together with a psychotherapist. Though each of the five is primarily concerned to solve certain problems of her own, these five form a collectivity of sorts. One day the therapist says: 'What I'd like now is for each of you, going round clockwise from Lydia, to summarize in one word what you personally think men are like. Please decide what you are going to say during a two-minute pause now, then I'll begin asking each of you what she thinks'. Two minutes later, she asks Lydia for her response. Lydia says, thoughtfully and sincerely, that she thinks men are selfish. It turns out that three of the others say the same. They all laugh. Everyone correctly believes that no one was influenced by anyone else in any way. I shall assume that when this has happened there is common knowledge in the group that most members of the group believe that men are selfish.

If these were all the facts, how appropriate linguistically would it be for Lydia to report to a friend: 'Our group thinks that men are basically selfish' or 'In our opinion, men are selfish'? She might in fact say this. But I suggest that there would be something off-colour about it. It is at least *somewhat* inappropriate. Meanwhile, if she said 'We all thought . . .' or (more accurately) 'Most of us thought . . .', that would be impeccable. The same goes for what the therapist might say. There is something not quite right about 'The women's group thought that . . .', as opposed to 'Most of the women in the women's group thought that . . .' Of course, until more is said about features that are missing from this situation, one might wonder, precisely, 'But what is missing . . ?' or 'But what else could one say this kind of thing about?' On the other hand, according to my sense of the meaning of ascriptions of belief to the group, whatever else is true, the situation here does not quite merit description in such terms.

There are possible hidden assumptions – none of which is intended as part of the example here – which could alter someone's sense of what descriptions are appropriate. For instance, a more positive reaction might obtain given the assumption of an explicit understanding among the group members that the aim of their expressing their personal views was to arrive at a a group view, which would be derived from the view of the majority, if there was one.

It is worth noting that given such an understanding, there is in principle an extra 'strain' on each individual with respect to her sincerely expressing her personal view. Each person now realizes that what she says may affect what view is taken to be the group's view. This could, in principle, move her to express a view other than her own. In other words, when the conditions become closer to those under which 'it's our view' is an appropriate reaction to a set of public expressions of view, it will be less certain that the views expressed are genuine personal views on the issue. In the group therapy case it is hard to imagine why each woman would not, in practice, go ahead and just express her real personal view in spite of knowing its potential influence on what will be accepted as the group view. But there are related cases in which it is not at all hard. This issue merits a brief excursus from the group therapy case.

Consider the case of parliamentary elections, as they proceed, for example, in Great Britain. Exactly how to characterize what goes on when such elections take place is a matter not just of theory but of delicate empirical findings. However, it is clear that this case is far from one where each individual vote can be presumed to be a straightforward expression of personal preference for a particular candidate. Almost everyone understands that the country is to be governed by whichever party gets the majority of seats in parliament, and that this majority is arrived at by summing the individual votes cast with respect to particular seats, so that the party with the majority of the votes wins that seat. There is therefore a very important end result to the voting process which everyone is aware of. In practice this clearly influences many votes. Often, three candidates are up for election. Therefore, someone who would prefer above all to elect candidate A, may in fact vote for candidate B, since A is unlikely to win anyway, and the real issue is whether B or C will be elected. Again, knowing that his preferred candidate will come second, someone might capriciously vote for one of the other candidates, feeling that it really does not matter how he votes. That such things can happen shows that we must view with scepticism the claim that two hundred thousand votes cast for X in an election of this sort means that two hundred thousand people personally preferred to see X in parliament. What it may rather mean is just that two hundred thousand people chose to vote for X, in the knowledge that votes were to be summed and whoever of X, Y, and Z received the most votes would be returned to parliament.[20]

I am not saying that the result of a British election is not properly described as a 'mandate from the nation' or 'the choice of the British people'. Nor am I saying that one is not supposed to vote for the party one would prefer to see in power. This may well be what is supposed, and it may even be that in general people vote accordingly. This was used as an example of a type of case where it may be appropriate to sum certain expressions (the votes) to give a 'group view', but where at the same time it is quite likely that the votes are not pure representations of personal view, given the understanding of what is going on.

Now suppose people were to vote in a mock election. I suggest that it would not be proper to take this as determining the 'choice of the British people': not because of a possible failure of sincerity, but because people did not think their vote was 'real'. Exactly how people understand their situation when they express their views is surely of the utmost importance to our deciding on the bearing of these expressions of view on the nature and existence of a view of the group.

To return now to the group therapy case, my own sense of things is that if the facts are simply and precisely as described, the test sentences are at least somewhat inappropriate. This may be because there is a strong reading of them in which they are *clearly* inappropriate. Whyever exactly it is, I propose that the open personal confession situation is not a paradigmatic verifier of the test sentences. This throws doubt on the common knowledge account of collective belief.

5.5 Assessment: (2) The issue of collectivity-involvement

Next, let me go to the test phrases. Does the phenomenon of 'commonly known general belief' within a group seem to be appropriately referred to by the label 'the belief of a group'? My own immediate reaction is negative. My intuitive understanding of 'Group G believes that p' is such that it is not entailed by: 'It is population common knowledge in G that p is generally believed in G'. Such intuitive reactions find support when we ask more specific related questions.

One such question is: is this phenomenon essentially collectivity-involving? Or could everything else be the same, but a population which is not a social group be involved? That this is so may seem obvious, since population common knowledge can apparently be a feature of populations which are not social groups. At this point, however, we should assess with care the following train of thought, which is of some interest in itself. A population as such can, admittedly, fail to be a social group: it can be a set of persons randomly selected by an observer, for instance, or a set of people whose sole link is the possession of some common attribute. Meanwhile, population common know-

270

ledge does not exist in all populations. It could be that where population common knowledge occurs in a given population, that makes the population a social group. In the previous chapter I proposed an account of social groups which goes against this idea. However, we may now consider an alternative hypothesis: is population common knowledge, specifically of a widespread belief in the population in question, enough to turn the population into a social group?

Some possible objections should be rejected. For instance, the ideas that if this were so, then the whole of humanity could, in principle, form a social group, that there can be highly transient – even momentary – social groups, that mere dyads could be social groups, that very hostile people could form social groups. These consequences are surely acceptable.[21] (My own account of a social group allows for all these possibilities in principle.) However, there are some excessively worrying aspects of the idea that population common knowledge of a widespread belief can make the people involved members of a social group. One problem involves common-sense propositions.

Suppose some people possess a feature F (like having brown hair) such that most normal adults will know that they have F, if they have it. Suppose further that F-ness does not carry with it any obvious special tendencies, attitudes, and so on. Now, all normal adult humans with F will believe many common-sense propositions. Given all this, if p is any common-sense proposition, it will be population common knowledge in the population of those who have F that everyone in the population believes that p. Surely, one might feel, whether or not the population of brown-haired people is a social group, it will not be for *this* reason.

Another implausible case of a social group is as follows.[22] Take some population, P, say, the population of brown-haired people, and some proposition p which is believed by some members of P. Suppose that it is reasonably believed by each P-member who does believe that p that he is at least not alone in believing that p (the proposition, say, that some men prefer brunettes). Now consider the population P', specified thus: P' is *the population of those P members who believe that p.* It will surely be population common knowledge in this population that most members of P' believe that p. For it is analytic or tautologous that all those P members who believe that p believe that p. Let us then assume that this will be open* to all P members who believe that p, and that all P members who believe that p realize this. It will then be population common knowledge in P' that most members of P' believe that p. It seems quite counterintuitive, however, to call this particular population a social group by reason of this belief. For how could the members' knowledge of analytic or tautologous propositions, albeit ones involving defining properties of the population, make a population a social group?

This contention, then, seems to stand: there can be population common knowledge of a generalized belief in a population which is not a social group. According to the account now being considered, then, group belief is not essentially collectivity-involving in the strong sense introduced earlier. For everything else could be the same and a population rather than a social group be involved. I take this to support the intuition that fulfilment of the conditions laid down in this account is not logically sufficient for group belief.

It is true that the belief of a group according to the account is such that as a matter of logic the people involved in the phenomenon of group belief must form a group. Moreover, this is not so in quite such a thin way as is the case on the simple summative account. There, there is a group G and everyone in G believes that p. Here, there is a group G and everyone in G knows that *there is a group G* and that *most members of G* believe that p. In other words, people's awareness of a group is an integral part of the phenomenon of group belief as defined here. Moreover, if population common knowledge in general is a property of the population in which it occurs, then in the case of group belief, it is a property of the group in question. The group as such, then, is arguably involved in this phenomenon in a relatively integral fashion. None the less one can question whether it is, intuitively, involved in such a way that the group can be said to have a certain belief of its own. For when all is said and done, what is commonly known here is a fact about what most people individually believe. Why, one might wonder, call this a *group belief* even if it involves a group in the way noted?

Is there a clear contrast, on this account, between 'the group believes that p' and 'the members believe that p'? Clearly, there is a contrast, because of the nontriviality of the common knowledge condition. The group's believing that p is not just a matter of all or most of the individual members believing that p. The contrast, however, is not that strong, since *what* the group believes about something simply reflects what the majority of the members personally believe about that thing.

It has been suggested that a widespread belief of which there was population common knowledge would be 'socially real' whereas a widespread but hidden belief would not be. Bach and Harnish have defined a concept from the common knowledge family which they call 'mutual belief that p in a collectivity G'. This involves a number of levels of beliefs about beliefs. They claim that if and only if something is mutually believed in a group G is it 'socially or intersubjectively real for G' (1979, p. 270). As will emerge by the end of this chapter, a different sense could be given to 'socially/intersubjectively real', corresponding to a different sense of 'collective belief' (or 'collective knowledge'). Meanwhile, that a group belief in the sense of the current common knowledge account exists is clearly an important thing. We do have here a phenomenon worth noticing, and therefore worth labelling in *some* way. The pertinent question here, though, is whether 'collective belief' is a good label. On present showing the answer is negative. But if there were no phenomenon more apt for this label, it might seem pointless to jib at its being used here. It would be good, then, to find a better candidate.

5.6 *The case of coextensive groups: a counterexample to both summative views so far considered*

A single rather special kind of case may be cited as important further evidence that neither of the summative views considered so far can be correct. This case concerns 'coextensive' groups – distinct groups with all their members in common.

Assume that there are two groups, say the Library Committee and the Food Committee of a residential college, which, by coincidence, have the same members. It seems quite possible to say, without contradiction, that (a) most members of the Library Committee personally believe that college members have to consume too much starch, and this is population common knowledge in the Library Committee; (b) the same goes, *mutatis mutandis*, for the members of the Food Committee; (c) the Food Committee believes that college members have to consume too much starch, whereas the Library Committee has no opinion on the matter. The obvious conclusion is that according to our intuitive conceptions it is not logically sufficient for a group belief that p either that most group members believe that p, or that there be population common knowledge within the group that most members believe that p.

6 A THIRD SUMMATIVE ACCOUNT: THE GROUP AS CAUSE

6.1 Introduction

One sympathetic to summativism might now argue that something about how the general beliefs in question come about is what is needed as an addition to or substitute for the summative view with common knowledge. If the beliefs themselves are in some way caused by the group, then it will be more intuitive to speak of them as the beliefs of the group. This suggestion ties in with ideas from both Durkheimian sociologists and contemporary analytic philosophers of social science. I shall develop this idea as sympathetically as possible and then test it. It will represent the most complex summative account dealt with here.

What is it for an individual's belief to be produced by a group? A well-known passage in the social science literature could be thought to throw light on this. After arguing that it does not in fact do so, I proceed to take the general notion of a group's production of a belief in an individual as a complex notion which is grasped intuitively provided that its components are grasped. As I shall show, some quite diverse mechanisms fall under this general notion. I shall develop a detailed account of one such mechanism, and derive from it a relatively precise causal account of collective belief. If the conditions posited by this account are not sufficient for collective belief intuitively, this will refute the claim that a 'production by the group' clause is sufficient to rescue the simple summative account, or the common knowledge version.

6.2 The Counterfactual condition of Mauss and Fauconnet

In their important encyclopedia article, 'Sociologie', Durkheim's followers Paul Fauconnet and Marcel Mauss write:

> it seems clear that the group, crowd, or society has its own nature, that it causes certain ways of feeling, thinking, and acting in individuals, and that *these individuals would not have had the same tendencies, habits, or prejudices, if they had lived in other human groups.* (My stress and translation from 1968–9, p. 141)

The stressed clause has been thought helpful in clarifying the nature of social facts in general.[23] However it was intended by its authors, let us examine whether it provides an acceptable explication of the idea of a belief's being produced by a particular society. Let us consider, that is, the following proposed analysis: a belief general in society S is *caused by S* if and only if *the individuals concerned would not have had the belief in question had they lived in other human societies*. Let us call this the *MF* (for Mauss and Fauconnet) analysis. This stands in need of clarification in various ways. I shall consider in turn the adequacy of two different conditions which could be intended.

Call the following the *First Counterfactual condition: the individuals concerned would not have had the belief in question had they lived in any' other actual human society*. This condition is surely too strong to be acceptable as a logically necessary condition on a belief's being a product of a given society. At least from a logical point of view there could be be two societies which independently produced a given belief in most of their members. And if two societies were sufficiently similar otherwise, their producing similar beliefs in their members would be something to expect.

At the same time fulfilment of the First Counterfactual condition does not seem to be logically sufficient for production by a society. Suppose that there is a general belief in society S that the moon is made of blue cheese. Suppose, further, that had the members of S been members of any other actual society they would not have had the belief in question. From these premises it does not seem to follow that anyone's belief that the moon is made of blue cheese is produced by S. Many other possibilities appear to be open. For instance, a stranger in the grip of a temporary delusion could have capriciously persuaded the individuals in question that the belief was correct.

Now the First Counterfactual condition hardly jibes well with the thought of Mauss and Fauconnet as a whole. For them, as for Durkheim, the existence of the same highly distinctive institution in different societies was practically the *raison d'être* of social science, indicating as it did that an explanation of a given institution's existence might be found in other general features of the society in which it occurred. (Institutions mentioned include the *couvade* and the levirate.) So let us look for another construal of the MF analyis.

The MF analysis could possibly be construed as requiring that had members not been members of their actual society, but of some other randomly chosen one, they *might not* have had the belief in question. So let us now consider the *Second Counterfactual condition: there is at least one other human society S' such that, had the members of S lived in S', they would not have had the belief in question.* Here practices shared by some societies are not ruled out. Practices which are universal are.

This is weaker than the First Counterfactual condition, so, if I was right about that, it will not be a sufficient condition for the production of a certain belief by a given society.[24]

It is not obvious that fulfilment of the Second Counterfactual condition is necessary if a belief general in a society is to be produced by the society. It seems possible that a universally general belief could be produced by some or all of the societies in which it occurs. If all societies develop some set of rules about sexual relations between members, and all forbid intercourse between biological parents and their children, then quite likely most people in each society will personally believe that this form of incest was a bad thing. It is by no means obvious that a given individual's belief cannot then be produced by the particular society in which he happens to live.

Now it may be suggested that when Mauss and Fauconnet spoke of beliefs people would not have had if they had been in other human societies, they were referring to beliefs which did not derive directly from what they call, in the text under discussion, 'the organic and psychic nature of the individual', that is, of human beings in general. The authors refer to 'the phenomena of sensation, representation, reaction, or inhibition' and write '. . . they are the same, whatever group the individual belongs to. If an isolated individual were conceivable, one could say that they would be what they are even outside any society' (my translation). Organico-psychic phenomena, then, are conceived of as completely unconnected with an individual's location in a particular society; they are the class of reflex actions, instinctive tendencies, innate concepts, and the like. Now, one can presumably argue that if there are organico-psychic beliefs, every normal member of every human society will have them. Hence, if a belief is not virtually universal, it will not be organic. However, the mere fact that a belief happens to be universal does not logically entail its organicness. Meanwhile, to speak of 'necessary universality' is unhelpful without specification of the type of necessity involved. At this point it looks as if the core notion here is, in any case, 'not organico-psychic' rather than 'not universal' or even 'not necessarily universal'.[25]

Finally, then, consider the following descendant of the original MF analysis: a belief which is general in a society S is produced by S if it is not determined by innate biological or psychological tendencies. This surely will not do. This negative characterization of the belief in terms of what it is not determined by simply does not tell us what it is determined by. Thus, from a logical point of view, it leaves things too open. The hypothesized generality of the belief does not close things up. The belief could be general because a single person persuaded the individual members of S of its truth. There seems also to be the logical possibility that the beliefs are not 'determined', in any obvious sense, by society or by anything else.

Perhaps it will be noted in defence of this condition that human beings do not in fact mature properly outside a social context; therefore a mature human being's possession of all but innate concepts and beliefs must be to some degree a causal consequence of his or her social context. However, the stated condition is being assessed as a purported explication of the notion of causation by a society. The truth of the claim made in the objection would not show that the very idea of a belief's being caused by society was replaceable by or equivalent to that of its being non-organic.

In the light of the above objection it is worth stressing that the question at issue here amounts to the following: when can it be said that a given society caused some individual to have a given particular belief? It is hard to see how one can argue for the causality of a society at this level from general facts about the dependence of the development of human faculties on a social context. To give an example, it could be that everyone in a given tribe believes that it is hot in the month of Mogg. It will presumably be true that they possess the idea that there are different months and so on as a result of their membership in the tribe. Even so it seems perfectly possible that each one personally holds the belief in question as a result of living through many hot Moggs. This particular belief will be caused by the weather, then, rather than by his society. In general, even if in practice many of one's concepts derive from one's society in some way, the concepts one holds can only be said to determine one's beliefs in a weak manner: they provide a boundary for possible beliefs, but do not determine which beliefs are held within that boundary.

I have argued for the unsatisfactoriness of certain ways of explicating the notion of a belief's being caused by a society. No reference to the incidence of the belief across actual societies seems to work. Nor does a negative characterization in terms of lack of organic origin. We are left where we started, with the unanalysed idea of causation by a society or, more generally, by a social group. This idea alone, however, gives no clue as to how causation by a group is possible; it provides no sense of what kinds of mechanism of production we can expect. Someone might be forgiven for wondering, indeed, whether it was an idea which could have any application. One might wonder in particular how it could have any application to the beliefs of the individual members of the group. This is an issue of great general significance. The idea that a social group or social forces can affect the beliefs and behaviour of individuals has seemed obvious to many. It has also seemed to pose significant threats to the idea of human freedom. One cannot properly assess the implications of the idea of social causation without attempting to understand the possible mechanisms by which groups can affect their members.

6.3 A central model of production by a social group (Model M)

Suppose that Jim becomes a member of a certain social circle, and discovers that it is open* to all the members of this circle that most of them disapprove of boasting. Jim may prefer not to boast given this open* general disapproval and hence not boast. Jim's attitude could be widespread. Thus it could be that most people in the circle currently refrained from boasting as a result of the open* widespread disapproval (in addition to their own personal disapproval).

In some contexts things could be more complex. In a multi-generational society disapproval of boasting could have been manifested to all when young, by parents and teachers. Thus at an early age people may have come habitually to refrain from boasting, perhaps never being consciously inclined to boast. Awareness of the open* general disapproval of boasting could still have some influence on behaviour. Thus though one may have ceased to think of boasting as a real possibility, one may know that were one suddenly to think of it this way, the thought would have to be suppressed. And this knowledge would presumably serve as an extra if not currently necessary force preventing one from boasting.

Now, particularly with respect to the first kind of example, it may seem natural to say that the open* generalized disapproval of boasting within a social circle produced or was at least in part responsible for someone's refraining from boasting. Do we yet have, intuitively, a case of production by a social group? More specifically, is production by the open* generalized disapproval within the group properly seen as production *by the group*?

This question leads us into the area of what might be called the *causality of things*. This is a somewhat delicate area. Let me make a few rather rough observations about it.

It appears that, in general, when we take it that some thing or entity E has produced some state of affairs S, we feel we can infer that E was in some qualitative state such that *E's being in that state* produced S. The converse, however, does not seem to hold.

Consider some examples. If I tell you that I hit the tennis ball over the net, you will assume that I did this by virtue of my being in a specific qualitative state, in this case, presumably, the state of swinging my racquet against the ball. However, at least in the case of a person, it seems that the causality of not just any state of the person will be deemed obviously to entail the person's own causality. Thus suppose I am in the following state: I have my back to the tennis court. Now suppose a ball bounces off my back onto the court, without my having any idea of what is happening. Someone might rather jokily say: 'Thanks for stopping the ball, Margaret!' Jokiness seems to be in place because it is not entirely appropriate to say that *I* stopped the ball. It seems more clearly right to say that my body or back stopped the ball than that I did. In so far as there is an intuitive difference in the kinds of states at issue in these examples, it apparently has something to do with the presence or absence of intention, of whether or not I intentionally produced the state of affairs in question. Exactly why intention is deemed to be relevant is a further question.

In any case the above considerations suggest that it is sometimes relevant to distinguish between a state of a thing in general and a state or feature of a thing whose causal efficacy counts as the causal efficacy of the thing itself.[26] Let us say that a state of thing T is a *T-causal state of T*, if whenever T's being in that state has some effect this means, intuitively, that T itself has that effect.

The discussion so far suggests the following model (model M) of a society's causing an individual to engage in a practice (where practices include courses of action, beliefs, and attitudes):

Model M: a person A's personally engaging in a practice Pr is produced (at least in part) by his social group G if some G-causal state of G provides one of the reasons for which A engages in Pr.

The following questions arise in relation to Model M. What kinds of phenomena will count as G-causal states of a social group G? Are there kinds of production of action by a group which do not correspond to this model, or does the model exhaust the possibilities? What is it, supposedly, for a state of a group to provide one of the reasons for which someone does something? Given that reasons for action are involved, is this a truly causal model?

What kinds of phenomena will count as G-causal states of a

social group G? Going back to the original example, does the existence within a social group G of open* general disapproval of boasting count as a G-causal state? More generally, is it the case that for there to be some open* general practice within G is for G to be in a G-causal state? In this section I shall assume for the sake of argument that this is so.

I myself am doubtful of the intuitive acceptability of what I shall call *the open* practice assumption*. But one with my reasons for doubt is unlikely to think that a causal model of collective belief can be the basic or primary model, as we are now supposing. For I find it plausible to suppose that it is only G itself doing, feeling or believing something that involves a G-causal state.[27] Meanwhile I take it that an open* general practice does not involve any of these things. Considerations in support of this assumption were adduced in discussion of the second summative account. However, if one is trying to give a causal account of the basic case of collective belief, it makes little sense to think of incorporating as an element a phenomenon one deems already to be a collective belief or a phenomenon of the same type. This will, in effect, force one to agree that there are two radically different types of collective belief, one of which is more basic, or primary, and that the one which is more basic is not captured by the causal account.

In spite of my doubts about it, the open* practice assumption has a degree of plausibility. The issue of when we have a G-causal state of a thing and when we do not is somewhat obscure, and the principle of distinction far from obvious. Meanwhile, open* general disapproval, say, within a group does involve a property or state of the group in some sense. We can correctly say that *G is such that* it is open* to its members that most of them disapprove of such-and-such. (Similarly, we can see simple general practices as features of a group: the group is such that most of its members disapprove.) Moreover many have presumed that open* general practices have a major influence on human behaviour.[28]

First, though, it should be made clear that the type of production by society characterized by the generic Model M is a special one – there are other processes which could fairly aptly be referred to as production by society, given the involvement of a society-causal state of society.

Consider the following imaginary case, which is not so far from home. Members of an island tribe T openly* desire that as much as possible of a certain local herb, H, be sprinkled in the rivers on the island, believing that this will be universally beneficial. As a result, H is regularly sprinkled in the rivers by those with access to it. The unintended, unforeseen result is that due to chemical changes in the water, everyone in T is seized with the (totally unfounded) belief that aliens are about to invade the island. Here, even given the open* practice assumption, the tribe T is not, intuitively, the *immediate* agent of the change in belief. The chemical change in the water was what really did it, we might say, assuming of course various consequent changes within the bodies and brains of the persons concerned. None the less, one might want to say that in a sense the change in the individuals' beliefs here was produced by T.[29]

The example indicates that the general notion of production by a society has application to real phenomena which are not covered by Model M. Some of these phenomena such as environmental pollution are of great importance in our lives. At the same time the example makes it clear that if we are interested in understanding the detailed mechanisms by which a society can influence people – in particular by influencing their beliefs – we need to develop relatively specific models of production by society.

I shall in what follows develop a version of Model M in which, in the context of the open* practice assumption, the social group exercises a maximally direct form of causality.

Something must be said about the reference to *reasons* in model M. When we say something of the form '(The fact that) F was part of X's reason for Q-ing', we understand at least that

(1) F;
(2) X believed that F; and
(3) this ((2) in particular) led X to Q.

Such references to reasons, then, involve implicit reference to a *belief* of the agent. Model M is obviously intended to apply to situations in which a true belief about one's social group leads one to perform or attempt a certain action. So a stab at articulating a more precise version of this model might run as follows:

(1) X is a member of social group S;
(2) S has feature F;
(3) X believes that (2);
(4) S's having F is all or part of the cause of X's belief that S has F;
(5) X's belief that S has F led him to Q.

Once the model is articulated in this way some important issues regarding its coherence and its status as a causal model become salient.

First, quite generally, can features of the world properly be said to *cause* someone's belief in their existence? They may cause us to have certain sensations or experiences, but do those cause our beliefs? Beliefs, it might be argued, are *founded* or *based* on certain impressions or experiences of the world, but being based on is distinct from being caused by. Second, are beliefs that a group has a certain feature (including an open* general practice) ever caused by (or based on experience of) the group's having that feature, as opposed to being caused by (or based on experience of) events which do not themselves amount to that – such as a few particular individuals doing and saying certain things?

Leaving aside these questions, there remains a crucial, famous question about the generation of action which bears strongly on the issue of whether Model M as articulated here provides a model of something properly called causation by a social group.

In the proposed articulation of Model M, clause (5) runs: X's belief that S had F led him to Q. Now, in so far as 'X's belief that p led him to Q' is held to be an implication of 'the fact that p was part of X's reason for Q-ing' it seems to be unpackable further in a way that can be applied to Model M as follows:

(5') X believed that S had F, and so could consider whether the fact that S had F was a reason or ground for Q-ing.
(5'') X took the fact that S had F to be a reason for Q-ing.
(5''') X did Q, in part at least for the reason that S had F.

Now it may be argued that to state that X Q-ed in part for the reason that p is not to state a cause of X's Q-ing. It may be argued that reasons are grounds for Q-ing or for attempting to Q, and that therefore the concept of the reasons for which one acts is clearly distinct from the concept of the causes, if any, of one's action. It has even been suggested that if one's act was done for a reason it *cannot* have been caused. This is an important, much-discussed, and contentious area of philosophy.[30] Luckily, we need not examine it in depth here. Regarding Model M and any developments of it involving a person's reasons for action there are two alternatives open. Either the sequence (5') to (5''') describes a causal sequence of events or it does not. If it describes a causal sequence, and the other questions just noted are answered in the affirmative, then Model M is a truly causal model of production by society. But suppose the sequence is not a causal sequence. Then, if people do act for reasons quite typically, Model M (including the sequence of statements (5') to (5''')) can be taken to involve an important type of chain of events ending in the action of an individual person, and in terms of which the action in question can be explained. Such a chain of events, if it is not strictly speaking causal, has apparent affinities to causal chains. The very applicability, intuitively, of the notion of a 'chain' of events is one of them. Similar things may be said regarding the possibility that negative answers to the other two questions may turn out to be correct. I shall not pursue these issues further here.

6.4 *Towards a causal account of collective belief*

The precise model of production by a social group that we are to focus on is Model M1, below. We are allowing that this is a special case of model M, given the open* practice assumption:

> *Model M1*: a person A's personally engaging in a practice Pr is produced at least in part by his social group G if some open* general practice Pr' provides one of the reasons for which A engages in Pr. (Pr and Pr' are not necessarily distinct practices, though they may be.)

Now, certain cases which may appear to fit M1 as it stands do not involve the most direct possible kind of production by a social group. Knowing that there is open* general disapproval of boasting in my group I may refrain from boasting not directly or simply for the reason that there is this practice, but rather because, for example, I predict that if I boast others will dislike me. In this and other such cases, then, I do not perceive the open* general practice as in itself providing a reason for boasting. If for instance I had known in advance that people were ready to laugh off my one instance of boasting, I would not, on this hypothesis, see any reason not to boast now. In such a case we can say that an open* general practice does not provide a *basic* reason, from my point of view, for doing something, and hence its productive role is relatively indirect. In a model of maximally direct production of action by an open* general practice this will be seen as reason in itself for doing something. This brings us to Model M2.

> *Model M2*: a person A's personally engaging in a practice Pr is produced at least in part by his social group S if an open* general practice Pr' within S provides one of the basic reasons for which A conforms to Pr.

It should be understood that there is a serious question as to the extent to which Model M2 is applicable to real processes. For it is reasonable to assume that when one is apparently moved by the fact of open* general disapproval, often the 'deepest' reason for action is neither that fact considered in itself nor even the probability of incurring others' disapproval or dislike, or of their making their dislike manifest. Rather, it is likely to be the expectation of personal pain. One may expect to feel pain as a result of learning of others' disapproval, or as a result of their infliction of the kinds of penalties that people who disapprove of one's behaviour are likely to inflict: ostracism, sarcastic words, harsh rebukes, and more violent forms of aggression. Hence it is to be expected, in practice, that in so far as people act in the light of open* attitudes of disapproval, their basic reason for action will be that personal pain is expected. But then Model M2 will not apply to the situation.

Similar things can be said about action in conformity to open* general practices, that is, to one's doing what the others are doing. Someone may well predict that he will be overcome with painful emotions if he is in the position of perceiving himself doing something different from others. Both adults and children sometimes do not want to do something because 'I'd be embarrassed.' This suggests that what concerns them is the fact that their own perception of the situation will, in the event, cause them to *feel* bad, perhaps in spite of their own better judgment. It is arguable, then, that Model M2 applies to the world more rarely than might be thought.

The virtue of staying with M2 for present purposes is the very directness of the connection it posits between the action in question and the person's group as represented by an open* general practice. Any modification of it to allow for cases of the kind just discussed will drive a wedge between the action and the group. Moreover, when one acts to avoid pain which will ensue if one does not respect or conform to an open* general practice, then one acts in a way which could naturally be seen as unfortunate, as alienated. One sees the society and its (other) members as something standing over and against one. If one's model of collective practices includes practices derived in this way, such practices may tend to be seen as bad things, as inevitably imposed upon and coercive of the individual. There is another type of model of such practices, however, which is such that the individual members of society have a less alienated relation to them. I turn to it after concluding my consideration of summative views.

Model M2 is couched in terms of conformity to practices in general. How should it be converted into an account of collective belief?

We can distinguish two kinds of reasons for believing. I may take a particular open* general practice as evidence for the truth of p, and come to believe that p as a result. Seeing that it is open* to everyone in town that almost everyone is wearing a raincoat, I may infer that rain is predicted, and that, hence, it will most likely rain. We could say in this context that my reason for believing that it will rain is that there is an open* general practice of raincoat wearing.[31] Let us say that in such cases an open* general practice is one of my *epistemic* reasons for believing something.

Clearly in the raincoat case the productive connection between the open* practice and my belief is indirect in the sense implicit in my discussion of non-epistemic reasons. Thus presumably I would not have believed that it would rain as a result of the open* raincoat wearing if I myself had heard a recent trusty prediction of sun. In other words the open* general practice might well not have had the effect it in fact had. Where my epistemic reason for believing that p is an open* general *belief that p*, one supposes that there is in general going to be a similar kind of indirectness. (The odd example out is where the proposition in question is: 'There is an open* general belief that p' or something entailed by it.) So for maximal directness of the connection between society and belief in our model of collective belief, it seems we should couch it in terms of *non-epistemic* reasons for believing or trying to believe. People often have such reasons for believing, as for having certain attitudes and performing certain actions. And one may come to believe some proposition as a result of accepting that one has such reasons.

Someone might wonder whether people really have it in their power to bring it about that they believe something, even given that they accept they have a sufficient non-epistemic reason for trying to believe it. The idea that one can just decide to believe something, compared with the idea that one can just decide to do something like turning right at the lights, does have something fishy about it. None the less, it surely is possible to bring it about that one believes something by using various tricks.

Often people are strongly motivated to hold particular beliefs: a child wishes to believe that his father is wise and good; an American without a definite political stance realizes that his social life would go more smoothly if he consistently thought along Republican lines; an agnostic wishes he could embrace the faith of his devout wife; a woman wishes to believe that her husband is faithful to her; and so on. One need not start off thinking that the view in question is false. Clearly, if one does one is faced with a special kind of conflict. But often one starts off in a neutral position, and the views one wishes to hold are not made clearly false by obvious evidence. It may then not be too difficult to arrange one's life so that one gradually comes to hold the belief in question: one attends a place of worship regularly; one deliberately avoids thinking about incidents where one's father behaved badly, so that one gradually forgets all about them; one goes to Republican meetings and switches off speeches by Democrats. There is nothing inherently unrealistic, then, in a model of the generation of belief through the acceptance of non-epistemic reasons.

Cases that will fit a model of belief-production through acceptance of non-epistemic, basic reasons include cases where a person regards the existence of an open* general belief that p as itself providing a non-epistemic reason for believing that p, or where someone regards the existence of an open* general preference that one believe that p as a non-epistemic reason for believing that p. As indicated, cases of this specific sort may not tend to occur in practice. Rather, one may appeal ultimately to the likelihood of one's feeling shame at one's difference or pain from sanctions deliberately imposed. However, the relative lack of realism of the model may be overlooked for present purposes for the sake of the directness of the society–belief connection that it posits.

6.5 A causal account of collective belief: statement and assessment

The following account of collective belief can now be proposed for assessment.

> A group G believes that p if and only if it is open* to all in G that most members of G believe that p, and an open* general practice Pr within G provides one of the basic reasons for which most of the members of G set out to believe that p.

Probably the best way to assess the account is to have before us some examples to which it applies. So consider an imaginary tribe, the Ti. In 1986 it is open* to all the Ti that most of them personally wish that everyone would believe that a saviour will come to the tribe in 2050. Let us stipulate that this fact has provided a basic reason for most members to bring it about that they personally believed in the coming of a saviour in 2050; so most members now have this belief.

Is it intuitively correct to say that the Ti tribe believes that a saviour will come in the year 2050? I suggest not. Consider that it is not clearly apt to say that we have here a case of a *group* believing something. It is true that there is relatively rich contrast, now, between the beliefs of all or most members, and what is said to constitute, on this account, the belief of the tribe. However, as in the previous accounts considered, it is individuals who believe that p, so that the 'group's' believing that p is at base a matter of its members having that belief. Someone may say, since only individuals *can* believe anything, must this not be the case? But it is not obvious a priori that some form of correlativism must be true. The possibility remains that there are phenomena for which the label 'group belief' is appropriate and in which the group's believing that p is not dependent on any of the members believing that p.

Consider, finally, the question whether the phenomenon described here is essentially group-involving. It seems that, importantly, the answer here is negative.

Consider the population of mushroom pickers first encountered in Chapter II. These folk live on the perimeter of a wood and it is open* to all that each one regularly picks mushrooms in it. They have, however, had no communication or interactions we would be inclined to consider social. Now assume that it is open* to all that the mushroom pickers all speak English: each one has obviously come from some part of England, the country in which the wood is located. Moreover, each mushroom picker has taken to talking to himself, fairly loudly, as he works. As a result of this, each one has observed each of the others expressing (to himself) the view that a red sky at night means a rainless tomorrow. The existence of this open* general belief about red sky provides each mushroom picker with one of the basic reasons for which he continues to hold this belief. (We stipulate that this is so for the sake of argument.) Assuming they did not constitute one initially, would this state of affairs make the mushroom pickers, intuitively, into a social group? I should say that as so far described, they do not form one even now. The occurrence of a self-perpetuating, open general belief is not, apparently, essentially group-involving.[32]

One more example may be useful. Imagine that in the tabloid read by everyone in Townsville, the headline on 29 March reads: 'Teenagers in Townsville all accept that it is better not to use marihuana.' Reading this true report, each teenager in Townsville feels that he now has a reason to continue to hold that marihuana use is bad. The reason is, simply, that he and his peers already openly* hold that belief. (This is something that we stipulate.) Each one therefore continues to hold this view, and to do so quite openly. Does this make the teenagers of Townsville constitute a social group of their own? (I assume that this age group did not form a collectivity in advance.) Once again, I find that, intuitively, this is not enough to give us a collectivity. (Recall that I am not presupposing my own account of the concept of a social group. I am trying to react to the example in terms of how I would label it without assuming any articulated version of the concept.)

As one might expect, things are no clearer if we posit that the real or basic reason people have for espousing or continuing to hold the belief in question is fear of personal pain were they not to do so. Consider a smaller-scale example. Suppose that each of Smith and Jones and Robinson believes his differing from the others' publicly expressed views will cause him pain, and for that reason each continues to hold and express a certain view himself. This does not seem to be enough, intuitively, to make the three into a collectivity.

I conclude that Model M2 does not capture a phenomenon which is really apt for the label of group belief. Nor is it at all clear that it captures the best possible candidate. More generally, the idea that our concept of a collective belief is the concept of a set of individual beliefs among group members which were somehow produced by the group looks doubtful. I shall now turn to a radically different account of collective belief. This account does not have a set of individual beliefs that p as the core of a group's belief that p.

7 A NONSUMMATIVE ACCOUNT OF COLLECTIVE BELIEF

7.1 A context for the ascription of group belief: the poetry discussion group

Consider the following fairly humdrum, commonplace kind of situation. A group of people meet regularly at one member's house, to discuss poetry. The format of their meetings evolved informally over time. A poem by a contemporary poet is read out. Each participant feels free to make suggestions about how to interpret and evaluate the poem. Others respond, as they see fit, to suggestions that are made. An opposing view might be put forward, or data adduced to support or refute a proffered suggestion. When discussion in this vein has gone on for a while a point is usually reached where a preferred interpretation has emerged. No one is voicing any objections to it. Someone asks if anyone wants to say any more. No one speaks up. The poem is then read out once more, stressed and phrased according to the preferred interpretation.

Suppose that the poem this time is 'Church Going' by Philip

Larkin, and that, according to the preferred interpretation, the last line of that poem is quite moving in its context. After the poem has been read for the second time, the group moves on to discuss another Larkin poem. The following dialogue then takes place. First person: 'The ending here is far more persuasive than that bathetic last line in "Church Going"!' Second person: 'But we thought that line was quite moving!'

Consider the second person's response. I take it that this would be very natural in the context described, and would naturally be accepted as true (or as possessing whatever truth-analogue was appropriate). It implies, crucially, that at some previous point remarks such as the following would have been acceptable:

'We are agreed that the last line is moving'; 'We think that, etc.'; 'In our opinion, etc.'; 'We decided that, etc.'; 'Our view at this point is that, etc.'; 'In the opinion of our discussion group, etc.'; 'The group thought that, etc.'

Presumably this point would have been reached at least by the time the second reading of the poem was completed.

Now it is possible that the case up to this point is as yet underdescribed, that some feature crucial for the truth of an ascription of group belief has not been explicitly mentioned. With this in mind, I shall take it that one way of arriving at an account of what it is for a group to have a belief or opinion, intuitively, is to try to isolate those features of the present context which seem to substantiate the statement that the group has a certain belief.

I suggest that what is both logically necessary and logically sufficient for the truth of the ascription of group belief here is, roughly, that all or most members of the group have expressed willingness to let a certain view 'stand' as the view of the group. Obviously more discussion of the nature of this condition is in order. However, let me quickly note some intended corollaries of the proposed hypothesis.

First, according to this hypothesis, the truth of the statement that the group has a certain belief would be perfectly compatible with the fact that even by the end of the discussion of 'Church Going' most members of the group, in their hearts, judged the last line of the poem to be far from moving. Most of them might personally be inclined to judge it jarring or bathetic. (Why, then, would they not have spoken out? Perhaps they were unwilling to, because a particularly sensitive person suggested that it was moving, and obviously set much store by this opinion. Clearly there are other possibilities. In any case, what is essential is that, for whatever reason, they *did* decide to hold their peace.) Second, the ascription of group belief could be true even though the majority of members of the discussion group had *no personal opinion* on the last line of Larkin's poem, either during the discussion or after the poem had been read out for the second time, after everyone had 'had their say' (as we put it).

More generally, if the proposed hypothesis is correct, no form of summative account of collective belief can be correct as a general account. That is, it is not a necessary condition on a group's believing that p that most group members believe that p. Indeed, it is not necessary that *any* group member personally believe that p.

Regarding the last corollary, I take it that once a certain point is reached, a given view is established as the group view, and this could remain the group view even if everyone subsequently came to have a contrary personal opinion. Hence, the group can believe something at a certain point in time without any member of the group believing it. Moreover, it appears not to be necessary that any member of the group ever believed it. Suppose everyone lets one person's suggestion stand unopposed and hence it establishes the group's view. The person in question need not have believed what she said. A variety of motivations could lie behind her saying something she disbelieved or about which she had no current opinion.[33]

That someone was not convinced of the truth of an established group view might later come out as in my imaginary dialogue. More likely, it would come out as follows: '*I personally* do *not* think that the last line of "Church Going" is moving.' That is, 'personally' would be added as a special qualifier, perhaps in contrast to 'as a person representing this group', or 'in my capacity as a member of the group'. Similarly, someone might deny having an opinion 'of their own'.

A summative theorist might raise the following objection to the proposed hypothesis. It could be that people feel free to speak of 'our opinion' in this case because the lack of voiced objection by the end of the discussion is good evidence that most members of the group personally believe that p. If subsequently people use locutions like 'I personally think that not p', this could be in contrast to the supposed group belief, that is, the supposed majority view. My own sense of the matter, however, is that people who say things like 'Our view was this' in such a context do not feel that the truth of their assertion depends upon facts about what individual members thought 'in their hearts' at the end of the discussion.

A further aspect of the situation is relevant here. The first person in my imaginary dialogue is evidently doing something slightly shocking. That this is so is suggested by the naturalness of

beginning the response: 'But . . .' One can imagine hearers
thinking to themselves with puzzlement or annoyance, 'How can
she say that!' The natural way to construe this 'But' is as a rebuke
to the speaker, a rebuke which is a response to the speaker's
plainly and without preamble expressing a view contrary to the
view of the group.

It may be queried why it is natural for the second person in the
dialogue to say 'But we thought' rather than 'But we think'. The
exact import of this is not obvious. Possibly use of the past tense
is in place here because, once the first person's bold remark has
been made, it seems to open the whole issue up again. Clearly a
group can be prevailed upon to change its view. In any case, the
past tense statement can still be read as expressing a reproof for a
bald assertion of contrary view, once a group view has been
formed. This is the most natural way to read it.

The existence and precise nature of what I shall call the
predicted rebuke is an important clue to the nature of our
intuitive conception of collective belief. We can usefully begin to
clarify the nature of the rebuke by considering the difficulty it
presents for a simple summative account of collective belief.

Suppose for the sake of argument that what a group thinks is,
by definition, a matter of what most members think. Then the
'But. . .' in the dialogue will have to be be explained in that light.
There are various ways the explanation could go. But none of the
obvious candidates properly respects the flavour of the response
as it is most naturally interpreted.

A summative theorist might interpret the response as an
expression of surprise. Then, however, it would not have to be a
rebuke at all. Two other possibilities are a conformist rebuke for
difference from the majority, and a rebuke for an evident lack of
shame at difference from the majority, given the willingness to
manifest such difference openly and without preamble. One
problem with these interpretations is that they make the
predictability of a rebuke dependent upon the conformism of the
respondent. Meanwhile a rebuke is predictable irrespective of the
attitudes of particular respondents.

Again, the response might be interpreted as a rebuke for not
having publicly expressed one's (unusual) point of view during
the discussion. This is inadequate for at least two reasons. For
one thing, the first speaker could successfully counter the rebuke
on this interpretation by saying: 'I didn't keep anything hidden.
I've changed my mind since the end of the discussion.'
Meanwhile, on its intuitively correct interpretation the rebuke
cannot be successfully defused by reference to a change of mind.
The rebuke is directed precisely at the first speaker's present

announcement, in the context of a particular group belief. A second, related problem with this interpretation is that the rebuke could be in place whether or not the first speaker had publicly expressed her view during the discussion. Suppose that she had indeed done so. Something presumably happened after that so that a different view was the one allowed to stand as the group's view. Perhaps after she spoke someone interjected 'How can you say that! The line is really quite moving!' No one gainsaid this. Given some such context, the first person will still be considered out of order, if she repeats her original statement without preamble.[34]

It appears, then, that the explanations suggested by the simple summative view are not acceptable explanations of a rebuking response which is generally appropriate in the context of a previously formed group belief. In short, it does not make the right prediction in this case.

Let me continue to describe how things are intuitively without concern for how they fit any particular theoretical mould.

It appears to be understood that, once a group view has been ascertained, it is incumbent upon the members either to presuppose that view in their subsequent discussions, or to prefix their statements with some qualifier or excuse such as 'I know that we thought that the last line of the last poem was moving; personally, though, I still have my doubts about that line.' In other words, the rebuke we have been discussing concerns the violation of an obligation which members of the group are understood to have taken on when and in so far as a group view was established.

In sum, there is reason to think that the following is a general feature of situations in which it is appropriate to speak of a group belief: once a group belief that p has emerged or been formed, members of the group will regard themselves as somehow *obliged* not to deny that p or to say things which presuppose the denial of p in further discussion with group members. If they do say or imply that not-p, they must give some sort of explanation, or qualify by saying something like 'in my personal opinion, not-p'. If they violate the obligation, they stand to be rebuked.

7.2 How paradigmatic is the poetry case?

The poetry case is, of course, special in various ways. None the less, as long as it involves the generation of group belief, one can use it as a basis for formulating an account of such belief. In fact it is less significantly special than might be supposed. Let me briefly argue this in relation to some specific concerns that have been expressed.

It has been objected that the poetry group is a special type of group, in that non-membership is a genuine option for the participants. It is thus unlike a family or the larger communities in which people are born and raised and moulded. The distinction appealed to here is less clear-cut than might be thought. There could be severe pressures on people to be members of a group like the poetry group: many may feel that they can do nothing else. In any case, however important it is in some contexts, the distinction at issue is not obviously relevant here. A family may negotiate its views in precisely the same way as the poetry group. How the members got together and why seems irrelevant.

Another concern with the poetry group has been that it seems too like a committee regularly meeting with the explicit purpose of reaching group decisions on various issues. It may appear doubtful whether what goes on in such a group can be very relevant to group belief in general. For a group may surely have a belief though there has been no conscious aim to arrive at one, nor any explicit acknowledgement that the group has this view.

Now, as my description was intended to suggest, it need never have been part of the explicit purpose of the poetry discussion group to arrive at a group decision on the poems discussed. The initial idea may have been to discuss poetry in a very general sense of 'discuss'. The format discussions now have could have developed spontaneously. Alternative practices might have evolved, for instance, a practice of what amounts to serial personal confession in which each participant reacts with her own personal reactions to the poem which has been read out: 'Oh, I *like* it!' 'Too sentimental for me!' 'Ah well, you can't please everybody!' 'Would you like some wine?' Even as things are people may never to this day have made the determination of a group view of the poems an explicit aim of the group, or of any given discussion. Nor need they ever explicitly acknowledge that a certain view is the group's view. In my example such acknowledgement was provoked only by the bizarre reaction of one member. In sum, the poetry case stands a good chance of throwing light on a wide range of cases of group belief including those where a group judgment is neither explicitly sought nor explicitly referred to as such.

Another problem suggested is smallness of scale. The poetry group, like a committee and a household, is a small group, whose members all know each other and frequently interact. Yet we also ascribe beliefs to large groups which are not like this, tribes, say, firms, and even nations. Can we expect an account of collective belief derived from the poetry group to cover such cases?

This is perfectly possible. We could have one basic concept of group belief which applies both to large and small groups. True, the processes of group belief formation may be expected to be different. (Compare the case of population common knowledge. As defined, this can exist in both small and large groups, but there will generally be different mechanisms by which it comes about.) Clearly, members of a large group may not be able to get together and discuss things in an open forum, letting everyone have his or her say. But this type of process may be inessential to group belief. My discussion so far suggests that the core phenomenon is something like expressed willingness to let a certain view stand as the view of the group. There is no reason to suppose that the members of large groups cannot participate in such expressions or know that others have done so.

It is also possible, and I think predictable, that our core concept of group belief will be one which applies clearly and unproblematically within small groups, the primordial social context, while one or more derived notions are available for some large group contexts. I say more about this later.

The poetry case, then, is not obviously so special that we cannot expect an account of group beliefs derived from it to be usefully general. In a more positive vein, I want next to connect it with one of the central phenomena of human life, conversation. Evidently, conversation is a standard mode of human verbal interaction. It is possible that other modes such as ordering and questioning are best understood in terms of the conversational mode. Conversation is almost as ubiquitous as gatherings of two or more people are. Conversations occur on the highway, at the family dinner table, in pubs and clubs and offices. I shall now argue that in everyday conversations things proceed very much as they do in the poetry group.

7.3 Another context: conversations

Consider two acquaintances, call them Eddie and Martin, who meet by chance on their way home from work and fall into conversation. 'Feels like summer's really begun, doesn't it?' says Martin, in a cheerful tone. Eddie, who is rather impervious to the heat, replies: 'I suppose it does.' He speaks pleasantly, but without any sense of conviction. The analogy to the poetry group case is apparently quite close. One person in a group – in this case a small transitory group – puts forward a proposition for consideration, and another reacts, in this case accepting the proposition in some way. Eddie might be described as 'going along with' Martin. But what is it to 'go along with' someone in such a context? As in the poetry case, we could speak, perhaps rather pompously, but quite intelligibly, of Eddie's deciding to let a certain proposition stand as the view of this little conversational group.

Another way to describe this situation is to say that Eddie implicitly agrees that this is the view he and Martin will *jointly accept*, at least for the duration of their conversation (which may end there). Consider that Martin might wonder if Eddie really thinks it feels like summer. Yet at the same time there seems to be something odd about his putting this thought in terms of Eddie's deceiving him. I would suggest that this is because they are doing something like negotiating a position they can jointly accept. In so far as this is their main aim it is not incumbent upon Eddie to 'tell the truth' in the sense of saying what he personally believes. What is sought is a view that can be accepted jointly: something that each is willing to presuppose together with the other, in the continuation of their discussion and perhaps in further discussions they hold together. This need not necessarily be a view either one individually believes. (I say more on the nature of such 'presupposing' later.) When this is so a charge of deceit will seem less obviously in place if someone expresses a view he does not personally hold (though charges of cowardice, lack of seriousness, hypocrisy, and the like might seem perfectly in place).

There are of course some conversational situations where a charge of deceit is straightforwardly in place. My point is that this is not always so. This indicates that conversation as such may best be thought of more as the negotiation of a position to be jointly held than as, say, an exchange of information about personal views. The cases where charges of lying and deception are in place will then be special cases.[35]

Here, then, is the beginning of a theory of conversation. When people talk together in conversation, at least when they make assertions as opposed to questioning, they 'put up' propositions for joint acceptance or rejection. Depending on how others react, a given proposition is jointly accepted or rejected. Wrinkle: some propositions may be kept on hold, so to speak. One person says: 'I think I should avoid all Sagittarians in the future.' His companion is sceptical of astrology and just says 'Hmmm'. in a definitely-not-agreeing tone. These two, one might say, do not (as a group) 'know what to think' about the proposition in question. A question might be seen as intended to elicit a proposition for consideration; an order as presupposing that the person giving the order is entitled to decide unilaterally on what is to be done.

This theory is in effect a model of what may be going on when people converse. It is a model, in particular, of how people may perceive their situation when they are engaged in conversation. In my view it is quite plausible as a model of what goes on in cases clearly falling under the folk concept of a conversation. There is no place for a thorough discussion here. But I should like to mention an occurrence which helped to suggest this theory to me long ago.

The following dialogue took place in Manchester *circa* 1967.

Me: 'I prefer strawberry ice-cream to any other.'
My friend Mircea: 'No, no, I prefer chocolate!'

Why did Mircea say 'No, no, . . .'? What was there about what *I* had said, about what *I* preferred, that prompted him to see what he was saying about what he preferred as contradicting or opposing it, as he evidently did? It seemed to me that his 'No, no' was quite bizarre. He surely knew very well how the pronoun 'I' is used. What could have tempted him to follow my utterance as he did?

It struck me then that the following would account for Mircea's sense that he must explicitly reject what I had said. Suppose, first, that it is a general assumption in conversation that views which are not challenged are considered to have been jointly accepted, and that it is incumbent upon one who jointly accepts a view with certain others to jointly presuppose that view in the future course of the dialogue, at least. Now, when I said 'I prefer strawberry ice-cream' the view expressed was, of course, a view about what I, Margaret Gilbert, prefer. Suppose however that, realizing that he was being asked, in effect, jointly to accept a certain view, my friend suddenly focused on the words I had uttered. It would then have seemed to him that he was being asked jointly to accept the view expressed by *his* potential utterance 'I prefer strawberry ice-cream.' This, however, was a view he knew with complete certainty to be false. He would quite naturally then feel it hard to accept my 'I prefer strawberry ice-cream' jointly with me, and, in his reply, take himself to be putting me straight about the view which should be jointly accepted.[36]

To propose that conversations may be characterized as, in effect, negotiations of jointly accepted views, is not to say that all verbal interactions are best seen in this way.[37] I have no need to argue this here. However, it is worth noting that the negotiation of joint view model can be argued to apply to verbal interactions beyond paradigm cases of conversation. A teacher, for instance, may make it clear that he wants his student to go ahead and express himself, while the teacher thoughtfully 'takes in' what is said, occasionally prompting the student further to develop his own thought. A psychotherapist may do something similar. Such cases seem rather different from typical conversations. These people are hardly 'talking to each other'. Rather, one talks and the other listens. None the less, it seems natural to think of them as involved in something much like a conversation. And the negotiation of joint view model can be argued to apply here, in the context of a rather special framework of understandings. It could be argued that in these cases it is understood that the central proposition that is 'up' for joint acceptance is, say, 'Betty is currently inclined to say that . . .' where Betty is the student or client, and it is also understood that since Betty is the authority on what she is is currently inclined to say, there is no serious 'negotiating' to be done.

To accept the theory of conversation adumbrated here is not to rule out the possibility of radically flawed or pathological cases of conversation. Indeed, this theory can help to explain why some interactions seem jarring and unfortunate. Clearly, if one person believes he is involved in negotiating a jointly accepted view, and the other does not, we have an uncomfortable sort of interaction on our hands, a kind of minor chaos.

It may be understood by all, to a degree, that 'negotiation of a jointly accepted view' is in progress, but one person may wrongly assume that in this group his word is law; he may therefore talk on, taking no notice of anyone's reactions, assuming that everything he says goes. Or someone may not want to participate in negotiating a jointly accepted view, even though he knows others do. He may ignore their wishes, and go ahead as if it were agreed that he would simply express his own thoughts and be listened to. (Compare Asquith on Churchill: 'his conversation . . . is apt to degenerate into a monologue.')[38]

The possibility of speaker–hearer interactions that do not fit the negotiation of joint view model does not, then, invalidate it as a model of conversations in general. Indeed, it may help to explain why some interactions, seen by some or all of the participants as conversations, can be quite uncomfortable.

My main claim here is that the negotiation of joint view model applies to and can help explain what transpires in clear cases of conversations. It seems also to fit the poetry discussion case. (In both cases 'negotiation' may seem too strong a term; nothing like hard bargaining may occur, or be in place. I keep this word for want of a better.) The model may, indeed, be taken to throw light on what it is to be willing to 'let a view stand as the view of the group', a description used in relation to the poetry case. This may be explicated as being willing to 'accept that view jointly with the others'. The poetry discussion case, then, may be argued to find a close analogue in many informal conversations. A model of group belief derived in part from the poetry case may be expected to apply to much less formal and more common kinds of situations of everyday life.

Conversational groups are typically transitory, and some conversations can be of the utmost insignificance. Yet families and even quite large groups will surely tend to derive their character from the many particular conversations that take place within them. Specifically, they may thence derive certain beliefs.

One mechanism by which this might happen is the following. Some individual might personally believe that p but wish to have this view ratified by some others before really going public about it. In a conversation among a few friends he might bring up the idea that p, and find that no one objected. Let us take it that the idea that p was thus jointly accepted by the participants in this conversation. This could embolden both the originator and the others to say that p in some other group, in a fairly confident way; their confidence may help to bring it about that it is endorsed there too. Other mechanisms for the generation of jointly accepted views in largish groups are possible. For instance, it could be open* to all in G that p has been jointly accepted in small private conversations throughout G. This could embolden someone to make a public statement to the effect that p, on the understanding that opposition is unlikely. And so it may come about that it is common knowledge in G that the members of G jointly accept that p.

7.4 On the conception of a jointly accepted view

(i) Joint acceptance versus individual acceptance of a view

Care must be taken with the interpretation of the phrase 'joint acceptance of a view'. I have written of group members being willing to let a certain view stand as the view of the group, and of group members' willingness jointly to accept a certain view. I see these two descriptions as virtually identical in meaning.

It must be clearly understood that the notion of joint acceptance of a view is distinct from the notion of the personal acceptance of that view by each person concerned. As a matter of logic, a view that someone jointly accepts with certain others in a certain context is not necessarily a view that he personally accepts. We might say that a view I personally or individually accept is a view that I accept *as my personal view*, or *as my own view*, while, in contrast, a view I accept jointly with another is a view I accept *as our view*, where the conception of 'our view' is distinct from, and does not include, the conception of 'my view'. Given the nature of the concepts involved, as so far noted, someone could in principle be willing to accept that p jointly with others even though he personally neither believes that p nor expects to come to accept that p as his own view.

Perhaps we would expect someone to be willing jointly to accept a proposition that he personally believed to be false only *in spite of* his personal belief. This will be so, of course, if he wishes that the jointly accepted view be true, all other things being equal. None the less, even given such a wish one may see it as preferable overall jointly to accept with certain others a particular view one does not personally hold. For instance, one may feel that it is above all important that some view or other be jointly accepted by group members. Meanwhile, joint acceptance of the proposition one personally accepts may appear impossible. So one goes along with something else. In the cause of smooth social interactions in general, people must often feel that arrival at some jointly accepted view is a matter of paramount importance.

In such cases the usual constraints of rational negotiation or bargaining may be expected to come into play. For instance, one participant may prevail because of a 'threat advantage'. Perhaps he alone personally believes the group view. Or a compromise view that no one personally believes may be settled on. (One may, of course, feel intimidated by another, and so on, for no good reason.)

Another possibility is that a person has reasons for wanting a proposition other than the one he believes true to be jointly accepted. That is, he is not simply willing to compromise for the sake of so-called unanimity. For instance, a commanding officer may want the members of his company jointly to accept that they have a good chance of success, and to discuss things in these terms. Meanwhile he personally may doubt whether this is true. He may believe, however, that if this becomes the jointly accepted view, and future conversations are conducted in terms of it, then the individual soldiers are more likely personally to accept it, and hence more likely to fight well. Everyone in the company could, in fact, be in a similar position; given their desires, joint acceptance that they have a good chance of success is possible. (Is this a case of deceit? Morally speaking it is not clear that honest talk is required in such a context, at least once the decision to engage in combat is made.)

(ii) *Joint acceptance versus majority acceptance of a view*

What relevance to an individual's decision about what to accept jointly with certain others is there in the fact that the majority individually believe that such-and-such? Supposing that in selecting a view for joint acceptance, discussants will standardly feel some constraints in the direction of truth, *this* does not provide clear grounds for accepting the view individually held by the majority. Of course someone might think that the majority are likely to be right. But that the majority in any group will be right on any matter is far from obvious. Moreover, someone may be completely convinced that his own view is correct. If such a person were to go along with the majority, this would not be because he thought they were likely to be right.

In a sense, someone who accepts some view jointly with certain others does 'go along with the majority'; but in this sense, *he* is one of the majority. For he accepts a certain view jointly with the others, and each of them jointly accepts it with the rest. Willingness to go along with the majority in this way clearly does not entail that one does something because one perceives that most people personally believe a certain thing.

Someone might feel that where there is a majority view, and a decision on what is to be jointly accepted must be made, joint acceptance of that view is the only feasible outcome of negotiations – the only just outcome, perhaps. Such a sense on his part may, clearly, lead him to be willing jointly to accept what, as it happens, most people personally believe. But as a matter of logic, 'the members of G jointly accept that p' neither implies nor is implied by 'most members of G personally believe that p.' Nor is it obvious that if there is a majority view, that view will in all real cases be the one which is jointly accepted. The 'logical wedge' is not purely notional, but marks a real possibility.

In discussing with precision the relations between a jointly accepted view and a particular view that most people hold, we should distinguish what can be called the *prior* personal view of the majority (the view of the majority at some time prior to the formation of the jointly accepted view) and the *concurrent* personal view of the majority (the view the majority holds concurrently with the jointly accepted view). Not only in logic, but also in fact, the jointly accepted view need not reflect the prior or the concurrent personal view of the majority.

As to the prior view, we need only consider that people can put their own personal views 'on hold' in negotiating a jointly accepted view. They may wish to hear what is said *in foro publico* before venturing any opinion about what should be jointly accepted. And they may find a view which is put forward acceptable enough, without having any idea who is in the majority and who is not, or even whether there is a majority view at all. (Clearly there need not be any prior majority view on the issue.) As a result, they can easily come jointly to accept a view with the others while at the same time the majority had always held the contrary view up to the time of joint acceptance. Even where it *is* known that there is a majority view, people may not feel bound to accept it. They may wish to defer to a vocal minority or to a single 'dictator'. One is going to need arguments to show that a view most people individually accept as their own *should* become the jointly accepted view. In any case, the many factors entering the negotiation process are such that there is no reason to suppose that in general what should be jointly accepted (if there is such a thing) will be. As for the concurrent personal view of the majority, one need not change one's own mind, as we say, just because one has been willing jointly to accept some view contrary to one's prior personal beliefs. Thus parents may have jointly accepted a compromise view. 'We think you should be home by 10 p.m.', they say, neither personally having changed her or his own mind.

None of this speaks, of course, to the issue of how a group view, once formed, may influence the views members of the group accept as their own. I say more about this shortly.

(iii) On the irreducibility of the notion of a jointly accepted view

Certain kinds of reductive analysis of the notion of joint acceptance of a view are not possible. I have stressed that joint acceptance of a view by certain persons neither entails nor is entailed by their personally accepting that view. Some further points should be stressed also.

One way of looking at joint acceptance of a view is in terms of a commitment on everyone's part to presuppose that view together with the other group members in future group discussions. Someone might query whether the notion of joint acceptance of a view does not then reduce to the notion of committing oneself personally to presuppose that view in future conversations. The idea is, rather, that when one jointly accepts a view with others, one commits oneself precisely to presuppose-together-with-the-others or jointly to presuppose the truth of the view in question.

It might be objected that jointly accepting that p with other members of a certain group commits one simply to talking and acting as if one personally presupposed or believed that p, when interacting with the other group members. (Note that collectivity concepts are not entirely eliminated from the commitment as it is conceived of here: it is understood that the behaviour or actions in question will take place only in a certain context, so far referred to as 'when interacting with the other group members'. Moreover, it is possible to argue that the only plausible specification of the context in such a case must indeed bring in a collectivity concept. Consider that by accepting Martin's statement that it feels like summer, Eddie may commit himself to acting as if he presupposes that the day is warm, *in further conversation with Martin*. But if he says goodbye to Martin and then meets Polly, he can surely take a different tack without violating his obligations to Martin. Again, if Eddie and Martin run into Polly, and she complains 'What a chilly day!' it is not incumbent upon Eddie or Martin to volunteer, in disagreement, their previous 'group view'. Not wanting to offend Polly, who holds a senior position in their organization, they may defer to her view, so that, in this current conversation, Polly's view is jointly accepted.)

Now even if a personal commitment to act as if one believed that p in a given context were a part or consequence of jointly accepting with others that p, that would not show that the notion of joint acceptance reduces analytically to the notion of a commitment to act as if one believed something. Again, even if all that seems to be going on behaviourally speaking when people jointly accept that p is that each proceeds to act as if he or she believes that p, in a certain context, this clearly does not show that the *notion* of joint acceptance of a view reduces to the notion of individuals committing themselves to behave as if they had a certain belief themselves, or to the notion of their actually so behaving. Presumably, all there is behaviourally to having a certain belief is behaving as if one has it, but surely the notion of belief does not reduce either to the notion of committing oneself to behaving as if one believes or to the notion of actually so behaving. It hardly could, if the latter notion was to make any sense.

It is of course perfectly possible that a set of people exchange promises or agree that each will act as if they personally believe that p, and carry out such an agreement. However, they do not thereby jointly accept the proposition that p. Quite simply, the understandings involved are different. People who jointly accept a proposition understand that this has consequences, in particular consequences about how each one should behave. The mandated behaviour, meanwhile, is not the same as that made mandatory by a set of promises to act as if one personally believes the proposition in question. For recall that while jointly accepting a proposition with certain others, it is possible to admit that *personally* one thinks differently. This seems to show that participation in joint acceptance does not even *carry with it* an obligation to act *as if one personally accepts something.* (It seems to show, further, that in committing oneself to joint acceptance of a view, one does not take it upon oneself *personally to believe that* view.)[39]

The notion of a view that I accept jointly with certain others can be equated with the similarly irreducible notion of a view which is *ours** or a view whose plural subject we constitute. Someone might query what the point of this notion would be. One consideration is this: the notion of a jointly accepted view, when it is believed to apply to a population to which one belongs, can *power* a certain kind of behaviour. An understanding that I have jointly accepted that p together with X, Y, and Z, that, in other words, *this is our** *view*, provides an *intelligible ground* for my acting in certain specific ways. (I say more about this aspect of plural subject concepts in general in the concluding chapter.)

An evocative general prescription indicating how one is to act as a participant in joint acceptance recalls the famous frontispiece from Hobbes's *Leviathan*: act as a constituent of a single person who accepts that p. Alternatively, act so that together you accept that p *as a single body.*

Those who have jointly accepted some view with the other members of a certain group will not, then, see themselves as acting as if they personally believed something. Rather, they will see themselves (possibly at a deep level and not consciously registered) as speaking as members of the group. 'I'm afraid you just didn't meet our needs' the chairman of the department says to the candidate he had favoured. Conscious of his role as a representative of the department, he may be aware of no insincerity, nor properly be characterized as insincere. It is tempting to use computer jargon here and say that he is now in the 'group representative mode', and, when in that mode, he does not have immediate access to, or interest in, his own personal views. When in the group representative mode, it is proper for him to express the views of the group, rather than his own personal views. He can of course *switch* modes, and say, for instance: 'Look, that isn't *my* view, you know that. But what can I do? My hands are tied.'[40]

There are, evidently, various ways of describing the situation of those who have jointly accepted a view with certain others. We may say they have undertaken to express a certain view when acting within, or as a representative of the group. One might even say that someone has accepted a view *qua member of a certain group*. Whatever one says, the notion of jointly accepting a view with certain others appears not to be reducible to that of undertaking personally to believe that view, nor to act as if one believes that view.

(iv) On the influence of a jointly accepted view

There is no need to deny that there may be a close connection between the joint acceptance of a belief and its generality at the individual level. If I do want the jointly accepted view to be true, then I am likely to push my own beliefs as those to be jointly accepted. Even if I am not especially concerned with the truth of the jointly held opinion, if there are no special constraints my own contribution to discussions is likely to be what I personally think. Hence we can assume that there will be many cases where a jointly accepted view reflects the view of at least some individuals.

Meanwhile, once formed, a jointly accepted view is likely to have an influence on the views of individuals. In the first place, one would expect the personal views of many people eventually to mirror those they jointly accept with others. For they have bound or committed themselves to 'speak that view' among the others when speaking in an unqualified manner. Presumably they must also act in terms of that view, on pain of being considered to have 'let the side down'. Given that you are acting and speaking for all you are worth in terms of the jointly accepted view, it would not be surprising if you were to come to hold that view on your own account. This move from joint acceptance to personal acceptance would presumably be easiest if one initially had no particular personal opinion on the matter. But it would be hard to lay down a priori that even one who *knows* that such-and-such cannot come to doubt it, and finally to believe its opposite, after participating in joint acceptance of the opposite view for a lengthy period.

This being so, it is obviously quite a grave thing to acquiesce in a certain view jointly with others, even if doing so does not automatically taint one, so to speak, in one's own heart. It is true that in some cases one's personal view is unlikely to be influenced because one's participation in joint acceptance is very short-lived. But generally speaking, one stands to be influenced.

If one already personally holds a view that conflicts with the jointly accepted view, one is in a particularly difficult situation. For one is committed to mouth the jointly accepted view and to act upon it, disagreeing with it all the while. Indeed, as noted, it can be said that one is committed to believing the proposition in question, *qua* one of 'us*'. I have argued that believing *qua* one of us* is not equivalent to believing period, or believing personally. *Qua* a member of Tom's family I may believe Tom should have got the job; *qua* department member I may be of the opinion that he was the worst candidate; as for my personal view, I may think he fell somewhere in the middle. None the less, the appositeness of speaking of believing *qua* group member, or in one's capacity as group member, indicates that in jointly accepting a view that one does not personally hold one in effect undermines one's *integrity*, one sets up a situation of internal conflict: *qua* group member I believe that p, but I myself think that p is pernicious rubbish (perhaps).[41] Clearly there will be a strong temptation to give up or change one's personal view in such a case. This will avoid the discomfort of inner conflict and allow for one's continued fellowship in the group. Such change could come about in various ways: avoidance of evidence conflicting with the doctrine; repression of doubts as they begin to surface, and so on.

An important aspect of the influence of jointly accepted views concerns their likely effect on growing children. Imagine that in 1942 Clarissa and Peter Peterson have jointly accepted, along with others of their circle, the view that a woman's place is in the home. Given this joint acceptance, Clarissa stays home, and when their child Emily is born they both naturally presuppose, in conversation with Emily and in the way they treat her, that she will grow up to find her place at home. Emily will most likely grow up personally believing that a woman's place is in the home. She will not give the question much thought. In such situations, a jointly accepted view can be the only view a person has access to, a view, moreover, which appears to be held by people she knows are older and believes to be wiser than herself. She is obviously likely to make that view her own, believing it true or at least plausible.

Does this mean, one might ask, that over time and through generations jointly accepted views disappear and are replaced by, simply, views that most people personally hold? The answer seems to be that, first, the fact that some jointly accepted views inevitably become mirrored in personal views does not mean that the views are not jointly accepted as well. Second, as we know quite well, people are not that fixed, and they can query the views they themselves have, if reason is presented for doubting them. After getting married, Emily perceives that she has become bored and miserable spending her time at home. It occurs to her, gradually, that this may not be *her* proper place. Perhaps there is no place proper for women as such. She reads her husband's copy of Plato's *Republic*, and finds that Plato is of that opinion. Other people are thinking about this very issue, and a new set of jointly accepted views begins to form. Under cover of these, Emily begins training as a lawyer.

7.5 A nonsummative account of group belief: collective belief as jointly accepted view

In the light of the foregoing I propose the following account of our everyday concept of a group belief:

> *A group G believes that p* if and only if the members of G jointly accept that p.

This in turn may be explicated thus:

> The members of G *jointly accept* that p if and only if it is common knowledge in G that the members of G individually have intentionally and openly* expressed their willingness jointly to accept that p with the other members of G.

(A way of putting this condition on joint acceptance which may be found helpful is this: members of G individually have openly* and intentionally expressed their willingness *to accept that p together with the other members of G as a body*.)

It is a corollary of the above (given in my particular account of common knowledge) that when there is joint acceptance of some proposition p the people in question know this. They will know that 'We* (members of G) jointly accept that p'. (Thus the 'members' knowledge principle' will be satisfied for group belief on this account of it.)

It should be understood that: (1) Joint acceptance of a proposition p by a group whose members are X, Y, and Z, does not entail that there is some subset of the set comprising X, Y, and Z such that all the members of that subset individually believe that p. (2) One who participates in joint acceptance of p thereby accepts an obligation to do what he can to bring it about that any joint endeavours (such as a continuing conversation) among the members of G be conducted on the assumption that p is true. He is entitled to expect others' support in bringing this about. (3) One does not have to accept an obligation to believe or to try to believe that p. However, (4) if one does believe something that is inconsistent with p, one is required at least not to express that belief baldly. Any denial of the proposition must be qualified by a phrase making it clear that one is talking *in propria persona*, and not in one's capacity of group member. Such qualifiers include: 'Personally, . . .'; 'In my personal opinion . . .'; 'Speaking for myself . . .'.

The account proposed does not require that anyone explicitly agrees to anything. Evidently one can communicate one's willingness to participate in joint acceptance in quite subtle, nonverbal ways. It will be understood in advance by all that once everyone has intentionally and openly* expressed such willingness, they do jointly accept that p. Thus joint acceptance can be brought about without explicit recognition of what has taken place.

The account does not logically entail anything about the reasons why members of G have indicated their willingness jointly to accept that p. Given the constraints of negotiation and other factors, even people who clearly prefer that the group belief be true may end up jointly accepting a view each one thinks is false.

Regarding the constraints of negotiation, various factors can come into play in the course of discussions. It is possible in principle that the proposed condition on group belief be satisfied even given a fair amount of intimidation and, in effect, psychological coercion of the parties. The following example is derived from a real case in which a subtle use of rhetoric by a person of high status led to a group's accepting an opinion which was by no means obviously the one most people felt was right. The action takes place at a meeting of a university department in England.

An outstanding student who had serious psychological problems prior to the written examinations in his field now stood to get a 'lower second' degree grade on the basis of these examinations. There was some discussion as to whether and how to raise the degree grade one notch. Claire, a department member who knew the student's work well, urged that this should be done, suggesting at the same time that it would not be good to raise the grade without asking the student to do some further task. She proposed that he be given a short oral examination, or 'viva', in which he would be asked a few questions on the topic of the examination. A more senior member of the department, Ben, questioned what would happen if the student did poorly on the viva. Claire suggested that this need not affect a decision to raise the grade. Ben exclaimed: 'I see! A *punitive* viva!' The force of the word 'punitive' was enormous. As it echoed around the room, people quickly agreed that the student's grade should be left as a lower second. As Claire saw it, they did this not because they personally believed that the student's grade should not be raised, but because they did not want to be accused of endorsing a 'punitive' policy.

I conjecture that the phenomenon of group belief as characterized here is ubiquitous in human societies. This is a phenomenon with important consequences, both good and bad. Among other things, group beliefs help to produce relatively harmonious interactions between people, providing a set of stable background assumptions for their conversations and discussions. On the other hand, group belief can have unfortunate, even horrifying results. Whole societies may be in the grip of false doctrines, their members given over to mouthing and publicly acting upon false and pernicious views. On a smaller scale, isolated individuals can be unfortunately affected by the views and conclusions not only of other individuals, but of groups, as was the brilliant student with the unrepresentative grade.

To use Durkheim's phrase, a collective belief on this account has 'coercive power' in the following sense: individual parties to a collective belief necessarily understand that their behaviour is subject to a certain constraint, the obligation to speak and act in specified ways. Moreover, they understand that they have granted to one another certain rights of enforcement.

Collective beliefs on this account may well tend to become correlated with the corresponding individual beliefs, though they need not do so. When they do not, there are two main possibilities. First, most people may have no personal opinion on the matter in question. Second, most have a contrary opinion. The latter looks as if in practice it will be a particularly unstable situation. (Recall Hans Christian Andersen's story about the emperor's 'new clothes'.) But its possibility raises important questions: how will things develop, and why will they go the way they do?

It is now time to assess this nonsummative account of collective belief, beginning with the usual tests.

7.6 Assessing the nonsummative account

Are sentences like 'We believe that alcohol weakens moral fibre' and 'the Zuni tribe believes the north is the region of destruction' appropriate when the conditions in the nonsummative account are fulfilled? In favour of an affirmative answer is the main consideration on which the account was based. In a situation such as the poetry group case, such locutions as 'Our group was of the opinion that . . .' and 'We thought that . . .' are likely to be made: they would come naturally to the participants in such a situation.

Someone might query: how can predicates like 'are of the opinion that p' be applied to a group when none of the individuals believes that p? Does the account not have as a consequence that a group G may believe that p even though no one in the world believes that p strictly and literally speaking? If so, then must not the account be unacceptable? If one holds that to have a belief literally speaking is to have a mind, and one also holds that to have a mind one must consciously experience something, then the nonsummative view does imply that a group can have a belief that p without there being anything with a belief that p literally speaking. For the nonsummative view does not require us to believe that groups have experiences or consciousness, given a certain natural understanding of those states. For present purposes, meanwhile, a full scale assault on the concept of belief in general is neither necessary nor possible.

Let us ask a question which is agnostic with respect to the proper account of the literal meaning of belief statements. Given our intuitive understanding of the belief statements we make about human individuals, would this account be acceptable as an account of something appropriately labelled 'group belief' *whether literally or in an extended or metaphorical sense?* In order for this to be so, and, in particular, in order for this to look at least like metaphor, we need to be able to discern some relatively strong analogy between the situation in which a group is said to believe that p and the situations in which individuals are said to believe that p. That there is an analogy is clear from the account of group belief.

Surely those who on this account are part of a group which believes that p have done as much as they can to *believe that p as a group.* When an individual believes that p, he grants the proposition that p the status of an assumption in his own private reasoning. When people jointly accept that p, they commit themselves to granting p the status of an assumption in their public reasoning, their discussions, arguments, and conversations with the relevant others in the contexts at issue.

It may be suggested that surely people would more appropriately be said to believe that p as a group, if they individually believed that p, as well as 'jointly accepting' it in my sense. I am not convinced that this is so. As far as their *believing that p as a group* is concerned, it seems that they have done all that can be done in jointly accepting that p. Anything else is strictly irrelevant, logically speaking, to that issue. Their own individually believing that p, even all of them doing so, is just that. In particular, it can hardly affect the degree to which they jointly accept that p, from a logical point of view. Of course there can be causal connections between individual view and jointly accepted view, but this does not affect the logical issue.

The nonsummative account provides a clear potential contrast between the belief *of the group* and the beliefs of all or most members. The belief need not be endorsed individually by members of the group, though each must jointly endorse it together with the other members of the group. Under such conditions it seems particularly apt to say that the group as opposed to the individual people who are the members of the group believe that p.

Could everything be the same but a population which was not a social group be involved? First, a particular social group is involved in intention, so to speak: the group members have to have certain thoughts about their group in order that the group have beliefs. This was true for some of the summative views. But here, unlike there, it seems that we can actually give an affirmative answer to the question whether we have here a phenomenon which is collectivity-involving in the strong sense. Should there be a population P, not initially a social group, its fulfilment of the conditions would make it into one. Joint acceptance of a view is just the kind of thing that would make people a group, if they were not a group before.

Consider an example. In a railway carriage where none of the passengers has yet interacted in any way, a guard enters and shouts out: 'Is it all right if I put a caged dog in this compartment?' One man, after looking around a bit, shouts back: 'Sure, we think that's fine.' The guard also looks around and asks 'Is that right?' Everyone nods. Let us assume that the joint acceptance conditions are now fulfilled for the population in the railway carriage. I suggest that from an intuitive point of view this population now constitutes a group, and does so because its members jointly accept that it is fine that there be a caged dog in the compartment. Another example: three people are talking. At one point one of them says something about how modest he is. One of the others winks at the third, who acknowledges with a wry smile. Such an exchange of gestures could achieve the joint acceptance by the two listeners of the proposition that the self-ascription of modesty is false. Intuitively, a temporary group of two would thereby be created. My own account of a social group accords with these intuitions. Group beliefs may thus be argued to be essentially collectivity-involving: they 'create' collectivities.

Out of all of the accounts considered, then, the nonsummative account of a collective belief does best on the intuitive tests. This is so even if we waive the last issue discussed. Given that this is so, the discussion in this chapter may be deemed to support the account of a collectivity given previously. For the phenomenon otherwise most apt for the label 'belief *of a group*' turns out to involve a plural subject at its base.

An important query should now be addressed. There are cases where we may feel that it is fine to talk of a group's belief, even when the conditions given in my preferred account do not hold. Let me mention two of these, and consider what consequences can be drawn for the status of this account. Is it fair to say that it gives the *basic case* of group belief, and the others are special or parasitic cases? Or are there several different kinds of group belief, with no significant common element?

Consider the following example. (This is derived from comments by Raymond Geuss and by Steven Wagner.) A committee may form a judgment at a meeting from which some of its members are absent. These members may not know of the judgment at the time. Indeed, they may never come to know it. Yet we judge that the committee as a whole did indeed form the judgment.

This kind of case is clearly special. I suggest that we presume that there is an understanding or convention among the committee members that absentees are to be considered as committed in the usual way by the outcome of a meeting, and hence as in effect having expressed willingness jointly to accept the judgment. In the absence of any such convention it is hard to see why we should feel entitled to say that the group as a whole believes something in this case. (The established quorum could be much less than a majority of the members as a whole, so this kind of case cannot be accounted for by the fewness of the absentees and relaxation of the idea that every member must express willingness jointly to accept a view.)

Another type of special case has been referred to before. Here the salient problem is not absenteeism but rather the possibility that a single 'special' individual or group believes or asserts something and the belief is considered ascribable to the group. An important example is the case where a government believes something and the belief is ascribed to the society in question. Here again it can be argued that our willingness to allow that the group as a whole thinks something depends on our assuming a group-wide convention or understanding that this person's or group's belief may be regarded as that of the group as a whole, group belief being construed as joint acceptance.[42]

311

In relation to both of these cases, then, it can be argued that the phenomenon characterized by the joint acceptance account is understood to be the basic case of group belief. For it is plausible to suppose that the reason we are willing to ascribe a group belief in these cases is that the participants themselves jointly accept that a group belief may be deemed to exist in the circumstances, where group belief is construed according to the joint acceptance account.

I contend, then, that group belief statements are standardly if inexplicitly interpreted in terms of joint acceptance, and that this is the most plausible construal considered in terms of the whole battery of intuitive tests used here. I propose, further, that this is the central or basic interpretation for such statements. Other standard interpretations can be argued to assume this as giving the basic case of group belief. This is not falsified by the fact that people's off-the-cuff attempts at *analysis* often go in a summative direction. After all the interpretation I argue for is not easy to articulate.

Of course any account of 'the' meaning of a phrase or term may run foul of loose or extended uses, not to speak of idiosyncratic ones.[43] At the end of the day what is most important about the joint acceptance account of collective belief is not that it allows us correctly to characterize the semantics of certain English sentences but that it focuses attention on the phenomenon of joint acceptance. The interest and importance of that phenomenon will not be diminished if collective belief sentences are sometimes given an unrelated interpretation.

7.7 Concluding comments: on the beliefs and knowledge of groups

At the outset of this chapter I noted that the very idea of a group *belief* might appear preposterous. Groups do not have minds – how can we speak of them having beliefs? By now these initially puzzling questions have received an answer, in that I have provided an account of conditions under which collective belief statements have an appropriate home. There is nothing suspect about these conditions. In particular, they do not contain any reference to a 'group mind' of any unacceptable sort. *This* is how we can speak of a group's having beliefs.

The propriety of the use of the term 'belief' in this context has been queried. One problem cited has been the apparent irrationality of group beliefs, in the sense of their frequent formation under pressures other than the motive of truth-seeking. This applies, however, to the beliefs of individuals also. While it may be that such beliefs should ideally be 'proportioned to the evidence' many are formed under pressures other than the motive of truth-seeking. Indeed, as I have argued, many of our personal beliefs, in so far as we have them, are direct reflections of collective beliefs in the sense adumbrated here. Evidently, some – Popper for instance – have thought that the best path to truth lay through public open discussion. While the fallibility of this method cannot be doubted, open discussion of the right sort can help to iron out biases and include needed information. There is, then, no obvious reason always to label what a group has as similar to but other than a belief, as a prejudice, say, or an ideology. A related point is that a group can have good reasons for believing what it does, though it need not, and it can have evidence for its beliefs. I touch on this again shortly.

Let me now say a word more on the analogy between collective beliefs on my nonsummative account and the beliefs of individuals. Both of these 'phenomena of belief' may be seen as essentially involving a relation between a proposition (the proposition believed) and a subject. In the case both of groups (plural subjects) and individuals (singular subjects) when a proposition is believed, it is given a special status in relation to reasoning and to action. The proposition figures in the life of the group, or in the life of the individual. In picking out beliefs, then, we may not primarily be concerned to pick out a special state of mind, so much as picking out a certain proposition as one which has an explanatory role to play in an account of the behaviour of individuals on the one hand and sets of individuals on the other. In the former case, an individual is guided by the proposition in question, in his personal reasoning and action. In the latter case, individuals in the role of group members are guided by it as they act within the group and as members of the group. If we look at things this way the analogy between collective and individual belief may seem, after all, to be quite close.

When do we have group knowledge, as opposed to group belief? Even without any general account of *knowledge*, one can still say something about the question of *our** knowledge. If there is a plausible concept of our* knowledge, it will presumably parallel the concept of an individual person's knowledge. In so far as knowledge seems to have to involve belief, then our* knowledge would have to involve our* belief. Obviously, the criterion that the thing known be true, perhaps the one criterion never disputed, can also be fulfilled for our* knowledge. Another criterion that has seemed to have something right about it is that in order to know something one must have some reason for believing it. And it is often added that one's reasons must be sound. (Edmund Gettier's famous examples have thrown doubt on the *sufficiency* of justified true belief.)

We* can have reasons for our* beliefs. These would be whatever we* jointly accepted *as* our* reasons. Clearly people can jointly accept that such-and-such is their* reason for a certain belief. Here is one type of case. In a cabinet meeting, the chairman says 'So, we are agreed that a tax on milk is the only viable policy at this time, since touching beer would be politically disastrous.' Everyone nods assent. Here is a less formal type of case. In a conversation, after one proposition has been jointly accepted someone might add 'and so, of course, no human will ever walk on the sun.' Everyone implies that they are willing jointly to accept this. And of course educators commonly teach their students the reasons for things. That these are the reasons for these things becomes something they jointly accept.

Evidently a definition of 'common knowledge' as 'our* knowledge' can be derived from these remarks. However, the former label might best be kept for the phenomenon it is currently generally applied to, so as to avoid confusion.

VI

SOCIAL CONVENTION

1 INTRODUCTION

1.1 A family of properties

People often justify their actions by reference to certain phenomena that seem to form a family. These include customs, traditions, rules, laws, and conventions. Clear signs of the importance of such phenomena for the social sciences can be found in the writings of both social scientists and philosophers. Max Weber's 'fundamental sociological concepts' include that of a convention and of a custom (*Convention* and *Sitte* in German).[1] Hart, 1961, sees his investigation of the concept of law as a contribution both to jurisprudence and to sociology. The central role in human social life of 'rules', 'socially established rules', and 'norms' has been widely stressed.[2]

Often no stipulative definition of the term in question is provided by a writer, and we are left with our intuitive understanding. Meanwhile, one supposes that explicit stipulative definitions of 'convention', and so on, such as Weber's, are often intended to capture existing everyday concepts, or to be close to coextensive with them. For these common notions of everyday life pick out phenomena of central importance to those who live that life. It would be good to have accurate accounts of these notions.

1.2 Social conventions

In this chapter I focus on the everyday concept of a social convention. That is, on the concept involved in English sentences such as: 'There's a convention in this department that we dress formally for department meetings' or 'In this country there's a convention that you may use a person's first name immediately after being introduced.' Social conventions would appear to be paradigm social phenomena. As in the previous chapter, I shall not presuppose at the outset the accuracy of conclusions reached earlier. In this case, I shall not take as my brief the working out of an account of social convention that accords with my previous account of a group's belief or of a social group, and so on. Rather, by starting afresh, I hope to confirm those accounts by showing how, in effect, an initially independent discussion of social convention tends in their direction.

In advance of analysis, there are a number of clear fixed points about social conventions. It will be useful to make something of a list at once, both to clarify the topic and to provide an initial framework for the assessment of proposed analyses. (In what follows I sometimes write of 'conventions', simply, instead of social conventions, trusting that the context will make my intention clear.)

Social conventions are undoubtedly both ubiquitous and influential. However local or temporary, they are always forces to be reckoned with. To give some examples: if there is a convention in my social circle that one send one's hosts a thank-you note after a dinner party, then I court censure if I never send such notes. If I arrive in a country where there is a convention that only close family members ever kiss in public, and I kiss an old friend on meeting her in a restaurant I risk being thought outrageous, alien, insane, or all three. Once I know that there is such a convention in the country where I am living, I have an argument for acting in accordance with the convention, though not necessarily one which will finally dictate how I act. The existence of a convention is, then, apt to encourage conformity to the convention.

Evidently social conventions do not only apply to situations involving people's 'social life' in a narrow sense, to situations such as dinner parties. Social conventions can relate to behaviour in public places, to behaviour at work, at school, in the market-place; to the behaviour of scholars and scientists, writers, artists, and politicians. They may also reach into the heart of a person's private life. There can be conventions about when and on what and for how long and with whom one sleeps, about the degree to which one's home is to be kept tidy, about the appearance of both the front parlour and the back bedroom. In short, there can be conventions relating to practically every activity a person can engage in, and to all aspects of action – to manner, time, location, and so on.

Conventions may differ radically from group to group. In some groups there may be a convention governing behaviour when waiting for a bus, in others there may be no such convention. One group may have the convention that women wear skirts and men wear trousers; another could have the reverse convention. Conventions may also change radically over time within a given group. A society's convention that one kisses friends on greeting could be replaced by a convention requiring a different kind of behaviour. Or a point may be reached where 'anything goes'.[3]

One rather striking thing about social conventions is that they may be tacit: they can exist among people who have never explicitly agreed to adopt them. For example, there could be a convention in a factory that one does not join a stranger at one of the tables in the cafeteria unless no other table is empty. Such a convention could have started without any explicit declarations or agreements, in the wake, perhaps, of a set of coincidental choices on the part of individual factory personnel not to join strangers at table. The current existence of the convention could be indicated in various ways: a newcomer who approached a table where a stranger was seated might be met with an unwelcoming stare; people may be noticeably careful to steer away from already occupied tables, and so on.

There are important verbal signs of convention. For instance, there will be reprimands for doing what one *should not* have done. More generally, normative judgments are part of what one might call the language of social convention. Much more will be said about this feature of conventions later.

On the face of it, there is a close connection between social conventions and collectivities. Thus we say that there is a convention 'in' a given group. We also say that the group 'has' the convention, and refer to the conventions 'of' the group. So at least some social conventions are conceived of as having an intimate relation to collectivities. Moreover, it surely sounds odd to say that a given population has a certain convention, but then deny that the population is a collectivity. This suggests that only populations which are collectivities can have conventions, intuitively speaking. This could be so if, in order for a population to have a convention it must first be a collectivity, independently of having any conventions. In this case, however, conventions would not *create* collectivities, so to speak. In fact, I would take it to be a mark against an account of a social convention if the fulfilment of the conditions it posits as sufficient for convention does not at the same time create a social group. Hence I take conventions to be essentially collectivity-involving in the strong sense defined in the previous chapter.

It is obvious that social conventions deeply affect the character of societies and smaller groups; they widely influence the actions and sufferings of individuals, and have their consequences for the course of human history. But though the ubiquity, diversity, and consequential nature of social conventions is easily agreed upon, it is not easy to say precisely what a social convention is.

1.3 David Lewis's game-theoretical approach to conventions

The philosophical literature contains an imposing and influential account of 'our common, established concept of convention', that of David Lewis in his book *Convention*. Lewis traces the lineage of his ideas to Thomas Schelling, and even further back to David Hume.[4]

Lewis's intricate discussion introduced a new level of thoroughness and clarity into philosophical discussions of the ways human beings relate to one another. A number of the key notions Lewis uses in the course of his discussion, such as 'common knowledge' and 'coordination problem', are of independent interest and have influenced and stimulated others working in related areas.

Lewis is clearly not concerned with 'convention' in the sense of 'gathering' (as in the Democratic Convention of 1980). Meanwhile, conventions for Lewis require for their existence a multiplicity of persons. Thus there is reason to perceive him as, in effect, pursuing the common, established concept of a social convention. My first task in this chapter will be to assess his account of convention in this light.

The account is of particular interest here for two reasons. First, in developing it Lewis invokes the conceptual framework of the mathematical theory of games. This theory is a popular tool in the quest to understand human social processes.[5] Discussion of Lewis will inevitably throw light on the theory's explanatory power. Second, Lewis at no point uses the concept of a plural subject.[6] But social conventions would seem to be paradigm social phenomena. Thus, if Lewis is right about conventions, the concept of a plural subject could be argued to have a less central place in an account of social phenomena in general than the argument of this book so far would suggest. Indeed, if Lewis is right it will be arguable that collectivities are not necessarily plural subjects.

My discussion of Lewis's analysis here will be critical, but quite detailed, given the interest of his account both in its specifics and in its general approach. My critique of Lewis prepares the ground for my own radically different proposal.[7]

2 DAVID LEWIS ON CONVENTION

2.1 Lewis's aims

The stated motivation for Lewis's enquiry in *Convention* relates to the nature of language. Lewis wishes to rehabilitate 'the platitude that language is ruled by convention' (p. 1).[8] Lewis explains that philosophers have attacked this platitude with the following argument: Conventions are created by agreement. We need language in order to make an agreement. Language, then, is needed to create convention. Hence language as such cannot be ruled by convention.[9] In response, Lewis disputes the first premise. Conventions do not require agreements.[10] In order to convince, he sets out to provide 'an analysis of convention in its full generality, including tacit convention not created by agreement' (p. 3). In other words, he aims to analyse 'our common, established concept of convention' (p. 3). As I have noted, there is reason to think that what Lewis in fact pursues is the concept of a social convention.

Evidently Lewis's account of convention can be assessed from a number of different standpoints. One pertinent question, obviously, is: does Lewis's account help to explicate an important platitude to the effect that language is ruled by convention? More important here is another such question: has Lewis in effect provided an account of the established concept of a social convention? (We should not be too quick to assume, as Lewis seems to, that if one of these questions has an affirmative answer the other does also.)

Lewis claims that however well he has succeeded in explicating the sense of an existing term, 'what I call convention is an important phenomenon under any name' (p. 3). Many share Lewis's conviction that conventions-in-the-sense-of-Lewis are ubiquitous, important phenomena, that human social life is run through with them. For this reason among others, Lewis's model of convention merits examination.

In what follows I shall examine carefully the logical space, so to speak, that Lewis's model of convention occupies. I shall argue that this is importantly different from the space occupied by our everyday concept of a social convention. Clarity concerning the differences will increase our understanding of both concepts and our ability to detail what goes on in everyday life.

2.2 *Lewis's source: the theory of games*

Lewis tells us that his theory of convention had its source in the theory of games of pure coordination, in particular in the work of Thomas Schelling. He also says that 'in the end the theory of games is scaffolding; I can restate my analysis of convention without it' (p. 3). The analysis can indeed be stated without using the technical terms of game theory. This is hardly surprising since these terms can in general be explicated, if lengthily, in everyday terms like 'preference'. Lewis's reliance on game-theoretical concepts and reasoning goes fairly deep, however. Possibly he feels that his account of convention stands independently of his game-theoretical reasoning. None the less, in so far as the reasoning is questionable, there will be less support for his theory. Further, game theory does not use the concept of a plural subject, so an account of a social process with its source in game theory may be expected not to use that concept either. Lewis's account of convention could be restricted in this way for various reasons, but its game-theoretical scaffolding would both suggest and support this significant restriction.

The following brief characterization of game theory may serve for the purposes of this chapter.[11]

The theory concerns situations ('games') in which a number of agents ('players') have a number of alternative actions open to them. For example, each person in a certain village can take an umbrella to work, or go to work without an umbrella. A possible 'outcome' of a given game is a particular combination of agents' actions. For example: everyone taking an umbrella to work; no one taking an umbrella to work; all but Smith taking an umbrella to work, and so on, through all the possible combinations of agents' actions. With each player is associated a ranking of the possible outcomes in the game, his 'preference ranking'. It is assumed that each player's preferences among the possible combinations of players' actions are linearly ordered, allowing indifference, and can be represented on a scale of arbitrarily chosen units so as to show the rank order and relative value (or 'payoff') of the combinations to the player in question. (It is not assumed that the payoffs to different players in a game can be compared as the same, greater, or lesser.) Each agent is presumed to be out to maximize his own payoff, that is, to do as well as possible in the circumstances, given his personal preference ranking.

This does not imply that game-theoretical agents are necessarily 'selfish' in the sense of having no concern for the well-being of others. That is, a player's rankings of the outcomes are not assumed to reflect only what he thinks will be best for himself in terms of his own personal well-being (health, wealth, productivity, and so on).[12] Thus it is quite consistent with the theory that someone most prefer, say, that he go to the concert and be bored, so that his mother will have company and thus gain even more pleasure from her evening out. In short, all the game-theorist supposes is that each player ranks the outcomes on some basis or other (not necessarily the same basis either). Only if a given basis is inconsistent with other assumptions of the theory or its spirit, is there any reason it should be disallowed.

It is also important to be clear that at the point where each must choose what to do, no individual player has an interest in the payoff ranking of any other agent, except as evidence of what the other will do. Each player's goal in playing the game is only and precisely to maximize his own personal payoff, irrespective of how others will fare according to their own payoffs.[13]

Game theory can be construed as providing advice to individual players faced with the question: 'what action should I, personally, perform now?' It should be clear at this point that the concept of a plural subject is no part of the theory. (I say more about game theory and plural subjects later.)

In the interesting games the values of at least some of the outcomes for at least some of the players depend not only on what the player in question does, but on what some other or others do. For instance, everyone in the village may prefer that on this occasion either almost everybody carries an umbrella or else almost everybody goes without. Then a given individual cannot, by his own choice (to carry or not to carry) ensure that he gets his most preferred outcome. As in the above example, it will often be helpful to an agent who wants to use his own power of action as effectively as possible to figure out what the others involved with him will do. To do so, he needs some understanding of what the others are like.

The agents with which game theory concerns itself are, by stipulation, *rational*. 'Rational' is a slippery term, but in the context of game theory the attributes of rational agents are standardly held to include the following.[14] (a) They are perfect reasoners. In particular, given the information available, they will make no mistaken inferences. They will, moreover, utilize all relevant information that is available. (b) Each will act as reason dictates, if reason does dictate a particular choice of action. (c) Each one is out to do as well as possible according to his individual ranking of the outcomes. (d) If reason dictates no specific choice, then an agent will choose 'freely' in a strong

321

sense: the actions reason allows will not be equally probable. Rather, no probability will be assignable.[15]

In the standard game-theoretical model, it is assumed that each agent has perfect knowledge of the 'payoff matrix', that is, of the ways outcomes are ranked by each player. In addition, it is 'common knowledge' between the players that each one is rational and has perfect knowledge of the matrix. The common knowledge condition at issue here may be simply defined as follows. It is common knowledge between player A and player B that both are rational if and only if player A knows that both are rational, player B knows that both are rational, player A knows that player B knows that both are rational, and so on. (In some situations none of this information need be used when a player reasons his way to a conclusion about what to do, in particular when each player has a strictly dominant strategy. In any case, all the possible premises about knowledge of knowledge of rationality, etc., are considered available if needed.)[16] Given these assumptions, each player is empowered to replicate the other players' reasoning. Moreover, each one's reason-replication can take into account the fact that the other agents know of *his* rationality and can replicate *his* reasoning. Such power is obviously important, for it may lead to the desired outcome of knowing what the other agents will do.[17] Finally, it is in general assumed that the players have no further information bearing on their decision problem beyond that already noted. Clearly, the theory will have application to actual human beings just in so far as they approximate in some way to rational agents as defined.

While the founders of the theory focused on the two-person 'zero-sum' game or situation of pure conflict, in which agents rank the outcomes in opposite fashion, games involving other preference structures, and more than two persons, have also been studied. In *The Strategy of Conflict* Thomas Schelling argues for the interest of (pure) 'coordination games', games in which 'the players. . . . rank all possible outcomes identically in their separate preference scales' (p. 84). Among other things, Schelling suggested that 'the coordination game probably lies behind the stability of institutions and traditions . . .' (p. 91). This is, evidently, an empirical claim. Schelling does not try to *define* 'tradition' or 'institution' or anything else in terms of coordination games. None the less, this suggestion comes close to the heart of Lewis's theory of convention.[18] As we shall see, Lewis argues that we implicitly define convention in terms of what he calls 'coordination problems'.

Lewis's account of what a coordination problem is, and his game-theoretical argumentation, are his own. I must next explain what these are. (The next two sections are mainly descriptive of Lewis's work. Those familiar with it could probably skip them, though they may want to check on the construal of Lewis that is at issue here.)

2.3 'Coordination problems': Lewis's examples and definition

For Lewis, a convention is a regularity in the behaviour of members of a population of agents when they are in a recurrent situation involving a specified structure of preferences. This abstract summary needs elaboration.

First, what kinds of situation does Lewis have in mind? He begins by giving eleven examples of the class of situations in question, which he calls 'coordination problems'. One example involves two people who are cut off while talking on the telephone. Both want the connection restored. It is no good if both immediately call back, since each will get a busy signal. It is obviously no good if both sit and wait. So each must choose what to do, where the desired outcome is that one and only one calls back. Not unexpectedly, another example has to do with language. (Here more than two people are involved.)

> Suppose that with practice we could adopt any language in
> some wide range. It matters comparatively little to anyone (in
> the long run) what language he adopts, so long as he and those
> around him adopt the same language and can communicate
> easily. (p. 7)

Clearly conventions can cover such situations. People whose telephone conversations were often cut off might come to have a convention that the original caller call back. There could be a convention in a group composed mainly of expatriate Welsh people that the members speak Welsh to one another. A convention, then, may cover what Lewis would call a 'coordination problem'. It is a further question, of course, whether this must be so.

Having given his examples, Lewis sets out to find an illuminating description of their common character.[19] As he proceeds, it becomes clear that what he is trying to characterize is this: a *nontrivial situation among rational agents with predominantly coincident interests*. (In what follows I shall refer to a 'nontrivial' situation, period, for brevity's sake. The qualifications just given should be understood.) 'Coincidence of interests predominates' is given a stipulative, game-theoretical interpretation; the rough idea of what Lewis means by this condition is clear from the phrase used.[20] The aspect of *rationality* that Lewis stresses is that rational agents follow the dictates of reason, if there are any. He does not go into the nature of rationality in any detail. It is natural to take him to be adopting the usual game-theoretical approach outlined above. Some problems which arise for him on this assumption will be detailed later.

Clearly, there is some reason to call the example coordination problems nontrivial. Someone in such a situation may well not know what to do, particularly if he cannot communicate with the others. For example, when our call is cut off there may be nothing in our situation or its background which makes it obvious that I should call back rather than wait. However, it is not obvious that in seeking a perspicuous characterization of coordination problems one should look, in effect, for a characterization of a nontrivial situation. Later I shall describe an underlying abstract argument about conventions which seems to have provided Lewis with a reason for seeking a definition of a nontrivial situation. For now, let me move on to the account of a 'coordination problem' that Lewis finally reaches.

As it happens, a key term in this account – 'proper coordination equilibrium' – is given an ambiguous definition.[21] I opt here for the construal that is reflected in Lewis's final definition of convention. According to Lewis, then, there is a *coordination problem* where coincidence of interests predominates, and there are at least two *proper coordination equilibria*. That is, there are at least two disjoint combinations of the different agents' actions, call them combinations C1 and C2, such that each agent prefers that if all but one person do their parts in C1, then the remaining person does his part in C1. On the other hand, each prefers that the remaining person do his part in C2, if all but one do theirs. Thus, in the telephone case, we have the combinations 'Player One call back, Player Two wait,' and 'Player One wait, Player Two call back.'[22]

2.4 Conventions

Having defined 'coordination problem' Lewis leads up to his definition of 'convention' by describing how coordination problems can give rise to a 'self-perpetuating system of preferences, expectations, and actions' (p. 42). He first considers how rational agents in a coordination problem may end up doing their parts in one of the proper coordination equilibria.

Given the definition of 'proper coordination equilibrium' it is clear that a rational agent will have no problem knowing what to do, all else being equal, if he knows that the other people involved are going to do their parts in a particular equilibrium of this type. (Suppose that a phone call between Lyndall and Anna has been cut off, but both want to go on talking. If Lyndall knows that Anna will call back, she will not call back herself, and so she will receive Anna's call.)

One way of knowing what another will do in a coordination problem involves knowing what that other expects you to do. In a variant of the last case, suppose Lyndall knows that Anna wants to go on talking. Suppose also that Lyndall happens to know that Anna expects her to call back. She can then infer that Anna will wait. Lyndall's knowledge of what Anna expects may in this way provide her with a reason to act in a certain way, in this case, to call back. Generalizing the point, Lewis writes: 'Circumstances that will help to solve a coordination problem. . .are circumstances in which the agents become justified in forming mutual expectations belonging to a concordant system' (p. 33).

Lewis notes that one highly effective method of forming such a system is agreement. Suppose Harry and Fred are the only drivers on a private estate, and they agree to drive on the left. Each thereby gives evidence of his preference for driving the way the other drives, and of his intention to drive on the left. 'By observing this evidence, we form concordant first-order expectations about each other's preferences and actions. By observing each other observing it, we may also form concordant second-order expectations' (p. 34). And so on, perhaps, for higher orders of expectation.[23]

Lewis wishes to stress that agreement is not the only way to produce a system of concordant mutual expectations. The means he focuses on is *precedent*.

Coordination by precedent, at its simplest, is this: achievement of coordination by means of shared acquaintance with the achievement of coordination in a single past case exactly like our present coordination problem. By removing inessential restrictions, we have come to this: achievement of coordination by means of shared acquaintance with a *regularity* governing the achievement of coordination in a class of past cases which bear some conspicuous analogy to one another and to our present coordination problem. . . . Given a regularity in past cases, we may reasonably extrapolate it into the (near) future. . . . We acquire a general belief, unrestricted as to time, that members of a certain population conform to a certain regularity in a certain kind of recurring coordination problem for the sake of coordination . . . our expectation of

future conformity is a reason to go on conforming, since to
conform if others do is to . . . satisfy one's own preferences.
(p. 41)

So there comes to be a 'metastable self-perpetuating system of
preferences, expectations, and actions, capable of persisting
indefinitely'. This, Lewis says, 'is the phenomenon I call
convention' (p. 42).

He then presents his first, rough definition of convention:

A regularity R in the behavior of members of a population P
when they are agents in a recurrent situation S is a *convention*
if and only if, in any instance of S among members of P, (1)
everyone conforms to R; (2) everyone expects everyone else to
conform to R; (3) everyone prefers to conform to R on
condition that the others do, since S is a coordination problem
and uniform conformity to R is a [proper] coordination
equilibrium in S.

Though logically speaking Lewis's definition leaves it open
whether there are some conventions which are not 'regularities in
the behavior of members of a population when they are agents
in a recurrent situation' it is clear that for Lewis the class of
conventions which are regularities of the above kind is the class
of conventions, period. Lewis does not make it entirely clear
when, precisely, such a regularity is to be taken to exist. The
impression one gets from his discussion, however, is that in *clear*
cases the situation in question occurs fairly frequently among
members of P, and *more or less as often* a particular type of
behaviour, B, occurs in instances of S.

An important amendment to the first definition involves the
addition of a common knowledge clause.[24] In order for there to
be a convention in a population, P, it must be common
knowledge in P that the other conditions on convention (the
conditions on conformity, expectation and preferences) are
fulfilled. Lewis's work contains three different accounts of
common knowledge.[25] For present purposes we need not worry
about the details or adjudicate between them. We can read Lewis
in terms of the account of common knowledge that I opted for
earlier, taking him to have a condition of *population* common
knowledge as I defined this in Chapter V.[26]

Lewis's final version of his conditions allows for cases in which
'situation S' is not in itself a coordination problem. It may call
only for the action of a single person. But when S is of this sort
each person in the population must be concerned in the usual
way to coordinate what he does in a particular instance of S with

what others do in nearby instances of S. So the people in question have a problem of coordination on their hands, and a structure of preferences parallel to that of people in self-contained coordination problems like the telephone case. Lewis means to include cases like that of his price-watching oligopolists: each one can reset his prices whenever he pleases. None the less when one resets his prices, he acts in the light of his expectations about what the others will do, preferring that he does whatever they all do (pp. 46–7).

Lewis also allows that there may be some abnormal instances of S, and so on. Thus his final account of convention runs as follows (p. 78):

> A regularity R in the behavior of members of a population P when they are agents in a recurrent situation S is a *convention* if and only if it is true that, and it is common knowledge in P that, in almost any instance of S among members of P, (1) almost everyone conforms to R; (2) almost everyone expects almost everyone else to conform to R; (3) almost everyone has approximately the same preferences regarding all possible combinations of actions; (4) almost everyone prefers that any one more conform to R, on condition that almost everyone conform to R; (5) almost everyone would prefer that any one more conform to R', on condition that almost everyone conform to R', where R' is some possible regularity in the behavior of members of P in S, such that almost no one in almost any instance of S among members of P could conform both to R' and to R.

Lewis's account of convention does not explicitly use the concept of a collectivity. His concept of a *population* appears to be wider than that of a collectivity, though he does not define this concept explicitly. Thus though his common knowledge condition requires that members of a population with a convention know certain things *about members of that population*, this appears not to entail that any collectivity concepts must be applied by them.

The game-theoretical source of Lewis's account is obviously intended to be reflected in both his first and in his final statements. In particular, the reasoning implicitly imputed to each agent is in terms of what he should do in order to maximize his own payoff. Given that an agent expects the others to do their parts in a particular proper coordination equilibrium, it follows that his own best course is to do his part, and so he does his part.[27]

Luckily for the agents in many coordination problems, the others are not trying to outwit or outfox them. Often, no one's gain is someone else's loss, but rather the players win or lose together.[28] But for all that, joint agency is not in question, nor is anyone interested in maximizing satisfaction to all parties, with respect to their personal preference rankings.

The relation of conventions in Lewis's sense to collectivities will be discussed more later. It should already be clear, however, that Lewis's account of convention does not explicitly use any collectivity or plural subject concepts.

2.5 *The underlying abstract argument*

Lewis seems to have based his coordination problem account of convention on an abstract line of argument which he never makes explicit. This underlying argument is fairly simple. It starts from the premise that 'it is redundant to speak of an arbitrary convention' (p. 70). Conventions, in other words, are *arbitrary* by definition. There are also the following assumptions. First, conventions are, again by definition, *regularities* in behaviour. Second, conventions hold among *rational* agents, in particular among agents such that if the balance of reasons for action lie with a certain action, A, then such agents will do A, at least in so far as they are acting rationally. Third, a convention is, to some extent and to some degree, in the interests of all parties to it: 'coincidence of interests predominates'. Finally, there is common knowledge among the agents of one another's rationality and of the structure of preferences among them.

The argument proceeds roughly as follows. (The general form of the argument should be clear without familiarity with the technical terms involved. The argument refers at all times to choice-situations involving two or more (ideally) rational agents with predominant coincidence of interests and common knowledge of the matrix of preferences and of each other's rationality.)

(1) Unless a choice-situation has multiple proper coordination equilibria it will be trivial. (If a situation is trivial, it will be common knowledge among the agents that each should do his part in a given combination of actions.)

(2) Let S be a trivial choice-situation. Let action A be what each rational agent should do in S. In a population of such agents a regularity of doing A in S, the regularity which we expect to occur, will not then be *arbitrary*, and hence it will not be a convention.

(3) Let S be a *nontrivial* situation, that is, one having two or more proper coordination equilibria. A regularity R of doing one's part in one of the proper coordination equilibria *will* be arbitrary. There will be at least one other regularity R' which might have been conformed to, that of doing one's part in another of the proper coordination equilibria.

(4) It follows that the only situation in which arbitrary regularities (and, hence, conventions) obtain among agents who are (ideally) rational is a situation with *two or more proper coordination equilibria*. Whatever regularities do arise in such a situation will be arbitrary.

(5) Now, there is a class of intuitively similar 'problem' situations which may be introduced by means of examples (like the telephone case) and which we may call 'coordination problems'. A consideration of examples makes it clear that a general, distinctive, and important feature of the members of this class is their lack of triviality. We may reasonably define 'coordination problem' in terms of whatever is responsible for this nontriviality. By premise (1) above, this is the possession of more than one proper coordination equilibrium. Hence we may define a 'coordination problem' as (roughly) a situation in which there are multiple proper coordination equilibria.

(6) In conclusion, then, conventions – arbitrary regularities in behaviour – depend on the existence of coordination problems. More specifically, a regularity is a convention only if it is a regularity of doing one's part in a particular proper coordination equilibrium in a coordination problem situation.

Some such argument does appear to be implicit in Lewis's text.[29] In any case, if it were acceptable it would be a powerful argument in favour of his account of convention. There are serious problems with it, however, as we shall see.

3 CRITIQUE OF LEWIS (1): A FLAWLESS MECHANISM?

3.1 Introduction

One of the striking things about Lewis's model of convention is how detailed and precise it is. A reader might well find it beautiful. Its wide acceptance as an articulation of our everyday concept of convention may have been facilitated by such features. In addition, it could appear that Lewis has detailed a flawless mechanism by virtue of which rational agents faced with an initially impossible situation (a nontrivial problem of coordination) may end up regularly reaching a happy conclusion.[30] More specifically, it could appear that we have a model of regularities in behaviour arising under the conditions of game-theoretical rationality, plus, simply, common knowledge of a successful precedent. In consequence one might suppose that we have a model of the emergence of regularities in behaviour in an especially interesting circumstance: the agents have and are known to exercise a strong form of free will. In particular they are not subject to any 'blind' tendencies or a-rational instincts. Such agency may appear to be an attractive ideal. Whether or not humans in general fulfil it, people commonly aspire to it. It is thus important to see how far such rational agency can take us, and under what circumstances.

In this section I show that the power of rationality is not as great as some have thought. In particular, it is not true that rational agents will inevitably come regularly to follow a successful precedent in a particular coordination problem, other things being equal.

3.2 The impotence of precedent: general remarks

One of Lewis's reviewer's, Richard Grandy, supposes that rational agents will follow a problem-solving precedent in a coordination problem. ('It would be rational to persist in these choices', Grandy, 1977, p. 131.) But common knowledge of precedent as such will not by itself automatically generate expectation of conformity or conformity on the part of rational agents.

Let us take the telephone case, assuming that it has the simple payoff matrix in Figure 1.

We start with the usual assumption that all that the agents have to go on is common knowledge of rationality and of the matrix. We now allow them common knowledge of a certain successful precedent: previously, whoever was the original caller has called back. Will rationality now dictate that precedent be followed?

Consider how a rational agent – call him Smith – might reason concerning precedent.

(1) Previously when Jones and I were in this situation whoever was the original caller has called back, and our problem was solved. The question is, what to do *now*? It does not seem obvious that I – the original caller in this case – should call

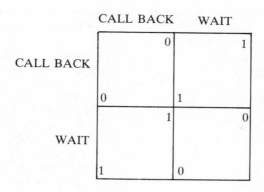

Key: A given cell of the matrix represents the combination of the action described at the head of its column and the action described at the left of its row. The numbers represent the payoffs to each agent. Payoffs to the agent who must choose between the actions described at the left of the row (Lewis's 'Row-chooser') are represented by the numbers at the bottom left of the cell. The other numbers represent the payoffs to the other player.

back this time, *just because* the original caller has called back with success in previous cases. It is obvious, however, that:

(2) *I should conform to precedent now, if Jones does.* So my next question is: will Jones conform to precedent? Let me try to replicate Jones's reasoning.

(3) Jones will realize, as I do, that though it is not obvious that he should wait now, just because previously the person called waited, it is obvious that he should conform to precedent if I do.

(4) If he starts reviewing my reasoning he will soon see that reason-replication will get him no further than it gets me.

In short, Smith's reasoning will get him nowhere.
In his review, p. 131, Grandy argues that

If e.g. by chance, they should on some round of the game end with a coordination choice, it is reasonable to expect that they will persist in that choice in all future rounds. This requires no communication – only the recognition that neither of them can unilaterally improve his position.

But the idea that 'neither can unilaterally improve his position' is irrelevant to *future* cases. By definition, if two agents do their part in any *equilibrium*, then neither could have improved his position unilaterally. Any other choice one could have made alone could not have made him better off. However, the fact that two agents have in the past done their parts in an equilibrium in itself says nothing about what *either one* will do in the future. So of course it remains true that *if* my opposite number will do his part in this equilibrium *then* I should do my part (or I might as well). But this has no logical consequences for what I should in fact actually do, or expect him to do, failing some further assumptions about our natures. I conclude that Grandy has not provided an argument to show that rationality dictates that one conform to precedent as such under the conditions stated.

3.3 On salience

Someone might argue that a successful precedent will make one particular combination of actions *salient* in the following sense.[31] It will be common knowledge among the agents concerned that this combination 'stands out from all the rest' or 'is the odd man out' in the estimation of all concerned.[32] There are two important questions to ask about salience here. First, does the fact that a given combination of actions is the combination which succeeded last time necessarily make it salient for rational agents as such? Second, if a given combination were salient, would this give rational agents a reason to do their parts in it? In what follows I explain why, in my view, the answer to each question is negative.

In the simple telephone case, the claim that a successful precedent will as such be salient surely depends on assumptions which need not be true of a rational agent. If calling back if and only if one is the original caller is distinguished by being the 'success-providing' precedented case, then, from a purely formal point of view, not calling back if and only if one is the original caller is distinguished by being the 'success-providing' unprecedented case. (Clearly there is more than one unprecedented combination of actions; but there is a unique unprecedented combination which would count as a successful solution to the coordination problem.) Only a specific psychology could make one combination salient in this situation. Thus in a society of highly nonconformist, or counter-suggestible, or determinedly creative people, the fact that something had been done in the past would make the other option the more attractive one for everyone, and so perhaps the one that would stand out from all the rest. Were one faced with a rational Martian, one would hardly know, on the basis of known rationality, what kind of psychological set one was dealing with. We can conclude that in general it is not the case that salience of a precedented combination of actions is generated by common knowledge of successful precedent, given common knowledge of rationality.

The psychological nature of salience might be queried for cases such as a colour matching case in which there are, say, seven colours with a unique successful precedent.[33] For here there are multiple success-providing unprecedented cases.[34] Even if this point is well taken – it may be – it leaves us the crucial question whether there is reason to do one's part in the salient combination of actions.

Contrary to asseverations of many,[35] no reason for acting can be directly derived from salience. Given that a combination of actions, C, is salient, our rational agent, Smith, can only argue as follows: 'Clearly C is the odd man out, in the estimation of both Jones and myself. But what should I do? Clearly, I should do my part in C if Jones does. But will he?' And so on, inconclusively, in the familiar way.

Heal argues that

Both A and B have good reason for choosing the salient, simply in virtue of the fact that, clearly, doing so is the only (or the easiest and most reliable) way of coordinating.[36]

This surely begs the question, at least if it is intended as an argument for salience in general. *Both* doing their parts in *any* acceptable combination of actions would be an equally good *way of coordinating*. The question is, does each one have reason to do his part in that combination? The same question must be asked of the salient combination. Looking at the simple telephone case, even if we assume that the precedented course will be salient for the agents, I see no way each one could argue that doing his part in the salient combination is the only (or the easiest and most reliable) way of coordinating. Doing one's part in the nonsalient combination, *if* both do their parts in it, is equally easy and reliable.

Discussions of the role of salience sometimes go like this. Assumption: rationality does not dictate an answer in a one-off case. Conclusion: what is needed is some 'clue' which enables the agents to coordinate their actions none the less. Now one way of looking at this conclusion is to see it as saying: maybe instincts or psychological propensities which have nothing to do with rationality could operate in a situation with this preference structure, so that beings of the relevant psychological type, at least, could cope with it. In itself this kind of move seems permissible. (I say more shortly about the role of assumptions about psychological tendencies within the framework of game theory.) What I am arguing is that *within the framework of game theory* the assumption that some point is salient gets us nowhere. That is, it does not move the agents' reasoning on to the conclusion: act this way.

Possibly this will be disputed on the following grounds. Rational agents will surely *realize* that what they need, given an otherwise 'unbreakable' matrix, is a clue, any clue, as to how to go on. In particular, they will surely realize that they need to look for a combination of actions that 'stands out'. But how can this last be so if once it is common knowledge that C stands out nothing follows from that? What they may realize, rather, is the different and quite trivial point that they need some clue as to *how they should act*, or as to what the other *will do*. But to know of mere salience (as defined here) is not, I suggest, to have *this* powerful a clue.

This suggests that hidden equivocations may lie behind the sense that salience can conquer all. Consider the claim that agents need to be able to 'single out' one combination from the rest. What they actually need to be able to do is to single out one combination as *the one each should do his part in*. Unfortunately, that a certain combination is uniquely conspicuous does not have the desired implication (even given that the conspicuousness is open to all). Redefining salience so that by definition one ought to do one's part in the salient combination clearly leaves the original problem unsolved. 'Salience' was supposed to provide a mechanism by reference to which the question 'how might rational agents discover what they ought to do?' may be answered. To answer this with 'by finding that they ought to do the conspicuous thing' is useless. How are they to find *that* out?[37]

Note that there are cases of the following kind. First, in a one-off case, reasoning which does not itself appeal to salience dictates a certain course of action to each agent. (By a 'one-off case' I mean a case where there is common knowledge of shared rationality and of the matrix, and no one has any other information to go on.) Second, the combination of actions which is the intersection of rationally required strategies is (by virtue of that fact) the salient combination.[38] Now even though the concept of salience may be properly applicable, there is no obvious reason to refer to salience as such in this connection. Presumably, it will have no role to play in the explanation of action here. In cases like this allusions to salience, though conceptually proper, should be made with care. Since by hypothesis the salient combination in such cases is also the one each ought to do his part in, the important conceptual distinction between combinations of these two types could become blurred. This is one good reason for not talking about salience in the kind of context in question.[39]

Of course, one might point out that if we were all to follow the maxim 'all else being equal, do your part in the uniquely salient solution' we would solve more problems than we would otherwise. Pointing such things out can be helpful. But it is important to realize that this maxim will *not* necessarily be followed by all rational agents as such.

A similar response is appropriate, I suggest, to an idea of David Gauthier's. Gauthier argues that salience 'does enable persons (in a coordination problem) to coordinate their actions' (1975, p. 210). He himself argues that in so far as salience as such does not alter the utilities it cannot 'in itself' be taken as providing a reason for acting by anyone. Meanwhile, he invites us to consider that salience enables players to 'substitute, for their original conception of the situation, a more restricted conception' as follows: each player has to choose between two options: (1) go for the salient point; (2) randomly choose, with equal probabilities to each, among all the available strategies. Gauthier argues that 'coordination is easily achieved' once the players so reconceive the situation, which has its own, derived payoff matrix. For present purposes I shall not dispute his general claim about the ease of coordination given the new matrix.[40] Sometimes, at least, a straightforward appeal to the utility numbers would indeed then be available. But there is a prior problem.

The logical structure of Gauthier's reasoning here seems to be as follows. A rational agent can reason: 'If each of us does this (reconceives the situation in such a way that it is obvious he should do his part in the salient combination of actions, and then makes his choice in the light of this reconception) then we will coordinate in one of the desired ways.' From this he is supposed to be able to infer that he *should* do this.

But this form of argument is open to the type of objection that I argued against the appeal to salience as such in the first place. It begins with a *conditional* about what will happen (a desirable outcome) if each player does a certain thing. But you only have reason to play your own part here if you have reason to think the other player will. But what reason can this be? He is in the same position that you are in.

Once again, then, we can agree that in certain cases it would be *good* if *all* rational agents involved followed a certain maxim (reconceive the situation and play the game envisaged there). All rational agents can recognize this, without that generating any confidence in a given agent that his opposite number, on this occasion, will act accordingly.[41]

I conclude that rational agents as such cannot be expected to do their parts in a given salient solution in an otherwise problematic coordination problem. This is worth stressing, because it is obviously tempting to deny it. If we deny it, we take the exercise of rationality to be a more useful tool than it is. It is important to be clear about the limits of reason.

3.4 Lewis on the force of precedent

Lewis's own discussion of precedent suggests something of a shift in perspective. Towards the end of his discussion he writes: '*we are entitled to expect* that when agents acquainted with the past regularity are confronted by an analogous new coordination problem, they will succeed in achieving coordination by following precedent and continuing to conform to the same regularity' (p. 41; my stress). This could be read as a claim that conformity to past successful precedent is sheerly a matter of rationality. The preceding discussion has a different flavour, however. Lewis characterizes precedent as the source of 'an important kind of salience: conspicuous uniqueness of an equilibrium because we reached it last time' (p. 36). Now he may assume (wrongly) that given no other clues salience will always be a result of precedent for rational agents. In any case, he does not seem to think that it is a simple function of rationality to follow salience or to follow precedent.[42] Thus he writes:

> We may tend to repeat the action that succeeded before if we have no strong reason to do otherwise. Whether or not any of us really has this tendency, we may somewhat expect each other to have it, or expect each other to expect each other to have it, and so on. . . . Each one's expectations that the others will do their parts . . . gives him some reason to do his own part (pp. 36–7).

(I take it that, according to Lewis, if an agent has a *tendency* to conform to successful precedent, then it is a law-like truth that, all else being equal, he will do so. A tendency may be called a 'brute' tendency if it is not a function of the exercise of reasoning; a 'brute' expectation will be similar.) In this and similar passages Lewis evidently considers brute tendencies to conform to successful precedent, or brute expectations of such tendencies, and so on, to be integral parts of his model of convention. Thus he appears not to presume that rational agents as such will have tendencies to conform to successful precedent or expect each other to have them.

3.5 *Rationality and tendencies*

Someone might try to defend Lewis's model as follows (Lewis himself may have slipped into this line of argument). Suppose you know that whenever they were confronted with the telephone problem certain rational agents did their parts in the successful action combination 'the original caller calls back, while the person called waits'. Surely you *are* entitled to infer that they will go on doing this, and hence will go on solving their problem in this way. The basis of the entitlement is our old friend, induction: we are in general entitled to presume that the future will be like the past, all things being equal.[43]

But there is a problem in applying inductive reasoning if the agents are assumed to be rational in the sense specified earlier. Such agents act on the basis of reasons, and will act freely if reasoning does not specify a determinate answer. That is, no probability is assignable to their acts in that case. In fact the use of induction is not only ruled out given the premise of free will. An assumption of the *equal* probability of all acceptable actions equally disallows the use of induction from a determinate past pattern of the kind in question.

An example will illustrate the point. Consider the telephone problem in its simplest form. In a one-off case it will be understood that each agent will make a free choice. Now suppose that, as luck would have it, a certain free choice on both sides brings the parties to a successful outcome. It is common knowledge between them that this is the case. Neither has any basis for ascribing any particular tendency to the other. Each is known to have acted freely. But then, when the next case comes around, each one must reason as if it is a one-off case. This will be common knowledge. Of course, nothing prevents a lucky outcome a second time, but nothing in the agents' rational nature suggests that one is more likely. Obviously, this line of reasoning will hold even for a million cases.

Now it could be argued that the following axiom should be added to the theory of rationality: if a certain strategy has been successful in the past in a given coordination problem, CP, then failing any reason to do otherwise, a rational agent will use it in future occurrences of CP. (A sophisticated version of this could increase the degree of probability of repetition with the number of successful 'trials'.) It is clear, however, that this can be no mere addition to the theory. It entails one's abandoning the original specification of rational natures, now endowing rational agents with a particular a-rational tendency. This may appear to be an extremely useful tendency. But, as I have argued, the original theory of rationality had no place for it. Talk of such a tendency immediately raises questions such as: where is it located? Is it a kind of habit that develops under the stimulus of positive reinforcement? Or what? Clearly such questions lie completely outside the conceptual map of game theory. It is important to see that we are taking a major conceptual step if we allow our rational agents to have and to think of themselves as having such tendencies.

When he refers to tendencies Lewis seems not to care whether what drives his agents is actual tendencies to repeat successful actions, or possibly false expectations that people have such tendencies. It is conceivable that he was not completely happy about endowing his rational agents with *actual* brute tendencies of the sort in question. Meanwhile, even rational agents can in principle be fed with false information without changing their basic nature. So the false-expectation-of-tendency option may actually seem more attractive in this context. (The change in the picture may seem less deep.) However, if the agents are allowed to be wrong about the springs of one another's actions, we have moved quite far from the original game-theoretical picture in which the workings of each agent's mind are available to the others.

In addition, the following should be noted. (This is my rendition of an argument from Saul Kripke.)[44] Let us imagine that the agents are rational as originally defined, but each has been given the false belief (perhaps by a kindly philosopher) that when reason does not dictate one particular course each has a tendency to repeat the action that led to a successful outcome before.[45] It is common knowledge between them that they have this belief. They now only have common knowledge of one aspect of their rationality: they act on the balance of reasons if this is determinate. It is not known to them any more that they act freely otherwise, since they believe that they have a tendency to conform to successful precedent unless the balance of reasons is determinate. But actually they are rational and act only on the basis of known reasons for action, or else they act freely. Consider how one such agent, call him Ishmael, may reason regarding a current telephone problem with his friend Sarah.

(1) Last time I waited and she called back. There is a single obvious way to describe this particular successful precedent: the original caller called back, the other person waited.

(2) It is not obvious what I should do, given knowledge of the matrix or the simple fact of successful precedent, and irrespective of her actions. So I must see if I can figure out what she will do.

(3) She has a tendency to conform to successful precedent if reason gives no determinate outcome.

(4) Before I know she will act on her tendency, I must look at her reasoning, to see if she has any reason to perform some determinate action.

(5) She will start like me, *mutatis mutandis*, with (1) to (3). She will then end up looking at my reasons to see if I will act out of my tendency. There seems to be no end to the amount of reason replication to be gone through here.

(6) Reason-replication will get us nowhere. In short, reasoning will give her (and me) no answer as to what to do.

So, I can conclude that: (7) she will act on her tendency.

But: (8) she will be at her analogue of (7). So she will have a reason to conform to successful precedent. So,

(9) She will not act on her tendency.

Now a contradiction has been deduced from the premises. Since this is so, a rational agent will realize that these premises are useless in combination. Since in the absence of reasons for action he will (by hypothesis) make a free choice, he will do so. Whether or not he conforms to precedent will be a matter of luck.

We may conclude that contrary to what might be supposed, common knowledge of a shared belief in a tendency to conform to precedent will not ensure that rational agents conform to precedent.

4 CRITIQUE OF LEWIS (2): LEWIS'S CONDITIONS ON CONVENTION

4.1 Introduction

The conclusions of the preceding section do not show that there can be no conventions in the sense of Lewis's eventual explicit definition. Here rationality is not mentioned. Indeed, conventions are not (necessarily) self-perpetuating structures, whether purely 'rationality-driven' or not.[46] They are simply regularities in behaviour which are *correlated with* certain preferences and expectations, such that given those expectations the people in question prefer to perform the action in question. They are, it is true, conceived of as law-like regularities, but the basis for the law-likeness is not made explicit and is not explicitly a matter of the consideration of precedent in the generation of expectations.[47]

Has Lewis captured the everyday concept of convention? Let us begin by considering the force of the implicit argument linking conventions and coordination problems in Lewis's sense.

4.2 *The implicit argument*

Recall that the argument starts from the assumption that 'it is redundant to speak of an arbitrary convention' (p. 70). It is by no means obvious that one should base a theory of convention on this assumption. Part of the problem is that the term 'arbitrary' can be interpreted in a variety of subtly but importantly different ways.

Lewis himself does not make an issue of the interpretation of 'arbitrary'. The closest he comes to a definition is as follows: 'Any convention is arbitrary because there is an alternative regularity that could have been our convention instead' (p. 70). There is reason to suppose that Lewis would expand this by saying that there is an alternative regularity that would have been more or less as good as the one we have. Not surprisingly, then, he has been read as thinking of arbitrariness as 'a certain indifference'.[48] Hilary Putnam writes 'What is arbitrary is that the agreed-upon side [on which one drives] should be the right side rather than the left side. . . . On the Lewis definition, something can *only* be a convention if it is *arbitrary*' (Putnam, 1981, p. 6). Putnam evidently thinks of Lewis as defining 'arbitrary' as something like 'having at least one equally acceptable alternative such that it matters little which is chosen'.

Now one can find standard examples of social conventions which do not automatically strike one as arbitrary in the sense of having an equally acceptable alternative. A convention that one send one's hosts a thank-you note after a dinner party, for instance, is surely not saliently arbitrary in this way. More importantly, one can be confident that there is such a convention without even considering whether there is an alternative which is 'more or less equally acceptable' from some point of view.

One of the fixed points about social conventions noted earlier was that they can and do vary from group to group. But this does not show that conventions are arbitrary in what I shall call

Lewis's sense. Views on many subjects vary between groups, and within one group at different times. This does not show that all (or any) of these opinions are arbitrary in Lewis's sense nor need anyone think that they are. It is true that people commonly say things like: 'That's just a convention.' But the connection of this with the idea that conventions are arbitrary in Lewis's sense is at best obscure.

There is no need to deny that *some* conventions are arbitrary in Lewis's sense. For the issue is whether it is redundant to speak of an arbitrary convention, where 'arbitrary' is so construed. If this is at best unclear, it is not a plausible basis for a theory of social convention.

It is natural to think of those with a convention as having something in some ways like an agreement. Meanwhile it is surely doubtful whether agreements as such must involve anything which is saliently arbitrary in Lewis's sense. They *may* do so. You say 'Shall we have cod or sole tonight?' I reply 'It really doesn't matter. Why don't we have cod?' It was a matter of indifference to both of us which agreement was made. But things need not be like this at all. Perhaps I know that the pills I am taking have made me violently allergic to cod. I explain this, and we agree to eat sole tonight. There is nothing about our agreement that is saliently arbitrary in Lewis's sense. We made it on the basis of what we considered to be weighty reasons. We rightly think we made the best possible choice. Similarly, people can explicitly search for the most appropriate convention: 'We have no convention about how to dress for meetings.' 'Why not quite informally?' 'I think that could lead people to feel too relaxed.' And so on. In the end one such convention may emerge as clearly better motivated than any other.

In so far as all agreements have an intuitive relation to arbitrariness of some kind, then, it is not to arbitrariness in the sense of indifference. Rather, it is to arbitrariness in an importantly different sense, in which the arbitrary is, roughly, a matter of judgment, decision, or will.[49] I say more about this type of 'arbitrariness' in relation to conventions later.

In sum, it is not obvious that arbitrariness in the sense of *indifference* is intuitively a property of social conventions as such. It would be best not to found a theory of social convention on the assumption that conventions have this feature.

I now turn to more specifically game-theoretical aspects of Lewis's abstract argument.[50] Recall that Lewis sets out to characterize with precision a nontrivial situation transpiring among rational agents with predominant coincidence of interests. It turns out that whichever construal we make of it, Lewis's eventual definition of 'coordination problem' does not effectively characterize situations of this kind.

First, it is not clear that only situations with Lewis's preference structure are nontrivial. One can construct examples of nontrivial situations of the kind at issue which lack the precise structure of preferences required for a coordination problem in Lewis's sense.[51] Second, it is not obvious that all situations with Lewis's structure of preferences are nontrivial. It is true that Lewis's structure excludes the possibility that either agent has a strictly dominant strategy. But it is at least arguable that this in itself does not entirely rule out triviality. (If it did, we would have an easy definition of 'nontrivial/trivial' in terms of strict dominance or the lack of it.) The issue here is a somewhat delicate one, for 'trivial' really requires definition.[52] One kind of case which may seem relevantly trivial but where Lewis's conditions are satisfied is a case like the simple telephone case, except that one of the two proper coordination equilibria gives each player a payoff vastly superior to the other, while the other gives each one a payoff little better than zero.

It could be argued that Lewis should have defined 'coordination problem' somewhat differently, insisting that no proper coordination equilibrium be a point superior to any other for both parties. But this device is quite strong, and rules out some nontrivial situations of the kind at issue.[53]

In conclusion, even if one accepts Lewis's premise that conventions are arbitrary regularities, and his linking of arbitrariness to nontrivial situations, one still cannot accept the detail of his conditions on preferences in so far as they are neither necessary nor, arguably, sufficient, for nontriviality of the kind at issue.

4.3 The precise preference structure.

Leaving aside Lewis's abstract argument and game-theoretical reasoning, it is clear from examples that social conventions as intuitively conceived can cover situations of interdependent decision which are not coordination problems according to Lewis's definition. The following example may serve.[54] Natalie and Anna often go to the theatre together. Natalie could wear either jeans or a print dress for her theatre visits. Anna, meanwhile, has trousers, a velvet dress, and a print dress. They might have the following detailed individual preferences regarding what is worn by whom. Natalie might rank as tied best her wearing jeans and Anna wearing trousers, and she and Anna both wearing print dresses. Next best might be her wearing a print dress and Anna wearing a velvet dress. The other possible combinations tie for worst case. Anna, meanwhile, most prefers her wearing velvet and Natalie wearing print. Next, jeans and trousers, and print and print, are tied. The other combinations tie for worst case. This situation does *not* involve two proper coordination equilibria. One can surely imagine that, by whatever process, Natalie and Anna arrive at a convention of wearing jeans and trousers, respectively, to the theatre. Even in advance of a precise account of what a convention is, then, one can conclude that the structure of preferences specified by Lewis is not necessary for convention. (The question of the sufficiency of his conditions as a whole will be dealt with later.)

4.4 Conventions and coordination

Do social conventions always cover situations which might naturally be described as interpersonal coordination problems? If so, then Lewis's general approach to convention could be accepted, in spite of the inadequacy of his account of the problems in question. If not, however, it will not be worth attempting to refine Lewis's account of coordination problems in pursuit of a general account of social convention. I next argue for a negative answer.

Note first that there are many conventions about what someone is to do when he, considered in isolation from any others, is in a particular situation. For instance, in one group there is a convention that one sleeps on a tatami rug, in another that one sleeps on a bed. Or consider conventions of dress. The convention in some societies that men do not wear skirts is not restricted to occasions when there are others present.[55] This seems to go against the idea that conventions must arise in the context of problems of interpersonal coordination.

Consider, however, a type of person I shall call a Conformist. A Conformist is primarily motivated by the desire to resemble any majority in his society. In a group of Conformists an analogue of a coordination problem will be involved even when people are in what we might call 'one-person' situations. When Conformists prepare to go to sleep, for instance, they wish to do whatever most other people in the group do when *they* go to sleep, if there is such a thing. Hence every situation in which he has to choose what to do is a kind of coordination problem for a Conformist: he wishes to do whatever most others in his society do when they are in this situation. In his or her own 'instance of situation S' each wants to do whatever the others do in their own 'instances of S'.

Now consider the convention that we sleep in beds. It could be suggested that such conventions are the outcome of Conformism. That beds came to be widely used in the first instance could have been the result of individual choice on grounds such as comfort, aesthetics, or conspicuous consumption. Then, when the common use of beds became known, Conformism could have made it all the more widespread, and then perpetuated it. Thus, preferences for coordination could in principle account even for those of our conventions which apply to one-person situations.

Though there may be something to them, such considerations do not support a coordination problem analysis of our concept of a social convention. For we can surely be clear that a society has a convention regarding a certain one-person situation without knowing whether or not the members resemble Conformists. We can even know that they do not. For there is no contradiction in saying that there is a convention in a certain group that one sleeps in a bed, even though each member of the group has always personally preferred that he sleep on a bed, whatever the others sleep on.[56] In sum, it is an empirical question whether a given convention derives from Conformist desires.

One should not be confused by the fact that once a group has a convention that one sleeps in a bed, this will encourage conformity to the convention. We cannot infer from this fact that the parties to the convention want one person's sleeping behaviour to be 'coordinated' with another's. The existence of a convention in a group could encourage conformity for some reason having nothing to do with coordinative preferences.

I conclude that the idea that social conventions must cover coordination problems in some intuitive sense is at best not proven.

4.5 Conventions and regularities

If we remove coordination problems from Lewis's theory, we are left with the question whether conventions necessarily involve regularities in behaviour which parties to the convention expect to continue. First, then, must they relate to situations which occur fairly frequently and in which parties to the convention almost as frequently conform to the convention? Various considerations militate against the idea. For instance, there could be a convention in a certain academic discipline that very eminent scholars are given Festschrifts at the age of sixty. It could also be the case that in this discipline, there are few very eminent scholars, or few reach sixty. If this were so, however, it is hard to see how the convention could be said to involve a situation occurring with fair frequency. Moreover, perhaps when the next eminent scholar reaches sixty no Festschrift is produced. It does not seem that this takes anything away from the existence of the convention, that there is anything less of a convention because there was no conformity. Yet it would seem that if conventions are regularities or require that something be done regularly in a certain situation, then there would be that much less of a convention here.

Even if one's notion of regularity allows exceptions, it seems to me, first, that each exception individually makes the regularity less of a regularity, but, second, that a given exception may make a convention not a bit less of a convention. Lewis in fact gives a definition of the 'degree of conventionality' of a regularity that implies, among other things, that each instance of nonconformity reduces the degree to which a given regularity is a convention. Intuitively, however, the degree to which a convention exists does not seem to be reduced. Just because there was no Festschrift for Jones we cannot conclude that the convention concerning Festschrifts has died or is fading away or even exists to a lesser degree. Jones might be known to hate Festschrifts, or to prefer not to have one produced in her honour, and so it may have been decided that, in spite of the convention, no Festschrift should be produced. Continued and widespread lack of conformity to a convention could presumably contribute to the demise of the convention. But this would be a causal rather than a logical contribution.

Consider another example. Say that there is a convention in my social circle that after a formal dinner party one sends a thank-you note. Assume that at a certain point in time people do conform to the convention, by and large. But as people get busier and busier, they keep forgetting to send notes until it seems too late; personal letter and note writing in general, let us suppose, go rather out of fashion; people are used to telephonic communications, it seems wrong to type a thank-you note, and one's handwriting is so illegible. So, on the whole, people do not send thank-you notes any longer. Some, with attractive handwriting, time, and stamps, do so regularly. Others do so occasionally. Many think about it but do not actually do it. Does it follow from all this that there is no longer a convention in my social circle that one sends a thank-you note after a formal dinner party? I do not think that it does. Of course, in circumstances like those described one might wonder how long a convention could survive. But this could be because conventions do not easily survive in the absence of conformity, not because conventions actually are or involve regularities in behaviour as a matter of conceptual necessity.

One might try modifying Lewis's account thus: conventions do not require that people regularly conform, but just that they would conform, all else being equal. But when must people conform to a convention they may properly be said to have? Is it provided they know of no reasons for not conforming? But it is not clear that one cannot simply decide not to conform to a convention, for no reason. Conventions seem to be the kind of thing which may not move actual human beings to action, though perhaps they must move ideally rational agents. If everyone were to feel perverse or to act irrationally a few times and not conform to the convention, that would not obviously show there was no convention. But then one seems to be left with the following 'regularity' for convention: people who have a convention must conform to it unless, for whatever reason, they do not. This also seems to be true for those who do not have a certain convention: they too will conform unless, for whatever reason, including no reason, they do not. In other words, this modified regularity condition is quite vacuous. Yet it also seems to be the only clearly acceptable regularity condition on the existence of social conventions.

On the issue of whether there is some nonvacuous regularity condition on the existence of social conventions, once again there must be a verdict of, at best, not proven. Conventions may tend to spring out of, or give rise to, regularities in behaviour, to distinctive patterns of action like the uniform wearing of clothes or speaking of Dutch. But it appears that a convention can exist without the correlative regularity in behaviour. It would be satisfying if some positive account of conventions could indicate how conventions were intrinsically independent of regularities in behaviour while at the same time tending to be correlated with such regularities. Before attempting to look for such an account, let me turn to the issue of expectations and convention.

4.6 Convention and expectations

Out of Lewis's complex account of conventions the following hypothesis is left: there is a social convention if and only if almost everyone in a certain population expects almost everyone else to perform an action of a certain type in certain circumstances, and this is population common knowledge. For instance, there will be a convention in my social circle that one does not telephone anyone after 10 p.m. if and only if it is common knowledge that almost everyone expects almost everyone to refrain from making phone calls after 10 p.m. Before assessing this view, let me draw attention to an important ambiguity in the notion of an expectation. Sometimes the sentence 'He expects her to come', for instance, has a normative sense, that is, it implies that he thinks it is incumbent upon her to come. Meanwhile, the sentence may also mean 'He believes that she will come.' Here the expectation is a belief about what someone will in fact do. Let us call such an expectation a *plain* expectation. It is important to be clear that the proposal under discussion concerns plain expectations.

There seem to be at least two problems in taking commonly known plain expectations of conformity as constitutive of social conventions. First, it is not obvious that there could not be a social convention in the absence of such expectations. Consider again the case of the convention that one sends a thank-you note after a dinner party. Let us allow that this might at some point in its history be accompanied by regular conformity. But suppose we have reached the point where conformity has dwindled, and most people no longer conform. There are two possibilities: it may be common knowledge that most people have stopped conforming, or it may not. If it is not, then people may well go on expecting conformity. But it is possible that there is uncertainty, say, about how many people actually still conform. If people are uncertain about this, then there is no common knowledge of general conformity nor of general nonconformity. Suppose, then, that there is no common knowledge concerning how many people act in accordance with the convention. Then there may equally be no common knowledge about how many people have plain expectations that most others will conform. Yet could there not still be a convention?

People may, at this point, still actually have plain expectations of conformity, by and large. But suppose they do not. Suppose that their views about what others will do are affected by their uncertainty about what others are currently doing. Then, it seems, it may well no longer be true that almost everyone expects almost everyone to conform. Does *this* mean that there is no longer a convention? If our concept of a social convention was such that social conventions existed only if the corresponding plain expectations of conformity did, we should have a clear sense that of course there was no longer a social convention. The present author, at least, has no such clear sense. Consider, for instance, that someone might say, 'I know I really should write that note, but this convention seems to be honoured in the

347

breach these days. I don't suppose anyone else will write one.' The naturalness of such utterances as this suggests that social conventions can exist in the absence of expectations of conformity. What may be true, as is the case where there is an absence of conformity, is that where there is an absence of expectations of conformity, there is now some evidence which suggests that the corresponding convention may no longer exist. But this could be because, social conventions being what they are, and being by their nature distinct and independent from plain expectations, they none the less tend as an empirical matter to bring regularities and plain expectations of conformity in their train.

A second problem with an analysis of social conventions wholly in terms of commonly known plain expectations is as follows. It seems intuitively clear that if there is a convention in your department that people have lunch together on Mondays, you have an obvious and quite strong reason for participation in the lunch, though one which may be overridden or ignored. Meanwhile, it is not clear that someone's belief that I will do something provides a reason of any kind for me to live up to it. It may be suggested that it is in general better to have true beliefs than false ones, and that reasonable people will in consequence want their beliefs about the future to be true, other things being equal. Even if this is so, the desire in question can be quite easily defused. There are countless plain expectations one would prefer not to have fulfilled. (Example: the expectation that one is about to fail one's driving test.) So I take the reasons suggested for satisfying any given plain expectation to be quite weak, certainly weaker than what is needed here. In sum, the claim that there is a commonly known, generalized plain expectation that people will do their parts in a certain practice does not seem to capture that aspect of social conventions which makes a social convention a moving force.

The upshot of these considerations is that, first, it is not obvious that social conventions *require* the correlative plain expectations of conformity in order to exist, and, second, it is implausible to *equate* social conventions with generalized plain expectations with or without common knowledge. Something other than plain expectations is necessary to explain the relatively powerful moving force of social conventions.

It is worth noting the implausibility of an account of conventions wholly in terms of commonly known plain expectations. Something very similar has been put forward by at least one writer proposing an alternative to Lewis's account.[57] Again, more than one writer on the subject has assumed, with Lewis, that commonly known, generalized plain expectations are a logically necessary requirement for the existence of a social convention. As I have argued, this weaker claim for social conventions is also implausible.[58]

5 CRITIQUE OF LEWIS (3): LEWIS AND THE 'OUGHT' OF CONVENTION

5.1 The 'ought' of convention

As I noted earlier, 'ought' judgments are part of the language of social convention. In this section, I say enough to enable an evaluation of Lewis's account of conventions from this point of view. After concluding my discussion of Lewis, I investigate the normative aspect of conventions further, and develop an account of conventions of my own which takes this aspect to be central.

As David Lewis stresses, social conventions may be tacit. Statements such as 'Our convention is that women do not wear trousers' need never be uttered. Meanwhile, when we consider how social conventions are typically manifested and discovered, it is clear that overt reactions of approval and disapproval play an important role.

To return to a previous example, imagine that you have just started work in a factory. In the cafeteria, you approach a table where two people you have not met are sitting talking. If they do not make you welcome, but on the contrary look put out at your implied intention to join them, you have some evidence that there is a convention among the factory workers that one does not join strangers at table. Now such a reaction is not conclusive. These two may be in the middle of an unusually personal discussion, and could be knowingly acting contrary to convention in discouraging your approach. Or their behaviour could be in total ignorance of the conventions, since they too are new here. They could be reacting with conscious or unconscious hostility to some feature of your appearance without even realizing that you have formed an intention to join them.

Imagine now that as you approach the table someone you do know taps you on the shoulder and says: 'You don't know them, do you? You shouldn't go and sit down with them just like that.' Now your evidence that there is a convention is a little stronger. It is not, in fact, conclusive. I say more about why this is so shortly. None the less, the linguistic expressions typically associated with conventions serve as powerful clues to their existence. And where there is a convention, we expect to come across locutions such as the following with fair frequency: 'You ought to wear a tie for an occasion like this'; 'It would be better if you did not take such an expensive present.'

Evidently, correlative with a convention there will be a set of attitudes of a special kind – prescriptive or proscriptive or permissive – in a word, normative attitudes, expressible in terms of the words 'ought' and 'ought not' and 'may'.[59] But to speak of 'correlation' is surely too weak. From an intuitive point of view the link is a conceptual one: normative attitudes are to social conventions as femaleness is to sisterhood.

Consider the following case. People in a certain community regularly take tea at four in the afternoon. Though this is population common knowledge no one affects any particular positive attitudes towards the practice, beyond generally conforming to it. In particular, it is not regarded as mandatory in any way. When Sally suggests to Charles that he come for tea at five, Charles may be a little surprised but has no sense of impropriety . If this is the way things are I suggest that we would not say that they have a convention that four o'clock is the time to have tea. That is, we would not say that people had a convention concerning the taking of tea at four unless they regarded taking tea at four as, in a certain sense, required, as something that to some extent or to some degree ought to be done.

The idea that certain normative attitudes are constitutive of social convention is supported by remarks in a large range of texts. For example, Jacques Barzun writes:

> The conventions governing these outside activities are more or less explicit. . . . These norms came out of pre-existing university customs. (1968, p. 50)

And Max Weber's account of the 'fundamental sociological concept' of *Convention* runs as follows:

> The term convention will be employed to designate that part of the custom followed within a given social group which is recognized as 'binding' and protected against violation by sanctions of disapproval. (1964, p. 127)

Let us now consider how we might develop the following hypothesis:

> in order that there be a convention in a social group that, say, men wear their hair short, it must be both true and common knowledge in the group that in general members of the group believe that, at least from a certain point of view, the men in the group ought to wear their hair short.

The qualification 'from a certain point of view' is necessary since there are many kinds of 'ought' beliefs – 'ought' beliefs which are seen as supported in specific ways – which do not seem to be constitutive of social convention.

5.2 *What the 'ought' of convention is not*

What I shall henceforth refer to as the 'ought' of convention must be distinguished from the 'ought' of intrinsic value. One who uses normative language may be meaning to mark a belief in intrinsic value: 'You ought to treat other human beings with respect (because) doing so is intrinsically valuable.' Meanwhile, it is not necessary for parties to a convention that one does such-and-such to believe that such-and-such 'ought' to be done, where the 'ought' is that of intrinsic value. To cite an example: that there is a convention in a certain office that inter-office memos are written in red ink does not entail that anyone in the office believes that there is anything intrinsically valuable about writing memos in red ink. Moreover, that people do ascribe intrinsic value to a practice does not appear to contribute to the conventionality of the practice. The presence of a social convention that men wear their hair short is not directly indicated by such remarks as 'men ought to wear their hair short, since short hair enhances the beauty of male facial characteristics' or 'it is part of virtue to look tidy'.

I am not saying that people's beliefs that such-and-such is intrinsically immoral or beautiful may not bear some interesting relationship to social conventions about such-and-such and related matters. One's normative attitudes may have a tendency to hang together. That we 'do not speak' about certain matters may, for instance, suggest that there is something unholy about such matters. Before embarking on any investigation of the relations which may hold between social convention and views of intrinsic value, however, we should be clear that from an intuitive point of view the 'ought' most closely associated with convention is distinct from the 'ought' of intrinsic value. (Perhaps this should be obvious, given the intuitive idea of intrinsic value. If something, a vase or a type of action or whatever, has intrinsic value, then it is valuable considered in itself, irrespective of any context, social or other.)

There is another important class of 'oughts', which is not at issue here. Let us return to the factory example. Your friend says: 'You don't know these people, do you? Then you really ought not to join them.' She then continues: 'You know how nervous you get when you meet strangers. You'll upset your digestion.' Or 'You'll get nervous and you know how you hate getting nervous.' In other words, the 'ought' is supported by reference to the needs or subjective preferences of the would-be agent. The action is evaluated purely in terms of these. At this point what would otherwise be (some) evidence of a social convention – your friend's initial remark – is now shown to have had a different explanation.

Consider now the natural assumption that the 'ought' of social convention is an 'ought' which is supported by reference to facts about the group in question. My discussion of Lewis's theory suggests that these will not be facts about shared preferences for coordinating actions, nor about plain expectations, nor about what everybody regularly does. Moreover, a consideration of examples indicates that the 'ought' of social convention can properly be uttered together with the denial of shared expectations, regular conformity, or preferences of the type in question. It cannot, then, be explicated in terms of these. The following examples may serve. 'No one really expects to get a bunch of thank-you notes, but you ought to send one'; 'I doubt very much if any of us ever cares to dress with the majority. In any case, we should all wear formal dress to the dinner this evening'; 'You know, we should be speaking French at this table, though we haven't been doing so.'

5.3 Lewis on conventions and norms[60]

Lewis finds nothing amiss in the fact that 'The definition I gave of convention did not contain normative terms: "ought", "should", "good", and others' (p. 97). He explicitly states that we have no reason to expect normative terms to occur 'in any equivalent definition'. This looks as if it is in conflict with what I have just been arguing. However, Lewis's meaning is not altogether clear.

Let me first clarify the status of my own conclusions. I hold that the parties to a social convention must themselves believe that certain things ought to be done. So I would expect any acceptable account of a social convention to use normative terms. This does not mean that the definer of convention must himself claim that something ought to be done. But in order adequately to characterize what others must think, normative terms must be used rather than merely put into quotation marks, or mentioned in Quine's technical sense. One senses that Lewis thinks it would be *undesirable* should 'normative terms occur in a definition of convention'. Meanwhile, there is nothing which should obviously trouble one about the necessity to use normative terms in the way I have in mind.

There is reason to think that Lewis meant to claim that one would not expect the definer of convention to commit himself to the view that anything, for whatever reason, ought to be done. Lewis may assume that no scientifically respectable definition *should* presuppose that anything ought to be done. He may assume in particular that no scientifically respectable definition should presuppose that something is intrinsically *good* or *valuable*. Such an assumption would, of course, hardly be unique to Lewis. Many have held that the social sciences in particular should be 'value-free'. The validity of this assumption need not be considered here.[61] For I have not been arguing that the definer of convention need himself claim that anything ought to be done.

As it turns out, Lewis goes to some length to argue that on his definition of convention, conventions are 'norms: regularities to which we believe one ought to conform' (p. 97). By 'we' in the last quotation he apparently refers to the circle to which he and his readers belong, as opposed to the parties to whichever convention. This lends some support to the idea that Lewis did not have intentional contexts in mind when he suggested that there was no reason to expect normative terms to occur in a definition of convention. It also suggests that his discussion of conventions and norms is likely to proceed in such a way as to avoid tackling one of the most important problems for his theory. This is the intrinsic inner normativity of convention according to our everyday conception, and the precise nature of this normativity. It turns out that what Lewis says goes no way to show that a proponent of his theory can find a satisfactory resolution of this problem.

Lewis claims that whenever an action would conform to a regularity of the kind he calls a convention, then there are 'presumptive reasons, according to our common opinions, why that action ought to be done' (p. 97). Lewis's idea is that for most individuals in a group with a convention in his sense, their conformity to the convention will, most of the time, answer both to their own and to most other people's current preferences. So according to our common opinions, Lewis says, they ought to conform: we presume that one should do what answers to one's own and to others' preferences, when everything else is equal.[62]

It seems that Lewis is talking here of the 'ought' of intrinsic value. According to our common opinions as Lewis reports them, doing what will answer to your own and others' preferences has intrinsic value, and hence should be done if all else is equal.

Lewis argues, then, that conformity to a regularity satisfying his conditions would be valued in a society sharing our common opinions on the relevant matters, and he may well be right. But Lewis writes as if he envisages that societies with other sets of values are conceivable. This may well be so. Suppose, then, that a society is conceivable in which a regularity satisfying Lewis's conditions would not be considered a matter of intrinsic value. In this society the people would not believe that they ought to conform to their own Lewisian conventions from the point of view of intrinsic value.

It now appears that one can accept what Lewis means to claim when he argues that conventions in his sense are 'norms' without agreeing that his account properly represents the normative nature of conventions. He argues that as a matter of contingent fact conventions in his sense may be viewed as being such that they ought to be conformed to as a matter of intrinsic value. Indeed, those in Lewis's cultural circle will so view conventions in his sense. He has by no means shown that it is a matter of conceptual necessity that conventions be judged as, in some sense, requiring conformity by the parties to the convention. (Given that, as I have argued, the 'ought' in question is not that of intrinsic value, one could have guessed at the outset that Lewis was barking up the wrong tree.)

A proponent of Lewis's theory might argue that there *will* inevitably be an 'ought' or 'should' of convention if Lewis's conditions are fulfilled. A rational agent with the preferences in question will know that he personally should conform to a regularity satisfying the other conditions. This does not help Lewis, however. I have already argued that the ought of convention is not of this type. I have argued, more generally, that the 'ought' of convention is not an 'ought' whose grounds are facts about the current personal preferences of the parties to the convention. In brief, conventions in Lewis's sense do not seem apt to give rise to the 'ought' judgments typically associated with conventions as ordinarily conceived.

Lewis argues for the normative nature of social conventions on the assumption that his coordination problem account of the concept of a social convention is right. I have, of course, been arguing against that assumption in various ways. I suggest that it is more plausible to start with the idea that it is somehow part of the concept of a social convention that the parties to a convention believe that they ought to do certain things in certain situations. This aspect of the concept seems to be more firmly fixed, rather minimal as it is, and better suited to serve as part of the foundation for a theory of social convention, than do any of

Lewis's conditions. Obviously, if social conventions are not logically required to cover coordination problems, their necessary normative aspect can hardly be explicated in terms of such an underlying structure.

At this point we already have reason to conclude that Lewis's conditions on convention are not logically *sufficient* to give us a convention in the everyday sense. Lewis's own explanation of their normative nature is not enough to show that they have the nature required for social convention. Failing some further argument, it appears there could be a Lewisian convention in a population without that population having the normative attitude that is definitive of social conventions. Thus Lewis has not given logically sufficient conditions for the existence of social conventions. I say more about the hypothesis of conventions as norms later.

6 CRITIQUE OF LEWIS (4): CONVENTIONS AND COLLECTIVITIES

6.1 The question of collectivity involvement

I have shown that Lewis's conditions on convention are neither individually necessary nor jointly sufficient for social convention in the intuitive sense. But an important issue remains, the question of essential collectivity involvement. Intuitively, one could not endow a population with a social convention without thereby, as a matter of logic, making that population a collectivity. An important test of an account of convention is whether it respects this judgment. We have not yet considered how Lewis's account of convention measures up to this test.

This issue would be of interest, in the context of this book, simply as a question regarding the relation of conventions in the sense of Lewis to collectivities. Lewis gives an account of a complex type of interaction between persons without invoking the concept of a plural subject. Should this set-up turn out to be intuitively collectivity-creating, and not somehow to create a plural subject, that would show that social groups are not necessarily plural subjects, as I have claimed.

Again, whether or not they have conventions in the everyday sense, populations in which there are regularities fulfilling Lewis's conditions might be thought to have thereby a degree of *structure* or *organization*, a degree of *common interest* or at least coincidence of interests, and to engage in a form of *cooperation*. In other words, the existence of Lewisian conventions in a population might be thought to endow that population with features standardly associated with collectivities in general. The relations of these features to collectivities will be usefully clarified if it can be shown that populations with Lewisian conventions need not be collectivities.[63]

So let us consider: when there is a convention in the sense of Lewis, is there for that reason a collectivity? The obvious method of answering is to review a case where the conditions are satisfied, and ask: is this, intuitively, a case of a collectivity? Is it a clear case, a borderline case, or, apparently, not a case at all?

I shall consider two cases of somewhat different types. An interesting feature of the first case is that the parties to the Lewisian convention need never interact or be in contact with each other in any intuitive sense. The case has features in common with one discussed in the last chapter (the teenagers of Townsville case), but is more complex.[64] The other case was judged not to be collectivity-creating. But that does not show that this case is not. In effect, we are now considering yet another type of complex of social actions in Weber's sense, this one more complicated than the last. We thus continue to test the hypothesis that the basic building blocks of social phenomena are social actions in Weber's sense, in this case social actions arranged in a rather special pattern.

The case involves two populations, social group G and population H (whose status as a social group will be in question). It can be described in two stages. First, it is population common knowledge in G that: (1) Everyone in G is a conformist of a special kind: each prefers that *if most others in a logical class that he is a member of* perform some salient act A in some recurrent situation S, then he does A in S also. More generally, within each logical class C to which he belongs, each prefers that any one more member of C perform A in situation S, if most members of C perform A in situation S. (2) Everyone in G reads the *Daily News*. The *Daily News* usually gives reliable information. (3) The *Daily News*'s headline yesterday was: in G most redheaded people clap their hands twice at dawn every morning.

Now for the second stage. Let us call the population of redheaded members of G, population 'H'. Given the truth of assumptions (1)-(3) above, it will easily come about that it is true, and population common knowledge in H, that: (4) Most members of H expect that most members of H will clap their hands twice at dawn. (5) Each member of H prefers that any one more member of H claps his hands twice at dawn, given that most other members do. (6) If it were the case that most other members of H clapped their hands twelve times at dawn, each member of H would prefer that any one more member of H did so also. (7) Each member of H regularly claps his hands twice at dawn.

Population H in the example fulfils Lewis's conditions on convention with respect to the regularity of clapping one's hands twice at dawn. Meanwhile, this population is not, intuitively, a social group by virtue of the above facts. At the same time, and perhaps in part consequently, it is hardly clear that there is anything we would naturally call a convention in that population.

This judgment on the matter of convention here squares well with my previous conclusions about Lewis's conditions on conventions in the everyday sense (the conditions are neither individually necessary nor jointly sufficient). In considering the question whether population H in this case is a collectivity, I have tried to call only upon inarticulate pretheoretical intuition, and not to consider whether this population met the conditions on collectivity existence posited in the account I gave previously, according to which social groups involve plural subjects. Meanwhile, my judgment on this case appears to jibe with that account. Before going any further, however, we should consider more carefully the relation between Lewisian conventions and plural subjects in the sense explained earlier.

6.2 Lewisian conventions and plural subjects

Recall that to be a member of a plural subject, in my sense, one must share in an action with certain others, where 'action' subsumes both actions narrowly speaking and beliefs, attitudes and other such attributes. In explicating what it is to share in an action narrowly speaking, I argued that each person must openly* manifest a conditional commitment of his will in relation to a certain goal, such that if others do the same, their wills are jointly committed to this goal. They then constitute the plural subject of this goal, and are in a position to share in an action, the pursuit of their joint goal.

Being a member of a plural subject has important practical implications. In manifesting willingness to be part of a plural subject of a given goal with certain others, one manifests willingness to grant specific rights and responsibilities to each person. Generally, each must facilitate and even encourage each one's promotion of the goal in question. (Thus it is incumbent upon someone out for a walk with another, if he finds he has drawn ahead, to do something about it. He might, for instance, stop completely till the other person catches up with him. He might shout 'Come on slow-coach!' to the other person. One who sets out on a walk with another and proceeds to stride ahead manifesting a complete lack of concern for the progress of his erstwhile companion, appears to have forgotten the name of the game. He may properly be rebuked for his insouciance.)

The conditions on plural subjecthood will be known by the participants to be fulfilled when they are fulfilled. As I put it, each will then appropriately view himself and these others as 'us*'. So much in recapitulation of what has been said about plural subjects so far.

Turning now to the case of the redheaded members of G in the foregoing example, I would suggest that nothing in the description of the case forces us to accept that these people appropriately (or inappropriately) view themselves as 'us*'. Let us consider this issue further.

We know that everyone has certain specified personal preferences. What, then, can we say about the goal each sees himself as trying to reach when he claps his hands twice at dawn? He need not have *the goal that most members of H* clap their hands twice at dawn, for nothing said so far implies that anyone sets any store by that state of affairs, or by any other state of affairs in which most members of H do the (saliently) same thing in some situation. A better candidate is that *any one more member of H perform a salient act A if most others do*. But must this be the goal anyone works toward in the case in question? One should note that there is no direct entailment between these people's preferences over the possible states of affairs and their conception of what they are trying to achieve in acting when they act in the light of those preferences. In particular, it seems perfectly possible for agents to have the *preferences* stated in clauses (5) and (6) in the example, but never to be *motivated* by them in acting. The description of the case and the satisfaction of Lewis's conditions entails that each does, regularly, clap his hands twice at dawn. Meanwhile, we are not forced to assume that any more goes on in anyone's head on a given occasion than this: most others will clap their hands twice at dawn, so *since I prefer that I clap my hands twice at dawn if most others do*, I should clap my hands twice at dawn.

In a given case, Lewis's conditions could be instantiated when each person believed that he had no right to act on his preference that any one other individual conform, given that most do. He may feel that all he is entitled to do is to make his own personal contribution in conformity, and that this is true of the others too. In other words, for all that they value maximal conformity with any majority, and know that their fellows do also, these conformists could at the same time be 'rugged individualists' who assume that one acts alone and independently of others. Thus each may come to act in order that he personally do what he expects most others to do, his act being conjoined, we may take it, with the hope that others will do likewise. It seems, therefore, that the description of the case does not entail that anyone is, or sees anyone else as, set up jointly to maximize overall conformity with the majority, or, indeed, jointly to do anything.

Lewis's conditions, then, can be fulfilled by agents who do not see themselves as acting together, and who are right not to see themselves thus. His conditions are stated without using the concept of a plural subject, and they can be fulfilled by people who do not possess this concept. In particular, they need not apply it when they act in such a way as to fulfil Lewis's conditions. They do not have to be rugged individualists, or have any other special ideas, in order to block their application of the concept of a plural subject. They may simply not be thinking in terms of that concept. However, if they do not do so, then they cannot form a plural subject in this connection. Thus it is clear that, as a matter of logic, those fulfilling Lewis's conditions do not thereby become plural subjects with respect to anything, in particular with respect to acts of maximizing conformity to whatever practice is at issue.

Someone may wonder whether the points just made about collectivities, plural subjects, and Lewisian conventions, do not depend on peculiarities of the example chosen, in particular the fact that members of the population in question need never interact with other members. So let us look at another example.

This case (adapted from Lewis) runs as follows. In a certain area telephone calls are automatically cut off after three minutes. After a while it comes about that residents of the area regularly wait for the other person to call back when they are not the original caller, and, equally regularly, the original caller calls back. Once this is common knowledge in the population of residents in the area, original callers continue to call back, expecting that the other party will wait, and wanting to reconnect the call. Had the original caller expected the other to call back, he would, of course, have waited himself. And so on. In other words, there is a Lewisian convention among the area residents.

These facts do not seem to make the area residents a social group or collectivity, intuitively. Let me now argue briefly that the residents do not form a plural subject of the relevant type. That they do not may help to explain the first intuition.

It may be noted that in an isolated case of the telephone coordination problem, as in some of Lewis's other cases, the situation that develops when the problem is solved involves a special feature. People talking on the phone usually constitute plural subjects. They are having a conversation, argument, or discussion, giving and taking orders, or whatever. But we should not let this confuse us here. Our question concerns the population of area residents. We can set aside the fact that particular sets of people from within this population regularly form temporary plural subjects.

If we consider whether the population of area residents as a whole ever constitutes a plural subject by virtue of having their Lewisian convention, it seems fairly clear that the answer is negative. First, what would these people be a plural subject of? There need be no interrupted calls that everyone in the area is a party to, so it need never be the case that all strive individually to restore a given call. What, though, of the general practice of reconnecting calls by employing the set of strategies: original caller call back, person called wait? Must the area residents constitute the plural subject of this practice? Must they think of it as 'Our* practice'? Must they think 'This is what we* do'? Surely not.

Consider what reasoning each must go through when faced with a disconnected call. Presumably all that need go on is something like this: I expect him to call back (because he called me and usually callers call back; because he will expect me to wait; or whatever); so I should wait, since I want to go on with the conversation. In other words, neither need allude to any facts about the plural subject-hood of the area residents.

It may be queried: by doing one's part in a certain combination of actions within a coordination problem, and in particular by doing it regularly and in a situation of common knowledge of general conformity, does one not imply one's willingness jointly to accept the practice in question with the other members of the population? Though one might be taken to do so, one would not necessarily be doing so, and one does not have to be so taken. There is no reason to deny that should a Lewisian convention get under way, members of the population could begin to assume that they have accepted, as a group, that they will support a practice such as reconnecting all interrupted calls in a certain way. After a reconnection one might manifest such an assumption by saying to another 'Well, we've done our bit as usual, haven't we.' In these circumstances, however, the other could reasonably express surprise at this way of putting things. 'Our bit in what . . . what do you mean?' This suggests that the assumption of plural subject-hood could have been premature in the circumstances. It has certainly not been given a strong justification. Such justification may be available when on numerous occasions a remark such as the first, in the above dialogue, has been accepted with a simple affirmative answer. However, it is hardly part of Lewis's definition of convention that any such justification is available.

An important general point has been highlighted once again. It is the fine grained description of a situation, in particular the details of intention and conception of the situation, which determine the application of the concept of a plural subject.

The main point in this subsection is that coordination problems and conventions in the sense of Lewis are not logically sufficient to create a plural subject.[65] In considering the collectivity involvement of Lewisian conventions we must be careful not to superimpose upon the agents, in cases where Lewis's conditions obtain by stipulation, the importantly special conceptual scheme of the plural subject, which, in real cases, may well as a matter of fact tend to be or become superimposed upon it.

The conclusion of the above discussion, then, is that Lewisian conventions as such are neither collectivity-involving essentially, nor do they make their populations plural subjects. It is arguable that the former lack is a function of the latter.

6.3 On the limitations of game-theoretical approaches to social convention and social phenomena in general

The foregoing suggests that in so far as social conventions and related phenomena are necessarily rooted in plural subjects, game-theoretical *definitions* of them will not be possible. The point is perhaps deeper than has yet been clearly brought out.

The game-theoretical scheme in general concerns a set of individuals who face each other, so to speak, while each sees himself as faced with a certain problem of his own: what should I do now? That this is so is implicit in the idea that in principle different players can have different rankings of the same outcome. Meanwhile, the conceptual framework of plural agency is different and the questions and answers relevant within it are different. We can see how for a given individual one action combination may be preferred to another, whereas, for a second individual, the order may be reversed. But if these two are engaged on a joint project, say, the project of rowing to the other side of the river, it may be indifferent to them in relation to that joint project, to them as 'us*' so to speak, which way things are done. Thus the group ranking of the outcomes may be distinct from the ranking of either individual. Moreover, from the point of view of 'us*' it may not even be obvious that the utilities of the individual elements of the plural subject are relevant to what we should do.

Suppose we wish to row to the other side. This is our sole goal, let us suppose. We can do so by: my rowing this hard; your rowing that hard – and so on. It may seem to be correct in such a case that, from *our** point of view, unless some (social) utility function sensitive to other parameters has been specified, all the possible combinations are indifferent, even if we both individually like some rowing schemes less, and like one most! By a social utility function here, I clearly do not mean a function which is by definition a function of individual utility functions, perhaps representing some intuitive form of distributive justice. I invoke a concept of 'our* preference ranking' where this is construed analogously to 'our* belief' as I construed this in the previous chapter. I assume that some such notion of 'our* preferences' is available, that is, is coherent and intelligible. I presume also that it finds instances in the real world.[66]

In what sense do *we** have a coordination problem in such a case? One cannot say that it is because each aims to maximize personal utility and can only do so if his actions mesh with those of another. For in the situation as so far specified, this may not be so. We can say: each is an element in a plural subject, fulfilment of whose goal requires that the actions of the elements (fractional agents) mesh *in one of a number of ways* which the plural subject may or may not rank indifferently. Given certain (liberal-democratic) values, and only then, it will be concerned with the embedded interpersonal coordination problem, with, that is, the relative value each personally assigns to a given outcome from his personal point of view.

Here is an example. Jules and Jim are out for a walk in the woods. They keep coming to forks in the path. One time Jules makes a turn and Jim follows. Next the reverse happens. Neither really considers the question 'What do *I* want to do here?' When Jules makes the turn he makes it since he perceives 'We need to make a choice' and takes it upon himself to do so. Jim follows because Jules has evidently made the choice *for them*, and Jim sees no need to think in terms of his own personal preferences. To do so would be very inefficient at this point, possibly leading to stalling the walk, and a vague, indecisive discussion as the two of them try to negotiate a fair outcome on the basis of the distinct individual preference rankings. Who needs that when out on a walk? Generally, at any given juncture letting one person 'take the reins' is best. (It need not be the same person at each choice-point.) He takes the reins of the cart bearing us along together. He may undertake his role in the spirit of wise judge or selfish autocrat or coin-tosser. The main thing for us, meanwhile, is that at every point someone takes the reins in this way – unless we have a convention, already established, that we shall always go by some particular route.[67] What a convention is, still remains to be seen.

6.4 Lewisian conventions and the nature of language

Before leaving Lewis's account of convention we should consider the relation of conventions in Lewis's sense to the nature of language. For Lewis's work on convention was motivated by a desire to explicate the platitude that 'language is ruled by convention'.[68]

What precisely does the platitude mean? I take it that the claim is that language by its very nature involves convention. What is meant by the term 'language' here? Note that we can distinguish between particular languages, considered as abstract objects, and language use. When he talks of 'language' Lewis is fairly clearly thinking in terms of the latter.[69]

Lewis's platitude is supposedly such that it 'commands the immediate assent of any thoughtful person – unless he is a philosopher' (p. 2). Meanwhile, various considerations suggest that conventions in Lewis's sense are not essential to language use from the point of view of prephilosophical intuition.

As argued earlier, it seems to be possible from the point of view of the concepts involved for a lone creature, a congenital Crusoe, to have a language. If we take this to be so, and if we also take it that language use as such involves *convention*, then it appears that this cannot be convention in the sense of Lewis: for it is clearly part of the spirit if not the letter of Lewis's definition that conventions reside, so to speak, in populations of at least two distinct persons. We need not restrict ourselves to congenital Crusoe cases. The fact that you or I, living in a society and speaking a common language, could invent a complex language (such as Esperanto) and be its sole user, seems to show that use of a given language does not have to involve Lewisian conventions. (Lewis has a response to the point that single-owner languages are possible. I turn to it shortly.)

A second observation which points against the claim that Lewisian conventions are involved in language use as such is this. Apparently people can adopt a signalling system or language-fragment for use on a particular, single occasion. For example, two members of an army accept the following arrangement: 'I shall only have time to come to the hill-top and signal once. I'll use a green flag to signal that the battle is lost, if it is lost. I'll use a yellow flag to signal that it is won, if it is won. As for any future signalling of any kind, we'd better leave the matter open. But we'll meet again before we need to use signals again, and can decide then what to do on future occasions.' Subsequently, the signaller waves a green flag to signify that the battle has been lost. Or someone who is asked to list her three favourite colours in order says: 'I've forgotten what the colour of this tablecloth is called, so for the purposes of making up this list now I shall call that colour "grue". My three favourite colours are yellow, grue, and red'.

Now this strongly suggests that Lewisian conventions are not an essential feature of language use. For a Lewisian convention is a regularity in behaviour in a recurrent situation. But no such regularity in signalling or linguistic behaviour is involved in the case of the green flag or of 'grue' above. Yet these are examples of language use (or, in the first case, use of a signal).

It is clear that Lewis himself does not regard single occasion cases as involving convention in his sense, strictly speaking. He explicitly considers the case of what he calls a 'one-shot' signal:

> Even the rising of the moon can be a signal – to begin an uprising, say – though it would be a prearranged, one-shot signal, not a conventional one. (p. 129)

and this is what one would expect given his understanding of what conventions are.[70] Meanwhile, it is important to note that in such cases we would in fact naturally talk of the adoption of a convention.[71] This suggests the following. First: language use and related phenomena such as use of a particular signalling system involves convention. Second: in so far as it does, it is not convention in the sense of Lewis that is at issue.

Consideration of the single *occasion* possibility also suggests that Lewis's explicit reaction to the single *person* possibility cannot be accepted. Let me explain. Lewis admits that, taking his definition of 'convention' literally, in the case of a language-using congential Crusoe 'there would be no convention' ('Languages and language', p. 26). He continues:

> But there would be something very similar. The isolated man conforms to a certain regularity at many different times. . .he has an interest in uniformity over time. (ibid.)

And he finally suggests that

> We might think of the situation as one in which a convention prevails in the population of time-slices of the same man. (ibid.)

In the case of a diarist (the case Lewis gives as an example) Lewis's suggestion has some attractions. Typically one writes a diary at least in part to make a lasting record of one's activities which one may read later. One wants it to be the case that if one uses a word in a given sense in making a certain diary entry, one will interpret that word accordingly when one reads the diary later. One has, in other words, an interest in uniformity of interpretation over time. However, an individual could surely adopt a linguistic convention for his own use on a single occasion, without any intentions regarding future uses. Such a procedure may seem likely to have little point, but the relevant consideration here is that it is conceivable. And a point is not unimaginable. Perhaps a poet is lying in bed and decides to make up a poem in her head about a certain man whose name she does not know. So she decides that for the purposes of her fleeting creation (in which the man will be named only once, of course) she will name him 'Twig'. She then begins to create the poem: 'Oh, Twig! . . .'.

In the case of a single use of language by a single user uninterested in coordination with herself over time, it is really hard to see how to view the matter as one involving a population with more than one member, or, more generally, as one in which a convention in Lewis's sense prevails. To say that this is the limiting case of something involving many persons, or beings, or indeed of speaker–hearer interaction, would seem simply to be question-begging. Perhaps the so-called limiting case should determine the law here. It should be stressed that this case does not have to be thought of in terms of a radically isolated person, one forever isolated from others. It is enough to imagine someone fully integrated into a society and party to a group's language, like the reader, who personally adopts a new linguistic convention for a single occasion. In so far as a single person can do this, and the sort of convention involved here is the only sort which is necessarily involved in all cases of language use, then the sort of convention necessarily involved in all language use is not convention in the sense of Lewis.

The foregoing considerations indicate that in so far as language use as such is indeed 'ruled by convention' it is not convention in the sense of Lewis. In particular, it is not a matter of regularities in the behaviour of members of many membered populations when they are in some recurrent situation.[72]

Let us now see how Lewis himself specifies his platitude further:

Words might have been used to mean almost anything. . . . We

could perfectly well use these words otherwise – or use
different words, as men in foreign countries do. (p. 1)

Now the point made here hardly seems specific to populations of
more than one person. (I could perfectly well use these words
otherwise, and in my private notebook, I do; we could use
different words – and after the revolution, we will.) One might
ask, then, what seems to be the real point being made here,
about the nature of language. What precisely is the force of the
platitude?

Prior to acquaintance with anyone's theory of convention, it
would be natural to construe the root idea here as concerning the
character of languages: of any language, used by any person. It
could be held to concern, in particular, the relation between
words – as yet uninterpreted – and the concepts which they
express in a given interpreted language. The idea is, roughly, that
any sound, mark or possible expressive vehicle could, in
principle, express any expressible notion. This idea is surely a
genuine platitude. Since it is a platitude about what we might call
the 'sound–sense link', I shall refer to it as the 'sound–sense
platitude'.[73]

The sound–sense platitude must be understood not to be tied
to the constraints and considerations which operate when people
are deciding what signs to use in order to express a certain
concept or thought. A given item may be too unwieldy to be used
as a sign by human beings. This does not seem to falsify the claim
that in principle the item in question could express any given
sense. Some signs will be such that something (onomatopoeia or
some other resemblance to a certain object, for instance) makes
them particularly apt to express certain concepts. Nothing like
this counts against the point about 'in principle expressibility'
being made.[74]

One thing about 'language' in the sense of language use follows
trivially from the sound–sense platitude. Suppose we use the
word 'white' in the sense of white. Then it follows from the
sound–sense platitude that we do not have to do so, at least in so
far as other words could in principle, at least, have been used in
this sense; similarly, we could have used the word 'white' to have
expressed any other expressible sense. Given that we in fact have
the capacity to use different words in different ways, then, given
the sound–sense platitude, we are at liberty to make the
sound–sense links that we please: we will still have a language.

The passage introducing Lewis's platitude, then, could quite
naturally be read as expressing a complex thought which starts
out from and takes a large part of its force from the sound–sense

platitude. It would be quite natural, evidently, to use the term 'convention' in expressing the thought in question, to say, with Lewis, 'language is ruled by convention'. An investigation of what 'convention' in general means would have to look further into what precisely the thought is and why it is appropriate to speak of a convention in this context.[75] It is clear, meanwhile, that the thought at issue does not include the idea that language use as such is a function of the existence of conventions in Lewis's sense. For it is precisely a thought about language use in general, and that includes its use by a single person, and its adoption for a single occasion.

7 TOWARDS AN ACCOUNT OF SOCIAL CONVENTION

7.1 Introduction

We already have many clues about how not to give an account of social convention. In discussing Lewis's account a number of popular candidates for necessary conditions have been rejected. Doubt has been cast on the likelihood of a game-theoretical account of conventions in which conventions are by definition a function of a certain structure of preferences among rational agents out to maximize personal utility. Such accounts are likely to suffer the same insufficiencies as Lewis's. On the other hand, we also have something positive to go on. There are two conditions which do appear to be necessary. First, conventions have a normative aspect. Second, they are essentially collectivity-involving: by virtue of having a convention a population becomes a social group or collectivity.

Where, then, are we to go from here? Let us start by investigating further the normative nature of social conventions.

7.2 Social conventions and agreements

I have argued for some negative points about the 'ought' of convention. A comparative point may now be added. There is a striking analogy between the 'ought' of social convention as so far characterized and the 'ought' of explicit agreement. When people believe they ought to do such-and-such and justify their ought judgment by reference to an explicit agreement, their judgment has all the negative characteristics noted for the 'ought' of convention.

In illustration, suppose Nell and Dan have agreed to meet at

Rudy's for dinner on Tuesday. Nell now judges that she ought to go to Rudy's. She does not think there is any intrinsic value in her going to Rudy's. She thinks she should go because she and Dan have agreed to meet there. Meanwhile these facts may obtain in the absence, and fail to obtain in the presence, of their meeting at Rudy's, of each one's personally preferring to go there, of each one's personally preferring to go provided the other does, and of each one's having plain expectations that the other will go. (Dan may not expect Nell to show up. He believes she wants to end their relationship, and realizes that if she does not honour their agreement this will hasten its demise. Nell meanwhile guesses that Dan will not expect her to show up, since she is aware of his suspicions. As a result, she may not expect him to show up, since she thinks he will decide not to risk the terrible pain her non-appearance would cause him.)

Now it is natural to judge that people would not have a fully-fledged social convention unless they were inclined to make ought judgments which they supported in a certain *positive* way. Thus in the context of conventions, 'oughts' tend to be supported by such locutions as 'That is what one is supposed to do.' In other words, the oughts associated with convention do not have purely negative characteristics such as those already specified above. They have this, too, in common with explicit agreements.

Now, it is a salient datum concerning our concept of a social convention that such conventions can exist in the absence of explicit agreements to conform to the convention in question: the 'ought' of convention is not the 'ought' of explicit agreement. Indeed, one may have a sense that agreements and conventions are in some important way at odds with each other.[76] To this issue I shall return. Meanwhile, the idea that the 'ought' of social convention presupposes a species or analogue of agreement is a natural one, and is suggested by the analogies between the 'oughts' of convention on the one hand and those of agreement on the other. What, if anything, can be made of this idea? The account I shall consider next is perhaps the most plausible account along these lines which does not involve the concept of a plural subject. It is a variant of a standard account of a central class of 'social norms' or 'social rules'.

7.3 Norms of quasi-agreement

Are there situations in which it would be natural to say of a set of people that, though they had made no explicit agreement about a certain matter, none the less their situation is such that it is much as if they had made an agreement concerning it? In pursuing this question one might come up with the following possible state of affairs.[77] In a certain social group, people generally make ought judgments, with respect to participation in a certain practice, in much the way they would if there had been an explicit agreement between them to participate, except that there has in fact been no such agreement, and they neither allude to one nor believe that one has occurred. Assume, more particularly, that if challenged to explicate their use of 'ought' they go at least this far: they characterize it negatively in the various ways referred to above. In addition, the general normative attitude to the practice in question, and the nature of this attitude as specified above, is common knowledge in the population. Such a situation could, presumably, arise by chance. We need not pause further now to consider other ways in which the situation could arise.[78] Since for obvious reasons it is somewhat fitting to describe such a situation as one in which 'it is as if they have agreed' to participate in the relevant practice, let us say that in such a population there exists a *quasi-agreement* to participate in the practice in question.

Now someone might suggest that if there is a quasi-agreement, then this fact could itself be perceived as supporting an 'ought': 'We ought to, because it is common knowledge that most people think that we ought to.' It could also come to be common knowledge that people think in this way, that they regard (what we are calling) their quasi-agreement as grounding an ought for them. In the light of this consideration, it may be tempting to speculate that our conception of a social convention is the conception of a quasi-agreement which is generally regarded as grounding an ought judgment, where it is common knowledge in the relevant population that this is so. I shall call this hypothesis about social convention the view of conventions as norms of quasi-agreement.[79] Let me summarize some obvious virtues of this account. First, it respects a basic intuition about conventions: the parties to conventions must believe that they ought to act in the ways which constitute conformity to the convention. Second, it respects the fact that parties to a convention will judge that they ought to act in a certain way, where their ought judgments can be characterized negatively in the ways which have been specified. Third, it respects the observation that parties to conventions do regard these ought judgments as having some positive grounding. Fourth, this account represents a possible development of the observation that there is a fairly strong analogy between agreements and social conventions. It was, after all, quite natural to label it as the view of conventions as norms of quasi-agreement. Fifth, it respects the idea that social conventions can be tacit: we do not need explicitly to formulate or to agree on our conventions.

There are two points of interest which are not matters of respect for the obvious data. The first is that the account uses no collectivity concepts essentially. To that extent, it may be found attractively parsimonious. The second point is that this account could be regarded as a development of a popular, even standard account of social norms, or social rules, in response to data relating specifically to the concept of a social convention.[80]

Another virtue of the account of conventions as norms of quasi-agreement should not escape notice. It is important to see that the account can be stated without using the technical term 'quasi-agreement', albeit in a cumbersome fashion. Roughly, there is a social convention in a group, according to this view, when and only when it is common knowledge in the group that most people think that any group member ought to do such-and-such in a certain context, and that this is so because it is common knowledge in the group that most members believe that group members ought to do this. In consequence, it appears that this view does not require that the parties to a convention must themselves think in terms of agreements. In particular they need not have the thought (or even the relevant concepts for the thought) 'it is as if we have agreed'. This is surely a desirable feature of the account. Irrespective of any desire to show that language or society could be founded on convention, one would have thought that social conventions are logically independent of explicit agreements and potentially prior to them in time. It seems equally plausible to suppose that the parties to conventions need not have the concept of an explicit agreement. In other words, though conventions and agreements may be analogous, it is not obviously necessary to think of social conventions as a species of agreements, or vice versa. They could be independent species of the same genus. I take it as a virtue of the account of social conventions under consideration, then, that conventions on that account are somewhat analogous to agreements, but at the same time it does not commit one to thinking of conventions as a type of agreement, or as being perceived as such.

7.4 Problems with the view of conventions as norms of quasi-agreement

There are serious problems with the account of conventions as norms of quasi-agreement, in spite of the excellent fit with many intuitive judgments.

Consider first the precise structure of the account. It posits two distinct levels of ought judgment, so to speak. First, there are the ought judgments constituting the initial or basic quasi-agreement, which is common knowledge: Most people just do or would judge without positive justification that such-and-such ought to be done. But in addition, most people believe that, given that this is so, one ought to do such-and-such, and this is common knowledge. Now, there is nothing obviously wrong with this structure, from the point of view of logical consistency. However, there are some problems with it from the point of view of our intuitive concept of a social convention.

First, recall the observation that when a set of people have a convention, they will back up their particular ought judgments by saying things like 'That's what one is supposed to do.' While this is right, one must also note that, given that they have a word for 'convention', they may back up their 'ought' by saying 'That's our convention.' Moreover, it is plausible to propose that these two ways of backing the 'ought' are virtually equivalent. Now, the account being considered does not reflect all of this.

The account is such that when people positively back up a (second-level) 'ought' of convention they do so by citing the fact that most people think one ought to act in this way (and this is common knowledge). Meanwhile, according to the account, this is *not* equivalent to saying that they have a certain convention, for their having a convention is not, on this account, simply a matter of a commonly known, generally endorsed ought judgment. It is by definition a matter of their predicating ought judgments upon such a commonly known, generally endorsed judgment.

I want now to suggest that what we should be looking for with respect to social convention, and indeed with respect to any true analogue of agreement, is a phenomenon or set of facts of a kind from which ought judgments *inevitably* flow, while at the same time the phenomenon is itself defined, so to speak, without necessarily referring to such judgments. This suggestion is supported by the observation that it is not clearly intelligible to suppose people acknowledging, with understanding, that they are parties to a certain convention (or agreement) and not finding themselves to have at least a prima facie reason to observe the convention (or agreement).

Can the present account be amended so as to cope satisfactorily with this observation? I think not. It may be suggested that we slim it down to a simple theory of conventions as quasi-agreements. But do quasi-agreements inevitably give rise to another set of ought judgments? One would think not. There are, it is true, various ways in which people could look at quasi-agreements so as to feel their existence provided a reason for action. They might wish to defend themselves against likely reproaches which would be personally unpleasant. Or they might act out of respect for the feelings of others, sensing that it is intrinsically better not to ruffle their feelings by doing what they think one ought not to do, and so on. But it seems that unless we explicitly stipulate that people do find a reason for action in the quasi-agreement, whether as such or by virtue of the likely consequences of deviance from its dictates, we risk defining convention in such a way that there are conventions that nobody thinks one ought to conform to. As I have argued, this seems to be wrong.

Another possible suggestion is to keep the account of conventions as norms of quasi-agreement and note that (third order) 'oughts' can be predicated of conventions in this sense. But here again we have the problem: is it inevitable that these 'oughts' will accrue? The answer here too seems to be negative.

Perhaps things are a little better in this case. Perhaps one could argue that, once people think they ought to do A because most people think they ought to, then in all consistency they should think that they ought to do A if most people think that they ought to do A because most people think that they ought to do A. Some sort of consistency in beliefs does perhaps demand this. However, though we might think people who did not predicate 'oughts' on norms of quasi-agreement strange, it seems we cannot accuse them of avoiding the inevitable. Once again, the connection between the necessary third-order 'oughts' and the putative phenomenon of convention appears not to be quite tight enough.

Two more problems with the norms of quasi-agreement view may be noted briefly. First, on reflection one may feel that the 'ought' of convention simply does not seem to be an 'ought' predicated on the existence of a norm of quasi-agreement. Though this was not one of the negative characterizations of the ought of convention that immediately came to mind, once it is mooted one may judge that it should be added to the others. To the extent that one is in doubt about this, of course, then other arguments against the norms of quasi-agreement view will be needed. But they do seem to be forthcoming, with respect both to the original account and the two amendments considered. Second, even though, once again, one may not find one's intuitions entirely clear on this, it seems that there could be a population which was not a collectivity intuitively, even though there was a norm of quasi-agreement within this population.

Though when there is such a norm members of the relevant population may be deemed to regard with respect the commonly known view of all on what ought to be, this does not seem to be enough to make them into a collectivity. Nor does common knowledge of this respect seem to change this. To allude to my own account of a collectivity, it appears that there can in principle be norms of quasi-agreement in a population whose members cannot yet be characterized as constituting a plural subject of any sort. It is arguable, then, that norms of quasi-agreement are not essentially collectivity-involving.

In addition to casting doubt on the view of conventions as norms of quasi-agreement the foregoing discussion has added to our understanding of what we need in an account of social convention. In the next section I propose an account which appears to pass all the tests so far arrived at, and which has greater intuitive plausibility than any of the other accounts considered.

8 SOCIAL CONVENTION

8.1 A proposal about social conventions

Suppose the following. It is population common knowledge in population P that all members of P have intentionally and openly* manifested their willingness jointly to accept a certain principle of action, which we may refer to as 'PPL'. This has occurred without anyone taking part in an explicit agreement to adopt PPL. The members now jointly accept PPL. (The notion of joint acceptance of a principle is explicated analogously to the notion of joint acceptance of a proposition in general, as characterized in the previous chapter.) PPL has the following form: whenever a member of P is in circumstance C, he/she is to perform action A. It is understood to be a *simple fiat*. That is, it is regarded as holding in the absence of any special justification which may be available. To accept a principle like PPL is to subject oneself to it. Joint acceptance of a principle by a given population entails that the population as a whole subjects itself to that principle. Thus PPL is a self-imposed decree, a *fiat* issued by the population itself.

Let us call this situation a situation of *tacit joint acceptance of a simple fiat*. In such a situation the members of P will know that they jointly accept PPL. In other words, they know that 'We* jointly accept PPL.' One consequence of this understanding on the part of any member of P is that the following reasoning is available to him: *We** accept PPL, therefore, *in so far as I am one of us**, I *ought to conform* to PPL.

Consider that it is hardly intelligible for an individual to ask: this being a principle I personally accept, do I have a reason to conform to it? As a matter of logic, *if* such-and-such is your principle, then, from your own point of view, you have a reason to conform. (Of course, if your principle is a bad one, it may not be true that you should conform to it, all things considered.) I take it that reasoning in terms of 'our* principle' will have a similar structure. Once someone's avowed willingness jointly to accept a principle has been observably met, so that he rightly judges 'We* accept this principle', he can infer that, as one of us*, he has a reason to conform to PPL, or ought to conform to PPL, all else being equal. (I say more in justification of such claims about reasoning from premises about 'us*' in the next chapter. I also claim that they parallel reasoning from premises about 'us', that is, from premises using the vernacular English 'we'. Given that this is so, it helps to confirm my idea that 'we*' and a central sense of 'we' have the same semantics.)

Even when each member has played his part in the joint acceptance of PPL, there is still room for any amount of what we might call *personal distance* from the jointly accepted principle. Suppose that for some reason I have jointly accepted with the other members of my department that we are to wear formal attire to department meetings. I may well feel that there is no intrinsic value in dressing up like that for our meetings. I may personally prefer always to dress less formally, and hence prefer to do so at our meetings. I may suspect that most others feel the same in their hearts. I may know that people have been influenced by the clear strong preference for formal dress of a much revered department member. I may wonder if there is some way of changing our principle to one more congenial to the tastes of the majority, our revered colleague notwithstanding. Should I come in wearing jeans and a T-shirt one day, maintaining a front of relaxed indifference?

In the case of joint acceptance of a proposition, the participants undertake to help make it appropriate to say that as a body they favour this proposition. As a consequence it is important that, roughly, when interacting with one another participants appear to take the proposition as a premise of their talk and action. Meanwhile, it appears that each may think as he pleases in his private reasoning. That would not be touched by his duties as a party to joint acceptance.[81]

In the case of joint acceptance of a principle, it may seem that there can be less divergence between the personal and the collective. Clearly I can act as if I believe that p, all the while thinking that not-p in my heart, but what would be the analogue in the case of action? If I act as if I accept a certain principle of action, then I conform to that principle. Is it possible, meanwhile, that I personally accept a contrary principle? It may seem odd to say that I can personally accept a given principle if all the while I am conforming to a contrary principle. With respect to the question of what principles one personally accepts, it may be thought, actions speak louder than anything else.

Consider, however, Jasper and Harriet's joint acceptance of the principle that Sunday is cold supper night. When Harriet is out of town, Jasper cooks himself a steak. Were Harriet out of town every Sunday, Jasper would cook himself a steak every Sunday night. Harriet brought the cold supper principle from her family of origin, and Jasper goes along with it in their marriage. But he thinks to himself: 'As far as I am concerned personally, steak on Sundays is the thing.' As we have seen, he follows this principle whenever circumstances allow. It seems, then, that after all a principle one accepts jointly with certain others can conflict with a principle that one personally accepts as one's own. It seems that this could be so even though in practice one always conformed to the jointly accepted principle.[82]

The case of Jasper and Harriet brings out an important possibility inherent in the case of both jointly accepted views and jointly accepted principles. It may be that if one jointly accepts a given view with certain others, one carries the relevant commitments at all times. But, in the case of jointly accepted views, it seems that these commitments need not go so far as to require that at all times the only view one expresses overtly and without qualification is the jointly accepted one. One is required to express the jointly accepted view only in the appropriate circumstances. Not only may parties to a jointly accepted view, then, at all times endorse a different personal position in their hearts, they may also publicly express this contrary belief without preamble or qualification in appropriate circumstances. There appears to be nothing in the nature of a jointly accepted view as such that prevents some circumstances from being appropriate.

In the case of a jointly accepted principle, it seems that, similarly, one may be able to carry out the obligations inherent in one's joint acceptance of a principle while not only personally endorsing a contrary principle, but actually conforming to that personal principle at certain times.[83]

According to the view of social groups as plural subjects, it is evident that when members of a population jointly accept a principle, they constitute a social group by virtue of that fact.

This jibes, of course, with what I said about joint acceptance of views in general, in the last chapter. It also seems intuitively right, given the understanding that collectivities can be very temporary and small affairs. But let me pause to argue independently for the intuitiveness of the idea that a population with a jointly accepted principle forms a collectivity.

Consider first the following case. The mushroom-pickers of Chapter II are at the stage where they have been bumping heads a lot, as they individually pick mushrooms in the wood with their heads bent down. One day one of their number blows a large horn, and all the mushroom pickers instinctively gather around him. It so happens all speak English, and so understand his suggestion that they adopt the following rule: after a mushroom picker has picked one dozen mushrooms, he must look up and make sure no one else is coming towards him. All agree on this idea. Then the little group disbands, and each goes back to his hut. So far a complex state of affairs has been described, involving verbal interaction and an agreement. But suppose that the mushroom pickers now continue to abide by the rule agreed upon, and to chide anyone who fails to abide by it. Gradually memory of the horn blowing and the agreement fade, but it is still understood among them that 'This is our* self-imposed decree.' They speak to one another and chide one another accordingly, when appropriate. Otherwise they go their separate ways and have no interactions, and jointly accept no other rules.

I would judge that, intuitively speaking, by the end of this story the mushroom pickers do form a collectivity, however poor in myths and mores. In other words, it appears that, from an intuitive point of view, having one rule they think of as 'ours*' determines that they may be referred to as a collectivity. This places them on a par – to a degree – with those cases of families, conversationalists, discussion groups, and so on, which provide our clearest, most undisputed cases.

To this point may be added the empirical one that sets of people are exceedingly likely to invent and jointly accept certain decrees about how to act when, unlike the mushroom pickers, they are already jointly engaged on some project. If two people are rowing a boat to the centre of a lake in order to save a drowning swimmer, it is incumbent upon them to arrive at a way of rowing harmoniously. Efficient fulfilment of their joint project demands it. They may soon come jointly to accept a principle as to how to row to the centre of the lake. This could come by trial and error, without words. A sudden change by one could plainly appear untoward, more than just a nuisance, more than something just contrary to plain expectation. The need for jointly accepted principles in larger populations with longer-term projects is equally obvious. Given that one accepts that to have a joint project is to constitute a group, this point can be rephrased as follows. Already-constituted groups with goals will be highly likely to develop self-imposed principles of action. Whatever analysis of a collectivity one gives, this point about groups is surely right.[84]

Evidently one can feel moved to take steps to change a principle one jointly accepts with others. But if one goes against the principle without obvious excuse or explanation, serious questions will be in order. Clearly one throws doubt on one's participation in joint acceptance of the principle. In so far as a group is wholly or in part constituted by its acceptance of this principle – is one still a member of the group? Does one mean to signal one's lack of interest in membership? How solid is this particular principle, as a principle held by the group? Can one rely on members continuing jointly to sustain the principle in question? How solid or real is the group itself? Clearly these are serious and disturbing questions, raising for everyone questions of their relationship to the others and of what behaviour is appropriate among them. Nonconforming behaviour of this kind, then, may be expected to provoke reactions of some force, depending, among other things, on the status of the principle in question (is it the one thing that held the group together?) and the degree of preference members have that the group survive.

I propose that our everyday concept of a social convention is that of a jointly accepted principle of action, a group fiat with respect to how one is to act in certain situations. As just noted, in my view social conventions on this account are essentially collectivity-involving: a population that develops a convention in this sense becomes by that very fact a collectivity. Further, each party to the convention will accept that each one personally ought to conform, other things being equal, where the 'ought' is understood to be based on the fact that together they jointly accept the principle. 'I ought to conform, in so far as I am one of us*, because that is our* principle.' So far so good, given the desiderata I have stressed for accounts of social convention. In the following sections I attempt to clarify and justify this proposal further.

8.2 *More on social conventions and agreements*

(i) *Concerning agreements*

One pretheoretically salient aspect of conventions was the existence of an analogy between conventions and agreements. The 'oughts' associated with both agreement and convention have a number of negative characteristics in common. Meanwhile, both are positively predicated on something, the agreement on the one hand, the convention on the other. Further, 'ought' judgments will *inevitably* be predicated on both the conventions and the agreements one is a party to.

We have seen that there is an 'ought' intimately connected with jointly accepted principles. Indeed, the connection is in no way contingent: judgments about what an individual ought to do inevitably stem from the joint acceptance of a principle. This is just what we want for convention. It is what we want for agreement also. But if conventions are jointly accepted principles, what are agreements? Is the 'ought' of agreement analogously non-contingent? I cannot attempt a full-scale assault on the everyday concept of an agreement here. But let me briefly argue for a characterization of agreements according to which there is an 'ought' of agreement of the same kind as the 'ought' of convention.

The issue of what an agreement is has considerable interest independently of the question how agreements and conventions relate. It is sometimes asked: whence comes our obligation to conform to agreements? Is there, indeed, any such obligation prima facie? If so, what precisely is its basis? Clearly, a proper answer to this question will depend on a correct understanding of what an agreement is. Two possibilities are suggested by David Lewis: 'an exchange of noncommittal declarations of intent' (p. 84) and 'an exchange of formal or tacit promises' (p. 34). As he points out, these are likely to be considered differently by the parties. They are indeed intrinsically different phenomena, generating quite different sorts of obligation.

If I happen to manifest to you my intention to wear my pearls by, say, fingering my pearl necklace as I prepare to dress, or even if I explicitly inform you of this intention, I can hardly be upbraided with any seriousness for ignoring this fact, changing my mind, and not wearing the pearls in the event. Things might be different morally speaking if I knew you would wear pearls now that you believed that I would, and that you would be sneered at by others if you alone wore pearls. Thus in special circumstances an expression of intent can generate serious moral obligations. Generally speaking, however, all that will (fairly) reliably occur if one does not carry out an intention one has manifested or reported to another will be an unsatisfied plain expectation on that other's part. But unsatisfied plain expectations are not necessarily matters for disappointment on balance. They are, it is true, matters of false belief. To the extent that false beliefs as such are intrinsically bad, then one always has some reason not to produce one. But both the badness and the reason here are weak at best. It is consequently implausible to characterize agreements as (simply) exchanges of noncommittal declarations of intent.

Intuitively, an exchange of promises is different from an exchange of declarations of intent. In making a promise one undertakes to perform a certain action. One has taken it upon oneself to do so. That one has *a* reason for fulfilling one's promise so understood seems obvious. There is no need to search for possibly debatable truths about intrinsic value. If someone acknowledges that he has taken it upon himself to do something, it is hardly intelligible for him to deny that he has sufficient reason to do that thing. Indeed, it appears he must accept that he has a strong sufficient reason to do that thing, one that can only be overridden in exceptional circumstances, if it can be *overridden* at all.[85] Thus it may be said that promising entails an obligation. One is now bound to perform an act of a certain kind. Of course one can ask whether it will be in one's interests (enhance one's personal health, wealth, and happiness) to fulfil a particular promise. But if one has promised to do something one must acknowledge that one has the corresponding obligation.

Standardly, a promise is made to someone other than oneself. My having promised you something apparently involves my granting you a special status, as well as putting me in a new position with respect to my reasons for acting. I cannot unilaterally release myself from my promise except by performing it. You can release me, however. If I promise to help you move house, and later tell you that I have a deadline to meet, you may kindly say that I should forget about helping and thereby release me from my promise. But it is not appropriate for me simply to inform you that I have decided not to help you after all. That is, if I were baldly to tell you this, apparently in full awareness of the fact that I did promise to help you, this will suggest that I do not understand what it is to promise. In practice it may sometimes look as if people baldly say that they cannot keep their promises after all. But implicit in the dialogue, standardly, is the fact that one awaits release from the promises. One may, of course, make it clear that one expects such a release, and it may be reasonable in the circumstances to expect it.[86]

The strength of the obligation generated and the inability of the individual to release himself from it unilaterally may suggest that an agreement is an exchange of promises. Consider however that to object to the breaking of an agreement one typically says: 'But we agreed' not: 'But you promised'. This suggests that something differentiates the structure of an agreement from that of an exchange of promises. And there is a notable difference. Promises are made by one person to another (or to several others at once). The promiser in effect binds himself to another. The binding, meanwhile, is unconditional and achievable independently of anyone else's vows. If I make my promise first, I am then obliged to keep it, whether you make me a promise in exchange or not. Agreements meanwhile are specifically devices whereby a set of persons (minimum two) can achieve the result that all are bound *simultaneously* and *interdependently* to enter upon a certain course of action. The binding of one is not effective independently of the binding of all the others.[87]

I suggest that an agreement may properly be seen as a *joint decision* on a certain course of action. (Possibly a quite complex course of action in which the different people will do different things. For instance, I will feed the cat and you will do the dishes.) That is, we will not go far wrong if we restrict our assertions that people have agreed on some course of action to cases where it seems apt to say that a joint decision has been made. I shall not try to spell out in detail what the relevant conditions might be. The following points may be noted, however.

The indebtedness we have to each other will be the indebtedness members of a group have to act as representatives of that group, all other things being equal. More specifically each is obliged to act as is appropriate for the members of a body which has decided on a given course of action.

If I personally decide to do A, I then have reason to do A, unless I personally change my mind. (I may realize that my decision was a foolish, immoral, or imprudent one.) If *we* decide to do A, then each of us has reason, in so far as he is one of us, to play the appropriate role in the performance of A. The correlative 'unless' qualification here is surely: unless we change our mind. We may do this by convening and agreeing not to do A after all, but to forget all that, or to do B instead. There may be other ways. But nothing I decide unilaterally can make it the case that *our* decision has been superseded by another one. It would hardly be intelligible, let alone acceptable, that I defend my violation of our agreement by saying: 'Well, I changed my mind'; meanwhile this is an acceptable defence of my not acting on a decision of my own.

Naturally, if much hangs on the agreement, if A sells his house on the assumption that B will sell B's house to A, then default on B's part will bear the heavy moral weight of causing A's homelessness. But this kind of consideration may not be present in the case of all and every agreement, any more than it must be present for all promises and all declarations of intent. Again, as with some personal decisions, not standing by a given agreement may be be the best course morally. None the less, the unilateral violation of an agreement always has something to be said against it: 'But we *agreed!*' This something has to do with something that *we* did. If agreements are joint decisions, this will be so. Each individual has at least a prima facie reason for conforming. This can only be rescinded altogether by the action of each one.

A personal decision is standardly something one formulates explicitly. One says to oneself 'I will do it' or 'No, I just can't'. Indeed, some such thought is seen as *constituting* one's decision. This helps to explain why the qualifier 'explicit' may seem practically redundant in the case of decisions. The case of agreements appears to be similar. In the case of agreements it is not necessary that the words 'I agree' or their equivalent be used. But an agreement is standardly set up by an exchange of words or gestures, and these are seen as together constituting the agreement.[88] It is a salient feature of typical agreements to do something that the gestures or words constitutive of the agreement do not themselves involve their utterers in already doing the thing in question. Like a decision, an agreement is a prologue to action rather than action itself. Thus a typical dialogue constitutive of an agreement might run: 'Shall we go swimming this evening?'; 'Sure.'

A note on the relation between agreements and plural subject phenomena may help to bring the notion of an agreement into sharper focus. Suppose that Aaron sees Pat is about to go swimming, says 'Wait a minute', and goes to get changed, after which they happily proceed to the pool. They have surely not at any point *agreed* to go swimming together. Meanwhile, their transaction was sufficient to enable them to do something together. Like many other cases considered, this shows that plural subject-hood can be created by means subtle enough for the notion of agreement not to be in place. Among other things, you can become the plural subject of an action with someone by starting to perform your part of such action, and they can complete things by doing their part.

That there is an important agreement-like phenomenon in human life that does not involve an agreement strictly speaking is indicated by the occurrence in many areas of discourse of talk of 'understandings', 'tacit contracts', and the like. (The areas are as diverse as mathematical economics and clinical psychology.) Though some political philosophers have been chary of talking of 'tacit agreements', many have appealed to them in attempting to justify the claim that one ought to obey one's country's laws. It is tempting to think that what these references latch on to in reality are plural subject phenomena of various types.[89] The exchange of conditional commitments of the will that I have argued is central to plural subject phenomena is of course not conceived of as involving understandings of the 'I promise if you promise' form. Nor is it of the form 'I promise to do A if you do B'. Like an agreement it is rather a device whereby a set of persons can simultaneously and interdependently become bound to act in certain ways. Hence there is a strong analogy between what goes on here and the making of agreements. At the same time the essentials of this case do not seem to be sufficient to give us an agreement proper.[90]

Agreements proper, then, can be argued to be analogous to conventions in that they too are phenomena of plural subject-hood, and they involve obligations of a similar general type. Agreements can appropriately be characterized as joint decisions on some course of action, conventions as jointly accepted principles of action. Further aspects of the relation of agreements to conventions are discussed in the next section.

(ii) Conventions and agreements contrasted

Given my analyses, conventions and agreements are distinct phenomena, though analogous. This accords with pretheoretical intuition. One can have an agreement without a convention, as in the following example. Suppose we agree to take tea in today's seminar break. Here is an agreement, but, intuitively, no convention is brought into being. My analyses accord with this, for we can have a joint decision to perform a particular action on a particular occasion, without doing anything which would intuitively be counted as the joint adoption of any *principle* of action. Again, intuitively, there can be a convention among us to do A in circumstances C, without our having agreed to do A in circumstances C. My analyses accord with this intuition. On my account, it is enough for convention that people jointly accept a certain principle of action, where it is sufficient for this that they openly manifest willingness jointly to accept a certain principle, and so on. That they have done this is not sufficient for their literally speaking having agreed to anything.[91]

It may be thought that agreements and conventions are somewhat at odds with each other. Lewis suggests that in so far as an agreement is an exchange of promises, an agreement to perform some action whenever a certain circumstance obtains will in effect prevent the corresponding regularity in behaviour from being a convention (p. 84). In his view this is because (and in so far as) each of the parties may feel personally committed to abide by his promise, no matter what the others do, and hence there will not be the right structure of preferences for convention. Of course, I accept neither Lewis's view of conventions nor his view of agreements. But it is worth asking whether agreements and conventions do stand in some kind of opposition intuitively, and whether my own account of conventions and agreements reflects any such opposition.

Intuitively speaking, if we do something because we agreed to do it, then we do not do it because there is a convention among us that it is to be done. This is a point about motivation which my analyses are capable of reflecting. Lewis suggests that if we continue to be motivated by our agreement (by the fact that we agreed to do such and such) then we do not have a convention that such and such be done. This is dubious as a point about our intuitive notions. If under some conditions an agreement can be said to have brought a social convention into being, then once those conditions have been satisfied people's motivations for conformity would not necessarily affect the existence of the convention.

Let us briefly consider whether and when an explicit agreement can create a social convention, intuitively speaking. In one kind of case we adopt what we quite explicitly characterize as a principle of action. For example we agree that we are to kiss on the cheek when we meet in public. It seems natural to say that we now have a convention, the convention that we are to kiss on the cheek when we meet in public. My analysis of convention clearly accords with intuition here. Another kind of case is like the following. We agree that we will lunch together once a week. Do we consequently have a convention to lunch together once a week? This seems less obvious, though one might have some inclination to say that a convention is created here. My analysis of convention suggests the following explanation: in making the agreement we apparently did not think in terms of adopting a principle of action, we just decided that we would do a certain thing on a regular basis. Accordingly, our agreement does not provide us with a principle, and hence (according to my analysis) we do not have a convention. None the less, to agree regularly to act in a certain way is about as close as one can come to agreeing to adopt the principle commanding such regular action, short of actually adopting the principle. This could account for any possible uneasiness about rejecting this as a case of convention-adoption. My analysis of convention, then, squares well with intuitive judgments in this area.

If what we have agreed on is, in effect, that our principle is to be: do A in C, it would be most coherent with this if we went ahead and did A in C for the reason that it accorded with our principle, rather than for the reason that we agreed that *do A in C* is to be our principle. For the agreement was intended to provide us with something other than itself, on the basis of which we would know what to do, and in terms of which we would act. On the other hand, in the case of an agreement that we will regularly do A in C, it would be in keeping with our thought in making the agreement if we subsequently do A in C for the reason that this is what we agreed we would do. Thus an agreement which founds a convention will likely not motivate in itself, unlike an agreement of the other kind.

In the case of an agreement to adopt a certain principle, it seems reasonable to speculate that we will eventually lose sight of our initial agreement. We will say things like 'Well, I guess we'll meet again next week!' 'Yes, *of course*', making it clear that we jointly accept a certain principle, but much less clear that we have it as a result of an initial agreement. Given this consideration it appears that an agreement regularly to do A in C is quite apt to spawn a convention. For dialogues like the above may well tend to occur here too, without explicit reference to the agreement that lies behind them. After a while it may become clear that we jointly accept the simple fiat 'A is to be done in C' irrespective of any prior agreement to do A in C. As in the previous case, the initial agreement may then tend to drop out of the picture altogether.

There is one way in which we allow that an agreement takes precedence over a convention. If there is a convention that one is to do A in C, it will be superseded by a subsequent agreement (among all parties) that one no longer need do A in C, or that A is no longer to be done in C. That is, we allow that an agreement against it destroys an existing convention. This is not to say that the convention may not, by dint of habit or attachment, reassert itself. But the agreement is judged to have killed any previously existing convention, as far as obligation goes. Why is this so? It is good to have a way of bringing a convention sharply to a halt. Suppose, for example, that we have a convention of speaking

Latin at the dinner table at home, but an aunt who cannot speak Latin and could not manage to learn it has come to live with us. Meanwhile, given that agreements are joint decisions, and that to have a convention is to have a jointly adopted principle, we would in any case expect this rule. Just as a decision has the power to cancel a previous decision, it should have the power to cancel the previous adoption of a principle.

8.3 Conventions and language: three issues

(i) Linguistic conventions and social conventions

Intuitively speaking, an agreement to act in a certain way on a single occasion is not sufficient to create a social convention. This accords with the view that a social convention is a jointly accepted *principle* of action. A reference back to something noted earlier is now in order.[92] We say that people have adopted a *convention* when they have agreed on signals for a single occasion. This was cited as a point against Lewis. I argued that he has not explicated the sense of convention involved in the platitude that 'language is ruled by convention' if this is understood as a commonsensically platitudinous claim about language use as such. For the sense of convention at issue is that which is involved when we speak of the adoption of a signalling convention.

What is the relationship between social conventions on my account of them and the type of 'convention' which is adopted when someone adopts a signal for a single occasion? It would be gratifying and supportive of my account of social conventions if a connection could be made out between social conventions on that account and conventions of the other type, which we can call 'linguistic conventions', 'signalling conventions' and so on. Let me argue briefly for a connection.

In order to do this, some sense of how 'convention' is conceived of when we speak of signalling conventions and the like must be developed.[93] If we ask what seems to be going on when we talk of a linguistic or signalling convention, we find that a natural way of putting things, eschewing philosophical worries about the terms, is that we have in mind something like a *rule* which 'binds' or links a sound or sign of some kind with a sense. When we adopt a certain signalling convention, we agree to abide by a rule linking a sign (a black flag, say) with a certain signification (*danger*, say, or *battle won*). What I am saying is that it is natural to put things this way, to rephrase or translate in this way talk about adopting signalling conventions or linguistic conventions in general.[94]

It is already obvious that there is a connection between social conventions on my account and linguistic conventions. It is clear that the general notion of a *rule* is common to both the specific notion of a linguistic convention and to the notion of a social convention as expounded here. (Evidently, a principle of the form 'A is to be done in C' is a type of rule.)

Another shared aspect which is quite salient concerns the content of the rule. We do not think of the rules involved in language as interpretable in terms of morality, prudence, or any sort of natural necessity. We do not imagine that such rules could be spelled out as 'It is morally required that "red" mean *red*' for instance, or as 'On prudential grounds "red" ought to mean *red*', or 'The nature of things dictates that "red" means *red*.' On the contrary, we think of this rule as having the form of a simple fiat, 'This word is to go with this sense.' As I noted earlier, it is uncontroversial that any possible expressive vehicle could in principle express any expressible notion. There is nothing in the nature of things, morality, or whatever, which precludes a particular sound from being linked to a particular sense, and thus *to have that sense*. It is quite predictable, then, that we envisage rules which link sounds and senses as having the form of a simple fiat. We seem to think of this as a fiat 'issued' as it were, from within the language in question. Here, then, is another obvious connection between conventions of the two kinds.

In sum, both linguistic conventions and social conventions as intuitively conceived involve rules or principles, and both involve rules which take the form of a simple fiat. A close connection between the two uses of 'convention' has been made out. Moreover, this particular connection cannot be drawn between linguistic conventions and conventions in Lewis's sense.

At one point Lewis refers to the concept of a *rule* as an 'especially messy cluster concept' (p. 105). He says there is much variation in what we would call a 'rule'. At one point he writes 'it is hard to show that there is *any* regularity which could not be called a rule in *some* context' (p. 104). This suggests that there is a use of 'rule' such that regularities as such count as rules. I find this doubtful. Consider one of the cases Lewis cites, from a cookbook: 'Here is a cardinal rule that has very few exceptions: *All* meat is more tender and juicy if cooked at *low* instead of high temperature' (p. 100). It seems to me that 'rule' may well be used here with implicit reference to the prudential maxim which is obviously and directly derivable from the generalization cited. One could imagine someone being very pedantic and complaining: 'But you haven't mentioned a rule, just a regularity!' Now suppose that the speaker attempted to defend himself by saying: 'Not at all, I was referring to a mandate from nature.' If this were the defence, then it rather obviously harks back to rules as prescriptions, proscriptions, permissions, and so on, and not to any regularity sense of rule.

Lewis refers at one point to rules which 'codify regularities' (p. 103). These rules, Lewis says, 'prescribe behavior'. . . are 'hypothetical imperatives'. It is not clear how such prescriptive statements can be said to *codify regularities*. ('Codify' usually means something like 'collect into a system'; what is thus collected is standardly a set of prescriptions.) Lewis can say that by 'codify' he means something like 'transmute into rules'. This is fine, but it has no tendency to suggest that mere regularities, as such, are themselves rules.[95] Meanwhile, there is little doubt that Lewis would very much like to be able to say that at least some regularities *are* themselves rules. For then conventions in his sense would be, or involve, rules. And, as I have argued, conventions involve rules according to our intuitive conception.

Now it may be that Lewisian conventions as such can count as rules in a sense. (Anything, of course, can count as a rule *in a sense*.) But in any case, it appears that the type of rule which is intuitively at issue where social conventions are concerned is not a rule in some regularity sense of rule. Nor is it a rule of the form 'if you want to achieve X, you must do Y', the type of rule most likely to occur to game-theoretically rational agents in coordination problems.

It is worth stressing this point. There could be a deep concern underlying rejection of the idea that social conventions embody rules of the fiat form, rules which we as group members prescribe for ourselves. That we have and exercise this capacity suggests that we are all continuously creative and responsible in relation to the way our lives go. This idea could be troubling or repellent. Whereas once Lewisian conventions get going we have (as Lewis hopes) a 'self-perpetuating metastable system' in which a given individual is little more than a cog in the wheel. Note that Lewis characterizes that system as a system of *expectations* and *preferences*. Facts about preferences are facts about what people want (and we can imagine these stem from natural objective needs). Facts about expectations are facts about what people believe (and we can imagine these beliefs reflect how things objectively are). It is facts of these kinds which, conjoined with what Lewis consistently refers to as regularities in *behaviour*, constitute conventions in Lewis's sense. There is no whiff of a rule regarding action in this particular, crucial conception of the

387

system. If any kind of rule is implied, it is a prudential rule each agent acts on in order to maximize his personal payoff. But, as I have noted, Lewis does not even require that members of a population with a convention act for reasons. They could act as a result of an inbuilt tendency to do whatever they believe has succeeded in the past.

Here, then, is another reason for thinking that Lewis has not captured our intuitive conception of a social convention. Conventions in his sense do not essentially involve anyone's accepting what they see as a rule regarding action. In particular, no one need accept any rule of the fiat form. It is important to note the great difference between conventions in Lewis's sense and regularities in behaviour which occur in response to the acknowledged existence of a certain group fiat. These are quite distinct 'possibilities of phenomena'. If our common notion of convention is indeed contoured to draw attention to regularities of the latter kind, this would suggest that the latter play a larger role in our actual lives.

In his discussion of conventions as rules (pp. 104–5) Lewis sounds very much as if he is talking about social conventions in the everyday sense and not in the sense he defines. For normative terms which have no obvious connection with conventions in his sense are introduced as if this is quite natural given the concept of convention. For example (referring to 'informal understandings' among players of the game of Jotto) 'Any group of players will develop understandings – tacit, local, temporary, informal conventions – to settle questions left open by the listed rules. What foreign words, slang, proper names . . . are admissible words? May a player have an earlier answer repeated. . .?' (p. 104). At the end of his discussion, though, it is clear that he has not changed his mind on how 'convention' should be analysed.

Here Lewis expresses the hope that his account of convention will enable us to rehabilitate the very notion of a rule, in relation to attacks on 'the philosophers' rules of language'. He cites William Alston's claim (1964) that 'what really demarcates symbols is the fact that they have what meaning they have by virtue of the fact that for each there are rules in force, in some community, that govern their use.' He also refers to Paul Ziff's attack (1960) on 'appeal to rules' in favour of 'the regularities to be found in a natural language'. He goes on: 'our rules will not just be regularities in verbal behavior; they will be regularities in verbal behavior, and in expectations and preferences regarding verbal behavior, and in expectations regarding these expectations and preferences, and so on' (p. 107). In so far as Lewis has yet described anything, however, he has not described anything that would be called a rule in any non-regularity sense. This seems to be a Pyrrhic victory over Ziff in so far as Lewis grants Ziff his basic point: regularities of some sort, not rules-which-are-not-some-species-of-regularity, are what are alleged to be at issue when we speak of the rules (or conventions) of language.

Are there philosophical grounds which might have led Lewis to eschew any reference to rules-in-intention, so to speak, in his account of conventions? He does appeal to preferences and expectations which appear to involve a variety of ideas. So why should he eschew a condition involving the conception or view that 'this is what is to be done'?

At one point in *Convention* Lewis displays an inclination to take up a behaviouristic stance about the mind.[96] (His work more directly in the philosophy of mind is more clearly oriented in this way.) If this is the way one wants to go, one may hope to take some preferences and expectations with one (though this may not be as easy as it looks). However, there is little hope of giving an adequate behavioural account of a belief that such-and-such is to be done whenever. How are we behaviourally to analyse the concept of what is to be done *whenever such-and-such*, as opposed to the concept of what is to be done in this instance, in that instance, and in all the instances one happens to come across? If one wanted an additional problem, one could try analysing behaviourally 'such and such *is to be done*' as opposed to, say, 'I prefer that such-and-such is done.'

Lewis displays a sensitivity to the point about universality in his discussion of precisely what one does have to have in mind in having a convention in his sense (pp. 64–8). This suggests that he may have had a strictly philosophical motivation for eschewing rules-in-intention, a preference for some type of behaviourism about the mind. Such a preference is not a clear philosophical imperative, however. And, in any case, the everyday concept of a social convention does appear to apply only to those who have the concept of what is to be done whenever certain circumstances arise.

(ii) Group languages and social conventions

What is the relation between social convention and a group's having a language? Lewis evidently envisaged a tight connection.[97] None the less it can be argued that a group's having a language is not, intuitively, a function of social convention in the intuitive sense, though it is a function of something in the plural subject family. I have already sketched what I take a group's language to be. Let me summarize briefly. The existence of a group language may now be characterized in terms of the joint acceptance of particular sound–sense links. That is, for a variety of terms, the people concerned must jointly accept that the term in question means such-and-such. If a group accepts that, say, 'red' means *red*, 'socks' means *socks*, and so on through the English dictionary, and given that they also accept that certain syntactical forms are correct, then we can appropriately say that English is the group's language.

This way of looking at things does not have as a direct consequence that in coming to have a given language the members of a population must have a social convention in the sense defined here.[98] Importantly, in this case no one thinks of anyone as having to *do* anything in particular circumstances. The understanding people have is of the form: (for us*) *this* is the sense of term 'x'. If this is so, then presumably individuals should act accordingly as best they can, in their linguistic behaviour. Presumably they should all hope to learn the language in the sense that they automatically use 'x' in the sense of such-and-such. Failing that, they can mouth the word in what they know is the right context, and get along fine from the point of view of social tact and communication. Another important feature of this view is that no one need envision that their language has any equally good alternatives. (That it is possible for people to view their language as God's language or the best language or the only language they could have accepted and hence not up to them to choose has been argued against Lewis's explication of the notion of a population's language, by Burge, for instance.)

As I would explicate the notion of a group's language, then, a group has a language not by virtue of accepting any fiat about what is to be done when. Rather, the group may simply accept a certain language, in the way proposed above. In this way it would be the group's language in a richer way than being the language most members happened individually to use, were known to use, and so on, without being its language by social convention in so far as this involves, by definition, a principle prescribing certain actions in certain circumstances. I believe that these aspects of my account recommend it.

(iii) An intuitive distinction explained

One of the data about our concept of convention in general involves a contrast between two kinds of case. Suppose we agree that at noon today I will stand at the top of the hill and, if we are winning, I will wave a black flag once, then descend immediately.

We would be thought of as having adopted a certain signalling convention. Meanwhile, if we agree to take tea together in today's seminar break, we would not be thought of as having adopted a convention of any kind.[99] As I have explained elsewhere, this intuitive distinction is relevant to Lewis's theory because an amendment which might have coped with the one-shot signalling case did not allow him to mark this distinction.[100] An explanation of the distinction can be derived, meanwhile, from my accounts of social convention, linguistic convention, and group languages.

First, *social* conventions are not necessarily involved when there is an agreement to adopt a given signalling system or language.[101] Nor is a social convention involved when a set of people decide to do something on a single occasion. Nothing occurs in the seminar break case that we would intuitively think of as the adoption of a *rule* about how one is to act. I take this to be because, intuitively speaking, a rule of action *mandates a regularity in action*, requiring that one do such-and-such *whenever* so-and-so occurs, and so on. (Thus rules are a particular species of command.) The presence or absence of a social convention, then, is not what distinguishes these cases with respect to the presence of 'convention'.

Second, we find convention in the one-shot signalling case not because of facts about agreement or the involvement of more than one person, nor because we find here a case of our adopting a rule about what we are to do when, but rather through our conception of what a language is. This is suggested by our finding convention even if only a single person sets up a temporary language. We see languages themselves as abstract objects involving rules of the fiat form, rules pairing sounds with senses.[102] Since we conceive of languages this way, we find it apt to say that we adopt a convention when we decide to use a certain word in a certain sense.[103] What then of the seminar break case? Given my analysis of the linguistic cases, there is no inconsistency in not speaking of convention here. In this case it is not obviously apt to say that there has been a decision to use an abstract object that encapsulates a rule of the fiat form. The cases get distinguished, then, because the seminar break case alone does not involve adoption of an abstract object of a certain kind. Neither case involves a social convention.

(iv) On convention in general

The discussion so far does not purport to be anything like the last word on the concept of convention in general. It shows, however, that social conventions and linguistic conventions can be argued to be part of the same family. The generic notion of convention suggested is that of a rule to the effect that such-and-such is to be so, a rule of the fiat form.

What about a single person adopting a rule, say, 'I am to brush my teeth every day at 9 p.m.'? Here is a fiat, issued by one person, so not a social convention. But would we be *at all* inclined to speak of a convention here, and, if not, does this throw doubt on the idea that conventions in general are essentially rules of the fiat form? It would not be totally bizarre for someone to say 'I have this convention' when referring to a rule like the one noted. But it would be more likely for him to say that he had adopted a rule. This suggests something that etymology suggests also. Suppose that the social convention sense of convention is the central sense. Social conventions on my account involve more than one person. From this social convention sense, the linguistic convention sense can be viewed as something like an analogical extension in which the 'fiat' which in the primary case resides in the group, now resides in the language. Now this extension involves a quite different realm of being, the realm of abstract objects. This kind of extension may occur more easily than would an extension to a significantly different case (one which does not involve a group) in the same domain (persons and their principles of action). Meanwhile, it is not completely bizarre to speak of 'my convention'. In so far as this is so, the facts already adduced can explain it as a derivative case of a somewhat awkward kind.

Obviously, what is important in all this is to see the phenomena as clearly as we can. In discussion of conventions and language it is crucial to stress that there is an important use of 'convention' which refers not to social conventions but rather to the kinds of rules we envisage as incorporated in languages. It is most important to get this clear, and not to be misled by our language of 'convention' to think that it somehow demonstrates that all language is social because it involves those paradigm social phenomena, social conventions. This slide has often been made, in what may be mistaken versions of Wittgenstein's objections to the idea of a language which is 'private'.[104]

8.4 On morality and convention

Intuitively speaking, our conventions are a different matter from our moral principles. My account of social convention accords with this intuition, and helps to clarify both the difference and the connection between these phenomena.

On my account we have a convention if and only if for some action A and some circumstances C, we jointly accept that, simply, we are to do A in C. This principle is regarded as holding independently of any justification which may be available: it is seen as a simple fiat. Meanwhile, to see something as a moral principle is surely to see it differently from this. The question of what makes a principle a moral principle is a debated and delicate issue. The following is a rough and undefended sketch of what I take to be involved in seeing something as a moral principle.

Principles seen as moral principles (such as: morally speaking, one should never tell a lie) are seen as principles with a particular type of ground, a ground in the nature of things. In particular, such principles are seen as grounded in objective facts about intrinsic value. In the following dialogue, the first speaker enunciates a principle that is viewed as grounded in obvious facts about value. 'It is wrong to do A.' 'Why?' 'Because it involves harming many people badly for a minor pleasure of your own.' 'Why would that be so bad?' *'If you can't see that*, there's nothing more I can say.'[105]

My account of convention, then, is not such that if a group has a convention to do A in C, then it believes it is morally required that A be done in C. Nor is it such that, if a group believes it is morally required that A be done in C, then, the group has a convention that A be done in C. Social conventions and collective moral principles are thus quite distinct phenomena.

A particular group could regard conformity to some or even all of its conventions as morally required. It could hold the general moral view that one (morally) ought not to violate the conventions of one's group. My account of convention allows for these possibilities.

Grounds for a general moral view that the conventions of one's group ought to be conformed to as a matter of morality might or might not be articulated precisely. Possible grounds do seem to be available. It might be argued that one morally ought to respect the conventions by virtue of their origin in 'the will of society'. It might be argued that it will provoke confusion and concern, on the whole, if existing conventions are violated, and confusion and concern are simply bad things, period.

There may, then, be some moral reasons for conforming to conventions, all things being equal. Meanwhile, the 'oughts' of convention are not themselves moral 'oughts'. The general conception of a jointly accepted principle of action entails that, by virtue of the nature of joint acceptance, each party to joint acceptance has reason to conform to the principle. That there are moral reasons for conforming to conventions may be so, but these will never be the only reasons people have for conforming to conventions. Conventions generate reasons for acting by their own force, so to speak, without appeal to considerations of intrinsic value.[106]

Now someone might accept that for there to be a social convention there need not be a collective moral view, but object that the reverse is not so clear. Suppose, it may be said, that in the village of Geeville villagers jointly accept that it is wrong morally for a man not to greet a lady by raising his hat. They do *not* think this as a result of recognizing that there is a convention, in my sense, that men raise their hats, etc. and of conjointly holding the moral view that one ought not to violate convention. Rather, they jointly accept that it is morally wrong for a man not to raise his hat, they think that it is intrinsically a bad state of affairs for men to keep their hats on their heads when greeting women. The question may be raised: don't we still want to say that they have a convention that men raise their hats, etc.? Well, do we? It is not at all clear to me that we do, or should.

Consider the claim: 'Heterosexuality is just a convention.'[107] Though taken at face value this implies that heterosexuality *is* a convention, it could have a different import in the context of an attack on a jointly accepted view that heterosexuality was morally preferable. The speaker could mean to urge that contrary to this jointly accepted view there are no grounds in the nature of things for prescribing heterosexuality and so the only kind of validity such a collective prescription could have is the validity of convention. If this were so the speaker need not be taken to imply that *in so far as* there is a joint view that heterosexuality is morally preferable, then there is at least a convention prescribing heterosexuality. And surely this would have been a doubtful claim.

But can a group have a convention and a moral principle enjoining the same behaviour, at the same time? It seems possible for these two social forms to coexist. People in a particular group could be aware that 'one is supposed to be heterosexual' as a matter of group fiat, and at the same time understand that in this group it is jointly held that 'heterosexuality is morally required'. People might understand the point of this set up in counterfactual terms: they could think that even were homosexuality not intrinsically wrong, and jointly believed to be so, there should be a group fiat against it. They could think this because they thought (perhaps truly) that there should be some group fiats, and (falsely) that no one would suffer much if this were one of them. Or they might have no views regarding the point of this set-up, but just understand that things were so. The situation envisaged appears to be possible as a matter of logic. It is allowed for by my account of convention.

It is worth pointing out how different intuitively the consideration that 'It's wrong (morally)' is from 'It's against our convention.' If I believe that something is morally wrong I may feel unable to do it when I find that it is expected of me in another culture. For instance, I may think that one who makes a practice of lively description of his own achievements shows a defect of moral character. Coming to a country where everyone does this, I may still feel unable to join in. If, however, I understand that in my country women wear skirts and men wear trousers as a matter of convention, I may more blithely switch my way of dressing when I come to a country where women wear the trousers. Of course habit can ensue from the prolonged following of convention, and there can be well-entrenched habits of embarrassment in certain contexts. I am not saying that adjusting to a new set of conventions is ever easy. But the blocks will surely be different for practices I find morally repugnant and those I view as a matter of simple difference of convention.

In the case of both a collective morality and a social convention an 'outsider' may suppose that the proscriptions or prescriptions involved are not derivable from the nature of things. He may suppose this because of the very diversity between groups. (He would be wrong, of course, to think that the existence of diversity showed that none of the prescriptions was grounded in the nature of things.) However, it is surely part of the logic of moral claims that if one personally believes some state of affairs is morally wrong, one cannot take this outsider's attitude to one's own view. Hence personal moral beliefs or beliefs about intrinsic goodness or badness seem by their content to have a stability precisely not possessed by beliefs that something ought to be done because it conforms to our principle or fiat. Our principle could be in conflict with morality and ripe for change.

I have been assuming in the last few paragraphs what I take to be an obvious distinction between one's morality (one's own moral beliefs) and the morality of one's society (the moral views jointly accepted by members of one's society). Clearly, one may personally find the morality of one's society repugnant, just as one may personally find any of its collective beliefs or conventions repugnant. Equally clearly, the morality of one's society can affect one's own personal morality strongly, in the usual way of collective beliefs. It is clear why one might speak of 'conventional morality' in this context, since this is the morality we have jointly accepted, a set of moral views sustained by the very mechanism that sustains mere convention. None the less, I think it a conceptual mistake to think of convention as providing a collective morality, and my account of convention does not entail that it does.

8.5 Further aspects of social conventions as group fiats

(i) The generation of conventions

In the case of Lewis's analysis of convention, the analysis itself incorporates an explanation of how something comes about: conventions are a type of regularity in behaviour, a regularity sustained by virtue of a certain set of expectations and preferences. The preferences explain why the regularity perpetuates itself, given the expectations. Thus coordination problems (in which preferences of the right type obtain) are apt to generate conventions in Lewis's sense, in so far as expectations of the right type arise within them. Nothing of this sort seems to go for conventions in my sense: the definition of convention does not incorporate an explanation of anything. This is not a fault in an account of convention, or of anything else. However, it would be satisfying to have a sense of the mechanisms by virtue of which conventions in my sense could arise.

I have noted that if and when a Lewisian convention was under way, members of the population in question might begin to assume that they have jointly accepted that they are to engage in a certain form of behaviour, such as reconnecting all interrupted calls in a certain way. I argued that the assumption of plural subject-hood could be premature, and might be shown false by people's reactions to explicit expressions of the assumption. I also indicated that the assumption of plural subject-hood might become justified if people tended to accept one another's explicit expressions of the assumption.

To take up this last point again, it seems that if people talk to one another as if such-and-such is a principle they jointly accept, and if such talk is accepted, then such-and-such is indeed a principle they jointly accept. Such talk could presumably arise in the context of conventions in Lewis's sense.

I have argued, of course, that if we are concerned with game-theoretically rational agents engaged in coordination games there are important restrictions on how expectations about future conformity and actions on the basis of these could arise, and hence on how conventions in Lewis's sense could arise. In particular, the existence of expectations based on the ascription of 'blind' tendencies to act in the way that was successful last time, seem to violate the premises of a game-theoretical model.

It is possible to model the emergence of regularities in the behaviour of rational agents within coordination problems in a way not referred to by Lewis.[108] This involves the plausible assumption that it is perfectly in keeping with rationality to *adopt a principle of action* in relation to a certain type of situation, as long as the principle in question does not go against any dictates of rationality. Therefore, we can consistently see someone as rational, and at the same time see him as having adopted a principle in conformity with which he will act, reason for doing otherwise not having appeared. A happy coincidence of choices arrived at by luck, within a coordination problem, allows us to assume that any such principles which were followed on the occasion in question will continue to be followed in the future. This may lead one who has not yet adopted an appropriate principle to do so. There may thus arise some reason for believing that everyone in a certain population has adopted a certain principle of action to govern their own actions in coordination problems of a certain type.[109]

Evidently, we would not yet have conventions in my sense. There would have to be a radical shift of consciousness in order that such a convention come to exist; it is not enough that everyone individually accepts for himself (and would like for everyone else to accept) a given principle of action. However, it is not improbable that such a shift of consciousness would occur in such a situation. People would, in effect, be emboldened to manifest their willingness jointly to accept the principle in question with others, to join forces with them in upholding this principle.

There would, for one thing, be reasons for wanting the principle to be jointly held as well as held individually. Given that it is desirable that some one principle be conformed to by all, and that the principle at issue is about as good as any other candidate, it is better that this principle be jointly held than that it merely be held individually. For a jointly held principle will be better enforced. That is because each will know that all think it legitimate for any given one to concern himself with any given other's conformity to principle, rebuking him for nonconformity, suggesting that he conform if he seems to waver, and so on. This is by no means so in the case of principles which are, simply, held individually.

Willingness jointly to uphold the principle in question could be manifested by what I have called *tendentious* references to 'our principle', and by acting in other ways as if the principle were jointly accepted. One might condemn someone for not adhering to the principle, 'as if one had the right' to criticize them in this way, and so on. If such tendentious references and behaviour are accepted or matched, and this is common knowledge, then a social convention in my sense will have arisen.

The concept of a social convention as I understand it, then, accommodates both the perception that conventions often cover coordination problems, and the understanding that they may arise tacitly, without explicit agreement.

One of the things I argued against Lewis was that conventions did not seem to have to involve coordination problems, though they might do. Generally, the relation of conventions to coordination problems was empirical rather than conceptual. This is true of conventions on my account. It may be useful to sketch a situation in which a convention in my sense could arise without anything with the flavour of a Lewisian coordination problem being present. So here is a case in point. Peter happens to have cooked spaghetti for dinner the previous three Sunday nights. This Sunday, he makes a tuna salad. His daughter, Anne, objects. 'No spaghetti!' Peter understands that she thinks they ought to be having spaghetti. Next Sunday, he produces spaghetti. The Sunday after that, he produces tuna fish, but with apologies. 'We were out of spaghetti.' The following Sunday, there are guests. Peter tells them: 'We have spaghetti on Sundays.' Two Sundays after, Anne is in charge of dinner. She makes tuna salad. Peter raises his eyebrows. 'Anne, I thought we were supposed to have spaghetti on Sundays!' Anne: 'I know, but I'm not sure how to cook spaghetti.' I suggest that some such course of events – some such sequence of statements and actions – will be enough to bring a convention in my sense into being, without any initial coordination problem, and without any explicit agreements.

The above example indicates that for there to be a convention in my sense, the participants must possess the concept of a convention. I see nothing untoward about this result. It is beginning to emerge that our collectivity concepts in general have this feature.

(ii) Conventions, expectations, regularities

I have argued that pre-existing coordination problems need not be involved in the genesis of conventions on my account, though they may be. Similar things can be said about the relationship of conventions to regularities in behaviour and to plain expectations of conformity. Here again, there is a contingent but intelligible connection. That is, on my account of them conventions can exist in the absence of these phenomena, but we can see why these phenomena should standardly accompany conventions.

A group fiat is clearly apt to generate conformity and expectations of conformity. Knowing that this is our principle provides me with a reason for conformity, and I know that the rest have a similar reason. Thus I can expect them to conform, in so far as they act on the balance of reasons and there are no reasons to counterbalance the reason provided by the group fiat. I can also expect them to expect everyone else to conform, with the same degree of confidence. None the less, it is not part of my analysis of convention that anyone expects anyone else to conform, or that there is any conformity. This is as it should be, for reasons noted in criticism of Lewis. Even in the absence of actual conformity or plain expectations of conformity, we allow that there can be social conventions.

(iii) On the arbitrariness of social convention

Insisting that social conventions as such are 'arbitrary' is likely to cause confusion. 'Arbitrary' is quite commonly interpreted as meaning 'indifferent' or even 'based on caprice'. Meanwhile, there are clear cases of social conventions which are not saliently arbitrary in these senses. So one cannot accept that arbitrariness in the sense of indifference is the key to social convention, as Lewis appears to have done. As I trust, I have now unlocked social convention with other keys. So let us consider whether social conventions on my account of them are inevitably arbitrary in some sense or from some point of view. (Though this question is worth pursuing, the main thing is to be as clear as possible about the nature of the phenomenon in question. The claim that 'social conventions are arbitrary' is neither clear nor obvious enough at the outset for one to think that something must be made of it.)

If we look at dictionary entries on 'arbitrary', we find that the term has been used to refer to a dependence on judgment, discretion, or will. This is primarily a legal usage, according to the *Oxford English Dictionary*. It is clear that in the usage in question a dependence on the exercise of will is not considered the same as a dependence on the capricious exercise of will. Here is a quotation to the point: 'the fines on admission to copyholds of inheritance, even if arbitrary, must be reasonable.'

Let us consider the question of *dependence on will*. If a social convention is a group fiat then, viewed from an external point of view, it is in a sense doubly dependent on will. For each member of a set of persons must have put his individual will into a pool of wills with the effect that these persons have jointly accepted a certain fiat.

Now from an external point of view a group's moral views, its beliefs in general, and its attitudes are as much a matter of *the exercise of will* as are its conventions. For a group to have a morality of its own, for instance, is for its members jointly to accept a certain moral view. The will of each is involved in the usual way. Meanwhile, it is a crucial feature of conventions on my account that they have a special 'inner' feature which can be used to distinguish the conventions of a group from its morality, its beliefs in general, and its attitudes.

On my account the parties to a convention must conceive of something as their rule or principle. This does not yet distinguish a group's conventions from its moral principles. In addition, however, the rule must be understood to have a quite specific form. This is the form: one 'is to do' A in circumstance C. I have called this the 'fiat form'. It is precisely the form appropriate to a rule or principle which is held to derive its validity simply from the fact that some person or body has decided to accept it. It is precisely not the *complete* form of a rule of intrinsic value or prudence. In those cases the appropriate rule would be more complex: 'One is to do A in C from the point of view of intrinsic value' and so on. (I note that one thing mentioned in dictionaries under 'arbitrary' is 'not based in the nature of things'.)

In so far as moral facts or prudential considerations *dictate* that one should act in a certain way, there is an important sense in which human will does not create the principle in question. It is a question of discernment rather than creation by a ruling. The fiat form is thus the expected form for *rules whose force is seen as deriving from judgment or will*. It is too strong, meanwhile, to say that use of this form implies that doing A in C is not something which *accords with* the dictates of morality. The basic *meaning* of the fiat form is as follows: this principle is to be conformed to irrespective of any special considerations, sheerly as a matter of decision. There is no alleged reason for conformity which is intrinsic to it.

Examples already considered suggest that one might consistently adopt a rule with this form even though one judges that it reflects or accords with morality or prudence. Consider a variant of an example which came up in relation to agreement. You and I decide that we are not to have cod for supper on any occasion. We have reasons for adopting this principle: you are allergic to cod. But we see ourselves as adopting a group fiat. This could be because we do not care if we lose sight of the considerations which prompted our decision. (We may assume that there will always be good reason to act this way. We may simply have no interest in recalling this aspect of our rule.)

Sometimes 'convention' is used to refer to the principle itself:

thus 'our convention is that . . .'; sometimes it is used to refer to the 'total phenomenon', as in 'in this society there are numerous conventions'. Clearly, my account of social conventions is an account of the total phenomenon, of when it is true that certain people 'have a convention'. In doing so I give, in effect, conditions necessary and sufficient for 'our convention' to have a referent. Given a notion of the arbitrary as that which is 'dependent on will, judgment, or decision', then, the total phenomenon of convention is arbitrary. And the principles that are conventions are principles perceived as arbitrary by those who hold them.

Tyler Burge (1975) develops a variant of Lewis's account of convention in which the arbitrariness of a regularity derives from there being an alternative, *not necessarily conceived of by anyone*, which fulfils the same 'social functions' more or less as well.[110] Burge is evidently willing to give up the idea of the inner or perceived arbitrariness of social convention. This seems somewhat unfortunate from an intuitive point of view, though I have not insisted on conformity to this idea as a test for accounts of social convention.[111] Lewis himself does feel that awareness of an alternative which 'would have done just as well' is essential to convention. Thus in his view the parties to conventions in his sense will and must be aware that they are arbitrary in a sense.[112]

As the above indicates, there are crucial ways in which social conventions in my sense are not arbitrary by definition. Consider the idea that social conventions are arbitrary in the sense that it does not much matter which convention one has. This is a misleading way of thinking of conventions on my account.[113] It may matter a great deal which fiat we jointly accept. Suppose in a given marriage it is jointly accepted that the wife is to defer to her husband at all times. Many would argue that this is importantly worse than other conventions they might have had. It implies an inequality of respect, and its psychological effects on the wife could be disastrous.[114]

Someone might query whether I am not talking about a morality here, as opposed to a convention. There is no reason to see the above case as involving a jointly accepted moral view, however. Presumably in such a case a convention might transmute into a morality, just as a moral view could change into a convention. Meanwhile, my sense is that in some ways conventions are more powerful, more tenacious, and more likely to be at issue in cases like the one under discussion. For they do not involve any purported factual claim, which could be disputed. Though the claim of moral fact is strong and loud it is open to the kind of disagreements all claims of fact are open to. But the claim that 'this is our principle' is less open to dispute as opposed to disavowal. And disavowal means moving at least to a degree outside one's group. Thus the constraining power of convention is considerable: the possibilities of dissent are limited, and the perils enormous. Social ostracism is a cross too great for most people to bear. Hence we hardly need a group morality if we have convention as a tool.

That a convention is distinct from a moral view does not, of course, rule out the moral criticism of conventions. It is interesting to note that most of Lewis's examples of conventions are such that in standard instances moral criticism is in fact irrelevant to them. Whether we are to drive on the right or the left, whether the original caller or the person called should be the one to call back, and so on, may seem to be paradigm cases of unimportant or inconsequential decisions. Focusing on examples of this kind may lead one wrongly to conclude that the choice between conventions is essentially trivial and that, in particular, moral criticism is unlikely to be relevant to them. My account of convention accords with intuition on this point, as the above example shows.

Let us suppose that a convention of equality of respect in a marriage would be the morally best convention. Must it not then be 'uniquely the best means' of fulfilling its social functions?[115] That depends of course on what its social functions are. Suppose we take its primary social function as that of indicating how fundamental decisions are to be made. This function is *served by* more than one distribution of respect. But can it be equally well served? Obviously that depends on our parameters. There seems no reason to think that the parameters here should exclude moral ones.

There is little point in trying to defend the idea that social conventions are ways of satisfying social functions which are matched by more or less equally good other possible ways. The only reason for concerning oneself with this idea is that one starts off with the (counterintuitive) notion that conventions are essentially arbitrary in the sense of indifferent. Possibly one could think this because one senses a distinction between nature and convention.

Given my account of convention, the concept of *conformity* to convention is distinct, in particular, from the concept of a biologically or psychologically necessary bit of behaviour. Meanwhile, one would expect conventions to arise and thrive precisely in situations where biology and innate psychological mechanisms made no rigid determinations. Thus one would expect that the conventional would come to be contrasted with the natural, *nomos* with *physis*, as it has been.

In sum, my account of social conventions endows them with a specific type of 'arbitrariness'. From both an external and an internal point of view, they are the outcome of acts of human will. They must be taken seriously, and cannot be regarded as necessarily a matter of caprice or of real or supposed indifference. They are susceptible of as many kinds of criticism as a human action is. They can be powerful forces in the world, for good or evil.

8.6 *Convention's relatives: custom, tradition, rule, law*

At the beginning of this chapter I noted that it is natural to list certain special properties of groups together: customs, traditions, rules, laws, and conventions. This list undoubtedly includes vague and ambiguous terms, terms with central and derived uses, and so on. 'Rule' in particular is very capacious, generally including at least conventions and laws. Is there an intuitive principle at work behind the list as a whole? This may depend on isolating certain core senses of the terms in question. In this short section, I suggest how it might be argued that these items do form a real 'family', with law being something of a black sheep. This can be done if we use my account of convention as a model of a type of group property. Let me explain very briefly what I mean.

My account of convention gives, in effect, a model of what it is for a group to accept a principle relating to action. The conventions of a group are, I say, principles the members jointly accept. They are, in this case, principles with the simple form of a fiat. 'Members of this population are to do A, in C, period.' No questions asked, no reasons given. Evidently, people can jointly accept principles of various kinds, the kinds differentiated by reasons explicitly understood to underlie the principles.

This possibility fits rather well with my own sense of what a group's customs and traditions are. The notion of a custom is (customarily) associated with that of a regularity in behaviour, of that which is indeed regularly done by the people in question. When people say 'Our custom is . . .' they certainly mean to imply that this is what they actually, standardly, do. Indeed, it may appear at first glance that this is all that is meant. But surely it is not. 'This is what members of this population regularly do' is, when you think of it, a very bland statement. If someone were to say this to you absolutely flatly, you might wonder if anything at all followed from it. It could quite naturally be said with resignation or with distaste or disaffection. One who says that something is 'our custom' would be expected to show more acceptance of what he was talking about, even to show a sort of approval of it. So the concept of a group's custom is not best thought of as the concept of what members of the group regularly do, or even what they individually regularly do as a matter of choice among viable alternatives. (This latter rules out such inevitable parts of life as eating and breathing as customs.) Nor is it the notion of a regularly chosen option of which there is population common knowledge.

The analysis that the model of convention suggests is this:

> Population P has the *custom* that one does action A in circumstances C if and only if members of P jointly accept that they are to do A in C, for the simple reason that that is what members of P (regularly) do.

If one accepts this, it distinguishes custom from convention, while maintaining the sense that if something is a custom in a group, members have a reason to conform. They have a reason because they accept that they have one. Thus the customs of a group are not equivalent to the things members happen to have chosen regularly to do. There could be many regularities, even commonly known regularities in a population, without that population having any customs.

Commonly known, chosen regularities may tend to become customs in the sense I have articulated. Dialogues like the following could start things off. 'I suppose we'd better ask them for five o'clock.' 'Why five?' 'That's what everybody does round here.' Once the people 'round here' come jointly to accept that they are to conform to this practice for this reason, then they have generated a custom. It may be tempting for observers to assume that mere regularities are customs when they come across them. If one does not talk to people or observe them closely enough to divine the nuances of their thought one will see nothing, after all, to distinguish regularities of the relevant sort from customs. Meanwhile, a type of mechanism alluded to earlier could tend to work here. The members of the population in question, seeing that this regularity in behaviour persists for no very good reason, could begin to assume that others have accepted it as a custom of the group, or at least would like to. This could lead to their acting and talking on this assumption, and as a result, to the existence of a custom.

Let me turn now to tradition. Clearly the concept of a tradition has to do with past behaviour. The simplest concept of tradition in the framework we are now considering has this analysis:

> Population P has the *tradition* that one does action A in circumstances C if and only if members of P jointly accept that members of P are to do A in C, for the simple reason that this is what they have (regularly) done in the past.

Clearly the difference between custom and tradition as described here is delicate. According to the accounts proposed a custom concerns what we regularly do, and a tradition concerns what we regularly have done in the past. There may be further wrinkles to be uncovered. But I shall not attempt to do this here. The difference between alluding to the past as such, and alluding to what we generally do at this point in time, is a real difference, and could well be the basic division intended by the distinction of terms 'custom' and 'tradition'. One can understand that some might find the idea of custom more attractive than that of tradition. Others might have the opposite sense. Someone with no particular reverence for the distant past, no wish to maintain links going far back, could well prefer the comforts of a stable environment here and now, and hence care for custom as such but not for tradition as such. Someone who was easily adaptable and had no fear of change might have a reverence for the past which made him more interested in maintaining traditions as such, rather than supporting whatever had recently solidified into custom.

What, next, of (social) rule? This I take to be generic, the parent of the others. Its analysis would go something like this:

> Population P has the (social) *rule* that one is to do action A in circumstances C if and only if members of P jointly accept that one is to do A in C, either for no reason, or for some specified reason.

This, of course, is an account of what has been called a rule of obligation, only. Parallel accounts can be given of other types of rule, such as rules to the effect that certain acts are permissible, or permissible only in certain circumstances, and so on.

What, next, of law? Tomes have been written on the concept of law, and obviously justice cannot be done to the subject in a short space. All I shall do here is note very roughly the kind of analysis suggested by the above account of a social rule in general, plus the assumption that to every law corresponds an accredited lawgiver.

A simple account of a law that might be proferred along these lines runs as follows: Rule R is a *law* in population P if and only if members of P jointly accept that: members of P ought to do A in C because L, a particular member of P or group of members of P, has enunciated R.

This account needs supplementation for a variety of reasons. In particular, first, it seems to be generally understood that individual members of a group with a given law may be ignorant of that law. Second, on this account it is not clear that L is precisely an accredited lawgiver, one who has been granted the authority to make rules for the group. What is jointly accepted with respect to a given rule is simply that L's enunciation of the rule in question is sufficient reason for each to obey it. This seems too simple. We can solve both of these problems at once by requiring that members of P jointly accept a special type of principle that may be called a *lawmaker-accreditation* or *ground principle*. A ground principle, G, will have roughly the following form:

With respect to all rules enunciated by L, members of P are to regard themselves as having jointly accepted those rules by virtue of their joint acceptance of this rule (G).

Importantly, G could indicate that the rules in question have to be enunciated in a particular context (such as a session of Parliament) in order that it be incumbent upon members of P jointly to accept them. It could also indicate that admissible rules must keep within certain guidelines. For instance, it might be required that conformity to them would not violate a given set of hallowed principles.

We have now arrived at the following account of what a law is:

Rule R is a law in population P if and only if L, a particular member or body of members of P, has enunciated R according to the conditions laid down in a jointly accepted ground principle G.

The account of a law that emerges from the framework of discussion here, then, is that of a rule such that everyone in the society can in principle figure out that he is to regard himself as having jointly accepted it together with the others. Such figuring may be quite complex. It must take account of precisely what ground principle he jointly accepts with the others, together with who enunciated the rule, and, possibly, the context in which it was enunciated, and the implications of the rule itself.

Naturally, in large nation states, it is going to be something of a fiction that all citizens know who is empowered to make the laws. But if *nobody* believes that anyone is empowered to make laws, if nobody believes, that is, that it is incumbent upon them to do what some person or persons say because they say it, then it is not clear that there can be a law. And it is natural to suppose that the closer we get to everybody both having a concept of law and helping to instantiate it in their society, the closer we get to the clear existence of law. Without these things there can be a threat, of course. But the concept of law is not equivalent to the concept of threat. The only other thing I am going to say about this brief speculation on the concept of a law is that the account sketched here allows that the only accredited lawgiver may be the whole population in session. It allows, indeed, that only what is unanimously agreed upon by those members when they have set aside considerations of personal interest is accredited law. It also allows that there be crazy, pernicious, and irrational laws. It all depends on what the population in question jointly accepts. The notion of joint acceptance that some person or body is authoritative, is, then, the core of the conception of law outlined here.

The notion of law characterized here may be instantiated by what would normally be called 'rules' rather than 'laws', by things such as club rules. Possibly 'law' in English usage is generally restricted to cases involving populations of a specific type, roughly, to 'laws of the land'. Yet, according to common parlance, clubs and other institutions (colleges, for instance) can have 'by-laws'. And we have the phrase, applicable in practically any context, 'His word is law.' I cannot pursue this issue here. Suffice it to say that further distinctions may need to be added to the type of account of law given here in order to differentiate laws proper from other kinds of 'law-like' rules.

Perhaps the main interest of this type of account lies in the fact that it indicates how a plural subject can regard itself as effectively subject to rules whose content is unknown to the individual members. It indicates, indeed, how the democratic fact that underlies all genuine associations can enable the wisdom or unwisdom of particular individuals to govern whole states.

VII

ON SOCIAL FACTS

Men are not, when brought together in society, converted into another kind of substance.

(J.S. Mill)

This *sui generis* synthesis, which constitutes every society

(Emile Durkheim)

1 THE STRUCTURE OF EVERYDAY COLLECTIVITY CONCEPTS: SUMMARY OF RESULTS

In this concluding chapter I first bring together and amplify somewhat the main results of my discussion so far. As I go on to show, these results are not only of interest in themselves. They enable us to deal more effectively with many significant issues.

I have argued that the general concept of a *plural subject* is involved in our everyday concepts of a social group, a collective belief, a social convention, and in a number of related notions. According to our everyday notions, social groups are plural subjects, collective beliefs are the beliefs of plural subjects, and social conventions are the 'fiats' of plural subjects.

It is clear that we have here a family of concepts with a similar underlying structure. We might call them the *special plural subject concepts*. I have played with two different types of account of these concepts in the course of the book.

In leading up to an account of the state of joint readiness for joint action, I noted that there was a sense in which a single individual cannot be ready for joint action. All that a given individual can have independently of the relevant others and openly* manifest to them is what I called his *quasi-readiness*.

408

Given that the necessary meshing expressions of quasi-readiness occurred under conditions of common knowledge, the people concerned would be *jointly ready* jointly to perform a certain action in certain circumstances. Each would then have a general obligation to participate in action appropriate to joint readiness of the relevant kind. There would be a variety of consequent obligations and entitlements for each person. The specific obligations and entitlements of one person would not be independent of those of the others. As long as joint readiness was maintained, all would have equal and correlated obligations and entitlements.

A similar way of putting things could be used for the other plural subject concepts. For example, in order that there be a collective or group belief, each of a number of individuals must have openly* manifested his quasi-acceptance of the view that p. When this is done in circumstances of common knowledge then we say that these individuals have jointly accepted the view that p. And so on. This, then, is one possible way of regimenting the accounts of plural subject concepts.

We need not use the technical terms 'quasi-acceptance', 'quasi-readiness', and so on. In each of the cases of doing something *jointly* (in a broad sense of 'doing') we can simply say that each of a number of persons must openly* express his *willingness jointly to do the thing in question with the others*, for instance, jointly to accept the view that p. Clearly we must bear in mind precisely what such an expression of willingness amounts to: it involves the understanding that if it is 'met' in a situation of common knowledge, then these people do jointly accept the view, and each of the parties has certain ensuing obligations and entitlements.

We can give an account of any of the special plural subject concepts, then, in either of two ways. The concept of a plural subject of belief, for instance, can be explicated in terms of a necessary set of expressions of *quasi-acceptance of a view*, or in terms of a necessary set of expressions of *willingness jointly to accept a view*. Clearly there is also a third option: there must be a set of expressions of *willingness to be part of the plural subject of a view*.

When we dig deeper into the nature of plural subject-hood we come to a description of a kind used by Rousseau. It seems that the concept of a plural subject is the concept of a pool or sum of wills dedicated, as one, to a certain 'cause', whether promotion of a goal or acceptance of a proposition or principle. As I have indicated, our concept of plural subject-hood includes an under-standing of how plural subjects are formed. Humans can express conditional commitments of their individual wills, on the understanding that in a situation of common knowledge a set of such conditional commitments results in a set of jointly committed wills, that is, a pool of wills. The 'nominal owner' of each will must understand that his will has been given over to a certain joint cause, and that this is common knowledge.

One could say that humans create plural subjects by volunteering for community service. This way of putting things is likely to startle because we do not usually think of ourselves as volunteering for community service all the time. Some of us regret that we, or others, never do volunteer for such service. Of course I am not using the terms 'volunteer' and 'community' with their commonest everyday referents. Usually we think of volunteering as involving public avowal. '*I* will help clean up after the service' someone says at a church meeting. This is a typical case of volunteering. 'I'm afraid I don't have time to help at the election this year' says someone rejecting the position of volunteer. But it is one of my crucial contentions that at the time of disclaiming the ability to help, this last person is a volunteer of sorts. Without any explicit preamble, she has volunteered her help in sustaining in existence a small, temporary 'community', that constituted by herself and the person or persons she is talking to.

Evidently there is a deep and rather special kind of 'voluntarism' at the base of everyday collectivity concepts. It is logically necessary and sufficient for the existence of collectives that each of a set of individuals volunteer himself, in the sense of his *will* (*voluntas*, in Latin). He must give over his will to the group – in order to constitute the group.

There is space here for a good deal of coercion. Clearly people may be pressured into joining a particular conversation, into getting married, into fighting in a particular war. The type of 'volunteering' at issue, then, is such that it is possible to be coerced into it. Meanwhile, in principle one's membership in a plural subject could in effect just 'happen', with little or no forethought on one's own part.

However much we may feel forced into participating in conversations, games, or marriages, we do *put into them*, if we enter them at all. We put ourselves into them, in a sense. This is what we have to do, to become members of a plural subject or collectivity.

I have spoken throughout of collectivities or social groups rather than communities. But we might think of any group as a 'community' in the sense that it is constituted by what can be thought of as a *communal will*, a sum or pool of wills which is dedicated to the support of certain goals, ideas, or principles of its own.

Being a group member takes work. Imagine writing instructions for a beginner in social life. In order to enter a group, however small and temporary, one must give over one's will to a sum or pool of wills which is itself dedicated to some cause (very broadly construed). This entails taking on or accepting a set of responsibilities and rights: it involves recognizing a new set of constraints on one's behaviour. (One also accepts certain new entitlements.) The rights and responsibilities most directly in question are neither moral nor legal. They could be referred to as 'associational', or, more familiarly, as political.

Simple examples suffice to illustrate the point. Going for a walk and having a conversation exemplify perfectly the structure of the concepts at issue, which are also at issue when we enter semi-permanent communities and societies. If one agrees to go for a walk with another person, one thereby accepts responsibility for doing what one can (within limits) to promote the aim implicit in such agreement. But of course one has also acquired a partner in pursuit of this aim. The other person has accepted equal responsibility. You have a right to his help, as he has to yours.

Reference to a theme in social psychology should help to clarify the point about *equal* responsibility. People have noted that, roughly, women often consider themselves as having sole or primary responsibility for the success of the personal relationships they have with men. Let me explain how the phenomenon of the 'hyper-responsible' woman can be squared with the claim that people understand they are all equally responsible for the promotion of whatever end, belief, attitude, or principle they serve together.

I first need some terminology to mark an important distinction. Suppose it is understood that there is an *initial basic* equality of responsibility among group members. Now let us take the case of going for a walk together. It is clear that where there are many choice points going for a walk could be troublesome for two people. How is it to be decided whether we turn right or left? Suppose the primary joint aim is just to go for a pleasant walk. It could be agreed that one person (who perhaps knows the terrain better) will make all these decisions. It seems appropriate enough to say that the main responsibility for the success of the relationship in question now devolves upon this person. (Note that it so devolves by virtue of an agreement, for whose fulfilment each is equally responsible.)

Let us now imagine that it is Ellen and Simon's joint goal that

411

the general tone of their encounters be pleasant. One can see that an initial presumed equality of responsibility for attainment of the aim could be combined with the emergence of a *convention* that Ellen alone is to focus on ways of keeping encounters pleasant. Simon may relax and act as he pleases. (If he attacks her, then, she may well try to placate him. She may restrain herself from 'answering back'.) Presumably the parties will assume equal responsibility for the maintenance of the convention. With deliberate naïveté, I have envisaged a situation in which a relationship between a man and a woman develops in a social vacuum. Consider next the case where there is a society-wide convention that women are to take care of the pleasantness of male–female encounters. At the entry point to their relationship, a particular man and woman will likely assume that each of them will uphold the society's convention in their encounters. In such a case there need be no explicit or implicit manœuvring about who has what job.[1]

Quite generally, then, even if everyone understands that in doing something together they share the ultimate responsibility for achieving the desired outcome, conventions may develop which ensure that, in effect, responsibility devolves more on one party than another. It may now be up to one person to do more, in order that things go right. Meanwhile, were the relevant convention to be abolished, everyone would presumably re-emerge as equally responsible. The idea of an acknowledged initial basic equality of responsibility in relation to a plural subject's 'cause' is consistent, then, with the fact that in particular cases one or more participants may come to be granted more responsibility than the rest. Precisely how things progress in a given case evidently depends on the personalities, needs, capacities, ideals, and expectations of the parties. Given an initial egalitarianism in both parties individually, equality of responsibility may emerge as a joint ideal. If we are following a trail in the woods, there will be no master and no slave, no one trying to keep up with or slow down for a regal pacemaker. Each of us will work to accommodate us both. We may happily feel that in our small community we have achieved true democracy and perpetual peace.

To say that each individual accepts a continuing responsibility for promotion of the joint enterprise may seem extreme. Are there no legitimate possibilities of exit? Just such a possibility is implicit in what generates the responsibilities and rights of the individual: the fact that there was a *joint* commitment to the success of the enterprise. Suppose that we have jointly accepted that Xavier Yawls is a louse. You suddenly beam and say (quite without sarcasm) 'Dear Xavier!' What am I to do? Recall the poetry discussion case. Am I obliged to demur on behalf of *our* view? I could say something like 'What do you mean?' Meanwhile, you have clearly violated your obligations in this matter. Your remark, your change of tone, has come quite out of the blue. Your behaviour is so bizarre that I may wonder if I should go on talking to you. My sanity may be at risk, since there is some evidence that you have lost yours. In a case like this, it seems that the party who has not yet violated any obligations has a range of options. He probably need not continue to act as one who jointly accepts the proposition in question. Certainly he need not do so for long. He could question the violator, and try to bring things back on track, or quite legitimately forget the whole thing.[2]

Such legitimate 'forgetting' can, of course, occur in contexts other than that of unilateral violation. In particular, if the parties agree to end their collusion, they will dissolve the set of associational obligations they had previously incurred.

The deep basis for the rights and responsibilities that accrue to one who enters a group is to be found precisely in the concept of a plural subject, the core conception here. (As I have stressed, neither moral nor legal responsibility is at issue.) My articulation of the concept of a plural subject enables us to explain how membership in a group can entail a set of *sui generis* responsibilities and rights, and to become clearer about their nature.

Consider first a person's own goals, principles of action, and so on. Intuitively there is a logical tie between this being my goal and my having a sufficient reason for bringing this goal about. To say: 'My current aim is to write a best-selling cookbook' and then to deny that one has reason to promote that aim is incoherent. To say that one accepts for oneself the principle 'do not ride on the Sabbath' and to deny that one has reason not to ride on the Sabbath is incoherent. We might summarize the force of these intuitions as follows: we take it that the will of a rational person is sensitive to the goals and so on of its owner. In other words, *my* will is sensitive to my goals, principles, and so on. In other words, other things being equal, my perception that I want such and such is enough to motivate my (rational) will.

Now, on my analysis, if there is a plural subject, then each of a set of persons has volunteered his will for a sum of wills to be used in combination in the service of a certain cause (broadly construed). These wills are now understood (by him and the others) to be jointly committed to the cause. The individual owners of these wills are now the members of the plural subject of the goal or whatever. They can refer to this goal as 'our* goal'.

413

Let us now hypothesize for the sake of argument that the logic of 'our*' parallels that of 'my'. It will follow that if our* goal is G, then *we** have a sufficient reason to achieve G as best we* can. What is it, though, for *us** to have such a reason? It seems plausible to hypothesize that the answer is roughly this: I have both a responsibility to promote *our** aim as best I can, and a right to be helped by you in this endeavour. You are in the same position.

Both hypotheses are supported by my account of plural subjects. This account predicts both the fact and the particular form of the reasons for action conjectured to be generated from the premise 'We* want G.' For to understand that your will is jointly dedicated with the wills of certain others to a given goal (which is equivalent to its being your* goal) is evidently to understand that your will is now (supposedly) susceptible to 'We* want G' in such a way that it will bring about appropriate movements. We can best indicate what is appropriate here in terms of the rights and responsibilities already alluded to. For it is not that each party to joint action must make an effort to reach G on his own; nor that he must make an effort to play some role in getting G. It is nothing like so restricted. Appropriate behaviour occurs when, for example, someone travelling with another feels entitled to ask what is holding the other person up, and obliged to wait for him (albeit impatiently).

It is tempting to argue that the concept of a plural subject is part of the genius of nature, and plural subjects themselves are its crowning glory. Along these lines, consider how a brief hypothetical account of the transition from a state of nature to a social state, in the tradition of political philosophy, might run. First nature (or God) produced a rational or reasoning being. Such a being moves by virtue of acts of will; these occur in response to an estimate of the 'balance of reasons'. This being was endowed with ideas of *its own desires* such that 'I want a drink' was understood to provide a reason to move towards a drink. Given that no other reasons intervened, and the being was not kinked in some way, an act of will would occur setting off motions towards the drink. Now more than one being of this kind was produced. What ideas could these beings be endowed with that might enable them to live together harmoniously?

Here is an idea (perhaps it is the most useful one). Give these beings not only the concept of *one's own* goals, but also the concept of *our* goal*. Let them understand that they can create a goal, a belief, and so on, which is *ours**. They can do this by individually openly* manifesting their willingness jointly to carry the relevant can. Once open* manifestation has occurred and been duly noted by all, there *is* a goal which is ours*. This means that there are complementary reasons for action for all parties, complementary rights and responsibilities which cease to be effective only under certain special conditions.

This story surely makes sense, crude as it is. It leads up to the plural subject version of social contract theory. One way in which this differs from the standard contract theories (and it is, after all, very close to Rousseau) is that it sees 'society' everywhere. Not only in families, but in conversational groups and in people going for a walk together. According to plural subject theory, society, or the human social group proper, begins at the moment that plural subjects are formed.

At that moment, a set of social or associational obligations are undertaken by the populace in question. They could not form a group, did they not consciously undertake these obligations. These societies can be small and ephemeral or large and historic. But their essence is the same. For this reason, a careful understanding of our vernacular social ontology is essential to a satisfactory discussion of governmental legitimacy and 'political obligation'.[3]

It follows from the equation of social groups with plural subjects that group membership is not 'normatively neutral'. That is, one cannot see oneself as being a member of a group (or that 'we are doing such-and-such', etcetera) and regard this as implying nothing for the way one's conduct should go. However, it does not follow from this that members of all groups must jointly accept some fiat of the form 'members are to do action A in circumstances C'. That is, it does not follow that every group must have a convention. Nor must it have a law, custom, or tradition. I stress this because some have taken it that social conventions and the like are not only constitutive of particular social groups but are also necessary to any group.

It is true that a necessary precondition of group existence is that everyone involved understands that *each is to do his part* in promoting some joint enterprise, whether joint acceptance of some proposition or joint acceptance of a principle of action, or whatever. The general form of understanding here, however, is not of the right sort to constitute *joint acceptance of a rule* of any kind. For the joint acceptance of a rule everyone involved must understand that each is to do his part precisely in jointly accepting a certain rule. Given the details of the conceptual scheme outlined here, then, groups can in principle exist without having any conventions, laws, customs, traditions, or social rules of their own. At the same time it can be and is the case that the existence of any group has normative implications for its members.

A related point concerns the notion of agreement, or contract. I have just referred to plural subject theory rather lightly as a type of social contract theory. But I am not arguing that full blooded contracts in the everyday sense are required to bring societies into being. Such a doctrine has long been considered problematic. An agreement or contract has seemed to be too sophisticated a thing on which to ground social reality itself. I agree.

I do, of course, posit a mechanism for the construction, so to speak, of social groups. And this mechanism can only work if everyone involved has a grasp of a subtle conceptual scheme, the conceptual scheme of plural subjects. Given that all have this concept, then the basic means for bringing plural subject-hood into being is at their disposal. All that anyone has to do is openly* to manifest his willingness to be part of a plural subject of some particular attribute. A meshing set of such manifestations creates a plural subject, and everyone who has the concept knows this. It appears that there need be no foothold here for the full-blooded concept of agreement or contract. None the less there is clearly some analogy. Agreements require the participation of a number of persons in an equal way. I cannot make an agreement with you, however grand I am, if you do not do your part. And agreements also generate simultaneous and independent obligations on all the parties. (This, I have suggested, is because to make an agreement is in effect to create a particular kind of plural subject, the subject of a decision regarding future actions.) There is therefore some justification, and much fun, in referring to the plural subject theory of society as a contract theory. As long as what the theory amounts to is clear, such reference should do little harm.

The results presented here bear on many issues. In the rest of this chapter I concentrate on three such issues from the philosophy of social science. First, I return to a proposed constraint of Weber's on admissible theoretical concepts of sociology. I said earlier that I both agreed and disagreed with that constraint. I am now in a position to explain my attitude to it. Second, I show how my results help us to come to grips with the classic issue of 'holism versus individualism' about social groups. Third, I return to the overarching question with which this book started – the question about the nature of social phenomena as intuitively conceived. I also briefly note a number of fields of thought to which these results are relevant.

416

2 'THE ACTIONS OF PARTICIPATING INDIVIDUAL MEN'

Weber wrote that the sociologist must reduce everyday collectivity concepts to 'the actions of participating individual men'. Alternatively, to 'the particular acts of individual persons'. He also wrote that 'there is no such thing as a collective personality which acts.' And, of individual persons: 'These alone can be treated as agents in a course of subjectively understandable action.' Now plural subjects can be said to do certain things, and, indeed, to think certain things and accept certain principles of action. So it may seem wrong to insist that a sociological description of events appeal only to the particular acts of individual persons. On the other hand, such insistence may still seem to have something right about it. I believe that some such point is indeed viable, but needs careful specification. What follows is relatively rough, but should clarify the nature of my stance on this issue.

I start with the following notions and assumptions. First, there is the general notion of a human being, a human being so far undifferentiated with respect to the particular ideas she holds. Then there is a plausible empirical claim of a crude sort: human beings behave as living human beings by virtue of their acts of will. For example, I type this sentence, go through these motions, by virtue of various acts of will. There is no room to discuss what an act of will is here. Another such claim, which I take to apply at least to adult humans, is that acts of will are exercised in a context of ideas, of perceptions of the world and conceptions of one's situation. We can sum up these two claims as follows: individual human beings are powered by their ideas and, ultimately, their acts of will.

One could see Weber's proposed constraint on sociological collectivity concepts as the outcome of just such a thought, coupled with the following. It is uncontroversial that the members of human collectivities are individual human beings. This surely means that in some sense human collectivities are *constituted by* individual human beings. Thus facts about collectivities will, at some level, 'reduce to' facts about individual human beings. These thoughts suggest what may be called the *human intentional states requirement*: viable sociological collectivity concepts will entail that facts about human collectivities, in particular about their actions, are constituted by facts about the ideas and acts of will of human beings. For human acts of will and ideas are what inevitably lie behind or power human social life. Possibly, then, Weber meant to propose the human intentional states requirement.

Given my account of our everyday collectivity concepts these do not seem to violate the human intentional states requirement. In so far as this is so, my account provokes no doubts regarding the acceptability of that requirement.

It is important to see, however, that there is another interpretation of Weber's proposal, and that on this construal the proposal is unacceptable.

On this second interpretation Weber's proposal is that viable sociological collectivity concepts must take groups to be *constituted* by the acts of *singular agents*. (Here I use a technical concept introduced briefly earlier.) Let me first say some more about what this proposal amounts to.

It is not possible to give a simple linguistic criterion of reference to a singular agent, but out of context the following statements would quite likely be construed as statements about singular agents: 'Sam decided to run for office'; 'Bob kicked Alan'; 'Maureen suddenly left the room.' One is a singular (human) agent at a given time if, at that time, one acts in the light of one's own personal goals, goals one sees as 'my goals'. That is, a given act of will results from the understanding that such-and-such is one's goal. The following exemplifies a crude model of the kind of thing that (by definition) goes on inside a singular agent's mind: 'I want to get Lilly's attention; raising my arm will best do the trick; so . . .'. There follows an appropriate act of will.

It is sometimes appropriate to say: 'Look, I don't *want* to do it, but I will.' It may be very important to me, and very significant psychologically, that what I do is not what I would have chosen to do, had I been 'left to myself', as we say. This is what utterances such as the one quoted may be intended to imply. Meanwhile, doing whatever it is may still serve an important personal goal of the agent, and that may be why he does it. Thus suppose your wife wants you to speak to her mother on the phone while you are not, independently of her desire, inclined to do so. None the less, you want very much to please your wife. What goes on in your head leading to your picking up the phone may then go like this. '(1) She wants me to talk to her mother; (2) I want to please her; (3) my picking up the phone will do that trick; so. . .'. There follows an appropriate act of will. (Other things, of course, may also go on in your head at this time.) You will count as a singular agent in this case.

There is some justice in thinking of a singular agent as an *autonomous* agent. Perhaps not all singular agents will intuitively count as 'autonomous' agents, since they may be doing something that, in a sense, they do not want to do. None the less, they will always be self-directed in a sense, in so far as such an agent always (by definition) acts in the light of his own personal goals. It may be both natural and pleasing to think of ourselves as essentially singular agents. Singular agents need not be selfish agents, though they may be. Like the agents of game theory, they may be deeply concerned about the welfare of others. Meanwhile, there may seem to be something intrinsically good and desirable about the kind of self-direction involved in singular agency. It may even be claimed that singular agency is the only possible kind of agency. If one thinks this, then the second version of Weber's proposal may look like an innocuous development of the intentional states constraint. But this claim about singular agency cannot be sustained, as I now argue.

It could come to seem that only singular agency is possible for humans if one accepts that the unique correct model of human action is one that might be dubbed the 'hydraulic' model.[4] According to this model, a physiological force, which we can call a Desire, causes people to do things. That is, acts of will are always caused by Desires.

Now as spelled out so far this model will not allow for singular agency in so far as it posits that Desires cause acts of will directly, without the intervention of conceptions or reasoning. As I have envisaged it, singular agency requires that someone's act of will is most directly a response to his understanding that something is the case.

A modified hydraulism may seem plausible, however. This could allow for singular agency, and indeed it implies that such agency is the only kind of reason-involving agency. According to this model, Desires are necessary causal conditions of action. Standardly one knows that one has a Desire. This understanding is expressed by 'I want. . .'. The Desire, in conjunction with this understanding, leads to the relevant act of will. Let us consider this reason-involving version of hydraulism. I shall briefly address two versions of it, which we can call the 'vivid' and the 'mild' versions.

The vivid version conceives of all Desires as phenomenologically like experienced hunger, thirst, and sexual desire. If this is what a Desire is, it is surely false that human acts of will *require* a propulsive Desire. Such conditions as hunger for food may indeed be so distracting that we feel we must act upon them. But it is simply false that this is always happening.

A proponent of the vivid version of hydraulism may start with the thought that a claim that one *wants* something is a claim that one has a propulsive desire of the sort at issue. Now the precise import of 'I want' statements is a delicate matter, one that I cannot go into properly here. Probably such statements can take more than one interpretation. It is obviously far-fetched, however, to think that generally speaking such statements are intended to refer to something like the condition of sexual desire or thirst or hunger. Suppose we accept that 'I want' statements refer to *desires*. We must then admit that not all desires are Desires. The desire to stick to one's diet has no manifestations like those of the craving for chocolate. I take it that 'I want X', in so far as this represents a standard premise in reasoning to an act of will, is not well understood as descriptive or expressive of a perceived state of excitation, or any sort of compelling or distracting force.

In sum, in so far as there is something to a model of action produced by states of perceived arousal, this model has a very narrow range of application. There is no obvious reason to take its scope to be as wide as the scope of singular agency in general. Its applicability where it does apply in no way supports the claim that singular agency is the only kind.

According to the mild version of hydraulism, Desires have no specific type of phenomenology. They are simply states of excitation in response to an object or the thought of an object. Suppose we were to concede for the sake of argument that humans require some physical arousal in order to act at all. It seems that we are not yet required to accept the uniqueness of singular agency. For that we would need a proof that the states that are necessary for and lead to action are necessarily reflected in reasoning in terms of what one personally wants.

A hydraulist may not feel particularly interested in giving such a proof. This depends on why one is a hydraulist in the first place. On the one hand, one might accept hydraulism because one assumes there must be a unique type of cause of human action. Given this general motivation, it would not particularly matter how the causes of action were reflected in reasoning, conscious or unconscious. It would hardly seem crucial to this picture that one should always be motivated in terms of what one saw as one's personal desires, preferences, or evaluations. On the other hand, one might be a hydraulist because one thought that the model of singular agency was the unique correct model of action, and intended by 'Desire' whatever type of state corresponded to sincere 'I want' statements. If this is one's reason for believing in hydraulism, one can hardly cite hydraulism as a reason for believing that the model of singular agency is the unique correct model of human agency. Given this rough discussion, I shall take it that we need not concern ourselves further with implications of the hydraulic model here.

Anything other than singular agency may seem impossible for another reason. Suppose one takes it that in human agency it is by providing *an intelligible ground for action* that some claim one accepts leads to an act of will. It may then be queried whether any relationship between premise and act is intelligible other than that between 'I want X; my doing A leads to X' and my doing A. Then it may be argued that, at least in so far as we are restricting our concern to acts based on intelligible grounds, the only kind of agency there can be is singular agency. I say more about this shortly.

The sense that any alternative type of human action must be morally odious is another reason one might cling to the idea that singular agency is the only kind there is. Use of a moral criterion like this is not appropriate to an objective appraisal of how things are. (With his emphasis on 'value-freedom' in sociology, Weber himself could not have approved of it.) One aspect of this issue may be noted, however. The 'opposite' of autonomy, in the sense of self-direction in general, would seem to be heteronomy, being ruled by another's desires. This latter tends to be viewed negatively, with intuitive justification. One who felt, with respect to any other, 'Your wish is my command' would be peculiarly unfree, a sort of slave.[5] Though one may think of virtuous people as caring for others one need not expect them to be subject to the wishes of others in this way. It is implausible to suppose admirable acts of charity, kindness, and so on, to be heteronomous. An account in terms of singular agency is more plausible (though not exhaustive of the possibilities). Suppose a friend sees that I am very unhappy and puts her arm around me. She does not need to be responding 'directly' to my perceived desire for comfort. She may want to comfort me if I need comforting. Thus she may act on her own desire. She will then be autonomous rather than heteronomous. In any case, what I wish to contrast with singular agency is not heteronomous agency. It is rather agency in one's capacity as a constituent of a plural subject. Such action is not best thought of as heteronomous, it has an intelligible ground (perhaps heteronomy strictly speaking does not: I shall not try to pass judgment on that), and in itself, as opposed to some of its concrete instances, it is not morally odious.

Consider an earlier example of a sentence which could be used to express a claim about a singular agent, 'Bob kicked Alan.' When one human being kicks another he may well be expressing a personal goal. He may personally be angry with the other and wish to hurt him. But consider what may happen when Bob is a member of a street gang. The gang sees Alan, a member of a rival gang, alone on the curb. Someone says 'Let's go, fellas!' Bent on attacking Alan, the gang rushes up to him. The following may go through Bob's mind. 'We* are attacking Alan; my kicking him will help do the trick, so. . .'. There follows an appropriate act of will.

I propose that the quoted reasoning is on the face of it as intelligible as the reasoning definitive of singular agency. The general type of reason scheme now under consideration is that which obtains, by definition, when one acts as part of a plural subject. Action as part of a plural subject occurs when someone rightly sees his act of will as an expression of the 'cause' of a plural subject of which he is a member. His act of will then expresses reasoning of the general form: 'We are performing action A; my performing action B will help to do the trick, so. . .'. For the sake of brevity, I shall sometimes call action as part of a plural subject *participant agency*.

Now the champion of singular agency might try to argue that the reasoning involved in participant agency is intelligible because we implicitly place it within a framework conforming to the model of singular agency. Though I do not think this can be shown, it is worth considering how this argument might proceed.

The example of Bob's kicking Alan, it might be argued, involved a situation of some complexity. If we unpack it into its components, we shall see how it is natural to presume singular agency is involved at every stage. First, Bob is a member of a gang. The gang, we may presume, is a set of young men who wander the city streets together at night, jointly engaging in various activities like visiting taverns and dance halls, and, where appropriate, defending members against rival groups, and attacking the members of rival groups. It is natural to assume that Bob joined the gang in the first place because he personally wanted to. Perhaps he wanted to be affiliated with some such group, and this was the appropriate one. Second, when one gang member says 'Let's go, fellas' on seeing Alan, and (let us assume) the rest (apart from Bob) start moving, Bob is faced with a choice: should he join them on this occasion, or not? He presumably knows that, if he chooses not to, he risks losing gang membership. He wants not to lose it (we naturally assume), so he joins the rush towards Alan. Third, in coming up to Alan himself, he is again faced with a choice of what to do. Given that he does kick Alan, we naturally assume that his reasoning includes the following: 'I want to retain membership in the gang, I risk losing it if I don't try to hurt this guy.'

As the case has just been described, then, Bob's joining the gang, his rushing with the others towards Alan, and his kicking Alan, ultimately issue from his conception of his own goals. The champion of singular agency may claim that the imaginary case of so-called participant agency that I described is rendered intelligible only by our implicitly filling in gaps in terms of the agent's understanding of his own goals, as has just been done.

I would argue that this claim is false. There is no need to claim that the facts are not sometimes as the 'singularist' describes. There is need to argue, however, that singular agency is not the only intelligible kind.

Part of such an argument may be indirect. There seems to be no way to argue for the priority of singular agency. Recall the idea that to every reasoned act of will there corresponds a Desire of the agent which is reflected in his understanding that he wants such-and-such. This view is either (in its vivid form) contrary to experience, or (in its mild form) both questionable and not directly supportive of the model of singular agency. The following points may also be noted.

The singularist case might gain plausibility if desires for continuing membership always in fact come into play in conscious prior reasoning, or in accounts proffered after the fact. Surely they do not. It is not plausible to suppose that such desires *have* to come into play when a group member acts. One may surely be totally thoughtless about the fact of one's membership, taking it as an unquestioned given of one's situation. One is most likely to become reflective about the desirability of one's membership when the goals of the group are saliently at odds with one's personal goals. Meanwhile, since humans are strongly influenced by the condition of the groups of which they are members, their personal goals will often be reflections of the goals of the group. In which case, it is unlikely that any strain will be felt when acting as a group member. In general, it is not necessary that one have a reason to consider acting contrary to the group's goal, and hence to reflect on the possibility of ejection from the group, and on one's desire to continue as a member.

As I have envisaged the singularist's argument, he accepts that we find the reason scheme for participant agency intelligible but argues that this is because we read into it a background premise about what the person in question personally wants. But do we? This is a factual question, a question about what has to be read into something in order to make it intelligible. I do not find myself reading anything about personal desires into the set of premises: 'We* are attacking Alan, my kicking him will further this aim' in order to make it an intelligible ground for an act of will. Given that I accept that I am one of 'us*', which is implicit in my use of 'we*', it seems to follow that I have reason to promote our* goal.

It could be hard if not impossible to find reasons for the intelligibility of something one finds intelligible. However, drawing on ideas introduced earlier, we can provide an argument in this case. We can meet the singularist challenge with the following conditional. If a person's own goals provide an intelligible ground for action (which the singularist does not dispute), then his group's goals should provide such a ground too. If 'we*' exist, then I have put my will at our* disposal in relation to some specific cause, broadly construed. (Presumably, I did not have to put my will at my own disposal. My will is my will.) This being so how can it not be intelligible that I find a direct *causa agendi* in our* cause? For I have dedicated or re-dedicated my will to us*. It can thus be argued that a human's will stands in a special, analogous relationship both to his or her own goals and values, and to those values he or she considers to be 'ours*'.

In Chapter IV I argued that in a central sense of the English 'we' it refers to a plural subject, just as 'we*' does, by stipulation. In arguing this I did not appeal to our sense of the role of 'we want' assertions in practical reasoning. But if we do look at that we find that 'we want' appears to licence just what 'we* want' licences, another argument in favour of the connection I have claimed. Surely, just as it seems intuitively obvious that *my* wanting X is a reason for me to exercise my will in order to get X, it seems intuitively obvious that *our wanting X is a reason for me to exercise my will in* order to get X. (As I learned after I first saw this, Wilfrid Sellars has argued in a number of places for the validity of the move, roughly, from 'We want X' to an act of will on my part.)[6] It is therefore plausible to suggest that the articulated concept of a plural subject can explain our intuitions on inferences licenced by 'we want' claims. It is not that our wanting X is identical, or includes as a part, my wanting X: it does not, or so I would argue. Rather, if I acknowledge that we want X, I imply that I am committed to using my force to help to get X. In so far as one's group's goals are perceived as 'our' goals, then one's group's goals *will* provide an intelligible ground for action, distinct from the ground provided by one's personal goals. I shall assume henceforth that 'we*' and 'we' (in a central sense) are identical.

In principle there can be conflicts between our wants and my wants. For example, our preference for this Sunday afternoon may be a trip to the beach, whereas my personal preference may be an afternoon in the garden. Though I shall not try to argue this here in detail, I suggest that the nature of acceptance of something as our preference is such that it implies acceptance of *the priority of our preference over my own.* Consider this example. Father says 'So we're agreed that an afternoon at the beach is best?' He then goes into the garden and settles into a deckchair with *The Golden Bowl.* Fathers may do this sort of thing sometimes, but such action is surely bizarre. According to the view of the matter presented here, this is because, in accepting going to the beach as 'our' preference, Father implicitly dedicated his own will to that project. But if he really has done this, then he understands that his will is not available for the pursuit of contrary projects. If the conceptual scheme I have elaborated here is roughly right, then, it would help to explain the bizarreness of actions like the father's in this case.[7]

The singularist spoke as if one can presume that someone's joining groups in the first place is an act of singular agency, based on a personal desire. But in principle groups can be joined for no reason.[8] In principle, then, they can be joined in advance of the development of explicit personal goals and evaluations.[9] This implies that a human could be a member of a 'we', of a mother–child dyad, say, without being self-conscious in the sense of self-ascribing goals, or evaluations. It seems possible, then, that the order envisaged by the singularist be reversed. Starting their conscious life perceiving themselves as group members with an understanding of group goals, values, and beliefs, humans could tend to use these as filters for selecting out acceptable personal goals.

It is plausible to suppose that each mature human being has a fund of knowledge of the goals of his group or groups, and of his own personal goals. It is not possible to say a priori what knowledge has come into play when an action takes place on the basis of reasoning. It is possible to argue, however, that participant agency as such is as intelligible as singular agency, and neither has any explanatory priority from the point of view of the concepts involved.

At this point an important aspect of the moral evaluation of plural subject-hood may usefully be noted, if only briefly. This has to do with accountability or responsibility. Does membership in a plural subject provide a means by which individuals can avoid being personally accountable for things they do? Can Bob, for example, effectively deny personal responsibility for savagely kicking Alan if he kicked Alan in his capacity of group member?

It seems plausible to suppose that as long as Bob (intentionally) kicked Alan, Bob may be held responsible for kicking Alan. This suggests that the conceptual framework into which the concept of responsibility fits is such that as long as Bob's act of will (intentionally) set a kick in motion, then Bob is personally responsible for what happened. The obvious contrast case here is with such familiar happenings as involuntary knee-jerks which are presumed not to involve acts of will (hence 'involuntary').

Is there some mitigation of responsibility for Bob in the fact that the kicking of Alan did not express his personal desires? He was not, we might say, *expressing himself* in kicking Alan. This could lead us to judge him less severely in himself, so to speak. Similar considerations may influence our evaluations of many things, such as acts performed in deference to local conventions that we find repugnant. None the less, as witnessed by reactions to the defence 'I was only acting under orders' in the context of the Nazi Holocaust, people are not convinced that one can evade responsibility for one's own acts by a simple appeal to one's participation in a group's action. This is particularly clear when there are strong and obvious moral motives for attempting to act otherwise.

It seems that someone acting in his capacity of member of a certain group attracts two different types of ascription of responsibility. If Bob himself kicked Alan, then he can be held personally responsible for this kicking. At the same time, Bob may be held responsible *qua* group member. For in so far as Bob's kicking Alan was part of an action of the group (the action of attacking Alan), presumably he can be held responsible *qua* group member for this kicking, as well as personally responsible. In being held responsible *qua* group member he is on a par with any other group member. Such 'being held responsible *qua* group member' appears to be equivalent to being held jointly responsible with the others, or to being a member of a group which is responsible. The above discussion indicates that in so far as a group can be held responsible for an action, this is not incompatible with a given member's being held personally responsible for that action. Meanwhile, it is not the case that all members need be held personally responsible.

Thought of the possibility of withdrawing from a group if one realizes that their goal is morally repugnant may suggest a new line of questioning to the singularist. At every stage of my membership in a group, can I not, in effect, leave the group just exactly when I please? So does my staying now not, after all, have to depend on what currently pleases me, on my personal goals? In a sense this is so. Say we are having a conversation. You could unceremoniously grab your hat and leave. You have that power. (You might say to yourself 'I've had it with this conversation. I'm leaving.' But if you do this, you have violated an understanding. You have, if you like, decided unilaterally to bring your will back under your control. Sometimes it is morally required that one do this, as I have indicated.[10] Sometimes the contrary is the case. (The person you are talking to may be desperately in need of the kind of reassurance only a long conversation can provide.) But moral considerations aside, once you have constituted yourself a member of a plural subject you violate an understanding and default on an obligation if you withdraw violently without leave. Surely such obligations are often honoured just because they are understood to be there. All that I want to argue here, however, is that in principle someone could be motivated by his understanding of what his group's goals are, without reference to what pleases him. This is a perfectly intelligible process.

Let me now summarize my position on the question whether sociology needs collectivity concepts which are explicable in terms of the 'actions of participating individual men'. I have said nothing to disprove the idea that according to a viable sociological concept human collectivities will be constituted by human beings in specific intentional states and by human acts of will. Meanwhile my conclusions do go against the idea that collective phenomena must be seen as constituted by the acts of singular agents. Collective phenomena are plural subject phenomena. The concept of a plural subject is the concept of a set of persons who are set up to act without reference to their own goals. This concept, meanwhile, appears to be a perfectly respectable one. (I add a brief note on its realism later.)

3 CONCERNING 'INDIVIDUALISM' VERSUS 'HOLISM'

3.1 Introduction

The concepts and distinctions articulated in this book provide a new way of approaching the opposition between 'individualism' and 'holism'. Though I have written of 'the' opposition, this controversy has been variously characterized, and distinctions between numerous different types of individualism and holism have been made.[11] In this section I concentrate on two central versions of the opposition in question, an ontological version and a semantic or analytic version. For my results bear most directly on these.

3.2 Ontological individualism versus ontological holism

Consider the following views: (1) social groups are nothing over and above the individuals who are their members; (2) social groups exist in their own right. Call (1) (ontological) individualism and (2) (ontological) holism. These views are crudely expressed. But such crude expressions or slogans tend to occur in discussion, and the views expressed have tended to appear irreconcilable. (It is common to associate Max Weber with individualism and Emile Durkheim with holism.) I shall show how these views may be reconciled, drawing on distinctions made earlier.

I shall argue that both (1) and (2) have two possible interpretations, and that there is one interpretation of each one, given which it is fairly clearly right, and one interpretation of each one, given which it is fairly clearly wrong. Reconciliation will consist in accepting the correct version of each view, and rejecting the incorrect version. Not surprisingly, the correct versions of these views are mutually consistent.

Any discussion of the versions of individualism and holism at issue in this section should make it clear that though these views have been associated with opposing moral and political doctrines, they are ontological doctrines. They have to do with what there is. Meanwhile, proponents of each doctrine, seeing proponents of the other doctrine as their opponents, and finding their own doctrine obvious, have tended to suspect their opponents as having false values which lead to their ontological blindness or foolishness.

Of course there is nothing to a society other than the individuals in it, an individualist may think. Anyone who says anything else must have a dubious motive for his view. Opponents of holism tend to link it with fascism, with a lack of concern for the proper treatment of individual human beings, with a hunger for power whose aims can be served by appeals to the needs of a 'supra-human' entity, the so-called state or nation. (And of course such appeals have indeed been made by fascists.) Meanwhile holists may think: obviously states, nations, families, and other social groups, exist in their own right. They may then seek for a disreputable origin for what they see as the individualists' blindness to this obvious fact. Individualism may be linked with an extreme kind of libertarianism, in which nothing but individual self-expression is seen as having any intrinsic value. Individualism, it may be argued, goes hand in hand with denial of the values of community, of sharing. False as it is, it probably derives any appeal it has from the biases of a capitalistic libertarian ideology.

Those who would align themselves with either holism or individualism have sometimes come up with conclusions which sound extreme. The individualist may feel moved to say: really there is no such thing as a 'state' or a 'nation'. These terms would be better expunged from our language. (Recall Weber's views on everyday collectivity concepts.) Holists, meanwhile, may argue that societies exist in their own right; it is their members that do not. Human beings are not 'individuals'. Such statements, puzzling at best, can only fuel the search for questionable motives.

If the original issues are ontological, they are separable in principle from questions of value. Moreover, if things are to proceed in their proper order, a clear understanding of what there is must precede evaluations. It may indeed be hard to see how, if individualism is correct, one can value a society as opposed to the particular individuals in it. In particular, it may be hard to see how societies and individuals could have conflicting claims on our care and concern. On the other hand, it may be hard to see how, if holism is correct, the flourishing of the individual members of a society could be of any significance compared with the flourishing of the society itself.

In spite of the extreme statements and passions which have been associated with both individualism and holism, when one dispassionately considers either view in isolation, one may find it rather trivially and obviously right. At the same time, taken together they may give one pause. Can it be true that (in some sense) societies are nothing over and above their individual members, and at the same time true that (in some sense) societies exist in their own right?

Let us consider individualism first: societies are nothing over and above their individual members. The ambiguity or vagueness here, as I see it, is similar to that of Weber's proposed constraint on acceptable sociological concepts. It concerns how the 'individual members' are being conceived. One whose act stems from his understanding that he has certain personal desires I have called a 'singular agent'. It is evidently tempting to think in terms of singular agents when one thinks in terms of 'individuals', 'individual persons', even 'individual human beings'. Perhaps this is in part because it is natural to suppose that in so far as there could be an 'asocial' state of humanity, a state in which people have not yet formed a collectivity, this would be a state of affairs in which there was only singular agency. Given the naturalness of *that*, it may be tempting to conclude that when human beings do form a society they go on being singular agents. To conclude, in effect, that singular agency is the natural, proper, and continuing condition of mankind.

It may then be difficult to see how a society can be anything very special. The relation between singular agents and collectivities may seem to have to be somewhat like the relation between a number of apples lying around in close geographical proximity and the 'thing' they form. One may be tempted to think of societies as mereological sums of singular agents, or as sets of singular agents, in the logician's sense of set. Though strictly speaking it may be correct, it may seem unnatural to say of societies conceived of as sets of singular agents or as mereological sums of singular agents that they 'exist in their own right'. This is also true of a society conceived of as a special complex of singular agents, for instance, as a set of singular agents who regularly perform actions which are responses to the actions of others.

In these cases the term 'society' may seem to operate somewhat like the phrase 'packed together'. Evidently societies so conceived, like uncemented walls of bricks, will not necessarily be causally unimportant, or even without value. They can have 'unintended consequences'. They can serve useful purposes. But there may well seem to be something 'insubstantial' about the so-called 'society' in relation to its components.

I have argued, so far, that, first, it is easy to construe ontological individualism as saying that societies are nothing over and above the singular agents who are their members. This implies, of course, that societies are indeed constituted by singular agents. One who has accepted this as correct is likely to find unacceptable the idea that societies exist 'in their own right'. This claim will be construed as meaning 'over and above their singular agent components'. The results in this book suggest that this 'singular agent individualism' is unacceptable. Meanwhile, an acceptable ontological individualism would be the view that human collectivities are 'nothing' over and above some special set of states of the individual human beings which are their members. This amounts to the view that all that is needed to produce a human collectivity is a set of human beings in some as yet unspecified states. This is clearly different from the view that a human collectivity is a set of singular agents.

Let me now turn to ontological holism. This will be unacceptable if it is construed as the denial of the acceptable form of individualism. If it is construed that way, it could lead to a belief in independent group minds or spirits, for which there is no empirical warrant, and which has tended to give holism a bad name. What, then, is the acceptable version of holism? I take it that one who says that societies exist 'in their own right' is saying that for a society to come into being is for there to be a substantial change in the way things are. Here 'substantial' is not meant in a technical philosophical sense, but rather in a vernacular sense. 'Change' is obviously change in relation to some implicit baseline. It is implied that the change produces something that is more than a conglomeration of things of the sort that there are at the baseline. It produces 'something new', indeed, a 'new thing'.

My account of social groups as plural subjects implies that a version of this doctrine is correct. In order for individual human beings to form collectivities, they must take on a special character, a 'new' character, in so far as they need not, *qua* human beings, have that character. Moreover, humans must form a whole or unit of a special kind, a unit of a kind that can now be specified precisely: they must form a plural subject.

We can see, then, that there is a way of reconciling individualism and holism. It works by making certain distinctions: between human beings, singular agents, and members of plural subjects, and by taking one of these categories and construing the doctrine in question in terms of it. Individualism in the acceptable sense can be seen to lie behind the criterion of human intentional states, a criterion one might find it reasonable to impose on an acceptable sociological collectivity concept. Holism in the acceptable sense draws attention, in effect, to the fact that social groups are plural subjects. In order to make a group human beings must be in special states and form a whole or unit of a special kind. A tempting but unacceptable version of individualism is a version in terms of singular agents which conflicts with holism construed as a way of denying that phenomena of singular agency are either necessary or sufficient for collectivity-hood. Finally, an unacceptable holism denies that the constituents of society are human beings in specific states.

Mill said that men are not converted into another kind of substance on entering society. He was right if he meant that human beings do not cease to be human beings. They are still the same natural kind of thing. He was wrong if he meant that human beings as such do not have to undergo a radical change in order to become members of social groups. In so far as it is true, his claim is rather trivial. Societies are real unities (said Simmel); societies are *sui generis* syntheses of human beings (said Durkheim). I agree. These are very natural ways of expressing the view I have called acceptable ontological holism. More specifically and concretely, it is the view that social groups are plural subjects.

3.3 A note on the reality of groups

Someone might say: you agree that at the base of society are individual human beings and their thoughts and acts. But thoughts and acts involve thinkers and agents, and any thinker or agent may properly refer to himself as 'I'. So the referent of 'I', the self, is prior ontologically, in your view, to the referent of 'We'. So whether or not societies exist in their own right, they are ontologically secondary to selves. This is surely the deep truth of ontological individualism.

The deep truth here may be put like this: in so far as thoughts and acts of individual human beings are the foundation of societies, and in so far as every thought and act can properly be accompanied by a 'self-referring' 'I', then at the foundation of societies there is an I, or self. The self involved here is a deep self. It may be a deeply hidden self. The 'self that acts', like Kant's 'self that thinks' need never think about itself in the usual way. I think about myself, when I represent to myself that I want such-and-such, that I am happy or hurting, that I am indeed thinking. We may find it appropriate to say that only when someone thinks in this way is he 'self-conscious'. The deep self that thinks and acts need not be self-conscious in this way, or so it seems: not all thoughts are thoughts *about the self*.

In my representations of the reasoning that leads to action when one acts as a group member, I have included a premise using a form of the first person singular pronoun. For instance, I suggested that one may reason 'We are doing so-and-so, my doing such-and-such will do the trick, so. . .'. This self-referring premise comes from a particular and restricted class. It could be rephrased as something like this: 'an act of will causing my body to move thus-and-so will do the trick.' This indicates that one who has the capacity to be a group member and act as such may yet lack the capacity to act as a singular agent. He may not yet ascribe *goals* and *thoughts* to himself. But one cannot act in the light of the fact that such-and-such is one's goal if one has no consciousness that such-and-such is indeed one's goal.[12]

The conclusion seems to be that humans *as singular agents* and humans *as members of plural subjects* are ontologically on a par. Neither is prior as far as ontology goes.

Given that it is clear what plural subjects amount to, one can decide on their reality in the light of one's own ontological preferences. I myself shall only hazard a brief word on this.

At base of both singular agents and plural subjects lies the human being, with his or her acts of will and conceptions of the situation. Out of this material, both singular agents and social groups are made.

Suppose I look at my mother and my niece, who are chatting, and I say: 'There's a plural subject for you!' Am I committing myself to the existence of anything which could plausibly be argued not to be there? Recall that there is a plural subject of a goal (say, the goal that you and I converse) if two or more people have openly* expressed willingness to be part of such a subject in a situation of common knowledge. Well, I take it that Natalie and Mother, chatting away in that absorbed fashion, have done just that. I take it that they have (inarticulately perhaps, but encapsulated in their use of 'we') the concept of a plural subject. Why should one deny of them that once they have fulfilled the conditions, they constitute such a subject? The only reason I can see, is if one has an ontology which is more or less restricted to stones.

We might say that for there to be a singular agent is for there to be a system which contains as a crucial element a conception of the system. This conception of the system powers the system in the sense that it is the precise nature of this conception which leads to acts of will and physical motions.

Now, how is this complex system, the singular agent, different in kind from the plural subject? Someone may say that it alone is 'self-contained'. It is, in the trivial way of having all its essential components packaged up in a single human body. But how can that fact contribute to a difference in the reality of one thing as compared with another?

Surely a plural subject, as characterized in this book, is the same kind of system as a singular agent. Its physical components are two or more human bodies. The movements of the system occur in response to the conception of the system which is contained contemporaneously in its physical parts, and which is based on the perception of what is taking place in each.

The pure case of a plural subject as a system is quite complex. The belief 'our* goal is G', for instance, which is embedded in and powers the behaviour of each physical part, is the outcome of a perception of the other physical parts and an inference that the other parts are each in a certain complex intentional state, one which meshes with an intentional state of the perceiver. There is also the perception of the openness* of this meshing.

The existence of the complex plural subject system does not entail the existence as a lower order component of two singular agent systems. In any case, it is hard to find a good reason for denying the reality of either type of system.[13]

Possibly someone will say, perhaps to me, 'There are no plural subjects *really*. It is a human *fiction* that there are.' What should I say? Am I to play ball and listen to this person? What's playing ball? What's listening to this person? *Is* there such a thing? You cannot *tell me* there are no plural subjects and be right. You cannot sensibly set out to tell me that. What is telling?

Plural subjects are a *special type* of entity, no doubt about that. But as far as I can see they are not illusory or based on illusion. They depend for their existence on people's possession of a certain rather special concept, and acting successfully so that the concept be instantiated.

The world would surely be less rich without plural subjects. In the end it cannot matter if they are sniffed at by those with certain restrictive ontological preferences. Plural subjects are surely with us* (tendentious 'we*').

In so far as for some reason students of human life feel that plural subjects are not a proper topic for *science*, perhaps the best advice to them will be: stop worrying about being a scientist in that case. Then you have a chance of being, at least, a student of human social life.

The ontological situation does not in itself lend obvious support to a proposed ideal of human beings striving at all times to realize their own personal goals, to speak their own minds, and to express their personal emotions.[14] It is at least a reasonable assumption that if there is any value in singular agency, or in collectivity, there is value in their substance, in what allows them to exist in the first place. How are human beings best to flourish? By joining groups, by talking to each other, by walking together, by dancing and making love? Or by developing and seeking personal goals, only connecting with others where necessary to achieve these goals? Or by some mix of these? These questions go beyond conceptual analysis and ontology, and beyond the scope of the book I have written here. For serious answers we need to go to empirical work, to the human sciences. Human beings are malleable and varied, and there may be no one right answer. However that may be, it would be wrong to think that there was no question.

3.4 Concerning analytic individualism

There is a distinct type of individualism which is couched specifically in terms of meaning or analysability. I shall call this type of individualism 'analytic individualism'. One version runs roughly as follows: everyday collectivity concepts are analysable without remainder in terms of concepts other than collectivity concepts, in particular, in terms of the concept of an individual person, his goals, beliefs, and so on. Let us call this strong analytic individualism.

A thoroughgoing strong analytic individualism implies two things. First, the concept of an individual person with his own goals, and so on, does not require for *its* analysis a concept of a collectivity itself unanalysable in terms of persons and their noncollectivity-involving properties. In Chapter III I argued in favour of such a position. This, however, does not make me a strong analytic individualist. For there is a second important aspect to that view, the claim that explication of the notion of a collectivity will not involve essential reference to *intentional states* the proper description of whose content involves concepts unanalysable in terms of individual persons, their goals, and so on.

Note that Max Weber may not have been a strong analytical individualist. (He is not really concerned with this issue.) His remarks on everyday collectivity concepts, quoted in the first chapter, and his definition of communal relations in terms of the sense of 'belonging together' suggest that he contemplates the possibility that some social phenomena, at least, could involve as an essential ingredient the exercise of irreducible collectivity concepts by human agents. Clearly one will tend to be a strong analytic individualist in relation to everyday collectivity concepts if one believes any irreducible collectivity concept to be unrealistic, and one does not wish to discredit the ideas in terms of which one conducts one's daily social life. This belief and desire may underlie assumptions such as those of Quinton on collective beliefs, as to 'what we are really saying' when we ascribe beliefs to groups.

The results of this book clearly go against strong analytic individualism. Our collectivity concepts are plural subject concepts. At a number of points I have looked in the direction of possible reductions of statements about plural subjects, and in no case have these reductions seemed right intuitively speaking. It is neither necessary nor sufficient for us to have a certain goal, that you have that goal, and that I do. Winning the war may be our goal, but it is unlikely that it is your goal, unless perhaps you are in charge of operations. That each of us wants to bring it about that each of us meets the Queen, does not entail that we form a plural subject whose goal is each one's meeting the Queen. If to simple analyses about what is true of most individuals in some set we add wrinkles about common knowledge or reasons having to do with everybody else we still do not get to plural subjectivity. It emerged that the best one can do by way of analysis of the plural subject concepts is to allude to a set of persons who understand their wills to be jointly committed to some cause. The notion of jointly committed wills comes from outside the conceptual scheme of singular agency.

The concept of a plural subject does not come from outside a more general scheme of what might be called the properties of human beings in general. Let weak analytic individualism be the view that our collectivity concepts are analysable in terms of a conceptual scheme appropriate to human beings, with all their possibilities and capacities for understanding. The results presented here do not conflict with this. But that is because the doctrine at this point is extremely vague. One virtue of the doctrine construed in terms of the conceptual scheme of singular agents is that it is relatively precise. But then its singular vice is that it is false.

Given that my analytical hypotheses are correct, one might wonder why proponents of strong analytic individualism should be wrong about concepts they themselves use all the time. Obviously this is no place to speculate on any individual's situation in this matter. But I suggest that what is at issue here is no mere logical nicety.

Plural subjects may have goals, beliefs, attitudes, and principles of action. These may conflict with individual goals, beliefs, and so on. Suppose I value spontaneity. In my capacity as member of a certain group, I may be committed to deride it. There is a potential for such inner conflict at all times, within each of us. This potentiality threatens the wholeness or integrity of the human being. It would clearly be comforting if this conflict could be thought away.[15]

My suggestion is, then, that the dichotomy between singular agency and participant agency reaches deep into human experience, and that attempts to deny its existence by focusing on one side only could ultimately stem, understandably but unrealistically, from a wish to simplify the ancient problem of how to live.

4 A SKETCH OF SOME FURTHER APPLICATIONS

4.1 Political philosophy

In order meaningfully to engage in political philosophy one needs an accurate social ontology. Political philosophy is the philosophy of the 'polis' or, more generally, of the collectivity or group. Traditionally, it has focused on questions of evaluation: what makes for a good polis, for a well-ordered group? These questions can hardly be answered if we do not know what a group is. (Another classic topic, the grounds of 'political obligation', has been mentioned earlier, and will not be discussed further here.)

Understanding that collectivities are plural subjects makes it plain that there are two radically different kinds of criteria of evaluation for societies, which we can call *relational* and *nonrelational*. On the one hand, political arrangements may be judged in relation to the individual persons who are members of the society. The criterion of distributive justice is of this (relational) kind. Has every individual received his fair share of the fruits of society? On the other hand, political arrangements may be judged in terms of the goals of the society itself, irrespective of the welfare of individual persons. Plato's criterion of justice in the *Republic* (Book 5) is of this kind: those best fitted to govern the society should do so, in order that its aims be most efficiently promoted.

There has been a tendency in recent analytic political philosophy to concentrate on relational criteria. It is important to realize, however, that collectivities can appropriately be judged according to the other type of criterion, and that these criteria can conflict. The most efficient way of winning a war may involve much curtailment of individual liberty, and so on. Plato's attempt to eradicate a sense of 'mine' and 'thine' altogether in the ruling class in his ideal city suggests an understanding of this problem, even if it does not represent a plausible solution. We need to consider not only how, say, individual liberty and distributive justice can be reconciled, but when and why it is politically proper to make collective goals subservient to such values, or the reverse.

It is unfortunate, but hopefully not inevitable, that those political theorists who have come closest to understanding the nature of human collectivities have also managed to earn the pejorative label 'totalitarian'. (The totalitarian, roughly, puts the group before the individual from the point of view of what is of value or importance. At the limit, the totalitarian denies that individual human beings have any value or importance except in their capacity as group members.) Perhaps this is because one cannot sensibly be a totalitarian without some inkling of the ontology of groups; whereas if one has no inkling of this ontology, one is not likely to elevate groups unduly in the scheme of things. Collectivities are indeed wholes, units, or 'totalities' of a special kind. And it is not entirely strange, given the details of their nature, that they should be valued types of entity (by virtue for instance of their 'organic unity'). But just as individual human beings can be admirable or otherwise, so can societies. Seeing collectivities as wholes of a special sort does not entail that we idolize them or cease to care about the welfare of the individual human beings who are their members. Some groups are simply bad, and it would be better if they changed completely, or ceased to exist.

This book has focused on small informal social units as opposed to nations and other relatively autonomous political units, the usual subject of political philosophy. Meanwhile, the vocabulary of politics, or most of it, is apposite to small informal units as well as to large. As soon as there are human collectivities, there are issues of good governance, questions about the need for inequalities and dominance, and issues relating to the needs of the individuals concerned. This thought is not original with me. Rousseau stressed the family as the original political unit, Mill argued that marriage was a locus of political reality, and so on. None the less the politics of small units is not usually addressed in political philosophy. Nor is the great range of something like Rousseau's notion of a human association noted.

At a late stage in writing this book I realized that I had come close to Rousseau's conception of what makes a collection of human beings into a genuine 'people' as opposed to a mere aggregate. Rousseau's concept is sometimes decried as hard to understand. However, one conclusion of this book is that something like Rousseau's conception of how a people is formed is implicit in our everyday mundane discourse about such acts as going for a walk together, and conversing. This does not make the conception easier to understand, but it does suggest that it must be understood, if we are to make good sense of ourselves.

To my knowledge I have not used any notion approximating to Rousseau's concept of the *general will*, which I make no attempt to characterize here. As far as I can see actual human associations may have little positive connection, real or perceived with the welfare of the individual members. Compare Rawls's initial characterization of a society in *A Theory of Justice*, which appears to suppose at least a perceived connection:

> Let us assume, to fix ideas, that a society is a more or less self-sufficient association of persons who in their relations with one another recognize certain rules of conduct as binding and who for the most part act in accordance with them. Suppose further that those rules specify a system of cooperation designed to advance the good of those taking part in it. Then, although a *society is a cooperative venture for mutual advantage*, it is

typically marked by a conflict as well as by an identity of
interests. (1971, p.4; my stress)

Rawls may not intend to characterize societies as such, as
opposed to societies we would consider minimally acceptable. In
any case it follows from my account of social groups that his
description is not acceptable as a general characterization of a
collectivity. This is surely so intuitively. (An example of a society
which was not perceived as aiming to promote the welfare of the
individuals in it would be one which saw itself (and was seen by
its members) as set up to promote the glory of a deity.)

4.2 Psychology

If human beings standardly view their environment and act in
terms of the plural subject concepts articulated here, then the
discipline of psychology, broadly construed, must obviously take
note of the detail of these concepts. (In 'psychology', here, I
include the fields of social psychology and clinical psychology.)
An understanding of these concepts may be expected to throw
light on a variety of phenomena, as well as suggesting new
avenues of enquiry.

Let me very briefly cite two specific examples in this
connection. First, consider the topic of 'social loafing'.[16]
Roughly, in certain experiments it has been found that someone
who exerts a certain amount of energy on a task he undertakes
alone will exert less energy when performing that task with
certain others. (The initial experiment involved pulling on a
rope.) A detailed grasp of the plural subject concepts should aid
our understanding of such phenomena in a very general way. For
it is already clear, given the structure of these concepts, that one
should not be confident of a constancy in an individual's
behaviour if he moves from undertaking a task alone to
undertaking it as the member of a group. It is a concomitant of
understanding that you are doing something with someone else
that you understand that responsibility for the task is shared or
joint. You are not personally responsible for the fulfilment of the
task, as you are when you perform it alone, but rather you
participate in joint responsibility. When the perceived locus of
responsibility changes from the individual to the group, this is
clearly a major change in the perceived structure of the situation.

A second example concerns the identification of problems.
One often reads in textbooks in social psychology of the problem
of why people seek affiliations with others. They are said to do so

in order to find out how they compare with others on various dimensions ('social comparison'), and so on. There is no equivalent concern with the reasons people seek to act independently of their affiliations, relationships, or groups. Yet this seems to be an equally important question. Once one realizes the *sui generis* nature of affiliation, in so far as this is equivalent to plural subject formation, one is more likely to see both the desire for affiliation and the desire for independent action as in need of explanation. One is also more likely to see as quite compelling the question whether there is a general human need for affiliation as such.

4.3 Questions of method

Analytical philosophy of social science has tended to focus on the question whether social studies can be scientific, and in this connection to raise questions about the types of explanation and methods of enquiry proper to social studies.[17] These concerns have been accompanied with a relative neglect of the nature of social phenomena. Clearly assumptions are made about the subject matter of social sciences in such discussions, and these may be made explicit and discussed somewhat. But the issue has not been the focus of concern.

Presumably in a logical ordering ontology precedes methodology. Weber and Durkheim saw things this way, and acted accordingly. I make no attempt here to enter the area of methodology, but clearly questions of method arise in relation to plural subject-hood. The nature of plural subject phenomena suggests that some sophistication will be needed in studying not only collective beliefs, and so on, but also the beliefs of individuals, their personal beliefs. For a given item of overt behaviour could express a person's own beliefs and goals, or the beliefs of his group, or both. Simply asking individuals what they think may not be enough. In particular, one may think that he is being questioned in his capacity of group member (as the member of a scientific research team, say, or as an American) and answer in that capacity. Hence the social ontology presented here has implications for the methodology not only of social studies but also of individual psychology, and for the gathering of statistics. In particular, investigation of 'consensus', in the sense of what most individuals in a particular population personally think, needs to be undertaken with special care.[18]

5 ON SOCIAL FACTS

5.1 Which are the 'social' phenomena?

How is the everyday intuitive concept of a social phenomenon to be explicated? If we consider the variety of accounts social scientists and others have given of their subject matter, we may conclude that the phenomena aptly thought of as 'social' are a motley crew, including, for instance, social actions in Weber's sense and Durkheim's social facts.[19]

Suppose we consider the questions: from the point of view of everyday linguistic intuition, do we have a social phenomenon when we have a social action in Weber's sense? Or when people act in terms of their expectations of what others will do? Do we have a social phenomenon if people act in terms of their expectations of what others will do, when they take it that those others are acting in terms of expectations about what they will do? Do we have 'social interaction' when we have any series of social actions in Weber's sense, such that perception of the first provokes the second, and so on? Are all situations of common knowledge social situations?[20] Suppose, for the sake of argument, that we say 'yes' to some or all of these. It is still incumbent upon us to note that there is another order of phenomena, phenomena of plural subject-hood, which are arguably involved in all of the clearest cases of: conversations, dancing together, telling people things, giving orders, meetings, greetings, and so on, not to speak of established relationships and groups such as friends, families, army corps, and so on.

There is little doubt that the plural subject phenomena are the most apt intuitively for the label 'social'. Etymology, which should not be the last word but whose blessing is pleasant, suggests that this is so, with '*socius*' meaning *ally*. In plural subject-hood, the members are in a clear sense 'in something together'.

Evidently phenomena of plural subjecthood involve alliances of a special type. 'We' can be fighting, quarrelling, at war. The basic features of plural subject-hood remain. In standard cases of war, there is a jointly sustained goal: that either X or Y win, or there is a tie. There may well be certain conventions about how to proceed. (If one participant falls, wait to attack him till he is standing up again, say.) Again, people may jointly accept that they hate each other, or that they are to avoid each other at all costs. Though such people are allies only from a special point of view, the very nature of plural subject-hood does involve a type of alliance. Whether or not the joint aims and so on make reference to conflict of any sort, there may be much antagonism at the personal level. Two people whose joint goal is a harmonious relationship may at the same time be full of hostility and resentment against each other. (Conversely, soldiers at war may or may not have a sense of personal antagonism for the individuals on the other side. And though our collective belief is that we dislike each other, each could personally experience strong positive feelings towards the other.)

Empirically speaking it is quite likely that plural subjects are involved in practically all face-to-face interactions among humans. Hence the construction of cases like that of the mushroom-pickers in Chapter II involves much artificiality. It is very easy to import assumptions about empirically ubiquitous phenomena into one's reading of a case. Similarly, it is easy not to notice such phenomena: they are part of the medium in which one exists, subtle and fine-grained and often tacit – easy to lose sight of, unlike physical bodies.

There is, then, an argument for seeing our general concept of a social phenomenon as equivalent to that of a phenomenon of plural subject-hood. Perhaps our concept is or has become more capacious than that. Even so, given the interest of plural subject phenomena and their special aptness for the label 'social' we may now want to reserve that label for them. If we do so we shall have a viable concept which is neither irretrievably vague nor unhelpfully capacious. Indeed, it cuts nature at the joints.

In the end it cannot be very profitable to worry about how or whether to limit the use of the label 'social'. What is of central importance is to bring plural subject phenomena into view as clearly as possible, and to explain their connections with and differences from phenomena of other kinds. I hope that the investigations in this book will have helped to achieve this aim.

5.2 *The Question of Animals*

This book has concentrated on human collectivities. This might provoke the following line of questioning. Are there not animal societies? Certainly many people, ethologists and others, talk as if there are. The literature is replete with references to primate societies, rat societies, and the like.[21] It may be argued: surely the animal populations referred to are not plural subjects. So our core concept of a collectivity must be distinct from that of a plural subject. In this section I consider the validity of this line of argument.

On social facts

The provenance of talk about animal societies merits investigation. It could involve an extension of the use of a term which is understood to have its home in the human domain. Or perhaps those who talk of animal societies implicitly presuppose that animals can and do form plural subjects. In either case, the prevalence of talk of societies of nonhumans would be consistent with the claim that the core everyday concept of a collectivity is that of a plural subject. How can we decide what is going on here? The following points may be noted.

It is no doubt apposite that we have a rich roll-call of names for groups of animals: a pride (of lions), a flock (of geese), and so on and on. At the same time, it is apparent that human beings, primates, and insects, say, do not all 'tick' in precisely the same way. Particularly as we get to the level of termites, for instance, the appositeness of ascribing thoughts and attitudes to individual creatures becomes less clear. Thus it looks increasingly probable as we go down the scale to less and less human-like creatures, that, to put it succinctly, animal or insect groups have a different nature, or have different natures, from human groups. It seems unlikely, then, that a concept of 'social group' that marks a significant phenomenon will cover both human and insect societies. Though this does not show that our core concept of a social group is not that capacious, it has some tendency to suggest this.

Now, flocks of geese flying north in formation look much as if they could be deliberately keeping together on the understanding that 'we are flying north'. Meanwhile it is hard to justify the claim that they really have such an understanding. Supposing that the core concept of a social group is the concept of a plural subject, then it seems likely that we call such flocks 'social groups' by virtue of a conscious extension of this central sense of the phrase. This accords with my own sense of what goes on when we refer to an animal group as a society or social group.

With respect to the needs of science, we can ask what a concept of a collectivity which singled out human and animal groups as a class might look like. The best way of specifying its conditions of application could well be something like this: wherever a set of creatures behaves in such a way that it would be appropriate for them to think 'We are doing A' where 'We' is the plural subject concept. But if this is so the concept in question is a derivative one, derived from the core concept of a (human) social group as articulated here.

Supposing that there is an alternative concept that gives no appearance of derivation from the human case, science will still need the concept of a plural subject in so far as human social groups are plural subjects, and their being so explains much of the behaviour of their members. The putative capacious independent concept will not attach to the essence of human groups, one might say. (I have in mind not a 'conceptual essence' of course, but rather a real essence in something like Locke's sense.) Perhaps it will fail to attach to the essence of anything.

Going back to the nature of our everyday concept, it is surely predictable that humans in groups will develop terms to express the essence of human collectivities. The terms 'social group', 'collectivity', and so on, construed as expressive of plural subject concepts, have a good claim to that status. Seeing oneself as a member of a plural subject with specific properties motivates one to behave in certain ways. These two ideas, then, are both quite plausible: the core everyday concept of a 'collectivity' is that of a plural subject, and the term is used of animals in what is understood to be an analogical extension.

Using terms like 'social group' for populations of humans and animals has obvious dangers. It could lead us to conflate importantly different phenomena, and lose sight of the very special nature of plural subjecthood. Whatever our terms mean, that would be a pity.

Concentration on the human case here has been productive. It led to the articulation of the concept of a plural subject. If, in order to cope with our talk about animals, the plan had been to articulate a general concept literally applicable without doubt to nonhumans or nonthinkers, it is possible the concept of a plural subject would simply have been overlooked. For the best way into it is by examination of a bit of human language, the first person plural pronoun.

It emerges that there is an available sense of 'social' in which man may be the only 'social animal'. That sense – in which social beings are plural subject forming beings – is important. It needs to be articulated and properly understood. Meanwhile, nothing in what I have said entails that animal populations may not be plural subjects. It is not essential for plural subjecthood that there be a group language. It is only necessary that, for instance, quasi-readiness with a certain content be openly* expressed in such a way that the participants are jointly ready to act in concert. Perhaps some or all nonhuman creatures are capable of this. This depends upon facts about the inner life of animals. No attempt to make a judgment on this matter need be made here.

6 AFTERWORD

I have argued that the plural subject concepts have a central place in everyday thought and talk about human social life, and, indeed, help to constitute that life. The details of these concepts are difficult to discern. Given the analyses presented here, perhaps further refined, many familiar questions should find more adequate answers, and many new questions find a voice.

NOTES

---

1 Mill, 1970, Bk. 6, ch. 7, sec. 1, p. 573. Note: Dates given in the bibliographic references in this book are those of the edition consulted by the present author. Details of those editions are to be found in the Bibliography at the back of the book. Where available, the dates of first publication of noncontemporary works are also provided there.

2 Mill, 1979, ch. 3, p. 31; Plato, 1974, sec. 462, pp. 123-4; Durkheim, 1982, p. 39.

3 Compare the opening remarks in Hart's *The Concept of Law* (1961). Hart characterizes the explication of the concept of law as not simply an exercise in semantics but as a contribution to theoretical sociology.

4 Unless otherwise noted, references to Durkheim's *The Rules of Sociological Method,* are to the Halls translation (Durkheim, 1982). This work will sometimes be referred to as the *Rules* for short.

5 Later in the *Rules* (p. 76), Durkheim allows that everyday concepts may be permitted to play a heuristic role in the location of phenomena for sociological concern. He stresses (more mildly) that we cannot assume their theoretical utility in advance of observation of the world.

6 This is one of the things argued for by Winch, 1956 and 1958; See also Taylor, 1971. To say that, in general, the observer must employ the concepts used by the person observed is to put things somewhat roughly. Some roughness need not trouble us here, but it may be useful to amplify the point in a note. In discussion below I refer to a child who is looking for a goblin. Now, assume that 'goblin' is a natural kind term, purporting to refer to a certain unusual type of creature. Kripke and Putnam have argued that in the case of genuine natural kind terms of a standard type, the qualities popularly associated with the term need not be either necessary or sufficient for an object to fall under the term, and hence cannot be thought of as defining the associated concept (see Kripke, 1980, and Putnam,

446

1975). Rather, the extension of the term is importantly related to certain crucial examples to which the term applies. Kripke has argued that, in the absence of such examples, not only is 'goblin' empty, but we cannot really say what goblins would have been. (See Kripke, 1980, remarks on unicorns, pp. 24, 156–8. There is a longer discussion in his 1973 ms.) At the same time, Kripke would not dispute that, in *some* appropriate sense, an observer may know what a child is doing when the child says he is 'looking for a goblin', and that to know what this is one must know what features are associated with goblins, something like what Putnam calls the 'stereotype' which is not, strictly speaking, the *concept* associated with the term. It should be stressed that, even according to Kripke, not all empty terms or phrases have this special logic – for example, 'ancient Greek scientist who knew modern superstring theory' is a reasonably determinate concept that happens to be empty. Though there were no such people, we know what such a person would have been, and in describing a deluded historian of science as looking for an instantiating example we really do employ the concept itself in a straightforward way. (I thank Saul Kripke for discussion of this issue.)

7 The quotations from *Economy and Society* in this section are from Weber, 1964, pp. 101-2.

8 Gerth and Mills, 1946, p. 55, translation from Weber, 1907 (p. 415).

9 Weber's idea that the sociologist will largely deal in so-called 'ideal types' may seem to go against the idea that realism is basic for him. This obviously depends on the precise import of Weber's doctrine of ideal types, which I cannot enter into in any detail here. Briefly, I do not think that Weber's notion of the 'ideal' was antithetical to the real. I believe Weber would allow that (1) things in the world could in principle conform exactly to an ideal type, while (2) most would not conform exactly but only partially. The ideal type was important precisely because of the messiness of reality, and the necessity, in effect, to think in terms of broad patterns and 'typical' cases if one was to explain anything. Thus one might define a 'bureaucrat', say, in terms of ten criteria (cf. Weber, 1964, pp. 333-4). In principle, there could be individuals who satisfied all ten criteria. Meanwhile, some actual individuals might satisfy most but not all of them. One would none the less expect their histories to bear some analogy to that of the 'ideal-typical' individual, and therefore to one another's lives. In this way ideal types could help us in our dealings with a wide range of material. In the context of such a doctrine, Weber could reject the idea of a 'collective personality which acts', for example, primarily on the grounds that there could be no such thing – a view he seems to have held. In addition, were an addition needed, the idea that something might 'approximate to' being a collective personality would presumably not seem very plausible to one who thought that there could be no such thing as a collective personality.

10 Weber, 1964, p. 102; Durkheim, 1982, p. 52; other examples include Homans, 1951, p. 1; Levy, 1952, p. 20; Pettit, 1980, p. 2.

11 Social scientists and others have, of course, given general character-

izations of a collectivity or social system. These characterizations often appear to be reflections of an intuitive concept. I shall consider some of these in what follows. Some accounts resemble my own in important ways. But I do not know of one which makes precisely the same articulations. In this area the detail is of great importance.

12 Such uses of 'his' and cognate terms are of course intended generically.

II 'SOCIAL ACTION' AND THE SUBJECT MATTER OF SOCIAL SCIENCE

1 Unless otherwise noted, page references to *Economy and Society* that follow are to Weber, 1964 (Parsons and Henderson's edition of Part 1).

2 See for instance Sprott, 1954, *Science and Social Action*; Douglas, 1967, ch. 13: 'Social actions as meaningful actions'; Skinner, 1972, '"Social meaning" and the explanation of social action'; Hollis, 1977, *Models of Man: Philosophical Thoughts On Social Action*.

3 A similar phrase 'social behaviour' also lacks any definitive meaning. I am certain that not everyone who uses this phrase agrees, for instance, with Homans's definition in *Social Behavior: Its Elementary Forms*, 1951, p. 2: 'the behavior must be social, which means that when a person acts in a certain way, he is at least rewarded or punished by the behavior of another person.'

4 Sometimes authors may erroneously believe that they use Weber's phrase in the sense in which he used it, for it is often misreported. See Inkeles, 1964, p. 7, for example. I have found it quite common for people to cite Weber's definition of 'action' *simpliciter*, when asked for his definition of '*social* action'.

5 For instance, Flew, 1985.

6 Cf. for instance, Douglas, op. cit.

7 See, for example, Parsons, op.cit., and in the article 'The role of ideas in social action', 1938. Weber himself does this also, which may account for some of the misreporting of his notion just noted. He, at least, does give an explicit definition of 'social action' so we know what he is supposed to mean by it.

8 Some philosophers have formulated arguments to the effect that all intentional action as such is social. I argue against such a conclusion in the next chapter. In any case, in advance of persuasion by such an argument one would surely suppose that actions as such do not have to have something social about them.

9 Cf. Weber, op. cit. pp. 124-30, on action oriented to a belief in the existence of a 'legitimate order'.

10 Regarding the thoughts of the agent, we may suppose that in cases of 'in order to' motives there will be a *belief* linking intended act and aim, the belief that chopping wood is the, or at least, a means of gaining a wage. Or, more generally, a belief of the form 'doing so and so is a means of achieving goal G' (and similarly for 'motives for

motives', and so on). Citation of such a belief of the agent will, in so far as it is citation of a component in reasoning which led to the action, contribute to an explanation of the action. A question which may be raised, and which is not as far as I know clearly answered by Weber, is whether such 'means–end' beliefs are part of the *meaning* of the action in question. I think this issue need not trouble us here. We are primarily concerned with the concept of *social* action, and whether an act is 'social' or not, in Weber's sense, is indeed, as must be stressed, a matter of its meaning's content, but the 'means–end' beliefs just referred to may be assumed to have a virtually unchanging content, except in so far as the other aspects of meaning (e.g. aim, motives) which we have noted, vary. What is more, this virtually unvarying content will not by itself make an action social. So whether we allow these beliefs to be part of an action's meaning or not, will not alter the 'socialness' or otherwise of any action.

11 Cf. James, 1984, who argues that one should be willing to question our 'prevailing intuitions about ourselves as agents' (p. 70) in the presence of certain doctrines of holistic explanation. In contrast to James, see Simon, 1982, for instance, who argues for the centrality of the concept of intentional action in the human sciences. It seems to me that if we question the assumptions I have just noted, at least, we might as well stop talking (and writing) to each other. If the powerfulness of intentional states is incompatible with certain doctrines, too bad for the doctrines. But I can waive appeal to my own sense of the matter here.

12 'Some categories of interpretive sociology', 1913, reprinted as Appendix 1 to *Economy and Society*, 1978, p. 1376. (I shall refer to this in what follows as the *Logos* essay, giving references to that edition.)

Parsons translates '*Verhalten*' as 'attitudes and actions'. In an editorial comment at pp. 88-9 of Weber, 1964, he contrasts *Verhalten* with *Handeln* (which he translates as 'action') as follows: '*Verhalten* is the broader term referring to any mode of behavior of human individuals, regardless of the frame of reference in which it is analyzed . . . *Handeln*, on the other hand, refers to the concrete phenomenon of human behavior only insofar as it is capable of "understanding" in terms of subjective categories.'

13 Cf. Weber's *Logos* essay, p. 1376. 'Empirically fluid is the transition from the ideal type of a meaningful relationship between one's own action and that of others to the case in which another person is merely an object (for example, an infant)'. When Weber writes of the 'empirical fluidity' between two types of case, I take him to mean, as he usually does, that the case at the 'other end' is not a case of the thing being defined or for which an 'ideal type' is being characterized (social action, in this instance).

Schutz, 1972, adopts as his starting point a concept similar to that I attribute to Weber, though he, following Sander, 1925, sees this as a refinement on Weber since 'We are leaving out of account intentional acts directed only to the other person's body as a physical object

rather than a field of expression for his subjective experiences'
(p. 144). It is clearly somewhat moot exactly what restrictions Weber
intended for his concept of social action. This is, equally clearly, in
part because he was clearly aware of, and at different times inclined
towards, a variety of different ways of drawing the boundary of his
concept (see below).

14 Even in *Economy and Society* some tension seems to have remained
in Weber's thinking. See his comments on *social relationships*. His
definition of 'social relationship', meanwhile, uses the (presumably
unrefined) concept of social action. I quote this definition and briefly
discuss it below.

15 See pp. 113-14. The classic discussion of crowds was that of Gustave
LeBon, *The Crowd*, to which Weber refers. What precisely goes on
in crowds is of course to some extent an empirical matter. (I say 'to
some extent' since the concept of a crowd may involve certain
constraints on what goes on.) Durkheim's initial instinct, in the first
edition of the *Rules*, was to treat 'crowd phenomena' as social
phenomena.

16 See p. 114. The reference to imitation occurs in response to
sociologist Gabriel Tarde's claim that imitation was the fundamental
social phenomenon (Durkheim stresses the difference between
himself and Tarde, in the *Rules* (1982, p. 59)).

17 The quoted phrase is from Weber's *Logos* essay, p. 1377.

18. In this essay Weber used the term *Gemeinschaftshandeln* with the
same definition as that later given to *Soziales Handeln*, standardly
translated as 'social action'. In *Economy and Society* Weber drops the
term *Gemeinschaftshandeln*. (On the change, see Roth's introduction
to *Economy and Society*, p. CII.)

19 Cf. the very general account of social phenomena as 'interorganism
behavior regularities' in Wallace, 1983.

20 In so far as there is a compelling logical argument from the existence
of a single *intention* to the existence of two or more persons, the
existence of a social action would of course logically entail that there
were at least two persons. I know of no such argument. See Chapter
III below.

21 See Nagel, 1961, p. 273: 'the subject matter of the social sciences is
frequently identified as purposive human action, directed to attaining
various ends or values.'

22 I have slightly altered Parsons's translation of the following passage
at the suggestion of F. H. Stewart.

23 Weber builds up more formal accounts of such concepts (like that of
a 'corporate group' on p. 145) on the basis of the complex notion of a
social relationship (p. 118). 'The term "social relationship" will be
used to denote the behaviour of a plurality of actors in so far as, in its
meaningful content, the action of each takes account of the others
and is oriented in these terms. The social relationship thus *consists*
entirely and exclusively in the existence of a *probability* that there
will be, in some meaningfully understandable sense, a course of social
action.' With regard to its facilitation of the analysis of intuitive
collectivity concepts, this notion can be criticized along the lines that

I criticize Weber's notion of social action, My discussion of the case involving 'demonstrative social actions', below, will be most relevant here.

As with the *Logos* definition and discussion of social action, Weber's notes to his definition of *social relationship* in *Economy and Society* suggest that a more restrictive definition might have served his own intuitions about central cases better. However, it is not my brief here to try to say what Weber 'really meant' or how he 'should have defined' social relationship. (I could argue that Weber should have defined 'social action' and 'social relationship' so as to bring them more closely into line with the accounts of everyday collectivity concepts that I shall give in subsequent chapters. There is even some reason to believe that this would not have gone totally against the grain of his own thought. However, in discussing Weber here I prefer to stick closely to his official definitions and positions.)

24 I owe the idea for this example to Raymond Geuss (personal communication).

25 It may, of course, constitute a population of some interest to demographers or to other investigators; neither possibility implies that it is, intuitively, a social group. See Chapter I.

26 Clearly, additional stipulations about the case could alter the picture. Suppose we were to stipulate that these people were originally at least members of a close-knit society, but hostility grew among them so that they unanimously agreed to fight it out, person to person, to the death. Against such a background we might judge (perhaps given further assumptions) that people formed some sort of social unit still. Evidently a given society or social group will often accommodate quite high degrees of hostility and conflict among its members. Without any such background, however, the people in this model need not together constitute a collectivity, intuitively.

27 Cf. Sander, 1925. I first looked at this thoughtful article some time after formulating my own critique of Weber's social action notion in relation to the everyday concept of a collectivity. Sander's approach to Weber's concept is quite similar to mine, and I find his criticisms congenial. He asks what one or both of two people have to do in order to form a *Kollectivum*. He starts with one person simply noticing the other's presence, and then goes through a number of examples of possible types of action on one or both persons' parts. His aim is both criticism of Weber's concept of social action and presentation of a positive thesis, using a refinement of that concept. In so far as I understand it, his positive view is, very roughly, that a pair of acts constituting successful communication of a Gricean kind gives us a collectivity. (He gets very close to Grice's model of speaker meaning. See H. P. Grice, 1957, 1969.) Having rejected Weber's official social action concept as a collectivity-theoretic tool for the reasons stated in this chapter, my own approach is to look at the question of collectivities from a different point of view, not attempting to refine Weber's concept further for the purpose. (See Chapter Four, below.) I thank Axel Buhler for discussion of Sander's article.

28 See in particular Chapter III, sec. 6, Chapter IV, and Chapter VI.

29 I argued this point about communication versus regular use in a paper presented to my philosophy of social science seminar, given jointly with Rom Harré, at Oxford University, Trinity Term, 1972. More recently Donald Davidson, 1982, has argued along similar lines. More specifically, he argues that *convention* is not necessary to communication, construing convention along the lines of Lewis, 1969, as a *regularity* in behaviour in a population. Our differences are largely terminological, I think. (I myself do not think there is a vernacular sense of convention, in which conventions are regularities. I would argue, meanwhile, that all language use does involve an element of convention, but not 'convention' in the sense of 'regularity of a certain sort'. See my 1983a, 1983b, and Chapter VI below.)

30 See Chapters V and VI, in particular the discussions of the 'causal' version of the summative view of collective belief, and discussion of Lewisian conventions.

31 Cf. Weber: 'A "state" for example, ceases to exist in a sociologically relevant sense whenever there is no longer a probability that certain kinds of meaningfully oriented social action will take place' (p. 118).

32 I do not want to rule out the possibility of a necessary condition which is illuminating though still not a *sufficient* condition. This is why I do not here simply say that a condition which is necessary but not also sufficient is not illuminating. Perhaps some necessary conditions might be enough to rule out clear noncollectivities. Possibly some set-ups in which animals coexist conform to such necessary conditions.

33 I return to the analysis of collectivity concepts in Chapter IV. When my own account of a collectivity has been given, the reader may judge whether I am in fact committed to W5. Suffice it to say that at that point it should be clear that W5 is a red herring in relation to the analysis of our vernacular collectivity concepts.

34 Douglas, 1967, p. xiii.

35 Cf. Durkheim, 1951, p. 46.

36 See Douglas, op. cit.

37 Durkheim's definition of suicide (1951, p. 44) has been criticized by Winch (1958, p. 111) and MacIntyre (1967, p. 107) among others. For a defence of Durkheim see Bryant, 1970, p. 100.

38 In Chapter V I say more about Durkheim's conception of social facts in general.

39 In *Suicide*, Durkheim discusses and rejects this explanation, which had been mooted by some criminologists, before adducing his own.

40 See the next section.

41 See, e.g. Hempel, 1965, sec. 5.

42 Dahrendorf, 1963, p. 159. I thank Frank Stewart for the reference and translation.

43 I was inclined to think I could take it as a datum that actions social in Weber's sense were social phenomena intuitively, and that any theory of the intuitive concept of a social phenomenon must therefore take this into account. I was definitely influenced by Weber's and his

followers' use of the label 'social action' for his concept. See Gilbert, 1978ms.

44 Recall that his original term for this concept was *Gemein-schaftshandeln*, which makes a presumed relation to collectivities quite clear. (Compare 'societal' versus 'social' in English.)

45 I would therefore argue that Wallace, 1983, is wrong to criticize Weber's dismissal of this case. See Gilbert, 1987.

III ACTION, MEANING, AND THE SOCIAL

1 See section 2.2, below. This is ostensibly a stronger thesis than the correlative thesis about language. Of course, if one assumed that the possession of a language was a logical precondition of thought and intention, one would presumably think this thesis followed from the correlative thesis about language, and so was not in fact a stronger thesis.

2 This phrase is used by Douglas, 1967, and Skinner, 1972, for instance. Another such phrase is 'shared meaning'. See Walzer, 1983. Doubtless these phrases themselves are susceptible of diverse interpretations. The term 'shared' in particular seems to allow for both a quite thin sense (a shared meaning is one two or more people individually express or possess or whatever) and for thicker, more complex senses. My discussion of the nature of a group language at the end of this chapter will in effect be an exploration of a *thick* sense of 'social meaning' or 'shared meaning'. See also Chapter Six, sec. 8.3, especially sec. 8.3.ii.

3 Cf. Geertz, 1973. What Geertz says there suggests he thinks 'meaning' in general is a matter of something like social convention.

4 For a further comment on this type of fact see sec. 5, below.

5 See the chapter entitled: 'Why not ask them?' in Harré and Secord, 1972.

6 Winch stresses a methodological point of this general sort when he says that the relation of the sociologist of religion, say, to the performers of religious activity 'cannot be just that of observer to observed. It must rather be analogous to the participation of the natural scientist with his fellow-workers' (1958, pp. 87–8). Winch evidently has in mind something like the need to 'know what religion is all about' whatever precisely that entails – possibly having been a participant in community religious practices.

7 See Nagel, 1961, p. 273, quoted here at Chapter II, p. 250.

8 All references to Winch's work in this chapter are to this book.

9 Winch gives it as an example of behaviour which is not rule-governed, p. 53. Since for Winch all meaningful action is rule-governed, one assumes that the behaviour will not in his eyes be meaningful. As MacIntyre (1967, p. 107) notes, it appears to be Winch's only example of non-rule-governed behaviour.

10 That is, as if 'acting in a way involving the participant in the observance of rules' (p. 52) is equated with 'having reasons for acting

as he does' (p. 53). If this were so, then, it seems, acting meaningfully would have to be doing something for a particular reason.

11 It has been a matter of debate whether the possession of a concept in some way entails the possession of a language. If it did, it might entail that we could not ascribe concepts to nonhuman animals, infant humans, and others – depending on where the boundaries of *language* lie. This might not worry Winch, who indicates that he thinks of meaningful behaviour as 'specifically human' (op. cit., p. 52). The point made in the text is independent of this issue.

12 A caveat: in discussion of his 'sociolinguistic' hypothesis of a 'division of linguistic labor' (1975), Hilary Putnam suggests that one can mean what is meant by a term in one's language, without having the relevant concept. I say more about the general idea of a division of linguistic labour in my discussion of the languages of groups in the last section of this chapter. Here let me just say that it appears that one who utters words which have a decided meaning in his group's language is not necessarily himself *using those words in any sense*, in the sense at issue here. Rather, he may simply intend to be taken in whatever sense is appropriate. (See especially section 6.4 below.)

13 Sherif and Sherif, 1956, p. 456, quoted at Winch p. 44.

14 I use the phrase 'general concept' with respect to concepts which are applicable to many different things. Thus action concepts such as those of eating, talking, getting hold of something, and so on, are general concepts, applicable to many different agents. The subjective meaning of an action will presumably always involve some general concepts of types of action. The point about concepts just made is in fact more general. It can be seen to apply also to what may be called 'particular concepts' (or, more perspicuously, concepts of particulars) such as the concept of Bertrand Russell as expressed by the use of his name, or the concept of the Zuni tribe. Concepts of particular persons or populations are not applicable to different things but only to the particular in question. They are, however, reapplicable over time. (Whatever concepts are expressed by Russell's 'logically proper names', these are special in not, by definition, applying at more than one instant in time.) However, we could in principle limit our discussion to general concepts here in so far as these are always involved in action. If the possession of a general concept presupposes membership in a society, then so will action.

15 The thesis will apply to all terms which can be counted expressive of concepts (see the previous note).

16 The above points recall the report of Wittgenstein's remarks in Moore, 1954, p. 7: 'One point on which he insisted several times . . . was that if a word which I use is to have meaning I must "commit" myself by its use. And he explained what he meant by this by saying "If I commit myself, that means that if I use e.g. 'green' in this case, I have to use it in others", adding, "If you commit yourself there are consequences."' Whatever Wittgenstein had in mind, his words go quite well with the rule thesis as explicated above. It is possible that

Winch had these remarks in mind when he made his point about the future relatedness of sense, quoted above.

17 I shall in fact argue later that not only do natural and vernacular ways of talking seem to suggest that concepts are 'real objects' of some kind, but even given any amount of neutral rephrasing, the best way to sustain the rule thesis is in terms of an ontology in which concepts are a type of real object. By 'the best way', I mean the only way that can be argued to have any philosophical viability.

18 One who has become sensitive to this issue may see a shift – or possible shift – within the quotations just made in the previous paragraph. From a question about 'what is meant by saying . . .', Winch shifts to a question about 'What is it about my utterance of the words "Mount Everest" which makes it possible to say that. . . .' This latter is rather a cumbersome statement, and one could wonder why anyone would put things precisely thus. However, with no special reasons to note subtle changes of language, most readers would probably take the cumbersome formulation to be asking the question about language which most closely parallels the initial question about thought – as a question, that is, about what is meant by saying that someone means something by his words. (As will emerge, Kripke's account of what Wittgenstein is up to suggests that Winch's tendency to mix the apparently rather distinct ways of talking of the kinds at issue here is traceable to the existence in Wittgenstein's thought of a sceptical argument to which Winch fails to give any special explicit attention.)

19 The issue of following a rule – in particular following *a given rule* on *many* occasions – becomes clearly important in the light of the 'sceptical' interpretation of Wittgenstein that Kripke articulates. What I have just said applies to how things look if we start with the idea of saying as much as possible about what it is to have a language, without special doubts about problems inherent in that enterprise.

20 See Winch, p. 29. Winch writes of any 'series of actions'.

21 Examples of complex predicates involving dates in this way were introduced into the philosophical literature by Goodman, 1973, especially pp. 72–81. Kripke, 1982, connects Wittgenstein and Goodman, see p. 20, pp. 58–9.

22 Winch does not make anything of his references to *saying* as opposed to believing or concluding, so I shall not read anything special into his locutions here. It is natural enough to construe him as intending a claim about justified belief, whether expressed or not. Possibly he takes it that all belief is 'said', in one's heart if not aloud. Or perhaps he has another reason for this language that is not spelled out. His restricted language here does read somewhat oddly and seem to call for an explanation. A quotation Winch gives from Wittgenstein also refers to what 'we would say', as if for some reason what is at issue is precisely what we would *say* rather than what we would judge, and so on. Kripke gives a context to such remarks in Wittgenstein, see below. In discussing Winch, meanwhile, I shall not try to read any special emphasis into the references to saying, since the text does not warrant any.

23 All references to Wittgenstein in this chapter are to this work. Where appropriate I give section numbers only (for the numbered sections in Part 1). Otherwise I give page numbers.

24 As Saul Kripke pointed out to me, according to Bertrand Russell, thesis (1) above would be false for Russell's 'logically proper names', which refer to momentary, non-recurring mental particulars, thus referring to something that no one else can have the right kind of access to. We do not take our everyday language of sensation types to be like this. Russell's is, evidently, a very special kind of language.

Kripke also suggested that Wittgenstein himself may have taken it that the meanings of the words of a hypothetical 'private' language in which one purports to refer to a certain type of sensation without behavioural correlates would be intrinsically unshareable, that is, that no one else could *have that language.* This presumably could not fail to encourage the view that such a private language was impossible. But this view surely contradicts what we would think at first blush, and certainly cannot be assumed as intuitively evident: rather, I have suggested, the contrary will be the natural assumption.

25 The nub of claims (1) and (2) may in fact be expressible in terms which do not mention individual people at all, as follows: (0) *Concepts (or meanings) are objective particulars.* Given that something is an objective particular, it would seem that it must be, as it were, 'open to all', provided that they have the requisite capacities and experiences, if any. Someone might object to (0) as begging the question in favour of platonism, and so perhaps as beginning to move away from 'prephilosophical' intuition. However, I suspect that whether any form of platonism about concepts is philosophically viable, a form of platonism accords well with intuitive understandings. I do not, of course, claim that any nonphilosopher you ask will say 'of course concepts are objective particulars' but that a view so expressible is naturally inferred from ordinary modes of thought and talk. I say more later about the way a form of platonism seems to accord with our intuitive understanding of what meaning is. There is no need to couch the discussion in terms of (0) at this point.

26 I have in mind such logical possibilities as one's being in touch with a machine that generally provides accurate information about the world. If the machine has proved reliable in the past, and it indicates that Jones has grasped sense S, then, arguably, I have reasonable grounds for thinking it correct. It seems I could then be said to have discovered, or to know, that Jones has grasped sense S.

27 One reason I have given Stella two types of ache is that it seems plausible that she might then want two special tags to help her record her phenomenological history. 'Ache' or 'that ache' might do if she only had one type of ache.

28 This is so at least if one is using the notion of 'sharing a concept' that is implicit in a plausible condition of meaning-shareability. (Distinct, thicker notions of shared meaning are possible; but these notions are not at issue here.)

29 Cf. Wittgenstein, sec. 358, where the interlocutor exclaims that

surely 'meaning' something by a word is what gives language sense, and is 'something in the sphere of the mind'.

30 See, for instance, Linsky, 1957, in Fann, (ed.), 1967, pp. 171-4; Pitcher, 1964, pp. 294–7. I say that the argument is seen as 'relatively' self-contained because some expositors address certain issues about the possible utility of memory, citing Wittgenstein, sec. 265. These discussions of memory, however, are not obviously relevant, at least as usually presented, to the thrust of the argument I consider in this section. I shall therefore not address them here.

31 See, for instance K.T. Fann, 1969, pp. 76–7. In these pages Fann closely echoes those parts of Winch's exposition that I focus on here.

32 Sec. 258. (I quote and discuss this passage below, at page 125.)

33 On Kripke's reading of Wittgenstein – which I discuss at length below – it is not so regarded.

34 The quotation is from Ayer, 1954, p. 70; see also Strawson, 1954.

35 Arguments such as those of Stich, 1971, for instance, could be addressed in a longer discussion. (Stich himself is concerned with syntactic rather than semantic knowledge.) Quite generally, I believe that proposed counterexamples to the content certainty thesis can be met in such a way as to leave what is true and important about the thesis intact. But I cannot go into this further here.

36 Winch may feel that what he has already said explains what the flaw in the picture is, at the point at which he responds to Ayer and Strawson. But he has not examined what from an intuitive point of view seems to be the nub of the issue – the intrinsic coherence of something like the natural view as characterized here – but rather skirts it (particularly within his second paragraph, p. 26).

37 All page references to Kripke in this chapter are to this book.

38 I thank Saul Kripke for discussing with me his interpretation of Wittgenstein. He should not, of course, be held responsible for the details of my exposition.

39 An account in terms of the *natural kind* this is, for some ostensions at least, seems wrong. Mustn't the fact that a given term does indeed refer to a natural kind – that it is a 'natural kind term' – be a part of its sense?

40 See Kripke, pp. 51ff.

41 See Kripke, p. 53. Kripke refers to Wittgenstein, p. 218.

42 Kripke discusses in detail a number of problems for dispositional accounts of meaning, see Kripke, pp. 22–37. This type of account is currently quite popular. Meanwhile, it clearly diverges from our intuitive conception on a *number* of dimensions.

43 Use of the term therapy, due to Wittgenstein, seems quite apt in both cases. What each philosopher does is close to some of the processes attempted in psychotherapy. Consider the following fast-motion sequence: 'Why do you cling to the belief that all men are to be feared? Because one man early in your life acted aggressively towards you. You are projecting your fear of him on to all men and are wrongly assuming your fears are properly based on your experiences of men in general. Now you realize that your beliefs about all men

are not properly based on your experience of them, and hence not properly based at all, you will (hopefully) be able to give up these beliefs, and proportion your beliefs about men to the evidence.' This may seem closest of all to Hume, who argued quite explicitly that we project an inner compulsion to expect event B after event A, having noticed their constant conjunction so far, on to the events themselves, so that we see A as necessitating B by 'natural necessity'. Meanwhile our experience of the events themselves gives us no warrant to speak of 'natural necessity'. In Wittgenstein's case, projection may be argued to come in as follows: certain vivid experiences are associated with language learning ('Now I know how to go on!'); we illegitimately transfer the power of our reactions to the experiences themselves, endowing them with the power to determine how we are to go on.

44 Cf. Kripke, p. 62, on 'Wittgenstein's main problem'.

45 The phrase quoted is in a passage from Wittgenstein (sec. 237) quoted by Winch at pp. 31–2.

46 Though see section 6 below, on group languages, regarding what seems necessary for a really high degree of confidence.

47 One might perhaps explain its possibility by reference to the very naturalness of the natural view. But then the question about the possibility of our language game arises again in a new guise: what makes the natural view so natural (granted it is at the same time so suspect)? In effect, Wittgenstein addresses this question also, as I have already indicated. It is obviously a good question.

48 Compare the simple or 'primitive' language games Wittgenstein describes in the early sections of *Philosophical Investigations*.

49 Of course for the natural view tallying reactions will be explained in terms of sameness of meaning rather than serving as the ultimate explanation of our talk of 'sameness of meaning'.

50 See the long note, fn. 83, pp. 102–4. Kripke's explicit references are to pt. 1, secs. 244 and 256–7.

51 I say more about this later, in section 4.5 below.

52 According to this weaker doctrine pure sensation terms can only be ascribed to one who is already an accredited user of terms for sensations that do have an appropriate behavioural correlate. If this is our way of proceeding, we still can be said to accept the condition that it is never the case for any speaker that whatever he calls 'right' is right. For anyone we allow to be the user of a pure sensation term must first have passed certain stringent tests.

53 Assuming that such uses themselves occurred only in the presence of the sensation in question. This may be presumed to follow from the definition of a pure sensation term.

It seems plausible to claim that something is assertable *now* only if in our current general circumstances we could get to be in a position to tell that the assertability conditions are satisfied. It will then be beside the point to suggest here that, if there are distinctive brain correlates of different types of sensation, then every type of sensation could in principle acquire its own broadly speaking 'behavioural' correlate accessible to all – a running neurological 'printout' of some kind, perhaps. Obviously distinctive brain correlates themselves, to the extent that there are such, cannot serve the present purpose, at least as long as they are hidden away inside a given person's brain.

54 Penny could be an accredited user of sensation terms already, and honestly say she has had the right sort of 'Got it!' experience, and so on, in relation to a putative pure sensation term. This does not seem to be enough to satisfy the assertability condition in question.

55 At note 85, p. 110, Kripke notes that 'If Wittgenstein would have any problem with Crusoe, perhaps the problem would be whether we have any "right" to take him into our community in this way.' Kripke refers to Wittgenstein, secs. 199–200, where Wittgenstein discusses a 'somewhat similar question'. There Wittgenstein asks, 'Should we still be inclined to say they were playing a game? What right would one have to say so?'

56 See Kripke, p. 52, for example.

57 Benacerraf, 1962, argues that logical impossibility has not been proved here.

58 The question, whether there can be infinite abstract objects, is one to which most practising mathematicians, at least, would give a positive answer with no qualms. The sequence of natural numbers is infinite. There is a simple proof that this is so, from the definition of natural number. It is not the place here to go further into the issue of the existence of infinite objects. (One might question whether an object with an infinity of normative implications has to be thought of as an 'infinite object'. I shall not pursue this issue here, since infinite abstract objects will not be adversely regarded.)

59 One of the unquestioned assumptions of transformational generative grammarians in the tradition of Chomsky has been that since a language (an abstract object) contains an infinite set of sentences, and our minds (brains?) are finite, we must contain finite grammars which can generate an infinity of sentences. But it may be questioned whether a human's knowledge of the grammar of a language must be a matter of knowing something finite rather than infinite.

60 See p. 52. 'Can we conceive of a finite state which *could* not be interpreted in a quus-like way?' (The quus function, invented by Kripke, is subtly different from the addition function, see below.) In spite of the reference to finitude here, the basic problem alluded to seems to be interpretability. See Kripke's note 34.

61 Cf. Wittgenstein, sec. 432, 'Every sign by itself seems dead.'

62 McGinn, 1984, pp. 98–101, echoes Kripke closely in his discussion of this issue.

63 This model has been discussed (sceptically) in Benacerraf, 1973, and (less sceptically – in discussion of Benacerraf) in Steiner, 1973. These authors are largely concerned with the supposed problem for platonism to be found in the assumption that we know and perceive as a result of some sort of causal commerce with the thing known, a problem I shall not discuss here. Both authors cite the great mathematician Kurt Gödel as a distinguished proponent of the view

that abstract objects are perceived. (Godel writes: 'we do have something like a perception also of the objects of set theory', 1964, pp. 271–2.)

64 I waive questions about the phenomenon of 'blindsight' here. The implications of this phenomenon are not entirely clear. People with blindsight do not, apparently, have the subjective experiences appropriate to perceiving, yet given certain criteria they could be held to be perceiving certain things. (Their behaviour may accord with the idea that they perceive a certain object, for instance.)

65 Is there a problem for the notion of concept perception in the fact that there are no organs of concept perception? (I believe that this has been argued by Elizabeth Anscombe.) I do not see that anything forces us to find a devastating problem in terms of our purposes here. First, maybe there do not have to be organs of perception in order for there to be perception, or some sufficiently close analogue to perception for our purposes here. There could be a process importantly analogous to the perception of physical things, which does not involve anything we would call physical organs of perception. Second, maybe there are organs of concept perception, but we do not know what they are: it might seem somewhat sensible to say this, if, say, it was found that humans with certain brain lesions could not learn to speak (that is probably so in fact) or even to think in very human ways. Finally, it could be argued that the stage at which we talk about organs is quite a late stage in the process of organizing the sensory data, so to speak, and that it is inessential to a basic notion of perception. One might allude to the following sort of picture of the way we think about physical object perception: there is all this buzzing sensible intuition and the thinking subject imposes the categories of physical external object and causality among objects in order to get things into shape. Part of the shape is one's own body and organs, and so on, part of the shape is the world other than that, and part of the shape is that one perceives the world via the organs situated in one's body. On the one hand, then, we have certain raw ('sensory') experiences which we take as the perception of physical things in space. On the other hand, we have raw meaning-experience (a special type of experience), and we take this as perception of concepts. The possibility of making this analogy suggests that there may be a general notion of perception which has nothing to do with having organs like eyes and ears. (Cf. the components of the Latin *per-cipio*.)

66 Kripke, p. 51. Cf. Alston, 1974, p. 29: 'the seductive picture of semantic facts involving a mysterious, sui generis kind of relation, connecting a linguistic element with an equally mysterious entity, its meaning'. Also see Putnam, 1978, p. 127: 'direct (and mysterious) grasp of Forms' (quoted and apparently endorsed in Millikan, 1986, p. 454).

67 I am not alone in so thinking. Since I came to this conclusion, two reviewers of Kripke's book have expressed a sense that a broadly speaking platonist conception of meaning may survive the scepticism

Kripke outlines. See Loar, 1985, and, especially, Feldman, 1986. (The form of platonism I defend here is somewhat different from that Feldman considers.)

68 There's a passage by A. A. Milne in which a character is trying to describe something he's just seen. The description goes something like this 'It was – like an elephant, like a jar, like a great big NOTHING.' Marvellously tantalizing. What on earth was it that he saw?

69 The fact that wuzziness is supposedly the quality of a *sensation* does not mean that 'wuzzy' is not a 'pure sensation term' in the sense at issue here. I am taking it that the central condition for being such a term is that there be no *distinctive* behavioural correlate associated with the relevant type of sensation. It is true that once they accept that 'wuzzy' names a sensation quality Sue's hearers have some ability to check her use of the term. For instance, if she says 'There's a big wuzzy bear over there' they may conclude something is wrong. But obviously this does not get them all the way they need to go. (If Sue supposedly used 'skuzzy' as the name of another type of sensation without its own 'individualized' behavioural correlates, others would be completely at a loss to differentiate between 'skuzzy' and 'wuzzy' sensations. Meanwhile, were Sue confidently to maintain that the two kinds of sensations were quite different, we should normally be content with her say-so.) I raise this issue with Wittgenstein, sec. 261, in mind ('What reason have we for calling "S" the sign for a *sensation?. .*').

70 I doubt, of course, whether it is really so very different in its fundamentals. One can feel that it is for various reasons incumbent upon one explicitly to deny something, while continuing to operate in terms of premises that imply that thing, in the course of one's life in general. (One could of course fail to be aware that this was so.)

71 If one were unaware of Wittgenstein's sceptical argument one might well wonder why assertability conditions were of much importance. Of course the argument provides a special motivation for the interest in assertability conditions regarding the 'meaning' game, in so far as supposedly intractable problems with the natural view suggest a motivation for concentrating on the 'use' of terms, rather than questions of meaning.

72 The quoted phrase is from *Webster's New Collegiate Dictionary,* (ed. Woolf, 1975).

73 Interestingly enough, each of these possibilities of confusion involves a possible slide in the same direction, since a strong meaning-identifiability condition for all terms appears to require outer criteria in at least the weak sense of 'outer correlate' for 'inner process' terms.

74 One well-known discussion is Albritton's regularly cited paper, 1956. Note the afterthought added when this was reprinted in Pitcher, ed., 1966. See also Strawson, 1954. Kripke does not, as he notes, 'enter into the finer exegetical points involved in Wittgenstein's notion of a criterion' (p. 99).

75 Wittgenstein, sec. 242.
76 Cf. McGinn, 1984, p. 89. McGinn's explanation of what it is to 'share a language' has it to be such that it would not necessarily enable seriously intended communication. Sharing a language in his sense certainly does not require behavioural criteria intuitively. Similarly, it only seems to require agreement in judgments in the trivial sense that those with the same language are indeed equipped to make the same judgments, all else being equal. Meanwhile McGinn seems to think that (a) communication requires a shared language, and (b) a shared language involves 'agreement in judgments' in some more than trivial way.
77 I say more about the notion of having a joint project, or sharing in an action, in the next chapter.
78 In Chapter VI, I discuss a more general class of situations into which the n-person problem of assigning the same meaning to a given term on a given occasion fits. I argue there that in general appeal to what happened last time – to precedent – is not going to be fruitful for free and rational agents in such situations.
79 Someone might question whether we could come to an *agreement* proper if we reached an understanding about what is to mean what by using such gestures and sounds alone. I would think that we could. What counts as an agreement strictly speaking is not altogether easy to pin down. (I discuss the nature of agreements as such briefly in Chapter VI, sec. 8.) But for present purposes this question is of only terminological interest. All that needs to be done can be done with gestures whose meaning has not been agreed upon. It can probably be done without anything that counts as an agreement strictly speaking. (Discussion in later chapters backs this up.) In any case, I see no harm in talking about both 'understandings' and 'agreements' in this section.
80 I shall not try carefully to specify the special status here.
81 Compare Wittgenstein, sec. 242: 'If language is to be a means of communication there must be agreement not only in definitions but also (queer as this may sound) in judgments' (p. 88e). It is striking how well this particular claim chimes in with my discussion here.
82 The general notion of a criterion could be broad enough to allow that what I have referred to as meaning-determining phenomena are criteria; in the case of sensations, however, the 'outward criteria' have a weaker relation to meaning, being as I have indicated. A criterion in general might then be thought of as 'meaning-determining to a greater or lesser degree'.
83 Putnam, 1975. See also Dummett, 1974. I make no attempt to review or discuss the literature on the 'division of linguistic labor' here, or to determine precisely what others have meant by such phrases.
84 There may be a rather general principle at work here, to the effect that if 'T' is to be a term in X's language, where X may be an individual or a group, there must be grounds of some appropriate type for claiming that X knows what 'T' means.
85 This perhaps accounts for my suspicion that it is possible to

understand a term (say, 'elephant') without being able to tell that a fairly good example of an elephant (in my idiolect) was an elephant. In so far as the fact of understanding the term is quite distinct from the fact of applying the term or the relevant concept to something experienced, it seems that it is logically possible to have a concept one lacks the capacity to apply in this way. (Thus it seems that one should distinguish, in principle, my not being able to apply a concept because I lack the concept in question, as in the case of 'emoting' referred to earlier, and the inability to apply a concept one possesses to experienced items.)

86 In using the word 'theorem' in this context I echo Kripke's discussion of Wittgenstein on 'criteria'. Kripke expounds what he takes to be Wittgenstein's overall assertability conditions approach to language first, and then explains how a kind of outward criteria doctrine falls out from it. (Criteria are probably not best described as *meaning-determining* in Kripke's account.) As noted above, I do not here dispute Kripke's interpretation of Wittgenstein in any way. He could be right about Wittgenstein, while I was right about group languages. In any case, the word 'theorem' is quite appropriate for present purposes.

IV SOCIAL GROUPS: A SIMMELIAN VIEW

1 Quotations here will be from the translation in Simmel 1971a.

2 These remarks were prompted by Raymond Geuss's comments on an earlier draft.

3 The case may look different given the consideration that, say, all those with this quality are openly stigmatized by those among whom they live, as in the case of Jewish people who live in openly anti-semitic populations, for example. Though I do not see the addition of open stigmatization as sufficient either, some phenomena which are likely concomitants of such stigmatization may be sufficient to bring a group into being. For instance, something like the mutually expressed intention to 'stand together' in the face of others' opprobrium, would, I think, be sufficient. The account I develop in this chapter accords with the intuition that it would be. (A remark of Jerome Shaffer's prompted this reference to the case of stigmatized populations.)

4 The remarks in this paragraph apply, *mutatis mutandis*, to the notions of a 'thing' and a 'whole' which appear to be equally capacious notions.

5 Nor would the addition that it was common knowledge – see below – that this was how each one viewed these people make them into such a group, intuitively speaking.

6 For instance Von Mises, 1949, p. 144 (quoted below at footnote 18). Von Mises seems not to believe that such things as feelings of sympathy and belonging together can be thought of as *producing or constituting* social relations. They are rather 'the fruits of social

cooperation'. Meanwhile, Weber's definition implies that a common orientation to the feeling in question is what is *constitutive* of a communal relationship, and that the question of any objective basis for the feeling is irrelevant to the existence of this sort of relationship.

7 In contemporary (or slightly past) common parlance someone might say that he and another 'belonged together' if he meant that they ought to live together in conjugal style. A sense that one belongs together with certain others in this sense is certainly too strong a condition on forming a social group with them. One can be a member of various groups without wanting to see the other members very often or having much interest in them personally.

The point about interest connects with another of major importance to the philosophy of politics. Writers often give the impression that societies as such are set up for the benefit of all. Yet it is clear that such purposes as members acknowledge as the purposes their group serves may have nothing to do with benefiting individual members, and members may have little concern to benefit either themselves or others in forming this particular group. (See Chapter VII, below, sec. 4.1, for more on this point.)

Weber sees 'communal social relationships' as just one kind of social relationship, to be contrasted with 'associative relationships'. In this he echoes Ferdinand Tönnies's *Gemeinschaft–Gesellschaft* distinction. (See Tönnies, *Gemeinschaft und Gesellschaft.*) He does not give the former kind of relationship a special pride of place, though he does speak of its elements being found everywhere, even in the context of (primarily) associative relationships.

8 Some recent writers have asserted or at least conjectured that there is no such thing as a belief. If beliefs do not exist, I grant that they cannot determine events in the real world. However, I suspect that those who claim to have some relation to the view that there are no beliefs have that same relation to the view that there are analogues of beliefs of some kind. I suppose, then, that they could be brought to have that relation to my views also, substituting 'belief-analogue' for 'belief' everywhere.

9 The idea that a pronoun can be used correctly or incorrectly should not in itself be puzzling. If a child says 'I am angry' when obviously intending to refer to his aunt by 'I', he is using the English pronoun 'I' incorrectly, that is, not in accordance with accepted English usage.

10 Quite a bit of work has been done on the semantics of pronouns in general. Perhaps best known among recent work is that of David Kaplan (see for instance 'Demonstratives' (ms)). The list of terms looked at in this area usually includes 'I' along with 'here', 'now', and others. But Kaplan, for instance, does not mention 'we'.

11 See for instance, Roderick Chisholm's book *The First Person*, 1981.

12 The *American Heritage Dictionary* (ed. Morris, 1969) reports the usage of 'I' as a noun, as meaning 'the self' or 'the ego'. What is a self, or an ego? Is thinking in terms of selves a matter of being misled by linguistic appearance into multiplying entities beyond necessity?

Clearly the temptation to think of one's self as an object whose existence is independent of the human body may be bolstered by desires to survive bodily destruction. This one could not do if one was one's body, or even if one was a body of a particular special kind, since presumably the kind could not survive the demolition of its substance. This one could perhaps do, however, if the self was a special thing existing in its own right. So there is some motivation from love of life (or fear of death) to believe in selves which are distinct from, and in no way mere modes of, body. There is also the thought that 'I' seems in some peculiar way to elude reference-failure. If 'I' necessarily refers to 'the thinker of this thought', and if all thoughts must have a thinker, then 'I exist' must be true, if thought. Then (it seems) there is a kind of thing (a thinker, subject of thoughts) whose existence can be known by any thinker, who may not know of any bodily facts. Hence logically speaking it is – apparently – possible that there be a thinker in the absence of body. Descartes argued along these lines. (That 'I' is immune to reference-failure has been challenged: see Evans, 1982; that I may necessarily be a body or dependent on a body for my existence, as a matter of metaphysical rather than logical necessity, is possible, given the conceptual tools provided by Kripke, 1980.)

13 The general line I shall take appears to accord somewhat with at least one lexicographer's opinion. The *American Heritage Dictionary* (ed. Morris, 1969) has as its first explanation of 'we': '1. Used to represent the speaker, and one or more others that share in the action of a verb.'

The *Oxford English Dictionary* (ed. Murray, 1971) has what could be taken to be a looser account: 'denoting the speaker and one or more other persons whom he associates with himself as the subject of the sentence'. Must the subject of a sentence 'share in the action of a verb'? Perhaps on some interpretations of the phrase that is so. In any case, I shall propose an account of the (or a) use of 'we' using in effect a rather strong sense of 'share in the action of a verb'.

14 Gilbert Harman reports that, in a comic strip, Superman once played tennis with himself, by flying over the net to return his own ball. Clearly a parasitic (extended ?) case. In any case, the claim that there are some action-terms in English such that one cannot be said to do A unless someone else did A with one is not crucial to anything I have to say here. The issue here is, rather, what it is for one person to do something with another, when this does happen.

15 Even when we have a term which connotes a necessarily partnered action, and a sentence with a plural subject, we do not imply that the people who are referred to by the subject term are partners in any action. It may be true that John and I are going to play tennis today, but we may not be about to play together. If John and I are going to play tennis, then he must play with someone other than himself, and I must play with someone other than myself, but we do not have to play with each other. Sentences of the kind in question can be disambiguated precisely by the addition of 'together' or 'with each other'.

16 In particular in the concluding chapter, where there is a general discussion of the types of reasoning associated with joint action.

17 I recall K. V. Wilkes once stressing, at a seminar we gave together at Oxford, *circa* 1972, that not only human beings could wash dishes, for example, but so could inanimate machines. I think the upshot intended for these and other examples was that washing dishes could not involve consciousness or intentionality – or *something* that human beings had while machines did not.

In any case, we certainly seem to refer to inanimate objects in terms of vocabulary also applied to intentional human behaviour. I suppose we would speak of robots raising their arms. Now, who is to say what is 'anthropomorphic' or an 'extended' use and what isn't? It may seem just too easy to speak of anthropomorphism or extension here. However, it surely can be argued that when we speak about humans (and perhaps some animals) we do make distinctions about what they are doing on the basis in part of their intentions. Is he raising his arm for fun? is he waving good-bye? is he producing a paradigm case of intentional action for some students of philosophy? That we draw distinctions in this way, by reference to intention and motive, suggests that there *is* a concept of doing which is a concept of intentional doing. Moreover, success conditions for such doing involve behaviour, and so the way is left clear for an extension or variant of the concept in terms of what is actually achieved behaviourally by a person or thing irrespective of intention – they are 'doing' what they would have counted as intentionally doing had they had a certain intention.

18 Cf. Von Mises, 1949, p. 144: 'Within the frame of social cooperation there can emerge . . . feelings of sympathy and friendship and a sense of belonging together. . . . These feelings . . . are not, as some have asserted, the agents that have brought about social relationships . . . they did not precede the establishment of such relationships.'

19 Someone asking 'What are you and X going to do?' could be taken to imply that he sees you and X as set up to do something together. (See below on how the idea that 'we' may refer to those who are set up to do things together conforms to my overall thesis.) The reply in terms of 'we' could be deferring to that representation of the situation, the use of 'we' itself carrying the implication that the two people are indeed so set up. I would suggest that when 'we' occurs in the answer we do tend to interpret it as 'we . . . together'. Such an interpretation could result in a wrong assumption about the facts, as might be brought out in a dialogue such as the following: 'Margaret and I are going to play tennis.' 'Together?!' (say Margaret is a much better player). 'No, of course not, with other people.'

20 Sec. 1170b25, 1985, p. 261.

21 This is not to say that paradigm cases of families do not generally 'share conversation and thought'. The question is, do the members see such sharing as their *aim*.

22 Cf. note 7, above, second paragraph.

23 These two perspectives – concern with functions which may not be mentally represented among the participants, and concern with those that are – can get mixed together. Cf. the discussion of families in Hoffman, 1981, p. 191. They involve quite different conceptual frameworks, however.

24 The context may not be sufficient. I owe to Martin Gilbert reference to outrage provoked by a government poster which, during the Second World War, attempted to enlist men with the words 'YOU CAN HELP US WIN THE WAR!' 'Us' was interpreted by some readers as exclusive.

25 Regarding the relation of 'you' to 'we', it may appear that in non-tendentious cases of the utterance of 'you' the addressee and addresser will be currently in the process of dialogue or verbal exchange, and will at least to that extent form a 'we' of sorts. However, to form a 'we' of sorts is not necessarily to be currently in the process of dialogue. It simply implies the logical propriety of the use of a certain possible pronoun, namely, an inclusive 'we', with respect to at least one person whom one could be in a position to refer to as 'you'.

26 Naturally what is counted as an especially intimate act will vary in different cultural contexts. In my discussion throughout I operate implicitly with a particular set of assumptions about my characters' cultural context. I do not see this procedure, which seems inevitable, as problematic. Regarding the notion of intimacy, I think there is something to the idea that sharing in any action whatsoever (in the strong sense of 'sharing' elaborated here) involves a degree of something we could call intimacy.

27 See Lewis, 1969, pp. 52–60, and 1975, p. 6; Schiffer, 1972, pp. 30–6; p. 131. Schiffer's term is 'mutual knowledge*'. In my ms. 1978, pp. 177–80, I criticize a number of the various accounts of common knowledge which have been proposed. See also Heal, 1978.

28 'Roughly' here indicates various issues connected with the notion of 'X would infer'. I count 'infer' here as having 'success-grammar'. One only *infers* p from q if q in fact follows from p. What follows from what is an objective matter. We are thus essentially talking here about what objective 'principles of inference' X has grasped, and *what they licence one to infer*. (I owe this sense of the nature of inference to Saul Kripke's graduate seminar on the nature of logic, Princeton, Fall 1974. I alone am responsible for the inferences I made from Kripke's talks.) Sometimes a mathematician 'creatively' proves an interesting theorem from well-known premises. It seems questionable whether one can give any nontrivial statement of conditions under which we all *would* have reached this theorem, given the inferential powers and concepts we already have. (That is, we may have to say something like: 'if we had been lucky enough to see it the way he did'.) In any case, the inferences which will be appealed to are entirely elementary.

29 See Schiffer, 1972; Lewis, 1975, Aumann, 1976. It is also usual to define 'common knowledge' in terms of the knowledge of the

ordinary participants rather than in terms of their smooth reasoner counterparts. In the idealized context of game theory, which in any case deals with smooth reasoners with maximally sophisticated mathematical reasoning powers, such a definition may be unexceptionable. (I discuss the conceptual framework of game theory more in Chapter VI.) Whether it is acceptable in other contexts is more of an issue. It depends a lot on when we allow ourselves to speak of (actual) knowledge. (See Schiffer, 1972; Gilbert, 1978, and Heal, 1978.)

30 But by the same token A', B', and C' will be able to infer that all the $Z(\alpha)$ obtains, and won't this start a new iteration too? Maybe so, but here we are getting close to the problems involved in the 'Burali–Forti' paradox. I take this not to vitiate the points made up to here.

It should be remarked that in the partition model of common knowledge used by Aumann, 1976, which has been widely used by subsequent game theorists as well, the property $Z(\omega)$ (in other words, the conjunction of all finite $Z(n)$) implies all the properties $Z(\alpha)$ for α greater than ω. More generally, the same thing holds for any model of common knowledge based on modal logic frames in (Kripke) 'relational' semantics. However, such an implication is not to be expected for all mathematical models of common knowledge (for example, even if we restrict ourselves to modal logic 'possible worlds' modellings, it would not hold in the 'neighbourhood' semantics). It is not clear to me that there is any intuitive reason why $Z(\omega)$ should imply the higher $Z(\alpha)$, and to the extent that it may not imply them, it would be desirable that a mathematical modelling should not prejudge the issue. In any case, whether the higher $Z(\alpha)$ are implied by the conjunction of the finite $Z(n)$ or not, it seems to be worth calling attention to them as significant properties of the intuitive situation that have not been discussed in the literature.

I thank Saul Kripke for advice on the set-theoretic formulation of my intuitive ideas and for the remarks on the properties of mathematical modellings of common knowledge.

31 This may not be strictly true for all cases. It depends on when one counts as 'having the concept'. Has one who hitherto lacked it, and then read and understood my definition, 'got the concept'? It seems that such a being, attempting mechanically to apply the definition to a situation he is in, may for a while at least not be sure whether or not it applies.

Evidently the kind of grasp of openness* I have in mind is the kind I presume normal humans to have, willy-nilly. If I am right, everyone possesses this concept, though most could not define it explicitly with any ease. I take such possession to go, generally, with the ability to apply the concept without hesitation when one is in a situation of openness*.

32 Note: given the power of assumptions (2) and (4), we can omit conditions (9) and (10) from a definition of paradigm situations: they follow from (2), (4), and (11). In the above discussion I wanted to

indicate that (11) is a reasonable condition, and this is presumably because we understand in advance that people have the concept of openness*, and so on.

33 See, for instance, Heal, 1978. See also (on the other side) Schiffer, 1972.

34 If they do not mean this they may be in trouble, since it is hard to be sure what anyone *would* infer, if his physical constitution were considerably altered. See Kripke's discussion of the dispositional view of meaning, 1982, especially pp. 22–37.

35 Heal, 1978, makes this point. Her own definition of common knowledge purports to fulfil the condition that 'infinite potential knowledge does enter into our account, but only as the object of a finite but actual thought'. Heal's own account does not in fact make any thought above 'infinite potential knowledge' on *explicit* requirement on common knowledge. The account I present here, in requiring knowledge of openness*, precisely requires knowledge of something which can be called infinite potential knowledge.

36 This has often been noted. See for instance Stalnaker, 1974, pp. 199 ff. See also Schiffer, 1972; Grice, 1967 ms.

37 What I have in mind is this. In the case of a single person, something like this seems to be rather obviously true: the 'whole' person has to say 'I' in order that the use of 'I' be valid, and self-reference be achieved. (In some special cases such as cases of multiple personality one might feel that a use of 'I' on a given occasion was not used by a 'whole' person and hence was of doubtful validity.) If there is something like a need for ratification of a given individual's use of 'we' by all the others involved in order that the use of 'we' be valid, then in effect the 'whole' referred to is, once again, required to be 'behind' the use of the pronoun.

38 A more direct way of describing the conditions on the *joint espousal of a goal* is that it must be common knowledge that each has in effect expressed his own quasi-acceptance of a certain goal in relation to the others in question. One's personal quasi-acceptance is as far as one can go alone, and the relevant complete set of commonly known quasi-acceptances constitutes actual joint acceptance. This type of account (which does not so much involve a joint disposition as a joint act) is what seems most appropriate to group belief, to which I devote a separate investigation in the following chapter. I shall not try to pick apart this way of putting things further here.

39 In response to a query I note that 'pool' is not intended to imply that wills are like drops of water, coagulating to form a liquid pool together. Think rather of the idea of our 'pooling' our resources.

40 Rousseau, 1983, p. 23. I shall not attempt to enter into exegesis of Rousseau here. Clearly the points made in the present volume as a whole are highly relevant to the interpretation and appreciation of Rousseau. See Gilbert, 1986ms.

41 Many who talk and write of 'shared beliefs', and so on, do not make any explicit distinction between sharing in the rich sense at issue here and the kind of sharing involved when everyone does the same thing.

As I make clear in this book, these are very radically different phenomena. If one does have the plural subject phenomenon in mind, one cannot make that clear simply by using the qualifier 'shared'.

42 I do not believe that my account presupposes any special assumptions about the nature of thoughts or cognitions.

43 In addition to Lewis and Schiffer, these include Gilbert, 1978; Bach and Harnish, 1979; Pettit and MacDonald, 1981.

44 See for instance the discussion of the opera goers in Taylor, 1980. Taylor's negative remarks about common knowledge helped to interrupt my own dogmatic slumbers.

45 A sensitivity to the kind of point I am making may be argued to be found in Plato's discussion of the virtue of 'moderation' in a city, *Republic*, Book 5. Plato allows that for a city to be wise only its rulers need be wise. Thus he does not have what may be called an aggregative or summative view of the wisdom of a city (or group). However, there has to be some way in which the rulers' wisdom attaches to the city as a whole. The virtue Plato calls moderation, in which every citizen is involved, brings this about: each citizen must accept the rulers as rulers.

46 See below on the reasonableness of talking of small and ephemeral groups as such.

47 I am reminded of a favourite scene in the film *The Graduate*. Ben announces to his parents that he is going to marry Eileen. His parents become enthusiastic and ask when the marriage was decided upon. Ben then informs them that the woman in question does not yet know of his plans. At this his father, quite irritated, says that Ben's plan seems pretty half-baked. (To which Ben replies stubbornly that it is fully-baked.) 'I plan to do X' may be ambiguous between something like 'I shall be doing X (and hence intend to)' and 'My intention is to do X (and hence I shall be doing X).'

48 The notion of joint acceptance of a proposition will receive more attention in Chapter V.

49 In an important but difficult passage in the *Phenomenology of Spirit* (B. IV. A., secs 178–84; 1977, pp. 111–12) Hegel appears to be concerned with something like the phenomenon of mutual recognition that is at issue here. As A.V. Miller's translation has it, the passage ends 'They *recognize* themselves as *mutually* recognizing one another' (Sec. 184; 1977, p. 112).

50 He writes: 'this consciousness [of sociating or of being sociated] is perhaps better called a "knowing" than a "cognizing". For here, the subject is not confronting an object of which he will gradually gain a theoretical picture. The consciousness of sociation is, rather, the immediate agent, the inner significance, of sociation itself' (p. 78). I confess I am not sure how Simmel himself would explain the difference between knowing and cognizing, nor, more generally, how he would spell out those of his pronouncements that I have found thought-provoking.

51 Termites, I believe, behave one way (independently) when there are

only a certain number of them around, but given a certain critical mass, they immediately go into a tight formation, behaving quite differently, and in a highly organized fashion.

52 Thus Kant: 'But if I yield myself completely to another and obtain the person of the other in return, I win myself back; I have given myself up as the property of another, but in turn I take that other as my property, and so win myself back in winning the person whose property I have become. In this way the two persons become a unity of will. Whatever good or ill, joy or sorrow befall either of them, the other will share it. Thus sexuality leads to a union of human beings, and in that union alone its exercise is possible. This condition of the use of sexuality, which is only fulfilled in marriage, is a moral condition' (1930, p. 167). Cf. Maslow on 'Love in healthy people': 'An ego now expands to cover two people, and to some extent the two people have become for psychological purposes a single unit, a single person, a single ego' 1953, p. 76. Use of the phrase 'to some extent' may indicate a certain unhappiness about this way of putting things. Clearly we need a means to make such points without a sense of intellectual embarrassment.

53 A version of this objection was made by members of the Frankfurt Institute for Social Research, 1973, in relation to an account of social groups from Theodor Geiger.

54 Its opposite might help to shore up capitalism, in so far as there is some tendency for people to value social groups as such (see below) and not want to destroy them, all else being equal.

55 See Lewis, 1976, pp. 113–14. Whether or not this is going on in a given case may not be an entirely easy thing to spot. See my comment on Lewis's remark in my 1983a, pp. 386–8.

56 See, for instance, Marx and Engels, *The Communist Manifesto* 1977, p. 214.

57 An issue to which I return at the end of the chapter.

58 Maybe I should simply call them Gilbert groups, in fairness, since Simmel is unaware of the particulars of my account.

59 The idea for this example came from a discussion in Mellor, 1982.

60 See Goleman, 1986.

V AFTER DURKHEIM: CONCERNING COLLECTIVE BELIEF

1 For a hypothesis linking fictional discourse and pretence, see Kripke, 1973ms.

2 It is interesting to note that though Quinton is explicitly talking about social objects and groups, the examples he gives are of economic classes. Such classes are not in general paradigm cases of social groups intuitively, as noted in the last chapter. They may well need to have their consciousness raised to the level of group formation. Should Quinton's account of collective beliefs be correct, semantic or analytic individualism could still have problems in relation to the analysis of the concept of a collectivity itself. Meanwhile, Quinton's examples – the French middle class, and the industrial working

class – could lead one to overlook this possibility. The 'French middle class', for instance, may indeed be just those French people with a certain degree of wealth.

3 In recent work on 'rational consensus' it is not always made absolutely clear whether what is talked about is the consensus as such, or what the consensus in a group ought to be, given the nature of the beliefs and attitudes of the people concerned. See Lehrer and Wagner, 1981.

4 Durkheim's *Rules of Sociological Method*, first published in 1895, was reissued with an important second preface in 1901. Unless otherwise noted, quotations from Durkheim in this chapter are from this work, using the Halls translation (Durkheim, 1982). The work will sometimes be referred to as *Rules*, for short.

5 The qualification 'fixed or not' is not directly important to my theme. Roughly, Durkheim saw some ways of acting as more 'fixed' or rigid and unchangeable than others. What might be called 'ways of being', for instance the design of dwellings, are only 'ways of acting', he says, which have been 'consolidated'. Meanwhile, 'a legal rule is no less permanent an arrangement than an architectural style'. No less to be counted among the social facts are ways of acting not yet 'caught in any definite mould' – which have not yet found any kind of physical expression in words or things, 'free currents of social life' (p. 58).

6 I shall not try to associate everything Durkheim mentions in Chapter I with social convention. One thing he talks of, not mentioned above, is the influence on people of being in a crowd, in particular the fact of being 'swept up' in the emotions of the crowd. What goes on in crowds or mobs is obviously somewhat special, and it is hard to know exactly how to characterize it. Quite possibly a mixture of different things goes on. I waive further discussion of this case here.

7 Compare the second edition preface, where he talks of his earlier references to constraint as stemming from a wish to indicate an 'external sign' by which social facts might be recognized.

8 One contrasting case Durkheim may have in mind is that of certain actions by individuals which have social aspects of various kinds, but none the less by virtue of their nature as actions by individuals appear to fall into the category of 'psychological' phenomena. For instance, a particular person's choosing to vote Democrat in a United States election. As noted earlier, Durkheim was particularly concerned to distinguish social from 'psychical' phenomena on the one hand, from 'organic' phenomena, on the other (see p. 52).

9 The chemical analogies, in particular, have been criticized by commentators. See for instance MacIver, 1917, pp. 86–8. Compare also Mill's statement that men are not, when they become members of groups, 'converted into another kind of substance'. Given current knowledge of the chemical and neurophysiological changes associated with emotional, psychological, and behavioural processes, the idea that there could be actual chemical changes in individuals associated with group formation has some plausibility. Durkheim himself makes

472

no such claims. However, his chemical *analogy* should seem less far-fetched in the light of their plausibility.

10 Cf. *Rules*, second edition preface, p. 46. 'Individuals are the only active elements' in society.

11 Compare the idea that something was the belief of certain people 'taken collectively'. It may seem that use of this particular phrase does not presuppose that the people in question constitute a social group. After all, it is the person using the phrase who is doing the 'taking' rather than the people referred to. Can one take a random assemblage of persons collectively? That depends, of course, how one construes the relevant phrase. 'Taking these people collectively' could be taken to mean 'considering these people, taken together, as the group they in fact form'. If it meant that, one could not take a random collection of individuals, or any non-group, collectively. My own exposure to the phrase suggests that it may be used to refer to non-groups in current discussions, when it is presumably taken to mean 'considering these people together', which would seem to come down to something like 'considering all of these people at once'. This could be a derived or bowdlerized use, however. The use of 'collectively' does not really seem to be in place.

12 Gellner 1956, in Brodbeck (ed.) 1971, p. 266. This quotation explicitly concerns decision rather than belief. The simple view seems less plausible for decision than for belief. In any case one might take it that there is some corresponding belief for every decision of the type in question (such as 'Jones is the person to appoint').

13 Cf. Durkheim and Mauss, 1970, p. 43. Needham's translation runs: 'The Zuni believe. . .'. Since I want to concentrate on explicit ascriptions to a tribe, I have my imaginary anthropologist explicitly use a collectivity term. (The Zuni are a tribe of North American Indians.)

14 The strict literalness of the use of 'belief' in such cases may be questionable. Can we distinguish here, for instance, between: 'you act/talk/feel exactly as if you believed' and 'you believe'? It seems plausible to suppose that believing, in the standard strict and literal sense, in so far as there is one, is conceptually distinct from behaving as if you believed.

15 If one wishes to think of a population as simply the set of its members one must use the term in some manner inconsistent with (1), (2), and (3). For example, someone might deny (3) and say that common knowledge is a property of a population only relative to some defining condition; in such a terminology, the single population comprised both of the dinner guests and Transylvanian spies is aware *qua* being the Transylvanian spies of the Transylvanian plans, but not *qua* being the dinner guests. There is room for more work in this area. Philosophers who have used the concept of a population (in particular David Lewis in discussion of conventions) have not devoted much discussion to its logic.

16 See Lewis, 1969, last para., p. 66, to p. 67, end of last full para. Schiffer, 1972, pp. 130–1, especially Comment 2, p. 131.

17 I take this assumption to be reasonable in relation to the account of common knowledge given here. I do not attempt to argue this in any detail here, nor to compare my account in this respect with others.

18 Cf. Schiffer, 1972, p. 131: 'I propose to borrow from a suggestion put forward by David K. Lewis, and to treat the mutual knowledge* condition as partially defining membership in group G.' I owe the criticism of this idea noted here to Saul Kripke.

19 Lewis (1975, pp. 5–6) appears to adopt such an amendment in his account of conventions; he does not explicitly acknowledge a change.

20 In this connection it is worth noting that there is a considerable literature on the possibility of manipulating various formal voting schemes by 'strategic voting'.

21 On the last two see Simmel's remarks on the marital couple: in 'small groups, such as the marital couple, . . . A certain amount of discord . . . is organically tied up with the very elements that ultimately hold the group together.' (1971b, p. 74)

22 This case derives from a point made by Saul Kripke at a seminar I gave on this topic at a regional workshop in philosophy held in Banff, Canada, June 1977. I was then putting forward a view something like the one I criticize here.

23 See Lukes, 1973, p. 14. 'By generality Durkheim was here seeking to identify factors that are specific to particular societies; that is, are neither strictly personal features of individuals nor universal attributes of human nature. Fauconnet and Mauss isolated this feature of social facts when they characterized them as "certain ways of feeling, thinking, and acting" which individuals would not have had "if they had lived in other human groups".'

24 Perhaps if a belief is general in many societies, it will look as if its occurrence in them cannot be entirely freakish: perhaps the hypothesis that it is a particular type of social structure which produces the belief will then look more plausible than in the case when the belief is unique to a single society. However, it is clear that in principle a belief could occur in the many societies in which it is general for a variety of quite different reasons having nothing to do with features of the various societies as such.

25 Thus Lukes's praise of Mauss and Fauconnet's counterfactual condition, quoted above, seems misplaced.

26 A form of this distinction may apply to standard physical objects. Consider the following example. My hat is blown off by the wind. It sticks on a thin branch at a far extremity of a huge oak tree. Did the tree itself stop the hat, or did the branch do it? Even if one is inclined to say that the tree stopped the hat, I think there is less of a sense of obviousness here than in the case where the hat was stopped by the trunk of the tree. If the trunk stopped it, so did the tree. The intuitive principle one is going on in making all such distinctions may be something like this: a thing T of kind K is itself a cause of X if X is caused by a state or feature S of T such that one cannot be a thing of kind K unless one is in states or has features of kind KS, where state S is a state of the kind KS.

27 This could be because a state of G is G-causal only if it involves G itself in some essential way. I cannot go into this issue here.

28 See for instance Lewis, 1969; Gilbert, 1978ms; Pettit and Mac-Donald, 1981.

29 This case may recall Karl Popper's claim that 'the main task of the social sciences is the task of analysing the unintended social repercussions of intentional human actions' (1961, p. 437). (Note that Popper says nothing explicitly about production by a *group*.) (Popper mentions the suggestion of Polanyi that Marx was the first to conceive of social theory as the study of the unwanted social repercussions of nearly all our actions.)

30 The large philosophical literature on reasons and their relation to causes includes Donald Davidson's well-known 'Actions, Reasons, and Causes', 1963, in which a view of reasons as causes is put forward. I note that Davidson's 'primary reasons' are pairs of beliefs and pro-attitudes. According to Davidson, X's believing that Q-ing will achieve end E, and his desiring or approving end E, are states of X which in combination may cause X to Q. Perhaps Davidson's point is most accurately put thus: explanation by reasons is or implies a causal explanation in terms of beliefs and pro-attitudes. It is perhaps unfortunate that this view has been labelled (with encouragement from Davidson's text) as the view that *reasons* are causes. This is not the place to attempt serious discussion of Davidson's views.

Opponents of some ideas of reasons as causes include Peter Winch, 1958, and A.I. Melden, 1961, both of whom acknowledge the influence of Wittgenstein. Exactly how the conceptual framework of 'reasons for action' maps onto others, if it does, is an important issue outside the scope of this book. Sympathy to the framework involves, in my case, the assumption that true explanations for human actions can be given in terms of what people have taken to be reasons for action: the framework is more than merely practical, whatever that might be.

31 The example is derived from one given in Lewis, 1969, pp. 119–20, with a different purpose.

The *openness** of the general practice could be relevant as follows. One reasons, perhaps wrongly: the practice of wearing a raincoat this morning is general and moreover it is perfectly open* that it is general. Evidently, no one has seen fit to remark to his neighbour that he, for one, is wearing his raincoat because he is on his way to Manchester, but the forecast for here was rather good, wasn't it? No one has, in other words, challenged another's raincoat wearing while explaining away his own. The fact that the general practice is open* and persisting is taken as confirmation, then, that almost everyone has good reason to believe that there is a good chance of rain here today. So everyone continues to wear his raincoat in part because raincoat-wearing today is an open* general practice in this community.

Compare a case of joke pointing to the top of a building, to see how many people you can get to look up. The more people there are openly looking up, the better it works on others. This may well not be just, if at all, because it is less likely that a whole lot of people will be independently wrong than that one will, but because one might expect those in the right, if there are any, to correct those they see making an error.

32 A related issue will be addressed in discussing the concept of a social convention in the next chapter.

33 I owe to John Tienson the following illustration: The current speaker's suggestion represents her guess as to what an absent member, whose side-kick she is, would say. Meanwhile this is something she personally does not believe. Nor does any other member, including the absent one, personally believe it.

34 The qualifier 'in some such context' is intended to allow that there may be related contexts in which someone has managed to guard herself against subsequent rebuke for expressing a view contrary to the group's established opinion. Thus if after her remark in discussion had been opposed, the speaker had said something like: 'Well, I think you'd better count me out of this. I simply cannot agree with where this is going' this may be sufficient to guard her against subsequent rebuke. I shall not pursue this matter further here. But it is clearly of some importance. The practice of allowing for a 'dissenting opinion' in the context of a court's judgment is clearly relevant here.

35 In one kind of case where a charge of deceit or lying is in place one person asks another what he thinks about some issue and is given a false answer.

Interestingly enough, the respondent in such cases can be argued to have acted especially badly within the negotiation of joint view approach to conversation. Suppose that someone asks: 'What is your personal opinion on that, Joel?' This case could be construed along the following lines. The parties (Joel and his interlocutor) are (at least) seeking *a jointly acceptable view of what Joel's personal opinion is*. Assume that it is understood that if Joel confidently replies, say, 'I think it's an interesting proposal', it will be jointly accepted that *Joel believes that it is an interesting proposal*. Given that there is a commonly known general preference that the jointly accepted view be correct, other things being equal (on this see below) it will seem reasonable to tax Joel with a relatively grave offence if he is discovered not to have expressed his own view on the matter. For in this case, his failure to express his own view amounts to his misrepresenting the truth of the matter in question. In general an individual participant's personal views need not play quite such a crucial role in the production of an acceptable joint view. Where this is so his failure to express those views or to dissent from views contrary to those he holds will not generate such a serious charge. In, as we say, lying, Joel will not only most probably have caused his interlocutor personally to believe something false. He will also have brought it about that the view he jointly accepts with the interlocutor is false. (This gives us, in effect, an extra line on the badness of lying. See Gilbert, 1985ms b.)

36 One might compare the way utterances of the form: 'I think that p' may appropriately be dealt with in conversation. They may be reacted to as descriptions of the speaker's state of mind. Or the 'I think' may be ignored, treated as a practically meaningless marker. There is thus a variety of appropriate objections from the point of view of joint acceptability. *Dialogue I*: Jones: 'I think Reagan's Star Wars policy is great.' Smith (focusing on what comes after 'I think'): 'But surely it's quite absurd!' or: 'I disagree.' *Dialogue II*: Jones, as before. Smith (focusing on 'I think'): 'No you don't! You're just saying that to shock me!' In the case of Mircea's reaction to me, the reaction appears to be of the second kind, the referent of 'I' and hence the precise nature of the view in question being momentarily misunderstood.

37 One must accept, of course, that many different things can be going on in any one interaction.

Other models are fairly standard in the philosophical literature. See for instance Grice, 1969, and Schiffer, 1972. These tend to suggest that whenever I 'utter' some sentence in your direction, my primary aim is to do something to you. The standard way of characterizing the basic roles in interpersonal verbal interaction as those of speaker (active) and hearer (passive) also tend to suggest something other than a negotiation of jointly accepted view.

The notions of speaker and hearer seem easy enough to apply through all conversational interactions. Yet – don't I (standardly) hear myself as well as speak? And doesn't my 'hearer' instantly endow my uttered sounds with his own meaning, thus being as semantically active as I? How central to what goes on must be the fact that I initiated the intrusion into the world of these sounds or marks?

38 See Martin Gilbert, 1971, p. 477. See also ibid., p. 384, where it is reported that Lloyd George urged Churchill to 'understand that conversation is not a monologue!'

39 If there were the last mentioned obligation, it would not follow, of course, that anyone had managed to live up to their obligation. That is, it would not follow that those who jointly accepted that p actually did believe that p personally. I take it to be harder to change one's views than one's actions, particularly if one is not aware of any new evidence against one's initial view.

40 These considerations have serious implications for the methodology of psychology and social science. See my Chapter VII below, sec. 4.3.

41 These considerations can be related to questions about the morality of lying (Gilbert 1985ms b). On lying see also note 35 above.

42 Cf. Plato's view that, roughly, in order for a city-state to be deemed wise by virtue of the wisdom of a small group within it, each citizen must accept that the members of that small group are those who are to do the city's thinking (*Republic*, Book 5).

43 It may also run foul of group belief ascriptions which use the sense explicated but involve false presuppositions or are otherwise false. Bas Van Fraassen referred to the usage discussed below in discussion

of my views on group belief at a colloquium of the New Jersey Regional Philosophical Association, 1984. A philosopher of science, for instance, may say 'The Greeks believed the earth was flat', knowing well that only the Greek scientific community had that belief, the rest of the Greeks being ignorant of questions about the earth's flatness, and even ignorant of the existence of a Greek scientific community. I suggest that in so far as the statement purports to claim that the Greeks 'as a people' believed that the earth was flat, it is simply false intuitively. So we have no counterexample to my account. But possibly both speaker and audience are only interested in Greek science in the first place. Thus for them 'the Greeks' refers to the Greek scientific community. If so, then the truth conditions of the original statement may well be as in the general joint acceptance account or in one of the special cases. In any case, the facts cited about most Greeks become irrelevant to a diagnosis of the usage in question.

VI SOCIAL CONVENTION

1 See Weber, 1964, on custom (pp. 121ff) and convention (pp. 127ff).

2 See for instance Emmet, 1966, *Rules, Roles, and Relations*; Ullman-Margalit, 1977, *The Emergence of Norms*, and Winch, 1958, who refers to 'socially established rules' at p. 33.

3 When 'anything goes' there are at least two possibilities. There may be no convention at all, or there may be a convention to the effect that each must be allowed to seek his or her own way.

4 Lewis cites Schelling, 1960, and Hume's *Treatise*, Book III, ii, 2. There is related material in Hume's *Enquiry*. I shall not attempt my own interpretation of Hume here. All references to Lewis in this chapter are to *Convention*, 1969, unless otherwise stated. The phrase quoted is on p. 3.

  Lewis's influence is explicitly noted in Schiffer, 1972, Bennett, 1976, Ullman-Margalit, 1977, Schotter, 1981, and Blackburn, 1984, among others. Developments from Lewis's work form a large part of the Schotter and Ullman-Margalit works cited.

5 Game theory was invented in its present form by John Von Neumann. One might count Plato among his forebears. In *Republic* Book 2, section 359a, Plato seems to envisage the structure of preferences now famous under the label 'Prisoner's Dilemma' (so-called because of the story attached to it by A. Tucker). For a diagrammatic representation of this structure see Lewis, Figure 9, p. 16. Hume also showed an implicit understanding of a branch of game theory in the discussion of convention that influenced Lewis. The theory is briefly characterized for those unfamiliar with it in section 2.2 below.

6 This second aspect of Lewis's theory is not surprising, given the first. See section 2.2 below.

7 I have published a number of previous studies of Lewis's work. See Gilbert 1974, 1981, 1983a, 1983b. See also 1983abs, 1983ms, 1985ms

a. Though I shall draw on some of that material here, the focus of interest is different, and my final proposal, touched on briefly in my 1983ms, is significantly different from the preliminary hypothesis sketched in my 1983a and 1983b, which is itself discussed critically below in section 7.4.

I thank David Lewis for discussions of his work dating back to the early seventies. He is of course not responsible for anything I have written here.

8 I take the platitude to be that conventions help to constitute language as such. At one point Lewis writes of 'The platitude that there are conventions of language'. This is very vague. One can take it as a reference to conventions constitutive of language. But it is also quite possible to read it more broadly as something like 'conventions connected with language'. This surface ambiguity may not be without consequence for Lewis's work on the conventionality of language. For it can be argued (see Gilbert, 1983a) that Lewis ends up attempting to give an account of a sense or type of convention such that it is by no means platitudinous that language as such is ruled by conventions of that sort, even though there obviously are conventions of that sort relating to language. I say more about this later.

9 Lewis cites the philosophers W.V. Quine (1936, 1960, and other writings) and Morton White (1950, 1956).

10 Lewis is surely right. The second premise of the argument cited can also be disputed. It depends on how liberally we construe 'language'. Agreements can probably be made without recourse to an already constituted *group language*. As in the situation envisaged in my discussion of group languages, it seems that people could reach an agreement using only gestures and sounds that they naturally interpret in the same way. It is not clear that there can be agreements without symbolization or expressiveness of *any* kind. But to insist that agreements require language seems to require that we construe the notion of language quite liberally. Be all this as it may, as far as convention is concerned Lewis appears to be on the right track.

11 This section is largely for readers otherwise unfamiliar with game theory. A classic textbook is Luce and Raiffa, 1957.

12 For certain purposes restrictions on and stipulations about what the payoff or utility numbers represent can be made. Thus one could use game theory to model the behaviour of agents stipulated to be entirely selfish. Or one could take the numbers to represent some objective measure of personal well-being, which the agents are presumed to be out to maximize. (Then the numbers would presumably be judged to measure the same quantity.) But such restrictions are not implicit in the theory at the outset.

The possibility of different stipulations about the payoff numbers is reflected in a somewhat confusing variety in the language used by Lewis and others. Thus sometimes Lewis refers to 'the outcomes the agents want to produce or prevent', sometimes to the agents' 'interests' as conflicting or coinciding. Must I always want to promote my own interests? It is rather natural to think not, given a nontechnical, everyday interpretation of 'my own interests' as something like 'what is conducive to my own well-being'. These two ways of talking, then, do not sit so easily together. Again, references to what 'is best' for one of the agents are somewhat ambiguous. They would rather naturally be interpreted in terms of what is best for the agent in terms of his own interests, as opposed to those of others. Meanwhile within the usual perspective of game theory, what would be meant is 'what the agent ranks highest in his preference scale' which may well not be in his own interest, intuitively speaking.

13 The nontriviality of the basic idea that one is out to maximize one's *personal payoff* may be demonstrated in various ways. In some situations it may be obvious to an agent out to maximize his personal payoff that he should do X, but for agents aiming for a relatively good outcome for all in terms of the given personal payoffs, X would not be the obvious choice. An example is the well-known Prisoner's Dilemma structure. With regard to the Prisoner's Dilemma, I take it that in an isolated case, at least, a rational agent aiming to maximize his personal payoff will opt for his strictly dominant strategy. Many agree with this, including Luce and Raiffa, op. cit., though it has been disputed.

14 These characteristics are at least implicitly ascribed to players in the literature.

15 Some theorists may query condition (d). But classical game theory operates in the framework envisaged here. 'From the Bayesian viewpoint, probabilities should be assignable to everything, including the prospect of a player choosing a certain strategy in a certain game. The so-called "game-theoretic" viewpoint holds that probabilities can only be assigned to events not governed by rational decision makers' (Aumann, 1987, p. 1, from the Headnote). In what follows (d) will be assumed without further argument. I take it to be worthwhile to explore the scope and limits of rationality according to the classical viewpoint. This is not the place to argue this. I might note, however, that, as far as I can see, arguments similar to those I give in section 3, below, could be formulated in terms of a Bayesian approach.

16 The definition of common knowledge just given became an explicit part of the theoretical apparatus of game theory with Robert Aumann, 1976. Apparently Aumann both named and defined this concept independently of Lewis's work. (This definition is simpler than the one used elsewhere in this book. Since we are dealing with a highly idealized model of action here, there is no need to attempt a definition with clearer claims to realism.) Note that in this connection as in others in game theory there is no need to move outside the conceptual framework of singular subjects of agency and cognition.

17 To take a simple example: suppose that in a two person game Player

One has a strictly dominant strategy. Knowing this, and knowing that Player One is rational, Player Two can infer that Player One will pursue that strategy. This will be enough to determine what Player Two should do himself, even though he does not himself have a dominant strategy.

18 See also Luce and Raiffa, op. cit., p. 105.

19 After giving his eventual definition Lewis says that he has taken the 'defining features of the class to be those distinctive features of our examples which seem important for an understanding of their character' (p. 24).

20 See Lewis, p. 14, second full paragraph. Aspects of Lewis's use of this condition on coordination problems are discussed in Gilbert, 1981, pp. 49–50. Lewis's own attitude to this qualification has evidently varied. It is dropped entirely from his restatement of his account of convention in Lewis, 1975.

21 See Gilbert, 1981, especially pp. 46–54, and p. 76, the first paragraph of 'Conclusions'.

22 See Figure 1, p. 330 below, for a matrix diagram of the telephone case.

23 This account of how an agreement would solve a coordination problem may strike one as rather strange. It is not an immediately appealing way of describing the way agreements between human beings work. In later discussion Lewis himself envisages a different mechanism coming into play where agreements are concerned. He remarks on how agreements may be seen to have a binding force, and thence gain their effectiveness. When this happens, according to Lewis, we do not have the complex phenomenon he takes to be constitutive of convention. The nature of agreements is discussed further in section 8.2 below.

24 That some such condition must be fulfilled is already implicit in Lewis's appeal to game theory in his discussion of coordination problems.

25 See Lewis, 1969, pp. 56; Lewis, 1975, suggests two possibilities.

26 At one point Lewis argues that the parties to a convention need not have 'the concept of a member of P' (p. 67; see pp. 65–7). All that is necessary, according to Lewis, is that they 'come up with the right particular beliefs regarding any new case that is presented in sufficient detail'. It is not clear why Lewis wants to say this. Should a set of 'creatures' behave appropriately, but turn out not to have the concept of a member of P, then it seems we should conclude that Lewis's common knowledge condition, at least as stated in his final definition of convention, was not fulfilled, since it would not be right to say that the members of P had any knowledge of the form: if anyone is a member of P then he does A.

Lewis's remarks could suggest a desire to explain concept possession in terms of convention, in which case the possession of a given concept cannot be among the conditions for convention. As far as I know Lewis puts no stress on the question of thought or concepts as opposed to language so it is hard to know how he thinks about this. Clearly if one does want to explain thought in terms of convention one must have some sort of behavioural, non-intentional account of convention itself. This type of line does not sit well with Lewis's theme of conventions as generated out of coordination problems among rational agents. I shall not proceed further down this particular byway.

27 That this is so could be obscured somewhat by the way the third clause in the statement of Lewis's first definition is formulated: everyone prefers to conform to R *since S is a coordination problem, and uniform conformity to R is a coordination equilibrium in S.* Assuming, as I do, that Lewis meant 'proper coordination equilibrium' rather than simply 'coordination equilibrium' (and there is every reason to assume this, including a personal communication from Lewis to that effect, 1977), each one's preference for his own conformity to R is in fact secured by uniform conformity to R's being a *proper* equilibrium, in the circumstances. (A proper equilibrium Lewis defines as a combination of actions each agent likes better than any other he could have reached, given the others' choices.) Meanwhile, it is unclear, as a matter of logic, how in the context of game theory anyone can be *motivated* to do his own part in a particular combination of actions specifically by the fact that it is a *coordination* equilibrium. (That is, by Lewis's definition, a combination of actions in which no one would have been better off had any one agent alone acted otherwise, either himself or another.) In any case, Lewis gives us no reason to think that anyone has to be so motivated, when doing his part in a particular proper coordination equilibrium.

28 There may be significant differences of preference, however. I might prefer that you call me back because I've already spent two dimes on the call. You may prefer me to pay again since you are very poor and consider that I ought to pay. I may know, meanwhile, that you are more anxious than I am to restore the call. Thus I could try to 'outwit' you by waiting, knowing that you will get tired of waiting before I do, and hence eventually at least, you will call and I will still be waiting.

29 We get nearest to an explicit formulation of the implicit argument at p. 70 of *Convention*, the passage beginning: 'This is why it is redundant to speak of an arbitrary convention.' Saul Kripke drew my attention to the fact that something like the argument just elaborated is implicit in Lewis's text, after I told him of some critical points I had developed concerning Lewis's game-theoretical claims. These points suffice to refute the implicit argument. See section 4.1 below, and also Gilbert, 1981.

30 Cf. the authors cited below. Also see Charles Fried, 1981, p. 15.

31 Authors who have appealed to salience in discussions of the generation of action in coordination problems include Lewis, Gauthier, Heal, Ullman-Margalit, Schiffer, and Kuflik, all following Schelling, 1960, who writes of 'focal points'.

32 Heal, 1978, uses this phrase, and also 'stands out'. Lewis writes of

'standing out from the rest by its uniqueness in some conspicuous respect'. He also writes of 'being unique in some way everyone will notice, expect the others to notice, and so on.' It is not clear that several different combinations of actions could not be salient in this sense. The definition of salience in this context should evidently be such that there can only be a single salient combination of actions in a given occurrence of a coordination problem.

33 The case with which Heal, 1978, was primarily concerned.

34 It may seem even more questionable in relation to a matrix containing an observable asymmetry. For instance, one of the generally more preferred outcomes is the worst, several tie for best. (The example is from Thomas Schelling. See Schelling, 1960, pp. 295–6.)

35 See Heal, 1978, p. 129, and Schiffer, 1972, pp. 145–47, among others.

36 Heal, 1978, p. 129, footnote. The argument is used '*contra* Lewis': 'we do not have to suppose that as a last resort A thinks that B has a tendency to choose the salient so that A himself has a reason for choosing the salient' (ibid.). Here I think Lewis is right. I say more about Lewis's own (somewhat mixed) attitude to the precedent issue in the next section.

37 I do not deny that there could be a use in a different context for notions of salience different from the one at issue here. Cf. McDowell, 1979, p. 335.

38 That rationality does dictate some course for each may not be sufficient for the kind of unique or maximal salience we are talking about. I suspect that it is not. That it is dictated by rationality presumably gives a course of action the property most closely relevant to what should be done. But the concept of unique relevance to what should be done appears to be distinct from salience in the sense at issue here. Is the intersection of dominant strategies the salient combination in the Prisoner's Dilemma? One might think that players are likely to 'notice' two different strategy sets: the one just mentioned, and the one where each player chooses his other option, and both are better off. Might this be a case where there is no salient solution in the strong sense at issue here, but it is still clear what rationality dictates? This issue need not trouble us now.

39 Cf. Schelling, 1960, p. 297. See also Kuflik, 1982.

40 In my 1983ms, I dispute the 'principle of coordination' to which Gauthier appeals.

41 Someone might defend Gauthier as presenting an account of how salience *could* work (if everyone decides to abide by a certain policy) or an implicit psychological account as to how it is salience often does seem to be *used*. His own discussion is perhaps slightly ambiguous on this, though he implies that 'successful coordination' which 'depends on conceiving a situation' in a certain way, is a 'matter of reason'. In the context of a discussion of game-theoretical rationality, in any case, I think we must conclude that his idea does

not show that rational agents as such will find (or derive) a reason for acting from the fact that one solution is salient.

42 See Lewis, pp. 35–6, on salience.

43 Cf. Gibbard, 1978.

44 I heard this argument from Kripke in 1983 (personal communication). Responsibility for the presentation of the argument here is my own. I thank Kripke for his permission to cite it here. Kripke also devised a version in which one can derive contradictory conclusions about what action a given agent will take, as well as about whether he acts on his tendency.

45 Lewis speaks of action on tendency in the absence of reasons dictating the contrary course. The difference of detail is irrelevant here.

46 See in contrast Schiffer, 1972, p. 149.

47 Compare Weber's reference to probabilities in his account of social relations in *Economy and Society* (1964, p. 118).

48 W. V. O. Quine, Foreword to *Convention*, p. xii. Not everything Lewis writes supports this idea. For instance the middle matrix in his fig. 20, p. 26, does not sit very well with it. (One of the two proper coordination equilibria gives each agent a far worse payoff than the other does, with no compensation in the security level of the corresponding strategies.) However, his verbal descriptions of coordination problems are mostly couched in terms of how 'it matters little' to the people concerned which of several preferable outcomes occurs. Lewis's game-theoretic definition of a coordination problem does not always capture the spirit of the majority of his examples.

49 See *The Oxford English Dictionary*, (ed. Murray, 1971), and others. The Latin derivation is stated as 'arbiter' or judge. Clearly the different senses of 'arbitrary' are related. But whether or not one judges something to be arbitrary will vary depending on which sense one has in mind.

50 For a more detailed discussion see Gilbert, 1981.

51 See Gilbert, 1981, p. 61, fig. 7, and discussion pp. 61–2.

52 For a discussion of the notion of triviality in connection with Lewis see Gilbert, 1981, especially pp. 63 ff. For defence of the claim that Lewis's definition is insufficient to rule out trivial situations at least given certain understandings of what triviality is, see pp. 71–4.

53 Such as the situation with the following payoff matrix:

$$(1.5, 1.5) \quad (0.0, 0.5)$$
$$(0.5, 0.0) \quad (1.0, 1.0)$$

(In this array, the first of a pair of numbers in parentheses represents the payoff to Player One, the second represents the payoff to Player Two. Each row represents a given action by Player One, each column represents a given action by Player Two.) This contains what I have elsewhere called an 'absolute best point', that is, a combination of actions such that each player gets his best possible payoff if each does his part in it. Some philosophers have written as if any example with such a point is trivial. See for instance

Gauthier, 1975, p. 201; Ullman-Margalit, 1977, p. 80. Lewis obviously does *not* think this, see his fig. 2 (p. 10) and his comments thereon. I have argued for the nontriviality of a situation with a structure similar to the above (my 'Guest's Dilemma') in 1983ms, see 1983abs. (The version here fulfils Lewis's coincidence of interests clause, my Guest's Dilemma doesn't.) This matrix, incidentally, seems less easy to solve than Lewis's figure where the absolute best point is at least arguably the obvious combination to do one's part in, having both the best security level and the absolute best point. My argument for the nontriviality of the Guest's Dilemma, which would apply to the above matrix, is based on the fact that to the absolute best point is opposed a choice preferable from the point of view of security level. In 1983ms I consider how the agents might try to reason their way to a clear decision either way, and argue that no dictate of reason is forthcoming.

54 For a diagram of this case see Gilbert, 1981, p. 85.

55 See also Rollin, 1976, p. 68.

56 For another expression of this intuition see Burge, 1975, for instance.

57 See Schiffer, 1972, p. 154.

58 In my view the considerations adduced in this section are hard to rebut convincingly. Further examples that suggest the lack of necessity of Lewis's three central conditions are to be found in Jamieson, 1975. Lewis's replies to Jamieson are found in Lewis, 1976. I shall not attempt to comment directly on that interchange here.

59 The clearest cases are probably of the first two kinds. 'You may go without a tie' can presumably sometimes be be construed as marking the absence of a particular convention, as opposed to the presence of a permissive convention. None the less the notion of a permissive convention is probably not an empty one. Myles Burnyeat suggested to me that such conventions are likely to arise in the wake of a prior proscriptive or prescriptive convention, where people may be expected to be alive to the issue of how things are to be done in a certain area. Another possibility is that people have something like a system of convention in which certain permissions are consciously contrasted with the presence of certain proscriptions or prescriptions. It seems natural to take the following description as referring to a complex of (three) conventions: one must wear a tie to department meetings; one may go tieless when teaching; one must go tieless at the departmental softball game.

60 See Lewis pp. 97–100. The term 'norm' is notoriously ambiguous. See Gibbs, 1965. Lewis has a separate discussion of 'so-called rules' which I refer to later.

61 Saul Kripke gave a strong and simple argument against it in discussion at a colloquium given by Richard Miller at Princeton University. See Miller, 1979, pp. 262–3.

62 This argument is echoed in Ullman-Margalit, 1977, p. 88, first full para.

63 Whether these features necessarily characterize populations with

Lewisian conventions depends, of course, on the precise nature of the features in question. The terms for these features are often used quite vaguely, so that they probably do apply to populations with Lewisian conventions. The following could be an argument for using the terms more precisely, or for the conclusion that populations could be structured and so on without being collectivities.

64 Section 6.9, in assessment of the causal account of collective belief.

65 Failure to see this in relation to coordination problems can be argued to lead some astray in their consideration of the dictates of rationality. See my 1983ms. Briefly, the usual game-theoretical assumptions do not support the supposition that when it will work out well for them the players in a given game will constitute a plural subject that aims to maximize the welfare of all. Some have written as if this were so. See for instance Gauthier, 1975, Kuflik, 1982.

66 Contrast A. Sen's opening remarks in his now classic *Collective Choice and Social Welfare*, 1970. I don't think that Sen considered the kind of interpretation of 'social utility function' that I am suggesting here. I believe that he was inclined to think that the only interpretation other than a derivative one would be something unacceptably mystical or unscientific. (This belief stems from a brief conversation with Sen, at the Public Choice Institute at Dalhousie University, summer 1984.) Given that there are such functions in my sense, however, it would be less than properly hard-nosed to ignore their existence.

67 Analogous examples that may occur to mind, apart from the politics of nations, are dancing and sexual intercourse. As it happens societal conventions have developed for both of the latter cases where the parties are a man and a woman, in which the man always leads, the woman is always a passive follower. That the man take the power, responsibilities and obligations of leadership in these cases can then come to seem, I suppose, the natural and objectively right thing to happen. See my remarks on heterosexuality in section 8.5 below. On the question of politics, see the final chapter.

68 I have discussed this issue previously in 1983a (see also Gilbert, 1974). Some of the points made there are repeated here.

69 In 'Languages and language', 1975, Lewis makes a similar distinction. At the outset he gives a strong characterization of language in the sense of language use, describing it as a social phenomenon. Here I do not assume at the outset that any user of a language must participate in society in some way. (Lewis himself implicitly denies this assumption in 'Languages and language' itself, in fact, in a passage I discuss shortly. He seems there implicitly to concede that there is no conceptual impossibility in a congenital Crusoe's use of language.)

There is obviously a close connection between the use of language and particular languages. In particular, since language use necessarily involves use of a particular language, one might accept that language use was 'ruled by convention' just in case languages were in some sense ruled by convention.

70 In 1983a I considered the possibility of amending Lewis's account of convention in general so as to allow for one-shot signalling conventions. The natural amendment, however, turns out to fall foul of an important type of counterexample, exemplified by my seminar break case. For a description and discussion of that case in relation to my own account of convention, see section 8.4 below.

71 We should not allow the phrase 'conventional signal' to confuse us. This phrase tends to be interpreted in such a way that one may adopt a signalling convention without adopting a conventional signal. See 1983a, p. 381, Romeo and Juliet example. (Lewis gives his own technical definition of 'signalling convention' (p. 135); here I intend no special technical sense. I believe that Lewis's technical sense does not correspond to the way the phrase would normally be interpreted.)

72 Must language use in many membered populations involve regularities in behaviour, and, more specifically, conventions in the sense of Lewis? Must it involve social convention as ordinarily conceived? As my discussion in Chapter III indicates, this question can be broken down into several distinct ones. Evidently, given the position I take in Chapter III, I do not take these questions to concern the nature of language use as such. I discuss what I take to be the relationship between a group's language and social convention as ordinarily conceived later in this chapter (sec. 8.3, ii).

73 A classic reference on this topic is Plato's *Cratylus*. For anyone who prefers to speak of 'uses' rather than 'senses' the basic idea here can be rephrased appropriately.

74 In fn. 31, Gilbert, 1983a, there are some examples that illustrate the points in this paragraph.

75 I hazard some thoughts on this in section 8.4, after presenting my own account of the concept of a social convention. The latter concept is, of course, the main quarry of this chapter.

76 A sense expressed by Lewis, pp. 83–8, where he contrasts conventions and agreements.

77 As I did in 1983b, p. 244.

78 Ullman-Margalit, 1977, pp. 88–9, suggests that the plain expectations involved when there is a convention in Lewis's sense (expectations she calls 'theoretical' expectations) are likely to give rise to correlative 'deontic' expectations. (She does not make it clear whether she thinks the original plain expectations remain alongside the new deontic ones.) This account of the generation of a generalized view that such-and-such ought to be done has the disadvantage of starting out from what I have argued is a suspect model of self-perpetuating regularities, at least if we are concerned with rational agents. It is unclear, in particular, how the plain expectations in question can be generated, given that it is doubtful whether salience, and in particular the salience of a past regularity, can generate expectations of behaviour among such agents. In Gilbert (1983ms), I sketched a model of the generation of self-perpetuating regularities in the life of rational agents in coordination

problems which involves an initial act of *principle adoption* on the part of the agents. If lucky, that is, if the principles adopted happen to cohere, the agents will have no reason to change or go against their principles, hence they will continue to maintain them. Presumably it could become common knowledge among rational agents that they individually hold certain principles, and, given they are in communication and the principles cohere acceptably to all, they will have no reason to negotiate a change. This suggests one way in which the situation at issue in this section may obtain among rational agents. I refer to this model again later at section 8.5 below.

79 See my 1983b, p. 245.

80 For what may be the standard account of social norms/rules see for instance Hart, 1961. For a group to have a rule, there must be a general habit of conformity in the group (p. 54) and 'some at least must look upon the behaviour in question as a general standard to be followed by the group as a whole' (p. 55). Cf. Ullman-Margalit: 'A social norm is a prescribed guide for conduct or action which is generally complied with by members of a society' (1977, p. 12). The concrete location of the prescription is left vague in this definition. See her pp. 88–9, where she is discussing 'coordination norms', for the implication that the people concerned must individually 'expect' conformity in a 'deontic' sense.

81 This appears to be so of joint acceptance in general. In some groups it may be clear that there are jointly accepted rules proscribing certain private thoughts and attitudes.

82 Of course, people who have learned to conform to a jointly accepted principle could develop a habit of conformity, so that they conform thoughtlessly at all times. They may also come personally to endorse the principle in question, by dint of conforming to it.

83 Evidently one may also act contrary to a jointly accepted principle without endorsing a contrary *principle*. Again, one may conform to a contrary principle that one accepts with a different set of persons.

84 This may help to explain a tendency in the literature to see conventions, rules, or norms as characteristic constituents of social groups. (See Emmett, 1966; Honore, 1973.) They may have also (rightly) been seen as constitutive of groups. On this issue see below.

85 I have in mind the following possibility. Not carrying out a promise could sometimes be *excusable*, while there was a sense in which it could not be rationally justifiable. This would be so just in case a promise is understood to provide a reason which cannot be overridden. A promise would be an *artifact* of precisely this sort. Kant's attitude to lying indicates that he feels we have a non-overridable reason not to lie. Perhaps we could have. Perhaps one could hypothesize some implicit contract among language-users never to lie. Even so, lying could sometimes be excusable. It could even be considerably better, all things considered, than its opposite.

86 This aspect of promising became salient during the discussion of a colloquium paper on promising presented by Thomas Scanlon, at the University of Connecticut, Storrs, in 1986. Cecily Hancock stressed the necessity of release by the promisee.

87 At one point Lewis refers to our agreeing by means of exchanging *conditional promises* binding us to conform to R only if others did' (p. 84; my stress.) But each one's saying 'I promise to go to Jackson tomorrow if you go', for instance, (the form of exchange Lewis seems to have in mind) lacks the force of an agreement that each will go to Jackson. Each has now bound himself conditionally, as one might say: only if the other goes to Jackson tomorrow is this one unconditionally obliged to go. But if we have *agreed* that each will go to Jackson tomorrow, everyone is now obliged to turn up tomorrow. Each is only obliged because everyone is obliged, or, rather, the simultaneous obligations of each have the same source. But each is unconditionally obliged at once. (Similarly, an exchange of conditional promises of the form 'I promise to go *if you promise* to go' is no agreement. Before anyone has any obligation to go, someone must first promise unconditionally.)

88 In special circumstances the 'gesture' of one party might be that of remaining silent or inactive. For instance, I say: 'If you don't respond negatively within an hour I shall take it that you agree.'

89 For more on the issue of 'political obligation' see the concluding chapter.

90 See also the concluding chapter, section 1.

91 See section 8.5 i. below for an example of a process whereby a principle comes to be jointly adopted without there being any agreement to do so.

92 Section 6.4

93 I previously discussed the nature of linguistic conventions in Gilbert, 1983a, also in 1985ms a.

94 As noted before, this point is not crucially dependent on thinking of sense or meaning as something other than 'use'.

95 Recall that the concept of a regularity is not presumed to involve the law-likeness of the regularity.

96 See pp. 67–8.

97 Cf. Lewis's (revised) account of when a given language, L, is the language of a given population in Lewis, 1975. There must be a convention (in Lewis's sense) of truthfulness and trust in L. In so far as the population in question is a social group, this account makes the basic fact something like the regular general use of the language by the individual members. The language in question may thus be well said to be the (or a) language of the individuals in question. It is not so clearly well said to be the group's language, the language of the group as such. This clearly counts against the idea that Lewis's or similar accounts adequately explicate our core intuitive conception of a group's language. For some other criticisms of Lewis's account see Gilbert, 1974.

98 See my discussion of the 'normative nature' of plural subject phenomena, in the concluding chapter.

99 I first noted this contrast in Gilbert, 1983a, pp. 381ff.

100 See Gilbert, 1983a, for a treatment of Lewis's work in this connection.

101 This could get obscured by the fact that if you and I agree on a

signal for a single occasion, or for our more general use, we may later refer quite properly to 'our convention' and say such things as 'we have this convention'. These could look like references to social convention. But this is just an instance of linguistic ambiguity. 'Our convention' can either refer to a social convention (principle of action) or to a linguistic convention.

102 I have argued earlier, of course, that to grasp a given sense or concept is to grasp a rule of a kind. As this idea was developed, it became clear that a concept is seen as a special, *sui generis* kind of object, one that has normative implications in that in order to apply it correctly one must do one thing rather than another. If you like, a concept rules some things into its domain, and ru!es others out. In any case it does not seem that concepts themselves are seen as 'rules of the fiat form'. In short, it seems that we see languages as abstract objects involving rules of two types: concepts or senses on the one hand, and the rules linking sounds and senses on the other. It is evidently a language's embodiment of the latter type of rule that is relevant in the present context.

103 More than one person has cited certain notions investigated by Paul Grice and his followers as providing a counterexample to the claim that use of a word in a certain sense involves convention intuitively. The sort of thing people have in mind is as follows. Suppose Molly leans out of the window, attracts Jason's attention, and points to her head. Jason realizes that by this gesture Molly means that he should wear his hat. In doing so Molly exemplifies the general phenomenon of 'speaker-meaning', which is referred to by the sentence form 'S meant that p by uttering "x"' where 'uttering "x"' can be a gesture, a sound, or whatever. Now someone might try to argue that (a) when there is speaker meaning there is an expressive vehicle which is used in a certain sense, yet (b) it would not be very natural to say that a convention had been adopted by the speaker or the speaker and hearer together. There are several issues here needing discussion. First, (a) is debatable. I do not find it obvious that if S meant that p by uttering 'x', it logically follows that S used 'x' in the sense of (or to express the proposition that) p. Gricean analyses of speaker meaning imply that rather than using 'x' in a certain sense, the speaker must essentially manipulate 'x' with a certain intention about what he wants the hearer to *believe*, as a result of recognizing his intention. Certainly the speaker must entertain the proposition that p, in intending that his hearer believe that p, but it seems logically possible that all of the Gricean type of conditions can hold without entailing that the phenomenon of S's using 'x' in a certain sense must occur. If (a) is indeed false, then we would expect our intuition to be that no language, and hence no convention of any sort, is involved in the phenomenon of speaker meaning. If, on the other hand, (a) is true (in which case the traditional type of Gricean analysis would be inadequate) then to that extent it would be legitimate intuitively to say that speaker meaning involves convention. We may not feel entirely comfortable saying that it involves

the *adoption* of a convention, since we may think of no explicit preamble or decision as being involved, and adoption may seem to have to be a rather deliberate thing. In fact I think it would be acceptable to say, of any case in which a speaker uses an expressive vehicle *in a certain sense*, that they have (implicitly) adopted a certain linguistic convention. We certainly could say that they are using a language that incorporates a particular convention.

104 See for example, M. Lessnoff, 1975, pp. 40–1, in a discussion of Winch, 1958. See also the quotation from Alston, 1964, above.

105 Of course, some philosophers would argue that if this is what a moral principle is, then there are no valid moral principles, since there are no facts about intrinsic value. See for instance Mackie, 1977. See also Harman, 1977, and elsewhere. Meanwhile, there is little doubt that many people see themselves as holding moral principles under this description of them, erroneous and misguided as some philosophers hold this to be. The issue here being how to distinguish a group's morality from its conventions, it does not matter whether or not moralities are all myths.

106 Intuitively, morality is no respecter of persons. One might feel that this idea can be explained in the following way. If lying in certain circumstances is intrinsically bad, then I ought not to lie in those circumstances, *whoever I am*. Now some have apparently found it hard to see how the fact that doing A in circumstances C is bad *from the point of view of intrinsic value* can entail, for each person, that that person ought not to do A in C. My account of our concept of a social convention suggests that, if one finds this hard to understand, one could be tempted to equate the 'ought' of morality with the 'ought' of convention. For one may find it easier to accept that as long as I am party to a convention that A is not to be done in C, I personally have reason not to do A in C. A view that moral 'oughts' are 'oughts' of convention rather than intrinsic value would be helped along, of course, by a denial that there is such a thing as intrinsic value. Cf. Gilbert Harman's discussion in *The Nature of Morality*, 1977. Roughly, Harman argues against the possibility of objective facts about value. (No evidence of such facts impacts upon our sense organs.) The search for the nature of morality then leads him to social convention. Harman finds the equation of morality and convention particularly attractive, because (roughly) the connection between 'morality' and a given person's reasons for acting becomes easy to understand when one makes this equation. (Harman's explicit account of a convention is not identical with my own.)

107 Once attributed to Adrienne Rich in conversation. Cf. Rich, 1980.

108 Referred to earlier, note 78 above. See my 1983ms for more details of the principle adoption model.

109 There will also, then, be reasons for expecting others to act in certain ways, that is, in accordance with principles already adopted. The proposed model, then, can be seen as suggesting a way Lewis's conditions could come to be fulfilled, as providing a mechanism for its fulfilment by rational agents with common knowledge of

rationality. However, in so far as agents are following principles of their own, they will not be acting predominantly by virtue of how they expect others to act. Hence this 'principle adoption' model does not suggest that Lewis's conditions on convention are apposite.

110 This development occurs in part because Burge (1975) feels that the parties to a convention need not be aware of any alternatives to their convention, and cites examples to that effect. In reading Burge I tended to agree that his examples could be used or developed in counter to Lewis, while disagreeing with his diagnosis or his own theory of convention. Among other things (such as its being an actual regularity theory) his theory depends heavily on a vague notion of 'social function' which may be manipulable in such a way that the theory is vacuous. For a more extended discussion of Burge, see Gilbert, 1978ms, pp. 281–3.

111 Burge, like Lewis, does not differentiate between social conventions and convention in general, and Burge's main interest is not really in our concept of a social convention (I would say). The kinds of distinctions I have been making here between types of convention have not been clearly marked in most discussions.

112 In fact conventions in Lewis's sense seem unlikely to be stable in this respect. For one would expect that as time went on, if expectations of others' conformity to a given regularity became reliable, people would lose sight of the fact that another regularity would have done just as well. They would simply cease to see themselves as in coordination problems. Thus facts about what went on in their minds would not indicate that there was any arbitrariness in the situation as a whole. In other words, once the 'mechanism' of Lewisian convention was well under way, there would most likely cease to be a convention on Lewis's definition.

113 This is true of Lewis's account also, from the point of view of the mathematics. From the point of view of the spirit of the theory, and most of the concrete examples given, however, such a characterization is relatively accurate.

114 Cf. the study by Broverman, *et al.*, 1970, which found a close correlation between the stereotypical 'female' character and features deemed to characterize a mentally unwell adult person.

115 The quoted phrase is from Burge, op. cit., p. 254.

VII ON SOCIAL FACTS

1 In neither case will there be reason to suppose that an individual woman has an unusual *nature*, or is 'hyper-responsible' if she 'takes' responsibility for the smoothness of a particular relationship. In the latter case, the wider society will have handed it to her. True, she is a member of the society. But the larger the group, the less chance an individual has of influencing the content of conventions, and the more likely it is that a given individual will have no option but to support a particular convention. Where the convention originates in a

given male–female dyad, there are many reasons why the woman might accept a peace-keeping role. It hardly has to 'come naturally' to her. (Of course, if it does come naturally to a given person, this could influence what develops in her relationships with others.)

2 A good example of someone who goes too far in maintaining his side of things is the cab-driver in the film *Airplane*. At the beginning of the film, he begins waiting for his fare, the hero, who has asked him to wait and then entered the airport and, without premeditation, proceeded to fly off on a plane. The driver is still waiting for his passenger at the end of the film.

3 See my 'Some footnotes to Rousseau', 1986ms. Some of the points made there have been alluded to in this section. Most relevant to the problem of political obligation here is the foregoing discussion of the special rights and responsibilities of membership. I hope to provide a longer treatment elsewhere. For more on how my results in this book relate to classic questions in political philosophy, see below.

4 The label is due to Thomas Nagel, I believe.

5 It would be rather natural to refer to one in this condition as *identifying* with the other person. This indicates that it is natural to see this kind of slavery as involving a deep confusion, as treating another person in a way uniquely appropriate to the treatment of oneself. These remarks only explain our intuitions against heteronomy in so far as they link them to our intuitions regarding which reason schemes are intelligible. (If the slavery were mutual perhaps the state of affairs might seem less unfortunate, though it could seem rather pointless, not to say inefficient.)

6 I only recently learned of Sellars's discussion of inferences involving 'we' statements. What I have so far understood of what he writes suggests a close correspondence with my own sense of the matter. To my knowledge Sellars does not isolate what I suggest is the model underlying this inference pattern, that is, the concept of a plural subject. Sellars also assumes a connection between the pronoun 'we' and groups. See Sellars, 1963, 1968, 1980. Another discussion I have only learnt of recently is Rosenberg, 1980. Rosenberg's discussion of the inferences generated by 'we' statements, which may derive from Sellars, also corresponds supportively in a general way with the conclusions reached independently here. I learned of these references from Tuomela and Miller's paper 'Group intentions', 1985ms, which draws its inspiration from Sellars's work. This paper alerted me to Tuomela, 1984, which it echoes to a large extent. I shall not attempt to discuss this development of Sellars's work here. As far as I can tell, the differences between myself and Tuomela and Miller are significant.

7 Some explanation of this chain of events would naturally be sought. The father could have been insincere in the first place, could have lacked understanding of the meaning of his words, could be strangely forgetful. Without some such explanation the chain of events described will appear quite mysterious.

8 I take it that an ungrounded, unreasoned act is conceivable. Perhaps

someone will argue that an act of will cannot intelligibly occur in the absence of any rational motivation, that is, of any implicit or explicit reason scheme which led to the act. But the notions of intelligibility and unintelligibility apply to the relation of reasons to acts. It therefore is not clearly intelligible to argue that an unreasoned act of will is unintelligible. Surely, if there were such an act, it would just happen. It would not be 'unintelligible' as opposed to 'without reasons'. (It would not be intelligible either.)

9 Social scientists sometimes presume as much and I see no philosophical reason for counting this an unintelligible presumption.

10 Note that this suggests that one is always to a degree personally responsible for the persistence of one's group. If one fails to exit the group, one perforce plays some role in sustaining it, and whatever ideals and goals it has. Similarly, of course, one is responsible to a degree for the joint acceptance of anything whose joint acceptance one is oneself party to. The degree of culpability (or praiseworthiness) at issue will depend on the plausibility of a claim that one was coerced into doing one's part in joint acceptance.

11 Perhaps the most famous qualifying label is 'methodological'. Von Mises, 1949, gives a careful and useful characterization of what he means by 'methodological individualism'. This phrase has been echoed by many writers. I shall make no attempt to distinguish or comment on the variety of individualisms which have been discriminated and discussed in the large literature. Hopefully the bearing of what I have to say here on these will be fairly clear. For a lengthy bibliography see O'Neill, 1973.

12 Some psychologists have suggested that the condition of women in some societies has been such that they practically lose self-consciousness, in the sense of being aware oneself of having one's own needs and goals. They are immersed in marriage or family and predominantly act in terms of the perceived needs and goals of the relevant group. Having little conception of their personal needs and goals, they may not consider them, so one member of the family may be frustrated and become depressed, in spite of that member's own efforts to 'please everyone'. They barely qualify as singular agents. They act on their own behalf on few and minor issues.

13 My talk of systems here does not imply that there can be societies of inanimate objects such as computers. That would depend on whether computers could fulfil the specific conditions proposed.

14 An ideal which has been attributed to the United States. See R. Bellah *et al.*, 1985.

15 The etymology of the word 'comfort' (from the Latin *confortare*, to strengthen greatly) recalls the notion of joining forces, something I have linked to the concept of a human collectivity. This indicates the depth of the risk involved in 'thinking away' the plural subject side of things. Evidently the alternative dismissal has special perils of its own from the point of view of human flourishing. In this context fears of engulfment in the group, on the one hand, and of isolation, on the other, are easily intelligible.

16 A classic paper is Latané *et al.*, 1979.

17 Winch, 1958, is still perhaps the best known instance. The 'science' issue has also been addressed by, for instance, Lessnoff, 1975, Braybrooke, 1987.

18 Cf. Pollock, 1955. This excellent discussion rightly casts doubt on the meaningfulness of questionnaire answers in relation to a summative conception of public opinion.

19 Wallace, 1983, defines a 'social phenomenon' as an 'interorganismic behavior regularity'. This definition is explicitly intended to expose what one might call the lowest common denominator in the plethora of accounts of the social that have been given by classic and contemporary sociologists. It does not purport to be a generic definition of social phenomena as such but rather an account of the phenomena actual social scientists take and have taken themselves to be studying. I am not certain that this account really does subsume all the definitions it is supposed to. But in any case, its great generality indicates how variously 'social phenomenon' has been defined in the social scientific literature. See also Gilbert, 1987.

20 See Ruben, 1985, for the view that 'nested expectations' are the key to sociality. Bach and Harnish, 1979, stress 'mutual belief'. See also my own 1978ms, ch. 6, in which I developed a theory of intuitive socialness as a matter of degree, on the assumption that a Weberian social action was something social, while situations of common knowledge, for instance, were more highly social. At that time I had not considered the phenomenon of plural subject-hood. Given the presumed scope and limits of the data, the conclusions I arrived at there still seem plausible enough.

21 See for instance Kummer, 1971, *Primate Societies*; Lore and Flannely, 1977, 'Rat societies'.

BIBLIOGRAPHY

Note: this bibliography lists all works referred to in the text. Dates cited are those of the edition used, not of first publication.

Albritton, R. (1956) 'On Wittgenstein's use of the term "criterion" ', *The Journal of Philosophy,* vol. 56.

Alston, W. (1964) *Philosophy of Language*, Prentice-Hall, Englewood Cliffs, New Jersey.

—— (1974) 'Semantic rules', in M. Munitz and P. Unger (eds) *Semantics and Philosophy*, New York University Press, New York.

Aristotle (1985) *Nichomachean Ethics*, tr. T. Irwin, Hackett Publishing Co., Indianapolis.

Aumann, R. (1976), 'Agreeing to disagree', *Annals of Statistics,* vol. 4.

—— (1987), 'Correlated equilibrium as an expression of Bayesian Rationality', *Econometrica*, vol. 55.

Ayer, A. J. (1954) 'Can there be a private language?', *Proceedings of the Aristotelian Society*, supplementary vol. 27.

Bach, K. and Harnish, R. M. (1979) *Linguistic Communication and Speech Act*, MIT Press, Cambridge, Massachusetts.

Barzun, J. (1968) *The American University*, Harper & Row, New York.

Bellah, R. N., Madsen, R., Sullivan, W. M., Swidler, A. and Tipton, S. M. (1985) *Habits of the Heart: Individualism and Commitment in American Life*, Harper & Row, New York.

Benacerraf, P. (1962) 'Tasks, supertasks, and the modern eleatics', *Journal of Philosophy*, vol. 59.

—— (1973) 'Mathematical truth', *Journal of Philosophy,* vol. 70.

Benacerraf, P. and Putnam, H. (eds) (1964, 2nd edn 1985) *Philosophy of Mathematics,* Prentice-Hall, Englewood Cliffs, New Jersey.

Bennett, J. (1976), *Linguistic Behaviour*, Cambridge University Press, Cambridge.

Blackburn, S. (1984) *Spreading the Word*, Oxford University Press, Oxford.

Braybrooke, D. (1987) *Philosophy of Social Science,* Prentice-Hall, Englewood Cliffs, New Jersey.

Bibliography

Brodbeck, M. (ed.) (1971) *Readings in the Philosophy of the Social Sciences*, Macmillan, London.

Broverman, I. K., Broverman, D. M. and Clarkson, F. E. (1970) 'Sex-role stereotypes and clinical judgments of mental health', *Journal of Consulting and Clinical Psychology*, vol 34.

Bryant, C. A. (1970) 'In defence of sociology: a reply to some contemporary philosophical criticisms', *British Journal of Sociology*, vol. 21.

Burge, T. (1975), 'On knowledge and convention', *Philosophical Review*, vol. 84.

Chisholm, R. (1981) *The First Person: An Essay on Reference and Intentionality,* University of Minnesota Press, Minneapolis, Minnesota.

Connerton, P. (ed.) (1976) *Critical Sociology: Selected Readings*, Penguin Books, New York.

Dahrendorf, R. (1963) *Die Angewandte Aufklarung: Gesellschaft und Sociologie in Amerika*, R. Piper, Munich.

Davidson, D. (1963), 'Actions, reasons, and causes', *Journal of Philosophy*, vol. 60.

—— (1982) 'Communication and convention', in his *Inquiries into Truth and Interpretation*, 1984, Clarendon Press, Oxford.

Douglas, J. D. (1967) *The Social Meanings of Suicide*, Princeton University Press, Princeton, New Jersey.

Dummett, M. (1974) 'The Social Character of Meaning', in his *Truth and Other Enigmas*, 1978, Harvard University Press, Cambridge, Massachusetts.

Durkheim, E. (1900) 'La sociologia ed il suo dominio scientifico', *Rivista Italiana di Sociologia*, vol. 4.

—— (1951) *Suicide: A Study in Sociology*, tr. J. A. Spaulding and G. Simpson, Free Press, New York. (First published, in French, 1897)

—— (1968) *Les Règles de la methode sociologique*, Presses Universitaires de France, Paris. (First published 1895)

—— (1982) *The Rules of Sociological Method*, tr. W. D. Halls, Free Press, New York. (Translation of Durkheim, 1968)

Durkheim, E. and Mauss, M. (1970) *Primitive Classification,* tr. R. Needham, Cohen & West, London. (First published as 'De quelques formes primitives de classification', *L'Année sociologique*, vol. 6, 1903)

Emmett, D. (1966) *Rules, Roles, and Relations*, Macmillan, London.

Evans, G. (1982) *Varieties of Reference*, Oxford University Press, Oxford.

Fann, K. T. (1969) *Wittgenstein's Conception of Philosophy*, Blackwell, Oxford.

—— (1967) (ed.) *Ludwig Wittgenstein: The Man and His Philosophy*, Dell, New York.

Fauconnet, P. and Mauss, M. (1968–9) 'Sociologie', in M. Mauss, *Oeuvres*, 3 vols, Editions de Minuit, Paris. (First published 1901)

Feldman, F. (1986), Critical notice of Kripke (1982), *Philosophy and Phenomenological Research*, vol. 46.

Bibliography

Flew, A. (1985) *Thinking About Social Thinking*, Blackwell, Oxford.

Frankfurt Institute for Social Research (1973) *Aspects of Sociology*, tr. J. Viertel, Heinemann, London.

Fried, C. (1981) *Contract as Promise: A Theory of Contractual Obligation*, Harvard University Press, Cambridge, Massachusetts.

Gauthier, D. (1975) 'Coordination,' *Dialogue*, vol. 14.

Geertz, C. (1973) 'Thick description: toward an interpretative theory of culture' in his *The Interpretation of Cultures*, Basic Books, New York.

Gellner, E. (1956) 'Explanations in history', *Proceedings of the Aristotelian Society*, supplementary vol. 30. (Reprinted in M. Brodbeck (ed.) (1971) *Readings in the Philosophy of the Social Sciences*, Macmillan, London).

Gerth, H. and Mills, C. W. (eds) (1946) *From Max Weber: Essays in Sociology*, Oxford University Press, New York.

Gibbard, A. (1978) 'Act-utilitarian agreements', in A. I. Goldman and J. Kim (eds) *Values and Morals*, Reidel, Dordrecht.

Gibbs, J. P. (1965) 'Norms: the problem of definition and classification', *American Journal of Sociology*, vol. 70.

Giddens, A. (ed.) (1976) *E. Durkheim: Selected Writings*, Cambridge University Press, New York.

Gilbert, Margaret (1974) 'About conventions', *Second Order*, vol. 3.

—— (1978ms), 'On Social Facts', unpublished D. Phil. thesis, Oxford University, Oxford.

—— (1981) 'Game theory and *Convention*', *Synthese*, vol. 46.

—— (1983a) 'Agreements, conventions, and language', *Synthese*, vol. 54.

—— (1983b) 'Notes on the concept of a social convention', *New Literary History*, vol. 14.

—— (1983c) 'On the question whether language has a social nature: some aspects of Winch and others on Wittgenstein', *Synthese*, vol. 56.

—— (1983abs) 'Some limitations of rationality' (Abstract), *Journal of Philosophy*, vol. 53.

—— (1983ms) 'Some limitations of rationality', paper given at the American Philosophical Association meetings, December 1983.

—— (1985ms a) 'More on one-shot conventions', reply to a paper by P. Weirich, given at the American Philosophical Association meetings, December 1985.

—— (1985ms b) 'On the morality of lying'.

—— (1986ms) 'Some footnotes to Rousseau', paper presented to the Philosophy Department, University of Connecticut, Storrs.

—— (1987) review of Wallace (1983), *Ethics*, vol. 98.

Gilbert, Martin (1971) *Winston S. Churchill*, vol. 3, Houghton Mifflin, Boston.

Gödel, K. (1964) 'What is Cantor's continuum problem?', in P. Benacerraf and Putnam, H. (eds) (1964, 2nd edn. 1985) *Philosophy of Mathematics*, Prentice-Hall, Englewood Cliffs, New Jersey.

Goffman, E. (1966) *Behavior in Public Places: Notes on the Social Organization of Gatherings*, Free Press, Glencoe, Illinois.

Goleman, D. (1986) 'Two views of marriage explored: his and hers', *The New York Times*, April 1986.

498

Bibliography

Goodman, N. (1973) *Fact, Fiction and Forecast*, Bobbs-Merrill, Indianapolis.

Grandy, R. (1977) 'Review of David Lewis, *Convention*', *Journal of Philosophy*, vol. 74.

Grice, H. P. (1957) 'Meaning', *Philosophical Review*, vol. 66.

—— (1969) 'Utterer's meaning and intention', *Philosophical Review*, vol. 78.

—— (1967ms) 'Logic and Conversation', William James Lectures, delivered at Harvard University. Partially published in D. Davidson and G. Harman (eds) (1975). *The Logic of Grammar*, Dickenson, Encino, California; and in P. Cole and J. Morgan (eds) *Syntax and Semantics 3: Speech Acts*, Academic Press, New York.

Gunderson, K. (ed.) (1975) *Language, Mind and Knowledge*, Minnesota Studies in the Philosophy of Science, vol. 7, University of Minnesota Press, Minneapolis.

Hacker, P. (1972) *Insight and Illusion*, Oxford University Press, Oxford.

Harman, G. (1977) *The Nature of Morality*, Oxford University Press, Oxford.

Harré, R. and Secord, P. F. (1972) *The Explanation of Social Behaviour*, Blackwell, Oxford.

Hart, H. L. A. (1961) *The Concept of Law*, Oxford University Press, Oxford.

Heal, J. (1978), 'Common knowledge', *Philosophical Quarterly*, vol. 28.

Hegel, G. W. F., (1977) *Phenomenology of Spirit*, tr. A. V. Miller, Oxford University Press, Oxford. (First published, in German, 1807)

Hempel, C. G. (1965) 'Fundamentals of taxonomy', in his *Aspects of Scientific Explanation and Other Essays in the Philosophy of Science*, Free Press, New York.

Hobbes, T. (1968), *Leviathan*, Penguin Books, Harmondsworth. (First published 1651)

Hoffman, L. (1981) *Foundations of Family Therapy: A Conceptual Framework for Systems Change*, Basic Books, New York.

Hollis, M. (1977) *Models of Man: Philosophic Thoughts on Social Action*, Cambridge University Press, Cambridge.

Homans, G. C. (1951), *Social Behavior: Its Elementary Forms*, Harcourt, Brace & World, New York.

Honore, A. (1973) 'Groups, laws, and obedience' in A. W. B. Simpson (ed.) *Oxford Essays in Jurisprudence*, 2nd series, Oxford University Press, Oxford.

Hume, D. (1978) *A Treatise of Human Nature*, ed. L. A. Selby-Bigge and P. H. Nidditch, Oxford University Press, London. (First published 1739)

—— (1980) *An Enquiry Concerning Human Understanding*, ed. L. A. Selby-Bigge, Greenwood Press, Westport, Connecticut. (First published 1758)

Inkeles, A. (1964) *What is Sociology? An Introduction to the Discipline and the Profession*, Prentice-Hall, Englewood Cliffs, New Jersey.

James, S. (1984), *The Content of Social Explanation*, Cambridge University Press, Cambridge.

Bibliography

Jamieson, D. (1975) 'David Lewis on convention', *Canadian Journal of Philosophy*, vol. 5.

Kant, I. (1930) *Lectures on Ethics*, tr. Louis Infield, The Century Company, London. (First published, in German, in 1924, from a student's lecture notes dated 1780–1)

Kaplan, D. (ms), 'Demonstratives'.

Kripke, S. A. (1973ms) 'Reference and existence', John Locke Lectures, delivered at Oxford University, to be published by Oxford University Press, Oxford.

—— (1980) *Naming and Necessity*, Harvard University Press, Cambridge, Massachusetts.

—— (1982) *Wittgenstein on Rules and Private Language*, Harvard University Press, Cambridge, Massachusetts.

Kuflik, A. (1982) 'Coordination, equilibrium, and rational choice', *Philosophical Studies*, vol. 42.

Kummer, H. (1971) *Primate Societies*, Aldine Press, Chicago.

Latané, B., Williams, K., and Harkins, S. (1979) 'Many hands make light the work: the causes and consequences of social loafing', *Journal of Personality and Social Psychology*, vol. 37.

LeBon, G. (1960) *The Crowd*, Viking Press, New York. (First published, in French, 1895).

Lehrer, K. and Wagner, C. (1981) *Rational Consensus in Science and Society*, Reidel, Dordrecht.

Lessnoff, M. (1975) *The Structure of Social Science*, International Publications Service, New York.

Levy, M. (1952) *The Structure of Society*, Princeton University Press, Princeton, New Jersey.

Lewis, D. K. (1969), *Convention: A Philosophical Study*, Harvard University Press, Cambridge, Massachusetts.

—— (1975) 'Languages and language', in K. Gunderson (ed.) *Language, Mind and Knowledge*, Minnesota Studies in the Philosophy of Science, vol. 7. University of Minnesota Press, Minneapolis.

—— (1976) 'Convention: reply to Jamieson', *Canadian Journal of Philosophy*, vol. 6.

Linsky, L. (1957) 'Wittgenstein on language and some problems of Philosophy', in K. T. Fann (ed.) (1967) *Ludwig Wittgenstein: The Man and his Philosophy*, Dell, New York.

Loar, B., (1985) Critical review of Kripke, 1982, *Nous*, vol. 19.

Lore, R. and Flannely, K. (1977) 'Rat societies', *Scientific American*, vol. 236.

Luce, R. D. and Raiffa, H. (1957) *Games and Decisions: Introduction and Critical Survey*, John Wiley, New York.

Lukes, S. (1973) *Emile Durkheim: His Life and Work*, Allen Lane, London.

—— (1982) Introduction to W. D. Hall's translation of Durkheim's *Rules of Sociological Method*, Free Press, New York.

McDowell, J. (1979) 'Virtue and reason', *Monist*, vol. 62.

McGinn, C. (1984) *Wittgenstein on Meaning*, Blackwell, Oxford.

MacIntyre, A. (1967) 'The idea of a social science', *Proceedings of the Aristotelian Society*, supplementary vol. 41.

500

Bibliography

MacIver, R. M. (1917) *Community*, Macmillan, London.

Mackie, J. L. (1977) *Ethics: Inventing Right and Wrong*, Penguin Books, Harmondsworth, Middlesex.

Malcolm, N. (1954) 'Wittgenstein's *Philosophical Investigations*', *The Philosophical Review*, vol. 63.

Marx, K. and Engels, F. (1977) *The Communist Manifesto*, in D. McLellan (ed.) *Karl Marx: Selected Writings*, Oxford University Press, Oxford. (First published, in German, 1850)

Maslow, A. (1953) 'Love in healthy people', in A. Montagu (ed.), *The Meaning of Love*, Julian Press, New York.

Melden, A. I. (1961) *Free Action*, Routledge & Kegan Paul, London.

Mellor, H. (1982) 'The reduction of society', *Philosophy*, vol. 57.

Mill, J. S. (1970), *A System of Logic*, Longman, London. (First published 1843)

—— (1979), *Utilitarianism*, Hackett Publishing Co., Indianapolis. (First published 1861)

Miller, R. (1979) 'Reason and commitment in the social sciences', *Philosophy and Public Affairs*, vol. 8.

Millikan, R. G. (1986) 'The price of correspondence truth', *Nous*, vol. 20.

Moore, G. E. (1954) 'Wittgenstein's lectures in 1930–33', *Mind*, vol. 53.

Morris, W. (ed.) (1969) *The American Heritage Dictionary of the English Language*, American Heritage Publishing Co., New York.

Murray, J. (ed.) (1971) *The Oxford English Dictionary*, (compact edition), Oxford University Press, Oxford.

Nagel, E. (1961) *The Structure of Science*, Routledge & Kegan Paul, London.

O'Neill, J. (ed.) (1973) *Modes of Individualism and Collectivism*, Heinemann, London.

Parsons, T. (1938) 'The role of ideas in social action', in his *Essays in Sociological Theory* (1949), Free Press, Glencoe, Illinois.

—— (1949) *The Structure of Social Action*, Free Press, Glencoe, Illinois.

—— (1964) (ed.) *The Theory of Social and Economic Organization*, tr. A. M. Henderson and T. Parsons, Free Press of Glencoe, New York.

Pettit, P. (1980) *Judging Justice*, Routledge & Kegan Paul, London.

Pettit, P. and MacDonald, G. (1981) *Semantics and Social Science*, Routledge & Kegan Paul, London.

Pitcher, G. (1964) *The Philosophy of Wittgenstein*, Prentice-Hall, Englewood Cliffs, New Jersey.

—— (1966) (ed.) *Wittgenstein: The Philosophical Investigations*, Doubleday, New York.

Plath, S. (1965) 'Daddy' (poem), in her *Ariel*, Faber & Faber, London.

Plato (1974) *The Republic*, tr. G. M. A. Grube, Hackett Publishing Co., Indianapolis.

—— (1982) *Cratylus*, in E. Hamilton and H. Cairns (eds), *Collected Dialogues of Plato*, Princeton University Press, Princeton, New Jersey.

Pollock, F. (1955) *Gruppenexperiment-Ein Studienbericht*, in T. W. Adorno and W. Dirks (eds) *Frankfurter Beitrage zur Sociologie*, Bd. 2, Europaische Verlaganstalt, Frankfurt. (A translated excerpt is in P. Connerton (ed.) (1976) *Critical Sociology: Selected Readings*, Penguin Books, New York.)

Popper, K. (1961) 'The Autonomy of society' (an excerpt from *The Open Society and its Enemies*, vol. II, Ch. 14), in J. Schneewind (ed.) (1969) *Mill*, Macmillan, London.

Putnam, H. (1975) 'The meaning of "meaning"', in K. Gunderson (ed.) *Language, Mind and Knowledge*, Minnesota, Studies in the Philosophy of Science, vol. 7, University of Minnesota Press, Minneapolis.

—— (1978) *Meaning and the Moral Sciences*, Routledge & Kegan Paul, London.

—— (1981) 'Convention: a theme in philosophy', *New Literary History*, vol. 13.

Quine, W. V. O. (1936) 'Truth by convention', in O. H. Lee (ed.), *Philosophical Essays for A. N. Whitehead*, Longman, New York.

—— (1960) *Word and Object*, The MIT Press, Cambridge, Massachusetts.

Quinton, A. (1975) 'Social objects', *Proceedings of the Aristotelian Society*, vol. 75.

Rawls, J. (1971) *A Theory of Justice*, Harvard University Press, Cambridge, Massachusetts.

Rich, A. (1980), 'Compulsory heterosexuality and lesbian existence', *Signs*, vol. 5.

Rollin, B. E. (1976) *Natural and Conventional Meaning: An Examination of the Distinction*, Mouton, The Hague.

Rosenberg, J. (1980) *One World and Our Knowledge of it*, Reidel, Dordrecht.

Rousseau, J.-J. (1983) *On the Social Contract*, tr. D. A. Cress, Hackett Publishing Co., Indianapolis. (First published, in French, 1792)

Ruben, D.-H. (1985) *Metaphysics of the Social World*, Routledge & Kegan Paul, London.

Sander, F. (1925) 'Der Gegenstand der reinen Gesellschaftslehre', *Archiv für Sozialwissenschaft und Sozialpolitik*, Band 54.

Schelling, T. (1960) *The Strategy of Conflict*, Oxford University Press, Oxford.

Schiffer, S. R. (1972) *Meaning*, Oxford University Press, Oxford.

Schneewind, J. (ed.) (1969) *Mill*, Macmillan, London.

Schotter, A. (1981) *An Economic Theory of Social Institutions*, Cambridge University Press, Cambridge.

Schutz, A. (1972) *The Phenomenology of the Social World*, Heinemann, London.

Sellars, W. (1963) 'Imperatives, intentions, and the logic of "ought"', in G. Nakhnikian and H.-N. Castaneda (eds) *Morality and the Language of Conduct*, Wayne State University Press, Detroit.

—— (1968) *Science and Metaphysics*, Routledge & Kegan Paul.

—— (1980) 'On reasoning about values', *American Philosophical Quarterly*, vol. 17.

Sen, A. (1970) *Collective Choice and Social Welfare*, Holden-Day, San Francisco.

Sherif, M. and Sherif, C. (1956) *An Outline of Social Psychology*, Harper, New York.

Bibliography

Simmel, G. (1971a) 'How is society possible?', in D. N. Levine (ed.)
Georg Simmel: On Individuality and Social Forms, University of
Chicago Press, Chicago. (First published, in German, 1908)
—— (1971b) 'Conflict and the web of group-affiliations', passages in
D. N. Levine (ed.). *Georg Simmel: On Individuality and Social
Forms*, University of Chicago Press, Chicago. (First published, in
German, 1908)
Simon, M. (1982) *Understanding Human Action*, State University of
New York Press, Albany.
Skinner, Q. (1972) '"Social meaning" and the explanation of social
action', in P. Laslett, W. G. Runciman, and Q. Skinner (eds)
Philosophy, Politics and Society (Fourth series), Blackwell, Oxford.
Sprott, W. J. H. (1954) *Science and Social Action*, Watts, London.
Stalnaker, R. (1974) 'Pragmatic presuppositions', in M. K. Nunitz and
P. K. Unger (eds), *Semantics and Philosophy*, New York University
Press, New York.
Steiner, M. (1973) 'Platonism and the causal theory of knowledge',
Journal of Philosophy, vol. 70.
Stich, S. (1971) 'What every speaker knows', *Philosophical Review*,
vol. 53.
Strawson, P. (1954) 'Review of *Philosophical Investigations*', *Mind*,
vol. 52.
Tarde, G. (1903) *The Laws of Imitation*, tr. E. Parsons, Henry Holt,
New York. (First published, in French, 1890)
Taylor, C. (1971) 'Interpretation and the sciences of Man', *The Review
of Metaphysics*, vol. 25.
—— (1980) 'Critical notice: Jonathan Bennett's *Linguistic Behavior*',
Dialogue, vol. 19.
Thompson, J. J. (1971) 'The verification principle and the private
language argument' in O. R. Jones (ed.) *The Private Language
Argument*, Macmillan, New York.
Tönnies, F. (1963) *Community and Society*, Harper Torchbooks, New
York. (First published, in German, 1887)
Tuomela, R. (1984) *A Theory of Social Action*, Reidel, Dordrecht.
Tuomela, R. and Miller, K. (1985ms) 'Group-intentions', given at the
American Philosophical Association meetings, December 1985.
Ullman-Margalit, E. (1977) *The Emergence of Norms*, Oxford Univer-
sity Press, Oxford.
Updike, J. (1981) 'Minutes of the last meeting', in *Problems and Other
Stories*, Fawcett Crest, New York.
Von Mises, L. (1949) *Human Action,* Yale University Press, New
Haven, Connecticut.
Von Neumann, J. and Morgenstern, O. (1944) *The Theory of Games
and Economic Behavior*, Princeton University Press, Princeton, New
Jersey.
Wallace, W. (1983) *Principles of Scientific Sociology*, Aldine Publishing
Co., New York.
Walzer, M. (1983) *Spheres of Justice*, Basic Books, New York.
Weber, M. (1907) 'R. Stammlers "Ueberwindung" der materialistischen
Geschichtsauffassung', in his *Gesammelte Aufsatze zur Wissen-*

schaftslehre (1922), Mohr, Tübingen.

—— (1913) 'Some categories of interpretive sociology', *Logos*, IV; reprinted as Appendix 1 to his *Economy and Society*, ed. G. Roth and C. Wittich, 2 vols, University of California Press, Berkeley, 1978, pp. 1375–80.

—— (1949) *The Methodology of the Social Sciences*, Free Press, Glencoe, Illinois.

—— (1964) *The Theory of Social and Economic Organization*, tr. T. Parsons and A. M. Henderson, Free Press, Glencoe, Illinois. (Part I of *Economy and Society*.)

—— (1978) *Economy and Society*, ed. G. Roth and C. Wittich, 2 vols, University of California Press, Berkeley. (First published, posthumously, in German, 1922)

White, M. (1950) 'The analytic and the synthetic: an untenable dualism', in S. Hook (ed.) *John Dewey: Philosopher of Science and Freedom*, Dial Press, New York.

—— (1956) *Toward Reunion in Philosophy*, Harvard University Press, Cambridge, Massachusetts.

Winch, P. (1956) 'Social Science', *British Journal of Sociology*, vol. 7.

—— (1958) *The Idea of a Social Science and its Relation to Philosophy*, Routledge & Kegan Paul, London.

Wittgenstein, L. (1953) *Philosophical Investigations*, Blackwell, Oxford.

Woolf, H. B. (ed.) (1975) *Webster's New Collegiate Dictionary*, G. C. Merriam, Springfield, Massachusetts.

Ziff, P. (1960) *Semantic Analysis*, Cornell University Press, Ithaca, New York.

INDEX

218; and summativism 260–73; surprise-avoiding 193–5; and use of 'we' 186–97; and we* 202–3

communal social relationships 151, 230, 232, 464

communication: and convention 452; linguistic, contrast to language possession 42, 134, 452; non-linguistic 143–4; seriously intended 88, 135, 462; as shared action 215–16; and social group formation 214–19; thin 87–9, 135, 216; and we* 215; and Wittgenstein's criteria 134–5

communities 410; *see also* social groups

concepts and concept-possession: and classification 69–70, 82–3, 94; content certainty thesis 96–7, 120–1, 457; and future behaviour 69–70; general 70, 454; grasp *see* grasping concepts; infinity thesis 94–5, 103, 112–3, 122, 459, 469; and language 68, 71–4, 454; in meaningful behaviour 68, 71; 'natural view' *see* 'natural view' of concept use; as objective particulars, 456; as objects 116–17, 122–3, 455, 459–60, 490; perception of 117–22, 460; privacy thesis 95–6; reification of 70–1; rule thesis 70, 94, 108, 454–5; as rules 66, 69–72, 74, 78–9, 94, 116, 122; shareability 80–3, 87–8; society-dependence, issue of 68, 90, 99; subjectivity thesis 96, 104; vernacular *see* social group, vernacular concept of; vernacular concepts; *see also* collectivity; language; social group; and other vernacular categories

conceptual analysis: of following a rule 72; methods 10–11

conflict: between individuals and plural subjects 423–4, 436; between social and individual goals 424–5, 434; between and within social groups 441–2, 451; *see also* coercion; individuals, beliefs of

conformity to social conventions: and arbitrariness 402; Conformism 343–4; coordination problems and 343–4; and Lewisian conventions 356; morality and 393–4; regularities in 344–6, 398–9, 488, 492

congruent behaviour condition on rule-following 82–3

consciousness, of unity 222–3; *see also*

feelings of unity; thought consensus 472

content certainty thesis for concepts: counterexamples proposed 457; in 'natural view' of language 96–7; and perception model 120–1

conventions (in general) 390–2, 452, 492; of an individual 392; one-shot 363–5, 367, 385, 487, 489–90; *see also* language, conventions; social convention

conversation 232; common knowledge in 194, 469; group belief in 294–8; and group formation 214–16; as negotiation of jointly accepted views 295–8, 476–7; lying in 476; models of 477; as a shared purpose of social groups 172; *see also* communication; jointly accepted views; language

coordination problems 480–2; agreement and 325, 481; Conformism and 343–4; equilibria 324–5, 328–9; game theory 320, 322–4, 341–2, 480–1; Lewis on 322–7, 329, 342, 481–3; plural subjects and 359–61, 486; social conventions and 323–7, 329–31, 337, 342–4, 396–8, 482

correlative individual beliefs 19, 239–40, 243, 287, 308

correlativism: definition 243; Durkheim and 253–4; inadequacy of 19, 288–99; and summativism 19, 243; *see also* jointly accepted view

'criteria', Wittgenstein's: and communication 134–5; definition and usage 133–4, 463; and group language 17, 133, 139–40, 142, 145, 462; meaning and 134; and pure sensation terms 110–11, 461

crime, Durkheim on 173

crowds 15, 450, 472

Crusoe cases; infants' need for society 131; language logically possible for 59, 72–3, 89–91, 93, 95, 98–9, 111–12, 363, 486; Wittgenstein on 109, 111–12, 459

custom 403–4; *see also* social convention

Dahrendorf, Rolf 53, 452

dancing: feelings of unity in 224; leadership 486; as shared action 165–6

Davidson, Donald 452, 475

Index

Index

Lehrer, K. and Wagner, C. 472
Lessnof, M. 491, 495
Levy, M. 447
Lewis, David 471, 489; on agreements 325, 378, 383, 481, 489; and collectivity concepts 327, 328; on common knowledge 188, 192, 195, 260–1, 326–7, 467, 470; concept possession 481–2; coordination problems 322–7, 329, 342, 481–3; game theory 15, 20, 320, 323–4, 327–9, 341–2, 479–80; on intentions 389; on norms 352–5, 378; on population common knowledge 262, 265, 473, 481; on precedent 336–8, 483; on rules 386–9; on social convention 20, 318–20, 324–8, 339–40, 386–8, 474, 475, 478–9, 481–2, 484–5, 487, 491; on social convention and language 319, 363–7, 479, 481–2, 486, 489; on tendencies 336, 338, 484; and vernacular concept of social convention 319
Linsky, L. 457
Loar, B. 461
Lore, R. and Flannelly, K. 495
love 225, 471; see also feelings of unity; intimacy; marriage
Luce, R. D. and Raiffa, H. 479, 480, 481
Lukes, Steven 246, 251, 474
lying 476, 477, 488; see also morality

MacDonald, G. 470, 475
McDowell, J. 483
McGinn, C. 459, 462
MacIntyre, A. 452, 453
MacIver, R. M. 472
Mackie, J. L. 491
majority opinion, in jointly accepted views 300–1
Malcolm, N. 80
marriage: discord in 474; feelings of unity in 225; Kant on 471; use of 'we' in 170–1; see also intimacy
Marx, Karl and Marxism 227–8, 229, 471, 475
Maslow, A. 471
Mauss, Marcel and Fauconnet, Paul 274–6, 474
meaning: of an action 62–3, 449; agreement on 137–9, 462; assertability conditions 108, 110, 461; behavioural correlates 84; 'criteria' and 134; definitions of 62–3, 67; dispositional accounts 457;

evaluability condition 108, 110; language game of 105, 107–12, 125–8, 129–30, 458, 461; human agreement condition 108, 110; imagist account 101–3, 113–14, 116, 122; intuitive concept of 90; language games 105–12, 125–30; and mental states 103, 107, 112; naming 126; 'natural view' 93–9, 116–17 (see also 'natural view'); non-platonist accounts 116–17; as involving perception 117–22; primitive state account 103, 112–14; shared 453; social 62, 453; by social convention 62–3, 453; society-independence 129–30; subjective experience 96, 104, 107–8, 112; teaching 106; *Verstehen* 26, 49–50, 51; Wittgenstein on 456–7; see also language; meaningful behaviour; thought
meaning-identifiability 84–91, 93, 461
meaning-shareability 80–9, 453, 456
meaningful behaviour: and concept possession 68, 71; general characterization of 66–8, 453–4; and rules 65–6, 70; and social science 33; society-dependence, issue of 58–60, 62–4, 68; subjective content 25–7, 67; as 'symbolic' 69; Weber on 24–7, 64–5, 66–7; Winch on 59, 62–7, 69, 453–4; see also action; concepts; intentionalism; rules; thought
means–end rationality 30–1
Melden, A. I. 475
Mellor, H. 471
member's knowledge principle for group belief 259, 261
memory 457
metaphor, group belief as 240–1, 309
methodology in social science 63–4, 440, 453; Durkheim's 4, 248–9; individualism and 494; summativism and 495; Weber's 4–7, 14, 22, 56, 417
Mill, John Stuart 3, 408, 431, 438, 446, 472
Miller, Richard 485
Millikan, R. G. 460
Milne, A. A. 461
mistakes: assertability conditions 110; in private languages 98–9; and rule-following 92–3; in understanding plural subjecthood 213–14; see also normative judgements; rules

512

Index

misunderstandings, in social groups 213–14
monotheism, and privacy thesis 95
Moore, G. E. 116, 454
morality: and agreements 378–9; and conformity 393–4; group belief and 395–6; of a group, relation to will 399–400; distinct from shared action obligations 162; individual and societal 395–6, 425–6; intrinsic value 393, 491; and plural subjecthood 425–6; reality of 491; of singular agency 421; and social convention 12, 21, 392–6, 399–402, 491; responsibility 425–6, 494; *see also* normative judgements
motive: for action 25–7, 166–7, 448–9, 466; agreement as 383; for talk of group belief 239; social convention as 383; and subjective meaning 25–6; for suicide 49–51; *see also* intention; reasons
multiple rules 74–5, 102
multiplicity constraint, on use of 'we' 174–5
mushroom pickers, the 36–9, 41, 287, 376, 442
mutual recognition, in social group formation 218, 470
'mysterious', as a critical term 123, 460
mysticism 123

Nagel, E. 450, 453
Nagel, Thomas 493
naming 126; *see also* meaning
nations 206, 212, 438
natural necessity 104–5, 458
natural units 151–2, 457
'natural view' of language use and concept possession: account of 93–9; and assertability conditions 124–5; attacks on 100; on concept grasp 115–17; content certainty thesis 96–7, 120–1, 457; and group language 134; infinity thesis 94–5, 103, 112–13, 122, 459, 469; and language games 106–7, 124, 127, 458; naturalness of 125–7, 458; perception model 117–22; and platonism 116–17, 124, 134, 460–1; primitive state account 112–14; privacy thesis 95–6; on pure sensation terms 125–6; and scepticism 101, 103–5, 112–24, 128–9; society-independence, issue of 128, 132–3; subjectivity thesis 96,

104; and 'therapy' 105, 457–8; Wittgenstein on 94, 104–5, 124–7, 458
necessarily partnered action 465
normative judgements and terms: and agreements 367–8, 371–3, 378, 380–1; and group belief 242; and intrinsic value 351; and language 386; in language games 108; levels of 371; and promises 379–81, 488, 489; and pure sensation terms 126; and social conventions 317, 349–55, 367–9, 371–3, 485, 491; and social group membership 415; *see also* mistakes; rules
norms 352–5, 378; *see also* social convention

objective particulars, concepts as 456
objects: concepts as 116–17, 122–3, 455, 456, 459–60, 490; languages as 391, 490
obligation: of agreements 378–82, 489; associational 209–10, 380, 381, 382; forgetting 209–10; of jointly accepted views 302–3, 477; legal 209–10, 411, 413; moral 411, 413; of plural subjects 357–8, 409, 411–14; political 382, 411, 414–15; rules of 405; in shared action 162, 409; of social group membership 411; *see also* morality; responsibility
O'Neill, J. 494
open* and openness*: in common knowledge 191–7; definition 191; practices, as reasons 283–5, 475–6; sense of 191, 193, 468; vernacular concept 191
open* practice assumption 278, 280
organizations, as social groups 230–1
ostension: agreement on 137–9, 143; ambiguity 73, 136; and group language 137–9, 143; pure sensation terms 85, 126; teaching via 73–4
'ought' *see* normative

paradigm cases for: common knowledge 188–94, 467–9; group belief 265; individual belief 260; social group 149, 212, 232, 471
Parsons, Talcott 23, 448, 449, 450
participant agency 422–5, 436
partnership: alliances 441–2; necessarily partnered action 465; in shared action 155–7, 161–4; *see also* plural subject; shared action
perception: of concepts 117–22, 460;

Index

introspectibilia 114, 120; experience of meaning 96, 104, 107–8, 112; feelings of unity 223–5; and language games 107–8; meaning and 103, 107, 112; and meaningful behaviour 25–7, 67; in 'natural view' 96, 114; not rules 114–15; in perception 119–20, 460; sense of openness* 191, 193, 468

subjectivity thesis, in 'natural view' 96, 104

suicide: Durkheim on 4, 45–6, 47–51, 452; motivation 49–51; rates 47–8; as 'social action' 45–51; social science subject matter, 45, 46, 47–8; vernacular notion, 45–6

summativism and summative accounts of group belief 19, 257–88; anti-psychologism about groups, psychologism about belief 242; causal 274–88; and common knowledge 260–73; and correlativism 19, 243; definition 241–2; Durkheim and 243, 247, 253; and essential collectivity involvement 258; simple 257–60, 272; and social science methods 495; support for 242–3

surprise-avoidance, and common knowledge 194–5

symbolic nature of actions 69; see also signs

system, plural subject as a 433–4

Tarde, Gabriel 450

Taylor, Charles 203, 446, 470

teaching: language 73–4, 106–7; meaning 106; by ostension 73–4; pure sensation terms 111

tendencies see psychology

tendentious use of 'we' 178, 180, 216–17, 467; defined 178; and generation of conventions 397–8

thin communication: defined 87; and meaning-identifiability 87–8, 89; shared language 135; status as social phenomenon 216

Thompson, J.J. 80

thought: and convention 481–2; development of, in infants 131–2, 144; of individuals 432; introspectibilia 112–15, 119–20, 122; and language 16; society-dependence, issue of 58–62, 129, 131–2; vernacular concept 16; we*- 201; see also belief; group belief

Tienson, John 476

Tönnies, F. 230, 464

totalitarianism 437–8

Toumela, R. 493

tradition 403, 404–5; see also social convention

travelling together 155–9, 161–4

Ullman-Margalit, E. 478, 482, 485, 487, 488

unit or unity: consciousness of 222–5, 235; natural 151–2, 457; perception that something is a 150; regarding sets of people as 150–2; see also feelings of unity

Updike, John 172

'us' see 'we'

usage, in conceptual analysis 11

values see intrinsic value

Van Fraasen, Bas 477–8

Verhalten 449

vernacular concepts: analysis methods 5, 10–11, 446–7; assumptions about 2; of collectivity in general 8–10, 12, 13 (see also social group, vernacular concept of); Durkheim on 3–4, 45, 446; of group belief 237, 238, 270; of intention 26–7; intuitive principles 8–9; in judgements of applicability 8–9; of language 16, 93–9; of necessity 104–5; of openness* 191; of 'social action' 23; of social convention 315–16, 319, 377, 383–4, 388, 390–1; of social groups see social group, vernacular concept of; of social phenomena in general 1–3, 22–3, 441–2; in social science 4–5, 55, 446–7; of suicide 45–6; of thought 16; Weber on 4–8, 34, 55, 56

Verstehen (understanding meaning): of an action 26; approaches to suicide 49–50, 51

voluntarism 410

Von Mises, Ludwig 224, 463–4, 466, 494

Von Neumann, John 478

voting 269–70, 474

Wagner, Steven 311

walk, going for a (together) 17, 164, 362

Wallace, W. 450, 453, 495

Walzer, M. 453

'we', 'us', and 'our': ambiguities 168, 174–5; animacy constraint 174–5; appropriate use 153, 174–99, 465,

519

Prepared with the help of M. Curtin

ERRATA

p. 190, line 18: read ''$(Z(\omega + n))$'' for ''$(Z(\omega) + n)$''
p. 416, line 23: read ''interdependent'' for ''independent''
p. 511, add index entry: **joint commitment** 198, 205, 382, 412-4; *see also* jointly accepted view; plural subjects

SELECT RECENT PUBLICATIONS BY THE AUTHOR

(1987) ''Modelling collective belief,'' *Synthese*, vol. 73.

(1989) ''Rationality and salience,'' *Philosophical Studies*, vol. 55.

(1989) ''Folk psychology takes sociality seriously,'' *Behavioral and Brain Sciences*, vol. 12.

(1990) ''Fusion: sketch of a contractual model'' in *Perspectives on the Family*, eds. R.C.L. Moffat, J. Grcic, and M. Bayles, Edwin Mellen Press, Lewiston, N.Y.

(1990) ''Rationality, coordination, and convention,'' *Synthese*, vol. 84.

(1990) ''Walking together: A paradigmatic social phenomenon,'' *Midwest Studies in Philosophy*, vol. 15, *The Philosophy of the Human Sciences*, eds. P. A. French, T. E. Uehling, Jr., and H. K. Wettstein, University of Notre Dame Press, Notre Dame.

(1990) ''Wittgenstein and the philosophy of sociology,'' in *Ludwig Wittgenstein: a symposium on the centennial of his birth*, eds. S. Teghrarian, A. Serafini, and E. M. Cook, Longwood Academic Press, Wakefield, N.H.

(1991) ''More on Social Facts: Reply to Greenwood,'' *Social Epistemology*, vol. 5.